VENETIAN NARRATIVE PAINTING IN THE AGE OF CARPACCIO

VENETIAN NARRATIVE PAINTING IN THE AGE OF CARPACCIO

Patricia Fortini Brown

Yale University Press · New Haven and London

BARR FERREE FOUNDATION

Published with the support of the Barr Ferree Publications Fund of the Department of Art and Archaeology, Princeton University.

Third printing 1994

Designed by Faith Glasgow

Set in Linotron Bembo by Best-set Typesetter Ltd
and printed in Great Britain by
BAS Printers Limited, Over Wallop, Hampshire

Library of Congress Cataloging-in-Publication Data

Brown, Patricia Fortini
Venetian narrative painting in the age of Carpaccio.

Bibliography: p.
Includes index.
1. Narrative painting, Italian—Italy—Venice—Themes, motives. 2. Narrative painting, Renaissance—Italy—Venice—Themes, motives.
3. Carpaccio, Vittore, 1455?–1525?—Themes, motives.
4. Bellini, Gentile, d. 1507—Themes, motives.
5. Art and society—Italy—Venice. I. Title.
ND1452.I8B76 1987 759.5'31 87–10669
ISBN 0–300–04025–3 (cloth)
0–300–04743–6 (pbk)

PREFACE

The foundation for this book was laid at the University of California at Berkeley where I received my formal academic training: as an undergraduate in the history of political theory and as a graduate student in the history of art. It was there that I determined that art could best be understood within a broad cultural context, and that the historical circumstances should be taken just as seriously as the art objects themselves.

Against this background, in 1980 I began research for my doctoral dissertation: 'The Painted Histories of the Scuole Grandi of Venice, c. 1494–c. 1534'. It focused on just two cycles of Venetian narrative paintings: the *Miracles of the True Cross* of the Scuola Grande di San Giovanni Evangelista and the *Life of St. Mark* for the Scuola Grande di San Marco. On completing it in 1983, I became increasingly aware that the cycles themselves, aside from the circumstances of their patronage and the society which produced them, needed to be placed within a yet larger visual context that included other narrative cycles painted in Venice during that period and, indeed, the tradition of narrative painting that preceded them.

What had begun as a study of patronage of two groups of paintings that shared a common institutional context – the Scuole Grandi – thus developed into an attempt to elucidate the birth, elaboration and decline of a whole stylistic movement – called here an 'eyewitness style' – within an even more comprehensive cultural and societal context. Hence the shape and title of the present book.

My dissertation research and writing was generously supported by fellowships from the Social Science Research Council, the American Council of Learned Societies, and the Gladys Krieble Delmas Foundation, and by a Fulbright-Hays fellowship to Italy. Further grants from the Ione May Spears Fund of the Department of Art and Archeology and from the University Committee on Research in the Humanities and Social Sciences at Princeton allowed me to expand my initial study into a book. I am also most grateful for a generous grant toward the cost of publication from the Barr Ferree Publications Fund of the Princeton Department of Art and Archaeology.

I would like to acknowledge my lasting debt to my mentors at Berkeley, each of whom contributed in a fundamental way to my academic development. L. D. Ettlinger, my dissertation supervisor, gave early and continuing support. Randolph Starn provided valuable historical and methodological perspectives. Loren Partridge, in whose graduate seminar I became acquainted with Venetian confraternities and the art which they patronized, insisted that I never lose sight of the integrity of the art object in the midst of so many social and historical distractions. He was kind enough to read the final manuscript of the book and offered throughout welcome encouragement. Svetlana Alpers, in whose graduate seminar I first became aware of the problematic relationship of words and images, encouraged all her students to question accepted models of interpretation.

It is a pleasure to thank the many persons who have helped me along the way as I researched and wrote this book. Among them are Bernard Aikema, Reinhold Baumstark, John Bernasconi, Vittore Branca, Angela Caracciolo Aricò, Linda Carroll, Howard Collins, Tracy Cooper, Gaetano Cozzi, Charles Dempsey, Rona Goffen, Peter Humfrey, Michael Hyman, Dulcia Meijers, Reinhold Mueller, Antonio Niero, John Onians, Debra Pincus, Wendy Stedman Sheard, Maria Francesca Tiepolo, Fred Travisano, Tullio Valery, Marino Zorzi and the staffs of the facilities in which I carried out my research in Venice – the Biblioteca Nazionale Marciana, the Archivio di Stato, the Fondazione Giorgio Cini and the Biblioteca del Museo Correr. I am especially indebted to Shari Taylor who tracked down the photographs with efficiency and good humor; to John Nicoll for his vision of the book as a book, and to his colleague at Yale University Press, my editor Faith Glasgow, who gave the manuscript exemplary care and attention.

I am particularly grateful to William Childs, Chairman of the Department of Art and Archeology at Princeton, who allowed me to arrange a teaching schedule which allowed time to complete the revisions for the book, and to those who read and offered valuable comments on various parts of the manuscript: Michael Baxandall, Marvin Becker, Richard Brilliant, Albert Elsen, Creighton Gilbert, Felix Gilbert, Thomas DaCosta Kaufmann, Patricia Labalme, Edward Muir, Mark Phillips, and Brian Pullan.

My deepest thanks go to four people: Glenn Most, John Shearman, Juergen Schulz, and my husband Peter Brown. Each of them contributed in a profound way to the completion of this book. Glenn Most considered the full text at an early stage from the outsider's perspective of the classicist. His advice was most valuable; his enthusiasm crucial. During the four years in which John Shearman was my senior colleague in Renaissance studies in the Department of Art and Archaeology at Princeton, he cast an incisive and exacting eye on much of the material that went into this book and offered sound advice and suggestions. His example as a teacher and a scholar has meant much to me. Juergen Schulz, whose own scholarship has contributed so much to our understanding of Venetian Renaissance art and culture, read the manuscript twice over. He challenged, corrected and encouraged. It was he who suggested a catalogue to disencumber the first draft of the text from the deadening paraphernalia of scholarly 'nuts and bolts'. His care and extraordinary generosity have helped to make this a better book in every way.

Peter Brown read every word of this book in its several redactions more times than I care to count. His patience, good sense, and singular qualities of mind and intellect sustained and inspired me through six years of research, writing and rewriting. The book is dedicated to him.

CONTENTS

Part Three: PAINTED HISTORIES

GLOSSARY

altana a wood platform, often serving as a terrace, on the roof of a Venetian house
archivio an archive or repository for documents and records, sometimes included in a *scuola* building
arte an artisan's guild
baldacchino a canopy or baldaquin, which may be an architectural structure built over an altar or a portable tent made of cloth that can be carried above a relic or holy object in a procession
barco an elevated gallery across the nave of a church, used in monastic churches as a *cantoria* or singing gallery
Banca the officers of a *scuola*, who served one-year terms. In a Scuola Grande they consisted of a Guardian Grande, Vicario, Guardian da Matin, Scrivan and twelve Degani. In a *scuola piccola* the Banca consisted of a Gastaldo, Vicario and two or more Compagni (companions) called Bancali (usually including a *masser* and a *scrivan*)
battuti members of a confraternity who practise the discipline, i.e. flagellate themselves
bottega (*botteghe*, pl.) a retail shop
broglio the Venetian nick-name for the Piazzetta, the area between the Ducal Palace and the present Biblioteca Marciana, where lobbying for state office took place and political deals were made
Bucintoro the ceremonial barge of the Doge
calle a narrow alley or street in Venice
campo a Venetian piazza. In Venice, only the area in front of the Basilica of San Marco was called a piazza
cartellino, cartello a card or label, typically bearing the artist's name or date, painted into a painting
cavaliere a knight
Chapter General the general assembly or legislative branch of a *scuola*, generally consisting of a quorum of thirty to fifty members, who elected the officers and voted on rules, procedures, major expenditures and allocation of charitable distributions
a cornu epistolae the side of the church from which the Epistle is read, i.e. the right side as one faces the altar
a cornu evangelii the side of the church from which the Gospel is read, i.e. the left side as one faces the altar
cortina a curtain that covers a *pala*
Degano (Degani pl.) a deacon, of which there were twelve on the Banca of a Scuola Grande, two from each of the six *sestieri* of the city, who provided a link between the Scuola administration and the brothers who lived in their respective districts – visiting the sick, reporting deaths, arranging burials, attending masses for the dead and investigating the reputations of girls proposed for dowry grants
doppiere a double candlestick, carried in processions
expectativa see *spettativa*
fondaco a headquarters for foreign merchants in Venice
fondamenta a street adjacent to the water's edge
Gastaldo the chief executive officer of a *scuola piccola*, with duties similar to the Guardian Grande of a Scuola Grande
garzone an assistant to a journeyman artist
Guardian da Matin the chief financial officer and supervisor of processions and other ceremonies in a Scuola Grande
Guardian Grande the chief executive officer of a Scuola Grande, who chaired meetings of the Banca, introduced proposals to the Chapter General, and was responsible for the day-to-day governing of the confraternity
incunabulum a book printed in the fifteenth or early sixteenth century
maniera greca in the Greek manner, denoting a Byzantine artistic style
mappamondo a map of the world
Mariegola a book containing the foundation statutes, amendments and rules of a *scuola*
masser (massaro) a treasurer or bookkeeper of fiscal accounts of a *scuola*
modello a preliminary drawing or cartoon for a painting
nazionale a *scuola* whose membership was limited to a particular national group: Dalmatians, Albanians, Greeks, Florentines, Germans, Milanese
onza (*onze*, pl.) an ounce, about twenty-four grams in fifteenth/sixteenth-century Venice
pala an altarpiece
penello a banner or processional standard
pescheria the fish market in Venice
piano nobile the main living-floor of an Italian palace, usually the next floor above the *pianterreno* (called the second floor in the United States and the first floor in most European countries)
pianterreno the ground floor of a building
portego a portico, usually a colonnaded porch attached to the front of a building
proto the supervising architect in charge of the construction or maintenance of a building
quadri riportati easel paintings in normal perspective that have been inserted into a ceiling decoration
relazione a report to the Venetian Senate from an ambassador or secretary on a diplomatic mission
rio a Venetian canal
riva a waterside street in Venice
sala capitolare the chapter hall in a *scuola*, used for meetings of the general membership or of the chapter
sansaria (sanseria) a sinecure, entitling an individual to receive a lifetime income from a brokerage (from a total of thirty)

at the Fondaco dei Tedeschi, for which he was expected to perform certain services to the state

Scrivan the keeper of the records of a *scuola*, who recorded the minutes and kept the membership lists up to date

secretario (segretario) in Venice, a high-ranking bureaucrat of non-patrician rank

Serenissima 'the most serene', a term denoting the Republic of Venice

Serrata the closure of the Great Council of Venice in 1297 and the formation of a hereditary aristocracy

sestiere one of the six topographical sections of Venice: Cannaregio, Castello, San Marco, Dorsoduro, San Polo, Santa Croce

ship's-keel ceiling a wooden ceiling constructed like the keel of an overturned ship, used in churches and public halls in north-eastern Italy

soffitto alla veneziana a Venetian decorated ceiling, typically composed of gilded wood compartments containing paintings or ornamental elements

spettativa the promise or expectation of a sansaria, normally granted in turn when one became available through revocation or through the death of a person who held one

spolveri charcoal dust, visible in infrared reflectographs, remaining from a preliminary sketch made under the painted surface of a painting

stato da mar Venetian territories in the east, particularly the Aegean

Terraferma Venetian territories on the mainland of Italy, including Bergamo, Brescia, Verona, Vicenza, Padua and Treviso in the late fifteenth century

tondo a round window or decorative panel

trifora three-mullioned window

trionfo, (*trionfi* pl.) in Venice, one of the Doge's 'trophies' or triumphal insignia, granted to him by the Pope in 1177 and thenceforth carried in processions

veduta a painted view, typically a cityscape

viaggiatore a voyager, i.e. a Venetian sea-faring merchant or a diplomatic envoy

Vicario an administrative assistant and occasional substitute for the Guardian Grande or Gastaldo of a *scuola*

telero, (*teleri* pl.) a painting on canvas in Venice

zonta (aggiunta) since 1521, by mandate of the Council of Ten, a body of twelve men who were elected yearly to sit with the Banca of a Scuola Grande when important business was transacted.

PHOTOGRAPHIC ACKNOWLEDGEMENTS

COLOR PLATES:

New York, Art Resource. Scala: II, III, XI, XII–XV, XVIII, XX, XXII–XXVIII, XXX, XXXIV–XXXVIII, XL, XLI, XLIII

Paris, Réunion des Musées Nationaux: XXXI

Venice, Osvaldo Böhm: XII, XIX

Venice, Cameraphoto: I, XXIX

Venice, Edizioni Storti: XVI, XVII, XXI, XXXIX, XLII

Venice, Museo Civico Correr: V–VIII

Washington, D.C., Dumbarton Oaks. Courtesy of The Byzantine Collection, Trustees of Harvard University: IV

BLACK AND WHITE PLATES:

Berlin (West), Staatliche Museen Preussischer Kulturbesitz. Skulpturengalerie: 9; Gemaldegalerie: 63, 118

Chatsworth, Devonshire Collection. Reproduced by permission of the Chatsworth Settlement Trustees: 119

Florence, Biblioteca Medicea Laurenziana: 99

London, British Museum. Reproduced by courtesy of the Trustees: 19, 25, 55, 66, 68, 69a–b, 85, 116

London, The National Gallery. Reproduced by courtesy of the Trustees: 2, 48

Madrid, Museo del Prado: 72

New York, Art Resource. Alinari: 1, 36, 44, 54, 64, 65, 70, 76, 90, 104, 105, 109, 112, 115, 117, 121, 122, 125, 126, 131, 143, 144, 145; Anderson: 30, 45, 46, 51, 52, 71, 107, 111, 113, 123, 142

New York, courtesy of The Frick Collection: 73

Paris, Réunion des Musées Nationaux: 21, 22, 49, 50, 53, 56, 61, 62, 67, 100, 132

Princeton, The Art Museum, Princeton University, Gift of Frank Jewelt Mather, Jr: 5, 7

Sacramento, Crocker Art Museum: 41, 42

Vaduz, Collection of the Prince of Liechtenstein: 120

Venice, Archivio di Stato: 27

Venice, Biblioteca Nazionale Marciana: 3, 6, 10, 141

Venice, Osvaldo Böhm: 8, 11, 13, 16, 18, 28, 47, 57, 58, 59, 60, 74, 75, 77, 83, 84, 86, 87, 91, 92, 108, 110, 114, 124, 133, 134, 135, 136, 137, 138

Venice, Fondazione Giorgio Cini: 4, 20

Venice, Museo Civico Correr: 12, 24, 31, 32, 33, 34, 35, 37, 38, 40, 78, 79, 88, 93, 94, 95, 96, 97, 98, 101, 102, 103, 106

Venice, Soprintendenza ai Beni Artistici e Storici di Venezia: 23, 39, 80, 81, 82

Venice, Soprintendenza per i Beni Ambientali e Architettonici di Venezia: 43

Washington, D.C., Photographic Archives, National Gallery of Art: 14, 15, 17, 26

Photographs not listed were furnished by the author.

The reconstruction drawings in the Catalogue were made by Voyislav Ristic and Simone Travisano of Mostoller and Travisano, Architects, Princeton, New Jersey.

Revised portions of my article, 'Painting and History in Renaissance Venice', *Art History* 7 (1984): pp. 263–94, appear in Chapters 5 and 6 with the permission of the publisher, Routledge and Kegan Paul.

1

Introduction: La Vera Historia

Few present-day visitors to Venice leave the city without falling under the spell of the paintings of Vittore Carpaccio. More than four hundred years after his death, the late twentieth century has appropriated him as its own. Reproductions of his works, or parts of them, can be had on calendars and notebook covers, as well as on the ubiquitous 'fine art' postcards. His color, his subject matter of ceremonial and popular life, his tapestry-like density of design all appeal to our notion of the culture of Venice as so many tableaux in an unfolding pageant. It hardly occurs to us to wonder whether his paintings may have had a serious narrative purpose when they were made. What we tend to prize most now in his works is their apparently factual replication of the splendid processions, the colorful assemblies and the many-faceted mosaic of persons and urban circumstance that made up the life of the Renaissance city.

Since the nineteenth century, travelers of a literary bent who have tried to characterize the appeal of such art have tended to emphasize the artist's non-discriminating 'innocent eye'. John Ruskin, who rediscovered Carpaccio after centuries of critical indifference, pronounced that the artist was

> never to be thought of as a responsible person, but only as a kind of magic mirror which flashes back instantly whatever it sees beautifully arranged, but yet will flash back commonplace things often as faithfully as others... a subject under Carpaccio's hand is always just as it would or might have occurred in nature; and among a myriad of trivial incidents, you are left, by your own sense and sympathy, to discover the vital one.[1]

Nearly all of Carpaccio's narrative paintings were made for the religious confraternities that Venetians called *scuole*, and hence they depict religious subject matter. Few of these works remain in their original settings. In Venice they can be found most easily in the Accademia Galleries: the nine canvases of the *Life of St. Ursula* made for the *scuola* of the same name, and one painting in the cycle of nine or ten canvases depicting the *Miracles of the True Cross*, originally made for the Scuola Grande di San Giovanni Evangelista. But one *scuola* does survive today as a corporate entity – the Scuola di San Giorgio degli Schiavoni – and here the nine canvases of Carpaccio that line the walls of the oratory on the ground floor give us some sense of the original effect of such works [Plate 1]. Even here, it should be noted, they have been transplanted from their original location.

To Ruskin, Carpaccio's paintings were essentially – if naively – pious. Modern writers deny him even this. In the words of Pietro Zampetti, writing of the *Healing of the Possessed Man* in the True Cross cycle of the Scuola Grande di San Giovanni Evangelista, 'the religious event ends up appearing like a pretext; or perhaps rather as passing unobserved among so very many occasions of life...'[2] And Jan Lauts adds: 'the actual subject of the narrative...takes second place; what captivates the eye immediately and remains indelibly impressed upon the memory is the view of Venice itself...'[3] Such observations reveal the modern consensus. In his painting, Carpaccio is said to have subordinated the goal of religious story-telling to other concerns: to glorify the city of Venice; to delight the viewer with extravagant and irrelevant detail; to record life as it happened, without editorial intervention [Color Plate XXII].

Carpaccio is not alone in receiving such assessments. For paintings by other artists who participated in the *True Cross* cycle – Gentile Bellini, Giovanni Mansueti and Lazzaro Bastiani – testify to a common narrative mode that embraced a broad range of talents and individual styles and yet called forth similar responses to the task of pictorial narrative construction. Few uninitiated observers of Gentile Bellini's *Procession in the Piazza San Marco* would be aware that it, too, was ostensibly intended to commemorate a supernatural event rather than a civic ceremony [Color Plate XVIII]. In the same way, in Mansueti's *Healing of the Daughter of Ser Benvegnudo of San Polo* [Plate 90], the ambient is so richly – even so verbosely – elaborated and is populated so generously with a secondary cast of characters that it obscures the miraculous healing embedded in it. Here again, the virtuoso display of detailed description and the portrayal of contemporary figures appear to be ends in themselves.

Three general views emerge from this brief look at the True Cross cycle. First, again, the images are regarded more as records than as artistic inventions, for they seem simply to present scenes of unedited 'life as it happens'. Second, religious events are dismissed as mere pretexts for representing secular life. Third, we have pictorial narratives that appear to fall short in what we might expect to be their primary purpose: to tell a story.

Although such observations may appear obvious, they might have seemed strange to a late Quattrocento Venetian. He knew that his life was not quite like the triumphant narratives of the True Cross canvases. He was certain of the religious character of the paintings and even regarded their commissioning as a pious act, in the same category as giving to the poor or lighting a candle for the soul of a loved one. And to him such a work was nothing less than an *istoria*: it was a document of silent history brought into his visual world by the artist. It is the purpose of this book to address these issues, recapturing some sense of what these paintings meant to viewers in their own time: why they were painted, how they were composed and what they signified.

The exercise is no idle one. Its implications go far beyond the True Cross cycle, for the works cited were themselves representative of a wider phenomenon. At least ten such programs of painted *istorie* with similar formal qualities, of which seven survive in good part, can be documented in the city during a fifty-year period beginning in the 1470s. Each of these was the product of corporate patronage, commissioned by governmental bodies or by the *scuole*. Each, therefore, reflected the will of a collective group of individuals and had been displayed to address a yet wider circle of viewers. Taken together they stood at the heart of Venetian public taste in those decades. Their popularity raises yet another question: what was the special appeal of this type of narrative representation – monumental paintings on canvas – at this particular time?

The answers to these issues are of interest because of what we have come to know about the central role of narrative in a society. It would not be too great an exaggeration to suggest that narratives are what keep societies sane. Even when masquerading as entertainments – fables, romances, secular dramas, 'naive' paintings – they function as mediating devices that help people to deal with the indeterminacies and insufficiencies of the real world. They are not 'magic mirrors' of reality. Real events are untidy and incomplete in comparison to the stories that we tell (or paint) about them. Narrative forms can make ambiguities tolerable, provide linkages and give structure to amorphous happenings. To confer coherence, wholeness, closure, and – perhaps most importantly – moral significance on the events that clutter our imperfect world, it is essential to narrate. Thus, narrative space – and this includes the most meticulously rendered painting of a historical event – is never filled with a simple replication of the real world; it always involves editing and selection. It mediates between life as it happens and as we wish to see it, for good or for ill.[4]

That such a mediation seems to us credible and real is often due to the note of authentication conveyed to us by the intervening narrator as eyewitness or self-proclaimed authority. Several of the canvases of the True Cross cycle are inscribed by the artists themselves with affirmations of their own devotion

1. View of interior, Scuola di San Giorgio degli Schiavoni, Venice

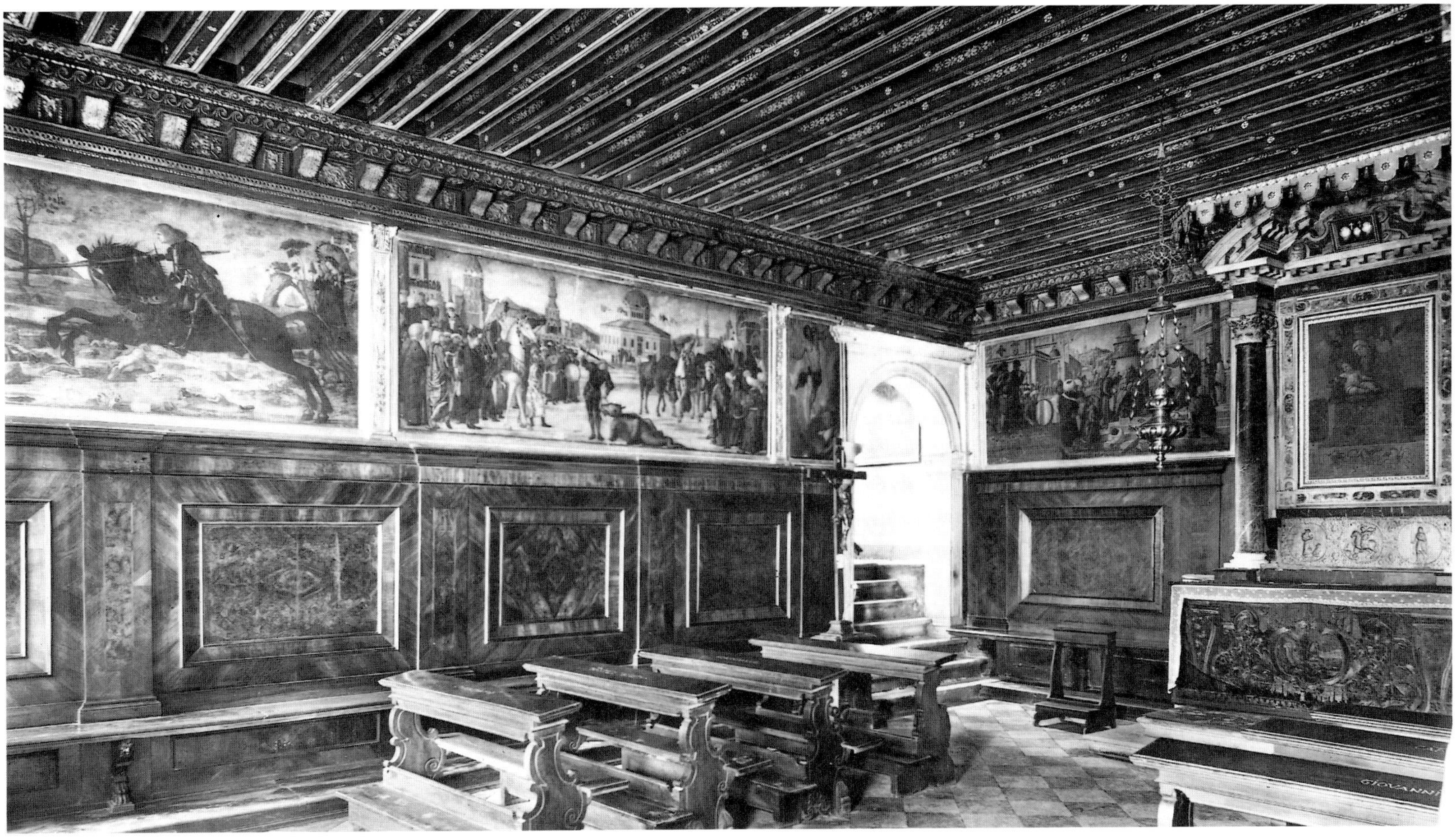

or even (in the case of Mansueti) their belief in the depicted event.[5] Similarly, a notary in the 1490s writing yet another redaction of a familiar episode of Venetian history, thus attests: 'this is *la vera historia*' – 'the true history': this is how it really happened.[6] Furthermore, pictorial narrative looks forward as well as backward. It not only creates the historical record; it also provides scripts for future action.[7]

As recently as the nineteenth century it was still possible for Pompeo Molmenti to write:

> Carpaccio with his brush was the most truthful chronicler of a people living in the full meridian of their glory, and some of his pictures illustrate in a marvellous manner those splendid ceremonies the fame of which remains, though in less lifelike and telling fashion, in ancient records at the Archives.[8]

But the archives have come to tell a different story. What we now know of Venice during this period makes us aware that its glorious aspect – the impression of 'a people living in the full meridian of their glory' – had its more anxious side. We may, therefore, question whether or not the tranquil *istorie* were even intended to reflect Venetian life as it truly was. The reverse may well have been the case: that they were intended to create an image of life as it should have been. To understand the original appeal of such images, we will have to look beyond their irresistible attractiveness and deceptive accessibility so as to take seriously the circumstances of the patrons, the painters and their viewers.

Before outlining the approach that will be followed in this reassessment of Ruskin's 'magic mirror', I would like to make clear the general scope of the study and to define the terms that will be used. My first decision has been to engulf Carpaccio within a school. The main contours of our inquiry will be defined by the activity of that group of artists which Jacob Burckhardt termed 'the second generation of Venetian painters'[9] – primarily Gentile Bellini and Lazzaro Bastiani – and the one that overlapped and followed it, most notably Carpaccio, but also Mansueti and others. Thus we will be focusing on a period that extended from approximately 1470 to 1530. In order to see it in context, however, it will also be necessary to look back to the visual narrative tradition that preceded it in Venice. The key figure in this tradition is Jacopo Bellini. As the foremost representative of the 'first generation', he also will receive considerable attention.

Secondly, allowing that art-historical labels are often misleading and are difficult to detach once affixed, we will refer to the common pictorial approach that binds these artists together as an 'eyewitness style'. The term is intended to embrace at the same time the more lyrical approach (and the stylistic development) of Carpaccio and the inventorial concerns of the others. Its appropriateness will become clearer in the course of the book. It is difficult to assess Giovanni Bellini's precise relationship to the group, since virtually all of his narrative paintings are now lost. Primarily through default, he will thus play only an incidental role in our inquiry. Similarly, Titian is peripheral to the central concerns of the study. Even though he was active during a good part of the period and introduced a competing narrative mode in the Scuola del Santo in Padua in 1511, the momentum of the eyewitness style was so great that the painters in the Venetian *scuole* paid him little heed. Indeed, when Titian painted the *Presentation of the Virgin* in the 1530s, his first and only wall painting for a

Venetian *scuola* [Plate 145], he conformed in a number of respects to the compositional habits of the eyewitness painters.[10]

Third, the term 'narrative mode' will refer primarily to the formal strategies which the artists employed to construct an *istoria*. It includes the construction of setting, the disposition of the actors, and the epitomizing of plot or narrative action. Like style, it can be assigned to individual artists and paintings as well as to broader groupings, for the narrative mode may vary from artist to artist and from subject to subject.[11]

Finally, although a pictorial narrative may be defined in several ways, here we will conform to Venetian terminology of the period. Any painting called an *istoria* – whether or not it contained sequential actions or was part of a larger cycle of several works – will be regarded as a true and proper narrative representation.[12]

The considerations outlined here will determine the form of this book, which will proceed through three levels of inquiry. The first section concentrates on the circumstances of patronage. In Chapter 2 we will identify the patrons of the *istoria* and look at the situation in which they found themselves at the end of the Quattrocento. The tradition of patronage for narrative paintings in Venice prior to the Great Council Hall campaign of 1474 will be discussed in Chapter 3. We will meet the eyewitness artists in Chapter 4 as they receive their commissions from the corporate groups of the city.

In the second section we will examine aspects of the visual culture which engendered certain expectations in the patrons and imposed certain restraints upon the artists. Chapter 5 will explore the intentions of the patrons as they were determined by the Venetian notion of the painted *istoria* as a visual document. In Chapter 6 we will consider affinities between pictorial narrative and dominant forms of history-writing in Venice during this period. The formal antecedents to the eyewitness style, as exemplified in the work of Jacopo Bellini, will provide the focus for Chapter 7. In Chapter 8, we will look at other eyewitnesses in Venetian society: travelers whose verbal accounts provide clues to perceptual habits and criteria of descriptive authenticity.

The first two sections will provide the foundation for the third, in which we will subject the *istoria* itself to closer scrutiny. Focussing on the formal strategies that artists employed, we will explore the ways in which patronage and artistic creativity came together in a series of solutions to fulfill the requirements of a successful painted history. Each chapter will deal with a different aspect of narrative representation. In Chapter 9 we will return to the True Cross cycle and discover how Venetian artists dealt with events that took place within a familiar and observable setting. In Chapter 10 we will consider how history could be constructed according to ceremonial paradigms. In Chapter 11 we will study the ways in which the eyewitness artists invented an unfamiliar setting for their painted histories and the developing concept of *fantasia* in narrative art. The patrons will return to the fore in Chapter 12, when we consider their appearance in the group portraits that were prominent in many of the *istorie*. As a coda to the study of the eyewitness style, the Epilogue will suggest some reasons for its demise.

A catalogue of narrative cycles documented in Venice prior to c. 1530 is placed at the end of the book. Its purposes are twofold: to provide a convenient reference to the works in their original programmatic contexts, with transcriptions of the original documents or sources referring to them; and to provide a chronological record of the development of monumental pictorial narrative in late medieval and early Renaissance Venice.

It is only against this wider background, I believe, that the paintings of Carpaccio which still charm us, as well as those of his contemporaries and co-workers whose attractions may become obvious only upon longer acquaintance, can be understood and viewed as appreciatively by a modern observer as they were by those who first saw their glowing and circumstantial canvases.

Part One

CIRCUMSTANCES

2

The Situation

Canon Pietro Casola, a Milanese priest attended mass in the Basilica of San Marco on the feast of Corpus Domini in 1495. He was particularly struck by the quality of harmony and order that informed the event. To his mind, it was extraordinary even for a religious celebration. Although the church was packed,

> a great silence was maintained – more than I have ever observed on similar occasions – even in seating so many Venetian gentlemen; every sound could be heard. One single person appeared to me to direct everything, and he was obeyed by every man without a protest. This filled me with astonishment, because I had never seen such perfect obedience at similar spectacles elsewhere.[1]

In the same year the sophisticated French diplomat, Philippe de Commynes, arrived in Venice and exclaimed: 'It is the most triumphant city that I have ever seen.'[2] We are in the world of Gentile Bellini's *Procession*: resplendent, but ordered, and eminently civic. To a Venetian, a visible show of concord and a triumphant aspect would not have been occasions for comment, for he took for granted the source: the Republic's divine foundation and destiny; its perfect constitution; its pious, dutiful and self-effacing citizens. Theirs was a *serenissima repubblica*. As the English knight Sir Richard Guylforde wrote in 1506:

> the rychesse, the sumptuous buyldynge, the relygyous houses, and the stablysshynge of their justyces and councylles with all other thyng^s y^t maketh a cytie glorious, surmonteth in Venyse above all places y^t ever I sawe.[3]

This is Venice as Carpaccio and Gentile Bellini plainly wished it to be seen.

The *Lion of St. Mark*, painted by Carpaccio for a government office in 1516, exemplifies the way in which Venetians thought of their republic [Color Plate I]. Its interpretation is well known, but it bears repeating. The lion symbolizes the protection ensured the city by its patron saint, Mark the Evangelist. Although powerful, the beast makes his pacific intentions clear with the inscription on the book that he holds: 'PAX TIBI MARCE EVANGELISTA MEVS' [Peace Unto You, Mark, My Evangelist]. This was the salutation given to Mark by an angel many centuries earlier. It stood for the extended message that followed, in which God designated Venice as the saint's final resting-place. No matter that the Venetians had fabricated the episode only in the thirteenth century. It was still cited as proof of the city's holy predestination. Standing with his front paws on the land and his hind paws in the water, the lion further signifies Venice's dominion over the land and the sea. The sources of Venetian justice and prosperity can be seen in the background: to the left, the Ducal Palace, a building of government and law; to the right, the sea-going galleys that made Venice the *entrepôt* of Europe.[4]

These features make up the basic contours of the well-known 'myth of Venice'. But as historians in recent years have been careful to point out, the reality was somewhat different.[5] The distinction is important, for it necessary to know something of both sides – myth and reality – in order to understand the compelling attractiveness of large-scale, public, visual narrative representation in this period. Indeed, it is in the disjunction between ideal and real perceptions of the same society or situation that narratives, whether written or visual, may find their most powerful appeal. The lack of a precise fit between the two views leaves a space which must be traversed by interpretative vehicles such as rituals, legends, chronicles and even diaries.[6] Among these devices, visual images are particularly effective in performing this act of mediation, since their non-verbal nature often allows for more flexibility, with multiple readings over time. So let us move on to look at a few concrete examples of the split between myth and reality, as experienced by the patrons of pictorial narrative in this period.

A vanishing peace

During the last decade of the Quattrocento the external political situation was uncertain, equivocal and far from serene. Venice had long been engaged in a series of delicate diplomatic manoeuvers, where defeats were masked as victories, and allies one year were enemies the next.[7] On the eastern front, the loss of Negroponte to the Turks in 1470 had profoundly shaken Venetian self-confidence in the ability of the Republic to control the Aegean Sea. The diarist Domenico Malipiero wrote of the news:

> it seems that these letters have put everyone in great terror, and it was suspected that following the victory of the Turk, the whole state would be lost.[8]

In 1474 he added:

> The ministers of the Signoria in the Levant very much fear the result of the war because of the greatness of the Turk and the small reputation of our soldiers and our government.[9]

It may not be any coincidence that this was the year in which it was felt necessary to replace the *Story of Alexander III*, a cycle of history paintings that had adorned the walls of the Great Council Hall of the Ducal Palace since the beginning of the century. They commemorated the notable events of the year 1177, when the Venetian Doge played a crucial mediating role between Pope Alexander III and the Emperor Frederick Barbarossa.[10] Writing about the paintings in the 1490s, Marin Sanudo, the tireless chronicler of Venetian affairs, had no doubts about their topical relevance to his own troubled times:

> And he [Pope Alexander III] returned to his seat in Rome with the help of the Venetians, who have always fought for the faith of Christ against all comers – especially Turks – who had prolonged the war such a long time...[11]

We will return to the paintings of the Great Council Hall in the next chapter. For the moment, we may simply observe that Sanudo's remarks reveal the resilient power of a painted *istoria* depicting events from three hundred years earlier to provide appropriate metaphors for viewers of a later day.

The year 1479 brought a peace treaty with Sultan Mehmed II, who ruled the expanding Turkish empire from Constantinople [Plate 2]. It was hailed as a triumph, but again there is a disjunction between the jubilant public posture and the facts of the matter. In reality, the armistice bought a tenuous peace at the humiliating price of the permanent losses of Negroponte, Scutari and other long-secure territories in Venice's Aegean hegemony.[12] Even this costly detente was to fall apart in 1499 when the Sultan's son and successor, Bayezid II, mounted an offensive against the entire Adriatic coast and hit hard at Venetian strongholds. Malipiero wrote bitterly in his *Diarii*:

> We were in good order of artillery and of brave men; but the captains of the galleys and ships have been so much more poltroons and traitors...All the good men of this armada, of which there are many, cry and shout traitor at the *Capetanio* who did not have the spirit to do his duty...[13]

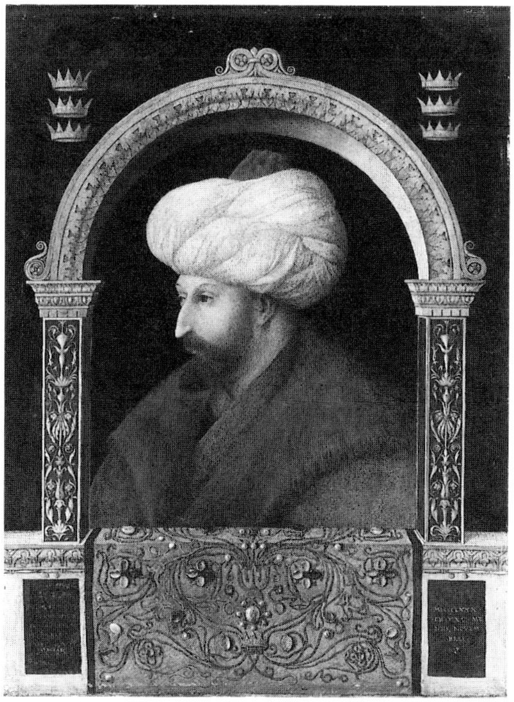

2. Gentile Bellini, *Portrait of Sultan Mehmed II* (London, National Gallery)

Venice's relations with Mamluk Egypt were becoming equally precarious, and in the course of ordinary statecraft enemies had to be treated as friends. In 1506 the Egyptian Sultan sent his Grand Dragoman, Taghri-Berdi, to Venice to negotiate a new commercial treaty. Although called 'most hostile...to our nation' in the Senate, the emissary was received into the city with full honors and entertained royally for nearly a year at Venetian expense.[14]

Whether in relation to the Ottomans or to the Mamluks, Venice still needed its ancient peace with the East, but this peace had largely vanished. As Alberto Tenenti puts it:

> The image of the *Serenissima* as Christianity's first line of defence, for so long mainly a convenient but empty publicity device for the use of western princes little inclined to support Venice's position in the East, was becoming a reality for Venice itself.[15]

Shifting alliances

The Republic was also pursuing a complicated diplomatic strategy with her Christian neighbors of the west. It was a time of constantly shifting alliances. At odds with the papacy in the War of Ferrara during the 1480s,[16] Venice became its ally in the Holy League in 1495, along with Spain, the Holy Roman Emperor Maximilian I and Milan, in the face of the French invasions led by Charles VIII.[17] But by 1499 Venice had again changed sides, joining the French against Milan in the Treaty of Blois.[18] Girolamo Priuli's observations on that occasion suggest the ambivalent and even fragile character of the statecraft of that period. The Venetians were surprised, he reported, when the French King, Louis XII, accepted all of their conditions; they concluded that Louis did so only to make war and take over Milan.

> Having learned this in Venice the Venetian Senate was not very much pleased, because they did not wish war at this time for any reason, doubting that Venice could support it even with great effort. [For] the city of Venice was very short of money. The whole thing having been concluded, they put the best face on it, hoping that the King of France would not come to wage war

> with Milan this year, because the Venetians more readily wished the Duke [of Milan] for their neighbor, even though he was a betrayer and most hostile to the Venetian state, than the King of France who was a friend of Venetians, knowing that he would be too powerful nearby, and the other was less powerful.[19]

In spite of such dangers, the Venetians concluded that the confederation was 'of great honor and glory to the Venetian State', noting with a certain satisfaction that it frightened the Duke of Milan and displeased the Florentines, 'and similarly all the rest of Italy'. Three days of feasting, fireworks and the ringing of bells were ordered for Venice itself, with the League to be published on the Feast of the Annunciation.[20]

That last decade of the Quattrocento, at once triumphant and treacherous, may be summed up by Priuli's reaction when a courier arrived in Venice in September 1499 and told of a victory over the Turkish armada at Porto Longo:

> Because of these words all the Venetian people ran to the Piazza, full of happiness, making the greatest celebrations, and the children, about 200 of them, ran through the Piazza with a banner shouting: Marco, Marco... But the letters having been opened, they did not find this news to be the truth... It is necessary to be cautious against wishing to believe so easily, because couriers carry the kiss in the mouth and the truth in the pocket.[21]

Such manoeuvers helped to create the climate in which the League of Cambrai was born in 1508. Four of Venice's powerful erstwhile friends (or enemies, depending on the time and place) – France, the Holy Roman Emperor, Spain and the Pope – joined together at that time to stop what they called Venice's ambition and imperialism in Italy. During the following year the Republic suffered through several dark months of military defeats, culminating in the Battle of Agnadello in May 1509. Losing Padua a few weeks later, Venice would not regain all the territories of the Terraferma lost in those months until 1516.[22]

The common good

Furthermore, internal tensions and contradictions, less visible, but potentially even more debilitating, lay close beneath the surface of Venetian society. If the physical cohesion of the Venetian empire was a problem, so too the social cohesion of the community faced new challenges. Before examining these challenges, we will look first at the institutions and values of the society that had earned it its reputation as a most serene republic. The genius of the ruling elites of the Republic is seen most powerfully in their successful promotion of a 'lifeboat mentality'. Every Venetian was expected to subordinate his or her own interests to the fragile man-made creation that was the city of Venice, surviving at God's pleasure in the middle of the sea.[23] The *sine qua non* of such a strategy, which gave it its coercive muscle, was the acceptance by each citizen that his personal fate was closely bound up with the common good.[24] What was taken for granted was the willing self-sacrifice of individuals of 'every quality and condition'. Heeding the same high call to patriotism and duty, they were expected to suppress individual ambition so as to ensure the harmonious functioning of the city's finely balanced administrative system.[25] The whole order hung together on this premise.

How the call to duty worked in practice may be observed in the fortuitous homecoming of the patrician Ambrogio Contarini. After a perilous state mission to Persia that lasted three years, and during which time he was given up for dead by family and friends, Contarini was finally on his way home to Venice in 1477. Yearning to reach *la terra sancta nostra* – our holy land – so that 'every day seemed to me a year', he detoured nonetheless, to the sanctuary of Monte Ortone in the hills south of Padua, to fulfill a vow made to a miraculous image of the Virgin. Again, entering the Canal of the Giudecca, he delayed his homecoming once more to fulfill a second vow at Santa Maria delle Grazie, a church on a tiny island near San Giorgio Maggiore housing another miraculous icon. As he sailed through the Canal, he met by chance his brother Agostino and two brothers-in-law, who then accompanied him to the church. But his home and family were still to wait. For it being Thursday, the Senate was in session, and, as Contarini observed, '. . . it seemed to me also my duty, before going home, to present myself to our illustrious signoria to make due reverence and also to report how I had carried out my commission.'[26] Contarini's contemporaries would not have questioned his order of priorities: duty to God and country clearly preceded any personal concerns.

Furthermore, the Republic's seemingly tranquil aspect and dutiful citizens – the envy of more turbulent polities like Florence – may be accounted for not only by its ideology, but also by two unique institutions: a social order that was based upon a large hereditary nobility and the *scuole* of the city which helped to mediate between the social groups who made up the hierarchy essential to that order. It is necessary to look at both to appreciate the situation in which Venetian patrons of the *istoria* found themselves in the last years of the Quattrocento.

The social order

Venetians of the late fifteenth century looked back to the *Serrata* of 1297 as the cornerstone of domestic peace and concord. At that time, their society had been shaped by law into a hierarchy of three estates. Participation in the Great Council – and thus any form of political activity – was limited to the patriciate, thenceforth a hereditary nobility. A good number of excluded families were equal in wealth and antiquity to those who were included in the Council, but they had been less active in government during that last critical decade of the thirteenth century. Although adjustments were made for another two decades, many of these old houses found themselves relegated permanently to a politically inferior estate.[27] They became simply citizens or *cittadini*, set apart in a separate middle order, as clearly distinguished from the larger group of *popolari* below them as they were from the *nobili* above. Citizens were further subdivided between those who were born in Venice (*cittadini originari*) and those who had obtained citizenship through a lengthy process of naturalization. In theory, any prospective *cittadino*, whether native-born or not, had to prove that neither he, nor his father or grandfather, had practised an *arte meccanica* or manual trade.[28]

Sanudo summed up the matter succinctly: 'There are three kinds of inhabitants: *zentilhomeni* – who govern the state and the Republic. . .; *cittadini*; and artisans or *populo menudo*.'[29] In the sixteenth century, it is estimated that the noble and citizen orders comprised, respectively, about 4 and 11 per cent of the population of the city, with a large mass of *popolari*, both native and foreign-

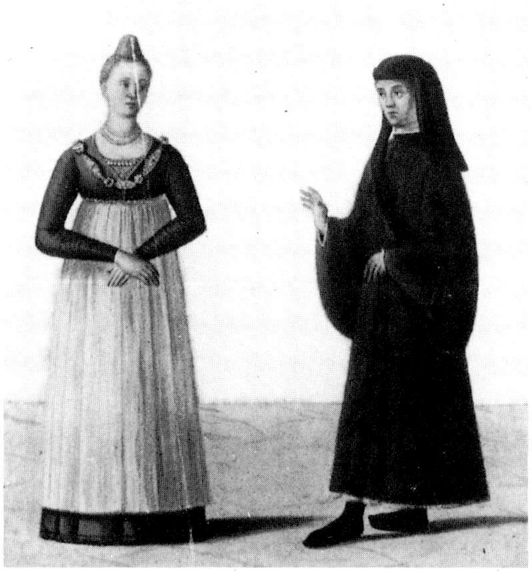

3. Pietro Baffo and Beatrix Freschi (Venice, Biblioteca Marciana: Cod. It. VII 165 [=8867], f. 6)

born, making up the remainder.[30] Although these groups are sometimes referred to as 'classes', the modern sense of the term is misleading and does not describe their composition and their dilemmas with sufficient accuracy. Venetians of the time often called them orders (*ordini*); or, following the historian Brian Pullan, we might call them estates or castes.

The hard legal edges that separated the orders were cushioned by areas of interaction or even of congruence. One major joining-point was in the marketplace. For, like patricians, most *cittadini* and many foreign residents earned their livelihood from mercantile activities.[31] A fiction of parity within the commercial sphere, embracing both patricians and commoners, was reinforced by a carefully maintained code of decorum. In a time when men looked closely at visible signs to determine another's status and condition, Sanudo made special note of the deliberately somber and unrevealing character of the merchant's dress:

> Gentlemen are not known from citizens by their apparel, because almost everyone goes dressed according to a [common] mode...long black robes to the ground with sleeves *a comedo*, black cap on the head, with a stole of black cloth...[32]

The *cittadino* merchant Piero Baffo is depicted in a family chronicle with his bride, Beatrix Freschi, the daughter of a prominent *cittadino* family who married him in 1476 [Plate 3]. He wears the old-fashioned headgear called a *cappuccio*, with the stole attached, and a toga that does not quite reach the ground. By the end of the century, togas were lengthened and Venetian men adopted the simpler *cappello*, wearing the stole (now detached) over their shoulder.[33]

Deportment was as important as dress. Sanudo's rival historian, Marcantonio Sabellico, made his own observations in the marketplace at the Rialto:

> Almost all the city comes together at this place morning and evening for their business, but the place being full of every manner of men, this presents an especially great marvel: that in such a crowd of men, one does not hear any voice, nor any din, no libels, no contentions, no injuries, no quarrels. Everyone speaks with a low voice, for clearly it is seen to be true that dictum that is said by many – that the correct mode of practising mercantile affairs has the need of few words.[34]

The soft voice, the measured speech, the controlled manner, the grave courtesy, the plain black toga: all were marks of the Venetian merchant which mediated and transcended legal divisions and tended to create a class of their own outside the hierarchical structure of the political and social order.[35]

This community of interest, generating outward from the nobility and based on like economic concerns, was reinforced within a second major arena of civic interaction by the special role allotted to the *cittadini* in government. From their ranks came the permanent salaried bureaucracy who provided continuity and stability in a state that was governed by 'noble amateurs', continuously rotating through the elective effices.[36] Given access to secret papers and, upon occasion, considerable authority in the execution of public policy, many Chancery notaries and secretaries thus participated to a substantial degree in affairs of state.[37] A notable exception to the patrician monopoly on real political power was found in the person of the Grand Chancellor. He was elected by the patricians from the *cittadini originari* to hold an office for life that was, in theory,

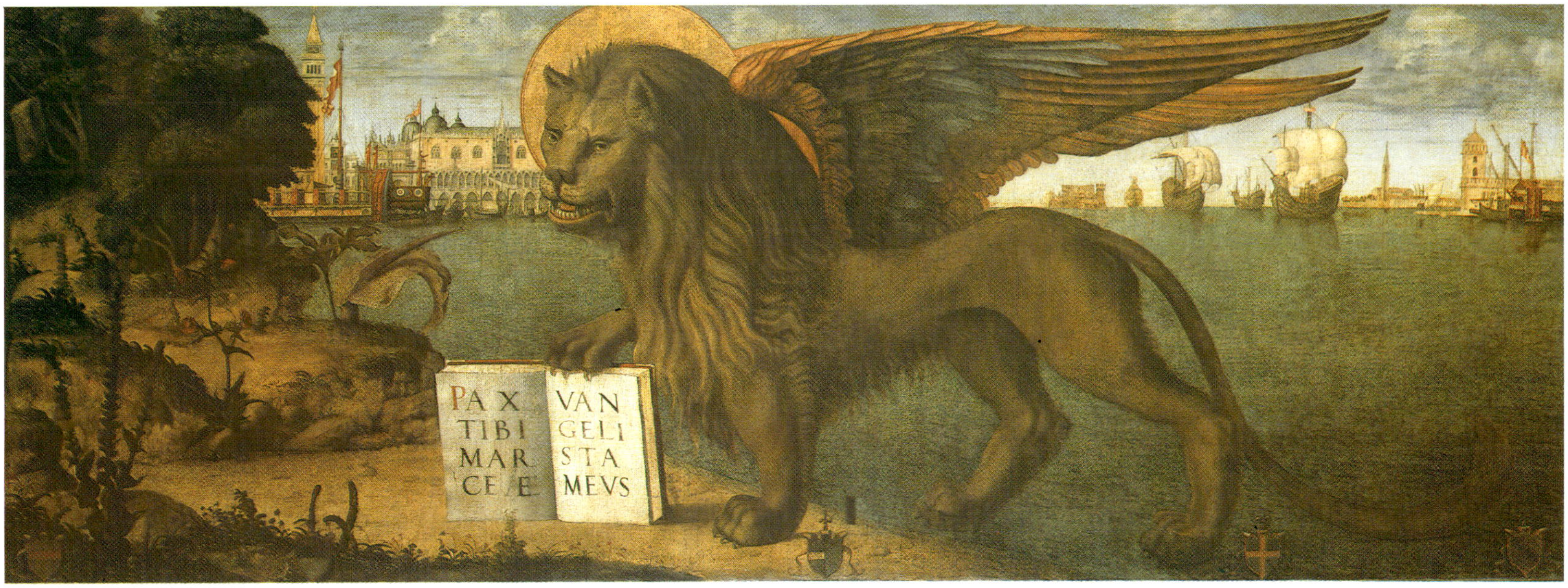

I. Carpaccio, *Lion of Saint Mark* (Venice, Ducal Palace)

second only to the Doge. Gasparo Contarini, a political theorist of the early sixteenth century, called him 'the prince of the common people'.[38]

Another opportunity for participation was to be found in the meeting-halls of the Venetian *scuole*. It was here in the lay confraternities that *cittadini*, *popolari* and even *stranieri* were given the opportunity to hold office and to engage in politics of a sort. The privilege was especially significant in the case of the Scuole Grandi. During the course of the fifteenth century, the *cittadini originari* were established exclusively as their ruling elites by government edict.[39] This move was later presented by Contarini as a wise concession on the part of the nobility, calculated to reduce the temptation of sedition by the disenfranchised, for

> such honours do the plebeians of eyther sort attaine unto in this commonwealth of ours, to the end that they should not altogether thinke themselves deprived of publike authority, and civil offices, but should also in some sort have their ambition satisfied, without having occasion either to hate or perturbe the estate of nobilitie...[40]

This role of the Scuole Grandi was a peculiar achievement of Venetian statecraft. It is essential to bear this in mind when we look at the paintings commissioned by them. Right down to the design of the halls in which these paintings were hung, the Grandi, and to a lesser degree the *scuole piccole*, were, in a sense, 'miniature commonwealths'.

Miniature commonwealths

As in other Italian cities of the later middle ages, Venetian confraternities were initially formed by men and women for purposes of mutual aid and devotion outside the institutional church. Typically, the groups adopted a patron saint, participated in collective prayer, visited the sick, accompanied the dead to the grave and shared in commemorative masses [Plates 4 and 5].[41] Some had an overtly penitential orientation and practiced group flagellation for the expiation

II (p. 16). Carpaccio, detail from the *Healing of the Possessed Man* (Color Plate XXII)

III (p. 17). Gentile Bellini, detail from the *Miracle at the Bridge of San Lorenzo* (Color Plate XX)

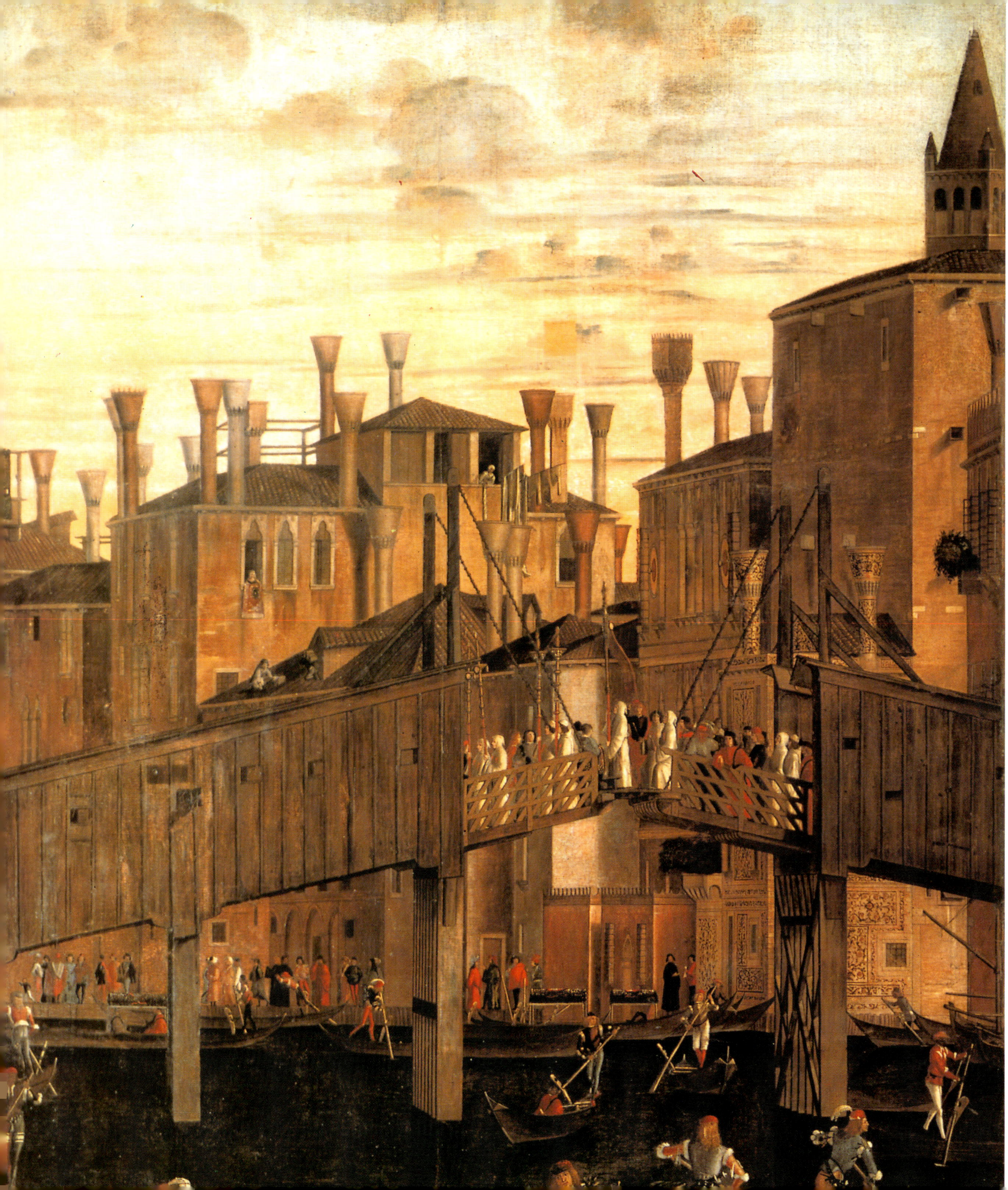

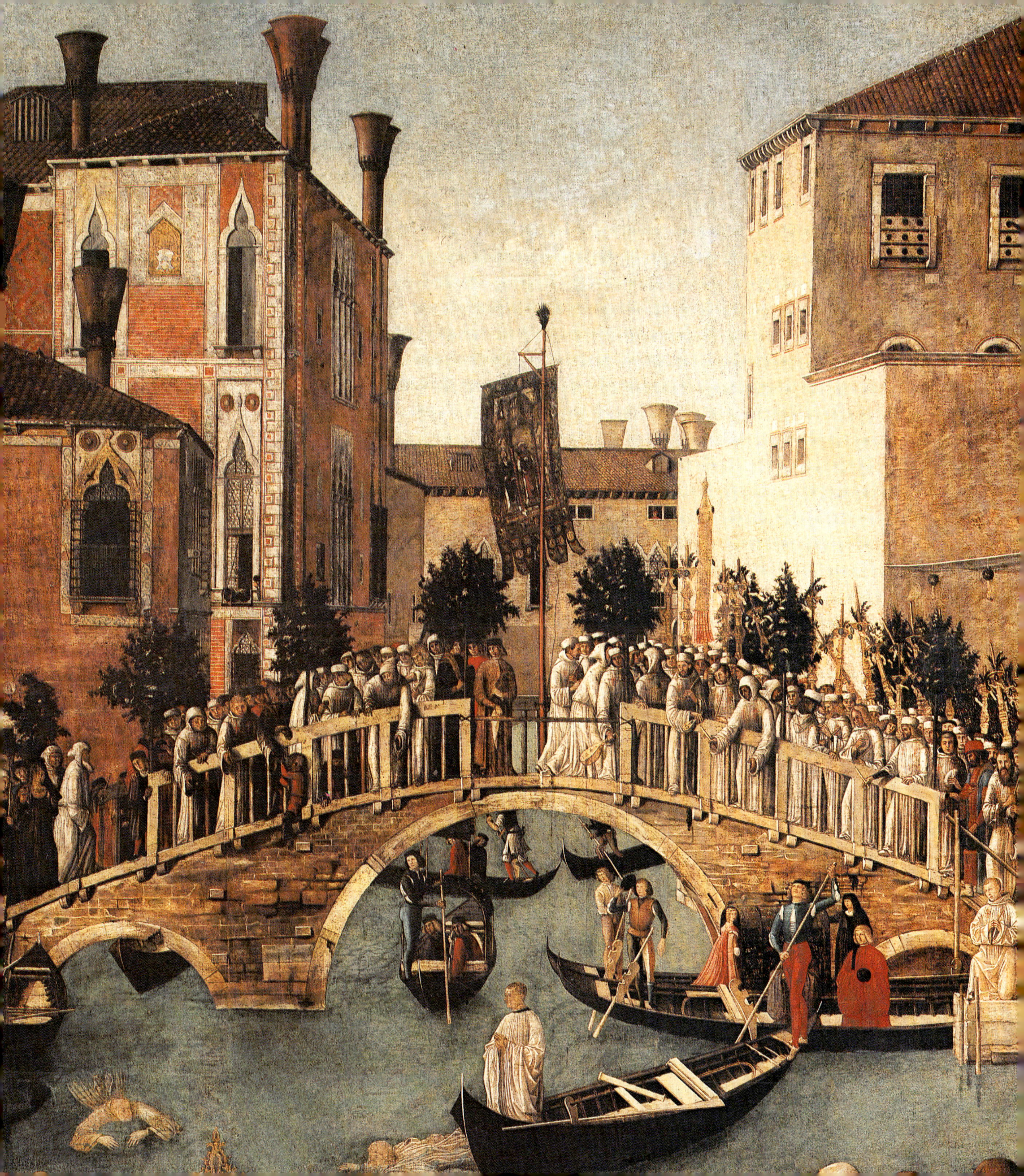

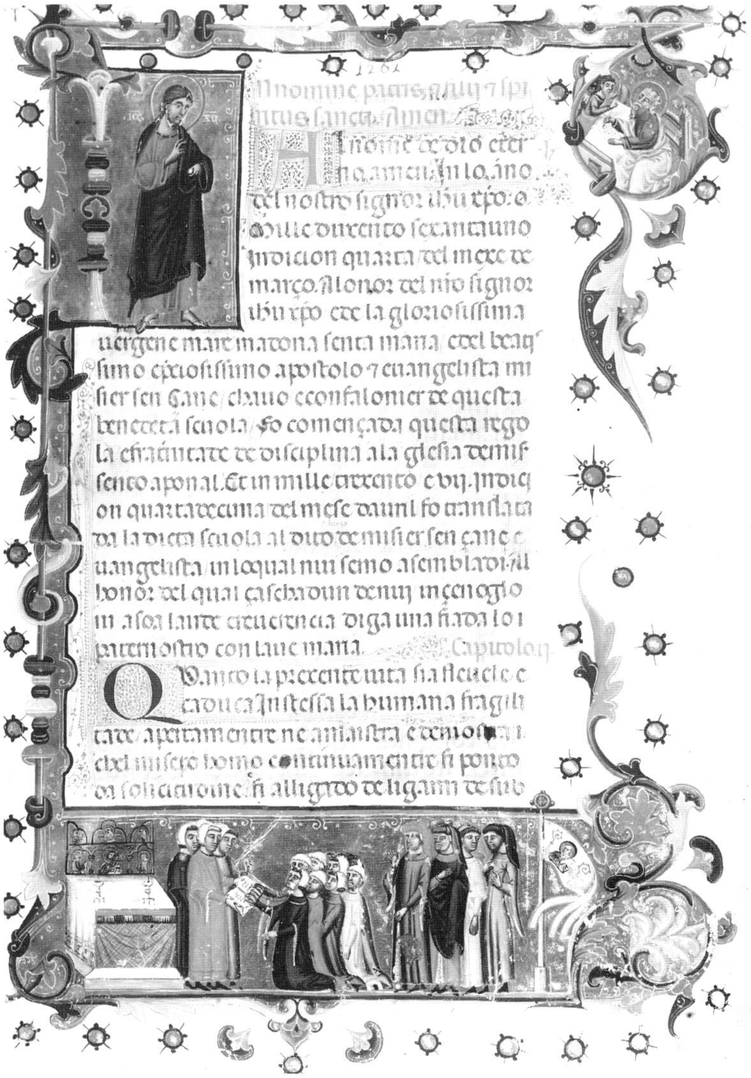

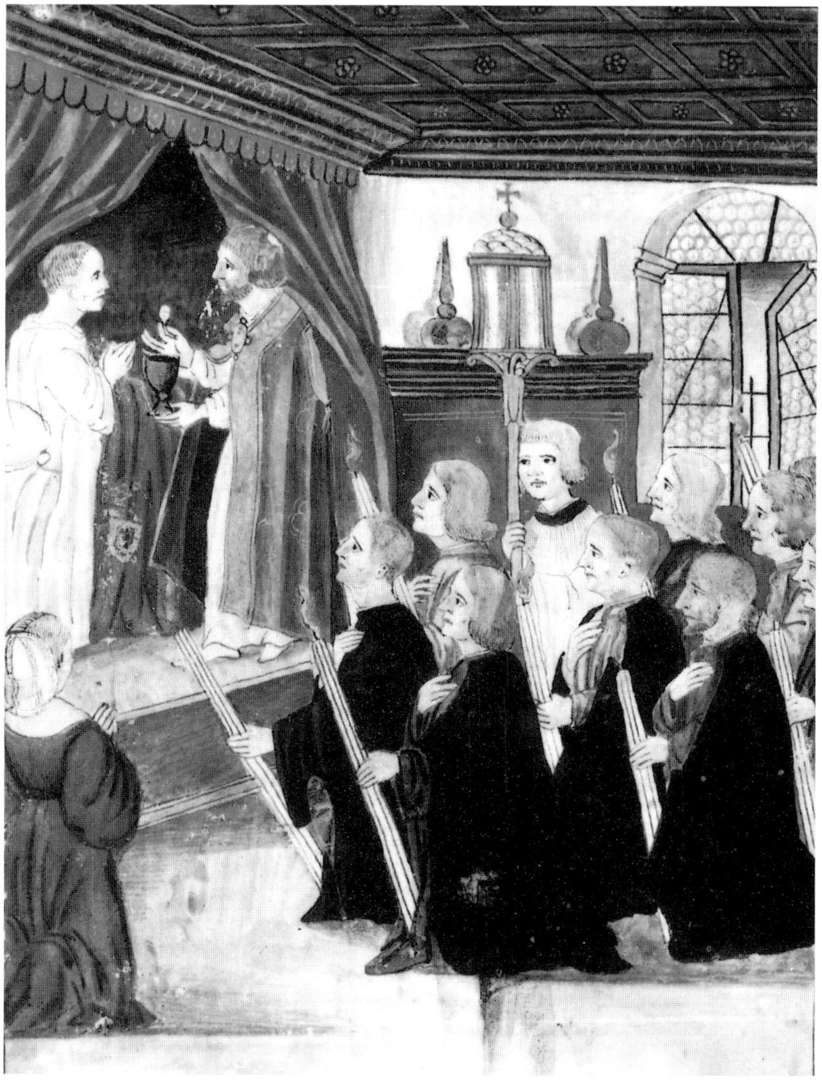

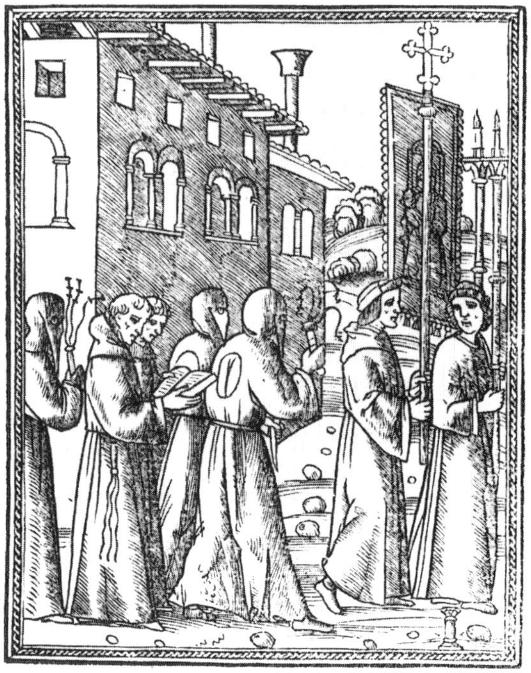

of their own sins as well as those of the group [Plate 6].[42] Over the years their financial resources grew, primarily through testamentary bequests, and they began to provide food, housing and medical care for their poorer members and to give dowries to their daughters. They often operated hospitals and the late-medieval equivalent of old-age homes.[43] What came to distinguish the Venetian *scuole* from their counterparts elsewhere in Italy was an additional civic role. Both in their numbers and in their close relationship with the state, they came to be regarded as a singular phenomenon, invariably remarked upon by visitors to the city.[44]

Overseeing the foundation of all the *scuole* since 1360, the Council of Ten came to intervene increasingly in their internal affairs. Protection by the state was linked to careful surveillance, with religious and political energies effectively channelled toward common civic goals.[45] Each *scuola* had an agenda of public processions, and its Mariegola – a bound volume in which foundation statutes, along with additional rules and amendments, were recorded – typically contained a provision like that of the Scuola di Sant'Orsola, wherein

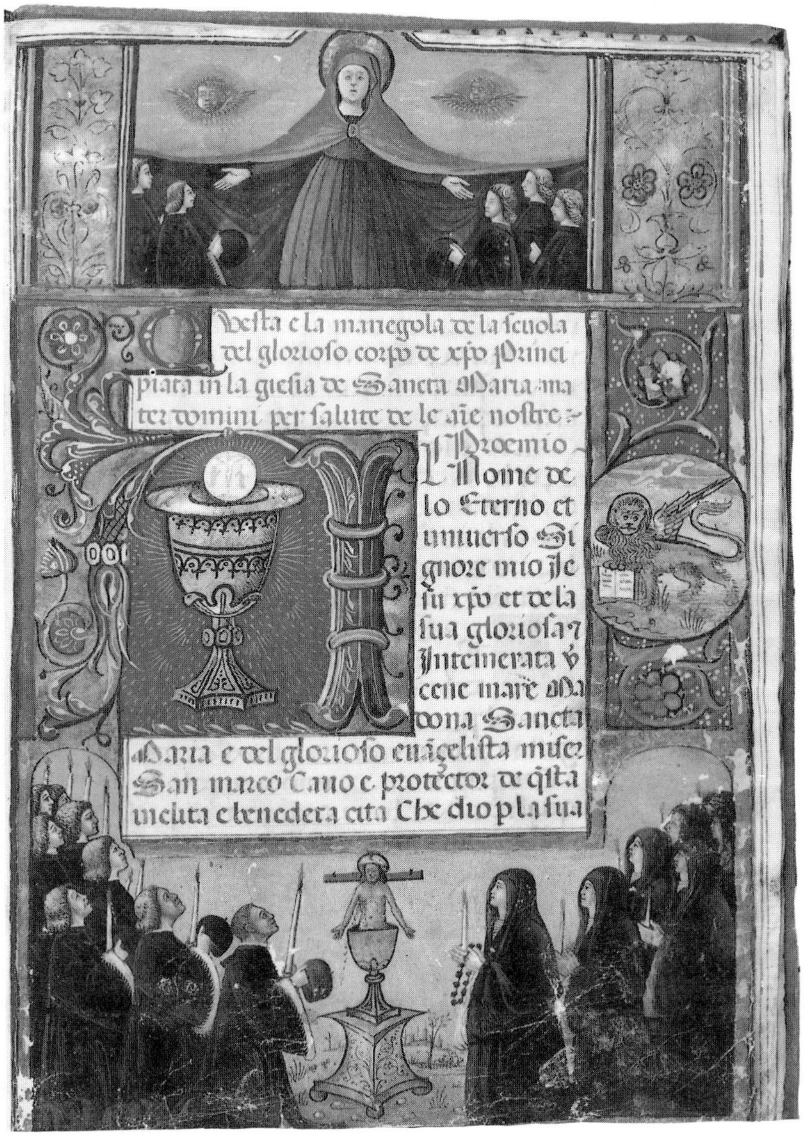

...any person of our scuola who would do or allow others to do anything that would be of injury, damage or contempt of *Miser lo Doxe* of Venice or of his council or of this blessed city, which was chosen by God the Father Omnipotent for the protection and sustenance of all the oppressed...would be denounced...to the doge and his council and would be expelled from the scuola in perpetuity.[46]

A manuscript illumination from the Mariegola of the Scuola del Corpo di Cristo that met at S. M. Mater Domini includes the Lion of St. Mark (in fact a political as much as a religious symbol) in the border of its first page, in a position opposite and nearly as prominent as that of the Holy Eucharist [Plate 7].

By 1500 there were more than two hundred *scuole piccole*, bound by similar rules, in addition to the five Scuole Grandi.[47] Their impact on the physical city was considerable. Francesco Scipione Fapanni, an amateur historian of the nineteenth century, looked around at the empty meeting-houses of once-flourishing *scuole* and saw them, somewhat romantically, as overspills of a religiosity so

4 (facing above left). Swearing in the new *confratelli*. Mariegola, Scuola di San Giovanni Evangelista (Venice, Fondazione Giorgio Cini)

5 (facing right). Visiting the sick. Mariegola, Scuola del Corpo di Cristo, S. M. Mater Domini, Venice, 1512, f. 14 (Princeton University Art Museum)

6 (facing below left). Flagellant procession. From *Triomphi, Sonetti, Canzone*, Venice, 1517, frontispiece (Venice, Biblioteca Marciana)

7 (above). Adoration of the Host. Mariegola, Scuola del Corpo di Cristo, S. M. Mater Domini, Venice, 1512, f. 3 (Princeton University Art Museum)

vigorous that it could not be contained within the walls of parish churches:

> For the most part, next to each of our churches, even attached to them, were one or more *scuole* of devotion, which invaded the free area that surrounded the ancient church – a curious appendage, as if the vastness of the temple would not be sufficient for the prayers and pious works of the good faithful.[48]

Indeed, a Venetian of the fifteenth century who sought some measure of religious and social solidarity through membership in a lay confraternity was allowed a range of options. Perhaps the major distinction was between the *scuole piccole* and the Scuole dei Battuti, the old flagellant confraternities of the city who are first named in state documents as the Scuole Grandi in 1467.[49] On the simplest level, the term reflected a difference in size. The Grandi were limited by law to a membership of five to six hundred each.[50] The *piccole*, by contrast, must rarely have exceeded two hundred members at one time and were usually considerably smaller.[51]

But just as important as size was the composition of the membership base. Although membership was confined to males, each Scuola Grande drew from the whole city and, in addition to patricians, encompassed every occupation and trade. A sampling of new members inscribed in the Mariegola of the Scuola Grande di San Giovanni Evangelista in 1482 yields a barber, a tailor, a fisherman, a book seller, a ship owner, a carpenter, a fruit vendor and merchants of silk, spices and objects of gold, with all six *sestieri* of the city represented.[52] Such a range was most probably no different for any other Scuola Grande.

By contrast, the *scuole piccole* generally included women, but their membership was sometimes restricted in terms of occupation or national origin. The recent immigrant, for example, would have been attracted by a *scuola* made up exclusively of members of a particular national group who lacked the benefits and protection of Venetian citizenship.[53] Patron saints or cults traditionally honored in the homeland also helped to maintain a sense of national identity and pride. Carpaccio painted *istorie* for two such *scuole*: the Scuola di San Giorgio degli Schiavoni, made up of Dalmatian sailors and immigrants, and the Scuola di Santa Maria degli Albanesi, filled at that time with poor refugees who had fled Scutari when the Turks took the city in 1479. The great majority of confraternities, however, were known simply as *scuole di devozione* or *scuole comuni*. They often had no specific membership requirements. Most accepted both sexes, as well as patricians, and in many cases the grouping would be determined by parish boundaries.[54] The Scuola di Sant' Orsola, probably Carpaccio's most illustrious patron, fell into this category.

There is evidence suggesting that many of the smaller *scuole* were patronized by one or more wealthy patrician families who acted as benefactors.[55] The situation was rather different in a Scuola Grande. The large cadre of patrician members in each, and their exclusion from Scuola office, tended to ensure by the weight of numbers and a balance of power that no single family would be able to exert undue influence upon the confraternity as a whole.

Apart from their size and their broadly based memberships, the Grandi also differed from the *piccole* in the prominent official role that they came to play in the ritual life of the city. This development stemmed in part from their origins as flagellant confraternities. What had begun as a form of personal atonement for oneself and one's *confratelli* soon became a means to expiate the sins of a whole community. The practice was not unusual in any Italian city of the time. What was unique to Venice, however, was the thorough incorporation of these penitential groups into the civic structure.[56]

To Jacopo d'Albizotto Guidi, a Florentine merchant who had immigrated to Venice, the marching *flagellanti* were a sign of the visible piety that helped set apart the Scuole dei Battuti from the *scuole comuni* as the 'other four *scuole* who are ordered by more nobility'. In 1442 he included their weekly processions in a long poem describing the city:

> Every Sunday not very far
> they go through the land with crosses in front
> with six *doppieri* and candles in hand
> All burning, each carrying one,
> and they are clothed above their doublets
> with a cape of rough appearance.
> And note this of their factions:
> all are in white and have a hood
> with the face showing discreetly
> And with cord belts so that no one would worry
> with a scourge in the hand for the discipline
> with shoes on the feet so that no one slips.
> At principal feasts they go in the morning
> through this land with devotion
> and at every church each one kneels.
> And they go also to all processions
> that this Signoria would order,
> with priests and brothers of religion.[57]

Processions similar to those described by Guidi appear in paintings by Carpaccio and Gentile Bellini [Color Plates II and III].

Each Scuola Grande had its own processional agenda, with major feast-days like St. Mark's Day, Corpus Christi and Good Friday common to all. But in addition there were times of crisis when their services were required by the Signoria. For in their new public role, the Battuti had become a ceremonial *corps de reserve* ready to march on behalf of the Republic for purposes of propitiation as well as celebration. Beyond that, since the middle of the fifteenth century they functioned as reserve corps in a broader sense, serving as conscription agencies to man the galleys of the state.[58]

By their very existence the Scuole Grandi celebrated the achievement of a Venetian consensus. They showed that it was possible to bring together in one miniature commonwealth the politically disarmed groups of artisans, citizen-merchants and citizen-bureaucrats with the politically potent nobility. Their leaders stood for all Venice. They were, indeed, Venice at its most reliable. A nucleus of 'mature and grave' males, they embodied the central social and moral values of the society.[59] As Guido Ruggiero writes:

> They came closer to embodying the myth of Venice, to fulfilling the ideal, than did the nobles. Rather than becoming a revolutionary class fighting for a place at the top, they remained an orderly buffer group contributing toward the preservation of the commune.[60]

The men of the banca

At this point let us narrow our focus to the ruling elites of the Venetian *scuole*, for it is specifically in the *albergo* or boardroom of a confraternity, rather than among the membership as a whole, that we encounter the patrons of Carpaccio, Gentile Bellini and the other narrative painters of the day. The decision to initiate a painting campaign would be made by a Chapter General, usually a body of thirty to sixty men, who were the most active and influential members of the *scuola*, many of them former officers themselves. After an affirmative vote, the commission was handled by the *banca*, who chose the artist and specified the subject matter.[61]

The *banca*, taking its name from the long bench at which it sat, numbered sixteen men in a Scuola Grande. The group was composed of four top officers: Guardian Grande, the chief executive officer; Vicario, his assistant and occasional substitute; Guardian da Matin, the supervisor of processions; and Scrivan, the bookkeeper and recorder. To these were added twelve Degani, two for each *sestiere* of the city, who oversaw the welfare of the members in their respective districts. The total number of officers was fewer in a *scuola piccola*, and its executive officer was often called a Gastaldo, but its *banca* functioned in a similar manner. After the contract was made with an artist, ongoing supervision of the actual work was typically delegated to a smaller committee of three to five members. Thus, even in a *scuola* with overt patrician sponsorship – as suggested by the Loredan family coat of arms in some of the paintings of Carpaccio's cycle for the Scuola di Sant'Orsola – group consensus was essential at the outset. Furthermore, continuing approval and support were necessary to carry through a project of any magnitude. Each member of the *banca* was limited to a one-year term in a single office, and each new year brought in a different slate of officers.[62] Paintings were paid for by donations, by assessments of the general membership or by subscription of a smaller group within it, such as the *banca*.[63]

One predictable consequence of this organizational structure for narrative painting was the reinforcement of a normative aesthetic. And as we become more familiar with those solemn toga-clad men who march across the Piazza San Marco in Gentile Bellini's *Procession* [Color Plate XVIII], or who cluster in the lower left corner of Carpaccio's *Healing of the Possessed Man* [Color Plate XXII], we may conclude that a structural bias toward conservatism in art was encouraged by occupational and personal factors as well.[64]

Generally speaking, we can assume that the men of the *banca* were drawn from the more affluent members of any confraternity – those who had the time and money to devote to activities outside their usual occupations. Most of the *cittadini originari* who held office in the Scuole Grandi were merchants, investors of various sorts, and bureaucrats, the latter group being made up principally of secretaries and notaries of the Ducal Chancery.[65] As the historian Ugo Tucci observes, their limited range of occupations 'tended to level out whatever was peculiar to the various attitudes of the *cittadini* apart from their purely technical aspects, and brought about a decided similarity of outlook, and therefore of life-styles and their social manifestations'.[66] The composition of the ruling elites in the *scuole piccole* is less well known, but again, the oldest, the most affluent, the most free to determine the use of their time, would in all likelihood have risen to office in their respective groups. The one segment of the population generally exempted from office was the nobility.[67]

Such were the members of the major corporate bodies who filled the city with their meeting-houses, and who commissioned the *istorie* that constitute the subject of this book. Although we cannot discount patrician influence and largesse in any given case, it can be stated with some certainty that these men had one thing in common: virtually all of them were members of one or another of the lesser estates. The reality created in the paintings is one that should be viewed with this fact in mind.

And yet, while they were not patricians, these men shared in the common 'lifeboat mentality' with which Venetians of every order faced the challenges and uncertainties of the outside world. Their well-being and very identity were closely bound to the pursuit of trade and the general financial and political health of the state. At the end of the fifteenth century, growing incongruities between the myth of Venice and the actuality of Venetian life fell upon the officers of the *scuole* in a special way and with particular force. We see this in three related areas: a widening division between rich and poor in Venetian society as a whole, but a source of more anxiety among the upper classes; sharper divisions between the estates of patricians and *cittadini*; and – most subtle, but most important for patterns of artistic patronage – a changing paradigm of honor.

Rich and poor

By the end of the Quattrocento, regardless of the pious intentions about humility and brotherhood expressed in their foundation charters, the members of any given *scuola* were not equal. Not surprisingly, patricians had held a privileged status in all the confraternities since the Trecento. In addition to their exemption from office, they were not required to perform the less popular duties required of the general membership, such as attending the burials of deceased members, or, in the case of the Scuole Grandi, practising flagellation (called the discipline). The attraction of membership for the patrician was to ensure for himself an honorable and well-attended burial, where in his final earthly journey he could be accompanied by a group of *confratelli*, sometimes numbering in the hundreds.[68]

In theory, the burdens of membership were supposed to fall equally on all the other members. But over the years, particularly in the Scuole Grandi, further distinctions were made. From time to time, groups of non-noble members were formed who were allowed exemptions similar to the patricians upon payment of a higher entrance fee and yearly dues. Exceptions to the original aims and ideals of the confraternities, they were clearly listed in the membership rolls as *exempti*.[69] But there were further, less obvious sub-groups forming as well. By the end of the fifteenth century, it appears that only a small proportion of the members, called *fradelli fadighenti* in the sources, were still marching in flagellant processions. Originally these brothers appear to have been probationers, new members who would be freed of the obligation once they attained full membership. But eventually they seem to have become a more or less permanent cadre of the poorer brothers. In return for the material benefits which the Scuola offered them, they performed the most unappealing physical duties of the confraternity: the penitential ritual of flagellation, the bearing of heavy apparatus in processions, attendance at the funerals of the poorest brothers.[70]

But – and this is the important point – a fiction of equality was still maintained

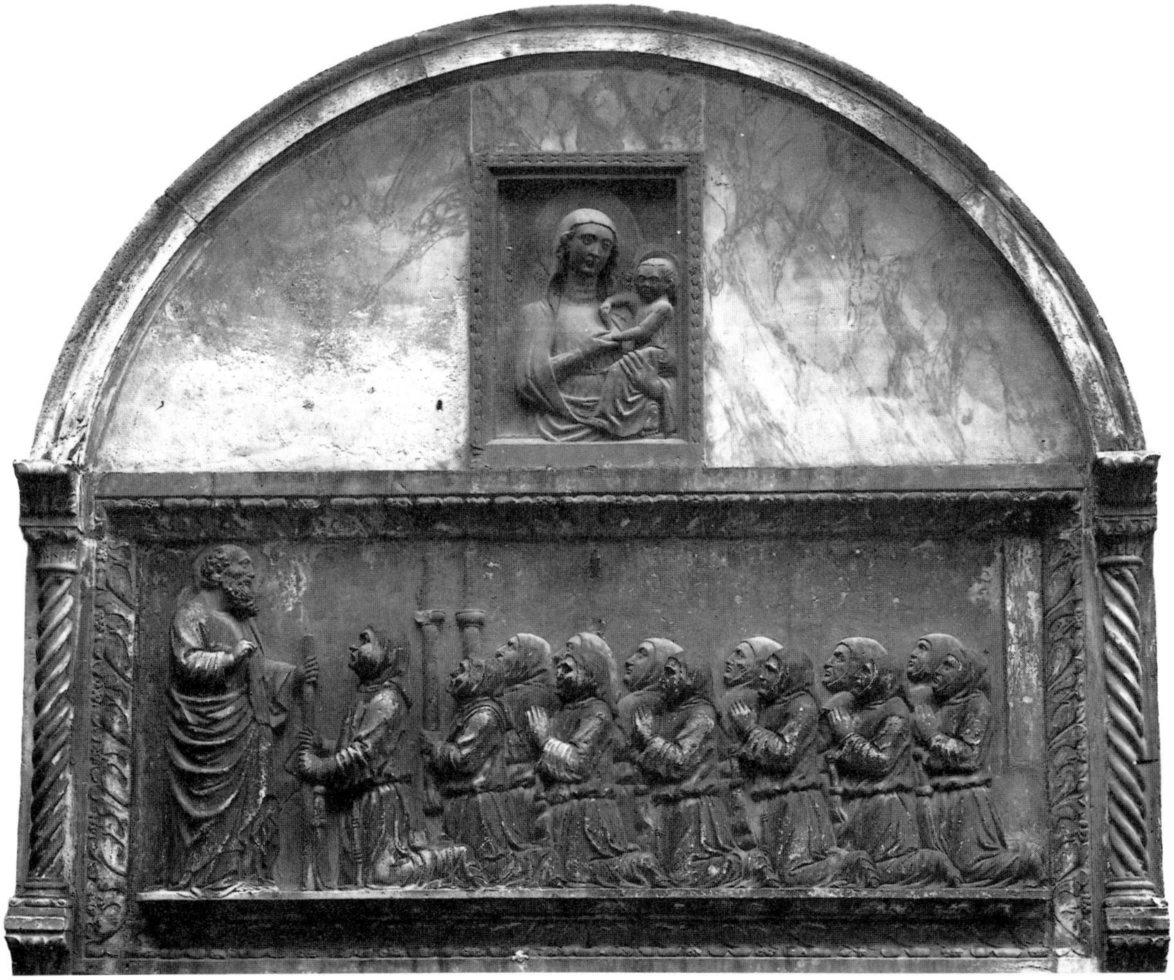

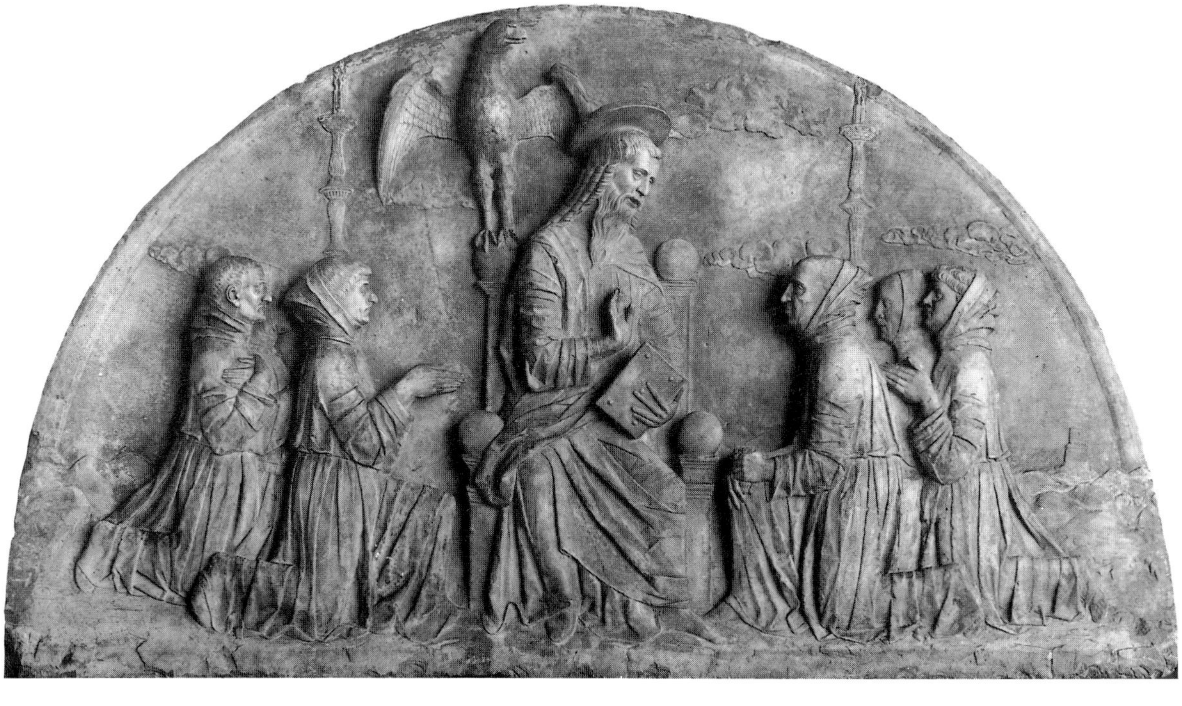

on the books. All the brothers, aside from the *nobili* and the *exempti*, were still listed in the Mariegola as *fradeli a la disciplina*.[71] Sharing in the sanctity of this activity, they were relieved of its discomforts. The change is graphically illustrated by two reliefs, about a century apart, from the Scuola Grande di San Giovanni Evangelista [Plates 8 and 9]. Each shows a group of the confraternity brothers – in all likelihood members of the *banca*, led by the Guardian Grande – grouped close to the patron saint. In the Trecento relief, each holds the scourge; in the later relief, dated to 1481, their hands are empty.

As Brian Pullan has shown, the frank recognition of economic disparity and a division of duties based on it was a symptom of the development of the Grandi into genuine charitable institutions. But this recognition brought with it an ethical dilemma. In 1498 the officers of the Scuola Grande di San Rocco recognized the morally ambiguous situation that had developed. Arguing that all non-noble brothers should be subject to the same obligations, they lamented distinctions of rank within the confraternity:

> This is a thing contrary to charity and to equal brotherhood, and has furthermore provoked scandal and mutiny among the brothers by making one a son and another a stepson of San Rocco, when all should be equal sons.[72]

The growing concern over the distinctions between rich and poor in Venetian society was not confined to the Scuole Grandi. It fell with special poignancy within the patriciate. While a natural nobility might expect to be naturally more prosperous than the lower orders, in reality this was in no way a foregone conclusion. Virtually the only remunerative occupations open to patricians were in trade and investments. The continuous warfare during the period exacted its toll in the form of high taxes and a recession in trade. While many of the richest families continued to add to their fortunes, those who had been of more modest means were simply squeezed out. Posts on the great galleys, traditionally the expectation of every patrician youth, were increasingly scarce. Those who were unsuccessful in business vied for state offices, but these had become insufficient in number to satisfy the demands of a burgeoning nobility for whom families of ten or twelve children were not uncommon. They were often forced to barter the only economic resource they had: their vote on the Great Council. By the end of the fifteenth century, the phenomenon of *broglio* – political intrigue, which often included the selling of votes – became a standard, if deplored, fact of Venetian political life.[73]

In 1497 Domenico Morosini, a highly placed Procurator of St. Mark's, responded to the situation with his treatise on ideal government, *De bene instituta re publica*. While avoiding a call to drastic reform, he saw a potential danger in the great disparities of wealth among the patricians who sat together in the Great Council. His remedy was to exclude the extremes of the too-rich and the too-poor from the Senate and to elect the Doge from the whole citizenry, embracing *cittadino* as well as *nobile* – a startling suggestion from a Venetian patrician.[74]

In 1509 Priuli estimated that three-fourths of the patriciate depended on state offices for their livelihoods and could be considered poor.[75] Resentment over great disparities of wealth surfaced also amongst the *cittadini* during the crisis associated with the war of the League of Cambrai of the same year. Martino Merlini, a merchant, wrote to his brother telling him to stay in the East because business was so poor in Venice. If he could sell something, Merlini complained, the profit all went to taxes. He was bitterly aware of a rich upper stratum of the

8 (facing above). *San Giovanni and the confratelli of the Scuola di San Giovanni Evangelista*, facade relief, 1349 (Venice, Scuola Grande di San Giovanni Evangelista)

9 (facing below). Pietro Lombardo?, *San Giovanni and the confratelli of the Scuola Grande di San Giovanni Evangelista*, portal relief, 1481 (Berlin-Dahlem, Staatliche Museen)

patriciate who continued to live in style, while the rest of the population suffered considerable hardships.[76]

Although sumptuary laws were passed condemning 'immoderate and excessive expenses... with great offense to our Lord God and the universal damage of our gentlemen and citizens',[77] there is little evidence that they were particularly effective. One suspects that their main value lay in making a visible gesture to pacify the less affluent elements in the patriciate without any serious expectation of compliance. The *poveri zentilhomeni*, as the poor nobles were called, were in a peculiar position. They were precluded from a wide range of occupations by their rank, and yet they could see around them a number of commoners with far more visible wealth.[78]

A 'REFINED NOBILITY'

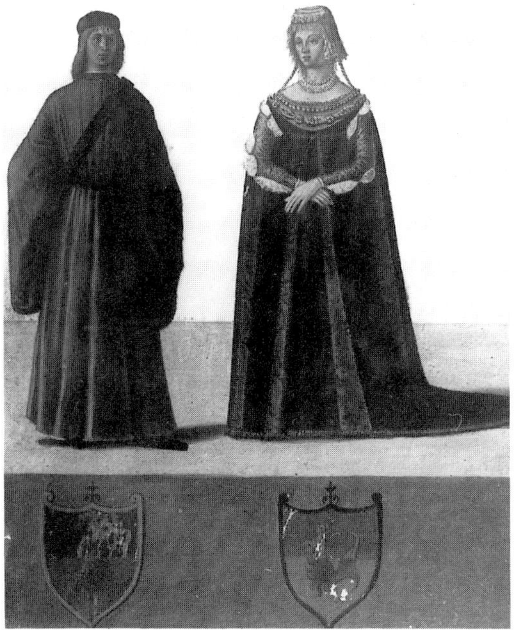

10. Zaccaria Freschi and Dorothea Zaccaria (Venice, Biblioteca Marciana, Cod. It. VII 165 [=8867], f. 7)

Alongside the growing concern over economic disparities within the patriciate, there developed a sharper definition of rank and its privileges. Although the aristocratization of Venetian society is typically seen as a phenomenon of the later sixteenth century, there are strong indications that it was well under way before the League of Cambrai. We see evidence of this in the level just below the patriciate with the succession of privileges granted to the *cittadini originari* during the Quattrocento. In 1410 the four top offices in the Scuole Grandi were reserved for them. By the 1440s the privilege was expanded to include all sixteen offices.[79] In 1478 they were given exclusive rights to chancery office.[80] Attention to their dress followed in 1485, when secretaries were required – one might read this more accurately as 'allowed' – to wear the red toga of the patrician senator.[81] The effect of such measures was to distinguish more firmly and more visibly the *cittadino originario* from all other commoners. The Chancery Secretary, Zaccaria Freschi, later named Secretary to the Council of Ten, is shown dressed in this manner in the family chronicle with his bride, Dorothea Zaccaria, as they would have appeared at the time of their marriage in 1486 [Plate 10]. In appearance they are virtually indistinguishable from any noble senator and his wife.

But in 1506, in legislation that marked a significant turning-point, a sharper line was to be drawn between them and their patrician counterparts. All parents and parish priests were required from then on to register noble births and baptisms with the Avogaria di Comun, and the official record thus compiled would become the *Libro d'Oro* of the nobility.[82] Marriages between poor noblemen and the daughters of wealthy commoners, with the children taking on noble status, had been a popular marriage strategy in the Quattrocento, but such unions were to be scrutinized more carefully in the future.[83] Legislation ordering stricter surveillance of patrician marriages came in 1526, as Sanudo noted, 'to keep our nobility refined and immaculate... and to provide for the peace and honor of our State, that men born of low condition would not come to the councils'.[84] Such provisions also had implications for the other orders, with similar requirements passed for the *cittadini*, who were eventually recorded in a *Libro d'Argento*.[85] As each order became more rigidly circumscribed relative to the others, those who were below the patriciate – particularly the *cittadini* – would have found it necessary to establish their positions more firmly within their own hierarchy.

A changing paradigm of honor

The sharper definition of rank and status was accompanied in the late Quattrocento by the emergence of a new paradigm of honor. Elsewhere in late medieval Italy, the merchant had often been cast in an unfavorable light. A culture still dominated by the ideals of a landed aristocracy, and cognisant of theological injunctions against usury, saw him as tainted by his material success and dubiously obtained profits.[86] But with the Serrata of 1297, Venice had achieved a unique coincidence of honor, mercantile wealth and political power. The 'natural' nobility formed at that time was a nobility of merchants.[87] Thus at the center of the Venetian paradigm of honor stood not the knight, but the merchant.

Traditionally, the common adherence to mercantile values by patrician and commoner alike had acted as a major area of congruence between them, and honor was there for the sharing. But by the end of the Quattrocento, there is evidence that the *cittadino* merchant stood on increasingly shifting sand in regard to his status within the larger society.

Donado da Lezze, for example, was very much a patrician of the new generation. Criticizing commanders of merchant galleys who had retreated from a naval encounter with the Turks in August 1499, he commented scornfully:

> It is one thing to be a merchant, another to govern states and fleets; and one never sees nor hears that a commoner does anything worthwhile unless it is making money.[88]

In denying civic and military virtue to the merchant, Da Lezze revealed the beginnings of a decisive shift of the patrician moral ideal toward aristocratic and humanist values. The development parallels the beginning of an actual geographical shift in the source of societal honor from the sea to the land. Priuli, no enemy of mercantile interests, nevertheless described the phenomenon clearly:

> Before these forefathers of ours had the Terraferma they devoted themselves to voyages and navigation to the great advantage and emolument of the city and they earned much money each year, and yet they were not renowned throughout the world and were regarded as fishermen. Whereas, having conquered the *stato* of the mainland, they have gained great reputation and name on that account and are much esteemed and appreciated and honored by the *signori* of the world and respected by all.[89]

Priuli thus reveals, perhaps unknowingly, that as the new century opened, a new competing paradigm of honor was in the making. The honorable status of the great merchant who ran galleys to Beirut or Alexandria would be increasingly challenged by the naval officer commanding military fleets, and the gentleman farmer – the *padrone* of a villa somewhere in the great fertile plain to the west. Along with the land had come the values of the landed gentry. Although this process became more obvious several decades later with the proliferation of villas in the Terraferma, its roots are clearly evident already in the last years of the Quattrocento. With the emergence of an increasingly non-mercantile nobility, many a wealthy *cittadino* would be pushed subtly into an implicitly second-rate occupational, as well as political and social, category. Even pilgrim galleys, formerly a lucrative patrician monopoly, could now be run (albeit with more peril and less profit) by *cittadini*.[90]

At the same time, divisions may have arisen amongst the *cittadini* themselves, between those who stayed in trade and retained traditional values, and the secretaries and members of the Chancery who had received a humanist education. In their daily contacts with patricians, the latter would be frequently reminded of the new notions about honor and the new divisions of rank. As members of the bureaucracy, they had further cause to align themselves with changing patrician standards. But even humanist circles tended to be segregated by the end of the fifteenth century, with patricians and commoners forming their own distinct, if overlapping, groups.[91]

The citizen secretaries continued to occupy a particularly sensitive position, increasingly astride two worlds, without identifying fully with either. Witnessing and recording heated debates in the most secret and sensitive councils of government, it was their task to give written form to the proceedings that would satisfy the spokesmen on both sides of any issue.[92] The fact that more rigorous proofs of citizenship were advanced first for the secretarial order suggests the elevation of a superior caste within the *cittadini*, with all the social tensions that would accompany such a development.[93] It is worth noting that a law of 1504, forbidding secretaries of the Chancery from holding office in a Scuola Grande on the grounds that it might interfere with their governmental duties, was frequently ignored.[94] Proportionally, they seem to account for the single largest occupational group on the *banche* of the Scuole Grandi.[95]

We are thus dealing with a period when rank became increasingly well demarcated and when the definition of honor underwent a subtle but significant change. While the concern with rank was, in all likelihood, related to the new assumptions about honor, it is important to distinguish the two problems. Rank – that is, a person's legal status and prerogatives as a *cittadino* or as a *nobile* – was inherently a less charged issue. It was a concrete thing, amenable to legislation. *Cittadini* could be granted special privileges, and noble births and marriages could be more reliably documented. Thus objectified by law, rank could be seen and felt, at which point it lost its capacity to charge relationships with indeterminacy. In theory, it simply defined an individual's place within the hierarchy, and once this had been re-established, he could feel secure in the very certainty of it. But the changing locus of honor was intrinsically more disjunctive. Ungraspable and labile by its very nature, honor was a valuation of worth and attached itself to individuals as well as to groups. As a question of reputation rather than a matter of law, it had to be constantly reasserted in visible ways.

There were, of course, sources of honor in the society other than one's occupation. Foremost amongst these were 'pious causes', such as those sponsored by the *scuole*. It often comes as a surprise to a modern reader that listed under this rubric in confraternity deliberations were not only acts of mercy, but also the patronage of art and architecture. In fact, to the men of the *banche* piety and material splendor were by no means antithetical; they were, in fact, indivisible. Although the lavish decorative campaigns undertaken by the great *scuole* of the city are often seen as examples of their declining piety and their unbridled competitive urges, it is important not to reject out-of-hand their avowed intentions. For such programs were consistently couched in terms of honor, necessity and civic duty. Whether or not one accepts the sincerity of the rhetoric, such pleas were convincing enough in their own time.[96]

It is precisely in the 1490s that an increased momentum of such programs in the Scuole Grandi can be documented; and earlier pleas for equality with the other Scuole were changing, with a new urgency to calls for outright superiority.[97] In commissioning a processional banner in 1506, the Banca of the Scuola Grande di S. Maria della Carità observed:

> All the confraternities of our noble city try with all means possible to them to exalt and glorify themselves in different ways, and have begun major adornments and furnishings of necessary things. . . And because for our confraternity. . . it is necessary first to honor God and then to be equal to the other confraternities, it is of great necessity to have a banner comparable to those of the others. . .[98]

By the following year, the officers insisted that the new banner

> would be more esteemed and would exceed the beautiful new banner of the Scuola of Misser San Marco. . . so that it would not be of less beauty and perfection, but rather would be better than it. . .[99]

In these tangible demonstrations of honor, the citizen was well advised not to act upon his own. The Venetian paradigm, while not always followed, was in theory one not only of group consensus, but also of group deportment – the low voice, the discreet gesture, the common black toga – which constituted a studied anonymity. The lavishly decorated private family chapel was thus not as common as one might expect in Venetian churches during the Quattrocento, and in no case is there evidence that it provided a setting for a cycle of personalized painted *istorie*, like those in Florence, Padua, Milan and many other cities in Italy.[100] Gasparo Contarini attempted, with some exaggeration, to explain the phenomenon in terms of the cherished 'myth':

> Our ancestors, from whom we received so flourishing a commonwealth, all united in a desire to establish, honor and augment their country, without any regard for their own private glory or advantage. This is easy to conclude. . . for in Venice there are to be found few monuments to our ancestors, though at home and abroad they achieved many glorious things to the advantage of their homeland. There are no tombs, no statues, no naval spoils, no enemy flags, after so many great battles.[101]

It is primarily for this reason that the *scuole* and the offices of government were the major patrons of the arts in Venice. Not only did pooled resources make more impressive programs possible, but also the corporate character of such initiatives allowed the individual to share in the collective honor of the group without drawing criticisms of individual pride and vainglory. The numerous portraits that occupied the foregrounds of Venetian history paintings were there in their public as much as their private guise. They showed men in terms of their bonds of membership, as *confratelli* of the *scuola*, rather than of kinship, as fathers and sons.

These men had been raised with an image of the world and themselves that had come under pressure. As they witnessed the tilt in relative importance of the Venetian geophysical world from east to west, they were also forced to accommodate to a new paradigm of honor that would shift them subtly to one side. It was in this far from tranquil mood that the sober men of the *banche* around the city may have found it even more necessary than had their fathers, the patrons of Jacopo Bellini, to display their honor. They went about this in the most visible way possible: through the acquisition of relics; through the loving attention to altars in parish churches; through the construction and adornment of meeting-halls, both large and small; and, most graphically, through painted histories. For on those canvases they could obtain a more coherent reality than that with which they were presented in their daily lives. Some could even make an appearance there in their corporate *personae*, as visible witnesses to the lives of the saints and the blessings of God and as active protagonists in the life of their city.

3

The Tradition

By the last decade of the fifteenth century, no Venetian man of affairs could have been unaware of the increasingly splendid effect of the Great Council Hall. One by one, the faded old frescoes were being replaced by fresh new paintings in oil on canvas. In 1493 Marin Sanudo completed the first draft of a guide for visitors to the city: 'De origine, situ et magistratibus urbis venetae', also known as the 'Cronachetta'. Not surprisingly, he devoted particular attention to the Ducal Palace, including it on his list of the twelve most 'notable things that one shows to lords in Venice' [Plate 11].[1] After observing that Venetians could be compared favorably to the ancient Greeks in learning and to the Romans in building, in arms and in virtue, he moved on to describe in some detail the huge room, where as many as eighteen hundred patricians came together each Sunday afternoon to conduct affairs of state:[2]

> Here is the most grand hall of the Great Council, and it is being renewed all around with paintings by the hands of those most excellent painters who are among the most worthy and the most famous in the world today: Gentil Belin

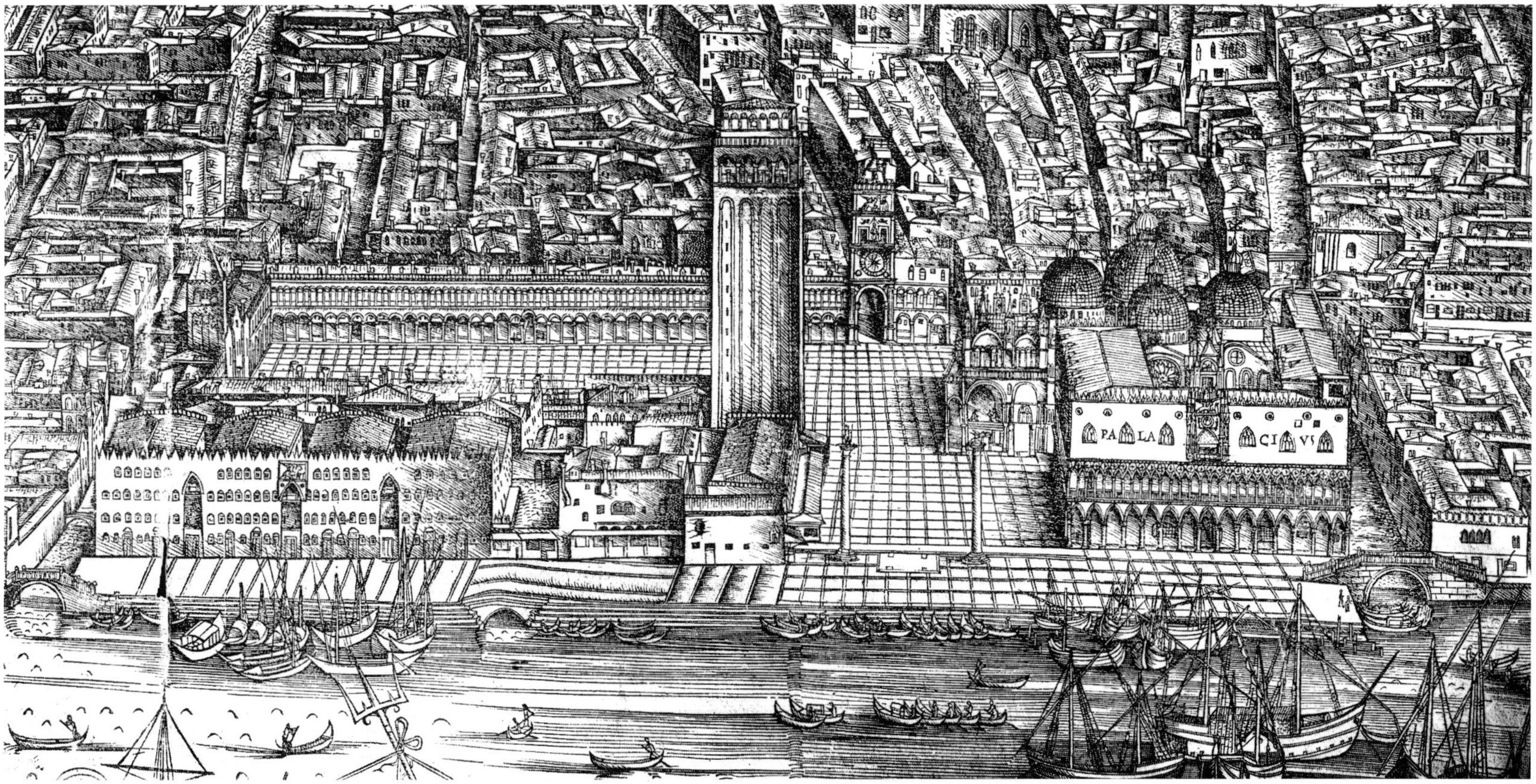

11. Jacopo dei Barbari, detail from *View of Venice*, woodcut, 1500 (Venice, Museo Correr)

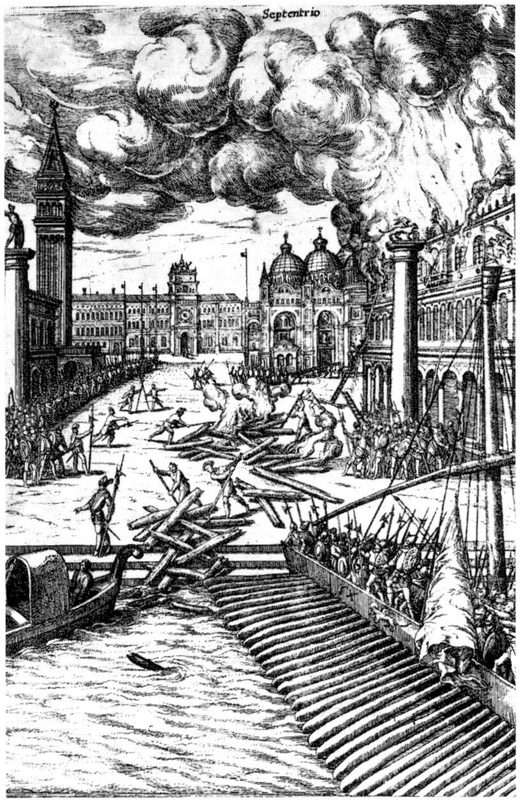

12 (above). *The Fire in the Ducal Palace of 1577.* From Giacomo Franco, *Habiti*, 1610, taken from an engraving by Jorg Hoefnagel, 1578 (Venice, Museo Correr)

and Zuan Belin, brothers, whose works show how much they should be esteemed...And continually they renew the said room, with the *historia* on canvases of the Roman Pope, Alessandro III, and of the Emperor Federico Barbarossa...[3]

He was referring, of course, to a painting campaign that had already been in progress for nearly twenty years. It dated back to 1474, when the members of the Great Council had voted to restore the great cycle of *istorie* that depicted the mediating role played in 1177 by Doge Sebastiano Ziani between the Pope and the Emperor. The official rendition of the momentous chain of events of that year was based on fact, but three centuries later it had grown in the telling to become one of the most cherished memories in Venetian history.[4]

The new campaign of decoration engaged the efforts of the leading history painters of the city, including Carpaccio as well as Gentile and Giovanni Bellini in the early years, and was eventually to involve Titian, Veronese and Tintoretto. In its finished state it constituted one of the great achievements of Renaissance history painting, comparable to the mural decoration of the Sistine Chapel. And yet we have only the vaguest idea of how it looked, for today it is but a memory. Its total destruction by fire in 1577 leaves a tragic void in the history of Venetian art around which any inquiry into the painted *istoria* must move with respect and even with some caution [Plate 12]. Of one thing we can be certain: its powerful exemplary role in the development of narrative painting in the late Quattrocento. We might allow that the history of the Venetian *istoria* as conceived by Carpaccio and his contemporaries begins in this room.[5]

But the Great Council Hall itself had a history. It grew out of a long-established tradition of pictorial narrative decoration in the public spaces of the city. Although most of these programs have also vanished, they were still visible

13. View of Cappella di San Pietro, mosaics, 12th century (Venice, Basilica of San Marco)

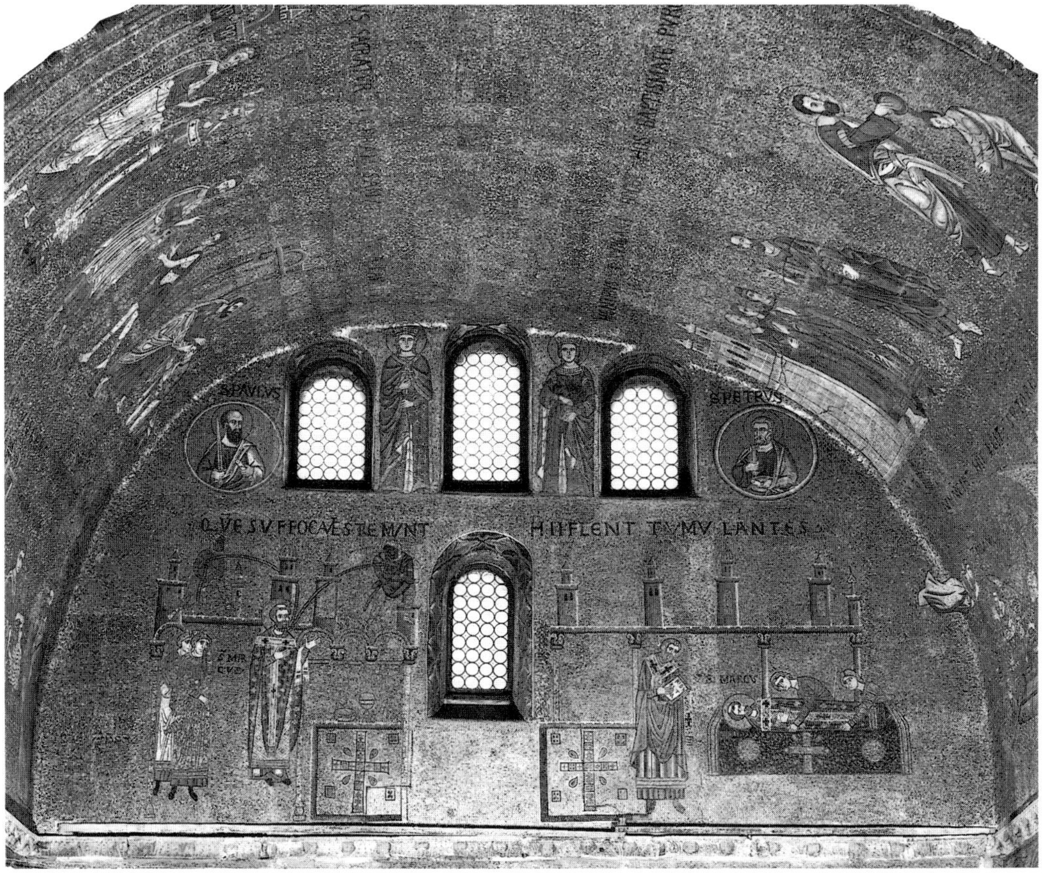

in the late Quattrocento to the men of the *scuole* and to the artists whom they patronized. Before turning to the Great Council Hall campaign of 1474, we will first look back at the history of the painted *istoria* in Venice to determine where and under what conditions its creation was felt to be appropriate, or, indeed, even necessary. The appearance of these works will not be at issue in this chapter, so much as their circumstances.

The earliest examples of large-scale pictorial narrative representation in Venice to survive in our own time, and probably in Sanudo's as well, are not paintings at all, but the mosaics of San Marco that date back to the twelfth and thirteenth centuries. Sanudo, again in the 'Cronachetta', recommended the building to his readers: 'San Marco is the second *sestiere*; it has a church most beautiful and rich, all worked with historiated mosaics, paved with the most beautiful stones, and all surrounded and invested with marbles, and it is a thing worthy to see.'[6] We are reminded that on the golden walls of the Basilica a number of monumental *istorie* from a distant age – so familiar that they merited only a passing reference – were continuously present to Sanudo and his contemporaries.

The genesis of the Venetian istoria

The vita of St. Mark

San Marco was not an ordinary church. It was the Doge's church and was thus the focus of civic as well as pious concern. Although later artists might have drawn inspiration from any and all of the *istorie* on its walls and vaults, it is in the elaboration of the life of St. Mark and the translation of his relics to Venice that we find the ancestor true and proper of the Venetian *istoria* of the late Quattrocento. This was a piece of local history whose composition and iconography were invented to suit Venetian needs, and as such it had to undergo revision and updating like any history, for it was represented not once but twice in the Basilica.

The earlier rendition of the legend of St. Mark and his relics consists of two mosaic cycles that cover the barrel vaults and back walls of the high chapels, now organ galleries, that flank the presbytery. The oldest *istorie* extant in the Basilica, they were made in the first half of the twelfth century. In the Cappella di San Pietro on the north side, the life or *vita* of St. Mark is shown in eleven scenes, beginning with his consecration by St. Peter and concluding with his martyrdom and burial [Plate 13]. In the Cappella di San Clemente opposite, the emphasis shifts to Mark's relics: here the *translatio* is represented in seven episodes, beginning with the removal of the saint's body from his tomb in Alexandria in 828/9 and culminating in the reception of his relics by the Doge, the Patriarch, the clergy and the people of Venice [Plates 14 and 15].[7] Whether or not the *translatio* was a piece of political propaganda as critics of Venice often claimed, the possession of Mark's relics was of central importance to the Republic in the twelfth century: the one concrete foundation on which the Venetian national church – a uniquely successful bonding of Church and State – was anchored.[8]

By the middle of the thirteenth century, Venice's place in the Mediterranean world had changed considerably. After her participation in the Fourth Crusade had culminated in a victory over Byzantium and the profitable sack of Constantinople of 1204, she entered the ranks of world powers, and for a time the Venetian Doge held the title 'Lord of a Quarter and Half a Quarter of

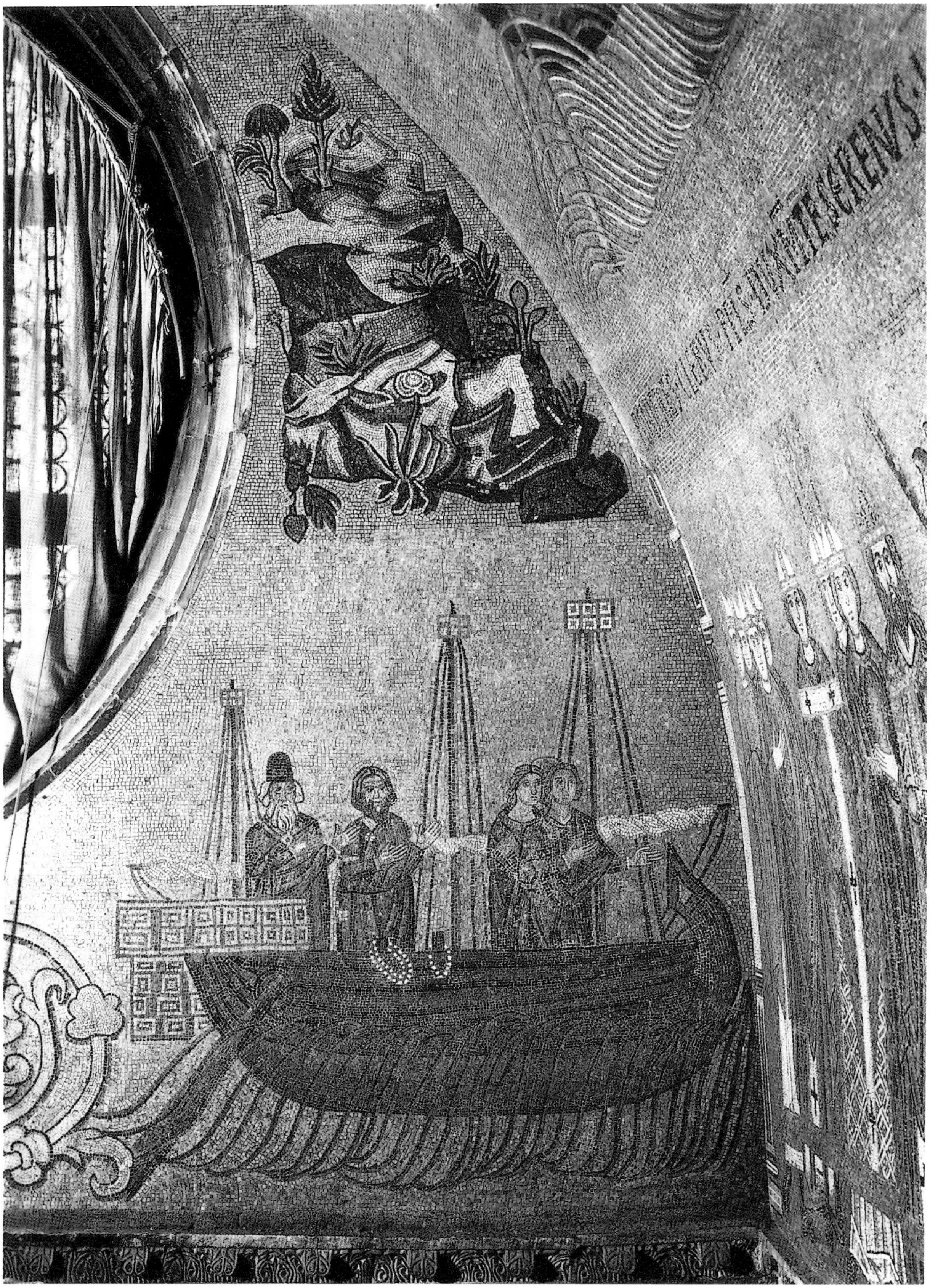

the Roman Empire'.[9] The Basilica that must have seemed sufficiently – even magnificently – adorned at the beginning of the century was now the focus of a new decoration campaign that was intended to reflect the rising status of the Republic. The re-elaboration of the story of St. Mark in a second mosaic cycle and its promotion to more visible places on the building were a major part of the undertaking.

Mark's life and martyrdom were now to be represented in twelve episodes along the barrel vault of the ante-vestibule of the south-west corner. We should remember that at that time the space was a main entrance to the Basilica and was remodelled into the Cappella Zen only at the beginning of the sixteenth century [Plate 16].[10] The scenes constituted more than a simple repetition of those in the presbytery, for several of the old episodes were edited out and replaced with new ones. Most important was the *praedestinatio*, whose inclusion in the updated program of the ante-vestibule would in itself, in the view of Otto Demus, 'have justified the monumental "reissue" of the legend'.[11]

An invention of the mid-thirteenth century, the new episode depicted the saint asleep, receiving a prophecy in a dream that his body would find its final resting-place in that very location in Venice where San Marco was to be built. No more convincing evidence of Venice's right to the saint's relics could have been wished for; it provided the justification and the rationale for the *translatio* that now moved triumphantly across the front of the church in the four lunettes above the doors of the west facade. This was, of course, the part of the story that was of paramount importance to the Venetians at this time. Demonstrating the

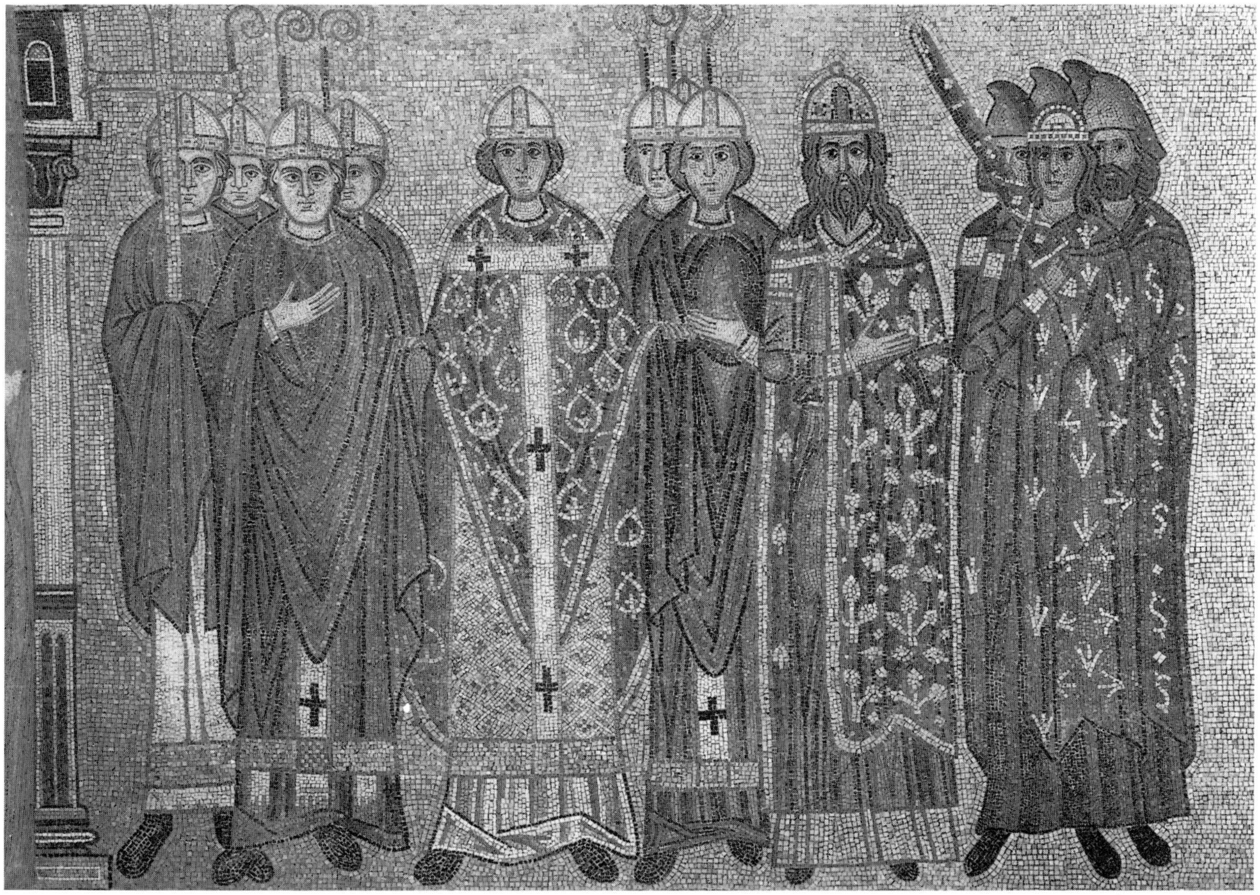

14 (facing). *Return of Mark's Relics to Venice*, mosaic, 12th century (Venice, Basilica of San Marco, Cappella di San Clemente)

15. *Reception of Mark's Relics in Venice*, left part, mosaic, 12th century (Venice, Basilica of San Marco, Cappella di San Clemente)

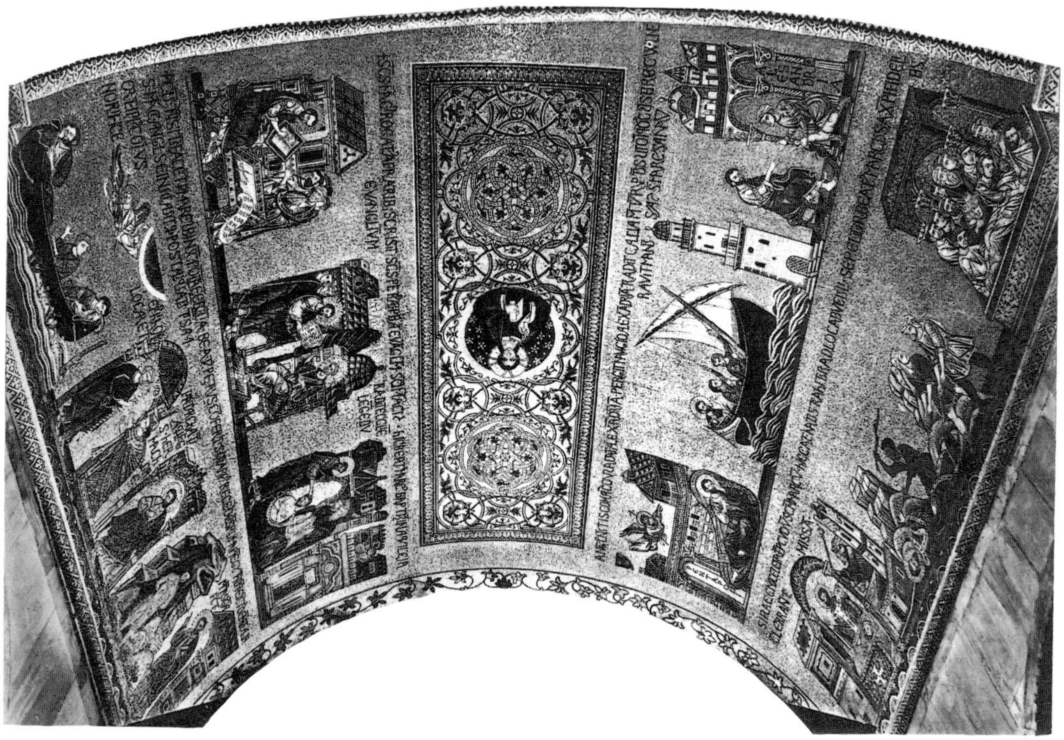

16. *Life of Saint Mark*, mosaics, c. 1267–75 (Venice, Basilica of San Marco, Cappella Zen, vault)

claim of the church to be the shrine of Mark's relics, *the translatio* served, in Demus's words, as the 'title page' of the Basilica. In comparison to this signal event, he observed, the saint's life was only a commentary.[12] By the end of the Quattrocento these facade mosaics were still part of every Venetian's visual patrimony. That artists were attentive to them is shown by their careful replication by Gentile Bellini in the *Procession on the Piazza San Marco* [Color Plate XII; cf. Plates 83 and 84], a rendering that is our only record of the three that are now lost.

The thirteenth-century campaign also added a third chapter to the *istoria* of St. Mark which expanded it into recent history and provided a coda to the events of the *translatio*. Placed in the south transept, it commemorated a miraculous event called the *apparitio*. According to tradition, the location of the saint's relics had been forgotten after a rebuilding of the church in the eleventh century. After three days of fasting and prayer by the Doge, the clergy and the whole Venetian community, a pillar in the church miraculously opened and revealed the body of the saint.[13] Thus depicted, the miracle confirmed in the most convincing way the continued presence of Mark's relics – with all the powerful resonance of divine mission that attached to them – in the seat of combined religious and political authority [Plate 17 and Color Plate IV].

The earlier redaction of the *istoria* of St. Mark in the presbytery remained to co-exist with the later version, and continued to hallow the east end of the Basilica. But it was by no means obsolete. By framing the sanctuary with its own foundation legends, it continued also to testify by its very age to the truth of the scenes that the new mosaics would recast in a more contemporary style. For the aim of the new program at the west end of the church was not to replace, but to augment. The venerable ancestry of those scenes retained from the first and replicated in the second cycle was an authentication to those that would be added. With the *istoria* of St. Mark brought up to date, the visual record had thus

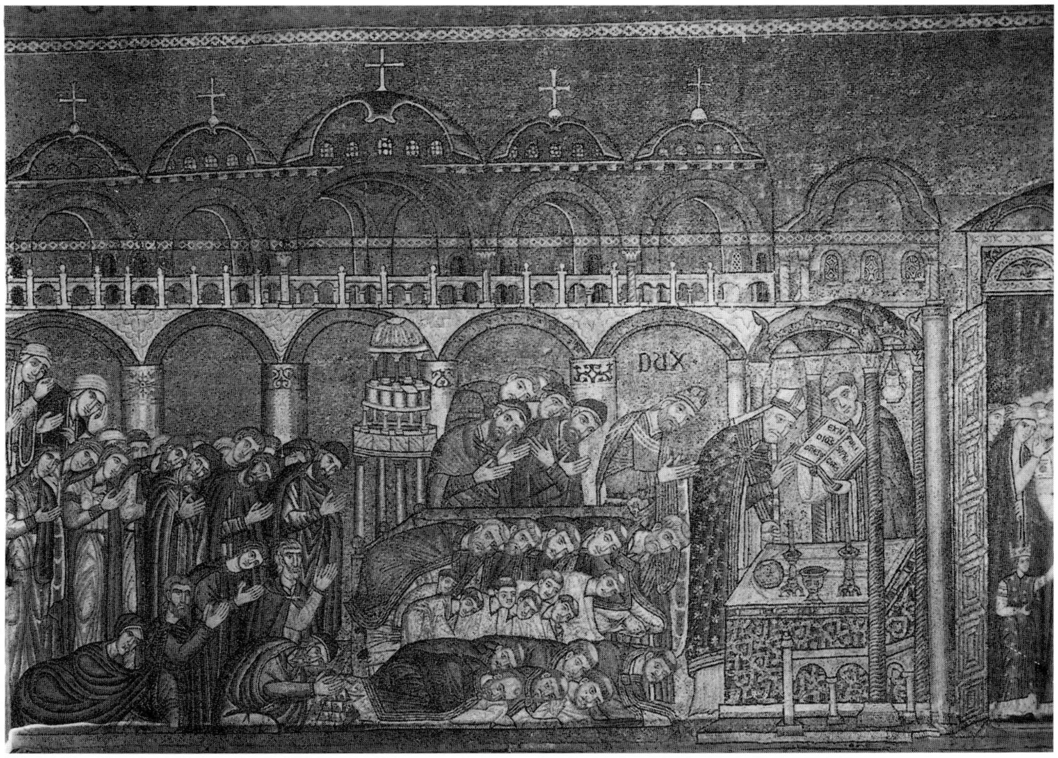

17. *Preghiera* (Venice, Basilica of San Marco, south transept)

achieved a satisfactory fullness. The decoration of the Basilica was again, for a time, considered complete.

The istoria of Alexander III

The first firmly documented cycle of history paintings – as opposed to mosaics – in Venice was commissioned in 1319 for the Church of San Nicolò in the Ducal Palace. An act of the Great Council described the chapel at that time as 'completely destitute of painting' and appropriated funds 'to be spent in the labor of painting in the said church, painting it with the history when the Pope was in Venice with the Lord Emperor and other things that will be seen'.[14] The theme has a familiar ring, for it is, indeed, the very legend of Alexander III that continued to hold such strong appeal for the Venetians of the late Quattrocento. There is evidence that the paintings, which must have been frescoes, were completed by 1329. They were still in place in 1400, although in poor condition and requiring repair. By 1525 (and perhaps before) they were destroyed, along with the church.[15]

Like the Basilica of San Marco, the Church of San Nicolò was no ordinary church. It too had a civic character. In 1362 Pope Urban V granted a special indulgence to those who prayed there for the souls of poor prisoners in the nearby prison. It was also a place where solemn contracts were witnessed. According to tradition, in the early years the Doge and Signoria attended mass annually together in the church. In the fifteenth century the Doge attended services there every Tuesday.[16]

At this point the Venetian *istoria* was as yet anonymous, for we have no certain knowledge of the authorship of these early paintings. But they were only one-half of an equation, for they were made in conjunction with a text. Around 1320, perhaps the year in which the paintings were actually begun, Bonincontro da Bovi, a notary in the Ducal Chancery, produced in Latin the first fully developed written account of the story. Bringing together earlier fragmentary versions of the event, it became the foundation text for numerous redactions and re-elaborations over the course of the next hundred and fifty years.[17] An illuminated manuscript version in Venetian dialect, dating to the middle third of the fourteenth century, derives from Bonincontro's text, and its eleven miniatures may well reflect the early frescoes [Color Plates V–VIII].[18]

Threatened by the aggressive military campaigns of the Emperor Frederick Barbarossa – so Bonincontro wrote – Pope Alexander III fled incognito to Venice and took refuge in the habit of a simple monk in the Convent of Santa Maria della Carità. His identity was soon discovered and was revealed to the Doge who, with the clergy and nobles of the city, proceeded to the Carità and honored him. In acknowledgment of such conspicuous support, the Pope granted an indulgence to the Carità. More importantly, he presented the Doge with the first of the *trionfi* (a group of triumphal insignia that would be used in ducal ritual until the end of the Republic): a white candle 'in sign of faith' and 'in sign of peace and of true love'.

Venetian ambassadors were then dispatched to the Emperor to sue for peace. They carried documents sealed with lead bulls by papal concession, instead of the usual wax, as a sign of Venice's sovereignty. The symbolic weight of this privilege was underlined by the fact that the seals bore the image of St. Mark, the patron saint of the city, just as the papal seals bore the images of Saints Peter and Paul.

Rebuffed by the Emperor, the Doge prepared to go to war in defense of the Pope. The latter presented him with a sword, affirming that 'in sign of reverence and honor of justice, you...should keep and carry the sword'. Against overwhelming odds, the Venetian fleet, led by the Doge, defeated the navy of the Emperor in a fierce battle and took his son, Otto, as hostage. The Pope presented the Doge with a gold ring and stated:

> We wish, Doge, that you would receive this ring and that every year in perpetuity you should marry the sea, just as a man marries his wife in sign of perpetual domination.

The Emperor was subsequently persuaded by his son to agree to a peace treaty. He traveled to Venice, where he prostrated himself at the feet of the Pope in front of the Basilica of San Marco. In gratitude, the Pope conceded a perpetual indulgence to visitors to San Marco during the feast of the Ascension. The three principals – Doge, Pope and Emperor – thereupon departed for Rome, but stopped first in Ancona where the Doge was granted a ceremonial umbrella to match those of the other two rulers. Aside from establishing the Doge's equivalence to the others, the umbrella also stood for one of the major themes of the Venetian 'myth': the city's admirable and unique setting – 'showing just as the shadow is a place of quiet, peace, concord and tranquillity, so is the place of Venice situated just as wonderfully'.

Finally, the group arrived in Rome, where the Doge was accorded a king's *adventus* to the city and received his final *trionfi*: gilded silver trumpets, signifying his regal dignity, and banners of different colors – *vexilla* – which carried a potent religious charge relating to sovereignty as well as to to divine protection, particularly in military campaigns.[19]

Bonincontro's literary labors and those of the anonymous painter of the Church of San Nicolò provided a satisfying narrative closure to two decades of political challenges. During that period unsuccessful military ventures had threatened to compromise the honor of the Venetian state in the eyes of the outside world. In the War of Ferrara of 1308 Venice had suffered one of her most devastating defeats in centuries. The Republic had unwisely become involved in a civil war and found herself pitted against the Pope who, as overlord of Ferrara, placed Venice under interdict and excommunicated many of her citizens.[20] Francesco Dandolo, the young patrician sent as Venice's orator to the court of Pope Clement V to plead for absolution, had been forced to prostrate himself on the floor and, Sanudo later wrote,

> to stay like a dog below the altar, making a great display of piety, and showing how much the Venetian men of God desired to be reconciled with the Church, pleading for absolution from the Interdict. . . . The said orator returned to Venice with the bull of absolution and from that time on was nick-named *Cane*. . .[21]

The emergence of a definitive script of the Alexander legend just a decade later may have represented a creative strategy to put an indirect gloss on the painful events of the recent past. Its new redaction in coherent narrative form, reinforced with a concrete visual parallel in the chapel of the Ducal Palace, allowed the Venetians to affirm their loyalty to the Roman Church while reasserting their claims to sovereignty and to a legitimate right to the Adriatic.[22]

The newly constituted legend also confirmed one of the great fixed points for the Republic's ceremonial calendar, the feast of the Sensa. The timing of the indulgence conceded by Pope Alexander III for the feast of the Ascension was no coincidence.[23] Already since the end of the thirteenth century the *desponsatio* or marriage to the sea was being celebrated each year precisely on this day, having itself grown out of a traditional benediction ceremony which dated back at least three centuries. By pulling together the venerable *desponsatio* with Alexander's donation of the ring, Venetians were now able to stage an even more richly symbolic event each spring – the feast of the Sensa – that proclaimed to the world the Republic's divinely sanctioned right to dominion over the entire Adriatic basin.[24]

The narrative thread of the story, thus enriched, became a vehicle to display, in painting and in living ceremonial, the imperial prerogatives of the Venetian Republic in a systematic and comprehensive fashion. It is a telling example of the dynamic relationship between an invented social script and the acted-out social drama.[25] For the granting of the *trionfi* provided the visual and ritual apparatus to make civic ideals concrete and to allow consensual participation in the celebration of those ideals on feast-days throughout the year. And the story could be played out again and again by succeeding generations of participants on the stage of the city itself, in celebration of the Republic's right to a maritime empire and her unquestioned devotion to the Church.

It was not long before the *Story of Alexander III* was depicted a second time in the Ducal Palace. Construction on a new Great Council Hall begun in 1340 was ready for decoration by 1365.[26] The fact that the same theme that already covered the walls of the nearby chapel was placed here as a repetition and not as a replacement underlines the prominent role it had come to play in public life. Almost certainly, the new program served as an elaboration and expansion of the earlier painting cycle, for it was based upon an enlarged text of the

Alexander legend that had been written by a certain Castellano da Bassano in 1331.[27]

The situation is analogous to that of the twice-told life of St. Mark in the Basilica, and we are again reminded of the need to rewrite – and repaint – important civic scripts over the course of time in response to new demands. In the chapel, the Alexander legend may have served as an inspiration and an *exemplum* – as well as a setting – for the Doge himself, but the audience at any given time would have been limited and without a defined character.[28] In the Great Council Hall, the larger cycle, comfirmed by the earlier, would provide an appropriate background for the deliberations of a legislative body composed of every patrician male in a city whose divinely sanctioned attention was turning toward the Terraferma at just that time.[29]

Again, this painting cycle is lost and our knowledge of it incomplete, but with it the first named artist appears on the scene of monumental history painting in Venice: Guariento da Arpo of Padua. It may be indicative of the great importance that was attached to this program that Marco Cornaro, who was Doge in 1365, sought a painter from outside the city, for Venetian artists had long been protected by legislation from 'foreign' competition.[30] A renowned master of fresco painting, Guariento had already demonstrated his abilities in pictorial narration in a cycle of *istorie* from the Old Testament which he had painted in the family chapel of Francesco Carrara, the Signore of Padua. He had also executed scenes from the lives of the saints in the Church of the Eremitani.[31]

Now badly damaged by fire and in a fragmentary state, the single work remaining today from Guariento's labors in the Great Council Hall is the *Paradise*. A huge fresco representing the Coronation of the Virgin surrounded by the heavenly hosts, it once stretched seventy-five feet across the east wall of the room above the podium [Plate 18]. We do not know how many scenes from the Alexander legend Guariento actually completed, for he worked in Venice for only two years, returning to Padua at the end of 1367. Aside from

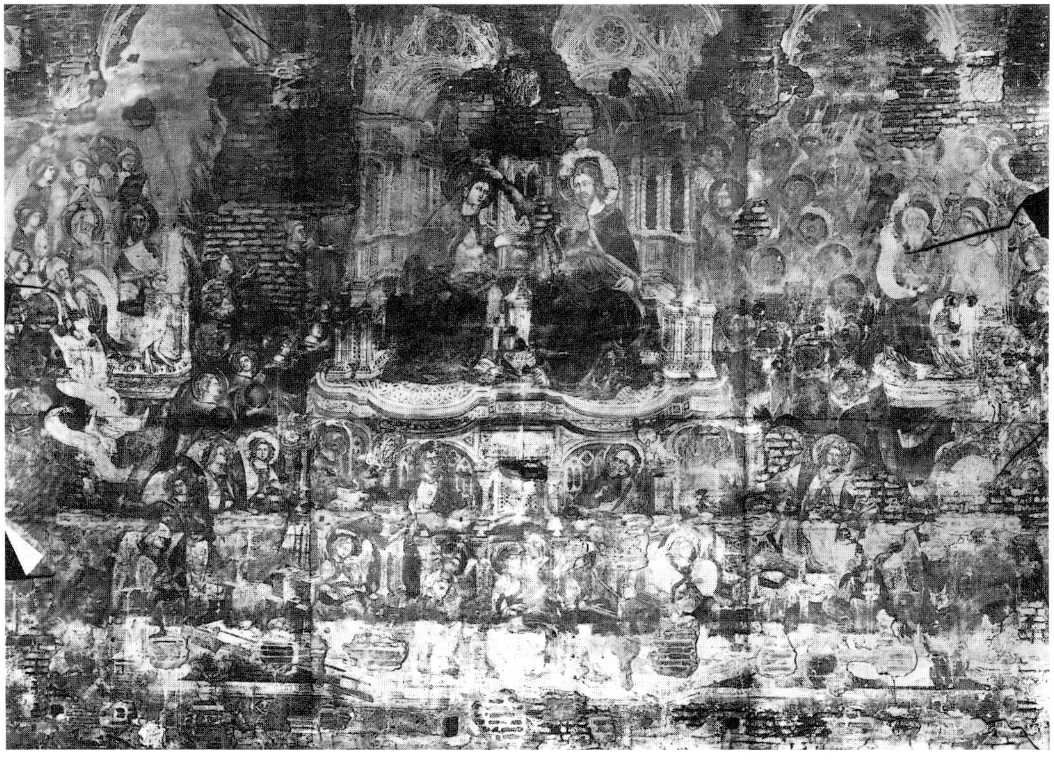

18. Guariento, *Paradise* (*Coronation of the Virgin*), detached fresco (Venice, Ducal Palace)

the *Paradise*, the only trace of Guariento's activity to survive is a drawing that may record a detail of one of the land battles painted on the south wall [Plate 19].[32]

Although Vasari also cited the participation of Antonio Veneziano in the program during this period, his observation, while credible, lacks outside corroboration.[33] A substantial amount of decoration must have been completed by 1382 when the Procurators of San Marco were urged to exert 'good care and diligence' in the as yet unused room, 'lest so much most solemn work in painting and other things be ruined'.[34] Completion of the program had probably been delayed by the War of Chioggia of 1378–81. Venice incurred crippling costs in naval battles against the Genoese in what was seen as a fight for the very survival of the Republic.[35]

By 1409 the Great Council had still not met in the hall. Reporting that 'much of the painting is destroyed', the body appropriated funds for its refurbishment.[36] The new campaign must have been nearing completion in 1415 when the Council observed that 'all lords and noble persons coming to our land' wanted to see the room that was by now 'famous for the beauty of the excellent works that adorned it'. More funds were voted at this time to construct a more convenient and grander staircase as a means of access, in 'consideration of so many beautiful works'.[37] In the summer of 1419, after more than fifty years of sporadic activity, the room finally became more than just a grand vision and an expensive curiosity when the Great Council began to hold its meetings there for the first time.[38] It is probably no coincidence that the impetus to complete the program and to allow the paintings finally to be on view came soon after the submission in 1405–6 of Vicenza, Verona and Padua to the Republic.[39] A suitably magnificent chamber of state for the lords of a quickly expanding dominion must have seemed imperative.

The new grandeur of the room was again the result of fresh talent brought in from the outside. Both Gentile da Fabriano and Pisanello participated in this phase of the decoration campaign, each painting at least one fresco on the north wall. In his *De viris illustribus* of 1456, the humanist Bartolomeo Facio cited these works among the major achievements of each artist.[40] Other painters of no interest to Facio may have participated as well in the renewal of the frescoes during this period.[41] The *historia* that informed the paintings seems to have been of particular interest to Francesco Foscari, who made his first public appearance as Doge when the Great Council Hall was officially inaugurated on 23 April 1423, for in 1425 all of the *tituli* or inscriptions on the twenty-two frescoes were recorded in a state document by public decree.[42]

The room continued to impress visitors to the city. Ignoring the contributions of Gentile da Fabriano and Pisanello, Michele da Savonarola of Padua described it in the 1440s and attributed the entire achievement to his countryman:

> And now Guariento painted with his own hands, with amazing artifice, the most magnificent, stupendous and superb hall of the serene dominion of Venice, which is called the Greater Hall, and he decorated it in an astonishing way; the viewing of it is awaited with so much eagerness, that when the solemn day of the Ascension draws near, when everyone is allowed entrance, there is no hour of the day when the room is not filled to over-flowing with an innumerable multitude of men from different countries; the delightful

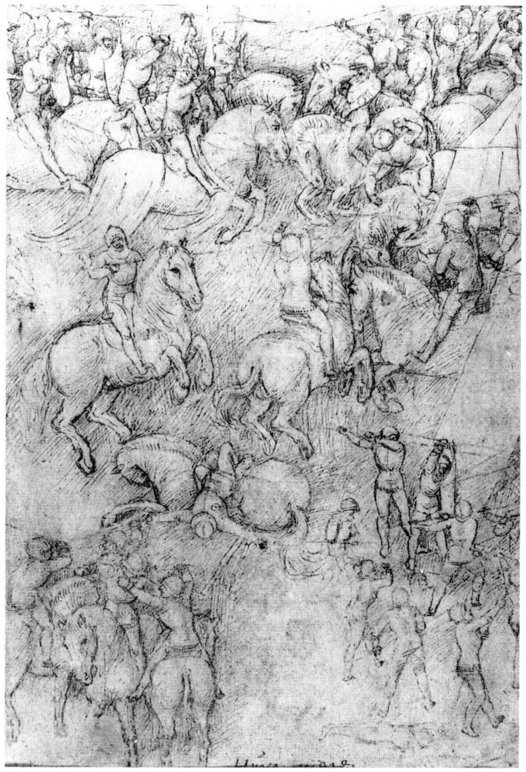

19. Northern Italian artist, copy after Guariento, *Battle of Spoleto*? (London, British Museum, Sloane 5226, f. 57r)

appearance of these figures and the representations of so many painted battles are so much to be admired, that no one wishes to leave.[43]

The decoration of the Great Council Hall with paintings of municipal history should be seen as a Venetian variant of a much wider European phenomenon of the later middle ages. In the north, audience halls were typically decorated with tapestries of the great deeds of history and legend. An inventory made in 1379 of the possessions of Charles V is typical. It included 'a great tapestry of the work of Arras, historiated with the deeds and battles of Judas Maccabee and of Antiochus. . .[and] a small tapestry historiated with the battle of the Duke of Aquitaine and of Florence'.[44]

Although tapestries were also used in Italy, large wall paintings were generally preferred for palace decoration. Princely halls would be fitted out with frescoes intended to glorify the family and person of the ruler. Cycles of famous men were particularly popular with courtly patrons, where contemporary heroes, and often the prince himself, could be included amongst the worthies of legend and antiquity. During the middle years of the Trecento, programs of this sort were sponsored by the Visconti of Milan, the Scaligeri of Verona, King Robert of Naples and the Carrara family of Padua. Painted *istorie* were often included as part of these cycles. In the Sala Virorum Illustrium in Padua, scenes from Roman history accompanied figures of the emperors.[45] The *istoria* of Thebes was painted in a nearby room. Marcantonio Michiel, a Venetian writing in the early sixteenth century, indirectly attributed its decoration to Guariento. He judged that the frescoes were painted by the artist 'who seems also to have painted the history of Spoleto in the Council Room in Venice. . .He was very clever at painting horses, but did not succeed so well in other subjects'.[46]

But the closest analogy to the Venetian situation is found in the communal, and not the princely, palace. The frescoes of the Palazzo Pubblico of Siena come immediately to mind: not only the famous 'allegorical narratives' of Good and Bad Government, but also historical events *per se*: battle scenes and even a local version of the legend of Alexander III, who happened to be a Sienese pope. Because so many similar programs have vanished, the Sienese achievements may seem to us now more unusual than they actually were at the time.[47]

In the Great Council Hall in Venice, the frescoes can be defined on one level as straight narrative: episodes of local history in which the Republic is placed in a more universal context that included the papacy and the empire. The inclusion of the *trionfi*, however, gave the cycle an added symbolic and allegorical charge. As Bonincontro's text indicates, each *trionfo* was a 'sign'. Altogether they provided a series of visual foci around which the *istorie* in the Great Council Hall were organized. They made visible and tangible the *idea* that underlay each scene in which they appeared, and lifted that scene above a level of discourse that was purely narrative.

Following the tradition

The Scuola di San Giovanni Evangelista

The inspiring example of the renewal of the *istorie* in the Great Council Hall during the second decade of the fifteenth century may have encouraged emu-

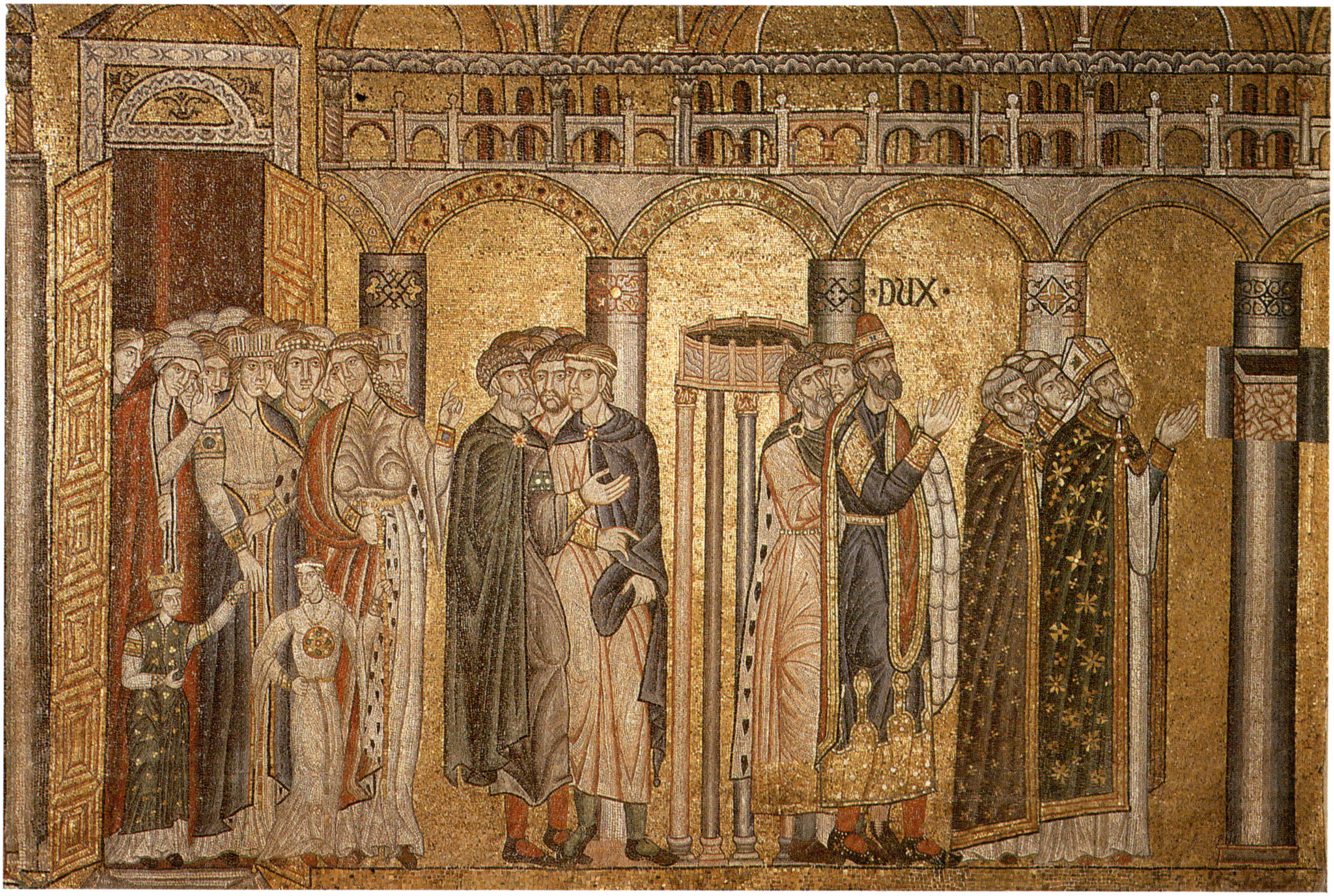

IV. *Apparition of St. Mark's Relics* (*Apparitio*), mosaic (Venice, San Marco, south transept)

lation. In November 1414, forty members of the Scuola di San Giovanni Evangelista came together in a chapter meeting and determined to commission their own cycle of history paintings. These works were probably intended for their *albergo*, the small boardroom where the officers held their meetings.[48] The Scuola was one of four large flagellant confraternities, later to be called Scuole Grandi, but at that time still known as Scuole dei Battuti.[49]

Two recent political developments could have stirred the brothers of San Giovanni to replicate (albeit on a reduced scale) the government initiatives. A law had been passed in 1401 ordering that the Mariegola of any Scuola dei Battuti could not be amended without the express permission of the Council of Ten.[50] It was followed in 1410 with the law reserving the four top offices to *cittadini originari* or to citizens by privilege who were members of long standing.[51] Clearly, the confraternities had achieved a new official status in Venetian society.[52] In the minds of their officers, tangible statements of cor-

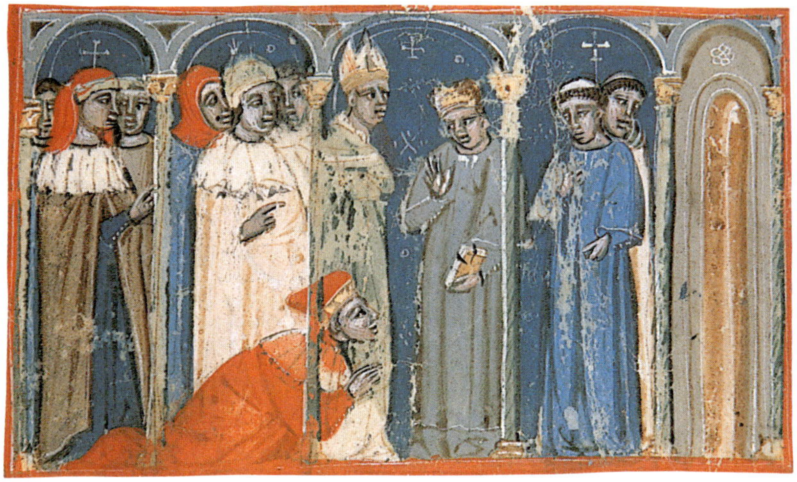

v. Venetian school, *Doge Ziani Kneels Before the Pope*, miniature (Venice, Museo Correr, Cod. Correr I, 383 [=1497])

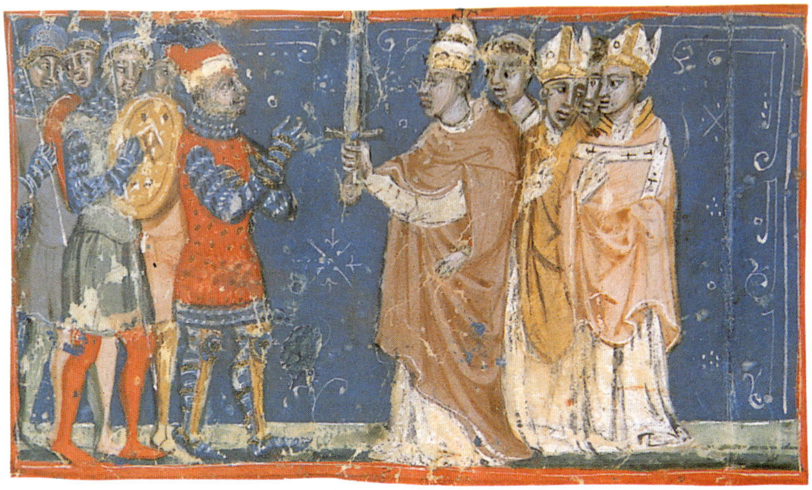

vi. Venetian school, *Consignment of the Sword*, miniature (Venice, Museo Correr, Cod. Correr I, 383 [=1497])

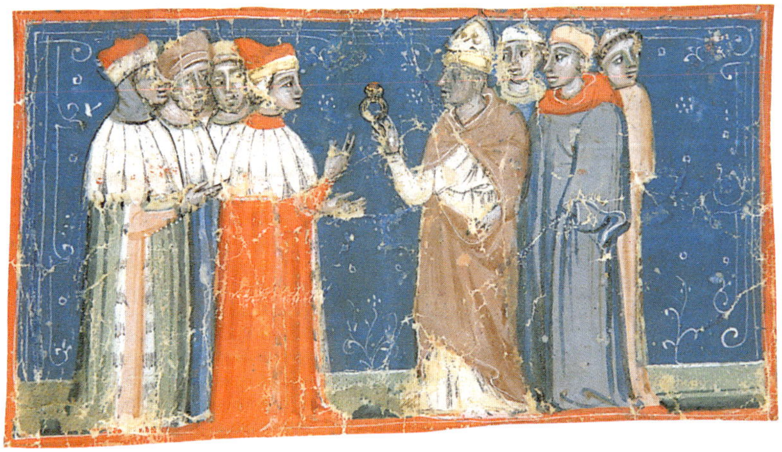

vii. Venetian school, *Presentation of the Ring*, miniature (Venice, Museo Correr, Cod. Correr I, 383 [=1497])

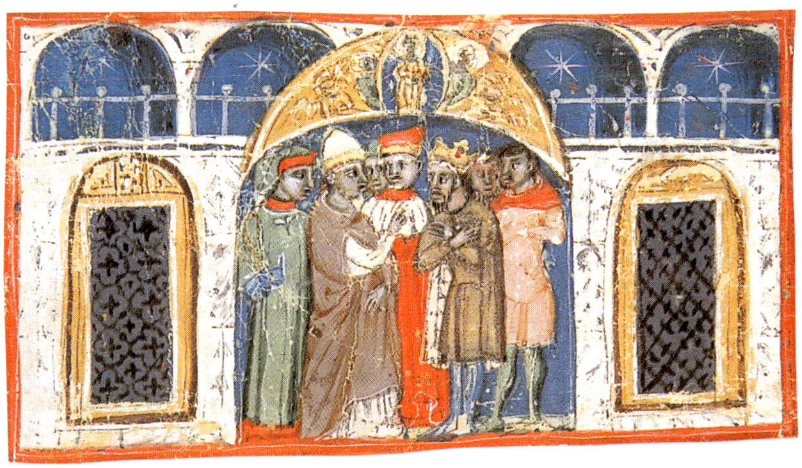

viii. Venetian school, *The Emperor and the Pope make Peace in Front of San Marco*, miniature (Venice, Museo Correr, Cod. Correr I, 383 [=1497])

porate identity centering on the embellishment of their meeting-halls may now have become necessary. In fact, from this time on, all four of these confraternities were engaged almost continuously in the expansion, rebuilding and decoration of their meeting-houses.[53]

However, the immediate impetus for the program of the Scuola di San Giovanni was a pious one. Earlier in the year of 1414 the young daughter of one of their members, Ser Nicolò Benvegnudo of San Polo, had been miraculously healed from a crippling affliction. The healing was attributed to the Santissima Croce, a prestigious relic of the True Cross that had been donated to the confraternity in 1369 by Philippe de Mézières, Grand Chancellor of Cyprus.[54] Since the relic had already demonstrated its powers on other occasions, the brothers decided to commemorate these events with paintings: 'the miracles effected by our Holy Cross in past times should be historiated in such a way that there would be notice of them [and] greater devotion by our brothers.'[55] The Santissima Croce was already a recognized symbol of the Scuola, for it was regularly carried in processions on feast-days [Plate 20].[56] The new civic affirmation of the confraternity may well have sparked the impulse to transform that symbol into a *trionfo* like those which informed the paintings of the Great Council Hall.[57]

In 1421, the officers of the Scuola di San Giovanni voted to continue the decoration of their meeting-house. They agreed to have the Sala Capitolare, the large hall used for assemblies of the entire membership, painted all the way around – *atorno atorno* – with histories of the Old and New Testament.[58] According to later sources, Jacopo Bellini was responsible for part of this program, although it is unlikely that he initiated it. Inscribed as a member of the Scuola in 1437, he seems to have completed at least a New Testament cycle for the room, perhaps around mid-century.[59]

The Scuola di San Marco

Meanwhile, across the city, the Scuola di San Marco, also a Scuola dei Battuti, had moved into a newly constructed meeting-house at San Giovanni e Paolo in 1438; it was to be involved in its adornment over the next four decades. After completing a ceiling of such splendor that the other Scuole dei Battuti were spurred to new decorative efforts, the Banca of San Marco would have looked jealously at the *istorie* of San Giovanni painted *atorno atorno*, which were so reminiscent of those in the halls of real political power. In 1444, they thus began the decoration of their own *albergo* with a program of painted *istorie* of unspecified subjects.[60]

Jacopo Bellini is the only artist who is documented in connection with this program.[61] That he was chosen may be an argument for prior experience and acclaim in the Scuola di San Giovanni and perhaps even in the Ducal Palace. He was now at the height of his career and his reputation. In 1441 he had earned the praise of several Ferrarese poets and humanists when he triumphed over Pisanello in a contest for the best portrait of Lionello d'Este, the Marquis of Ferrara. One writer proclaimed both artists 'the best painters of our times',[62] while another called Jacopo 'the new Phidias' and added in typical humanist panegyric: 'Thus to all others he taught the true way of the divine Apelles and the noble Polyclitus'.[63]

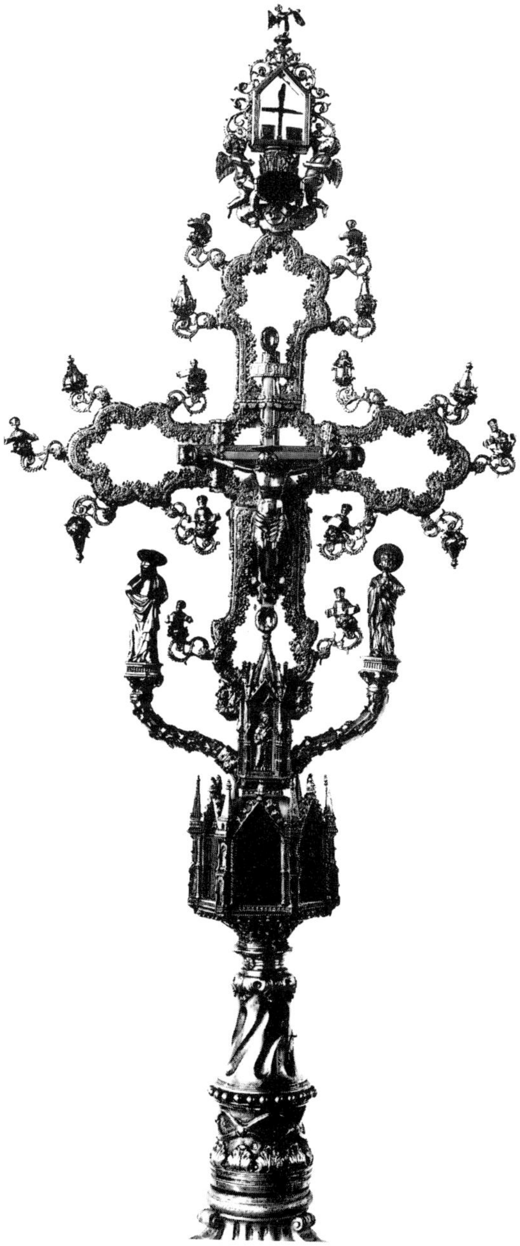

20. Reliquary of the True Cross, Scuola Grande di San Giovanni Evangelista, Venice

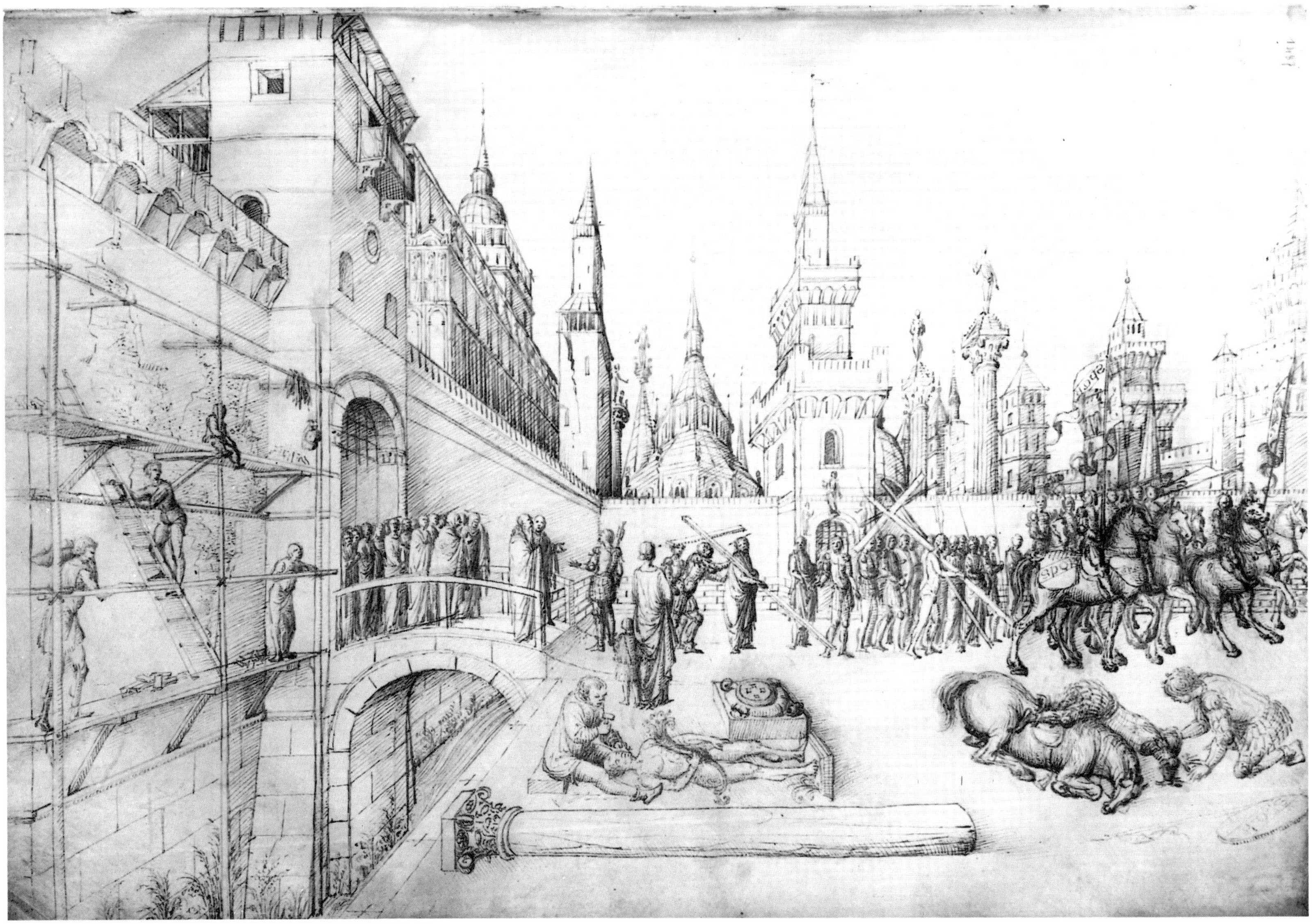

21. Jacopo Bellini, *Christ taken outside Jerusalem* (Paris, Louvre Album, fol. 19)

A refurbished albergo

Not to be outdone by the brothers of San Marco, the men of the Scuola di San Giovanni responded in turn, and in 1453 refurbished their own *albergo* with work of an unspecified nature. Four years later they decided that 'it would be necessary to have completed, gilded and decorated an altar made in the *albergo*. . . in which that most sacred and gracious cross of ours is kept, with all the other relics.' The Council of Ten allowed the confraternity to take in thirty extra members over their quota, whose entry fees would be applied to the project – a concession that in the future was to prove a popular means to finance decorative programs.[64] It is possible that an altarpiece which Sansovino later saw in the *albergo* and ascribed to Jacopo Bellini was made at this time. According to Ridolfi, the subject was a *Pietà*: 'the figure of the Savior and two Angels who piously support him'.[65]

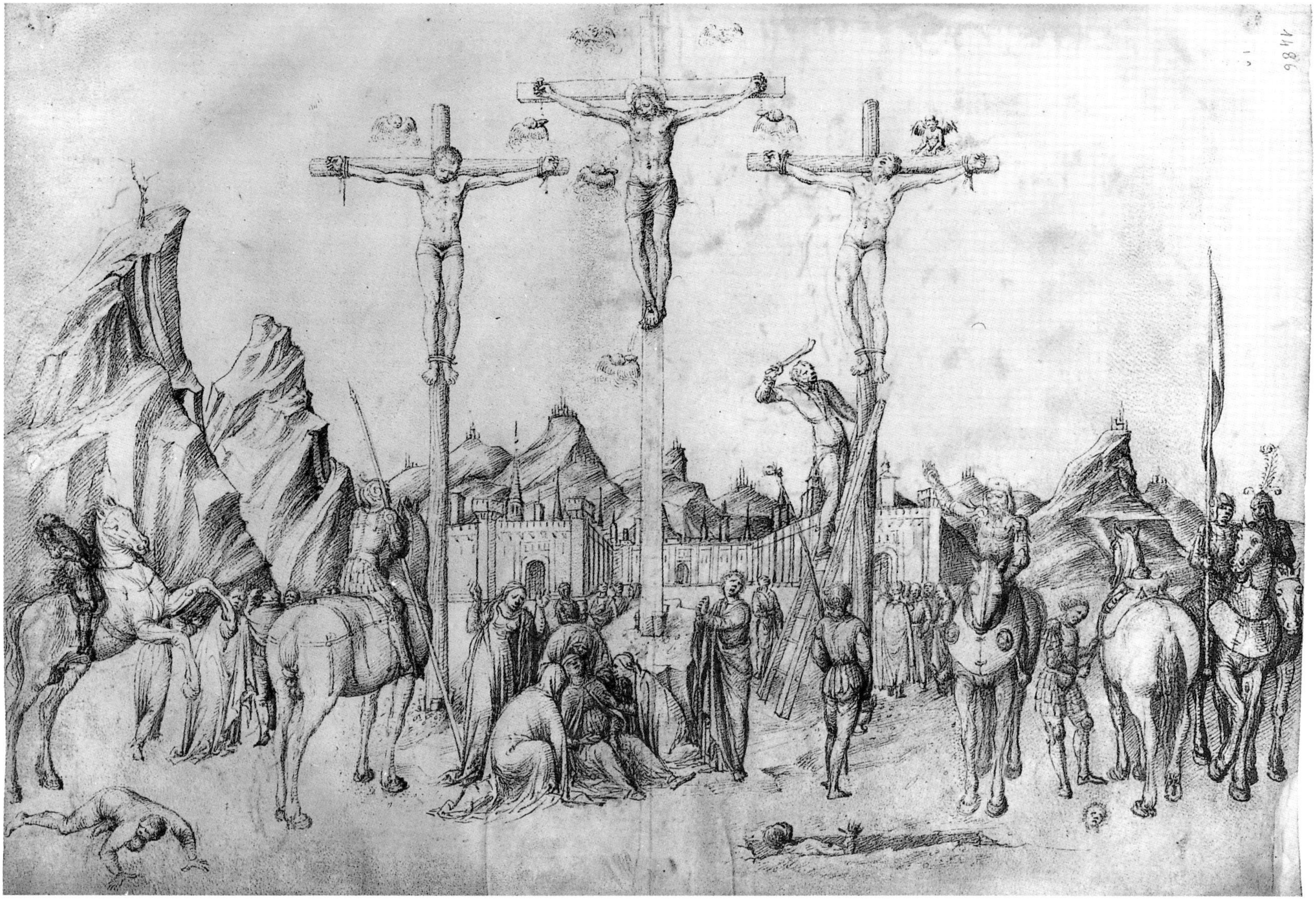

22. Jacopo Bellini, *Passion of Christ with Thieves* (Paris, Louvre Album, fol. 18)

The decoration of a Chapter Hall

Emulating the sequence established by the Scuola di San Giovanni, the officers of the Scuola di San Marco decided in 1463 to follow the decoration of their *albergo* with a second campaign in the larger Sala Capitolare. Only two or three *istorie* were comissioned at the outset. Again Jacopo Bellini's name appears in the sources. In an inventory of 1466 we find two paintings of unspecified subjects on canvas [*teleri*] by him, which were hung in the Sala at the altar of San Marco, although it is not clear whether they resulted from the decision of 1463.[66]

In July of 1466 he received a further commission to paint two more large *teleri* after the chapter of the confraternity expressed the desire 'to do that which would be in praise of God and in honor of this glorious city and of this blessed Scuola'. He was to be paid the considerable sum of 375 gold ducats for 'a Passion of Christ on the cross, rich with figures, and other things that would be fitting', to cover the entire south wall at the end of the room, and 'the story of Jerusalem with Christ and the thieves' – surely that of the Road to Calvary – that was to hang as a prologue immediately adjacent to it on the east wall.[67] Similar subjects appear in his drawing-books, although no direct connection can be established [Plates 21 and 22]. The canvases for the Scuola di San Marco probably marked Jacopo Bellini's last activity as a narrative painter, for he died in 1470/71.[68]

The remainder of the campaign in the Sala of the Scuola di San Marco involved paintings on canvas with scenes from the Old Testament. It is probably not by chance that the mixture of Old and New Testament scenes followed the model set by the Scuola di San Giovanni. At this point Gentile Bellini, Jacopo's son (probably the eldest), stepped into the arena of monumental narrative painting. In December 1466 he was commissioned to paint two scenes from the life of Moses: 'In one the *istoria* how Pharoah left the city with his army and how they were drowned and in the other how his people were drowned and how the other people of Moses fled in the desert'. These subjects, as well as the fee of three hundred ducats, again indicate large paintings with many figures.[69] In language increasingly typical of contracts of the time, the artist was obliged to equal or exceed the paintings of his father. It is worth noting that under the constraints of the family workshop system, so strong in Venice, neither Gentile nor his slightly younger brother Giovanni achieved true artistic independence in a professional sense until shortly before their father's death. In all likelihood, they would by this time have been journeymen painters for a good fifteen years.[70]

Gentile was followed in the Scuola by a succession of other artists, who were given contracts with similar terms to paint *istorie* focusing on major figures from the Old Testament. A month later, Andrea da Murano and Bartolomeo Vivarini were commissioned to make an *istoria* in two fields with scenes from the life of Abraham. In January 1470, Lazzaro Bastiani was assigned the story of David, again on a canvas with two fields. In April of the same year, Giovanni Bellini was commissioned to paint another two-part canvas with scenes from Genesis: Noah's Ark and the Flood. The latter painting was not finished by August 1482, and perhaps not even begun, for at that time the officers of the scuola were moved to hand over the commission to Bartolomeo Montagna. In any event, the cycle whose execution had been drawn out for such an extended period was truly 'finished' in 1485, although not in the manner envisioned by the members of the Scuola. On Good Friday of that year, a devastating fire consumed the entire building and all the works of art within it.[71]

Even with the loss of the paintings, the unusually well-documented campaign of the Scuola di San Marco is in itself a textbook example of a typical program of decoration in a Venetian Scuola Grande. It illustrates how they could extend over long periods of time to become collective enterprises on the part of both patrons and artists. During the twenty years in which the various canvases were commissioned, the successive *banche* of the Scuola brought together painters from the two major family workshops in the city – the Bellini and the Vivarini – as well as Bastiani, who was influenced by both, and Montagna, who had recently arrived from Vicenza. One might expect that the joint enterprise tended to enforce a normative style and the development of a common narrative mode.

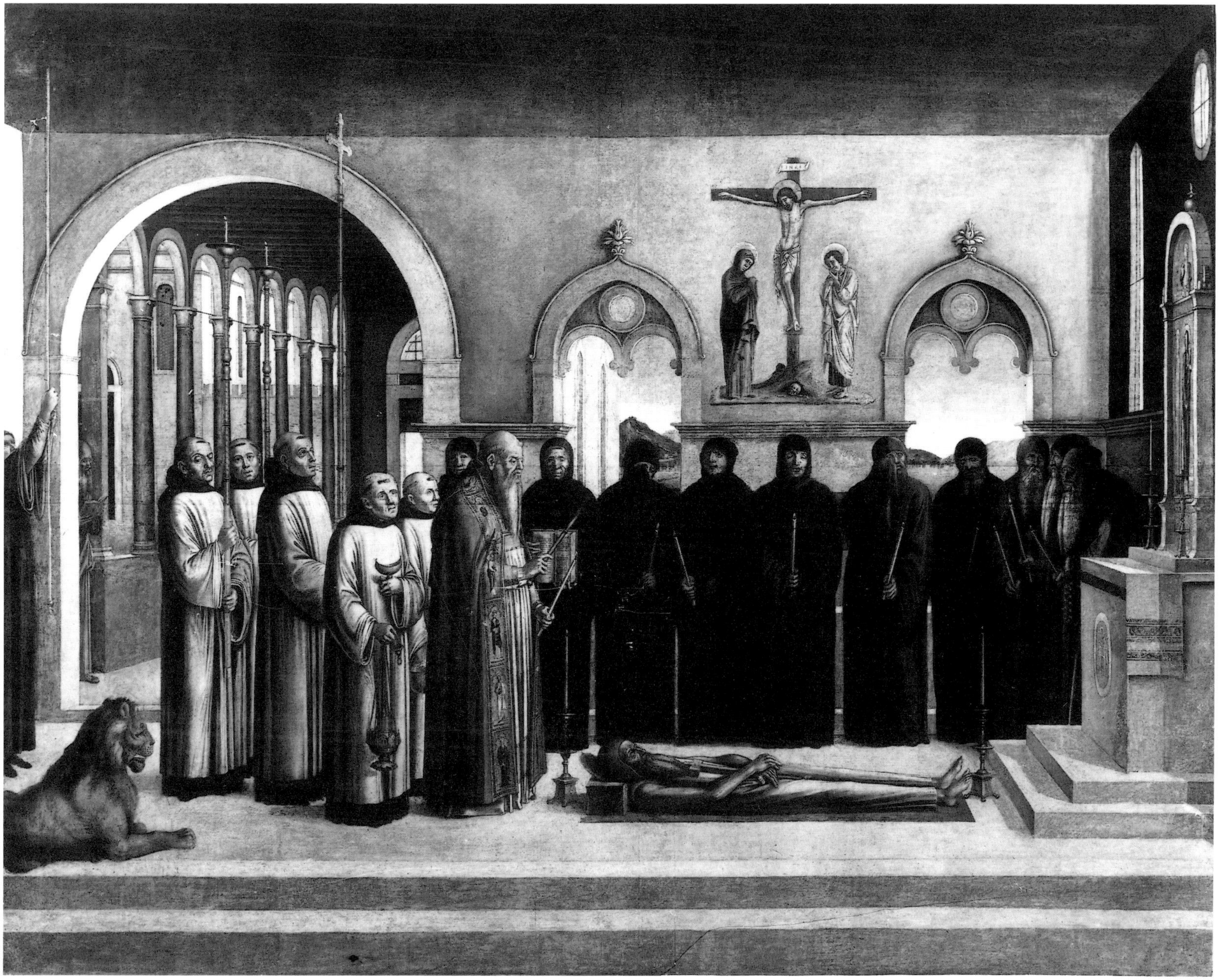

23. Lazzaro Bastiani, *Funeral of St. Jerome* (Venice, Accademia)

The Scuola di San Girolamo

Running virtually parallel in dating to the program in the Sala of the Scuola di San Marco was a narrative cycle in the Scuola di San Girolamo. A *scuola di devozione*, drawing members from various occupations, the confraternity owned a meeting-house next to the Church of San Girolamo in Cannaregio. In the series of five scenes from the life of St. Jerome painted on canvas we find the immediate forerunner of Carpaccio's hagiographical programs. As with the Scuola di San Marco, the campaign was a joint effort. Begun around 1464, it extended for ten to fifteen years and included works by Giovanni Bellini, Alvise Vivarini and Lazzaro Bastiani. Only Bastiani's canvases survive [Plate 23].[72]

The call in 1463 for the decoration of the Sala of the Scuola di San Marco, and the completion date of at least one of Bellini's paintings for the Scuola di San Girolamo in 1464, suggests a causal relationship between the two programs, with the smaller confraternity perhaps even taking the initiative. It is not improbable that the officers of San Marco had been moved to action at the prospect of a Sala with bare walls at a time when not only the Scuola di San Giovanni Evangelista was fully *istoriata* – to use their own term – but also when one of the lesser *scuole piccole* was beginning to adorn its meeting-house as well.

* * *

If we pause for a moment to consider the emergence and the early elaboration of the monumental painted *istoria* in Venice between 1320 and 1470, the insistently corporate nature of its patronage becomes obvious. Allowing that the fragility of fresco paintings in the Venetian climate may have deprived us of a full view of the evidence, we may conclude that the Venetian patron of history painting was invariably not a man but a group: either a government body or a religious confraternity. Furthermore, the setting of the *istoria* was determined by the collective nature of the patronage. It was found in public places that had a status somewhere between the sacred and the profane: neither wholly civic nor wholly religious.

The Great Council Hall – the political heart of the Republic – was dominated by Guariento's great fresco of the *Coronation of the Virgin*. The meeting-halls and even the chapels of the *scuole*, of whatever size, provided the setting for matters of a business and social nature as much as of liturgy and religious observance. The only churches in which we can place the *istoria* with certainty during this early period are the Basilica of San Marco and the little Church of San Nicolò in the Ducal Palace.[73] And these again are spaces that were virtually as much civic as they were religious. With this tradition in mind, in the next chapter we will return to the program of pictorial narrative decoration with which we began this one: the Great Council Hall campaign of 1474.

4

Artists and Occasions

In 1474 the Venetian Senate voted 126 to 6 (with two abstentions) to accept the offer of 'Maistro Gentile Bellini, eminent painter and excellent master' to restore and repair where necessary the paintings in the Great Council Hall 'which is one of the principal ornaments of our city'.[1] In lieu of a fixed salary, the artist would receive for his labors the next vacant *sansaria*, a brokerage at the Fondaco dei Tedeschi that would provide him with a fixed yearly income.[2] As the son of Jacopo Bellini, one of the leading artists of the city, Gentile was the natural choice for such a responsibility. Jacopo, who had died four years earlier, was himself the son of a tinsmith, but also a *cittadino originario*. It was a rank not claimed by every artist, nor was it to be taken for granted by the son of an artisan who had also worked with his hands.[3] The honor was passed on to his own sons, for Gentile and Giovanni were each called *fidelis civis noster* in the *Deliberazioni* of the Great Council.[4]

But Gentile held a further distinction. In 1469, he had been granted the title of *Comes Palatinus* – Palatine Knight – by the Emperor Frederick III, who paid a visit to Venice that year during the last days of Carnival.[5] Little evidence remains of Gentile's artistic activity before this date, aside from the paintings in the Scuola di San Marco, and one wonders what achievements had brought him to the attention of an emperor.[6] A portrait of Frederick has been suggested, although his busy stay of thirteen days in Venice may have allowed little time for one to be completed.[7] In any event, none survives.

But another possibility comes to mind: a cycle of *istorie* depicting the *andata* (journey) of Doge Cristoforo Moro to the port of Ancona in 1464. There he was to join forces with Pope Pius II in a crusade against the Turks. Although Pius died just as the Doge arrived, and plans for a military campaign were quickly set aside, the Venetians were not averse to turning the inconsequential event to their political advantage by commemorating it in pictorial form. The story was painted around the walls of the Sala dele do nape in the east wing of the Ducal Palace, where the Collegio, the steering committee of the Senate, received distinguished visitors.[8] Santo Brasca, a Milanese pilgrim on his way to the Holy Land, saw the paintings in 1480 and wrote that the room was 'the most beautiful of the entire Palace', where 'audiences are given to ambassadors and to other honorable men'.[9] The room and its contents were destroyed by fire in 1483.

Gentile's participation in this program cannot be proven, for no documents associating him with it have come to light. But the circumstances suggest it. A link between Venice's Turkish strategy and Frederick III can be traced in the letters of Michele Colli to the Duke of Milan. Colli described the Emperor's visit in 1469 and observed how lavishly the Venetians feted their guest. He suspected ulterior motives:

I believe, however, that these people have the eye to make him spend hugely on the Turkish venture; and I believe so many of these caresses are [intended] to incite him. However, those who know him are very certain that once he has turned his shoulder, he will never spend a cent, but he will take from them what he can, yet will return no more to Italy.

Up to this point I cannot find out what is discussed; according to public opinion it is about the Turks.[10]

If the paintings were already in place, Doge Moro and his counsellors would have made sure that Frederick saw and admired them.[11] A knighthood for Gentile Bellini, if he was the artist, might well have been an astute diplomatic ploy on the Emperor's part to pay honor to his hosts without putting himself in their debt. The case for Gentile's role in all this is only circumstantial, but it may help to explain his seemingly sudden elevation to knighthood.

Gentile Bellini and the Great Council Hall

A renewed recognition of the potential benefit of history paintings as instruments of statecraft may also have prompted the Signoria in 1474 to call for the refurbishment of the old paintings of the Grand Council Hall. From the report of Bartolomeo Facio in 1456, we know that the old frescoes had already been in poor condition for nearly twenty years, with the *Battle of Salvore* of Gentile da Fabriano barely intelligible. As the largest interior ceremonial space of the Republic, the room had been in continuous use during that time, not only for regular meetings but also for great banquets and balls honoring foreign dignitaries like Frederick III.[12] An engraving from the middle of the sixteenth century, showing only Guariento's *Coronation of the Virgin* at the east end, may give some sense of the room of the late fifteenth century before the paintings on the side walls were replaced [Plate 24].

As we saw in Chapter 2, the political atmosphere in 1474 was particularly tense. Although the whole city was soon to rejoice over the successful breaking of a six-week Turkish siege of the fortress at Scutari [Shköder] in upper Albania, few of those voting in the Senate to restore the paintings of the Great Council Hall 'for the honor of our Signoria' could have deceived themselves that the threat was over.[13] The main concern of the government that autumn was to gain western supporters, but its complicated diplomatic manoeuvers resulted only in a new treaty with Florence and Milan at the expense of alienating its former ally, the Pope. Angered over what was viewed as papal obstinacy, Venice withdrew its ambassador from Rome, 'in order that the world may know what manner of shepherd it is who looks calmly on as his flock is being devoured and does not come to its help'.[14]

A rather different mood can be observed here from that of the humble Venice of 1313, when Francesco Dandolo (*il Cane*) had grovelled beneath the papal altar in sackcloth to seek absolution from the interdict on behalf of the Republic. A century and a half of territorial expansion into the Terraferma, and rule by a well-entrenched patriciate, had produced a new generation that was prepared to deal with the Pope as an equal. In short, it was a likely time for a restatement of those civic ideals that were so clearly and eloquently expressed in the images and text of the Alexander legend.[15]

24 (facing). Anonymous, *The Great Council Hall before the Fire of 1577*, engraving (Venice, Museo Correr)

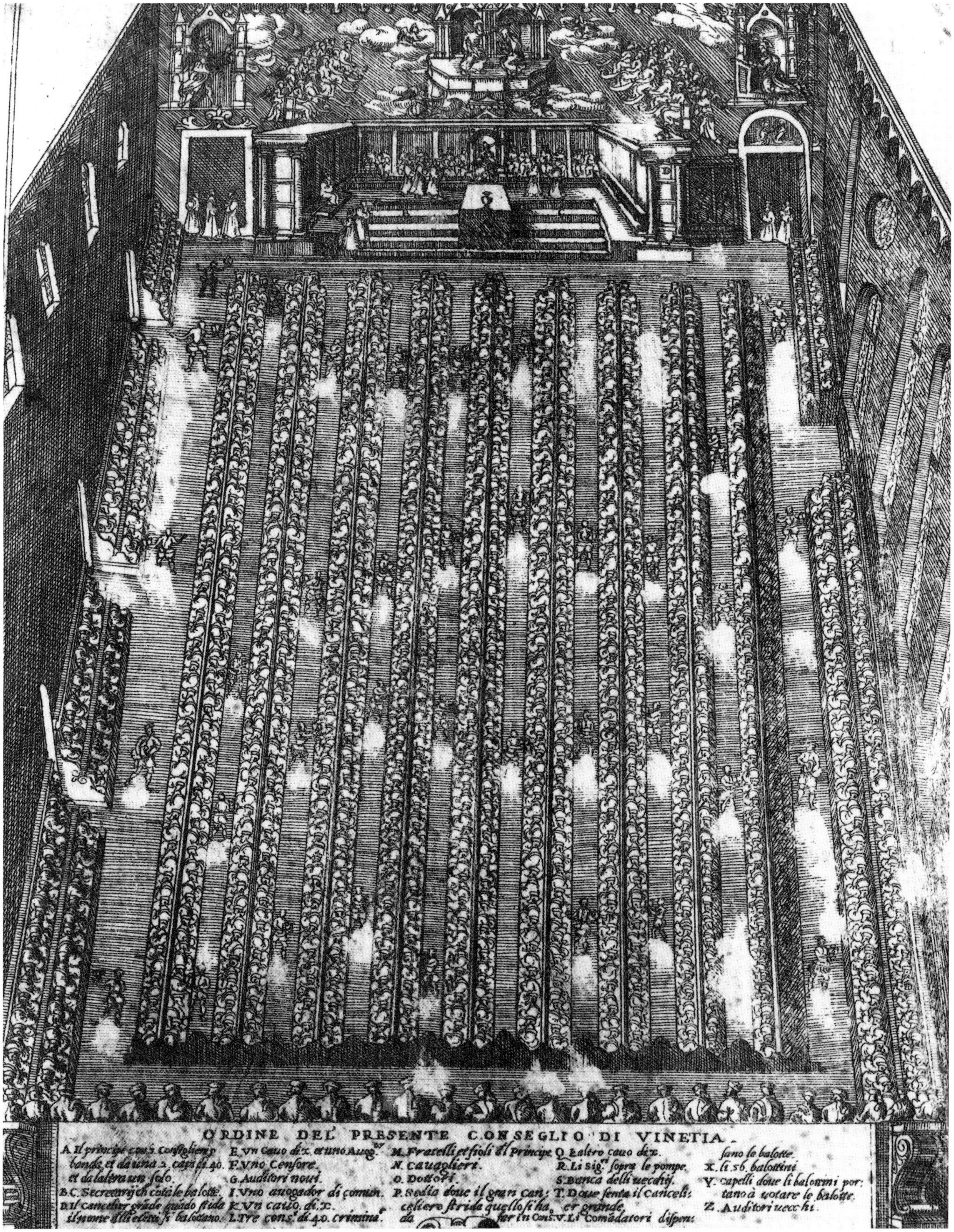
ORDINE DEL PRESENTE CONSEGLIO DI VINETIA.
A. Il principe con 3 consiglieri p banda, et da una 2 capi di 40. et da laltra un solo.
B.C. Secretarij che cota le balotte.
D. Il Cancelier grãde quado stida il nome delli eletti si balotano.
E. Vn cauo di x. et uno Auog.
F. Vno Censore.
G. Auditori noui.
I. Vno auogador di comun.
K. Vn cauo. di. x.
L. Tre cons. di 40. crimina.
M. Fratelli et fioli del Principe
N. cauaglieri.
O. Dottori.
P. Sedia doue il gran Canceliero strida quello si ha da far in Cons.
Q. Laltro cauo di x.
R. Li sig. sopra le pompe.
S. Banca delli uecchij.
T. Doue senta il Canceli: er grande.
V. Li Comãdatori dispensano le balotte.
X. li 56. balottini
Y. capelli doue li balottini portano à uotare le balotte.
Z. Auditori uecchi.

To move from the realm of hypothesis to that of documented fact, it was not long before Gentile was called upon to make his own *andata* on behalf of the Serenissima. On 25 April 1479, the feast-day of St. Mark, the peace treaty that the Venetian secretary Giovanni Dario had negotiated with Sultan Mehmed II was publicly proclaimed with a great celebration in the Piazza San Marco.[16] Two days later, Lutfi-Beg, the ambassador of the Sultan, dressed himself in two gowns of gold and was taken to the Great Council Hall where he would have seen the work under way on the new paintings by Gentile Bellini.[17]

Lutfi-Beg's report to the Sultan upon his return to Constantinople may well have led to an unusual request a few months later. As Sanudo recalled it:

> On the first day of August a Jewish orator from the Lord Turk arrived with letters. He wished for the Signoria to send him a good painter, and invited the Doge to go to honor the marriage of his son. [The Signoria] responded, thanking him, and sent Gentile Bellini, an excellent painter, who went with the galleys of Romania; and the Signoria paid his expenses, and he left the third of September.[18]

Malipiero noted that the Sultan had specifically requested 'a good painter who knows how to make portraits'.[19] Gentile had already completed several ducal portraits by this date, and probably also a number of private ones, although few survive.[20] In addition, according to later sources, one of the paintings that he would have finished in the Great Council Hall by this time, *The Presentation of the White Candle to the Doge*, contained a number of portraits, including Cardinal Bessarion, two Procurators of San Marco – Leonardo and Bernardo Giustiniani – and other cardinals, prelates and senators.[21] The only visual record of Gentile's compositions to survive with some certainty is a drawing by an unidentified artist of his *Consignment of the Sword*. Although it records only a portion of his composition, it gives a sense of the crowds of spectators that would have populated many of the scenes [Plate 25]. Before Gentile's departure, the Great Council, holding that work in the hall must continue, appointed Giovanni Bellini to replace his brother in the painting campaign, but obligated Gentile to resume his labors there upon his return.[22]

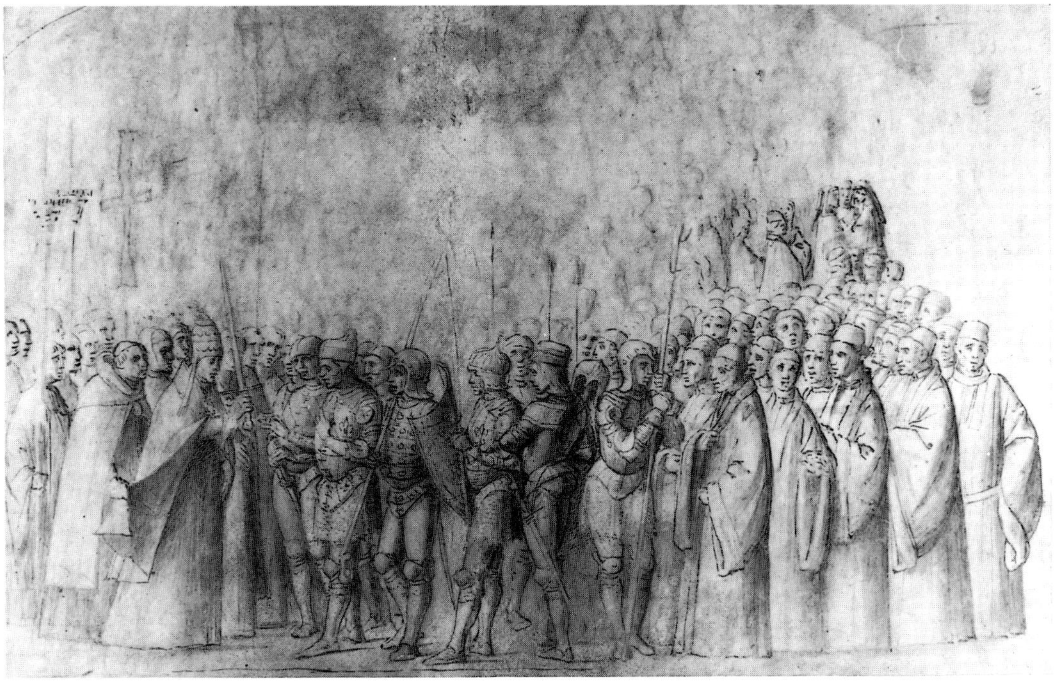

25. Copy after Gentile Bellini, *Consignment of the Sword*, drawing (London, British Museum, 1891-6-17–23)

Gentile did not travel alone. His entourage included two associates, as well as a bronze-caster, Master Bartolomeo, with two assistants of his own.[23] As a gift to the Sultan, the painter seems to have brought the book of drawings made by his father, Jacopo Bellini, that eventually ended up in the Louvre.[24] Gentile spent just over a year in Constantinople. According to Gian Maria Angiolello, a western observer, Mehmed 'wished him to make a drawing of Venice and to make portraits of many persons. . . . Gentile made various beautiful paintings, and especially *cose di lussuria*, in some things beautiful, so that there was a great quantity of them in the palace.'[25] We do not know what these *cose di lussuria* were. Usually translated as 'things of a lascivious nature', there is no reason to believe that they were necessarily erotic paintings. They may well have been scenes of banquets and other festive occasions at the Ottoman court. Only a handful of works survive from Gentile's Turkish sojourn, most notably a portrait of Mehmed II, which is probably original, and a medal of the Sultan, which the artist may have made after his return to Venice [Plates 2 and 26]. Sanudo later reported: 'And he was well regarded by the Signor Turcho and was made a knight; and he had him paint some things, especially a Venice.'[26]

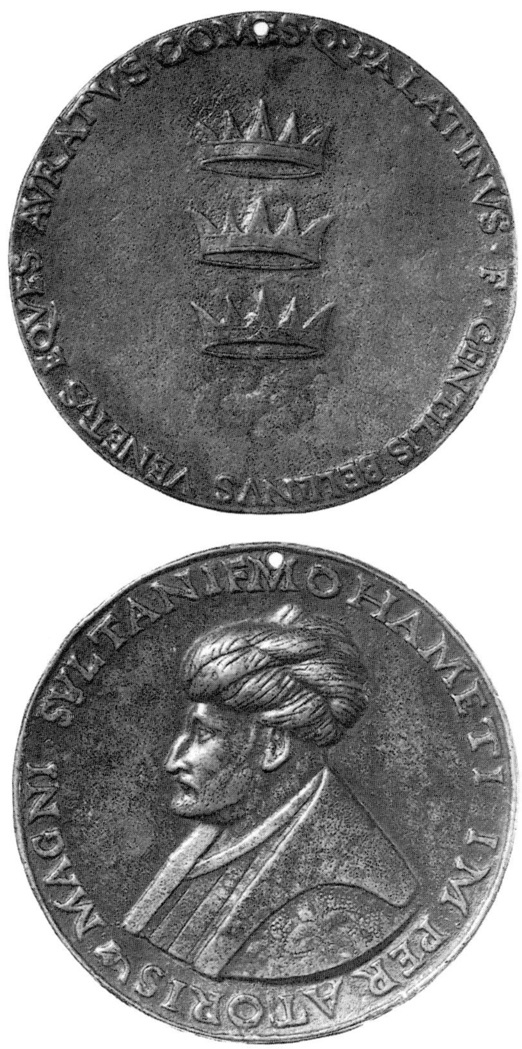

26. Gentile Bellini, *Sultan Mehmed II*, medal, recto and verso (Washington, D.C., National Gallery of Art, Samuel Kress Collection)

Gentile was honored by Mehmed with a heavy necklace of gold and an additional title: 'Eques Auratus'.[27] He lost no time in inscribing the title on a medal portraying the Sultan, conjoining it to that which he had already received from the Emperor in 1469. On one side it bears the profile image of Mehmed with the inscription: MAGNI SVLTANI F. MAHOMETI. IMPERATORIS. On the reverse are three crowns, surrounded by the legend: GENTILIS BELENVS VENETVS EQVES AVRATVS COMESQ. PALATINVS F.[28] When he resumed his work in the Great Council Hall, probably early in 1481,[29] he also proclaimed his new status on his next painting, *The Departure of the Venetian Ambassadors to the Court of the Emperor*. As Sansovino later described it:

> And because the said Gentile had returned from Constantinople, where he had made the portrait of the Turk, by whom he had been made a knight (as I have seen his privilege) with many rich gifts, he wrote under the aforementioned painting the following verses:
>
> Gentile Bellini has given this monument to his country, Having been called to the Ottoman, and made a knight as a reward.[30]

Gentile's fame continued to grow. In the *Supplementum Chronicarum*, published in Venice in 1486, Jacobo Filippo Foresti recorded the most significant events and people year by year from the time of the Creation up to his own day. His selection of distinguished men was usually limited to rulers, scholars and prelates, but under the entry for 1483 Gentile was cited and was, in fact, the only Venetian listed for that year:

> Gentile Bellini, Paduan born [*sic*], the most celebrated painter of these times, [and] not only in the region of Venice, for I would say his unusual and admirable painting is now seen to adorn the whole of Italy as well; to whom is given such a gift for painting, that he could be compared to any of the ancient and exquisite painters, Greek as well as Latin, without injury to merit.[31]

In 1488, another artist saw the participation in the Great Council Hall campaign as a certain way to gain prestige. Alvise Vivarini volunteered his services for a portion of what remained, affirming that it was a good opportunity to demonstrate some product of my skill in painting [so that] your sublimity . . . would see and recognize that my continuous study and diligence has not been in vain, but to the honor and praise of this illustrious city.[32]

Vivarini's offer was accepted, and he worked in the Council Hall until his death in 1503/5. Gentile Bellini was not listed among the five journeymen painters who, in addition to Giovanni Bellini and Vivarini, had received monthly salaries for painting in the room during the period 1489–95.[33] But Sanudo's notices in his 'Cronachetta', presumably up-to-date in its first redaction of 1493, indicate that Gentile was still engaged on the project.[34] The growing splendor of the room, in addition to the perception that Venice's constitution had divine sanction, may well have inspired the Florentines to begin building their own council hall in 1495, in direct emulation of the Venetian prototype.[35]

Carpaccio and the Scuola di Sant' Orsola

The first major campaign of narrative painting to follow that begun in the Great Council Hall was initiated not by one of the wealthy Scuole Grandi, but by a *scuola piccola*. According to its foundation statutes written in 1300, the Scuola di Sant' Orsola had been organized 'because the holy scriptures say that it is a good

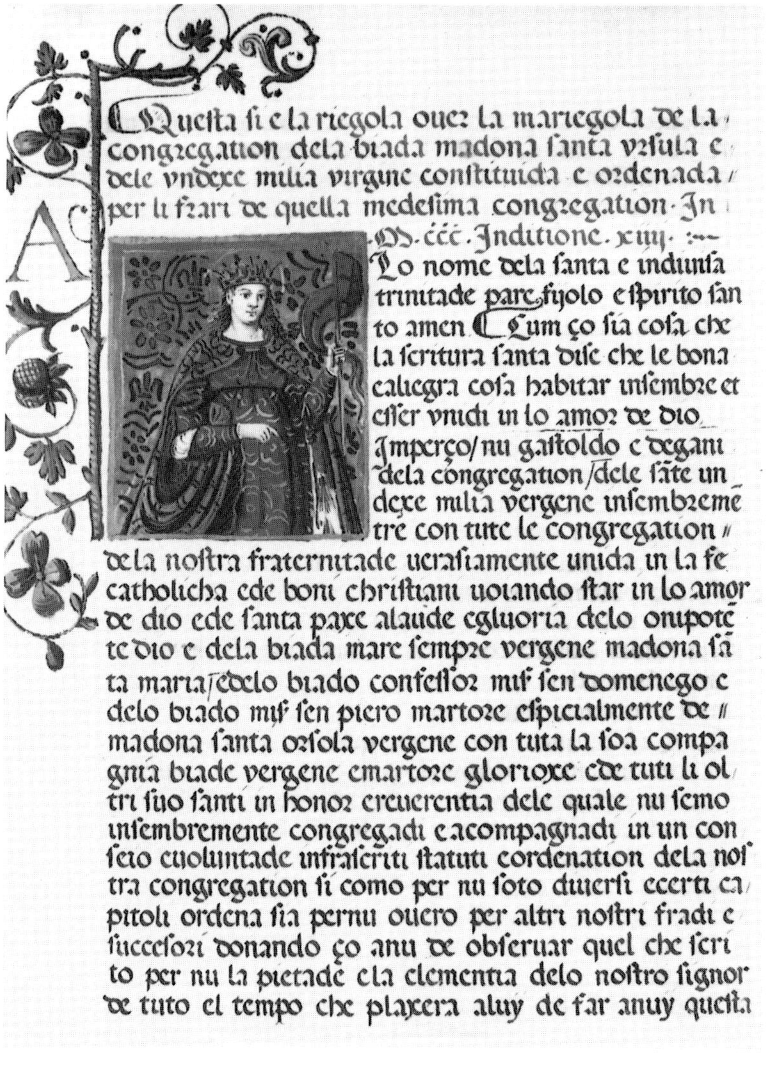
Questa si e la riegola ouer la mariegola de la
congregation dela biada madona santa vrsula e
dele vndexe milia virgine constituida e ordenada
per li frari de quella medesima congregation · In
M. ccc. Inditione. xiiij.
Lo nome dela santa e indivisa
trinitade pare, fyolo e spirito san
to amen. Cum ço sia cosa che
la scritura santa dise che le bona
e aliegra cosa habitar insembre et
esser vnidi in lo amor de dio.
Imperço/ nu gastoldo e degani
dela congregation/dele sãte un
dexe milia vergene insembreme
tre con tute le congregation
de la nostra fraternitade uerasiamente unida in la fe
catholicha e de boni christiani uoiando star in lo amor
de dio e de santa paxe alaude e gloria delo omnipotẽ
te dio e dela biada mare sempre vergene madona sã
ta maria/e delo biado confessor mis sen domenego e
delo biado mis sen piero martore especialmente de
madona santa orsola vergene con tuta la soa compa
gnia biade vergene e martore gloriose e de tuti li ol
tri suo santi in honor e reuerentia dele quale nu semo
insembremente congregadi e acompagnadi in un con
seio e uoluntade infrascriti statuti e ordenation dela nos
tra congregation si como per nu soto diuersi e certi ca
pitoli ordena sia per nu ouero per altri nostri fradi e
successori donando ço anu de obseruar quel che scri
to per nu la pietade e la clementia delo nostro signor
de tuto el tempo che plaxera aluy de far anuy questa

27. St. Ursula. Mariegola, Scuola di Sant' Orsola, 1488 (ASV, Scuole piccole, B. 597, f. 1)

and joyful thing to reside together and to be united in the love of God'. The members – both men and women – agreed to pursue the common goals of charity, mutual assistance and Christian devotion, under the protection of the Virgin and Saints Dominic and Peter Martyr and 'especially of the *madona santa orsola verzene* with her company of blessed virgins and glorious martyrs'.[36]

At a chapter meeting in 1488, the Banca of the Scuola discussed the decoration of their meeting-house. Serving also as a chapel, it was located next to the Dominican Basilica of SS. Giovanni and Paolo. The officers determined that a special fund should be established, supported by a monthly tax levied on members of the Banca and by fines assessed against ordinary members for infractions of the rules, such as swearing or non-attendance at funeral processions. The funds thus collected would be spent on the meeting-house, either to decorate it or to have canvases painted with the story of St. Ursula.[37] The project may have received additional financing from a group of patrician members, who had recently joined the Scuola and paid a higher than usual entry fee.[38] The decision was duly recorded in a newly transcribed Mariegola bearing a miniature of St. Ursula on the opening page [Plate 27].

The program was a bold one for a *scuola piccola*, envisioning a far grander scheme than the medium-sized paintings that had been painted recently for the Scuola di San Girolamo.[39] It was probably more equivalent to the decoration of the Sala Capitolare of the Scuola Grande di San Marco that had been consumed by fire three years before.[40] The huge *teleri* eventually painted by Carpaccio for the Scuola di Sant' Orsola measured about nine feet high, varying in width from eight to twenty feet, and wrapped around the room just like those in the Great Council Hall [Plate 28].[41]

The artist chosen for the project was not one of those experienced in the Ducal Palace campaign, but the young Vittore Carpaccio. From our distant vantage-point nearly five hundred years later, he appears abruptly on the Venetian artistic scene at about the age of twenty-five, seemingly as if from nowhere.[42] Few works securely attributed to him survive from the years before, and none involves an *istoria*. If Gentile Bellini made his reputation with the history paintings in the Ducal Palace, Carpaccio made his here, with eight narrative scenes and an altarpiece commemorating the life of a virgin saint who, along with her eleven thousand companions, probably never existed. It is the earliest surviving painting cycle in the Venetian 'eyewitness style'.

Ursula's *vita* had found its canonical form at the end of the thirteenth century in the *Golden Legend* of Jacopo da Voragine.[43] Featuring her as the beautiful and virtuous daughter of the Christian King of Brittany, it is often likened to a chivalric fairytale. It was, however, not a fairytale to Venetians in 1488. It was a true history, preserved as 'legend': that is, as an 'authorized' narrative that could be read in authoritative books.[44]

The grand design of the painted decoration may have been a consequence of aristocratic influence within the membership. The Scuola had been popular with patricians from the beginning. In 1370 they were required to pay a higher entry fee than commoners, since 'many persons entered the Scuola in the condition of nobles; through [their] being exempt from the offices...the Scuola has thus come to lack good men to make officials.'[45] The Gastaldo in 1488 was a certain Antonio di Filipo, who listed himself on the rolls as a nobleman, although his lack of a patrician surname would cast doubt upon his actual social rank.[46] An inscription and a coat-of-arms in two of Carpaccio's paintings appear to carry

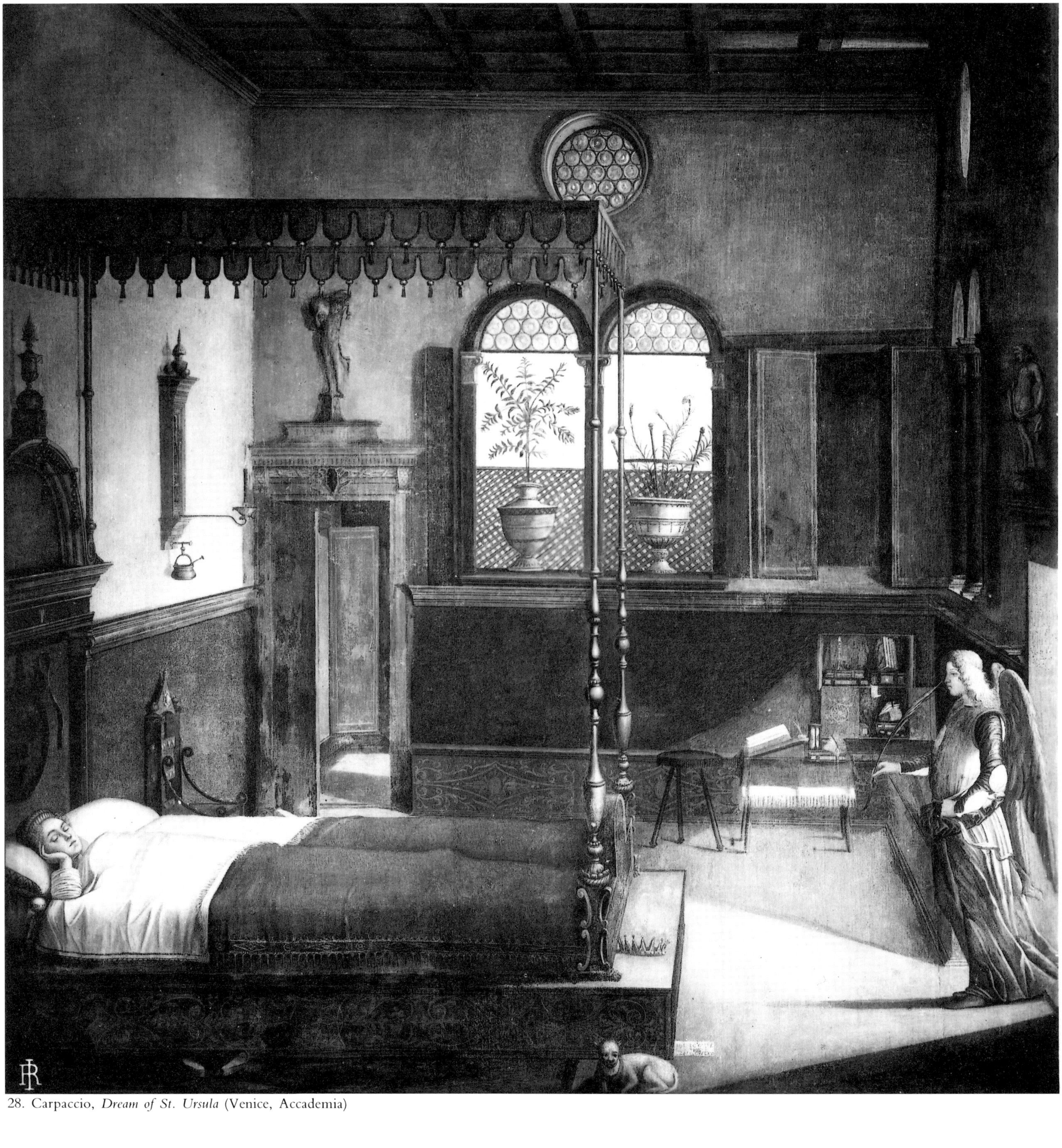

28. Carpaccio, *Dream of St. Ursula* (Venice, Accademia)

specific references to the Loredan family. This fact, along with the placement of the tomb of Pietro Loredan in the center of the meeting-house in 1508, suggests the family's financial support of at least part of the program.[47]

One should envision these works in their ritual context, with the entire membership assembling for mass in front of the altar of their meeting-house on the second Sunday of each month. In 1499 an office of St. Ursula and the eleven thousand virgins was published in Venice and was duly copied into the Mariegola of the Scuola. The opening prayer invokes:

> Oh God, glory of virgins and lover of them, who granted to the blessed Ursula in the palm of martyrdom the company of the eleven thousand virgins: Grant to us by their multiple interventions, efficacy in our petitions, constancy in our faith and purity in our good works.[48]

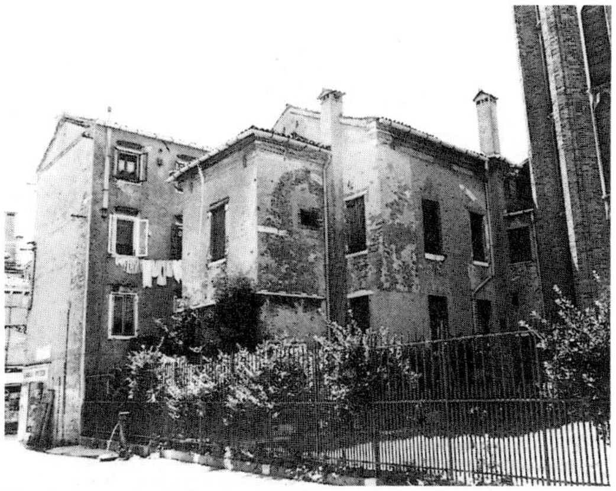

29. Apse end of the Scuola di Sant'Orsola in its present state

During the service, each brother and sister held a candle and joined in a procession around the room at the reading of the Gospel, perhaps following the progress of Ursula and her eleven thousand companions in the painted histories. At the *sanctus* the candles were lit, and were kept burning at the elevation of the Host.[49]

The members could then return home, reassured in those uncertain times by the sheer weight of numbers of their patrons and intercessors.

Carpaccio's paintings were clearly a success and a matter of pride for both the Scuola and the city at large. Sanudo, in the 'Cronachetta' that he kept updated until 1530, listed only three programs of painting among the 'notable things' of Venice, aside from that of the Great Council Hall: the altarpieces of Giovanni Bellini in San Giobbe and of Antonello da Messina in San Cassiano, and 'la capella de Santa Orsola, le historie et figure che è atorno bellisime'.[50]

30. Carpaccio, *Apotheosis of St. Ursula* (Venice, Accademia)

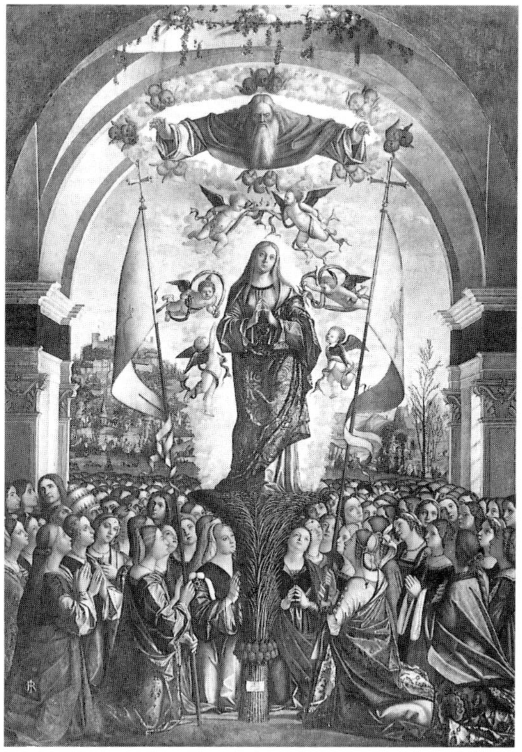

Each year on 21 October, the feast-day of the saint, the Scuola spilled out into public space with a celebration lasting three or four days. The meeting-house was decorated with garlands, and altars covered by tents were set up on the *campo* outside. On the eve of the feast, trumpeters and pipers went in boats to the Rialto and to the Basilica of San Marco. The next day the Dominican brothers of SS. Giovanni e Paolo celebrated a *missa cantata*, preceded by a solemn procession, and small woodcuts with images of St. Ursula were distributed.[51] Carpaccio's decoration campaign, probably completed by 1500, may have attracted more visitors than the meeting-house could comfortably hold, for in 1504 the convent ceded land to the Scuola to construct a new chancel. The addition extended the building by about three meters on the east end, and the main altar with Carpaccio's *Apotheosis of St. Ursula* was moved into it [Plates 29 and 30].[52]

There are indications that Carpaccio's talent was by now well-regarded outside the halls of the *scuole*. In 1496, when the Ursula cycle would have been nearing completion, Girolama Corsi Ramos, a poetess of noble lineage and wife of a *condottiere* in the service of the Venetian Republic, wrote a sonnet in praise of the artist. Her manifest delight in a portrait he had painted of her evoked the familiar humanist commonplaces by which artists had come to be eulogized by the *eruditi* of the period:

> That which his genius could put forth by tracing here my very features, all art and care in work he showed to cause my lips to utter ready speech. Yet heaven would not have this be that mortal man usurp and steal all

omnipotence that nature hath possessed, who from a piece of wood would make a living thing.[53]

Carpaccio was busy with more than portraits and the St. Ursula cycle during this period, for he had also completed an *istoria* for the other major narrative painting campaign of the decade: the *Miracles of the True Cross* of the Scuola Grande di San Giovanni Evangelista.

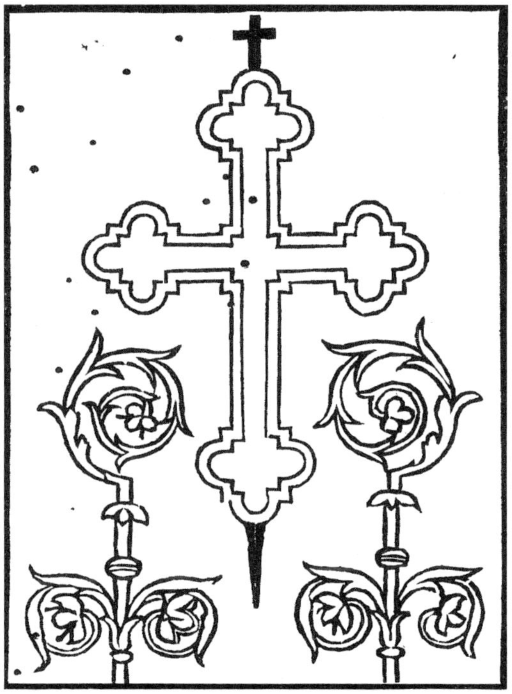

31. The Relic of the True Cross of the Scuola Grande di San Giovanni Evangelista (Venice, Museo Correr, Inc. H222 bis, frontispiece)

The eyewitness painters and the story of the True Cross

By the 1490s, the pre-eminence of the True Cross of the Scuola di San Giovanni in relation to similar relics was firmly established in the Venetian consciousness.[54] Sanudo listed five relics of the True Cross in his 'Cronachetta', but only that of the Scuola di San Giovanni was designated as 'miracolosa'.[55] In addition, he referred to the relic once again in his separate list of 'notable things' in different churches, along with the paintings of the Scuola di Sant' Orsola. The citation reads: 'It is a most miraculous cross, with the wood of the cross, which makes and has made many miracles'.[56] None of the other Scuole Grandi were credited specifically with miraculous relics of any sort.

The devotion of the brothers of the Scuola di San Giovanni to their venerable relic of the True Cross had not diminished over the years. It had been responsible, a member now observed, for 'almost innumerable miracles... recalling to memory and occupying the thoughts hereafter, that all things whether of man and of dignity, whether of goods and of resources, are bestowed on us by God'.[57] A small booklet, an *incunabulum*, was printed during this period (c. 1490–1506), recounting the history of the relic: how it had been presented to the confraternity back in the fourteenth century by Philippe de Mézières, and how it had begun immediately to demonstrate its miraculous powers [Plate 31]. Just nine of the miracles that occurred during the period 1369–1480 were described in some detail, but as the anonymous author of the treatise was careful to point out: 'This blessed cross has made many other miracles that are not written here, and it makes them day by day'.[58]

Thus, it is not surprising that the relic of the True Cross would be chosen not only as the rationale but also as the central theme for a new decorative scheme for the *albergo* of San Giovanni in the last decade of the fifteenth century. It had been some forty years since the room had received serious decorative attention. Indeed, in 1490 Sabellico was rather dismissive about the interior of the meeting-house, 'whose entrance is decorated in marble, in such a way that the other things inside being less ornate, in any event in the front it displays splendor'.[59] The new entry court, completed in 1481, set a higher standard that the rest of the building had yet to match [Plate 32].

It is not known precisely when paintings were first planned for the room, but in February 1491 the Scuola was given permission by the Council of Ten to admit twenty-five extra members, 'so that they could perfect their *albergo* and do other pious works'.[60] Further funding was obtained in September 1492, and in the following February a second petition to the Council of Ten for extra members referred to the completion of a new raised ceiling in the *albergo*, to the satisfaction of those who gathered together in devotion to the relic of the Cross.

IX (facing above). Carpaccio, *Presentation of the Virgin* (Milan, Brera)

X (facing below). Carpaccio, *Marriage of the Virgin* (Milan, Brera)

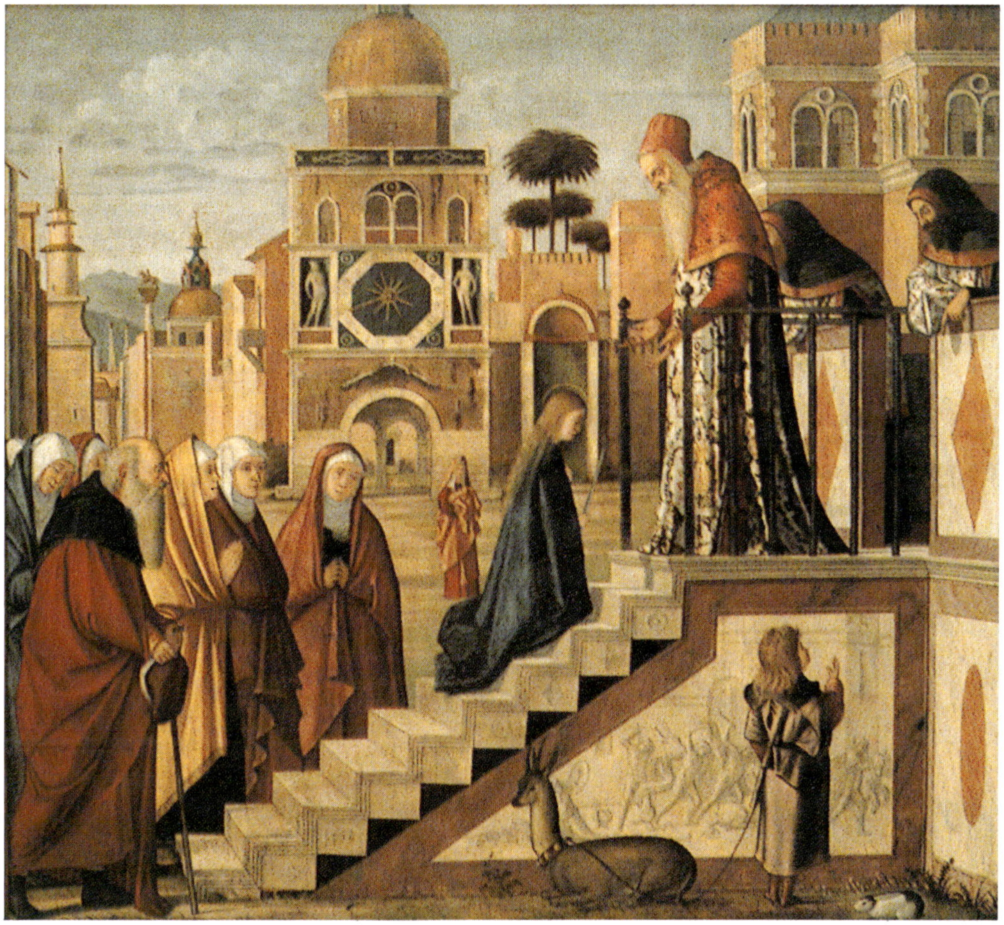

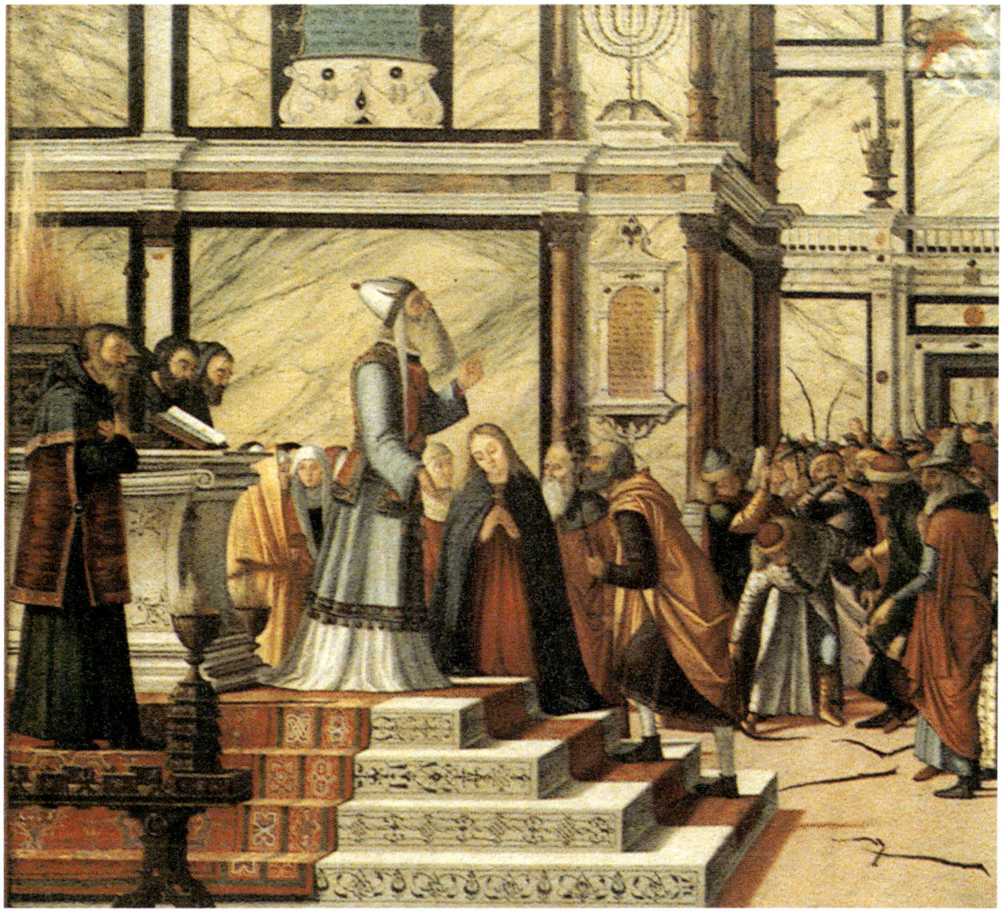

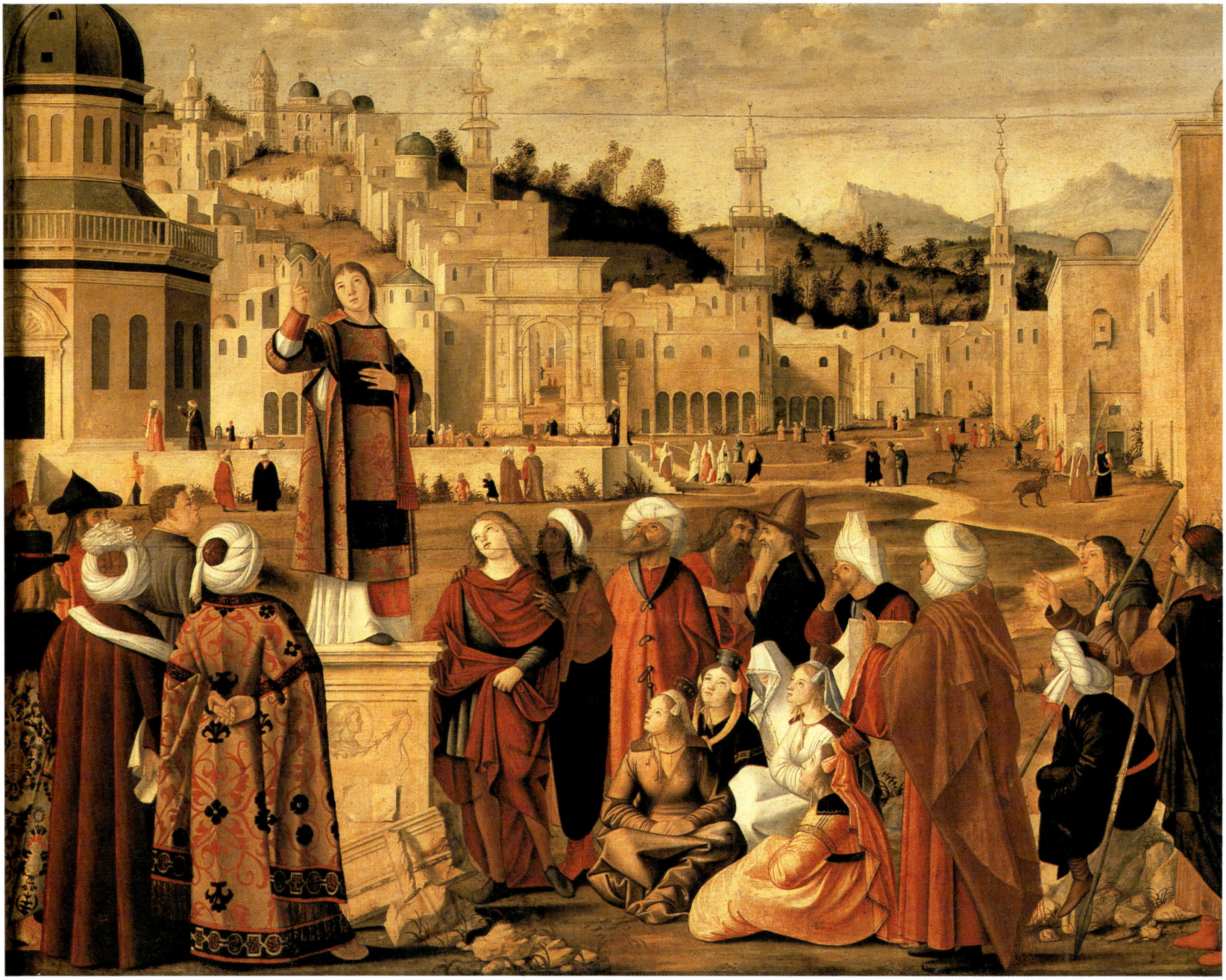

XI. Carpaccio, *St. Stephen Preaching in Jerusalem* (Paris, Louvre)

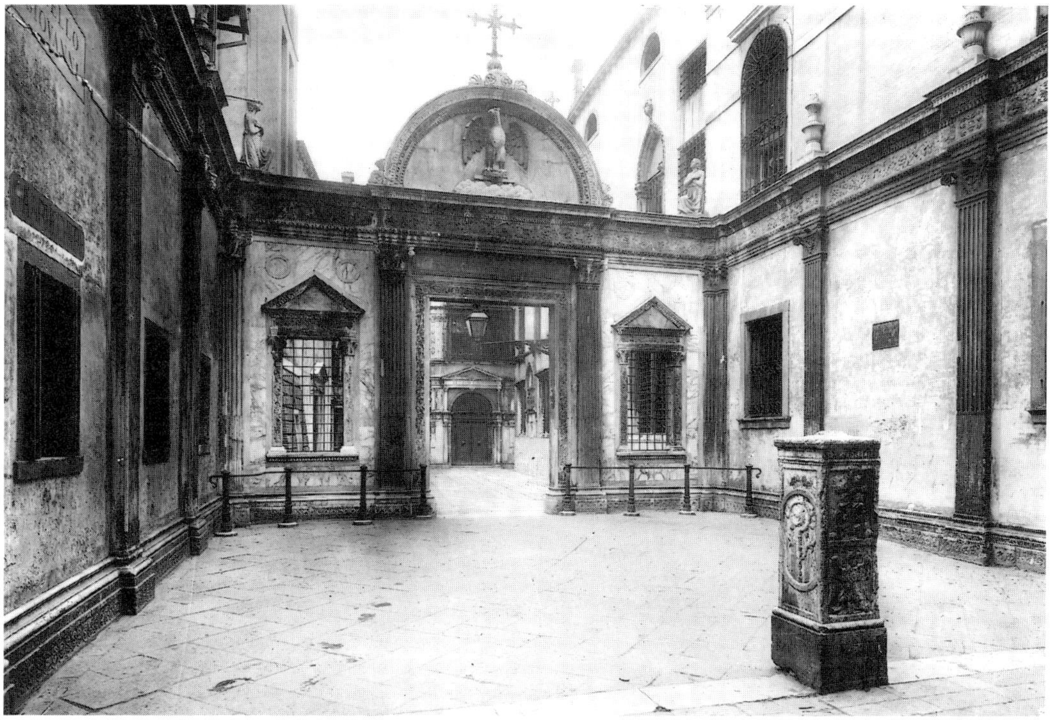

32. Pietro Lombardo, entrance court of the Scuola Grande di San Giovanni Evangelista, Venice, 1481

These worshippers included 'ambassadors and many famous persons, foreign as well as local...'[61] The concession granted at this time was for further unspecified works in the *albergo*, as well as for raising the ceiling of the *sala capitolare*. It was probably during this period that paintings of *The Miracles of the True Cross* were planned. The program, comprising at least nine canvases by six artists, was completed about 1505/10. It consisted of three paintings by Gentile Bellini, two by Giovanni Mansueti and one each by Carpaccio, Lazzaro Bastiani, Benedetto Diana and the Umbrian artist, Pietro Perugino.[62]

Leaving Gentile Bellini aside for a moment, let us consider the choice of the other artists. Carpaccio's first work for the St. Ursula cycle, the *Arrival in Cologne*, was signed and dated September 1490, just five months before the first documented appropriation of funds for the refurbishment of the *albergo* of the Scuola di San Giovanni. The *Apotheosis* and the *Martyrdom* were dated 1491 and 1493 respectively, and would have given further proof of his abilities in the construction of pictorial narratives.

Bastiani and Mansueti were both stylistically rather eclectic. They freely adapted their styles to suit a particular program. Here they painted under Gentile Bellini's formal influence and probably under his professional patronage as well. About the same age as Gentile, Bastiani seems to have been influenced at one moment by the Vivarini, at another by painters in Padua, and at yet another by the Bellini. Already in the 1470s, as we have seen, he had demonstrated his skill in the painting of *istorie* in his works for the Scuola di San Girolamo.[63] It may be difficult for modern readers to believe, but upon at least one occasion, a patron preferred his work to that of Giovanni Bellini. In 1473, Ser Antonio de Corradi, a jewel merchant in Pera, wrote to his brother-in-law in Venice and asked a favor:

> ...go to Lazzaro Bastiani...and have him make for me a painting the size of a half-sheet of small paper with the figure of Jesus Christ, that would be

beautiful [and] about which I have already written to him; or if by chance God caused his demise, or if he would not wish to make it, go to Giovanni Bellini and show it to him, and tell him that I want [it] in that manner, with that smoothness, of gold, polished and beautiful, and of this do not fail...[64]

Giovanni Mansueti was more closely connected to Gentile Bellini, acknowledging himself as a BELLINI DISCIPLI [sic] in an inscription in the *Miracle at the Bridge of San Lio* of 1494 [Color Plate XXI]. It is his earliest surviving *istoria*.[65] As far as we know, no one wrote sonnets about Mansueti, and yet he produced more paintings for *scuole* than any other artist of his time, with the exception of Carpaccio.[66] Like Mansueti, Benedetto Diana was probably of the same generation as Carpaccio, but he is known to us more through his altarpieces and *sacre conversazioni* than through his narrative paintings. The work that he painted for the Scuola di San Giovanni is his only certain surviving *istoria*.[67]

As for Perugino, he had been in Venice on several occasions during the 1490s. In 1494 he was commissioned to replace one of Guariento's frescoes on the south wall of the Great Council Hall. Assigned the second field from the west corner, he was to paint the *Battle of Spoleto* and the *Pope's Escape from Rome*. His fee of four hundred ducats attests to the high regard with which the Signoria assessed his talents.[68] He never executed the fresco, however, and it was later painted by Titian.[69] There is no reason to doubt that Perugino actually painted the canvas for the Scuola di San Giovanni, even though it no longer survives, having been destroyed in a fire in the sixteenth century.[70]

By now in his sixties, Gentile Bellini's heavy share of the campaign is surprising, even considering his unrivalled experience in pictorial narrative decoration. To all indications, he had more commissions than he could handle during this period.[71] Only special reasons would have moved him to take on such a heavy assignment from the Scuola di San Giovanni. Perhaps friendship was decisive. While a personal link between Gentile and Giovanni Dario, Guardian Grande from 25 March 1492 to 10 March 1493,[72] cannot be proven with certainty, a good circumstantial case can be made for it. The scenario follows.

A *cittadino* bureaucrat, Dario was the Venetian secretary of the Senate who had concluded the peace treaty with Mehmed II in 1479. Those negotiations had brought him three robes of gold and a knighthood from the Sultan, and acclaim and financial recognition from the Serenissima: a parcel of land near Padua and a generous dowry for his natural daughter, Marietta.[73] As Malipiero had put it, 'the land proclaims itself well satisfied with him, having concluded the peace with the Turk'.[74]

As we have already seen, one consequence of the new treaty was the Sultan's request for a Venetian painter. Dario's modern biographer, Franz Babinger, has further conjectured that the secretary may have discussed the proposal with Mehmed before returning to Venice in the spring of 1479. 'It would be difficult', he concluded, 'to find another explanation for the visit to the Conqueror's court of Gentile Bellini, the famous Venetian master...'[75] In fact, in a proceeding of the Senate of 13 August 1479 (not cited by Babinger), Dario was directly implicated in the Sultan's plans to obtain a sculptor and bronze-caster: '...just as also this desire of his is confirmed by his orator, who is departing from here, and by our faithful secretary, Joannes Darius'.[76] This link only reinforces Babinger's view that a close friendship between Dario and Gentile Bellini, at least in Venice, was 'as good as certain'.[77] But, indeed, the two can be placed in closer proximity than that, for Dario can be documented in Constantinople in August 1480 during the period of Gentile's service to the Sultan.[78] He may have arrived there as early as mid-May.[79] As two Venetian *cittadini* abroad at the Ottoman court, their relationship at the time could not but have been a familiar one.

From the distance of five centuries, Giovanni Dario is an elusive figure. A native of Crete, his service to the Venetian state began when he was already about fifty years old, and took him not only to Constantinople but also to Persia, Egypt and other exotic lands. We find him in 1484, for example, at the age of seventy, writing wearily to Doge Giovanni Mocenigo from Constantinople:

> I would gladly wish, most serene Prince, to be at home at my leisure, because by now I have entered the eighth decade, and I am so stout that I do not feel that by virtue of my age and the illnesses of my person, that it will suit me to celebrate carnival for long, and I should like to do it in my home and with my people, in that holy city [of Venice], and if I were there I would be silent as is suitable to my station, and I would leave speaking to those whom it is given from above, and I would sleep secure and without thought on my mattress.[80]

The Venetian paradigm of duty, however, transcended his own desires. Sent to Persia in 1485, to Istanbul and Adrianople in 1487, and to Albania in 1488, he returned home for good only in 1489.[81]

Dario must have amassed a substantial fortune, for he married his daughter Marietta to the patrician Vincenzo Barbaro, and built Ca' Dario on the Grand Canal at San Vio [Plate 33]. The palace bears an inscription that, if original, offers testimony to his classical learning and to a love for the city to which he had come only in late middle age: VRBIS GENIO JOANNES DARIVS. Four of the *istorie* of the True Cross cycle are dated by a later publication of the Scuola to 1494. Perhaps at least one of them was completed by the time Dario died in May of that year, at the age of eighty.[82] In any event, the die had been cast, and the program in the inception of which he probably played an instrumental role proceeded to a successful conclusion a decade or so later.

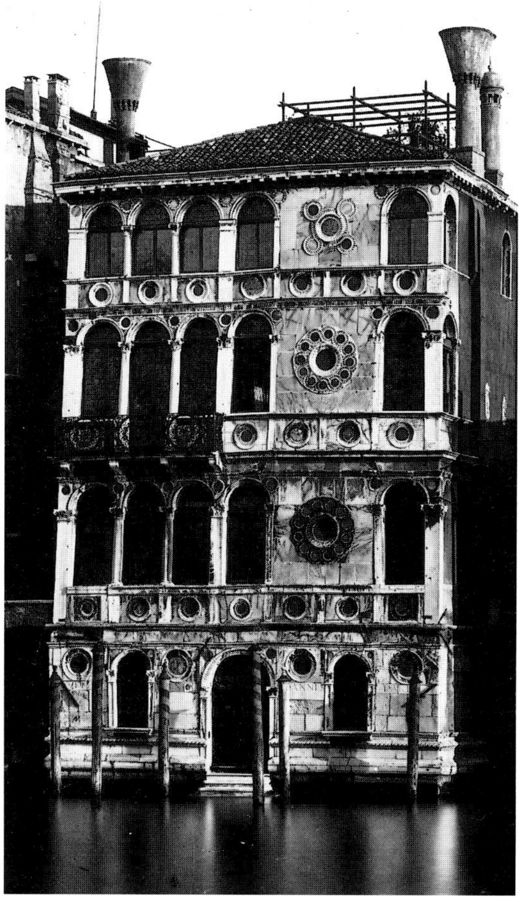

33. Ca' Dario, Venice.

We have given much attention to Dario, not only because he may have been instrumental in initiating a program of pictorial narrative decoration for a Scuola Grande, but also because he personally embodied something of a consensus of the old values of *cittadino* Venice. Merchant, secretary and pious layman, he combined in his single person the essential qualities of the typical member of a *banca* that were outlined in Chapter 2. His promise of silence befitting his station in his letter to the Doge speaks eloquently of the experience of an entire stratum of Venetian society. Although his own deepest motivations for supporting the painting campaign may have been personal – the approach of death and the desire to commemorate in a concrete and visual manner his position in Venetian society by the inclusion of his portrait in one or more of the paintings – his values and aesthetic preferences can stand in a broad sense for those of other members of any *banca* of a *scuola* during this period.

No portraits of Dario are known to exist, but a suggestion can be made. In the *Procession in the Piazza San Marco*, a white-haired man in a red toga stands between two figures credibly identified as Gentile and Giovanni Bellini [Plate 34].[83] A break in the row of marchers in front allows us to view him in full length. An old man, he wears the *cappuccio* headgear that was already out of

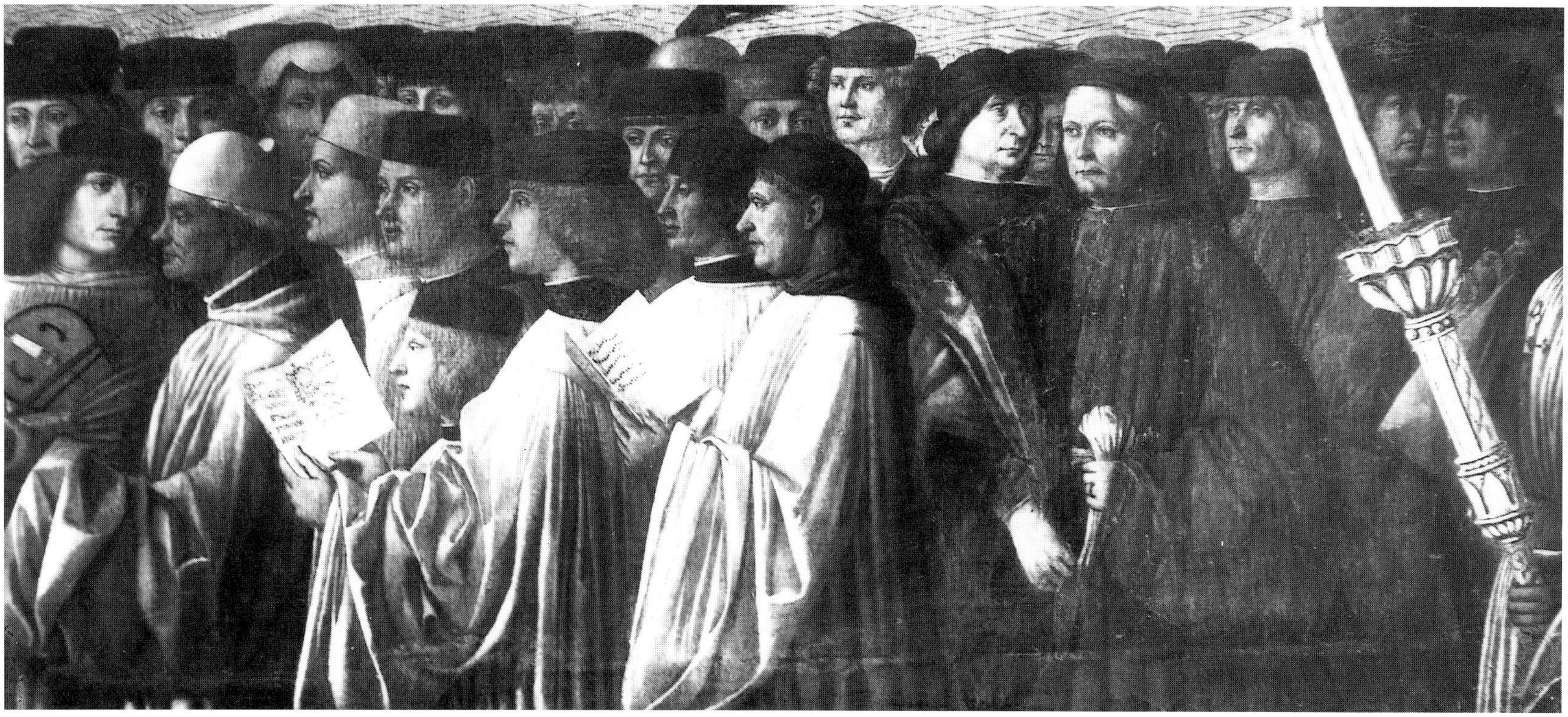

34. Gentile Bellini, detail from the *Procession in the Piazza San Marco* (Color Plate XVIII)

date. He holds in his hand a handkerchief, an affectation still more common at that time at the Ottoman court than in Venice. His right sleeve cut *alla ducale* was a privilege allowed to a Guardian Grande. It is (exceptionally) turned back, perhaps to show a robe of gold beneath. Is this Dario, then? It is possible but not proven.

Passing up the Grand Canal, we can see to this day the sumptuous whitish-gold marble facade of Ca' Dario, richly encrusted with red and green marble roundels. One scholar observed that 'the closest similarities to it are found in the settings and background architecture of contemporary paintings, particularly those of Carpaccio. . .'[84] This was one of the most extravagantly decorated facades of its day, similar to the Church of Santa Maria dei Miracoli. And it was owned not by a patrician, but by a *cittadino* – by definition on the periphery of Venetian civic life – who had moved to the center and had come to enjoy remarkable prestige in the city. It might be suggested that this prestige spilled over on his younger acquaintance, Gentile Bellini who, also by his skill and talent, had risen as far as his station would allow.

Divided loyalties

An appeal from Dario on behalf of the Scuola di San Giovanni, although backed by a decade of friendship, may have put Gentile into an awkward position in relation to the Scuola Grande di San Marco, of which he was then a member of the Banca. For in July 1492, he made his own *confratelli* a seemingly gratuitous offer. The *scrivano* recorded the motion:

> Motivated by inspiration more divine than human [Gentile – at that time Guardian da Matin – and his brother Giovanni, were] desirous and eager to

> make a beginning, with their praiseworthy *virtù* and skill in the art of painting, on the canvases which should be made in the albergo...

Two reasons are given for the proposal:

> ...in devotion and memory of their late father Jacopo who worked in the said *albergo* before the burning of the Scuola; [and] not from desire for gain, but only to the end that it would be for the praise and triumph of the omnipotent God.[85]

It was a peculiar time to make such a proposal. The rebuilding of the Scuola following the fire of 1485 was still under way. Construction of the staircase and installation of the pavement of the lower hall were not even to begin until the next year. The ceiling of the *albergo*, begun in 1491, was still unfinished in 1495, only to be replaced in 1504 with a new one.[86] Furthermore, in addition to its physical disarray, the Scuola was also experiencing severe fiscal constraints. Extraordinary measures to fund the rebuilding of the Scuola fabric had begun immediately after the fire and, despite a large grant from the Signoria, had to be repeated with monotonous regularity.[87] By 1495, the Guardian Grande would declare that the Scuola had little money left, for it had spent 'un texoro' – a treasure – on the construction.[88]

It has been suggested that since the balance sheet of the Scuola must have been well known to Gentile as a ranking member of the Banca, his offer was an affirmation of loyalty to San Marco after receiving the San Giovanni commission.[89] Indeed, in spite of its specificity as to details of payment and materials, the proposal appears to be a *pro forma* statement of intent, rather than a call to immediate action. And it goes beyond affirmation: the final paragraph of the document is most revealing in its promise that 'the said work cannot be given to anyone else to do, either in part, or in any way at all, provided that the said brothers [Gentile and Giovanni] perform their duty'.[90] This interesting stipulation reverses the common injunction against an artist *himself* contracting out work to others during the execution of a contract. Here the patron is bound to reserve the project – which in the full text envisions other paintings, that is, a full cycle – for these specific artists.[91] Thus, the Bellini brothers were given a virtual monopoly on the pictorial decoration of San Marco – a monopoly that they proceeded to exercise only in 1504.

Thus, while filial piety may well have moved Gentile Bellini to make his inopportune proposal in 1492, his inspiration may have been just as human as it was divine. If our scenario is close to correct, he may have been under irresistible pressure from his friend, Giovanni Dario, to take on the project at San Giovanni. Dario, now established in Venice, his 'holy city', as builder of Ca' Dario in his private life and frequenter of the Ducal Palace in his public one, would scarcely have settled for a lesser artist. But Gentile may have wished to maintain control over the situation at San Marco. He would have known that his confraternal brothers would be anxious to begin their own project when they saw the canvases beginning to cover the walls of the other Scuola and thus earning a disproportionate share of communal honor. There are indications, in fact, that the decision of San Marco in 1495 to abandon the unfinished ceiling in their *albergo* was prompted by sidelong glances at newly completed ceilings in the *alberghi* of both San Giovanni and the Carità.[92]

By the end of the century, Gentile had earned a reputation that went beyond a simple recognition of his artistic competence to embrace his moral qualities as well. Shortly before 1498 and soon after the painter had completed the *Procession* for the Scuola Grande di San Giovanni Evangelista, the humanist Francesco Negro finished writing a political treatise entitled *Peri Archon* or *De moderanda Venetorum aristocratia.* In it he held up both Bellini brothers as moral exemplars for Venetian patrician youth:

> servants of nature, one of whom professed the theory and the other the practice of painting; day by day they embellish not only your palace with the most beautiful paintings, but also decorate almost the whole city...[93]

He paid particular attention to Gentile's achievements in Constantinople at the court of Mehmed II, and recalled that having been granted the dignity of knighthood, Gentile

> was given gold in reward for his virtue, also an embroidered mantle, a tiara, boots and a gold necklace, that he brought back to his homeland. Therefore, under the leadership of such men, your adolescents should dare to imitate this [practice of painting], that it would be the remedy for excessive study and no less an approach to virtue and an honorable relaxation of the mind and the body.[94]

The honor of the *scuole* was no less Gentile's honor. In praising him for his mastery of the *theory* of painting, Negro was commending him not only as a gentleman practising an honorable profession, but as a scientist whose aim was, as well shall see, the convincing representation of pictorial truth. But what pictorial truth in particular? By the time Gentile Bellini turned back from the Scuola di San Giovanni to take up his offer to San Marco, a new visual element had entered the Venetian awareness.

Toward the East

Up to the middle of the last decade of the Quattrocento, the Venetian narrative painters had tended to interpret history within the embracing frame of the city itself. Painted *istorie* of events set in Venice, as in the Ducal Palace and the Scuola di San Giovanni – as well as events set in lands to the north, as in the Scuola di Sant'Orsola – were for the most part populated by people of the west and set against a familiar Venetian or 'venetianizing' backdrop. But all of this was to change, for by the end of the century one observes an abrupt shift in attention. The eyewitness painters virtually turned their backs on the west and focused thenceforth almost exclusively on the east.

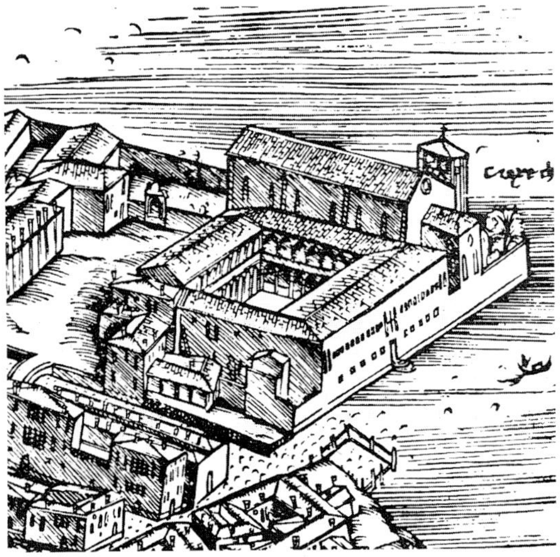

35. S. M. dei Crociferi. Detail of Jacopo dei Barbari's *View of Venice*, 1500 (Venice, Museo Correr)

Between 1495 and 1500 the Guild of the Silk-weavers (the Arte dei Setaiuoli) carried out a modest decoration campaign for their chapel in the Church of Santa Maria dei Crociferi, located at the northern edge of Cannaregio [Plate 35]. Like the Scuola di Sant'Orsola, it had ordered its Mariegola to be rewritten in 1488 in elegant lettering *alla cancelleresca* – in Chancery script – and now planned a campaign of pictorial narrative decoration.[95] The program consisted of an altarpiece of the Annunciation, with four *istorie* of the life of St. Mark by Cima da Conegliano, Lattanzio da Rimini, Giovanni Mansueti and a fourth artist whose name is unknown.[96] It is the earliest surviving cycle painted in an 'oriental mode'. The choice of artists was perhaps a function of availability rather than of demonstrated proficiency with the theme. Cima had arrived from Conegliano in the 1480s and specialized in altar paintings rather than mural decorations. He never did become a painter of *teleri* and seems to have worked almost exclusively on wood.[97] That the *istorie* of the Silk-weavers were also painted on wood – unusual for narrative paintings in Venice – suggests that he was the lead artist for the project. Lattanzio da Rimini and Mansueti were both experienced in traditional Venetian methods of painting on canvas. Lattanzio, another immigrant to Venice, was already working alongside Giovanni Bellini in 1495 on the *teleri* of the Great Council Hall;[98] and Mansueti, a native Venetian, would by now have completed his first painting for the Scuola di San Giovanni.

Iconographically, these *istorie* of the silk-weavers represent an artistic resurgence of the cult of St. Mark and the full-blown arrival of orientalism in Venetian narrative painting. While the translation of Mark's relics to Venice had received the main attention in the mosaic decoration of the Basilica di San Marco in the late thirteenth century, now it was his ministry and those of several other saints in the exotic lands of the east that exercised the talents of Venetian artists.[99] No documents remain concerning the program, and the specific interests of the patrons are unknown, but the cycle should be viewed as one manifestation of a general cultural interest in the Islamic world. As it became more of a threat, it also became something of an obsession.

Carpaccio and the Orient in the Scuole Piccole

To Carpaccio was to fall the distinction of being the greatest orientalist painter of the day. He was responsible for three complete cycles in *scuole piccole* in which eastern settings played a large role. Two of these were in *nazionali* – *scuole* limited to specific national groups: the Scuola di San Giorgio degli Schiavoni and the Scuola di Santa Maria degli Albanesi. In general, their memberships were made up of poor immigrants, many of them direct victims of the Turkish drive through the Balkans. These cycles were probably both begun around 1502.

The Dalmatians

The Scuola di San Giorgio degli Schiavoni had been founded in 1451 by nearly two hundred Dalmatian [*Schiavoni*] immigrants. They placed themselves under the protection of SS. George and Tryphon, later adding St. Jerome to their dedication.[100] The confraternity, which cited the service of Dalmatian sailors to the Venetian fleet in its foundation petition, was intimately involved with Venetian shipping and defensive measures against the Turks during the last half of the fifteenth century. Upon one occasion, the Guardian of the Scuola was ordered to report to the membership at chapter meetings on 'our many brothers outside of Venice on the sea and in mercantile trade, that everyone must pray to God that he would conduct them to a good port and to safety, and that they would escape from corsairs and robbers and be conducted safely home.'[101]

The confraternity was an integral part of Venice's plans for a Crusade in 1464. In anticipation of the event, Cardinal Bessarion granted the Scuola an indulgence for the feast-days of St. George, the Corpus Domini, St. Jerome, St. Tryphon and the first Sunday after the Assumption. In 1481 it received a

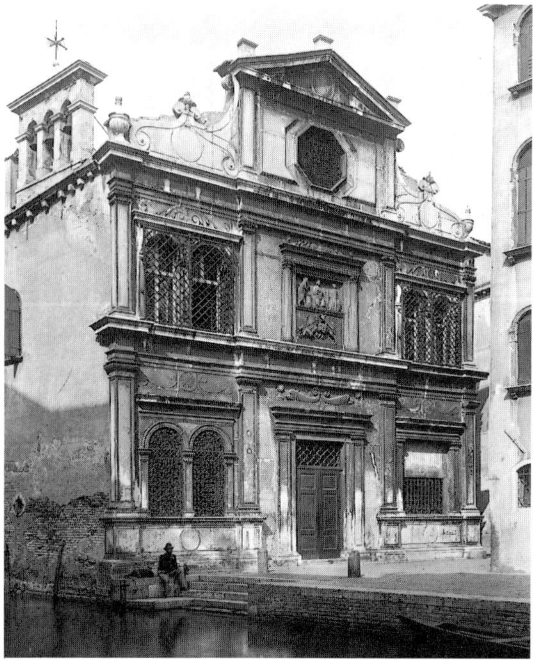

36. Scuola di San Giorgio degli Schiavoni, Venice

further indulgence from Pope Sixtus IV, who cited the Scuola's great generosity in collecting funds for an expedition 'against the perfidious Turks in the defense of the island of Rhodes and of the Catholic faith'.[102]

By the first years of the sixteenth century, the Scuola was wealthy enough, or (more likely) had received sufficient outside support, to undertake an extensive remodelling and decorating campaign for their meeting-house. It was located in the *sestiere* of Castello, in a building owned by the Order of the Knights of St. John of Jerusalem [Plate 36]. By 1503, the project had already cost 'several thousands of ducats'.[103] Carpaccio played a large role in the project, although no document from the period refers directly to his paintings. The nine canvases by his hand that still hang in the Scuola were probably painted between 1502 and 1508.[104]

The subject matter of the San Giorgio paintings breaks down into four mini-cycles: two paintings from the life of Christ; three canvases relating to the life of St. Jerome, a native son and special protector of Dalmatia, one of which depicts St. Augustine experiencing a vision following Jerome's death; three works depicting the exploits of St. George as a dragon-slayer; and a single scene from the life of St. Tryphon, the patron of the town of Cattaro [Kotor] on the Dalmatian coast.

Whether or not the paintings were originally intended as a unitary cycle in one room is not known. Most scholars are puzzled by the inclusion of the scenes from the life of Christ. But the conjunction of Christ with the patron saints recalls Bessarion's indulgence of 1464, which honored the Corpus Domini as well as each of these holy figures. Indeed, the indulgence itself may have been commemorated with Bessarion's probable portrait in the painting of *St. Augustine in his Study* [Color Plate XIII].[105]

As with the Guild of the Silk-weavers, the primary motivation behind the decorating campaign is not known. But one suggestive coincidence has been pointed out. In 1502, the year of Carpaccio's first dated work for the program, the *confratelli* of the Scuola received a valuable relic of St. George from the patrician Paolo Valaresso. A commander of the Venetian fortresses of Modone and Corone when they fell to the Turks in 1499, Valaresso had strong family ties with Dalmatia and had received the relic as a death-bed bequest from the Patriarch of Jerusalem. On 24 April, the feast-day of Saint George, it was carried with 'the greatest devotion' in a procession to the Scuola, 'with many priests with trumpets and fifes, together with the said magnificent missier Polo'.[106]

Valaresso, along with a number of his relatives, was taken into the confraternity as a member, a privilege that he would remember as he wrote his last will and testament. In it he requested that 125 brothers from the Scuola di San Giorgio, along with 250 more from the Scuola Grande di San Marco (of which he was also a member), should accompany his funeral procession.[107] The gift of the relic may have prompted the new program of decoration, with the *confratelli* and their benefactors resolving that a more distinguished setting was necessary to pay it due honor.

The Albanians

The Scuola di Santa Maria degli Albanesi had been founded in 1442 for the special benefit of the Albanian community. Following the fall of Scutari to the Turks in 1479, a number of refugees fled to Venice, where they received assistance from the Signoria.[108] Many of them would have swelled the ranks of the confraternity. In 1497 the group resolved to build a meeting-house next to the Church of San Maurizio, observing that 'even the Armenians have their own hostel and we have none'.[109]

When it came to the decoration of the building, Carpaccio was again the chosen artist. His six scenes from the Life of the Virgin indicate, however, that other commissions may have had first priority on his attentions [Color Plates IX and X]. The paintings of the Albanesi are of low quality by comparison with those of the Scuola di San Giorgio, and were probably carried out to a large degree by his workshop. They perhaps reflect necessary economies on the part of the confraternity. A document of 1503 noted that the majority of the members were artisans and mariners, indicating that the financial resources of the Scuola were probably very meagre.[110] In 1508 the chapter voted to grant six dowry subventions each year to daughters of poor members, to the humble sum of six ducats apiece.[111]

In a final decorative flourish that documents their long memories and continuing concern for the fate of their homeland, the *confratelli* of the Albanesi completed the facade of their building around 1530 with a relief sculpture commemorating the sieges of Scutari in 1474 and 1479 [Plate 37]. The Sultan Mehmed II, turbanned and crowned and accompanied by his Grand Vizier, stands holding a scimitar below a cliff on which is perched the fort of Scutari.

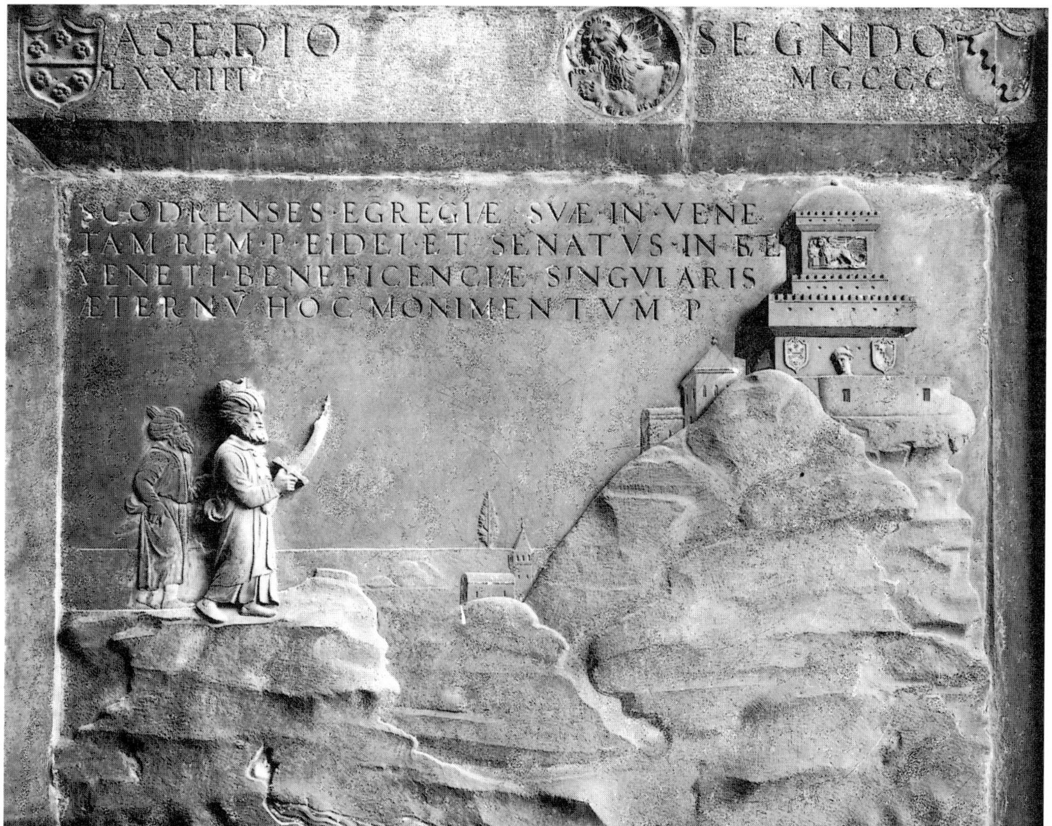

37. *Siege of Scutari*, relief sculpture on the facade of the Scuola di S. M. degli Albanesi, Venice

The heroes of each battle – respectively, Antonio Loredan and Antonio da Lezze – were honored by the inclusion of their coats-of-arms.[112]

Carpaccio must have been at the height of his fame during the years in which he painted for the Dalmatians and the Albanesi. In 1501 he contracted to paint a canvas of unknown subject matter for the Senate Hall in the Ducal Palace.[113] But it was only in September 1507, probably around the time he was completing the canvases for the Scuola di San Giorgio, that Carpaccio finally joined the ranks of artists painting the walls of the Great Council Hall. He was commissioned, along with Vittore Belliniano and a Hieronimo depentor, to assist Giovanni Bellini in completing two paintings left unfinished with the death of Alvise Vivarini. Of the three new painters, only Carpaccio was to be paid at the same rate as Giovanni himself: five ducats per month and a *sansaria* when one became available.[114] And yet, a few months earlier, Carpaccio had been narrowly edged out by Benedetto Diana, a more 'classical' artist who painted in the manner of Giovanni Bellini, in a competition to paint a new *penello* – processional banner – for the Scuola Grande di S. M. Della Carità. The confraternity had specified on that occasion that they wished 'the most sufficient painter in the land to make an excellent thing'.[115] It is apparent that tastes were beginning to change, in at least some of the Scuole Grandi. There is a certain irony in the fact that just a year later Carpaccio was called with Belliniano and Lazzaro Bastiani to make an official appraisal of the frescoes completed by Giorgione on the Fondaco dei Tedeschi.[116] They were looking at – and assessing – an artistic future that would not be theirs.

St. Stephen in the Holy Land

Carpaccio was still working in the Great Council Hall in 1511, when he completed the first canvas of the life of St. Stephen for the Scuola di San Stefano, in his final cycle of painted histories. A very old *scuola di devozione* dating back to 1298, it had met since 1476 in its own building opposite the church of the same name and under the protection of the Augustinian monks of the adjacent convent.[117] Its membership seems to have been primarily drawn from the artisan class. At a later time it was also called the Scuola dei Lanieri (woolworkers) because so many of its members followed this trade. In 1506, possibly with sidelong glances at the increasingly magnificent Scuola degli Albanesi a few steps away in the next *campo*, the officers obtained permission from the convent to 'freely adorn the altar, to make benches around, and to make other repairs, improvements and decorations in their chapel'.[118]

No documents have come to light concerning Carpaccio's role in the enterprise, although his works in the earlier cycles would have offered ample testimony as to his predilections and capabilities. Evidence indicating that the Scuola di San Stefano was under the protection of the da Lezze family has been found in some records relating to the confraternity.[119] Not only might we suspect a link to the Scuola degli Albanesi, who regarded Antonio da Lezze as a national hero and honored him on the facade of their building, but we may also see Carpaccio as the artist of choice for groups who had a particular interest in re-appropriating an oriental world within the confines of their *alberghi* (Color Plate XI).

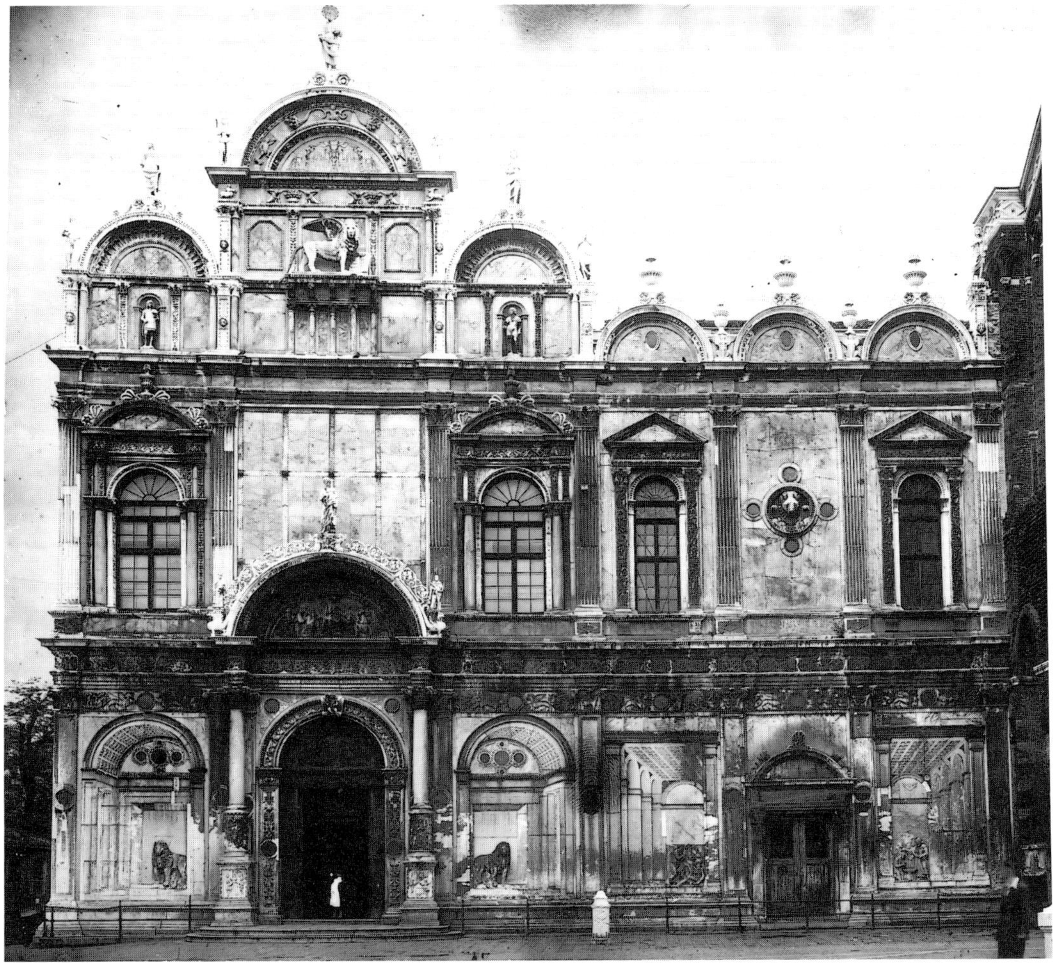

38. Facade of the Scuola Grande di San Marco, Venice

St. Mark in Egypt

During these years the Scuola Grande di San Marco took up the offer made by Gentile Bellini back in 1492. The *albergo* of its newly rebuilt meeting-house was finally ready for decoration [Plate 38]. On the first day of May in 1504 he was commissioned to paint a canvas that initiated the final surviving program of narrative painting within the compass of the eyewitness style. It took thirty years to complete, and in the beginning it too was set in the East. The subject of Gentile's painting was not defined in the contract, but the artist promised that 'it will be of more perfection and goodness than that of the *albergo* of San Giovanni [Evangelista] that is above its door. . .':[120] that is, his own *Procession in the Piazza San Marco*.

Although the True Cross cycle may have been the formal model for the new undertaking, the immediate impetus for San Marco's action was more likely a painting commission given to Pasqualino Veneto by the Scuola di Santa Maria della Carità in January of the same year. The Banca of the Carità declared on that date that it was

> . . .inspired more by Madonna Santa Maria, our Mother of Charity, than any other reason to wish to have a canvas painted to put in the end of the *albergo* above the door, and to make the *instoria* [sic] in praise of Our Lady

as she was offered in the temple, which according to the drawing will be a most noble thing...[121]

Pasqualino had obtained his contract in open competition with other artists, and the officers of the Scuola affirmed that 'by the invention of the design... the one made by him appears much better than the others that have been put to the test'.[122] The notion of an artistic contest was new in Venice. It is one sign of the changing times, when Venetian society as a whole was becoming more overtly competitive.[123] Pasqualino's drawing does not survive, and the names of the other contenders are unknown. However, it has often been suggested that a drawing in the Uffizi by Carpaccio, of the Presentation of the Virgin, was one of the unsuccessful submissions.[124] By the end of the year Pasqualino had died, and the hopes of the men of the Banca to obtain an '*ornamento bellissimo*' for their *albergo* would have to wait another thirty years for fulfillment.[125]

Stimulated by the example of the Scuola di San Giovanni and the potential threat to its honor by the projected campaign of the Scuola della Carità, the Scuola di San Marco had a wide range of subject matter from which to choose for its portrayal of the life of St. Mark. The facade of the Basilica, for example, offered pictorial models in the *translatio* which could have challenged directly the Scuola di San Giovanni, with large-scale representations of the city of Venice itself as the setting for the dramatic translation and reception of St. Mark's relics. Furthermore, Gentile Bellini had already amply demonstrated his skill in portraying the local urban landscape.

But times had changed, and the interests of the Scuola along with the personal aspirations of the artist conjoined to seek a new vision. Now around seventy-five years old, Gentile rejected the safe course and chose instead to follow the lead of the Guild of the Silk-weavers – and possibly the first orientalizing canvases of Carpaccio – by beginning the cycle with a scene from the *passio* set in Egypt: *St. Mark Preaching in Alexandria* [Color Plate XXXV].[126] Although the artist had gained fame and much of his reputation from his trip to Constantinople, up to this point, so far as we know, he had never painted an *istoria* with an oriental setting. The new painting would be a true demonstration of his *virtù* and a fitting end to a long career.

Furthermore, an oriental context for St. Mark would have had particular appeal to the members of the Scuola di San Marco. The membership was made up of a much higher percentage of seafaring men than that of the Scuola di San Giovanni,[127] and three of the greatest *viaggiatori* of the fifteenth century who left written records of their travels had been *confratelli*. These were Ambrogio Contarini – who had recently endowed the Scuola with a relic of the True Cross brought back from Constantinople – Giosafat Barbaro, and Alvise da Mosto.[128] The peaceful scene of St. Mark preaching to an orderly crowd of Mamluk Egyptians, as witnessed by the assembled ranks of toga-clad Scuola members, was only a beautiful fiction of an oriental world where few Venetians of the year 1504 could conduct their affairs with the ease of past generations.[129]

By March 1505 the first painting of the cycle was well under way, for Gentile returned before the Banca, stating that he had made good progress, and proposed a second.

For not without great care, misser Zentil has prepared a certain model in drawing that is a beautiful *fantasia*, to make another canvas...in our *albergo*

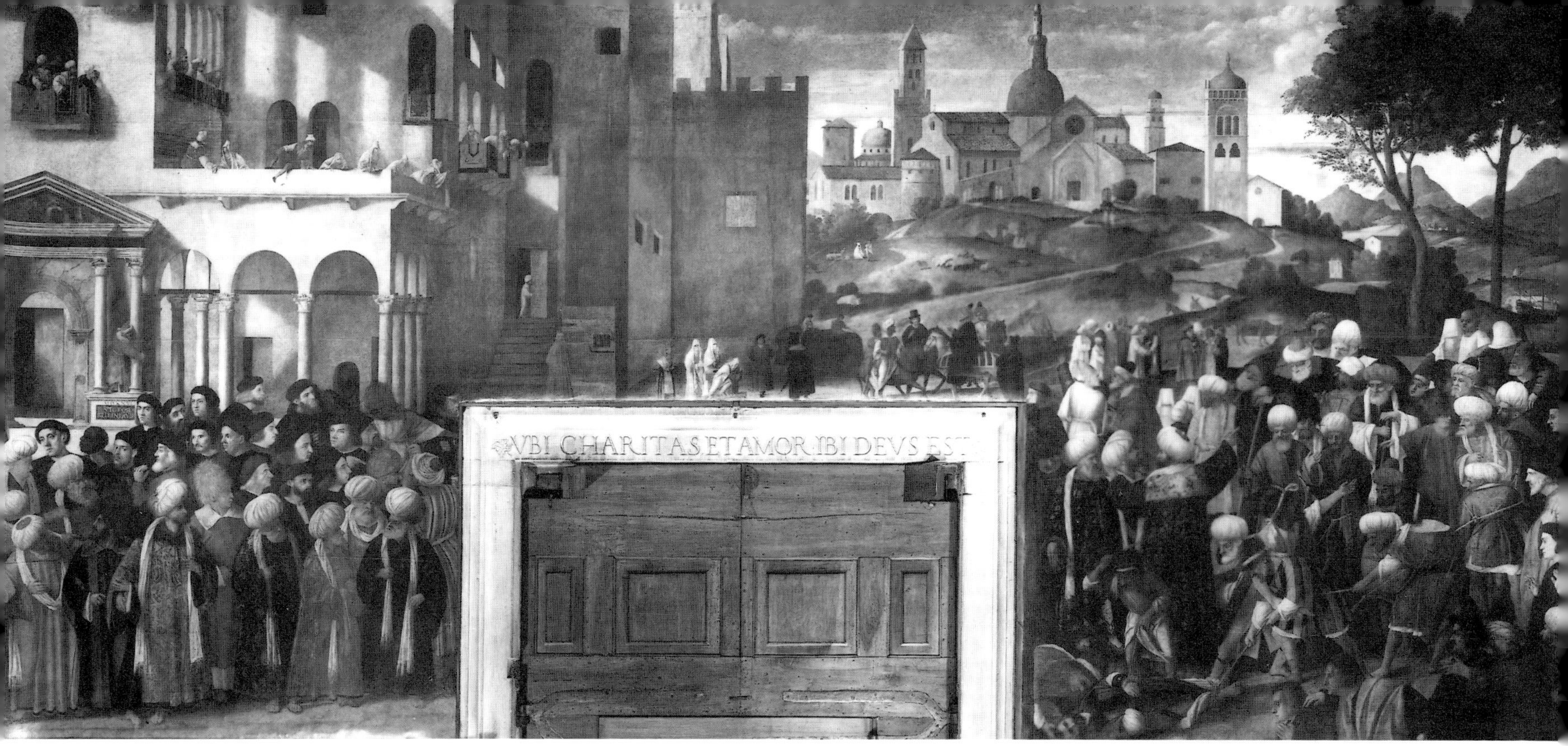

39. Vittore Belliniano, *Martyrdom of St. Mark* (Venice, Ospedale Civile)

above the door, on the wall opposite to the [one with the] first canvas . . .[130]

No record survives of the Banca's response to his offer, but the painter died in less than two years, leaving the first painting still unfinished and no certain work done on the second. In his will of 18 February 1507, made five days before his death, he referred only to the first work, and requested his brother Giovanni to 'complete the work begun by me for the Scuola di San Marco'. In return for this favor, Giovanni was to receive a book of drawings that Gentile had inherited upon the death of their father, Jacopo (most likely the book now in the British Museum). Giovanni completed the painting (making minor changes), probably within the next year.[131]

No further reference to the paintings appears in the Scuola records until July 1515, when the Banca voted to continue the cycle of *istorie*, commissioning Giovanni Bellini to make 'a painting on canvas on which he should paint a history of messer San Marco when he was in Alexandria, [and] how he was dragged on the ground by those infidel moors'. The *Martyrdom* was to hang above the entrance to the room in the same position as that envisioned in Gentile's offer of 1505 for a second painting, indicating that little, if any, progress had been made on that project before his death. Giovanni's new canvas was supposed to include 'buildings, figures, animals and everything that occurs . . .'[132] Again the execution of the painting was fated to be delayed, for Giovanni himself died the next year. Vittore Belliniano, a member of his workshop who was already assisting him in the Great Council Hall, took over the project. Possibly using drawings already made by his master, he completed the work only in 1526, three years before his own death [Plate 39].[133]

Giovanni Mansueti also contributed to the program, painting no less than three paintings during the period 1505–26. Like the two Bellinis who preceded him, he died before completing his last canvas for the Scuola.[134] By the end of the decade, the second generation of eyewitness painters had died: Carpaccio in 1525/6; Mansueti in 1526/7; Belliniano in 1529. But the decoration of the *albergo* of the Scuola di San Marco was still not complete.

In January 1533 a new Banca voted to 'commission one or two canvases that are lacking in our *albergo* and to have them made by the best painter or painters that it would be possible to have...'[135] In November of the following year, it was reported that a painting 'will be furnished in a few days to complete the cycle'. It could have been the *Presentation of the Ring to the Doge*, painted by Paris Bordone, who joined the Scuola in 1535.[136] He also seems to have completed the *Sea Storm* during this period, probably commissioned from Palma Vecchio and left unfinished at the latter's death in 1528.[137] These last two works were set once again in Venice, and the age of eyewitness orientalism in Venetian painting was virtually over [Plates 142 and 143].

As David Rosand observes, Paris's activity on behalf of the Scuola di San Marco may well have provided the motivation for the *confratelli* of the Scuola della Carità finally to revive the long-dormant project of *istorie* for their own *albergo*.[138] In August 1534, the officers of the Carità decided to commission 'such painting and decoration as are required for the dignity of our *albergo* and as are to be seen in the other *alberghi* of the *scuole grandi* of this most illustrious city'.[139]

Forty-odd years had passed since the Scuola di Sant'Orsola and the Scuola di San Giovanni had begun their ambitious campaigns of painted *istorie* modelled on those in the Ducal Palace. A new generation had come to maturity. During that long period, Venice had changed. The language of the *scuola* commissions had become more blatantly competitive,[140] and the artistic climate had changed as well, both in its stylistic tastes and in its subject matter.

By the middle of the sixteenth century, Gentile Bellini, along with his brother Giovanni, was already considered old-fashioned. Francesco Sansovino observed in 1561:

> They were much esteemed in their own time....Their manner was very diligent and almost in a miniaturist style, but they erred in too much diligence, because their figures were neither soft nor well modelled.[141]

Sansovino's lack of appreciation for Gentile's diligence would have been surprising to his patrician patrons of the late Quattrocento, as well as to men like Giovanni Dario who met in *alberghi* throughout the city and voted to commit their resources to expensive programs of painted histories. Their expectations were formed in a very different visual culture.

Part Two

THE VISUAL CULTURE

5

Intentions

The painted histories that began to line the walls of Venetian *scuole* in the late Quattrocento were commissioned and produced according to a set of unspoken assumptions about just what an *istoria* was meant to be, or rather, perhaps, what it was meant to do. The term *istoria* was applied loosely and broadly during that period to denote not only written accounts and visual representations of historical events proper, but also a wide range of scenes from the Bible and apocryphal sources, legends, and even literary romances. Up to this point, we have used the term in a similarly undifferentiated manner, but for the discussion that follows we will use it in its narrowest sense: the history painting as a visual cognate of history-writing. The narrative mode of Gentile Bellini or of the young Carpaccio cannot be understood without due recognition of the importance, to a Venetian artist, of tradition and of the peculiar documentary status given to a history painting by the Venetian viewer. It is a question of intentions: the fulfillment of certain narrative goals and pictorial values that were based upon specific notions about the status of the painted *istoria.*[1]

In an episode that reveals the very heart and meaning of the painted *istoria* for the Renaissance Venetian, two members of the Vendramin family made a gift of some houses to the Scuola Grande di San Giovanni Evangelista in 1484. They referred in the act of conveyance to a miracle at the Bridge of San Lorenzo in which their ancestor, Andrea Vendramin, had played a principal role, and added:

> Public documents, ancient paintings and histories in the said fraternity also give testimony to other almost innumerable miracles.[2]

To the Vendramin brothers, a painting was clearly more than an evocation of the past, or a vehicle for inciting religious devotion through the representation of a miraculous event. It was, in fact, a piece of testimony with a status equivalent to a public document or written history: an instrument of proof that such an event had actually happened. This documentary function of painting was a notion whose roots pushed deeply into Venetian soil.

The chronicler, Martino da Canal, wrote *Les Estoires de Venise* in the French language during the period 1267–75. To Martino, the proper business of the historical writer was the recounting of *res gestae* – deeds performed in the service of church and state. Credibility was his foremost concern. He continually underlined his efforts with promises of strict adherence to demonstrable truth: 'I will recount only what is the pure truth'. Challenging the reader to test his statements about contemporary events, he called forth the principals involved as outside witnesses:

And if you interrogate those whom I have mentioned to you, they will tell you the same things that I have told you here before.[3]

Of course, events of the distant past required another kind of testimony, and here he turned to the visual image as a form of corroboration. At one point he recounted in detail the story of the translation of the relics of St. Mark from Alexandria to Venice in 828/9 – the *translatio*. He then invited the reader to ascertain the truth of this most seminal event of Venetian history:

> . . . and if some of you wish to verify that those things happened just as I told you, come to see the beautiful church of San Marco in Venice, and look at it right in front, because this story is written there just as I have told it to you.[4]

Martino referred here to the newly completed mosaics in the lunettes above the four portals that flank the central entrance on the facade of the basilica. Although only one remains today, Gentile Bellini has left us a record of the other three in his *Procession* [Plate 83 and Color Plate XII. Taken together they constituted a narrative cycle, each scene depicting an episode in the *translatio*. Of this pictorial record, the chronicler could use the term *est escrit*: 'it is written'.[5]

The capacity of painting to transmit historical fact was further spelled out by Martino in the prologue to the second part of his history:

> I will tell you the deeds and battles that the Venetians carried out in those days [of Doge Ranieri Zeno] just as I have recounted the deeds and undertakings of their ancestors, because there are many people in the world who would like to know of these things, and this is not possible – for one man has died, a second is dying and a third is being born, and thus one cannot recount to everyone what has happened in those times – unless it is made known to them by means of writing or painting.
>
> We see writing and painting with our eyes, so that when one sees a story painted or hears a naval or land battle recounted or reads about the deeds of his ancestors in a book, he seems to be present at the scene of battle. And since events live, thanks to paintings and oral accounts and writing, I have undertaken to occupy myself with the deeds that the Venetians have accomplished in the service of the Holy Church and in honor of their noble city.[6]

An ability to render present the scene of action to the imagination of the absent viewer was thus a quality intrinsic to the painted history as well as to one that was spoken or written. It ensured that the event would live on in a transient world where people come and go: are born, live out their lives and die.

Martino da Canal was, of course, not alone. A similar stance had been taken since the early middle ages by writers elsewhere in Italy and Europe.[7] But its survival in Venice well beyond Martino's time carried with it decisive implications for Venetian attitudes toward the painted *istoria*. Indeed, the use of paintings as forms of historical documentation remained particularly appealing to Venetian chroniclers and historians because of their special approach to the past.

Throughout this period, their writing displayed three basic traits. First, it was myopically parochial in viewpoint. Whether or not an event would be included in a chronicle depended more upon its direct relevance to the political concerns of the city than to its general or global interest. Accounts began with the foundation of Venice, not with the Creation or the Flood.[8]

Furthermore, it betrayed a strikingly defensive and apologetic character. The concern for reputation, natural to any mercantile society, was joined to the political needs of an imperialistic power to justify present and past actions. Venice faced a hostile outside world: political sceptics, who resisted the seductive logic of the Venetian myth, and haughty neighbors, whose chivalric ideas of honor placed the patrician merchant of Venice in a distinctly inferior position.[9]

And finally, it was characterized by a pervasive religious sentiment, an almost magical belief in the very existence of the city as a manifestation of divine providence. Civic history in Venice was, in a very real sense, sacred history, for not only the body politic but also the physical city was seen unambiguously as *la terra sancta nostra*.[10] To the generally dour Priuli, in the midst of the travails following the Republic's traumatic defeat by the armies of the League of Cambrai in 1509, Venice with its disciplined and loyal citizens still appeared as '*una sacrestia de santimonia*'.[11] Such attitudes were rooted in an awareness of the city's physical fragility.[12] Venice was, indeed, in words which Francesco Sansovino was later to put in the mouth of a visitor, 'the impossible in the impossible'.[13]

The circumstances which helped to shape Venetian history-writing in this manner also fostered in the early Venetians a singular sense of the practical value of history for the education and civil preparation of their own citizens and for the edification of the outside world.[14] It was incumbent upon Martino da Canal and his successors to marshal *all* the evidence available – including fabricated and self-serving visual evidence – to buttress the official version of key historical events. Martino knew that in Venice, the commercial emporium of Western Europe, with its many visitors coming and going whose knowledge of Latin, Italian or Venetian could not be assumed, the public pictorial image took on an added weight. It is no wonder, then, that the painted *istoria* came to be seen and designated as the exact complement of the chronicle or written *istoria*, and to share with it the burden of demonstrating that the glorious – or miraculous – past had happened and would continue to be known to have happened.

Nothing reveals such an approach more clearly than the succession of paintings in the Ducal Palace that recorded the role of the Venetian Doge in resolving the differences between Pope Alexander III with the Emperor Frederick Barbarossa in 1177, and the attitude of generations of Venetians to those images.[15] The seminal importance of the Great Council Hall campaign of 1474 for the paintings of the *scuole* transcended purely formal influence, for the Ducal Palace frescoes provided, as well, the basic definition of the *istoria* that would underlie the attraction of an eyewitness style.

Marin Sanudo had the new paintings before his eyes as he completed his *Vite dei Dogi* in the 1490s. Like Martino da Canal two hundred years before, he used whatever proofs he had at hand to convince the reader that the event had transpired just as presented. After recounting the story of Alexander III, he referred first to a fresco by Spinello Aretino in Siena and then to the paintings in his own Council Hall:

> And for verification of such history, you will find it painted in Siena in the chapel of the Palazzo Pubblico, because the said Pope was Sienese; it was also

painted in our Great Council Hall, which if it had not been true, our good Venetians would never have had it painted.[16]

Like Martino da Canal, Sanudo cited the paintings as visual authorities by which he could corroborate the truth of his written discourse. For him and for the Vendramin brothers, a history painting or an *istoria* was thus much more than just a colorful and entertaining way of covering the walls. It also functioned as testimony, as reliable as the word of those long-silent witnesses who had commissioned it.[17]

There is a corollary to this approach, implied by Sanudo's invocation of his 'good Venetian' forefathers. In Venetian eyes, the antiquity of a painting and its close proximity to the action depicted gave certain weight to its reliability as testimony. This assumption also underlies a belated attribution to Petrarch of the *tituli* or inscriptions that had accompanied the painted histories begun by Guariento in the Trecento. When these inscriptions were recorded in the Chancery in 1425, no author had been cited for them. But in the last decade of the fifteenth century, when new paintings and amended inscriptions were going up on the walls of the Great Council Hall, the original *tituli* to Guariento's paintings were suddenly given a distinguished humanist past by the chronicler, Pietro Dolfin:

> But in the Great Council Hall the said history is painted in a series, with the inscription in each compartment composed by misser Francesco Petrarca, poet laureate, in the year 1341;. . .from the time of the event up to the time of Petrarca, 163 years had passed, [thus] to Petrarca this was a recent history; who, being a diligent inquisitor of truth, he wrote the events of the said history in these grave and ornate compartments not in order to applaud the Venetians, but in order not to be silent about the truth. . .[19]

This gratuitious ascription of the *tituli* to Petrarch is rejected by modern scholars, but it offers a revealing glimpse into the workings of the fifteenth-century Venetian mind. To Dolfin, Petrarch's authorship was important on two counts. First, he was a known seeker of truth and was therefore a man to be trusted. As an outside witness he could be expected to offer objective and unbiased corroboration to a Venetian story, giving confirmation to Sanudo's 'good Venetians'.

Second, he was considered to have been close to the event in question. We might find Dolfin guilty of stretching a point, given that a time-lapse of 163 years may be considered as something more than recent. Yet Dolfin was a better judge of the sufficiency of such criteria for his own contemporaries. He sought to weave a convincing fabric of authenticity around the inscriptions and paintings – and for the Venetian version of the story – based on a known reliable witness. In 1490 the *tituli* were rewritten for the new cycle in a more up-to-date humanist style by the historian Marcantonio Sabellico. Dolfin was careful to emphasize the fact that although the style had changed, the intent was to restore and not to replace: 'it has been described with another style in the restoration of the writing made in the Great Council. . .'[19]

The attitude continued. To Sansovino, the collective nature of the patronage was the telling circumstance:

> One should also give consideration to the painting of this history in the Great Council Hall, in which one should have faith as a public thing. It was

commissioned not by a single *capo* [head of state], and by his will, but by deliberation of a most grave and prudent Senate.[20]

Fra Girolamo Bardi, writing in the 1580s, claimed (probably without foundation) that an even earlier rendition of the Alexander cycle had been painted in the room as early as 1226. Like Sanudo and Sansovino, he stressed the reliability of the early patrons, again a 'Senate of grave men', who would not 'have determined to show to the world that which had not really happened'. This would have been particularly true, he added, since many of those present and voting would have been alive when the events occurred. The freshness of the memory (only fifty-one years old), and the integrity and size of the group, would have prevented the seduction of posterity, as Bardi put it, with a less than accurate visual record of the events in question.[21]

Such views imposed restraints on the artist, for they implied that the first painting representing a given event was the most accurate and that later renditions should be faithful to it. Similar concerns may account in part for what has often been characterized as conservatism at the expense of innovation in Venetian narrative painting. Just as many of Giovanni Bellini's half-length madonnas were painted in such a manner as to suggest an unbroken line of descent from the original Byzantine icon,[22] so too the Venetian *istoria* was ideally an element of continuity in the faithful transmission of historical truth.

The importance of repetition in historical images is best revealed in contracts for their refurbishment or replacement. Let us look at an example of this concern. Flavio Biondo had once observed a painted *istoria* in the center of Venetian commercial life: 'A distinguished painting, made two hundred years ago', he wrote, 'can be seen in the portico of the merchants at the Rialto, showing horsemen beginning a battle on this bridge.'[23] He was referring to one or more scenes of the Battle of Canale Orfano, a signal event of the early ninth century, in which Venice withstood the aggressive intentions of Pepin, the son of Charlemagne. In 1459 the paintings had to be destroyed to make way for a new loggia. A Senate motion spelled out the priorities:

It is proposed that a certain loggia be built at the Rialto for the convenience of our noble citizens and our merchants [and] that the histories that had been depicted on the old wall, be painted and placed on the new one, for the purpose of conserving the memory of these ancient histories; [we propose] that they should be removed and copied before the present decorated wall is demolished, so that they can be painted precisely and restored on the new . . .[24]

The replacements, so carefully preserving the old images, were probably destroyed by fire in the early years of the sixteenth century, when their further repetition no longer seemed important.[25]

But the principle of continuity remained viable in Venetian public art right up until the end of the century. After the disastrous fire of 1577 had reduced to ashes the efforts of the Bellini brothers and other artists in the Great Council Hall, the Signoria called in Bardi, as a recognized expert on Venetian history, to plan a new pictorial program. He solemnly conducted an expedition into the burnt-out hulk of the hall in company with 'many gentlemen, Venetian as well as foreigners'. He attested that on the walls once covered by the big canvases he could now see the earlier frescoes, painted in *maniera greca*, and asserted that they conformed exactly to the order of those that were begun in 1474. His purpose in examining these works, he affirmed, was that it was 'necessary to have such histories repainted that the same elements that were there before would be returned'.[26]

But what exactly was the nature of this continuity? Some years ago, Erica Tietze-Conrat was struck by the Venetian use of the word *ristaurare* to indicate the outright replacement of paintings; strictly interpreted, such a term denotes

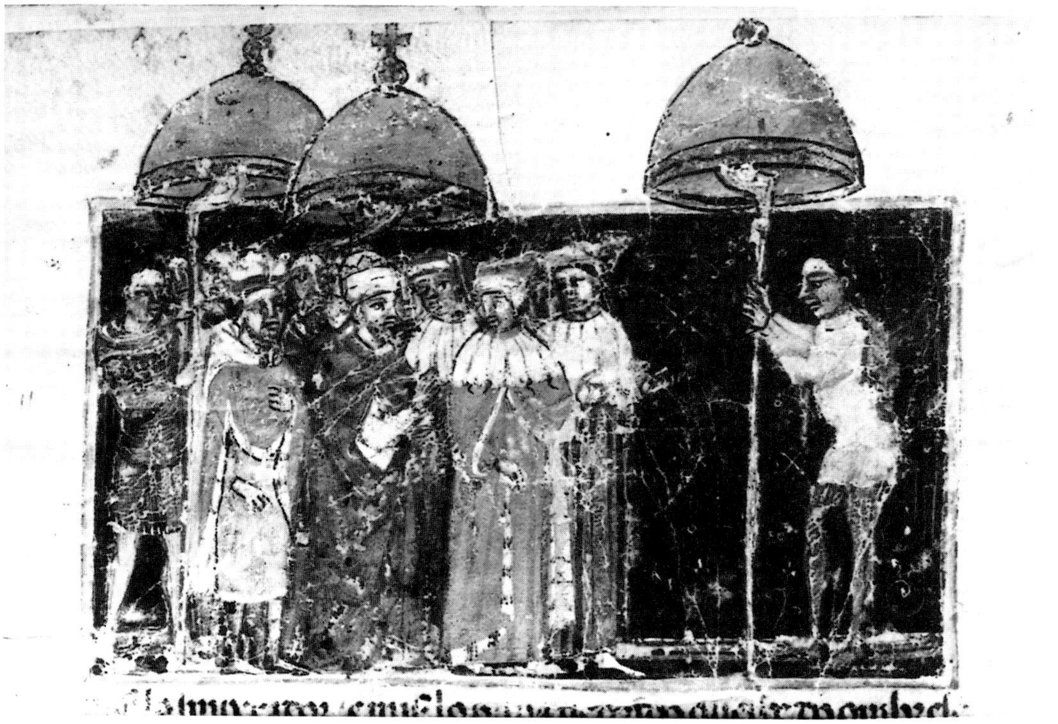

40. Venetian school, *Consignment of the Umbrella*, miniature (Venice, Museo Correr, Cod. Correr I, 383 [=1497])

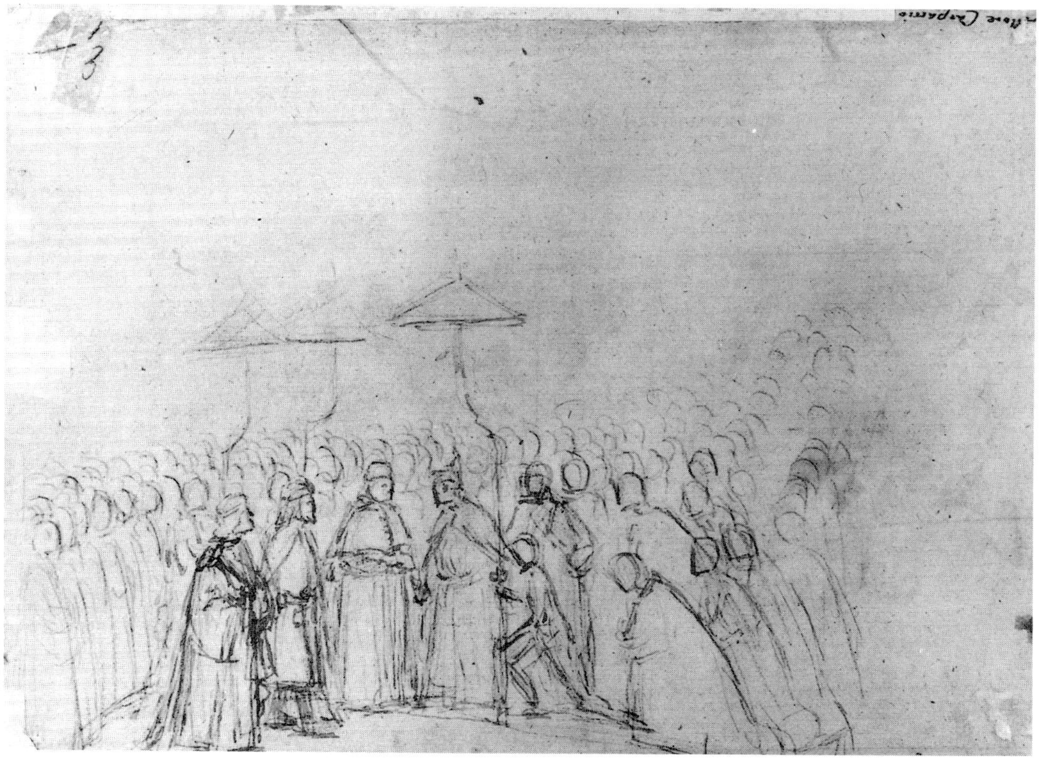

41. Carpaccio, *Consignment of the Umbrella*, preparatory drawing, verso (Sacramento, Crocker Art Museum)

repair. She stressed that in actual practice, this did not mean the technical restoration of an old painting, as we would understand it today, but the substitution of an entirely new work for another that was in poor condition or simply out of style.[27] We might also point to the characteristic use of the synonyms *reconzare*, *reparare*, *instaurare* or *renovare* to denote the repetition or repainting of the same subject by another artist.

The implications of these linguistic conventions may be seen by following the development of a selected theme from the Alexander cycle. The earliest surviving visual representation of the story is found in the fourteenth-century manuscript in the Biblioteca Correr already discussed in Chapter 3. While the precise relationship of its illustrations to the lost cycle of painted histories in the Church of San Nicolò is uncertain, the miniatures, for all the limitations of subject matter and detail that their size might impose, are still useful.[28] At the very least, they provide examples of the minimal criteria thought necessary in that period for the presentation of the theme. In the discussion that follows, we will use this assumption as an enabling factor, to make some general observations about the changing formal criteria for painted historiography in Venice over an extended period of time, rather than to establish the direct transmission of a particular composition.

One of the Correr miniatures depicts the *Consignment of the Umbrella*, where the Venetian ruler is given symbolic equivalence to the Pope and the Emperor through the presentation of a ceremonial umbrella of his own. The same event was painted by Carpaccio in the renewal campaign of the Great Council Hall cycle begun in 1474, for which two of his preparatory drawings remain, and later by Girolamo Gamberato after the fire of 1577.

The manuscript version is schematic, with no indication of a setting or locale [Plate 40]. At the left, the Emperor and the Pope stand under the imperial and papal umbrellas. Next to them is the Doge, who gestures toward an umbrella held by an attendant standing alone on the right. A crowd is gathered behind the three rulers.

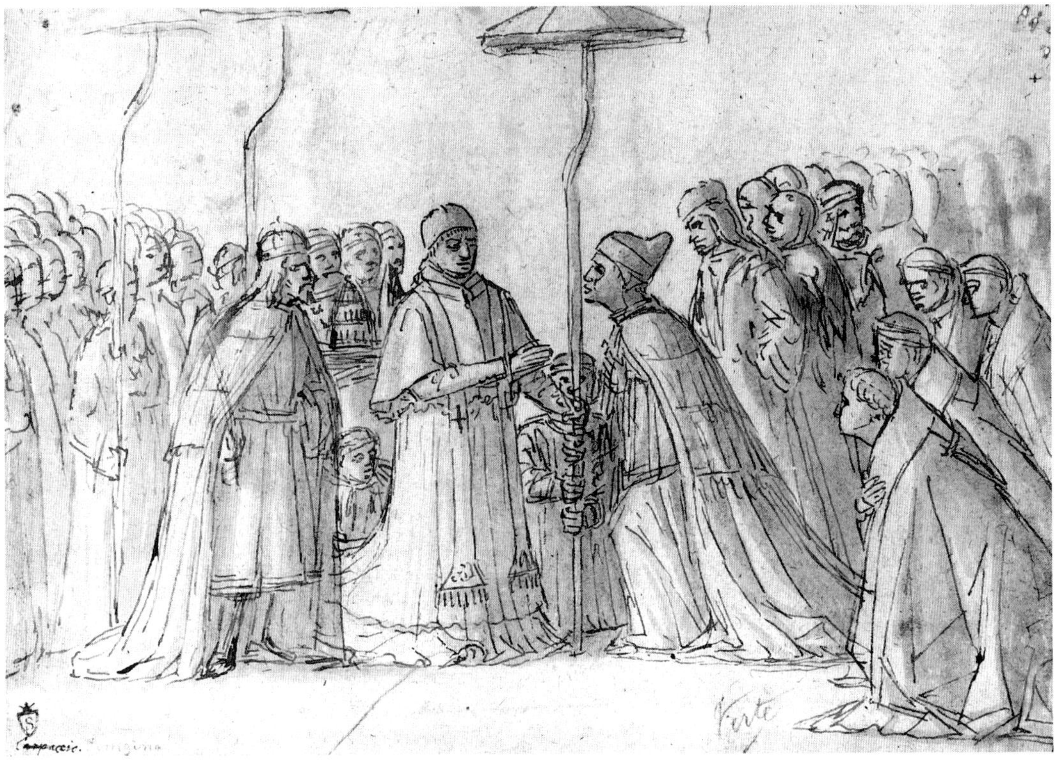

42. Carpaccio, *Consignment of the Umbrella*, preparatory drawing, recto (Sacramento, Crocker Art Museum)

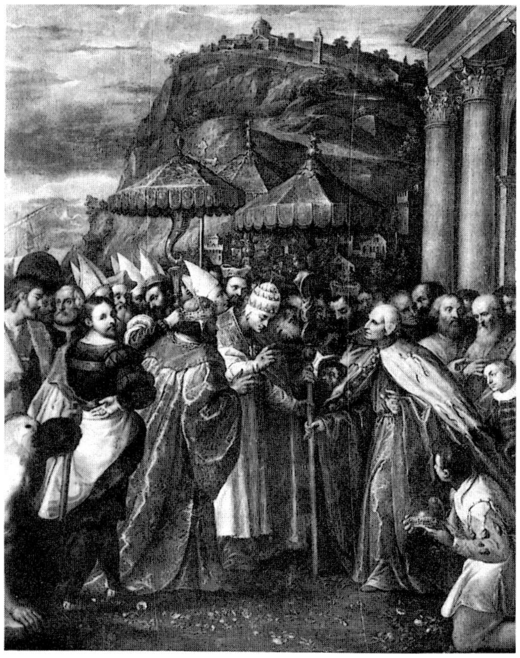

43. Girolamo Gamberato, *Consignment of the Umbrella* (Venice, Ducal Palace, Great Council Hall)

In both of Carpaccio's drawings, the umbrellas are grouped in a manner similar to those in the manuscript. In the earlier sketch, the Doge stands near the Pope with the umbrella held to the right [Plate 41]; in the later version, however, Carpaccio has moved the third umbrella to separate the Pope and the Emperor from the Doge, with the latter genuflecting [Plate 42]. Both sketches reveal the inclusion of a large number of spectators. Vasari wrote of Carpaccio's finished painting:

> One sees the Pope in his rochet [sleeved tunic], who gives an umbrella to the Doge; after having given another to the Emperor and reserving two for himself.[29]

Although Vasari's arithmetic is faulty in regard to the four umbrellas, he affirms quite unambiguously that the moment depicted in the final version has changed from that prior to presentation, as shown in the manuscript and Carpaccio's first drawing, to that afterwards.

In the extant painting by Gamberato of the late sixteenth century, the artist followed this latter arrangement, although again there are changes [Plate 43]. The Doge's posture has now become almost upright and his *corno* – the horn-shaped ducal beret – is carried by a page. The setting of Ancona is highly particularized – as it may well have been in Carpaccio's completed painting – with the church of St. Cyriacus high on a hill in the background and the masts of ships visible in the harbor.

Over the course of two hundred years, the schematic narrative core, constituted by the primary human protagonists in the scene, remained fairly consistent, but the changes are striking. Costumes changed to conform to prevailing fashion; gestures changed to reflect shifting nuances in the relationships between the principal figures or new ideas of decorum and protocol; the setting became more elaborate and particularized; and the participants and bystanders proliferated. We observe all this in works that are notionally 'faithful' copies of what was there before. In fact, it becomes apparent that the issue here is not *primarily* one of formal dependence of a later image upon an earlier version, although an earlier rendition would undoubtedly serve as a model and a restraint for a later one.[30] It is rather that, given a central event – in this case the reception of clearly recognizable, because familiar, *trionfi* and a series of solemn encounters where the participants are bound to each other by unambiguous gestures of submission, investiture, greeting – those elements that constitute indicators of the historical authenticity of that core event, and that weave around it a web of veracity, change over time. Moreover, the current conception of what those elements should be influences what will be included in the most recent painting of a given event: hence the incorporation in Carpaccio's painting of the view of Ancona, the numerous witnesses, the increased number of attendants for the Doge.[31]

Thus, while the documentary function of pictorial narrative imposed its own limitations, stylistic and iconographical change could still be accommodated within the paradigm. Just as styles in history-painting changed, so too did styles in history-writing. In order to follow the trajectory of the 'eyewitness style' of painting – its rise, its flowering, its decline – we must look more closely at history-writing in Venice and its structural affinities with history-painting. For the intentions of each were virtually identical: to provide a convincing testimony appearing true to past events.

6
Affinities

To Konrad Escher, writing in 1919, the canvases of the eyewitness painters and the chronicles of the period appealed to the same turn of mind:

> The chronicle mode of presentation was, however, provided with many genre-like details, according to Quattrocento taste; the portraits of contemporaries were particularly enjoyed, along with the colorful views.[1]

Others have repeated his telling insight, but it has remained just that. Its implications have not been much explored. yet a closer look at the formal characteristics of Venetian chronicles, and how these changed over time, can bring us to a better understanding of the stylistic qualities of the painted *istorie* whose aims, as we have seen, were so similar.[2]

The chronicle

Venetians clung to the chronicle long after other major cultural centers of northern Italy had turned to the humanist history as their dominant form of history-writing.[3] A good thousand chronicles in manuscript form survive from the Trecento alone and attest to their extraordinary popularity in Venice. Despite sporadic humanist attempts to produce a new type of Venetian history, they remained a standard part of the domestic inventory of the typical upper-class family throughout the fifteenth century.[4] Even the completion of the first humanist histories by Bernardo Giustiniani and Marcantonio Sabellico in the later Quattrocento failed to discourage the city's chroniclers, who continued to produce texts well into the following century. As Marco Foscarini, the eighteenth-century historian of Venetian literature, later complained of these chronicles: 'Who would dare risk drowning himself in all those interminable volumes?'[5]

Venetian resistance to a form of historiography that had received such a warm reception elsewhere can most plausibly be accounted for by the specific social context within which humanism developed. As Margaret King has shown, humanist studies in Venice were the handmaiden of patrician rule. They were decidedly the preserve, and sometimes the refuge, of a relatively small group of noble amateurs. Those Venetian *cittadini* who received a humanist education at state expense were trained in its technical aspects for service in the Chancery and not for creative pursuits. The professionals came from elsewhere; the most talented generally remained in Venice long enough to teach a few courses and perhaps to find out that their opportunities, both social and professional, would always be carefully circumscribed. They then departed for locales with more open boundaries and possibilities for participation.[6]

There were exceptions. Carpaccio's probable portrayal of Cardinal Bessarion – formerly the Archbishop of Nicaea – as St. Augustine, in a painting for the Scuola di San Giorgio degli Schiavoni, reminds us of the Greek presence in Venice [Color Plate XIII]. Other Greek humanists were accorded the not insignificant honor of inclusion in paintings in the Great Council Hall. Immigration had begun even before the fall of Constantinople in 1453, and swelled to make Venice the main center of Greek studies in Europe by the end of the century. But much though they contributed to the knowledge of Greek and the dissemination of Greek literature by their teaching in Venice and Padua, these learned immigrants remained *stranieri* – outsiders – from a sociological point of view: foreign transplants who remained to one side of civic life.[7] The official neglect of Bessarion's great library of Greek manuscripts, donated to the city with great fanfare in 1468, is telling. The codices sat around in boxes, subject to mold and pilferage, for nearly a century before they were installed in the newly built Biblioteca Marciana in 1565. Like the humanists who were honored in the Great Council Hall, the collection remained an ornament – highly praised, but in many ways unassimilated – of Venetian culture.[8]

The patrician humanists of the Quattrocento, a number of them quite learned, tended to view the *studia humanitatis* not as an end in itself nor even as a means toward individual expression and intellectual liberation. Rather, they employed it in training the young men of their own caste to rule, and in sustaining the ideology that legitimized that rule. The prevailing theme, as King has argued so powerfully, was the ideal of *unanimitas*. Humanism in Venice was thus less a creative force than a controlling one. Throughout the Quattrocento, historical writings of Venetian humanists maintained the themes of uncritical and apologetic civic self-adulation and deep respect for established authority, whether religious or political, which had characterized the Trecento chronicles. As King put it: '. . . the task of Venetian humanism was to affirm, not challenge, Venetian culture'.[9] It has been suggested that such writing was not to the taste of visiting professionals, and that before Bernardo Giustiniani produced his history no native-born writer with adequate credentials had stepped forward to satisfy these traditional requirements with good Latin prose. Rhetoric, furthermore, had never become a primary concern of Venetian humanists. It is not surprising, then, that the chronicle, deeply entrenched, satisfied the needs of an equally entrenched patrician class.[10]

Allowing for some notable exceptions like those of Zorzi and Piero Dolfin, the Venetian chronicle was often anonymous. Typically a family of means ordered its own redaction, similar to, but not exactly like, any other. It would bear the family coat-of-arms and occasionally the name of its patron, as well as that of the scribe who copied it. The scribe, a professional writer, borrowed the primary text from an earlier version, perhaps belonging to another family, and then made his own abridgements, additions and alterations. The revision would then be passed down to succeeding generations within the family, receiving further emendations without crediting any source.[11]

Focusing on civic affairs, the Venetian chronicle or *cronaca* thus became a means to define family identity within the context of the larger community. The Florentine *ricordanza*, a family history *per se*, had few counterparts in Venice until the sixteenth century.[12] Rather, it was the possession and preservation of civic history that was a personal affair, a circumstance which helped to ensure the tenacious hold of the chronicle form on the average educated Venetian. The study of local history was not simply a passive enjoyment, but one which was experienced actively by members of a whole stratum of society, if only in the physical act of patronage.

What, then, was the precise nature of the relationship between these textual forms of historiography and their pictorial counterparts? We might first note that the *modus operandi* of the chronicler – selection, abridgment or elaboration, and transmission – is virtually congruent to that reflected in the three successive renditions of the *Consignment of the Umbrella* that were discussed in the previous chapter.

Furthermore, the mobilization and deployment of information in the Venetian chronicles evolved during the fourteenth and fifteenth centuries in a manner stylistically parallel to their visual partner, the painted *istoria*. As both were documents, changing expectations of what should be included in an authentic document are revealed in both. With the exception of Martino da Canal's *Estoire*, which had no immediate successors, Venetian chronicles before the middle of the fourteenth century had been marked by a lack of descriptive details. The setting or precise ambient of an event was rarely described, nor was the internal life of the city.[13]

The basic text of the Alexander legend as written by Bonincontro da Bovi in 1320 had a similar character. It was a straightforward account, written in early medieval church Latin on a biblical model.[14] Allowing that a manuscript style would be different, within a given period, from that of monumental painting, one thinks immediately of the miniatures of the Correr manuscript: simple, clear and direct, with minimal setting and detail.[15] The reciprocal influence between such images and their related texts can be documented in at least one instance early in the Venetian tradition. A *parte* of the Great Council of 1331 thus reported a new written rendition of the familiar legend by:

> . . . Master Castellano, who compiled a book in meter about the history of Pope Alexander and the Emperor Frederick, about the war and peace held between them, and afterwards confirmed in Venice, according to what is painted in [the Church of] San Nicolò in the Palace and in a chronicle, to the honor of the lord Doge and the Commune of Venice, with great zeal and labor.[16]

Here we see plainly that Castellano – a poet from Bassano who put the story written by Bonincontro da Bovi into Latin hexameter verse – was credited with adhering not only to the manuscript of the chronicle but to the painted image as well. Whatever scenes an unknown artist had painted on the walls of the church in the Ducal Palace had now become an influential part of a continuous historiographical chain.[17]

A comparison of the accounts dealing with the *Consignment of the Umbrella* may give us an idea as to how this would have worked. Bonincontro had reported that the Doge added ten galleys to those of the Emperor and, together with the Pope, the two rulers departed in the direction of Ancona. He gave no description of their arrival there. Of their departure, he reported only that they left for Rome.[18] Castellano, on the other hand, described how these things took place. Upon nearing Ancona, he wrote, the ships dropped their sails and the group was rowed into the port. Upon leaving the city, the Doge and the

Emperor rode on horseback and the Pope on a snow-white mule.[19] We cannot know for certain, but the added visual details could well have been taken directly from the paintings.

A generation later, around 1350, the chronicle form was further transformed and enriched, with the appearance of the first texts in Venetian dialect. Prior to that time they were written either in Latin, the curial language, or in French, the language of the court (as used by Martino da Canal). Both reflected the restricted circles in which they circulated. Now a new, mundane thread was introduced into the basically formulaic chronicle tradition: the elements of the citizen diary. The old chronicle was thus, in the words of the historian Antonio Carile, contaminated with a 'multiplication of facts'. These facts were, so to speak, jammed into its annalistic fabric. Events were recounted in an anecdotal way, as a series of picturesque happenings noted down in a diary. To use another well-turned phrase of Carile's, the vernacular form that resulted was dependent upon the '*gratuità dell'evento*': the 'gratuitousness of the event'.[20]

For example, when Luchino dal Verme, a *condottiere* of the Republic, arrived in Venice after putting down a rebellion in Candia in 1364, the attention of an anonymous chronicler was all on the celebrations and not on the military victory. He wrote of the bonfires set in every neighborhood; of the pardons granted to all prisoners, both from fines and from prison terms; of the brigade of forty noble youths who invited an equal number of ladies for a dance in the *parish* of San Luca. He described the separate celebrations of the *popolari* and of the jewelers' guild, whose members made

> a very beautiful crown of great value and a belt of silver and a *chapello* [hat] wrought with great value; and they had a beautiful platform made in the Piazza San Marco with the ladies of the said jewelers. And the cry went up that those who jousted and were the winners of the joust, should have the *chapello*...
>
> In that same year, when the king of Cyprus came to Venice, the Doge of Venice with the gentlemen of Venice went to meet him on the *bucintoro* [the Doge's ceremonial barge], with the greatest of honor. And when the *bucintoro* had reached San Luca many knights went on the bridge with the king. That bridge broke into pieces, and the king with his baron went into the water. And then the king said: 'Now I am well and truly a Venetian.'[21]

In a chatty, discursive style, with one observation leading to the next, and each carrying equal weight, the writer painted a panorama of citizen life that could be experienced visually by the reader as if he himself were on the scene. The past and future of the events described – their political and diplomatic implications – were all but forgotten in the fascination with the here and now.

The vernacular chronicle was used to record the world into which Jacopo Bellini was born around 1400. His written and oral experience of local history would have come to him in that form. Remaining dominant in Venice during his own lifetime, it reached its full elaboration during the late maturity of his sons Gentile and Giovanni, in the various writings of Sanudo.[22] As the historian Gaetano Cozzi observed: 'The most important aspect of the work of Marin Sanudo resides in the sense that he has of the piece of news as a document of life, in his conception of history as an objective mirror of life...'[23] To create such a mirror, Sanudo found it necessary to recount 'innumerable particulars, at the risk of losing oneself and of making his prose clumsy and laborious to read'.[24]

The most credible account was thus one that looked the least edited and that supplied the reader with the most detail.

Seen against this tradition of 'thick reportage', the True Cross paintings emerge as a characteristic expression of a broader cognitive style. Mansueti's cluttered gatherings appealed to a taste for 'innumerable particulars', an issue to which we will return in Chapter 8. And Carpaccio's almost casual insertion of the central narrative event of his *Healing of the Possessed Man* – a miraculous exorcism – into the commercial life of Venice no longer seems so surprising [Color Plate XXII]. As in the *cronaca*, so too in Carpaccio's painting there is little apparent sense of a hierarchy of importance between the primary actions and the genre detail. A chronicler might have noted that a group of *omeni da ben* – men of honor, both nobles and commoners – had gathered that day beneath the loggia of the patriarch; that a procession of white-robed confraternity brothers was made across the Rialto bridge; that business was conducted in the marketplace with the usual decorum, despite rumors of new threats in the east; that the weather was fair; and that (incidentally) a prodigy had occurred by means of a certain miraculous cross. To Carpaccio's viewers, like Sanudo's intended reader, the slice of life in all its fullness signified uncontrived authenticity.

The humanist history

But one can take the analogy between text and image one step further. For Carpaccio's style did not remain static, nor did tastes in history-writing in Venice. The late Quattrocento was, in fact, a time of transition for Venetian historians, with the old chronicle tradition on its way out. Marin Sanudo, who prided himself on writing in the *sermon materno*, the vernacular mother tongue, was perhaps the last great practitioner of the genre. Civic pride called for something new. As the last decade of the century approached, two humanist histories finally appeared. The Venetian patrician, Bernardo Giustiniani, who is credited with the first serious account of humanist history worthy of the name, was still copying out his final draft when he died in 1489.[25] He had written in Latin, on the model of Thucydides, but the patriciate clearly wanted something more unreservedly adulatory. They got it in Marcantonio Sabellico. In 1486 he set out to write the definitive history of the Republic, using Livy as his exemplar. Published in 1489, *Rerum Venetarum ab Urbe Condita libri XXXIII* was an immediate success. Even the renowned humanist Ermolao Barbaro hailed it for making the chronicles obsolete.[26] Sabellico, a professional humanist from outside the city, was granted a generous bonus and a well-paying professorial chair with state subventions for future publications. As Cozzi put it, 'the Serenissima Signoria admired in Sabellico the aulic style, pompous, solid, that literary culture that refurbished the deeds and the personages; it appreciated, above all, his fashioning of Venetian history as a monument where the myths of glory and liberty shone forth'.[27]

One would like to view his achievement as a culmination of sorts, as a sign of Venetian humanism having finally come of age. But as King observes: 'Venetian humanism, not yet old, had begun to exhaust itself by the end of this period.'[28] She points to the foundation of the Aldine Press by Aldo Manuzio, and the publication of Francesco Colonna's *Hypnerotomachia Poliphili*, as visible signs of the two paths that the humanist movement would follow, for the most part, at the end of the century: narrowly philological on the one hand and escapist on the other. As was typical of most things in Venetian life, they divided also along social lines. Most of the humanist members of Aldo Manuzio's circle were commoners, practitioners of the technical tendencies long present in Venetian humanism and emphasized in secretarial training. Although the high-principled patriotism and ideological tone of patrician humanism were lacking, it was here that the real vitality lay. For the patricians, in great part, began to emphasize contemplative interests over public service. The *Hypnerotomachia* was perhaps a symptom of a deeper malaise – one might call it moral crisis – within the group. Less disciplined and less austerely moralistic than their fathers and grandfathers, patrician intellectuals became consumers: collectors and antiquarians, who provided the readership for the output of the presses.[29]

The *cittadino* order of secretaries, who were so influential amongst the ruling elites of the Scuole Grandi, played a supporting role in all this. Several wrote their own chronicles, with varying degrees of humanist pretension, and others transcribed parts of them in the course of their work. One may cite Andrea Ziliol, who wrote *Storie dei suoi tempi* in 1508 and whose brother, Vettor, was twice Guardian Grande of the Scuola Grande di San Marco.[30] Or we may point to the historical interests of Gianpietro Stella, Chancellor Grande of Venice from 1517 to 1523 and a member of the same confraternity. Naming two of its officers as executors of his last will and testament, he left a substantial library which included a preponderance of history books.[31] Perhaps more revealing was the experience of Lodovico Zamberti, twice a member of the Banca of the Scuola Grande di San Giovanni Evangelista in the 1490s and the notary for Giovanni Dario's first two wills. Coming across a chronicle of the fourteenth century, written in crude Lombard characters, that recounted the Alexander legend, he carefully transcribed it for the Doge and wrote to him:

> . . . knowing how gladly your illustrious serenity reads the ancient things, and especially those which concern the observance of religion of which your serenity is a special defender . . . [this is] the true history . . . which in these times I have had recorded in your Chancery so that posterity in some [future] time would not have any doubts, against the opinion of many people who say that such history had not been true; thus it has appeared well to me to keep a copy of it for your serenity and to exert myself to write it in the same antique tongue in which it was written in your Chancery; I am certain that your serenity, reading it, will have the greatest consolation, seeing in it how much gratitude would have been given by his sanctity [the Pope] to your serenity . . .[32]

Sabellico died in 1506, but only in 1516 did the Signoria create the new position of official historiographer of the Republic. The appointment of Andrea Navagero to the post was a further resounding rejection for Sanudo's *sermon materno* and all that it represented. In choosing Navagero, a young and inexperienced patrician, the Council of Ten opted for literary style and reputation over a simple commitment to historical observation and seemingly artless accessibility.[33]

We should make a few observations about the essential formal differences between the chronicle and the humanist history. Accuracy was not the issue, for each could be quite reliable as a record of current events. Nor was subject matter, for, as we have noted, the Venetian chronicle, like the humanist history, often focused exclusively on civic affairs and on the historical mission of the city A key distinction lay, rather, in the explanatory purpose of the humanist history. Guarino Guarini had advised Tobia del Borgo, about to take up the post of historian at the court of Rimini in 1446, to follow the Ciceronian model, taking care to concern himself not only with events but with their causes and consequences: 'First the intentions, then the event, and [finally] what is anticipated afterwards'.[34] Toward this end the historian was expected to find a cause-and-effect structure in the events that he described.

As a result of such a demand, the humanist history could be seen as the *invenzione* of a single mind: the product of an individual who wrote in a specific time and place. This view regarded the historical text as something created and constructed. It was grounded in truth, but it was proleptic and went beyond a written record of observed events. By weeding out extraneous details, the historian discovered the hidden order in a seemingly disordered world. Futhermore, following Petrarch, the purpose of history-writing was to give moral, spiritual and intellectual uplift not only through the content, but also through elegance in the telling. Capturing this mood as he wrote in the late Trecento, Salutati thus celebrated the written *historia*: 'Nothing is more ornate, nothing more elegant in expression, and [hence] nothing is so capable of moving while delighting the spirit.'[35] The humanist history, then, was intended to be a work of literature, as well as of truth. Unlike most of the Venetian chronicles, it had a named author. It was complete in itself and was not meant to be added on to by others – at least without due credit given – as the years went by. It was art.

The *istorie* of the Florentine artist Domenico Ghirlandaio might be considered as pictorial analogues to this narrative mode. Sharing a similar taste for genre detail with the Venetian eyewitness painters, he too was required to portray recent events in local settings with a good number of contemporary bystanders. And yet his works maintain a hierarchy of dramatic action, with every element of the composition arranged to maintain narrative focus [Plate 44].

The shift in dominant modes of history writing in Venice was paralleled by innovations in pictorial narrative composition. The criteria of authenticity – those elements in a painting that made it appear a truthful rendering of a true event – began to change: away from the ambient and toward the actor. Convincing testimony was increasingly to be found in the clear exposition of men's actions that were thought to reveal the 'motions of their minds', as Alberti had put it.

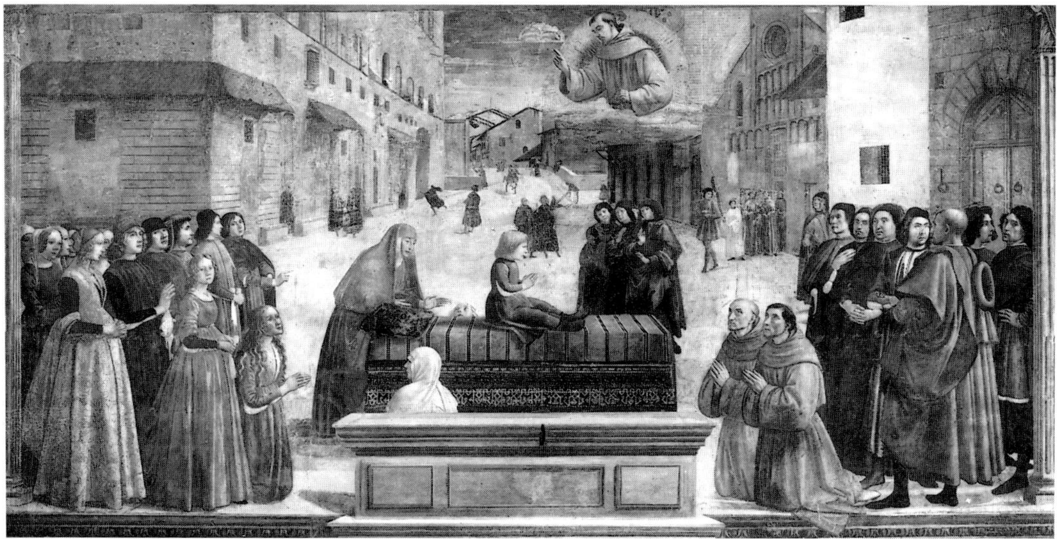

44. Domenico Ghirlandaio, *St. Francis Healing the Injured Child*, fresco (Florence, S. Trinità, Sassetti Chapel)

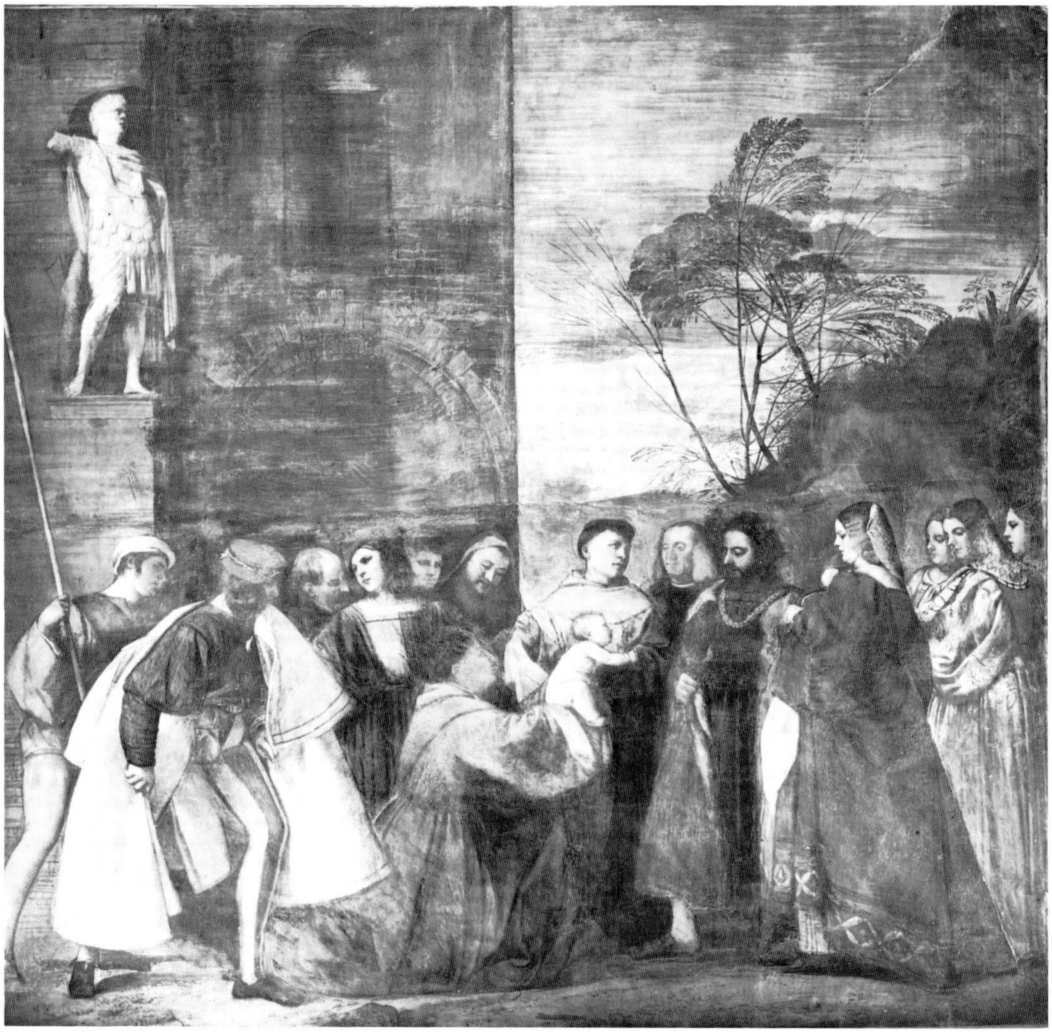

45 (right). Titian, *Miracle of the Speaking Babe*, fresco, 1511 (Padua, Scuola del Santo)

46. Titian, *Miracle of the Wounded Woman*, fresco, 1511 (Padua, Scuola del Santo)

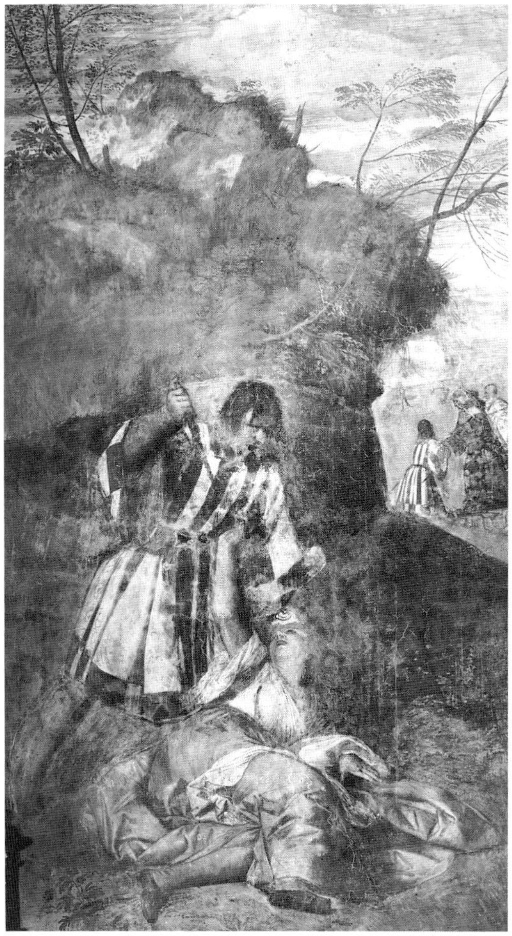

Titian's frescoes in the Scuola del Santo in Padua, painted in 1511, mark a watershed in Venetian narrative composition.[36] In the *Miracle of the Speaking Babe*, the compositional frame has contracted so that little remains but the actors essential to the central narrative event [Plate 45]. Grouped across the front plane on a shallow stage, the human figures take on a monumental weight within the scene. Each gesture is telling, none trivial; the landscape and architecture are disciplined by the most severe economy to heighten the focus on the essential human drama. Titian allowed no accident of mundane life to distract attention from the dramatic moment in all its fullness. One ponders the causes, the miraculous action of the child, the consequences.

In the *Miracle of the Wounded Woman* in the same cycle, the drama is heightened [Plate 46]. The husband is poised, about to stab his wife a second time. Again the cause – the woman's supposed adultery – is not shown. It is the violent action – the psychological and physical high-point of the story – that is given primacy of place in the front plane. But the foreshortened body of the victim leads us into deeper space toward the religious core of the story in the background: St. Anthony's merciful forgiveness and, by implication, the miraculous healing of the woman. Here Titian (exceptionally) breaks the unity of time, place and action and reverts to the medieval technique of continuous narrative so that he can show the consequences of the event. But this act of pardon is embedded within the landscape for reasons quite different from those intended by the eyewitness painters in the True Cross cycle when they 'lost' their miraculous healings within the urban panorama. Here St. Anthony's action is not supposed to appear as if it was simply part of ongoing life. Rather, the reduced scale of the figures in the background is intended to set up a formal hierarchy that will define the temporal sequence. The eye moves from the present to the future as it moves from front to back within the picture space.[37]

But like the chronicle, which survived in force, the eyewitness style was to continue for a time as an alternate view of truth, while betraying accommodations to the new measure of credibility. We see the two modes already appearing together in Carpaccio's paintings in the 1490s, with the tableau arrangements and processional movement of the St. Ursula cycle. In the proleptic sequence of the *Martyrdom of the Pilgrims and Funeral of St. Ursula*, the narrative action unfolds across the front plane, and the most significant events are no longer deliberately obscured in the background [Plate 47]. Another violent act is about to happen right before us. But the descriptive details remain to draw away our attention. In the many small figures in the distance we find a plenitude of circumstance, but not much consequence.

Likewise, in his later work, painted in the first two decades of the sixteenth century, Carpaccio moved further away from gratuitousness and the sense of a 'slice of life', toward a more rhetorical and immediately legible narrative message. The triumphant St. George holds the dragon front and center, with onlookers balanced left and right. St. Stephen preaches to his small congregation or disputes with the Jewish elders right before our eyes. St. Augustine is blessed with a miracle in subtly direct and natural terms [Color Plates XXXVIII, XI, XV, and XIII]. In each case the number of figures is limited, the gestures are clear and simple, and the narrative core is well defined. As we shall see in Chapter 10, such groupings were informed to some degree by the living ceremonies of

47. Carpaccio, *Martyrdom of the Pilgrims and Funeral of St. Ursula*, 1493 (Venice, Accademia)

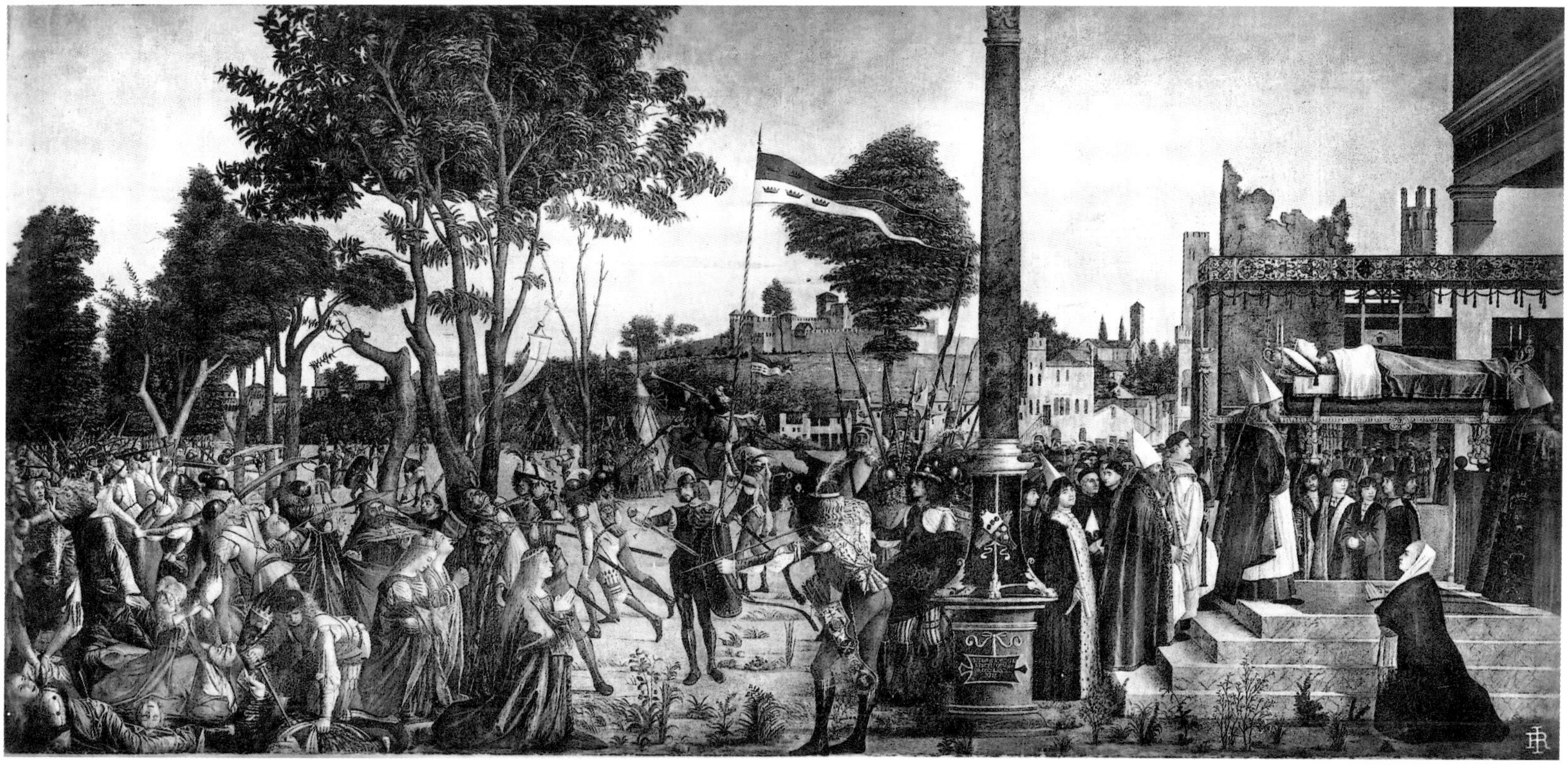

Carpaccio's time. That, however, was as far as he would go. He sacrificed much of the sense of happenstance, of small events taking place in a big world, but the concern for circumstance persisted. The carefully observed small detail and architectural peculiarity remained in his works until the end of his life.

Thus far we have ignored the role of Giovanni Bellini in the elaboration of the eyewitness style, simply because so few narrative paintings survive from his hand. The small scale of the handful of predella panels attributed to him make comparisons with large canvases inconclusive. But one might wish to continue a little further with the theme of violent acts and consider the *Martyrdom of St. Peter Martyr* in the National Gallery in London, which is generally ascribed to Giovanni's workshop if not to the master himself [Plate 48].[38]

St. Peter falls mortally wounded on the left; to the right, his companion is about to be stabbed. As with Carpaccio, the temporal sequence unfolds in a lateral manner. The main protagonists are given primacy of place, and yet the clear formal hierarchy of action shown in Titian's frescoes is missing. Our eyes move from one pair to the next and back again. And then they fix on the woodcutters in the background. These latter figures exist in a separate plane of space and, seemingly extraneous to the story, recall one of the most favored strategies of the eyewitness artist. Actively engaged in their own work, the woodsmen are seemingly oblivious of the tragic actions taking place close by. Somewhat unconvincingly, they seem intended to draw these actions into the rhythms of ongoing life. Unlike Titian's St. Anthony and the pardoned husband in Plate 46, they are not the result of the foreground action. But like Titian's characters, they seem to have a function beyond the setting of the stage. Replicating and (surely) commenting symbolically upon the narrative, their actions have more narrative relevance than one perceives at first glance. Giovanni Bellini thus seems to strike a compromise between the deliberation and consequentiality of Titian and the seemingly indiscriminate descriptive tendencies of the eyewitness artists.

We may conclude that the narrative mode of Carpaccio, Gentile Bellini and the other True Cross painters (and even, to a degree, of Giovanni Bellini) was initially grounded in a persistent chronicle-based taste for positing and apprehending significant historical events within the rich context of daily affairs. This taste informed history-painting *per se*, but it spilled over into the *istorie* of

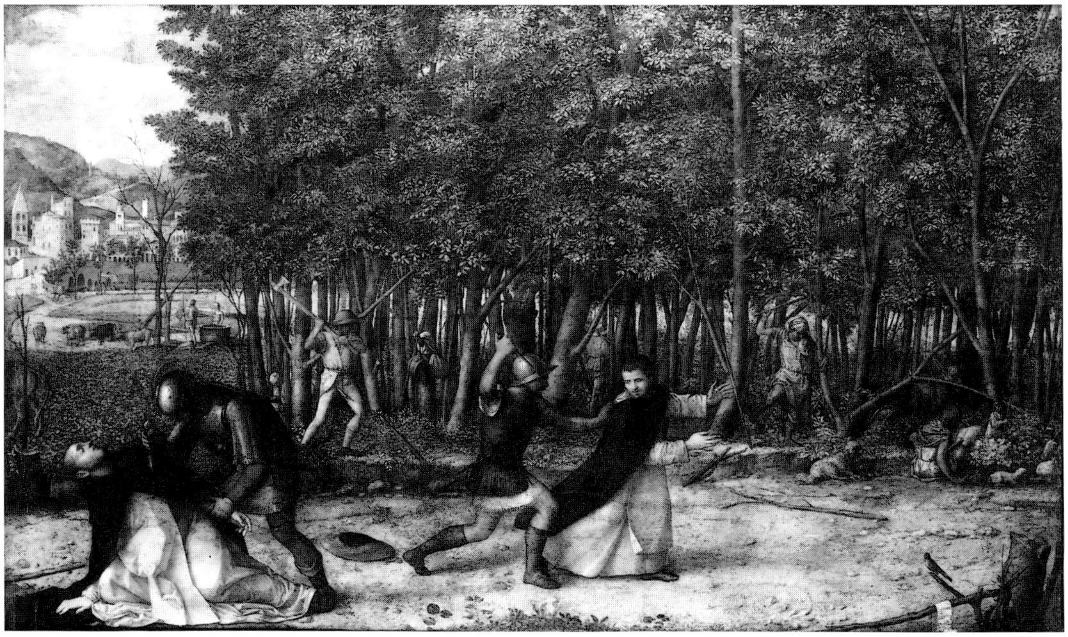

48. Giovanni Bellini, *Martyrdom of St. Peter Martyr* (London, National Gallery)

other subjects as well. It did not remain static, however, and soon developed toward a more consequential mode in consonance with new fashions in historical writing.

Naturally, such a suggestion leaves a number of questions unexplored. Allowing that affinities can be observed between certain formal properties and intentions of written history and painted history, one would not wish to press too hard for a direct causative link between them in whatever direction. It would, however, be fair to say that both historian and artist were bound by the common goal of documentation in their efforts to transmit a particular vision of a historical moment. The tenacity of the chronicle helps us to understand the popular appeal of the eyewitness style of painting to its patrons – many of whom were owners, and others transcribers, of personal copies of that circumstantial and discursive form of civic history.

Along with the emphasis on the literary form had come a growing awareness of its visual presentation: its actual appearance on the printed or handwritten page. A cursive form of humanist handwriting called *cancelleresca*, a Chancery hand developed by antiquarians, had become popular in the 1470s and 1480s. It is elegantly legible and immediately recognizable in the proceedings of government councils recorded by the secretaries of those years. In 1492, the Senate appointed an official penmanship instructor, Antonio de' Taglienti, to train new Chancery scribes in its use.[39] The men of the *scuole* were not oblivious to such aesthetic concerns. During the waning years of the Quattrocento, a number of *scuole* had their Mariegole rewritten. Thus in 1497, the Guild of the Cheese Merchants allowed that their existing Mariegola had been written and corrected in ugly *littera marchadantescha* (mercantile writing) that was 'difficult to read'. They voted to remake it, ordering that 'it should be written in large and well-formed letters, so that everyone could read it'.[40] The Scuola di San Girolamo, whom we met briefly in Chapter 3, incorporated a similar ruling into their own Mariegola in 1504:

> The great failing of Gastaldi and officers of our *scuole* of Venice, having beautiful Mariegole of great value and written with beautifully formed letters, [lies in the fact that] they allow letters to be written in their Mariegole in diverse hands in such an ugly manner, common and crude, and ruin their Mariegole in this way.[41]

This attention to visual form by the consumers of pictorial narrative should remind us of the visual tradition of the artists themselves, which had its own momentum. Indeed, the acceptance of the humanist history in Venice was probably more a symptom than a cause of changes in cognitive tastes. Just as it signaled a new openness of the Venetian ruling class to new modes of historical writing, so too there was a new openness of Venetian artists and patrons during the same period toward pictorial models from elsewhere. Indeed, as we shall see, the eyewitness style of painting in its several forms had not developed in isolation. Its stylistic and compositional particularites can only be understood as both an accommodation to and a rejection of the challenge of Tuscan art.

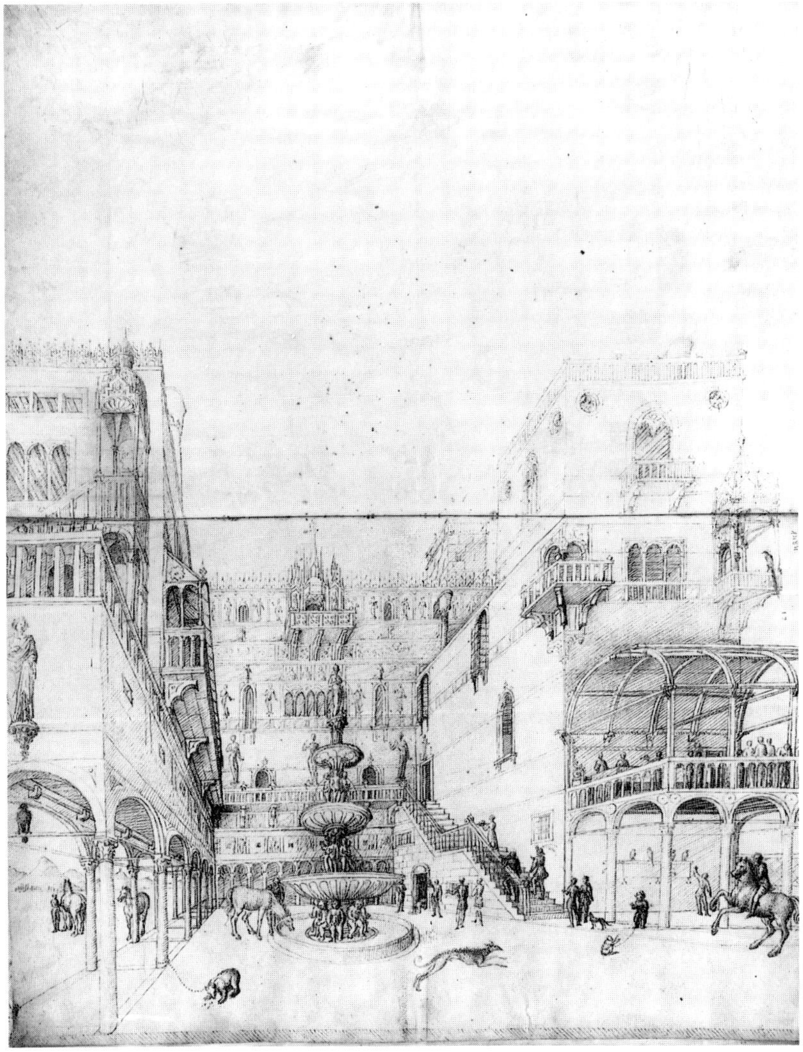

49. Jacopo Bellini, *Feast of Herod* (Paris, Louvre Album, fols. 15v–16)

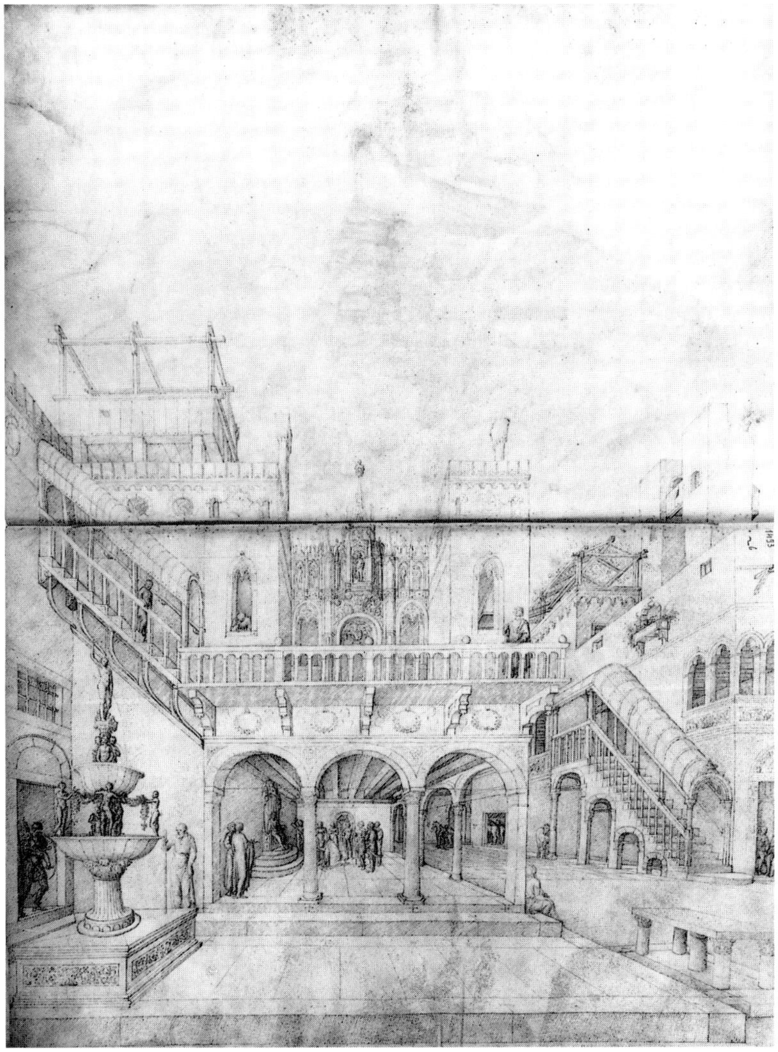

50. Jacopo Bellini, *Judgment of Solomon* (Paris, Louvre Album, fol. 25)

7

Antecedents

Many of the formal properties that made the Venetian *istoria* of the late Quattrocento seem so akin to the Venetian chronicle can be found in painting elsewhere in Europe: the delight in color and pattern, the emphasis on the surface at the expense of spatial depth, the down-playing of dramatic focus, the intrusion of secular trivia in the sacred story, the solemn little groups of patrons interspersed with the narrative actors. One thinks immediately of Flemish paintings and tapestries. As Panofsky wrote of the various anonymous artists, such as the Master of the Legend of St. Lucy, who painted in Brussels and Bruges in that period:

> Never before had the legends of individual saints, preferably female, and the sagas of such Biblical characters as Joseph of Egypt and Job been told at such length, with so many little figures and with such an abundance of 'local color' and entertaining detail; the very names under which most of these masters are known are eloquent proof of their passion for story-telling.[1]

But parallels could be cited just about anywhere in Italy. Even the frescoes of the Sistine Chapel, painted by a team of Tuscan and Umbrian artists in the early 1480s, exhibit many of the same characteristics. Altogether they testify to the lingering attractions of the International Gothic style in the face of the new spatial rationalism of Masaccio and his successors. And yet, the way in which these properties coexist in a Venetian *istoria* remains quite unique. One cannot mistake a painting by Carpaccio or Gentile Bellini for a work made elsewhere. The human actors are often caught up in a large and busy world of quite extraordinary light and color, almost in the northern manner; but it is a measured world. Herein lies the crucial difference: by the end of the Quattrocento, as we shall see, Venetian artists had achieved a synthesis that combined two kinds of realism: the structural realism of the south, wherein the picture space became a measurable three-dimensional world constructed according to mathematical rules, and the empirical realism of the north, wherein the details of the observed world – surfaces and the effects of light upon them – were reproduced with a high degree of fidelity to optical experience.

We may lament the loss of the late fifteenth-century canvases of the Great Council Hall of the Ducal Palace as a major piece of evidence for the precise nature of the early emergence of the *venezianità* that we see in the paintings of the *scuole*, but, in fact, much can be learned from the generation that came before that campaign: from Jacopo Bellini in particular. An examination of his drawing-books suggests that the paintings of his son Gentile, as well as those of Carpaccio and the other eyewitness artists, were the direct beneficiaries of

Jacopo's own efforts to effect an accommodation between traditional Venetian criteria for a history painting and the innovations of artists in Tuscany.

In page after page Jacopo can be seen responding to a wide range of compositional problems for any number of subjects in ways predictive of the paintings of the True Cross cycle. The narrative core of each scene is often pushed to one side, as in the *Feast of Herod*; or it is embedded in the background, as in the *Judgment of Solomon* [Plates 49 and 50]. Often it is overpowered by the extravagance of the architecture, and one is more aware of the virtuoso display of linear perspective than of the human actors in the scene. Some observers have thus concluded that perspective itself was the 'real' subject matter of Jacopo's drawings, and that the stories or themes depicted were of secondary interest.[2] Others argue that the stories were exactly the point: that the artist delighted in pictorial narration for its own sake and used the personal medium of the compositional drawing, unencumbered by demands of patronage, to indulge his pleasure in storytelling and in recalling the Venetian landscape.[3] So some call it science and others pure fantasy, and the result is simply narrative confusion. Such judgments may be precipitous. Jacopo's drawings, carefully gathered and preserved perhaps for the use of his sons and, indeed, for posterity, may well be viewed as visual records of a series of experiments in which the artist attempted to come to terms with new models for pictorial narrative, and thus for pictorial truth, in a cultural milieu which took such matters quite seriously.

Jacopo Bellini's earliest mentor in the construction of the *istoria* was surely Gentile da Fabriano, whom he would have met as a youth when the master painted in the Great Council Hall in the first decades of the fifteenth century.[4] They were probably also together in Florence in the early 1420s when the older artist was working on the *Adoration of the Magi* for the sacristy of Santa Trinità.[5] Jacopo later acknowledged his debt, signing two frescoes in the 1430s as 'Discipulus Gentili da Fabriano', and possibly even giving Gentile's name to his firstborn son.[6] It is thus with Gentile da Fabriano that we must begin.

Gentile da Fabriano

Evidence for Gentile da Fabriano's approach to monumental wall-painting is hard to come by. Since just fragments remain, it can only be reconstructed by analogy, aided by the occasional leap of the imagination. A ruined fresco by one of his followers in the cathedral at Pordenone is sometimes cited as a dim echo of the Great Council Hall frescoes. It features an urban skyline of crenellated towers and elaborate Gothic arches and pinnacles.[7]

More telling indications surfaced recently, however, during restorations of the old Palazzo del Capitano in Brescia. Two lunette-shaped pieces of fresco (each two metres high by one metre wide) were discovered on the upper part of two walls beneath the present ceiling. They have been identified as remnants of Gentile da Fabriano's well-documented fresco cycle of the life of St. George, painted in 1414–19 in the private chapel of Pandolfo Malatesta.[8] Sanudo visited the chapel in 1483, calling it 'most beautiful, worthy and elegant', and reporting that it cost '14,000 ducats to complete'.[9] The newly discovered frescoes show segments of fortified cities painted in a hilly landscape against a background of lapis lazuli. The architecture and spatial treatment are so similar to that in Gentile da Fabriano's *Adoration of the Magi* that we may be permitted to make a few

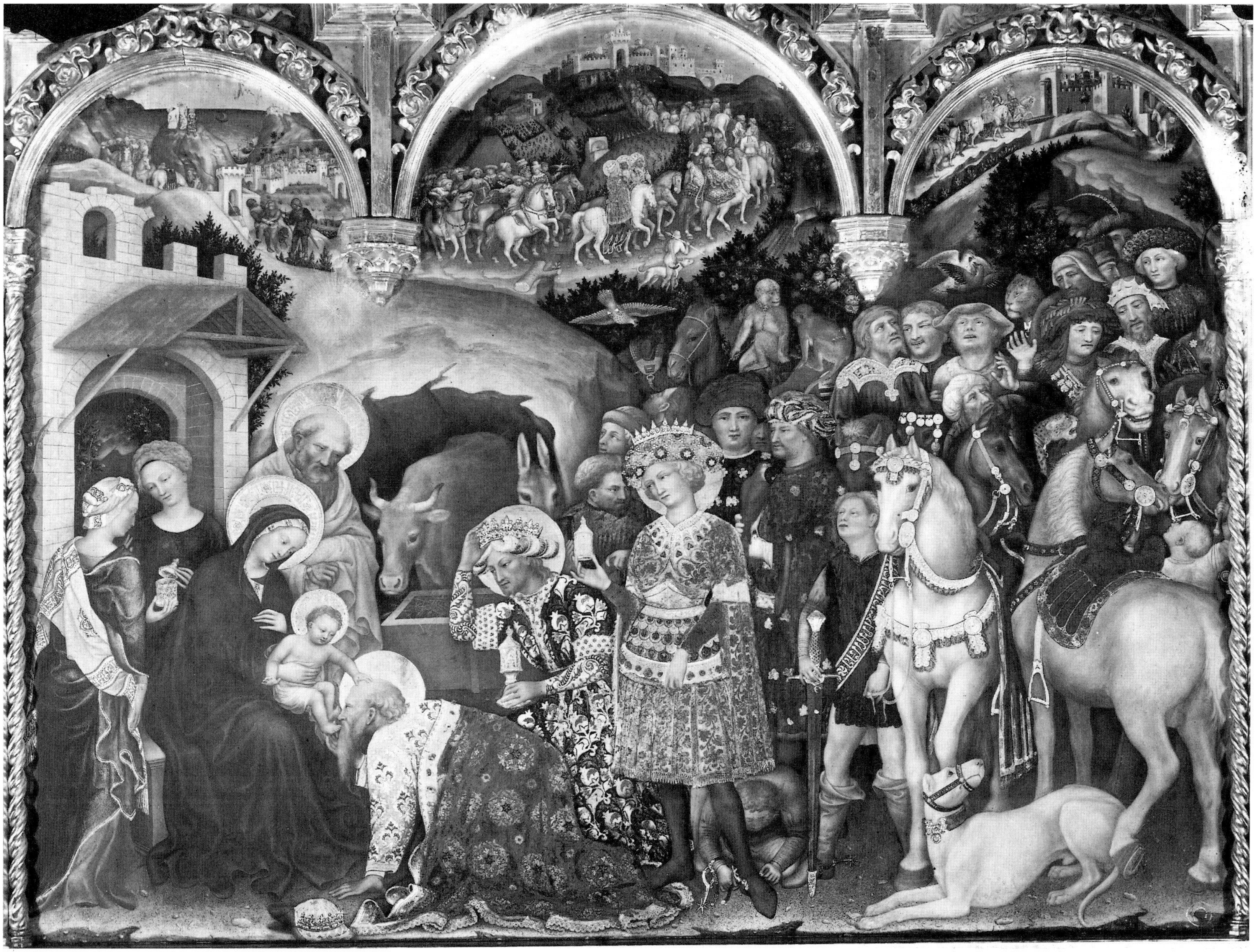

51. Gentile da Fabriano, *Adoration of the Magi*, 1423 (Florence, Uffizi)

further analogies. The *Adoration* [Plate 51] is his only surviving example of large-scale narrative composition. Bearing in mind that it is an altarpiece, with all the specific requirements of media and format of that genre, we will now turn to it as a reflection, if once removed, of his mural painting.

The *Adoration* would surely have satisfied the tastes of the most avid reader of chronicles. Presenting the event with all the dazzle and display of a courtly pageant, Gentile da Fabriano offered a full visual account of the principals of the occasion, as well as those in their entourage: costumes, colors, patterned stuffs and equipage, all generously garnished with gold. The pictorial field of the main panel, just like the narrative range of a chronicler, tends to a comprehensive expansiveness. A close examination of each portion of the painting repays the viewer with small but satisfying discoveries: exotic animals, a scene of brigandage, pomegranate trees and cultivated garden plots, a huntsman with his dog, a hat made of peacock feathers, the play of light across a rocky cliff, a colloquy of horses on the right who seem to balance the ladies-in-waiting behind the Holy Family on the left.

As Keith Christiansen pointed out in his recent monograph on the artist, Gentile da Fabriano's technical skill has tended to blind us to the extent to which all of these small details are based upon the direct observation of the natural world. Indeed, the painted surface has become here the direct extension of the viewer's own visual experience.[10] It was the reality of the careful and attentive observer, however, and not of the geometer. For although the pictured world is not flat, its depth cannot be precisely measured. Figures and objects are simply piled up the picture plane, one above the other, and the bits of architecture function more as decorative backdrops than as stages for human action.

The Veronese contribution

Although none of Gentile da Fabriano's surviving work deals with a battle scene like the fresco that he painted in Venice, if we turn to Antonio Pisanello of Verona, Jacopo Bellini's second important model for pictorial narrative, we can propose further analogies. Pisanello's Venetian activity may have followed rather than coincided with Gentile's, but he remained closely linked to him

52. Pisanello, *St. George and the Princess*, fresco (Verona, S. Anastasia)

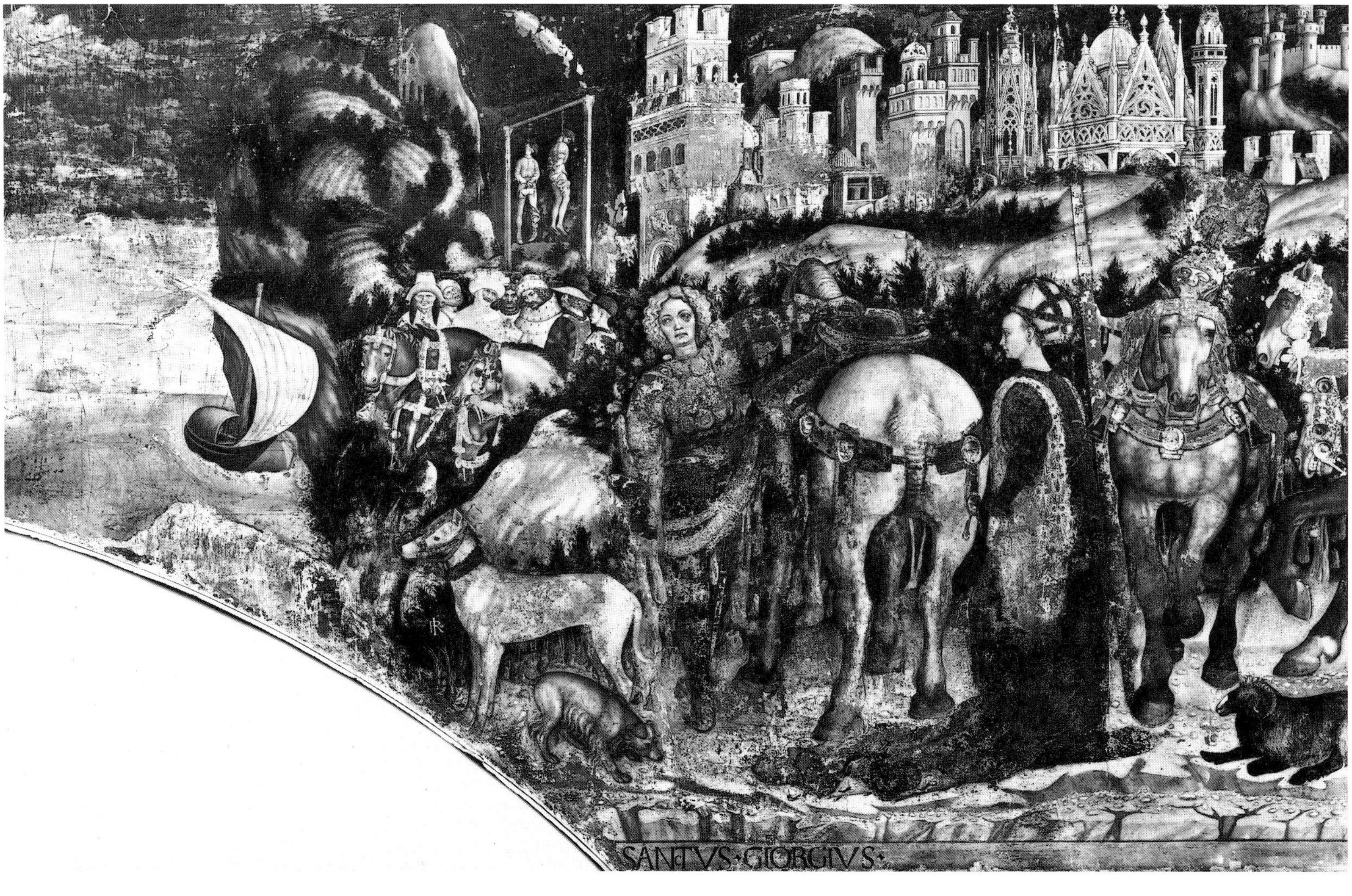

stylistically and even completed a fresco cycle begun by the older artist in San Giovanni Laterano in Rome.[11] There were, however, important differences traceable to his own stylistic formation within the Veronese tradition.

Pisanello's *St. George and the Princess* in S. Anastasia in Verona (1436–8) [Plate 52] is directly continuous in its basic compositional principles with Gentile's *Adoration*. Here again, the main protagonists fill the foreground of a landscape. The ground plane is defined in the front by the edge of a cliff, and mountains rise up in the rear, with city towers forming a skyline. There is a similar close attentiveness to every detail, as Pisanello bestowed a chronicler's indiscriminate regard upon the corpses hanging from the scaffold, the cluster of men of different races in front of them, the fashionable dress of the princess, the armor of the saint, the accoutrements of the horses.

But this is a pictured world which is becoming more convincingly three-dimensional. As line gives way to mass, the figures of humans and animals no longer pile one in front of another in layers, but generate their own volume and weight. The extravagant architecture, although based upon no consistent geometry, has become more constructable. While still only a backdrop, it is no longer perched on top of a mountain, but rises up behind it and implies an intervening atmosphere that was absent from Gentile da Fabriano's composition. By pulling the architectural elements closer to the front plane, Pisanello has reduced the infinite expansiveness of the landscape. He has made it more finite, but it is still not measurable. The same is true of Pisanello's chivalric scenes, painted about a decade later in the Ducal Palace at Mantua, that may provide a distant echo of the battle frescoes in Venice.[12] An apparently rising ground plane in all these compositions, rationalized by mountains and architecture to the rear, solves with finesse the problem of filling the middle ground.

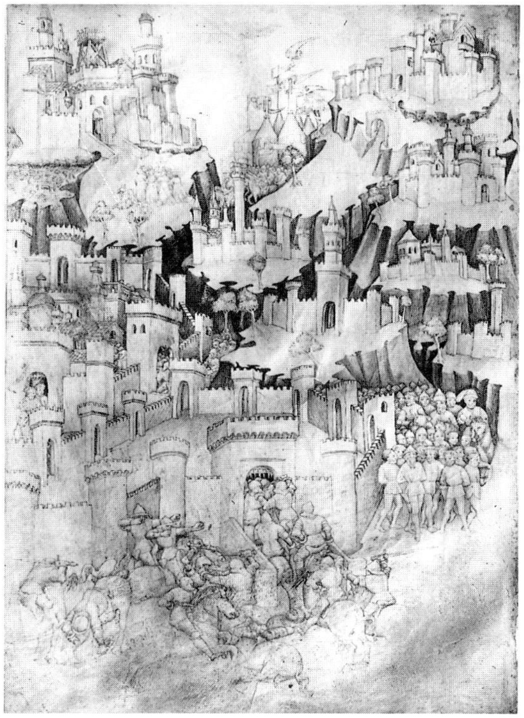

53. Altichiero, *Battle Scene*, drawing related to the lost frescoes in the Scaligeri Palace in Verona (Paris, Louvre)

A similar strategy is to be seen in a late Trecento drawing attributed to Altichiero that has been related to his lost frescoes in the Scaligeri Palace in Verona [Plate 53]. Like his frescoes in Padua in the Basilica del Santo and the nearby Oratorio di S. Giorgio (1376–84), it exemplifies the Veronese ambient in which Pisanello's own narrative style later developed.[13] Perhaps offering the best surviving indications of the general appearance of the early Quattrocento frescoes in the Great Council Hall of Venice, the Paduan paintings depict not only battles outside a city, but views within it.

Altichiero's *Council of Ramiro*, with the King enthroned in the center of a portico surrounded by members of the council [Plate 54], is a possible antecedent to two drawings that have been related to the frescoes of the Great Council Hall. One sketch, appearing to represent *Otto before the Emperor*, may record the fresco by Pisanello later described by Bartolommeo Facio:

> . . .he painted Frederick Barbarossa, the Roman Emperor, and his son as a suppliant, and in the same place a great throng of courtiers with German costume and German cast of feature, a priest distorting his face with his fingers, and some boys laughing at this, done so agreeably as to arouse good humor in those who look at it [Plate 55].[14]

We may also note in the sketch a dog and cat playing in the foreground, typical elements of *gratuità* in Pisanello's descriptive repertoire.

The second sketch, attributed to Pisanello himself, is generally identified as a preparatory drawing of the same scene [Plate 56].[15] A comparison with the other drawing, however, reveals a different formal conception and suggests another

54 (right). Altichiero, *Council of Ramiro*, fresco (Padua, S. Antonio, Cappella di S. Felice)

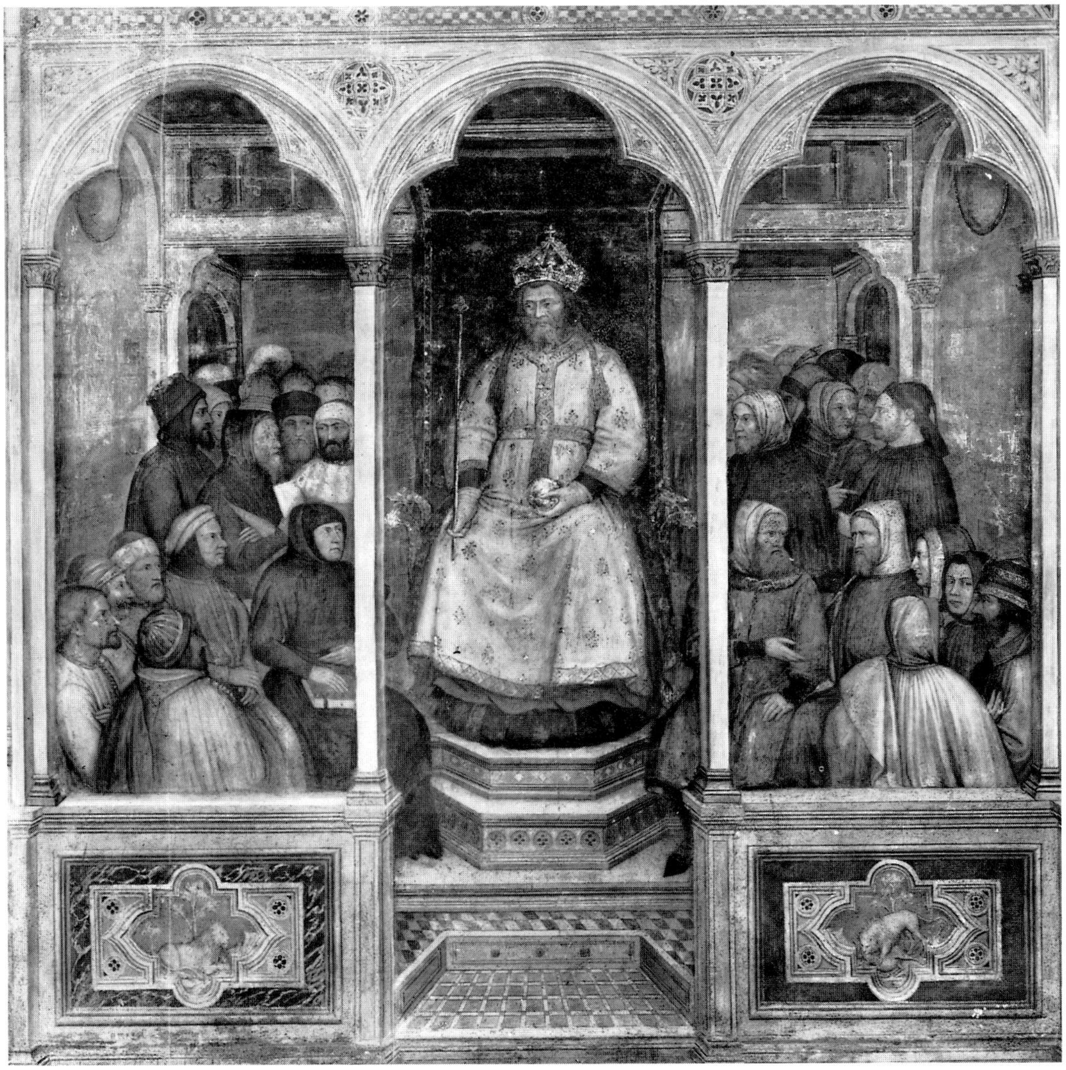

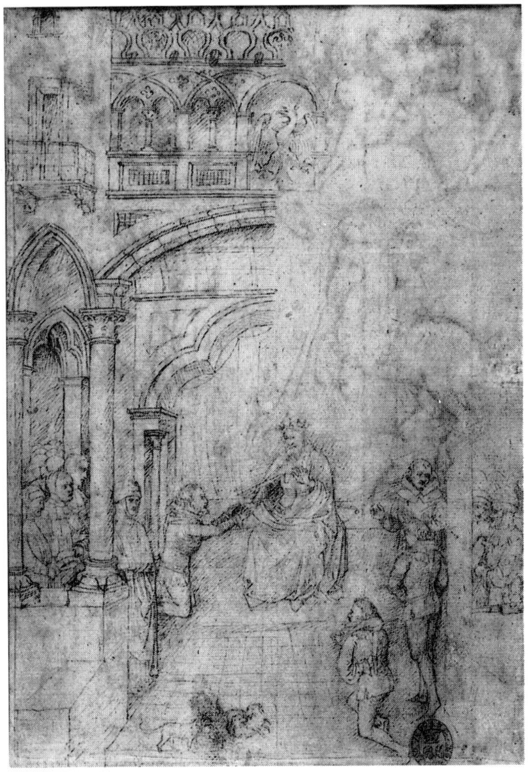

55. Northern Italian artist, *Otto before the Emperor* (London, British Museum, Sloane 5226, f. 57v)

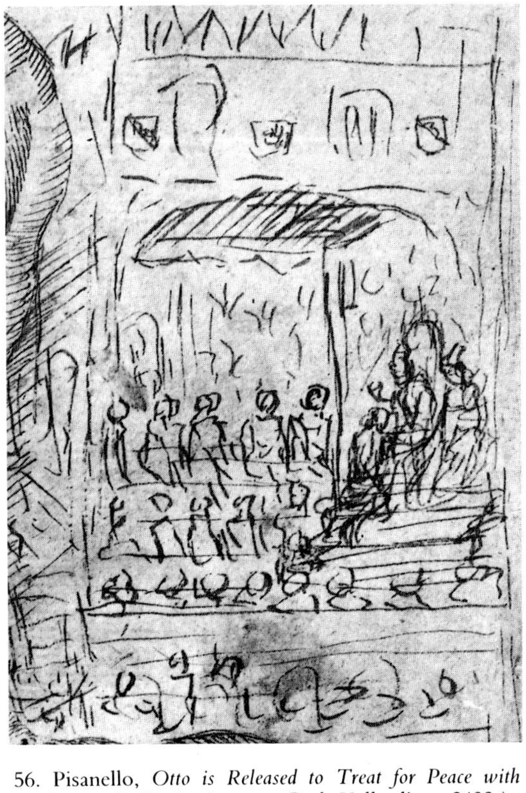

56. Pisanello, *Otto is Released to Treat for Peace with Barbarossa* (?) (Paris, Louvre, Cod. Vallardi, n. 2432r)

subject altogether: Otto kneeling before the Pope and the Doge while still in Venice, before he is dispatched to the Emperor.[16] Like Altichiero, the artist or artists responsible for these compositions has placed the human figures in and around an architectural structure, but the relative proportions in the drawings are notably more rationalized than those of Altichiero. Although we cannot know for certain, a comparison with Altichiero's frescoes suggests that these sketches encompassed whole scenes rather than just portions of them. If this is so, the problem of the middle ground is again avoided because of the close cropping of the scene. Indeed, in all compositions of Gentile da Fabriano and Pisanello that we have considered up to this point – and this is also true of their work in general – the artists did not attempt to come to terms with the problem of placing the narrative drama on a level ground plane within a spatially deep and mathematically rational setting. The protagonists are either placed against a hill, in the case of a landscape setting, or they are carefully framed, in the case of an urban environment. The creation of a rigorously consistent three-dimensional ambient was for them not a major concern.

Aside from providing a most conspicuous example of the seductive elegance of the courtly international style, Gentile da Fabriano had challenged Florentine painters with a new mimetic approach in his *Adoration of the Magi* of 1423. What he offered was empirical realism. Moving beyond the pattern books to a close observation of nature, he rendered with precision the surfaces of the physical world. But during the same critical decade, we know that Brunelleschi, Donatello and Masaccio offered another model, later to be adumbrated by Alberti: the structural realism of linear perspective, based upon a scientific approach to spatial construction and using the human body as its basic unit of measure. Italian artists for the remainder of the century labored to bring the two visions of reality into a satisfying and convincing balance.

The experiments of the Florentine artists were codified and elaborated by Alberti around 1435 in his treatise on painting.[17] Praising the painting of an *istoria* as the highest calling of an artist, he called for a return to the economy, restraint and narrative relevance of Giotto. As Michael Baxandall has shown, Alberti's structural model was a vehicle of impeccable humanist credentials: the Ciceronian periodic sentence. His system of pictorial composition was based upon a hierarchy of forms which were composed into a unified and interdependent whole, tending toward a single narrative purpose. Like the periodic sentence, the picture space was now (ideally) to be structured in a symmetrical or counterpoised arrangement. It had a scientific basis as well, for the representation of three-dimensional objects on a two-dimensional surface could now be formulated exactly with the help of Euclidean geometry.[18] Allowing that *varietà* – different kinds of figures, gestures, colors and things – was also an absolute value, he called for caution in the matter of *copia*: the quantity of these things. For while the ingredients of the *historia* should be *ornata* [out of the ordinary], its composition should also be *gravis* (grave and restrained), and, applying the classical concept of decorum, tempered with dignity and modesty. To achieve this goal, the number of figures included should be few – optimally nine or ten. The attitudes and movements of these human actors should express their inner feelings – preferably a variety of them – and should in turn produce like feelings in the viewer.[19] Alberti stated his case in carefully hedged terms:

> I will praise every kind of copiousness so long as it is appropriate to the action of the *historia*. For it often happens that when a beholder lingers to look at things, closely, the painters's copiousness wins favour. However I would wish this copiousness not only set off by a certain variety, but also tempered and moderated by a sense of dignitas and restraint. Certainly I condemn those painters who, because they wish to seem copious or want nothing left empty, follow no composition but scatter everything around in a confused and unconnected way, so that the *historia* shows less action than commotion. The painter who above all desires *dignitas* in his *historia* should perhaps maintain a certain solitariness in it.[20]

Uccello's *Flood* in the Chiostro Verde of S. M. Novella in Florence [Plate 65] demonstrates a close adherence to and perhaps even the fulfillment of Albertian prescriptions for the *istoria*.[21] By contrast, the paintings of Pisanello sometimes come uncomfortably close to all that Alberti was criticizing, although the writer never mentioned the artist by name.

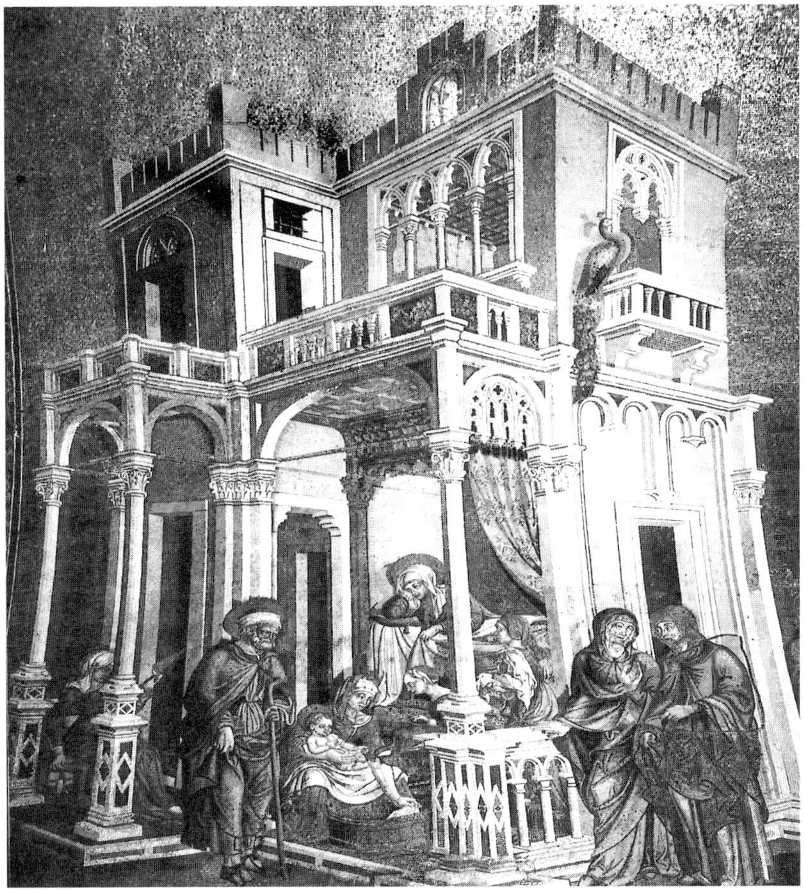

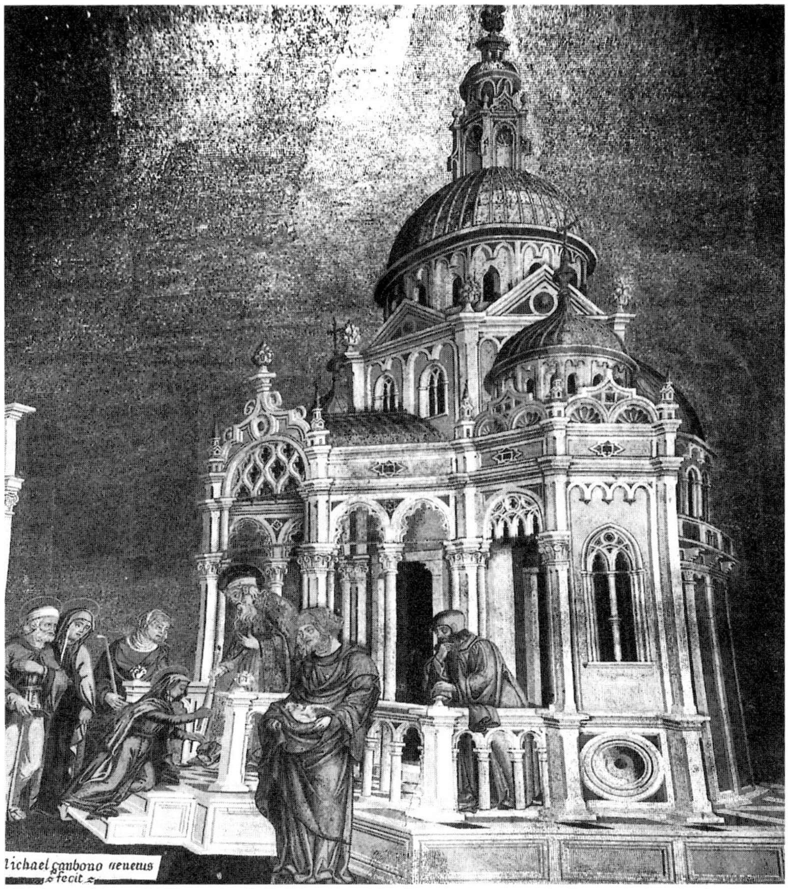

57. Giambono, *Birth of the Virgin*, mosaic (Venice, San Marco, Mascoli Chapel)

58 (right). Giambono, *Presentation of the Virgin*, mosaic (Venice, San Marco, Mascoli Chapel)

The crisis in Venetian art

The achievements of Florentine artists that formed the basis of Alberti's theoretical statements challenged the Venetians with intriguing new paradigms. What may be seen in retrospect as a crisis in Venetian art is summed up in the mosaic decoration of the Mascoli Chapel in the Basilica of San Marco, a project that began in the 1430s and continued for about twenty years. On the left vault of the chapel one sees two episodes from the life of the Virgin, the *Birth* and the *Presentation*, signed by Giambono, a leading exponent of late Gothic painting in Venice [Plates 57 and 58].[22] The fanciful architecture, obliquely placed, recalls the backgrounds of compositions by Gentile da Fabriano or Pisanello. Its sumptuous decorative elements give a superficial impression of complexity and detailed observation.

On the opposite side of the vault, in the *Visitation* and *Dormition of the Virgin*, however, we see the emergence of a different taste: in architectural style, in the treatment of the human body and in the conception of spatial reality [Plates 59 and 60]. Here the buildings feature the classical pediments, round-headed arches and Corinthian capitals associated with the Florentine Renaissance style. Their centralized and symmetrical facades are aligned parallel to the mosaic surface, behind which a three-dimensional structure appears to recede in a rational and measurable manner. The direct intrusion of central Italian influence is particularly evident in the structurally more coherent *Dormition*, with the two figures on the left betraying a Tuscan grandeur of form. Although clearly more than

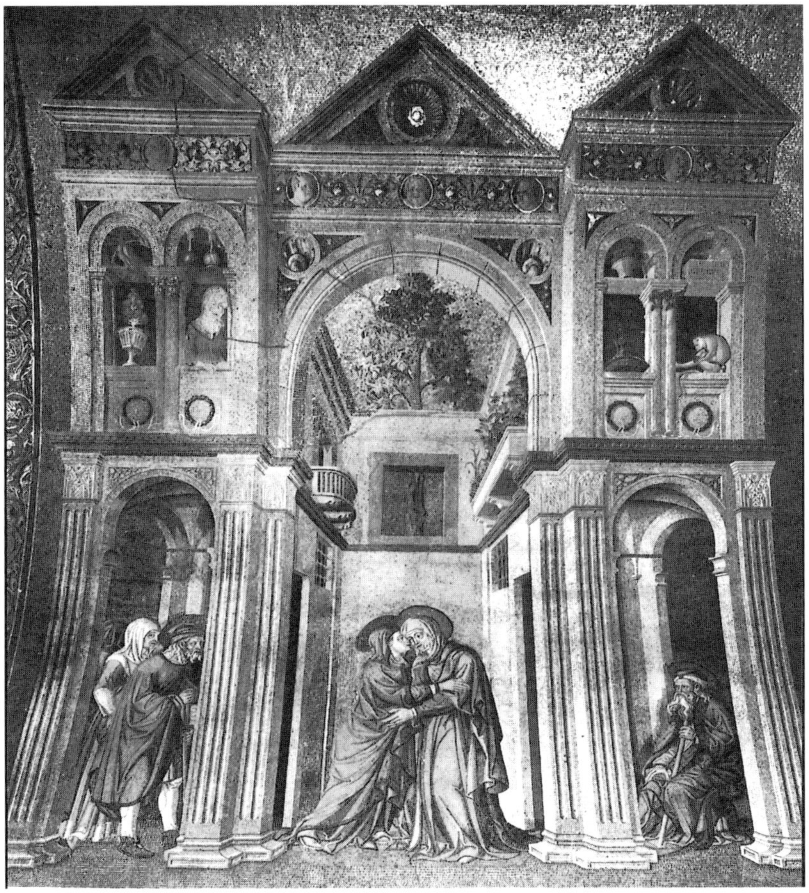

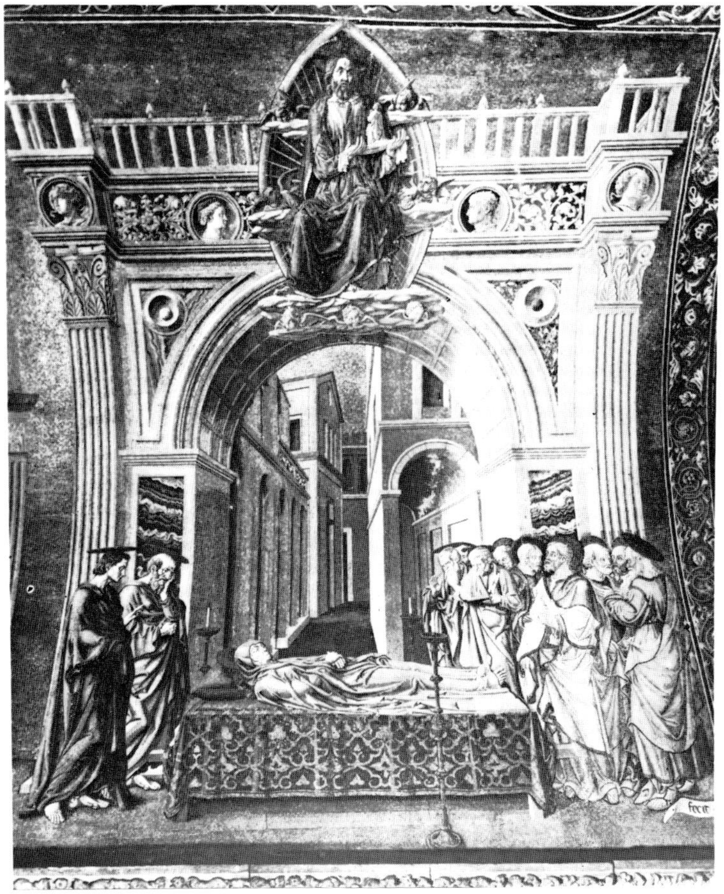

one artist was involved in the development of the cartoon, the postulated participation of Andrea del Castagno, documented in Venice in the 1440s, seems completely in keeping with its Florentine elements.[23]

Whether or not Jacopo Bellini was one of the principals involved, along with Giambono, is not known, but the architecture in both scenes on this side of the vault has cognates in a number of sketches in his drawing-books.[24] The main lesson of the Mascoli Chapel for our purposes is its lucid demonstration of the disjunction between two competing aesthetics in Venice during this period: the familiar and the 'modern'. It is clear that a reconciliation was necessary. Jacopo Bellini emerges as the pivotal figure in such an accommodation.

What was the nature of his dilemma? Jacopo Bellini was caught between two stylistic worlds. On the side of tradition, there was the specifically Venetian concern with authenticity and credibility in its history paintings. Such values were by now associated with the frescoes of Gentile da Fabriano and Pisanello in the Great Council Hall. The prestige of these artists remained high outside Venice as well, for they continued to enjoy the custom of courtly patrons and draw praise from humanist writers in the same circles. On the side of modernity, the new Florentine models of composition clashed head-on with familiar Venetian stylistic norms and made paintings in the Gothic style seem increasingly out-of-date. The notion of progress was by now gaining acceptance even in conservative Venice, and perhaps a 'truer truth' was possible to achieve in pictorial narrative composition.

59 (left). Giambono with Jacopo Bellini (?), *Visitation*, mosaic (Venice, San Marco, Mascoli Chapel)

60. Giambono, Jacopo Bellini and Andrea Castagno (?) *Dormition of the Virgin*, mosaic (Venice, San Marco, Mascoli Chapel)

So few paintings survive by Jacopo Bellini, that any observations on changes in his painting technique or in his treatment of color and pattern during this period remain conjectural, at least for the *istorie*. But his albums of drawings in the Louvre and the British Museum allow us to examine with more certainty his development of compositional formulae for pictorial narratives, and the implications of his preoccupation with spatial construction. The original function of these drawings is unknown. Although some have called them sketches, it seems more accurate to consider most of them finished works of art, for they represent compositions that are fully worked out and complete in themselves.[25] And yet there are no known paintings with which we can identify them. One point should be stressed. Whether or not any of these compositions were ever painted on walls, they were born of a mural aesthetic. Although often highly detailed, the full compositional drawings for the most part have nothing of a miniaturist quality to them, nor can one easily imagine them on predellas. They offer solutions for large surfaces.

In recent years, scholars have generally agreed with Marcel Rothlisberger's approximate dating of the books to a fairly narrow period between 1450 and 1455. Degenhart and Schmitt's new arguments, however, for a more prolonged period of execution (1430–60s), with the Louvre album the earlier, are more convincing from a stylistic standpoint. Following Degenhart and Schmitt's re-ordering, one can trace Jacopo's early reaction to his own training in the manner of Gentile da Fabriano with the testing of exaggerated spatial strategies, toward a more moderate and controlled approach in the later drawings, when he responded positively to the rationalizing examples of Mantegna and Donatello. The manner outlined here, in which Jacopo developed toward the style of the eye-witness painters, thus relies upon Degenhart and Schmitt's dates for the sequence of the drawings.[26]

In two versions of the *Adoration of the Magi*, probably drawn in the late 1430s, Jacopo was already making a critique of sorts of his old mentor's masterpiece back in Florence [Plates 61 and 62]. Bearing in mind the obvious fact that a drawing is inherently less dense than a painting, one still sees an opening-up of the spatial ambient. The shed and the mountains, essentially environmental stage props for Gentile da Fabriano, became for Jacopo important vehicles for generating space. The shed, conceived in both drawings in a radical and not quite convincing perspective construction, was intended as a measurable three-dimensional element within the unmeasurable landscape. The surrounding mountains helped further to define the limits and the volume of that space.

Jacopo also rejected the traditional solution of the rising ground plane and chose instead to tackle head-on the difficult problem of figural placement on a level surface within an expansive format. In Plate 61, he clarified Gentile's handling of the narrative tableau arrangement of procession and arrival, a scheme that was later used to good effect by Carpaccio. The cavalcade still coming down the hill is perceived as part of a temporal progression. It leads continuously into the group in front and is not simply placed above it on a separate mountain range or sandwiched behind it in the foreground.[27]

In Plate 62, we see a vast expansion of three-dimensional space, with the Holy Family and the Magi embedded deep in a huge landscape. It features not one, but two processions: the first leading down a mountain road of quite precipitous

61 (facing above). Jacopo Bellini, *Adoration of the Magi* (Paris, Louvre Album, fol. 31)

62 (facing below). Jacopo Bellini, *Adoration of the Magi* (Paris, Louvre Album, fol. 30)

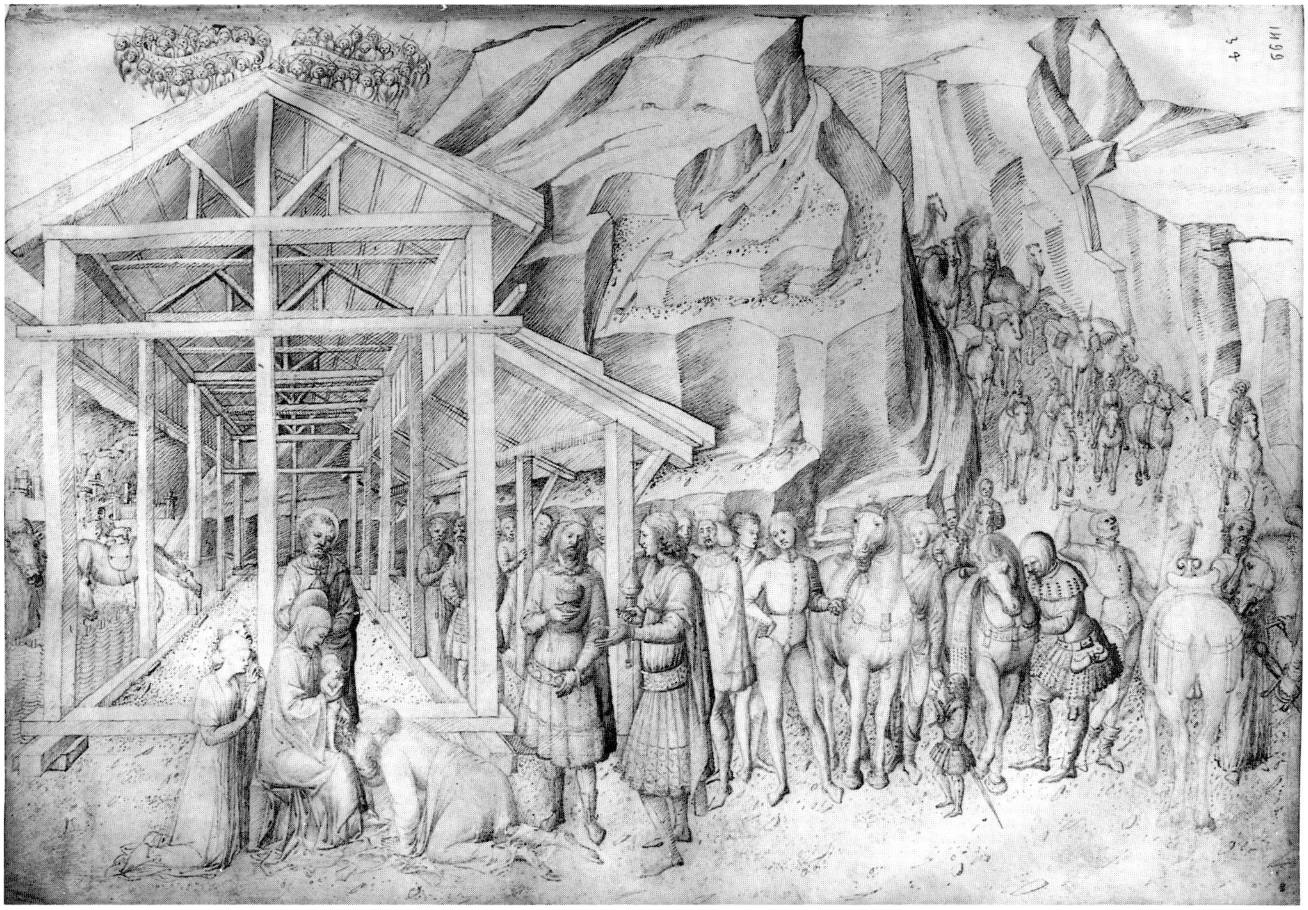

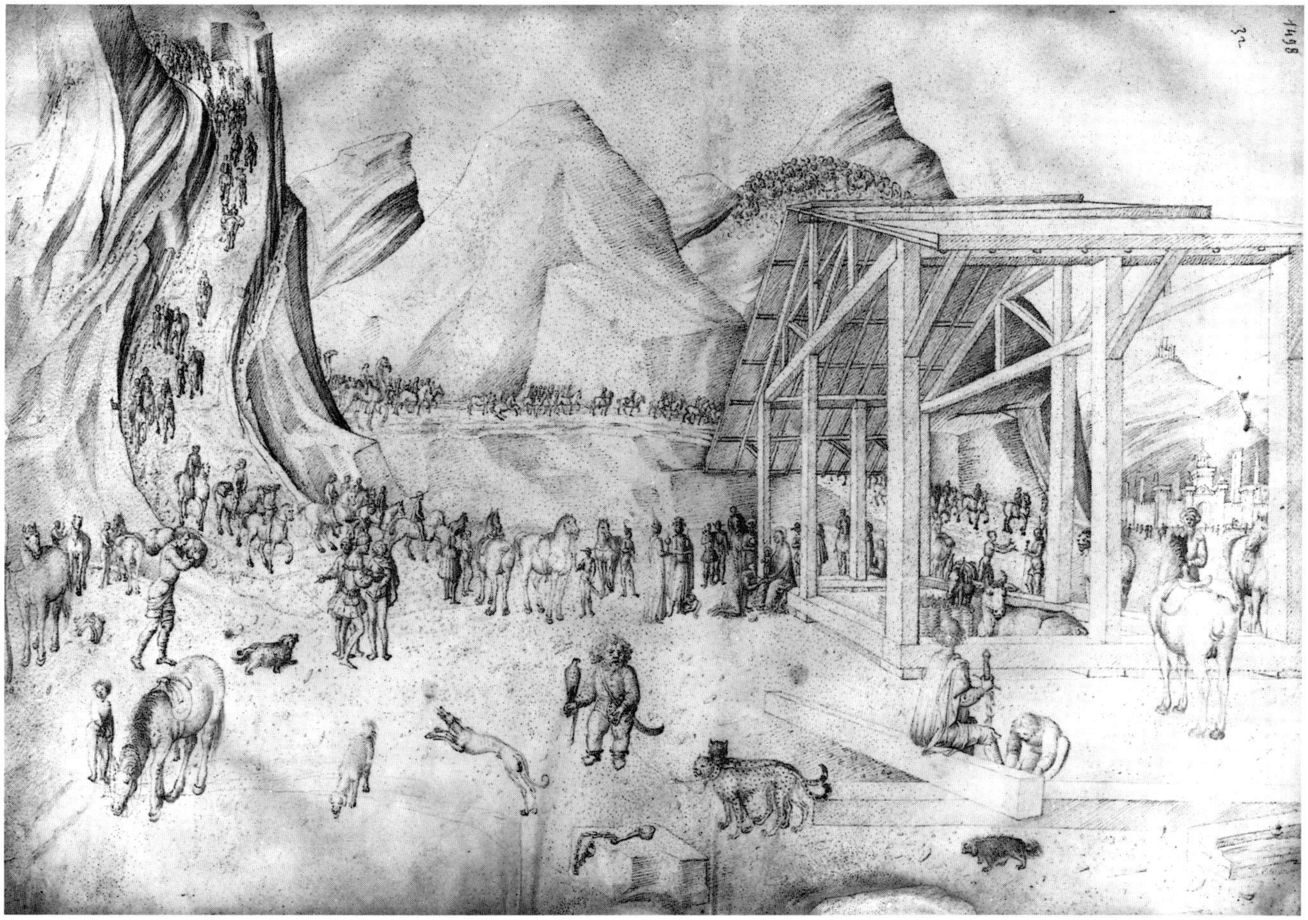

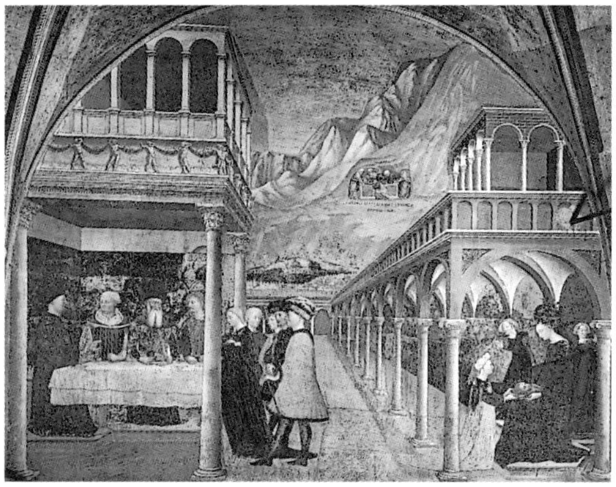

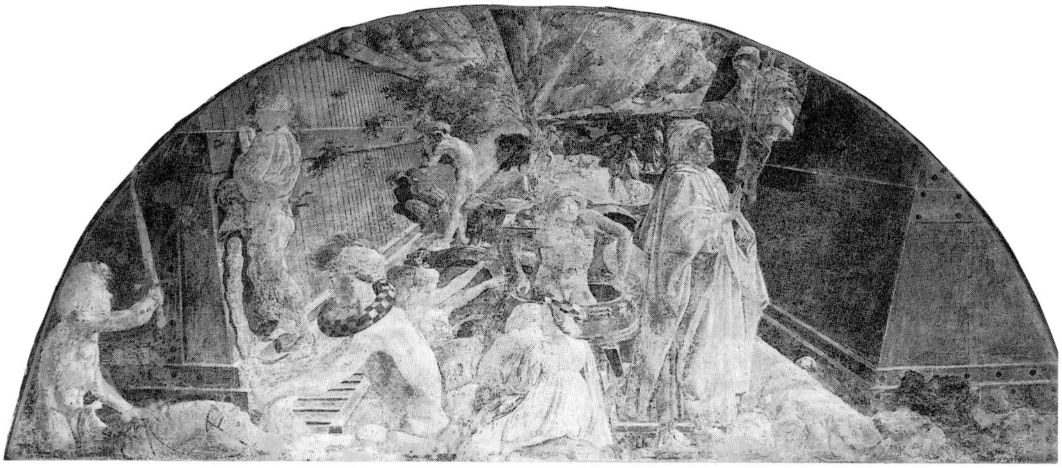

64 (above). Masolino, *Feast of Herod*, fresco (Castiglione d'Olona, Baptistery)

65 (right). Paolo Uccello, *The Flood*, fresco (Florence, S. M. Novella, Chiostro Verde)

63. Antonio Vivarini, *Adoration of the Magi* (Berlin-Dahlem, Staatliche Museen)

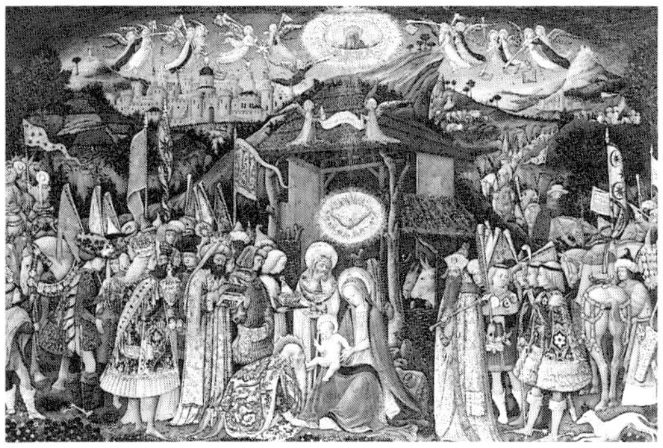

steepness, the second moving along the base of the mountain in the background and providing a certain measure of its distance. Figures and animals – dogs, cheetahs, and even a dwarf with a falcon on his arm – are scattered across the front plane, all contributing to the plenitude of the scene. Jacopo's strategy here might well be called the 'fullness of ongoing life'. But in his attempt to encompass the whole of the visible world, he came perilously close to losing its cohesiveness. The critical balance was one which continued to challenge him in his other drawings.[28]

That the courtly – rather than the naturalistic – aspects of the International Gothic style retained their attractions for Venetian patrons is indicated by Antonio Vivarini's *Adoration* in Berlin (c. 1440–45) [Plate 63].[29] Although we cannot deny that Jacopo's mural paintings would have retained some of the preciousness and refinement of their stylistic antecedents, it is apparent that his conception of a pictorial ambient was fundamentally different.

Jacopo's contributions in landscape compositions were taken up later by his son Giovanni, but Gentile Bellini and the other eyewitness painters found their most powerful models in his treatments of the built urban environment. In the *Feast of Herod* and the *Judgment of Solomon* [Plates 49 and 50], Jacopo rejected the easier solution of the shallow urban view often used by his predecessors, and opted for the deepest spatial recession within an expansive format. The illusion of depth was not achieved through overlapping planes, as was customary with Gentile da Fabriano and Pisanello, but through the linkage of primary structural elements into a single visual pyramid that tied foreground to background. The human protagonists in such scenes, although no longer packed into a dense layer of space and now free to move, were themselves secured within the cohesive linear network.

Jacopo's initial introduction to linear perspective may well have come in the 1420s when he was in Florence, but his understanding of it would have been enriched by continuing contacts with Tuscan artists who came through the Veneto. Analogous attempts at exploiting exaggerated perspective recessions can be seen in the frescoes of Masolino at Castiglione d'Olona (completed 1435) and Uccello in the *Flood* (c. 1450) [Plates 64 and 65]. Direct contacts between Jacopo Bellini and the other two painters are not recorded, but both were documented in Venice during the period preceding their fresco commissions.[30] However, a comparison between their compositions and those of Jacopo reveals

XII (facing). Gentile Bellini, detail from the *Procession in the Piazza San Marco*, (Color Plate XVIII)

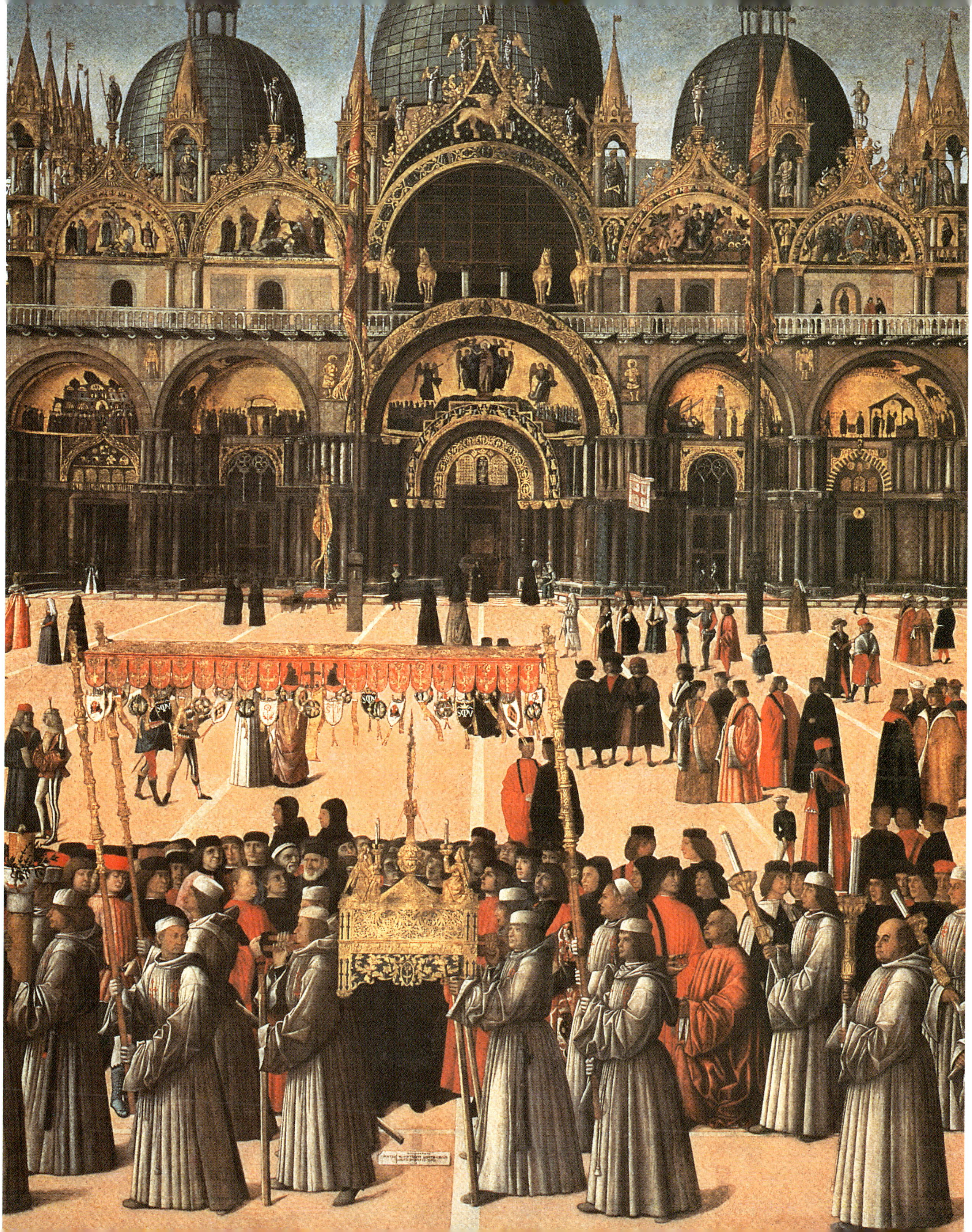

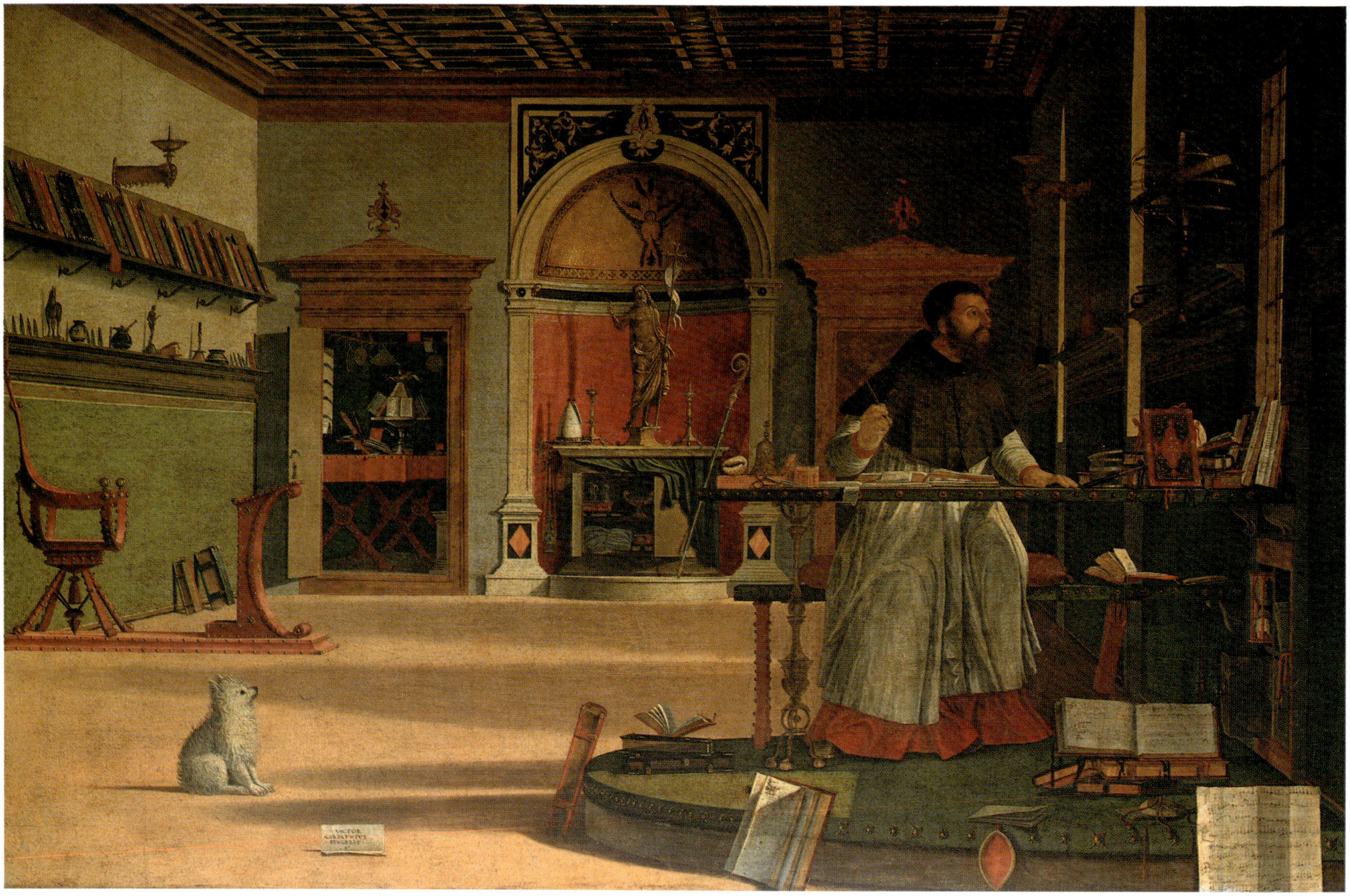

XIII. Carpaccio, *St. Augustine in his Study* (Venice, Scuola di San Giorgio degli Schiavoni)

XIV. Carpaccio, detail from *St. Augustine in his Study* (Color Plate XIII)

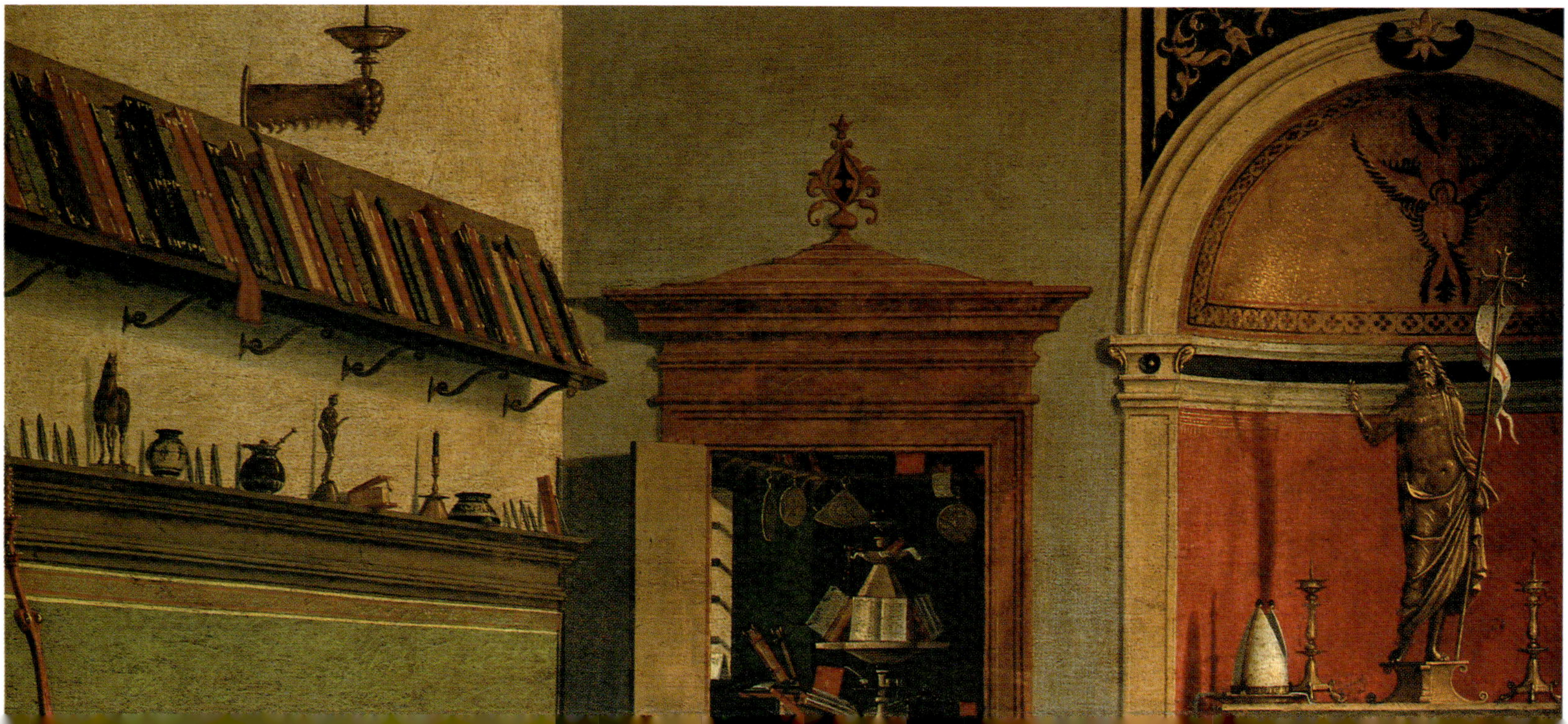

immediately a different emphasis. The Venetian artist captured the *gratuità* of a Venetian chronicle by embedding his protagonists deep within a panoramic world of incident and complexity. The Florentines, by contrast, placed their human actors in the front plane, thus assuring them monumentality and primacy within the scene as a whole.

The perspective effects were also achieved and functioned quite differently in each case. Jacopo and Masolino developed them through an empirical approach, while Uccello's method was rigorously geometrical and reflected a long acquaintance with Alberti's treatise on painting.[31] For Uccello, the deep recession was a means for conveying drama and expressive force; for Masolino it worked as a patterning device to distinguish two narrative episodes within a single scene; for Jacopo Bellini it brought together a whole universe of things – persons, animals, architectural fancies – into a certain relationship within the pictorial field. In all these examples, the artists employed perspective construction with all the passion of recent converts. The resulting recession is so assertive as to draw attention away from the narrative action at hand.

Jacopo drew the *Feast of Herod* again in the 1460s [Plate 66]. The spatial recession is now controlled through contraction of the pictorial field, but a panoramic expansiveness is not entirely sacrificed. The asymmetry remains, and the narrative focus is no less diluted, but the actors are more visually accessible, because closer, and the viewer's attention is more concentrated on the event through less competition from distractions.

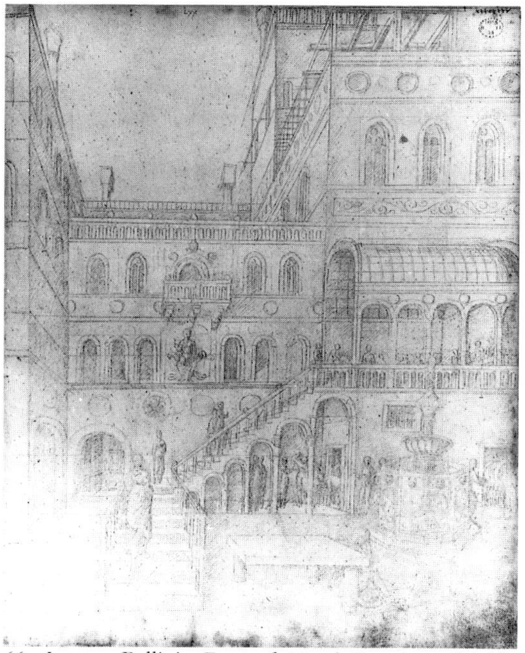

66. Jacopo Bellini, *Feast of Herod* (London, British Museum Album, fol. 75)

67 (left). Jacopo Bellini, *Dormition of the Virgin* (Paris, Louvre Album, fol. 27)

68. Jacopo Bellini, *Dormition of the Virgin* (London, British Museum Album, fol. 79)

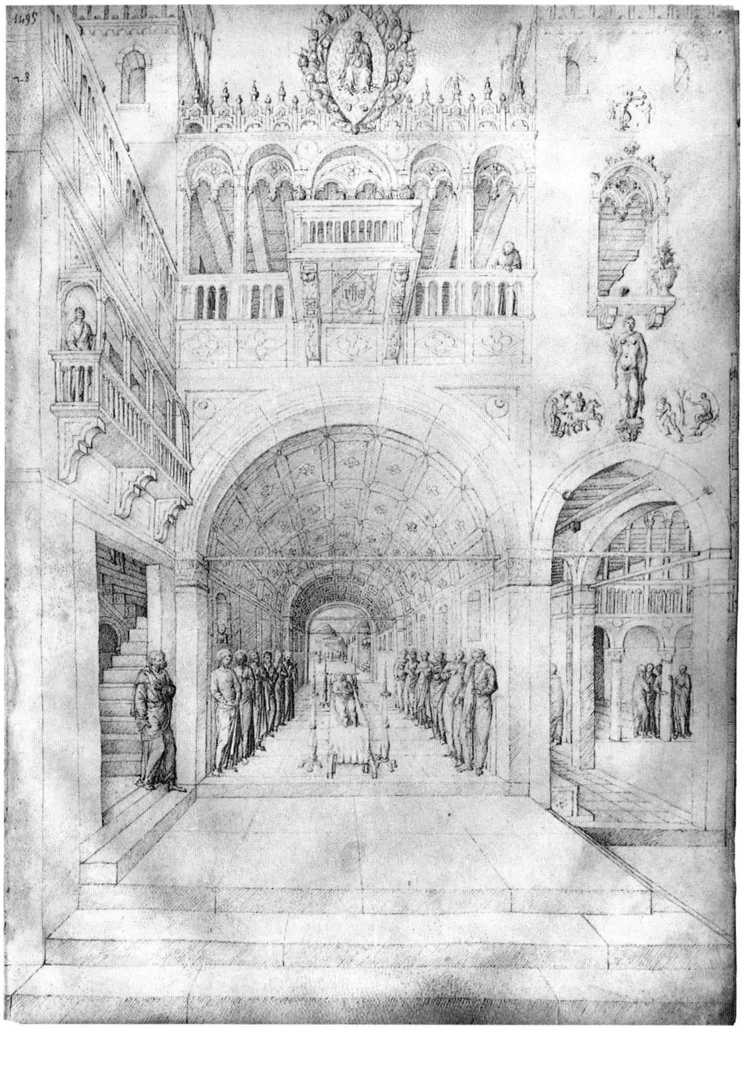

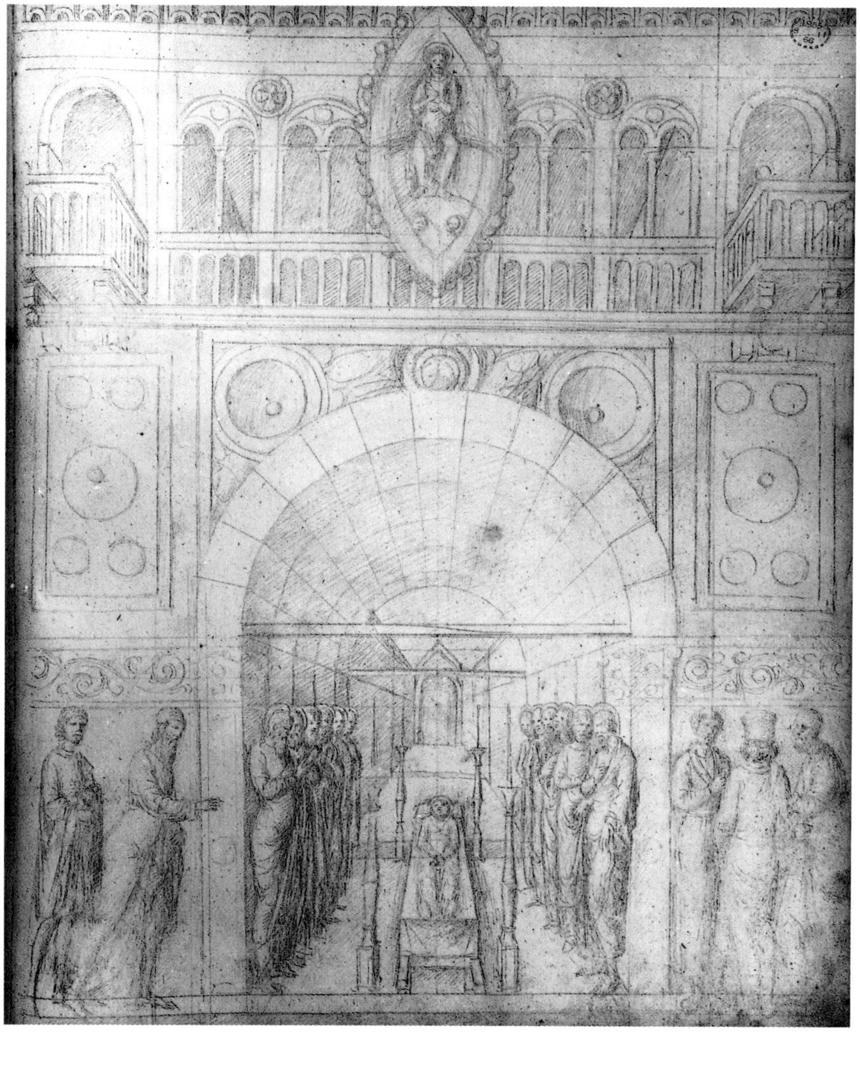

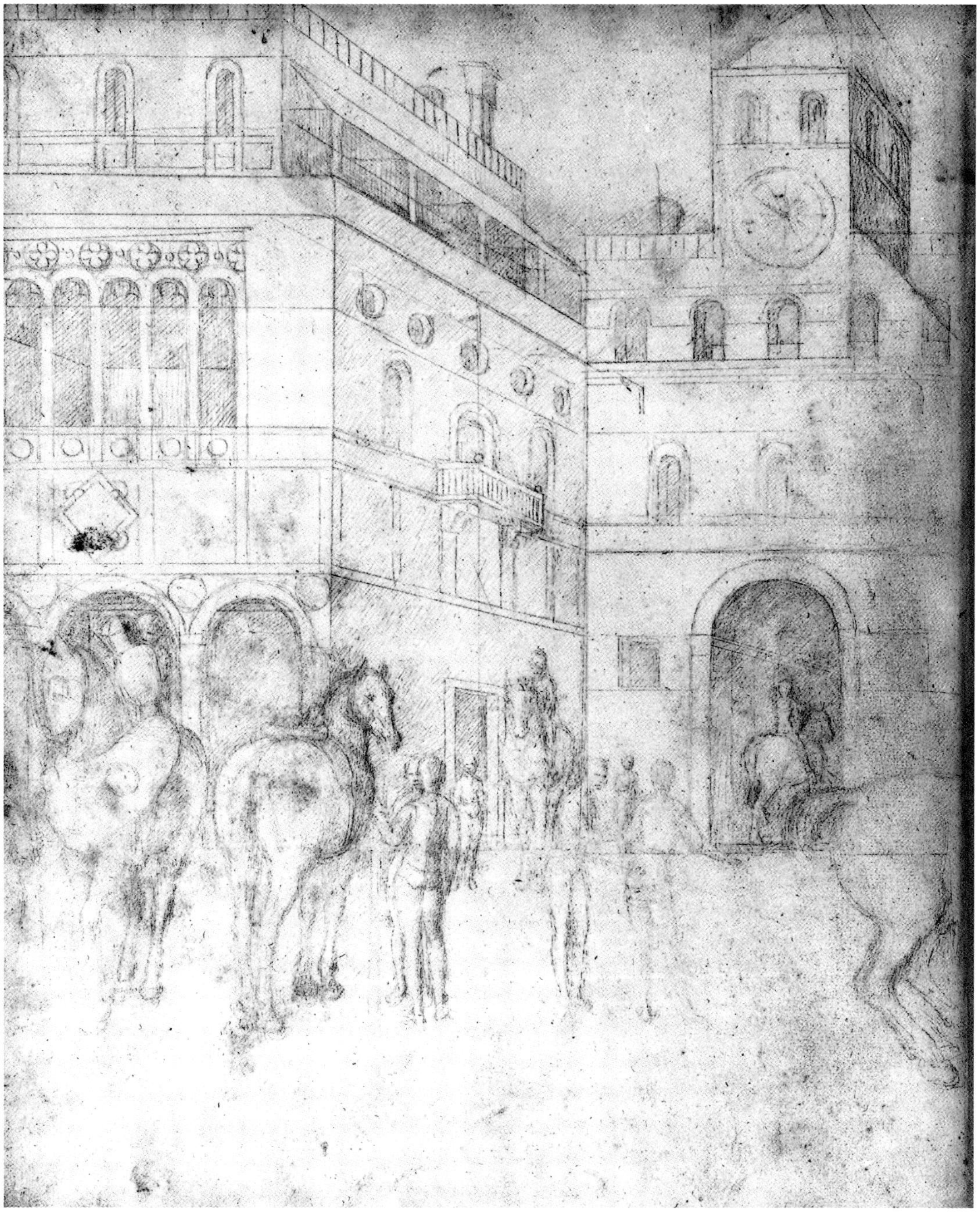

69a–b. Jacopo Bellini, *Tournament Scene* (London, British Museum Album, fols. 54v–55r)

A similar development can be seen in two renditions of the *Dormition of the Virgin*. The Louvre drawing [Plate 67], dated by Degenhart and Schmitt to the 1440s, encompasses a complicated aggregation of architectural structures: a stepped platform in the foreground; a central arch in the middle ground which forms a tunnel leading into deep space; a staircase and balcony on the left; an open portico on the right; a loggia above. The artist has attempted to distribute figures throughout the spatial continuum, but none are in the front plane. In the second version in the British Museum album [Plate 68], which probably dates to the 1460s, the field is reduced to the archway and its surrounding structure, reminiscent of the corresponding scene in mosaic on the vault of the Mascoli

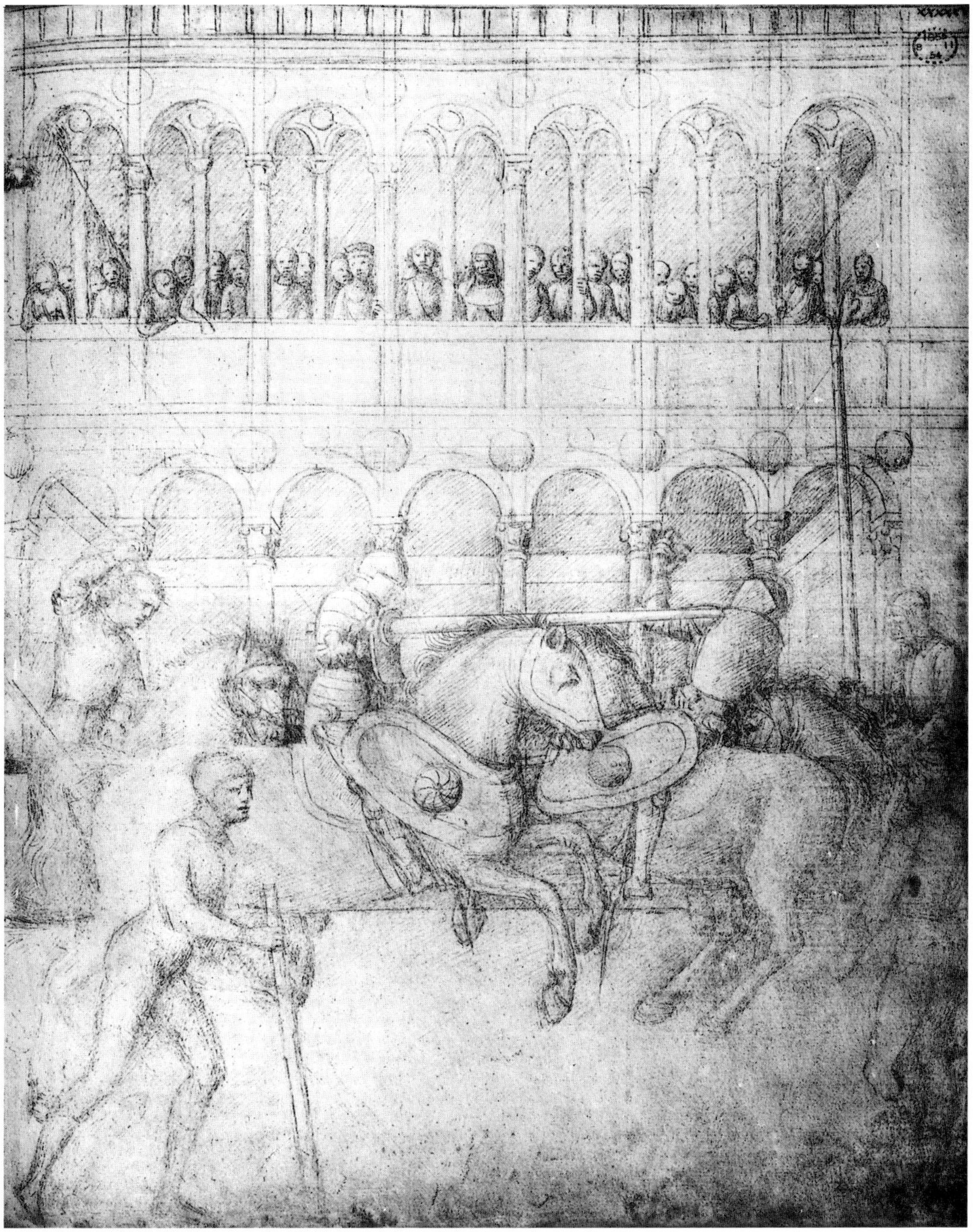

Chapel. The architecture is more austere, with a dependence upon geometric shapes. The recession is controlled by an altarpiece at the end of the archway, and the figures are grouped, for the most part, in the front plane.

The tendency toward anchoring figures in the foreground zone, with a consequent diminution of deep spatial effect is characteristic of Jacopo's later drawings in general. The double-paged *Tournament Scene*, with its frieze-like effect and observers in the windows above [Plate 69], is another variant of the processional format that was to re-appear, albeit with different subject matter, in the canvases of the *scuole*. There is a new spatial density in the drawings of the 1460s that was picked up by the eyewitness painters. It is not the tapestry-like

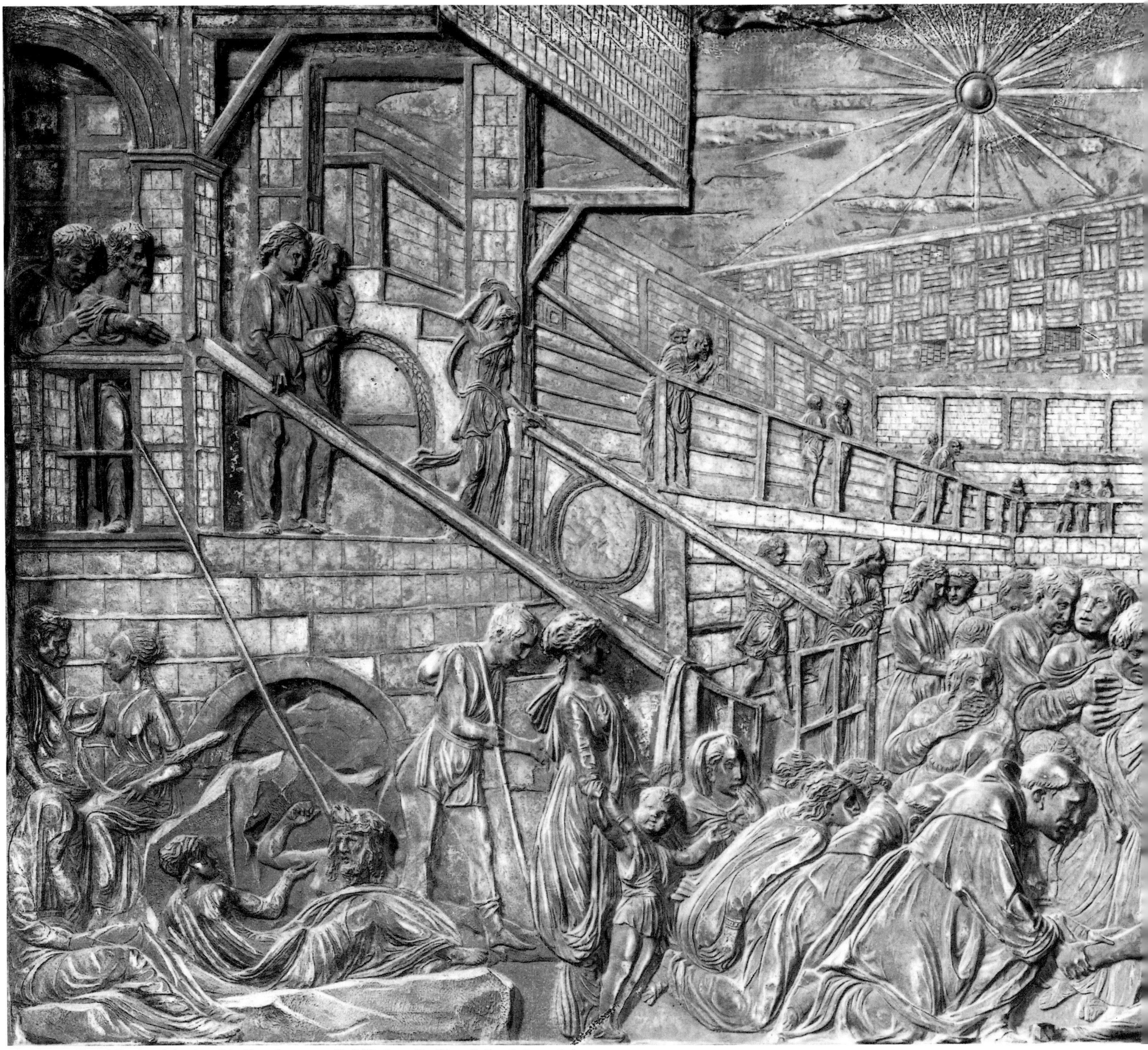

70. Donatello, *Miracle of the Irascible Son*, bronze relief (Padua, Basilica di Sant' Antonio)

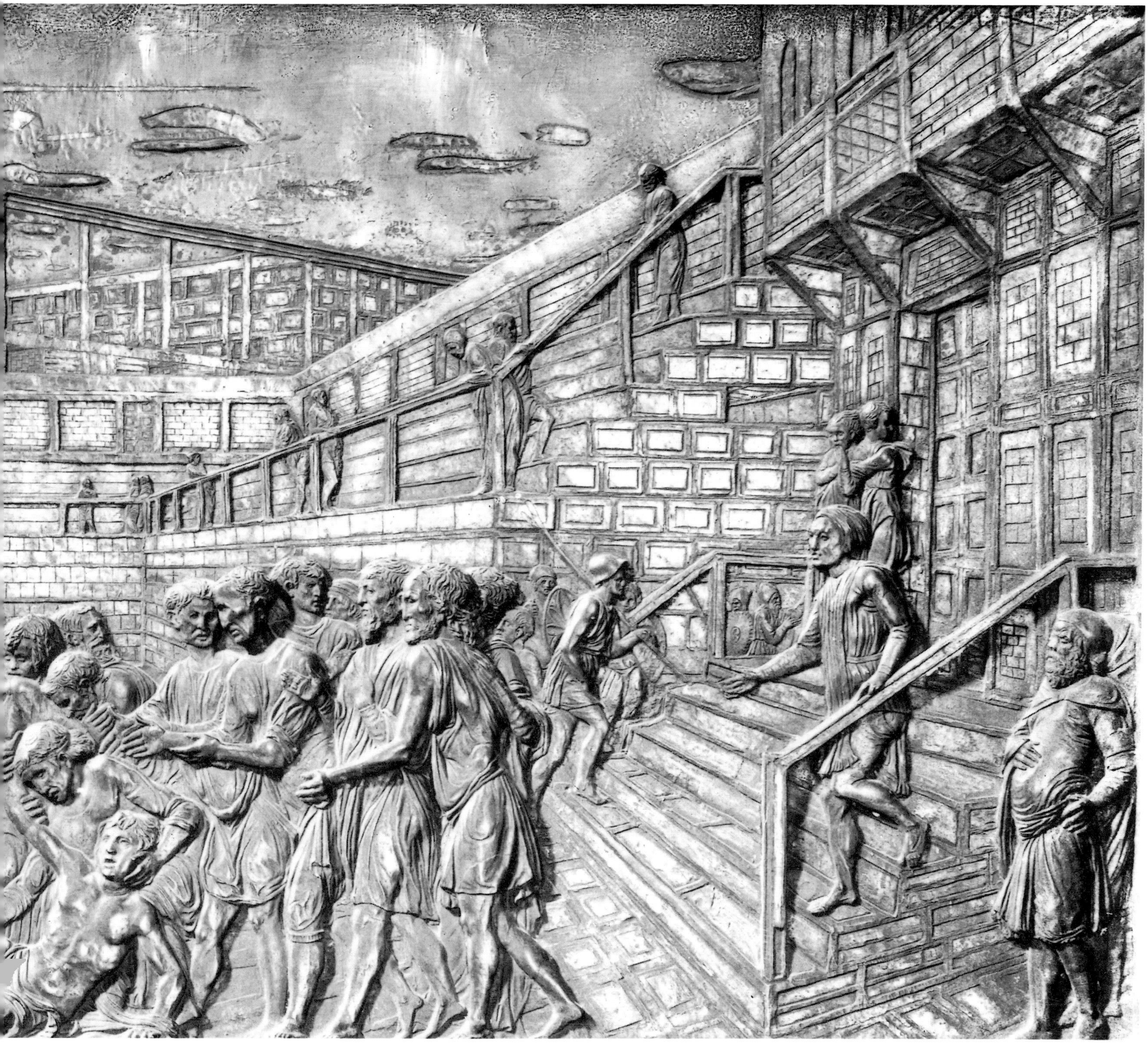

density of Gentile da Fabriano, but a cohesiveness that allows for the volume of space to be caught and held within a kaleidoscopic range of luminous colors and surfaces.

Jacopo did not lack for local models to stimulate his own powers of invention. Donatello's four large bronze reliefs for the high altar of the Basilica del Santo in Padua (modelled in 1447) also featured *istorie* with elaborate and detailed architectural settings, populated with many figures.[32] But the build-up of a climactic movement in each of the scenes reveals a deep difference in intentions from those of Jacopo Bellini. Only in the *Miracle of the Irascible Son* did Donatello risk a dispersion of focus with a wide perspective view and figures distributed into the depth of the pictorial field [Plate 70]. But even there he placed the narrative event prominently in the center of the front plane, where the viewer's attention was held by the vigorous gestures and movements of many of the figures.

By the early 1440s, Jacopo's ingenuity in perspective construction had been sufficiently celebrated to merit the dedication of a treatise on the subject (now lost) by the Paduan inventor, Giovanni da Fontana.[33] But for all his demonstrated proficiency in such things, Jacopo may have been less attuned to Albertian precepts than appears at first glance. While he could have had personal contact with Leon Battista Alberti on one or more occasions,[34] his relationship to the new scientific rules for perspective was demonstrably more visual than theoretical. As others have observed, he sometimes employed Alberti's prescriptions for linear perspective construction, but he did not apply them consistently.[35]

Although Alberti has to be reckoned with in any consideration of the *istoria* in the fifteenth century, his direct influence on artistic practice should not be overemphasized. With some notable exceptions, like Uccello and his *Flood*, by the 1450s only Piero della Francesca and Mantegna had begun to take seriously the Albertian model of composition in its entirety, particularly in its injunctions against excessive *copia* and in favor of decorum.[36] It was not drawn into the mainstream of central Italian art until around 1500, most notably through the works of Leonardo and Raphael. Before that time, only Alberti's Book One – the concept of the picture as a window and the construction of linear perspective – made a significant impact on the compositional habits of central Italian artists.

Jacopo Bellini rarely adopted the window concept in his own work, and his obsessive experimentation with perspective solutions seems to have been stimulated far more by the work of other artists than by any theory expounded in a book. It is only in the later drawings of the British Museum album that he evolves toward a more Albertian simplicity, and one must recognize here the exemplary role of his son-in-law, Andrea Mantegna.

A NEW MONUMENTALITY

Mantegna's frescoes of the life of St. James, painted in Padua in the 1450s and mostly destroyed in the Second World War, reveal concerns similar to those of Jacopo, but offer different solutions. Whereas Jacopo had populated his architectural fantasies with numerous figures, Mantegna constructed the setting – solid and massive, but no less imaginary – around a limited number of protagonists, each of whom took on relatively greater importance. Further-

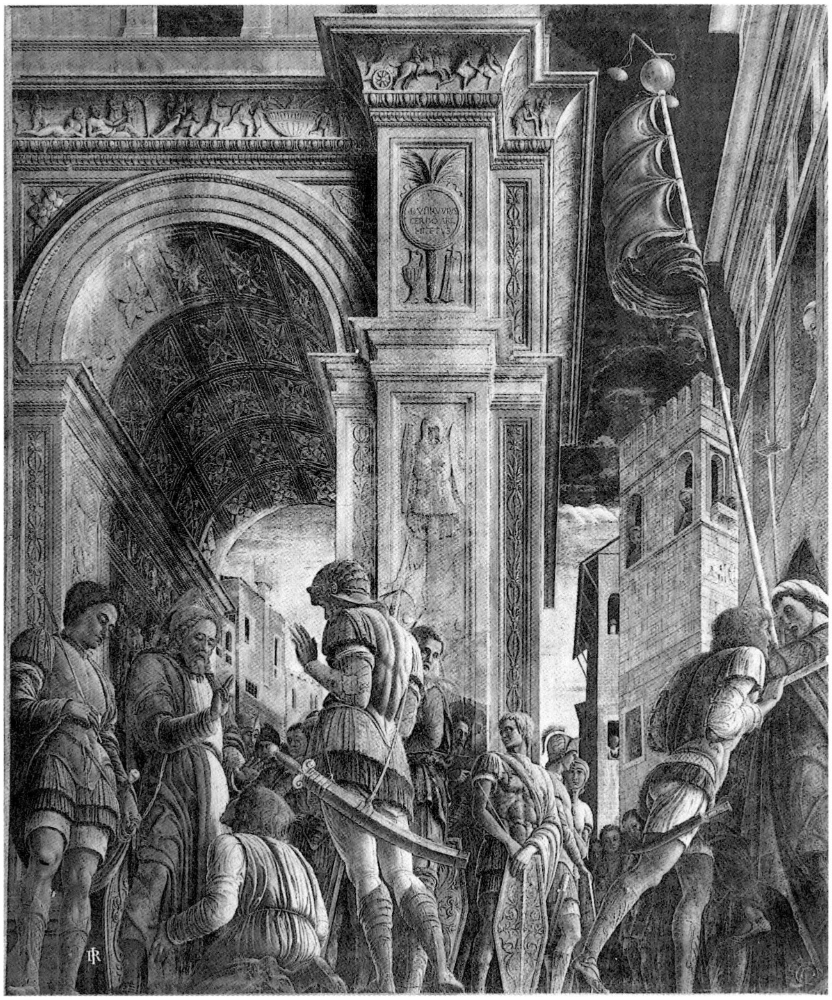

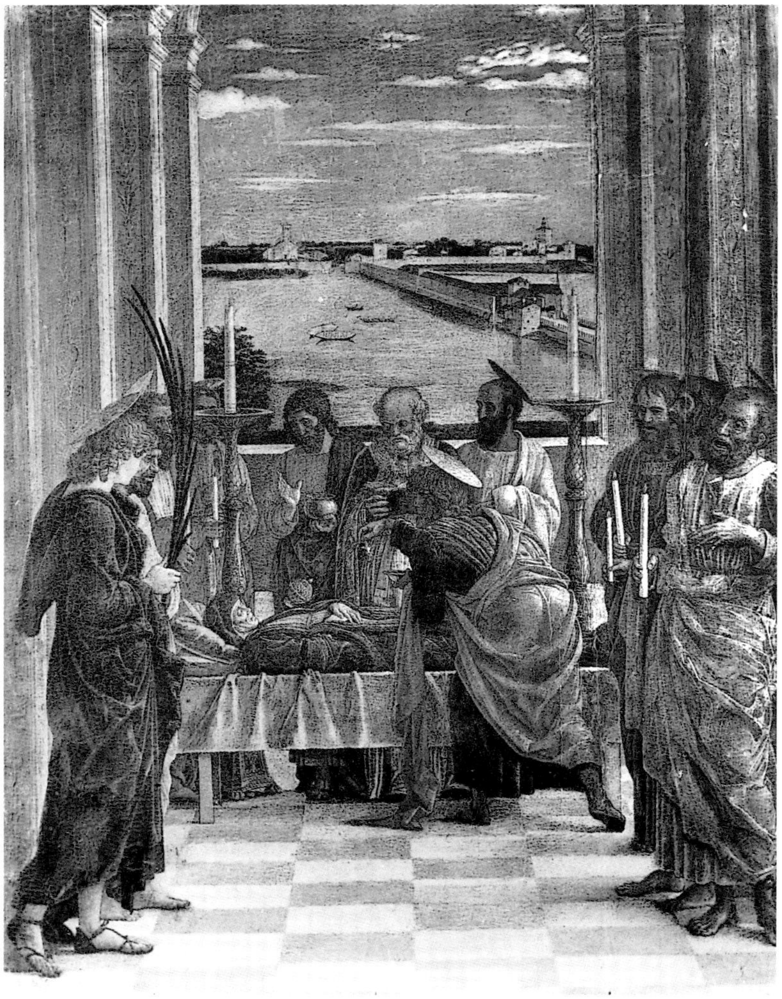

71 (left). Mantegna, *St. James Led to his Execution*, fresco (Padua, Eremitani, now destroyed)

72. Mantegna, *Dormition of the Virgin* (Madrid, Prado)

more, his genuine mastery of linear perspective was coupled with a sensitivity to its limits. He avoided drawing uncontrollable diagonals that extended improbably into deep space, and carefully limited the depth of the pictorial field.

In *St. James Led to his Execution* [Plate 71], the weighty classical architecture remains subordinate to the human figures which always constitute the dramatic focus of his compositions.[37] With a horizon line below the bottom edge of the painting, a worms-eye viewpoint heightened that drama and directly engaged the viewer who looked up at the fresco from the floor level below. Mantegna eschewed the soft, delicate modelling typical of late Gothic Venetian painting in general, in favour of a stonier, lapidary treatment of form. No less committed to a north Italian taste for detail and description, Mantegna made his own accommodation between it and Tuscan rationalism and order.

In the *Dormition of the Virgin* (c. 1461), Mantegna offered another way to achieve a unified and spatially deep pictorial field [Plate 72]. The surviving panel in the Prado is only a fragment. Now about two-thirds the height of the original painting, it originally culminated in a high barrel vault with Christ in a mandorla in the center.[38] Mantegna's figures are typically monumental and prominently placed, but here an expansive landscape – the lake that surrounds Mantua – is included in the background. By means of the window and the high horizon line, the artist was able to retard the spatial recession and hold the eye in the front plane, but also to include a view into deep space.

The northern element

The use of the window to bind interior and exterior views had been pioneered in the north by Jan Van Eyck.[39] Its adoption by Mantegna brings us to the role that Flemish art played in the eyewitness style. It has often been observed that Venetian artists throughout the Quattrocento were indebted to northern models for the development of portraiture, for the oil painting technique, for luminous effects of color, and for a pathetic quality in their religious paintings.[40] Flemish paintings were said to be in Padua as early as the 1430s, prompting Millard Meiss to call the city 'a sort of Eyckian outpost'.[41]

Meiss made a further observation which has particular relevance for the issue at hand. He noted Mantegna's borrowing of an iconographical element from Jan Van Eyck in his *Crucifixion* predella in the Louvre (1454–9). Some of the soldiers, now finished with the event, have turned their backs and are simply walking away from the scene. As Meiss put it,

> The death of Christ on the cross, far from darkening the sun and the moon, scarcely affects the tenor of life of a multitude of visible people. Never before was the event immersed so deeply in the flow of time.[42]

The motif was picked up by other artists in north Italy, but it rarely appeared in Florence. Mantegna used the element simply as a genre motif – it was surely one that appealed to viewers already accustomed to the dispersion of narrative focus in many International Gothic paintings – but he did not allow it to undercut the drama of the event. By contrast, for Jacopo Bellini and for the painters of the True Cross cycle of Mantegna's own generation, a concept of ongoing life 'immersed so deeply in the flow of time', analogous to that of Van Eyck, would become the informing motive of the composition as a whole.

An ekphrastic taste

There is another factor which may have reinforced in Jacopo Bellini a pre-existing tendency toward copiousness and descriptive richness: humanist esteem. Even though the Ciceronian orthodoxy of the Latin version of his treatise on painting had been aimed precisely at a learned audience, art criticism of the middle third of the century accorded the highest praise to artists like Pisanello and Gentile da Fabriano, whose *copia* and spatial inconsistencies seem to have fallen rather short of Alberti's ideals.[43]

As early as 1427, Pisanello had drawn the attention of no less eloquent a writer than Guarino of Verona: 'What understanding of light and shade! What diversity! What symmetry of things! What harmony of parts!'[44] Such enthusiasm had little to do with Venetian notions of an *istoria* as a historical document. It probably stemmed more from Pisanello's dazzling descriptive technique and the appositeness of his narrative mode to the literary requirements of *ekphrasis*, an antique rhetorical form recently imported from Byzantium by the Greek humanist Manuel Chyrsoloras and popularized by Guarino.[45] In the *ekphrasis*, the writer describes a work of art to an absent viewer and demonstrates his descriptive skills by enumerating an assortment of visually engaging objects within it. The *ekphrasis* was, as Michael Baxandall explains, 'a tendentious form; it depends for its existence on pictorial variety, it cannot operate without a fair number and diversity of items to list.'[46] The internal harmony of these individual objects was desirable, but their strict narrative relevance was of little consequence.[47]

By 1441, Jacopo's relationship with Pisanello had changed from slightly younger observer, and perhaps imitator, to outright competitor. It was probably in the summer of that year that his portrait of Lionello d'Este, the new Marquis of Ferrara, was chosen over Pisanello's entry in a contest recorded in a sonnet by the poet Ulisse de' Aleotti.[48] Some years later, Angelo Decembrio referred again to the event in his *De politia litteraria*. Set in Ferrara in the 1440s, it was conceived as a monologue addressed by Lionello d'Este to Guarino. While Alberti had written as an artist, Decembrio spoke for the courtly patron. Speaking through Lionello, he praised the artists of antiquity who cooperated in perfecting each other's work, and observed how times had changed:

> whereas nowadays, as we know, they are consumed by rivalry with one another. You remember how Pisanello and Bellini, the finest painters of our time, recently differed in various ways in the portrayal of my face. The one added a more emphatic spareness to its handsomeness, while the other represented it as paler, though no more slender; and scarcely were they reconciled by my entreaties.[49]

One may infer from Lionello's remarks that competition in and of itself encouraged stylistic variations to the end that the mimetic aims of art were at risk. For how could such disparate portrayals both be true representations?

Also revealing is his criticism of weavers and designers from north of the Alps, who 'are far more concerned with the opulence of colour and the frivolous charm of the tapestry than they are with the science of painting'.[50] Since Pisanello's paintings are particularly notable for their color and charm, we may take it that their attraction for Lionello must have lain in their science. But what did he consider as science? Part of the problem with the tapestries had lain in their depiction of fabulous historical events which Lionello called 'popular absurdities, pandering to the extravagance of princes and the stupidity of the crowd'. But even more serious were their deficiencies of draftsmanship when it came to the new criteria for empirical realism:

> Certainly it would have been more elegant to have represented these subjects, however legendary they may be, accurately, even if only with one single quick line from a pencil or brush.[51]

In this judgment a courtly humanist taste conjoined for a moment with Venetian notions of the *istoria*: a true event, convincingly rendered.

The world of Jacopo Bellini, however, was not really the world of a princely court. Despite his success in Ferrara, Jacopo's own notions of science were formed within a different context of patronage: that of a collectivity of citizens – patricians and commoners alike. Their interests would have moved him toward a vision of reality different from the refined and ornamental one perfected by Gentile da Fabriano and Pisanello. And yet, we cannot conclude that his labors represent a rejection of the international style, which probably retained for him and other Venetians many things appealing to eyes accustomed to the shimmering golden surfaces of the Basilica of San Marco: jewel-like color and descriptive richness, elegant line and pattern, the preciousness of gilding, and a special quality of light. It may also have retained a resonance similar to that of their own concern for credibility and truth. But neither do Jacopo's experiments represent an inability to break free of the style. They constitute, rather, a series of attempts to incorporate new techniques of composition and spatial representation within the old tradition.

It was partly a question of different narrative interests. While Jacopo still included landscape settings in his drawing-books, as well as some of the courtly and chivalric subjects that were central to Ferrarese tastes, the actual Venetian environment was resolutely civic. The proper depiction of an urban space, such as Florentine artists were painting in family chapels throughout their city, also required from Venetians in attentiveness to the new norms of 'correct' spatial construction. Although Jacopo's architecture may have been fantastically grandiose and far from the actual experience of the citizen, it was still grounded in the totally man-made environment of Venice.

And for Jacopo Bellini, as opposed to the Florentines, linear perspective was not a means of focusing attention on a narrative situation within a geometrically consistent environment so much as it was a way to rationalize a whole world of disparate activity. Plotting the random observations of the chronicler with the efficiency of a scientist on a graphic model of urban space, he virtually invented the *veduta* – the painted view – grounding the inhabitants of a city within an embracing and apparently circumstantial urban panorama. In his drawings of the urban scene we are brought close to the milieu of Gentile Bellini, Mansueti and Carpaccio. They also bring us back to the issue with which we began this discussion: just what distinguishes the artists of the north from the Venetian painters of the *istoria*?

73. Jan Van Eyck, detail (about 2 × actual size) from *Madonna and Child with Saints* (New York, Frick Collection)

74 (right). Carpaccio, detail (about one-half actual size) from the *Lion of St. Mark* (Color Plate 1)

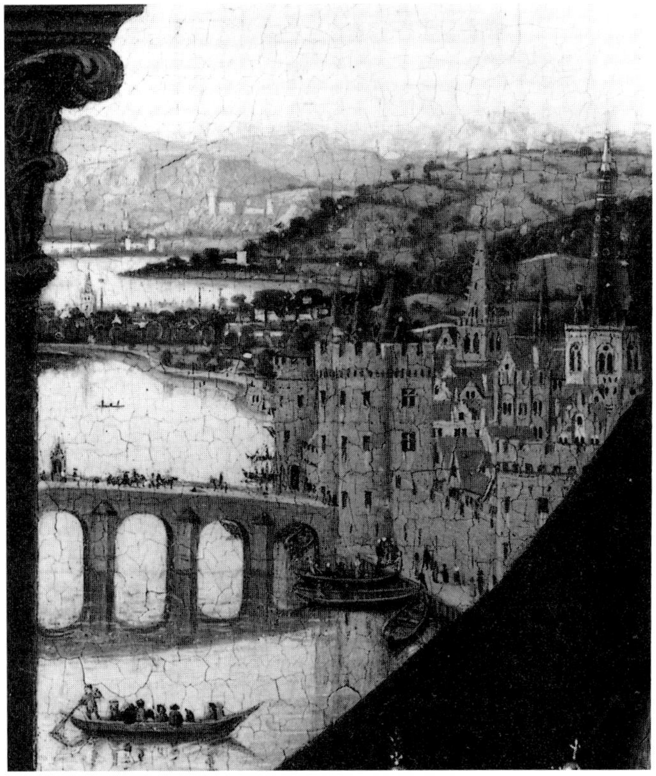

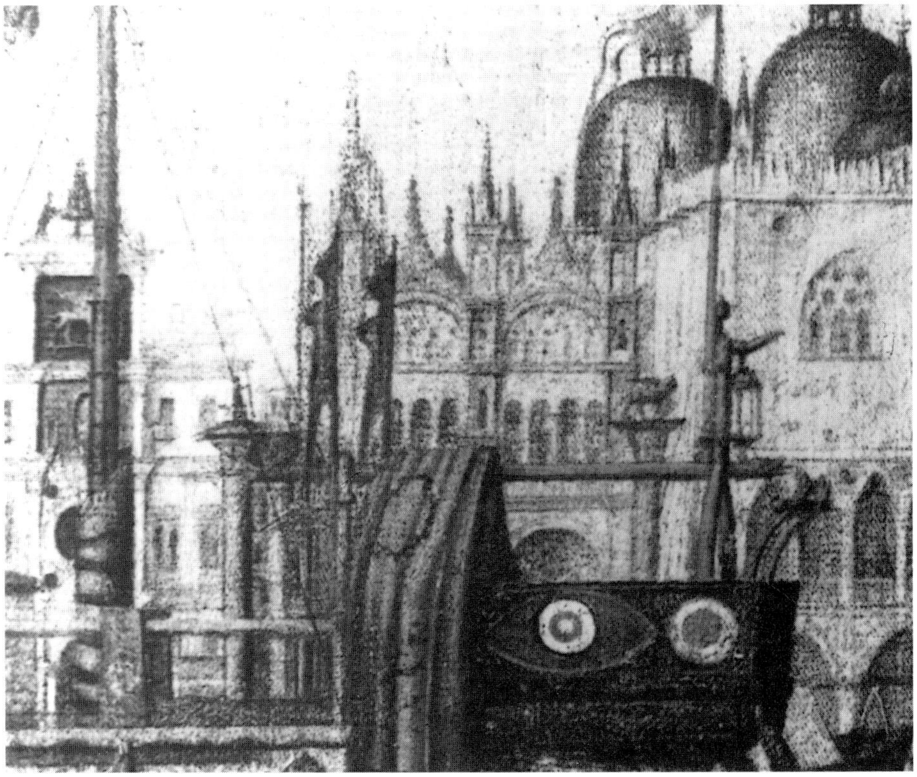

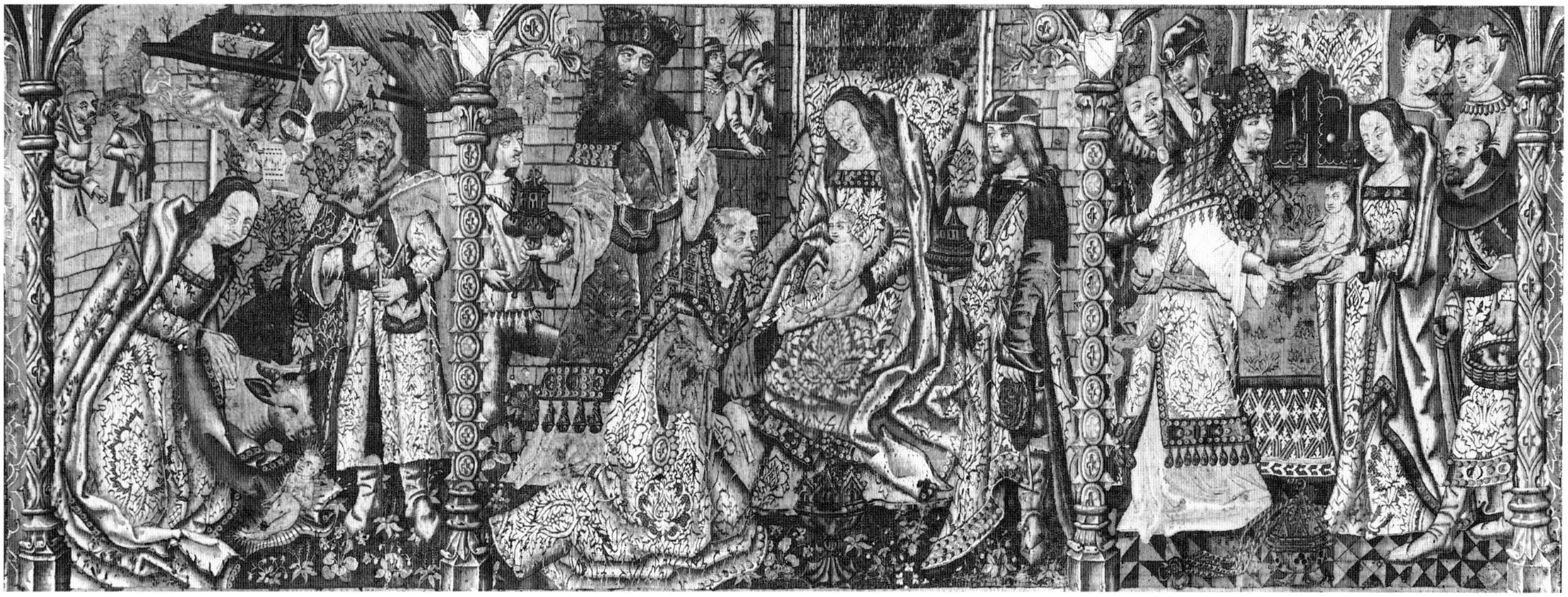

75. Flemish School, *Infancy of Christ*, tapestry (Venice, Galleria Giorgio Franchetti [Ca'd'Oro])

* * *

Our first impression of a painting by Carpaccio may be one of Flemish microscopic detail and infinite space. But upon further examination, we see the hugeness of space subjected to a rigorous geometric order, and we are offered only the illusion of precise delineation. A comparison of details from paintings of Carpaccio and Jan Van Eyck should make clear the difference [Plates 73 and 74]. With Van Eyck, the closer one looks, the more one sees; with Carpaccio, as one moves closer, the image dissolves into canvas and blotches of paint. Panofsky once defined 'the great secret of Eyckian painting: [as] the simultaneous realization, and, in a sense, reconciliation, of the 'two infinites', the infinitesimally small and the infinitely large. It is this secret that intrigued the Italians, and that always eluded them'.[52]

But it is also a question of origins, intentions and functions. The central medium for Italian narrative art was the monumental fresco. Carpaccio's paintings are rooted in a mural tradition, by way of Jacopo Bellini, and not in the art of the miniaturist like the altarpieces of the Netherlandish painters. *Istorie* that were woven into tapestries in the north were put directly on the walls in the south in the form of mosaics and frescoes. Tapestries made no real pretense to three-dimensional illusionism and the extension of physical space, as we plainly see in a fifteenth-century tapestry now in the Ca d'Oro [Plate 75]. But Italian walls were increasingly being 'painted away' as windows to an alternate painted reality. Jacopo Bellini's drawings represented large-scale solutions for large surfaces. Here the task of Carpaccio and the other eyewitness painters, building upon Jacopo's experiments and responding to new initiatives from central Italy, was to create the idea of comprehensiveness and the impression (but not the actuality) of perfect fidelity to surface detail within a large pictorial field. As we shall see, their aim was to satisfy the perceptual habits and tastes of a citizen's world that was itself one of dedicated eyewitnesses.

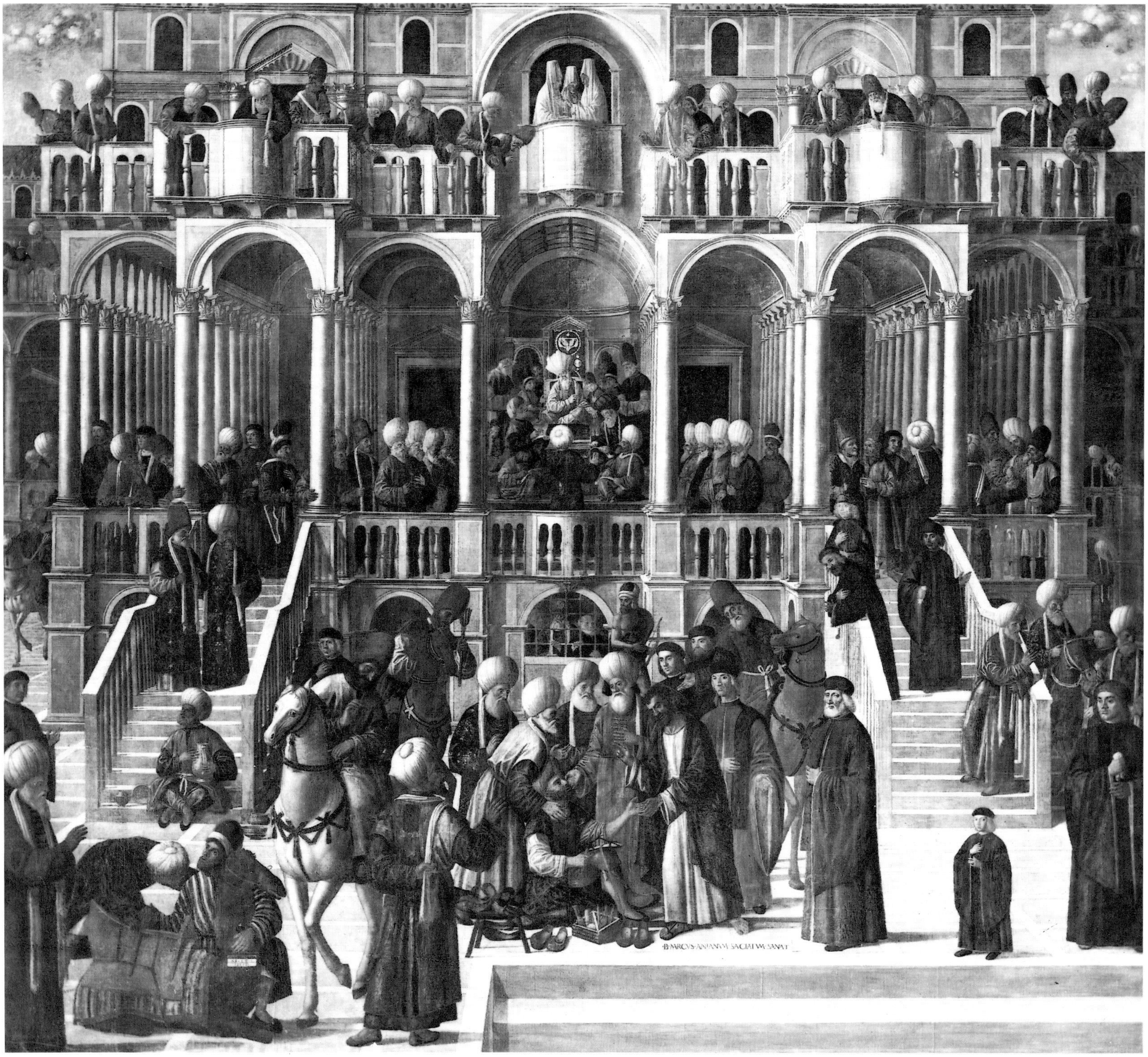

76. Mansueti, *St. Mark Healing Anianas* (Venice, Ospedale Civile)

8

The Eyewitness

Venetian artists remained particularly resistant to Alberti's counsel on decorum and the restraint of *copia* in the *istoria*. As Carlo Ridolfi later complained of Mansueti's *St. Mark Healing Anianas* [Plate 76], painted for the Scuola Grande di San Marco:

> . . . [the painter] would introduce too much tedium in recounting minutely the friezes and the many carvings, with which the columns and the cornices of that palace [in the painting] are adorned; so that it seems that Mansueti would have no other intention than to make one see how much he would be accurate and diligent in similar labors.[1]

Ridolfi was referring to the often cluttered quality of Venetian *istorie*. It is what Francesco Valcanover has termed the 'inventory style'.[2] Indeed, in the case of the painting in question we see that Mansueti's diligence was not confined to architectural details. Although he had learned the virtues of a centralized narrative focus, he did not hesitate to distract the eye through the generous addition of descriptive detail and whole congeries of bystanders. Only a few of these are portrait figures of his Venetian patrons. The vast majority are turbanned Mamluks, inhabitants of a fanciful Alexandrian setting, but accurately arranged according to oriental protocol for court audiences, even down to the scribes who record the pronouncements of the Sultan. The elaborate architecture itself functions as a display case for the supporting cast of characters. Mansueti, moreover, even included a row of balustrades and balconies across the upper zone of the canvas, specially constructed so that he could add another whole tier of figures.

Yet, as we have seen, the implicit charge of the Venetian painter of an *istoria* was to create a painting that looked as truthful as possible, according to prevailing standards of evidence and proof. One aspect of this goal favored works that conveyed a sense of the fortuitous, with the artist appearing to have just happened upon the scene – by accident, as it were. Furthermore, we may assume that even if this quality was achieved (or attempted) with a hand as heavy as Mansueti's, every element that the artist included in the composition was put there for a purpose: to confer upon a particular version of an event a look of documentary authority. So if we balk at the 'trivial detail' or irrelevancy in one of these works we may be missing the point.

In order to understand the taste for an inventorial quality in painting, we will turn now to a vernacular mode of writing that was an ongoing complement to the chronicle in Venice: the eyewitness account of the *viaggiatore* – the Venetian who travelled abroad for business or diplomacy. Instead of great deeds of the past, the *viaggiatori* recorded the minutiae of the present in cultures far removed from the *terra sancta* of Venice. These accounts, as well as the official *relazioni* of the ambassador, exhibited a certain candour, immediacy and all-inclusiveness.[3] Through them we may learn how a travelling Venetian described a seen ambient that was unfamiliar to those at home, and discover just what visual data he felt were important to include for accuracy and reliability.

The patrician *confratello* of the Scuola di San Marco, Josafat Barbaro, combined in his person both merchant and diplomat. Admittedly his experiences may not have been typical of the average Venetian of his day, but his accounts of journeys to Tana and Persia provide a vivid portrait of the East as seen by a man of the West who was well aware of his own culture. The sixteenth-century translation retains the exotic flavor of the original:

> . . . seeing that I have spent all my yowthe and a great parte of myne age in ferre cuntries, amongst barbarouse people and men without civilitie, much different in all things from our customes, wheare I have proved and seene many things that, because they be not vsed in our parties, shulde seem fables to them (as who wolde saie) were never out of Venice.[4]

Barbaro was aware of the fantastic quality of his narrative – 'Nowe shall you hear wonders and things almost incredyble' – and took pains to affirm: 'I that have seen it do not only believe, but also knowe it.'[5] Simplicity and directness were equated with reliability; Ambrogio Contarini, who succeeded Barbaro as ambassador to Persia, concluded his own account by assuring his reader:

> I might possibly have written in a more elegant style, but I preferred stating the truth in the way I have done to adorning falsehood in fine and elegant language.[6]

Such a claim to artlessness appealed to deeply-held Venetian sentiments about reliability. It created in the readers just the same impression that the Venetian chronicler, and the Venetian painters that concern us here, sought to achieve through the appearance of happenstance and inventorial completeness.

This taste was manifest not only in the reports of the great *viaggiatori*, in a literary tradition that goes back to Marco Polo, but also in the day-to-day communication of government functionaries. The *relazioni*, or reports of Venetian representatives at foreign courts, became known throughout Europe for their completeness of description. As we read an extended passage written by the Venetian secretary Giovanni Dario from Persia in 1485, we seem to enter the exotic world of the eyewitness painters [Color Plate XXXII and Plate 77]. Here Dario described the solemn arrival of an ambassador sent by the Ottoman Sultan Bayezid II to the court of the Lord of Persia. Sitting next to the Hungarian ambassador, he carefully observed the diplomatic ritual of gift-giving:

> And then for a good length of time, the presents of the Sultan began to come; and first of all there was a large animal like a lion with varied stripes, black from the head to the tail, who was a terrible thing to see; then came six very beautiful horses, the first with a saddle and bridle of gold and with a harness of worked *lamé*, and then the other steeds unequipped. Behind [them] there came three racing camels, with three saddles and cushions of silk cloth, and covered in their [Ottoman] manner. And behind these came small presents: three most beautiful parrots with cages, and four black eunuch boys, and two decorated

swords and four undecorated swords; two very beautiful maces of iron, two axes with the tips decorated, helmets [and] shields of iron. And behind these were many saddles, belts, Indian cloth [and] clothes of silk that in truth at two pieces per man were more than eighty by count of who carried them.

Behind the presents came the ambassador with a cap on his head and a green damask gown and sleeves embroidered with gold, and his entire back down to the ground was covered with sable. And immediately when he presented himself in that circle, the courtiers came out of the pavilion with their entourage and went to meet him there; after the greeting, they took him under the pavilion, and with Dawud Pasha below, and the others seated in the middle, and talking for a good time, they were called by the lord; and the three pashas went with the ambassadors and that great man of learning of his who came from Constantinople. And the Lord having entered, they stayed less than a quarter of an hour and went outside, and then returned to sit under

77. Mansueti, detail from *Episodes in the Life of St. Mark* (Plate 123)

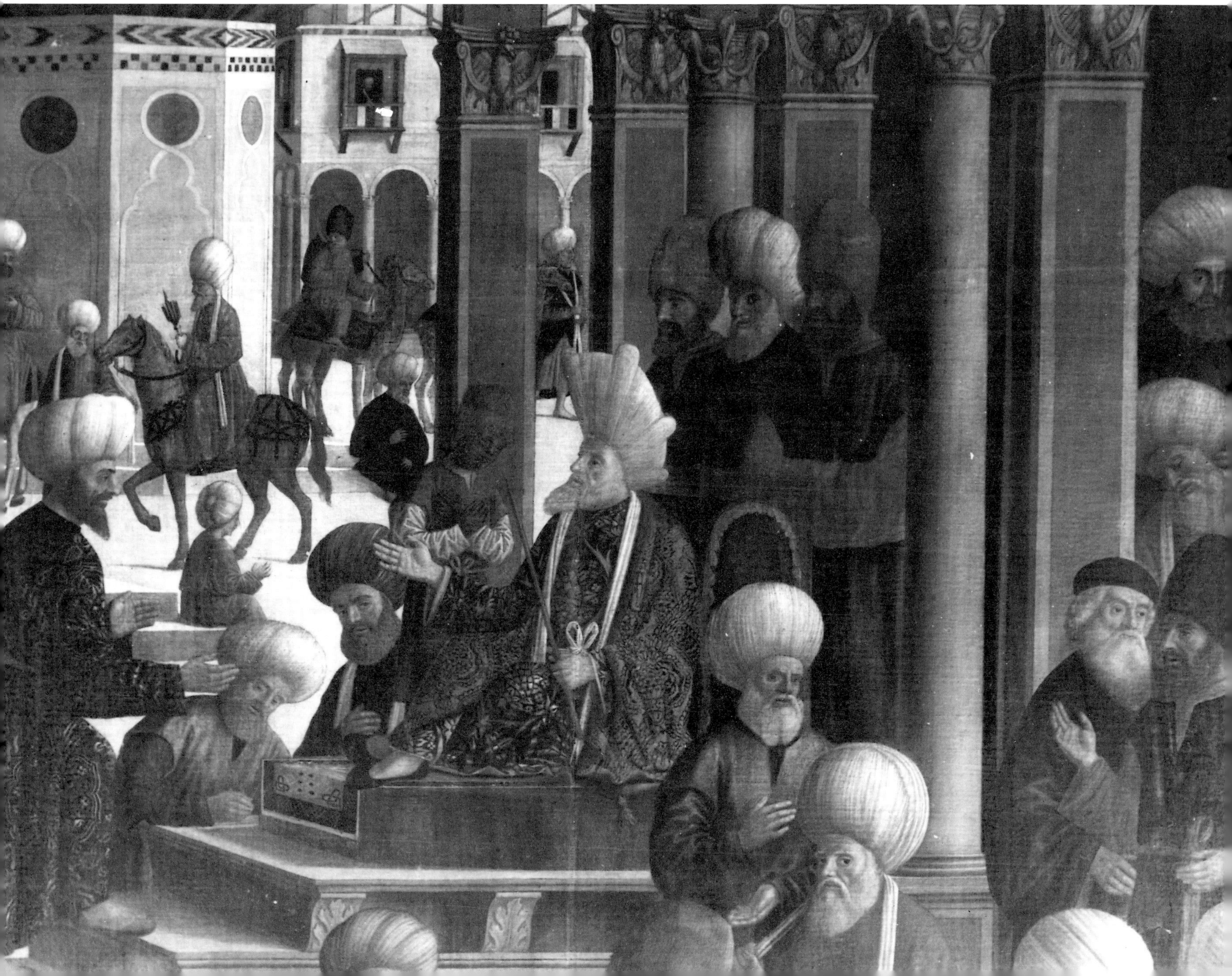

the pavilion, and they carried outside a great roll of writings, which they had cut open, and the man of learning read them, and it was a very long reading.[7]

In his *relazione*, Dario attempted to paint a picture in words, with the quality of a careful drawing. It is the cumulative weight of his observations rather than his description of any single thing which is significant. His mobile eye constantly measured and assessed: the sizes, shapes and material of objects; the number, condition and relative placement of men; the color and quality of clothing; the expressions and gestures of the principal actors. It is important to remember that such an account is not a *unicum*. We need only leaf through a few pages anywhere in the *Diarii* of Sanudo to see similar mentalities at work – concrete, reportorial, particularizing – and not only from the hand of the diarist himself, but also from those contemporaries whose words he recorded.

Three tendencies can be discerned in all such accounts that seem to be of direct relevance to the inventory style of the painted *istoria*. First, while one gets little sense of the topography of a city, there is a tendency to use Venetian monuments as a measure for specific buildings. Describing the route from Aleppo to Tauris in the second decade of the sixteenth century, a Venetian merchant passed through the town of Orfa [the ancient Edessa] and instinctively compared the dimensions of unfamiliar monuments to those in Venice. He observed 'a magnificent castle with walls of immense size and thickness. . . and in it there are two fine lofty columns, equal in size to those of Venice, in the Piazza of St. Mark. . .'[8] In the city of Caramit [Kara Amid] he compared the size of the churches to those of SS. Giovanni e Paolo and the Frari in Venice. Of particular interest was the church of St. Mary, 'built up with vaults above vaults', and 'having columns upon columns, like the palace of St. Mark [Ducal Palace] at Venice'.[9] His use of the city of Venice as a standard of measurement would have been, perhaps, only a natural habit, but such frequent reports tended to reinforce a mentality that constantly gauged the oriental world by a Venetian yardstick, thereby subtly annexing that world to the lagoon city.

Secondly, as Dario's letter demonstrates, the informants were very concerned with the color and quality of materials and adornment. To quote from the report of an attache to the Venetian ambassador to Cairo in 1512, which describes the palace of the Sultan:

> The floor was composed of a mosaic of porphyry, of serpentine, of marble and other precious stones. This mosaic was nearly entirely covered by a carpet. The ceiling and rafters were carved and gilded; the window grills were of bronze instead of iron.[10]

The commitment to historicity in the painted *istoria* would have required specific visual elements – costume as well as topographical features – to be rendered in detail to provide the particularity of place and moment.

A third factor common to eyewitness accounts of foreign places was their quantitative perspective. The *viaggiatori*, as well as state envoys like Dario, enumerated the particulars of exotic lands with the care and conscientiousness of census-takers or tax-assessors. Shipwrecked off the coast of Norway in 1431, Pietro Querini had been given shelter in a nearby village. He carefully noted in his diary that the inhabitants numbered 120, of whom 72 took communion at Easter.[11] In the 1440s Nicolò dei Conti travelled all the way to Java, where he observed three types of parrots: a red one with a yellow beak, another that was

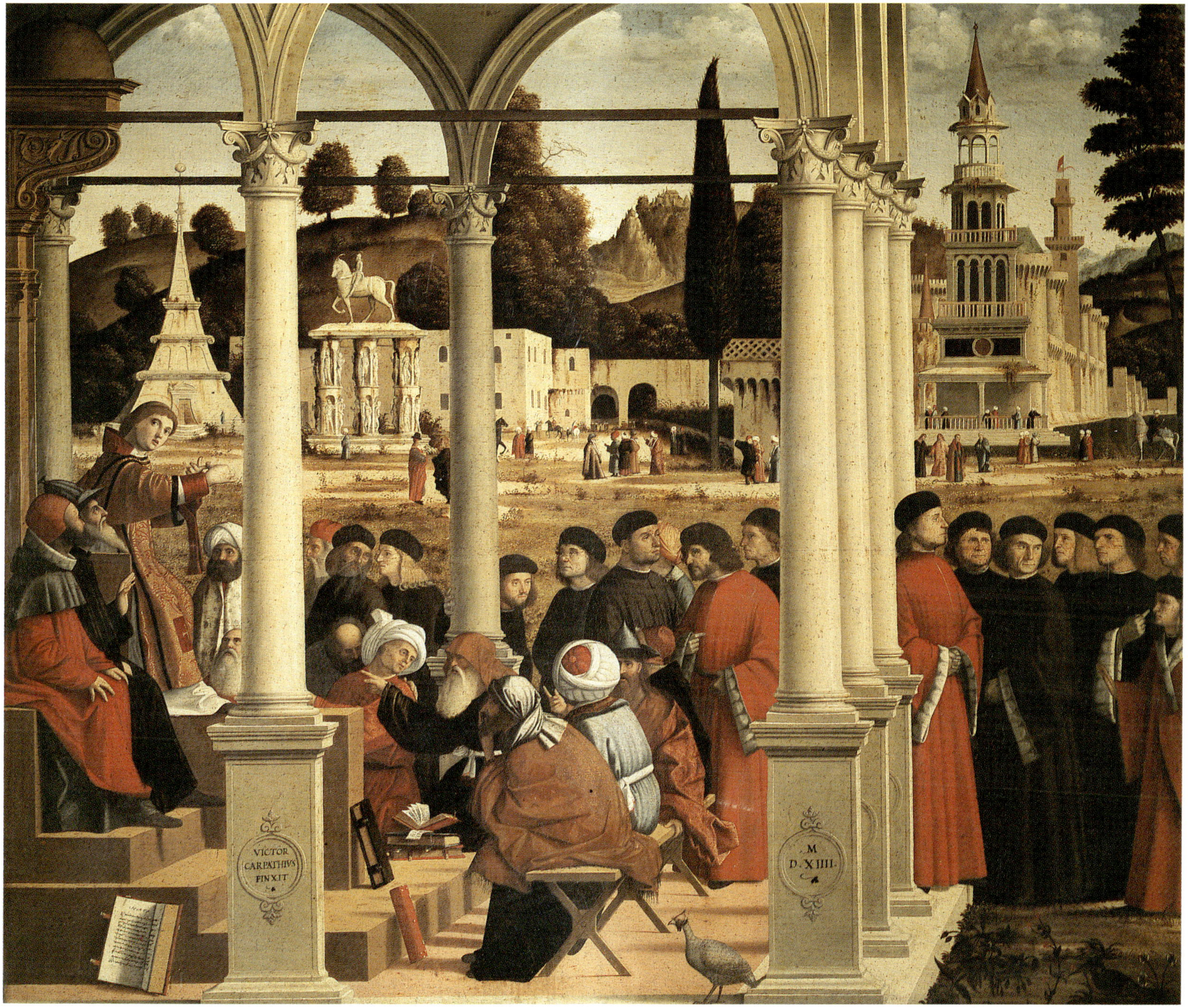

xv. Carpaccio, *Disputation of St. Stephen* (Milan, Brera)

multi-colored, and a third that was white and more highly prized than the others, 'because they learn to speak admirably, and respond to what is asked them'.[12] Giosafat Barbaro described the town of Camara (now Or Kinara) on the Persian coast where he had seen

> a rounde hyll which on thone side seemeth to be cutt and made in a fronte of vj paces high: on the toppe whereof is a plaine, and rounde about xl pillers . . . everyone whereof is xx yardes longe and as thicke as iij men can embrace; but some of them [the pillars] arr decaied.[13]

The penchant for all-inclusiveness also indicates a lack of hierarchical ordering similar to that which we frequently encounter in the paintings. What was important was that each item should be included, for each item was equally necessary.

XVI. Lazzaro Bastiani, *Donation of the Relic* (Venice, Accademia)

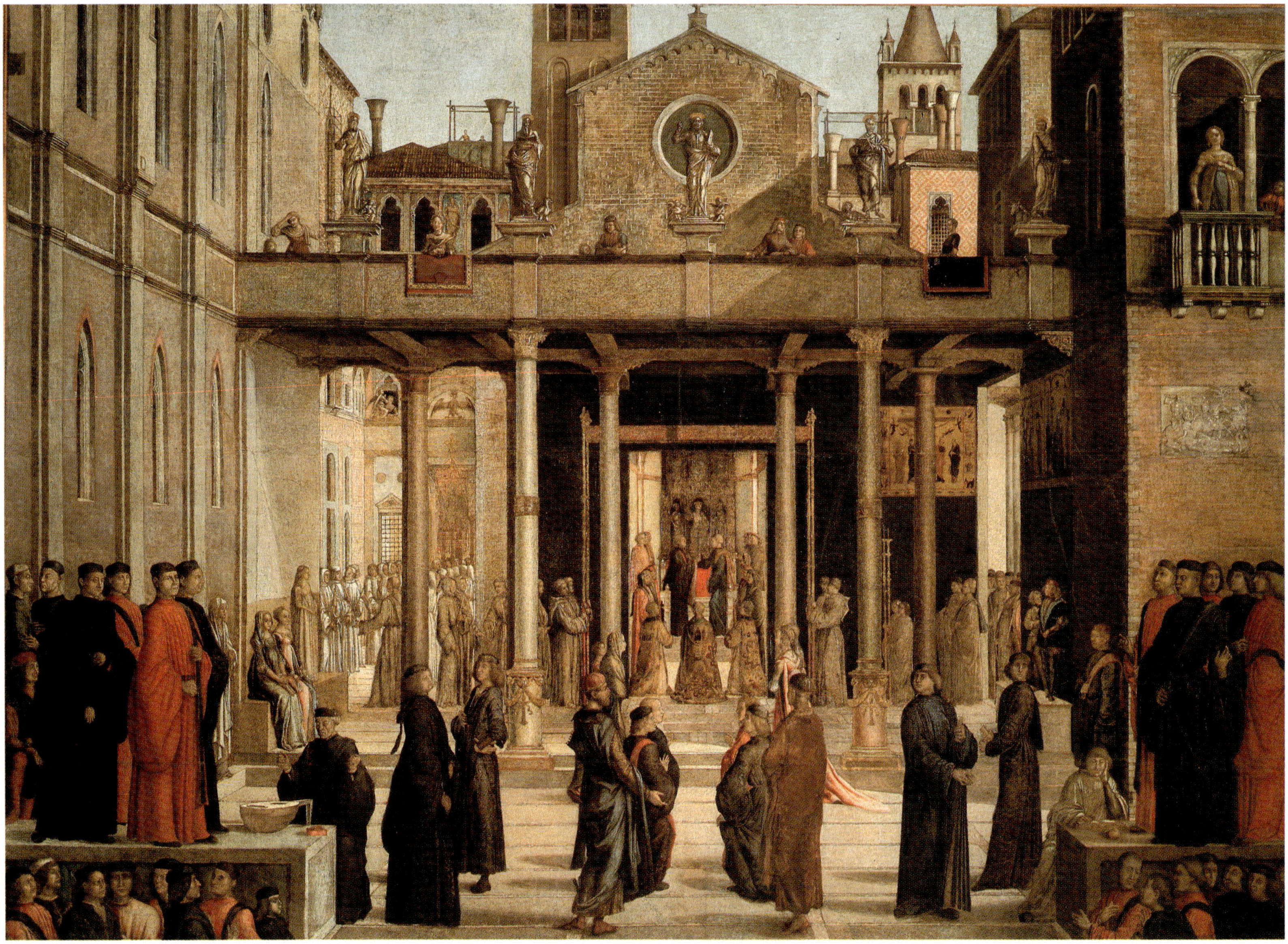

In the Venetian *viaggiatori* – whether merchants or diplomats of high or low rank – we have discriminating viewers. The point to remember is not so much that they influenced the perceptual modes of their untravelled brothers in Venice, as that they reflected a common cultural taste for the particular: for determining the quality and quantity of things, for savoring the odd detail.[14] Perhaps such a bent had emerged from necessity in a mercantile culture that depended upon written communication over long distances, for written reports on merchandise or trading conditions in distant lands could ill afford to be ambiguous, unclear or incomplete.

While such circumstances were not unique to Venice, they would have preponderated in that city. Not only had a good proportion of the male patrician and *cittadino* population experienced foreign travel themselves on an ongoing basis, but those who stayed at home were subjected to weekly descriptive reports as they sat together in the councils of government – the Senate or the Great Council of which every patrician male was, in theory at least, a part. In Venice such documents were not private information. They were the object of immediate public reading, debate, decision-making and further recording. As Gaetano Cozzi once observed:

> Sanudo registered everything, took count of everything, holding that completeness of information would be a presupposition of truth and that truth would be the indispensable element of history. . . For Marin Sanudo, the historic work is a moment of life that should be narrated in all its complexity.[15]

The same can be said for the paintings made by his contemporaries.

* * *

The special look of Venetian Renaissance art has often been linked to its physical environment. In the rich color, the quality of light and the impression of a tangible atmosphere in *istorie* as well as in altarpieces, viewers see mirrored the ever-changing, moisture-charged sea air and the mutable shades of the city itself. And in Venice, the time-hallowed tradition of brilliantly colored mosaic *figurae* that floated on a skin of glittering gold *tesserae* in the city's central monument are seen as formative models of the taste for sumptuous color in painting as well. Such observations are legitimate; but they hold true for a Titian as well as for a Carpaccio and do not explain the fundamental differences in style between two such unmistakeably Venetian artists. Nor do they explain the earnest quality of the eyewitness in the narrative paintings of Gentile Bellini, Carpaccio and the other artists who worked with them in the *scuole*.

For these reasons, the point of departure for the inquiry in these chapters on the visual culture of the period has been provided by Michael Baxandall's work on the relationships between language and perception and on the formation of a 'period eye'. In *Giotto and the Orators*, he reasoned that observation is linguistically enforced with a set of criteria and concepts by which our attention may be focused. That is, the language that we use – Sanudo's *sermon materno* – controls how and what we can perceive, by giving us the words to describe it; it thus controls the expectations imposed on painting by patrons and artists alike. Baxandall was referring primarily to rhetorical practice and humanist Latin as a model for art criticism and for Alberti's notion of *compositio*. Here we have sought to extend his insights to the vernacular tradition, with a consideration of chronicles and the written accounts of *viaggiatori*.

The chronicle was close in aim to the *istoria*, for it too sought to preserve the memory of an historical event. Allowing that text and image are inherently different, we can still discern formal affinities between the two: the seeming absence of design in recording the actions of the protagonists – in which the narrative event is sandwiched inside the context of ongoing life without a 'heroic focus' – and a taste for description and detail.[16] Although it is by now a commonplace that Italian art of the period was textually based, there are indications that the painted *istoria* was linked to the chronicle in a reciprocal relationship, with influence in both directions. Indeed, it is probably just as likely that the chronicler referred to a painting to get his information as the reverse. Hence, while the painter and chronicler alike shared a common mentality based upon common cultural values and a common language, it would be wrong to push too far the debt that any artist owed directly to any chronicle account. They simply, as it were, shared the same table.

In the same way, the eyewitness account is probably more of an indicator of existing perceptual skills that Venetians exercised in recording the world around them, than a specific influence on the artist. It gives us an idea of what artist and viewer both saw and what they wanted others to see. It also provides a kind of index of credibility: the subject matter and description that were considered sufficient in a full account of men and places unseen.

The insistently denotational character of the paintings of Gentile Bellini, Bastiani, Carpaccio and Mansueti is thus a symptom of a whole complex of cultural concerns of which the paintings are no more than a tangible and concrete deposit. But there is more to it than that. It is not only a 'period eye', but a 'period eye' mobilized to create a 'period' version of truth. For it was the commitment to historicity in the painted *istoria* which required specific visual elements – costume as well as topographical features – to provide the particularity of place and moment. We are dealing, in fact, with what Quattrocento Venetians considered to be sufficient indicators of the reality of an event.[17]

The Venetian *istoria* thus developed its particular artistic profile in a precise cultural setting and with precise perceptual habits, tastes and literary models, echoed in a precise artistic tradition. Having attempted to restore some of this setting, let us now proceed to examine some major themes and concerns of these paintings and to consider how the individual artists sought to resolve them.

Part Three

PAINTED HISTORIES

9

The Sacred in the Profane

> Amongst the other worthy relics that one presently finds in Venice, truly the cross of the scuola of misier San Giovanni Evangelista is the most worthy and the most excellent; which most certainly and undoubtedly is believed to be the wood of the cross where our savior hung to save us, and this is proven by many miracles that happened in diverse times which are noted in order here below.[1]

The first page of the *incunabulum* that proclaimed the miracle-working powers of the True Cross of the Scuola Grande di San Giovanni Evangelista stated the relic's credentials without equivocation. The pamphlet lacks printers' marks, but was almost certainly published by the officers of the Scuola. They were well aware that the possession of an efficacious relic – one that was not only genuine, but that also demonstrated an ability to mediate between the human and the divine – was a powerful means by which to enlarge their share of civic honor.[2]

Only through visible signs such as miracles could the authenticity of the relic, with all the honor that attended it, be established. While the *incunabulum* – a *liber miraculorum* – was one way to refresh failing memories about the prodigies attributable to it, the great canvases of Gentile Bellini, Carpaccio and their associates were surely most potent and present reminders of the special favor enjoyed by all Venetians in regard to divine power and the special place of the Scuola within the *sancta città* of Venice.

It has been suggested that a lack of charismatic objects like relics within the religious confraternities of Florence accounted for the inconsequential ritual position of these groups in the city.[3] Such was not the case in Venice, however, where the *scuole* owned many such items of spiritual power and regularly paraded them in public space throughout the year. We may recall that in 1493 the officers of the Scuola di San Giovanni reported a continuous flow of visitors who came to the *albergo* in devotion to the holy relic, and that for this reason it was necessary to expend funds to adorn and 'to perfect' their meeting-place.[4] Without a suitably decorated setting, the relic would have lost a good part of its charisma. As Richard Trexler has observed: 'The value of image or relic depended on the value set upon it by a patron. Patronage determined what was institutionally holy just as surely as it bestowed fame upon an artist.'[5]

The *albergo*, therefore, was really a frame for the miraculous fragment of the True Cross donated to the Scuola back in 1369; and its pictorial decoration was intended not only to authenticate the relic by documenting its past acts of power, but also to increase the devotion of the present visitors. The *istorie* were more than simply representations of the relic and its prodigies; 'relics' in

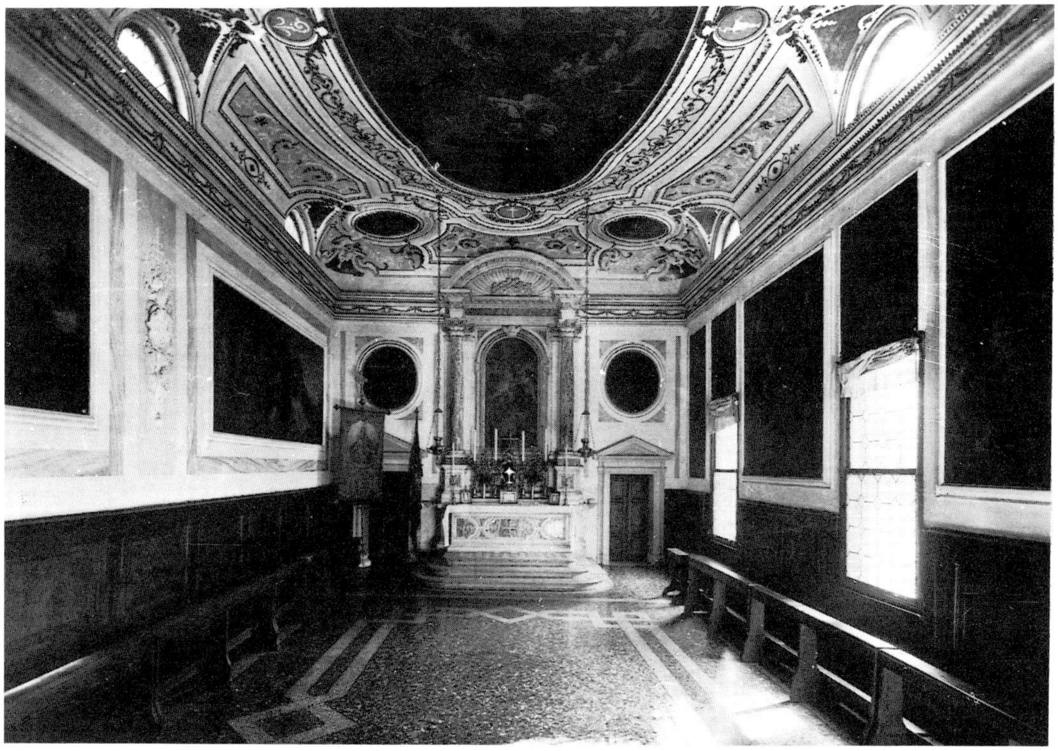

78. Sala della Croce, Scuola Grande di San Giovanni Evangelista, Venice, in its present state

themselves, they bore a silent message of vows made and prayers answered. They offered the means to capture and to amplify the holiness of the relic for the benefit and reputation of the confraternity within the full ritual context of the city.[6]

The sancta città

The Scuola building has survived to this day, and the former *albergo*, now called the Sala della Croce, remains more or less intact in its basic structure [Plate 78]. The ceiling was remodelled into the present coved form, with framing for *quadri riportati*, in the seventeenth century.[7] Judging from the surviving *soffitti* of the Scuola della Carità and the Scuola di San Marco, the original ceiling would have been flat, probably with gilded compartments containing rosettes. A *confratello* of the period approached the room on the *piano nobile* by means of the magnificent new staircase designed by Mauro Codussi. Upon entering through a door in the west wall, he would have found himself in a large room more than two stories high. Looking to the far end he would see its spiritual focus: an altar holding the reliquary of the True Cross, kept there in a locked case along with other relics owned by the Scuola, and above or behind it, probably the *Pietà* painted by Jacopo Bellini.[8]

Our *confratello* would then become aware of the monumental canvases that lined the walls just above his head – *atorno atorno* – and that ranged in height from 10.5 to 12 feet. The lower part of the walls would have been lined with wooden benches, as they are now, their backs forming a wainscot about six or seven feet high.[9] Like magnificent tapestries the *teleri* literally replaced the upper walls of the room, but unlike tapestries they were painted with such convincing particularity and such veristic attention to the most minute detail as to create a whole alternate reality – or a choice of alternate realities – that gave ritual resonance to the most mundane tasks or the brotherhood.

Indeed, the *confratello* would now find himself in the quiet center of civic ceremonial space. All around him the walls celebrated the physical face of Venice: the Piazza San Marco, the Rialto Bridge, the Campo San Lio, two private courtyards, the bridge near the Church of San Lorenzo, the *cortile* of the Scuola and the Church of San Giovanni Evangelista. Packed with color and contingency, these canvases offered the promise of new discoveries every time the member returned to the room.

Familiar faces vied with known landmarks, tempting the eye to wander and threatening to distract our observer from the business at hand. For the room had a secular focus as well. To the left of the entrance sat the four top officers of the Scuola on a dais behind the large bench – the *banca* – that gave them their name. The dual function of the *albergo* – at once shrine and boardroom – eventually caused a certain confusion, and the uncomfortably close proximity of spiritual and administrative exercises led to the addition of a new *albergo* to the east of it in 1544. Here the business of the Scuola was transacted, and the old *albergo* became the Sala della Croce, serving solely as a place of worship.[10] But at the end of the Quattrocento, such distinctions may have been far from the minds of the men who sat on the *banca* and who closely identified their charitable activities with their pious practices.

The civic landscape of the narrative canvases was a product of a similar attitude about the indivisible nature of the sacred and profane. As Juergen Schulz has observed, the depicted topography of a city was often connotative in this period; it took its meaning from the story that was enacted within it.[11] Similarly, the *View of Venice* of Jacopo de' Barbari of 1500 can be understood not only as a detailed record of the physical city, but also as an emblem of the commonwealth of Venice as a mercantile and maritime power [Plate 79].[12] The *istorie* of the Scuola di San Giovanni, when regarded as a whole, respond to an analogous interpretation, but with a less secular tone. In them, the well-known squares and byways of the city are not simply presented for themselves. They aim also to convey the certainty that Venice was, indeed, a *sancta città* in which miracles could and were known to take place.[13]

The awakening interest in the urban scene also found literary expression in Venice during this period. The guidebooks to the city, written by Sabellico and Sanudo, came out within a few years of the beginning of the True Cross campaign and the Barbari map. They, too, may be seen as products of a common desire to display the city in all of its *sestieri*. In his *De origine*, Sanudo moved away from the encomiastic perspective of earlier panegyrists like Sabellico, toward a concrete approach which portrayed the city as an organic and realistic totality.[14] And what did Sanudo think of as notable? The public and private places of Venice: not only the churches, the Basilica, the Ducal Palace and the Rialto, but also the warehouses, the bridges and the family palaces. Yet Sanudo was concerned with more than real estate, for he also portrayed the city in terms of the people who lived there: the sober merchants who traded at the Rialto and the jewel-bedecked matrons:

> There is not such a sad and poor patrician woman who would not have 500 ducats in rings on her fingers, without large pearls, that it is an incredible thing to believe, but seeing, you will believe.[15]

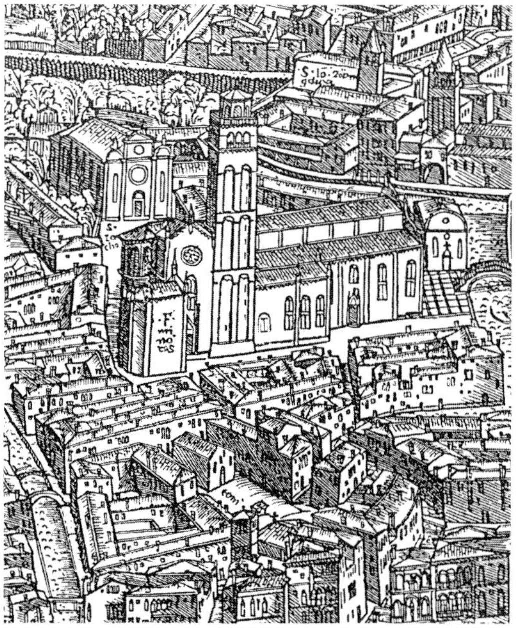

79. Jacopo dei Barbari, detail from the *View of Venice*, 1500, with the Scuola Grande di San Giovanni Evangelista at the upper right (Venice, Museo Correr)

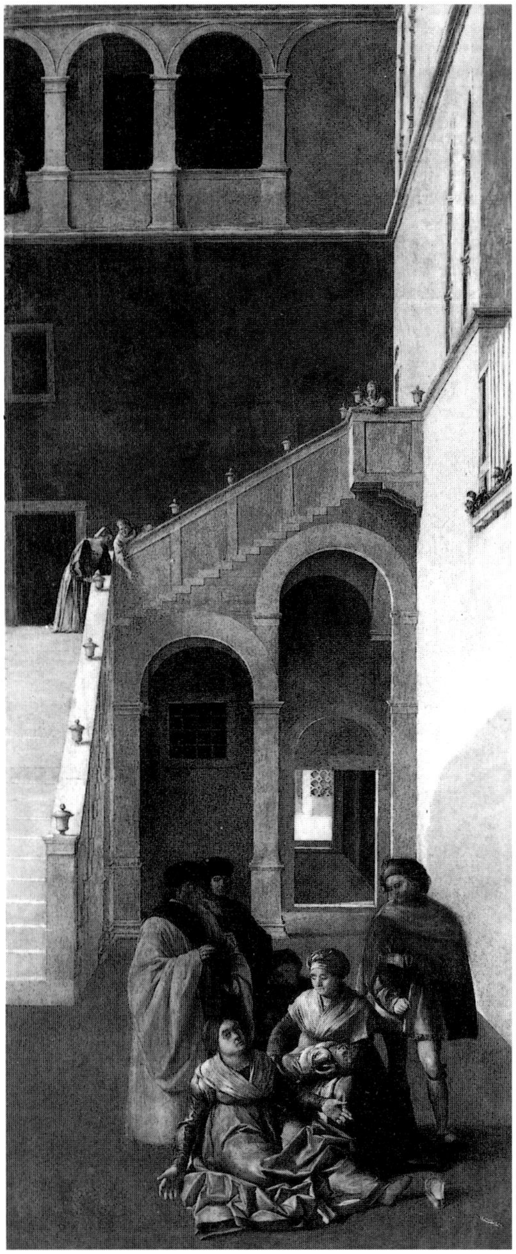

80. Benedetto Diana, *Healing of the Son of Alvise Finetti* (Venice, Accademia)

In short, it was the same civic world of Venice that was brought into the *albergo* of San Giovanni to be displayed on the *teleri* – the citizens along with its buildings.

If we look more closely at these paintings, we can see that they offer more than photograph-like reproductions of the passing scene. They present a strikingly unified city, despite the participation of at least five artists and the range of settings required for the different *istorie*. This is achieved not only through adherence to a common 'eyewitness' style, but also through a correlative geometry, scale and color.

First, structural consistency is obtained by locating the vanishing-point of the perspective system on the central vertical axis of each work, with only one exception. This stabilizing factor is immediately apparent in those paintings in which the architecture is centralized – for example, Gentile Bellini's *Healing of Pietro de' Ludovici* and *Procession*, and Bastiani's *Donation* – but it is also utilized in counter-balanced compositions like Carpaccio's *Exorcism* and Bellini's *San Lorenzo*. It is even more surprising of observe it in Diana's narrow *Healing of Finetti's Son*, where its use gives weight to the argument that the work maintains its original format and was never cut drastically at the left side as some have suggested [Plate 80].[16] The single departure from the norm is Mansueti's *Miracle at the Bridge of San Lio* [Color Plate XXI]. Here there are two vanishing-areas, balanced more or less symmetrically on each side of the vertical axis. We will consider the reasons for this exception in more detail below.

Second, the paintings share, for the most part, a common figural scale. The use of the adult male figure in the front plane as the measure for the perspective system, customary in Italian Quattrocento painting, brought the surrounding architectural settings into relative correspondence as well.

Third, a common palette tending toward the warmer colors – rich reds, golds and ochres – provides a coherence and harmony which binds the paintings together chromatically. The blues are warm as well. The aquamarine blue of the domes of San Marco is picked up again in the *ciborium* of the Church of San Giovanni Evangelista, in the waters of the Grand Canal and the canal at San Lorenzo, and in the background sky of most of the paintings. And finally, the black togas worn by the great majority of Venetian citizens, and the white robes of the brotherhood, provided a form of 'sartorial continuity' which linked each painting to the next to create the illusion of an apparently seamless narrative.[17]

The predominating tendencies toward unity are qualified, however, for the cycle as reconstructed displays no consistent light source.[18] Nor, indeed, is there any rational way in which the existing corpus of paintings could be arranged to achieve this effect. Such an inconsistency was unusual during this period.[19] While several explanations come to mind, such as an expansion of an original program which had envisioned a different placement of the canvases, it may well be that the effect was intentional: that each scene was meant to be illuminated separately as the true depiction of an event that happened in a particular place at a particular time. Six of the extant paintings depict episodes which took place out-of-doors in identifiable locations in Venice. The direction of sunlight would thus indicate the precise hour of the day in each. Following this assumption, the attentive viewer would know that the *Donation* had taken place around midday, the *Exorcism* near the Rialto bridge in the morning, and another four miracles in the afternoon.[20] If this hypothesis is correct, then we might conclude that the appearance of historical accuracy was of greater importance than full aesthetic unity.

Moreover, the miracles depicted do not follow the chronological order of the *incunabulum*. Here the choice may have been determined by formal considerations. Gentile's decision to paint the miracle of Jacopo de' Salis in its full ceremonial setting in the Piazza San Marco must have been based upon an awareness of the potentially splendid effect that it would make as a wall-to-wall backdrop for the Banca. It is more than likely that something similar to the 'retracto de Sancto Marcho, cum tutta la piaza et pallazo de venetia', drawn by Jacopo Bellini and offered by his son Gentile to Francesco Gonzaga, Marchese of Mantua, in 1493, had already been seen and admired by various members of the Banca of San Giovanni.[21]

The synchronic nature of visual art is made manifest here, wherein the entire message can be perceived and absorbed all at once or in a number of different sequences. The apparently random arrangement of the separate canvases recalls Nelson Goodman's observations on Memling's *Life of Christ*. Here many episodes are arranged on a single panel without consistent orientation or direction to indicate the order of telling. Goodman concluded that such events were regarded as eternal and emblematic rather than episodic and transient, and thus their precise arrangement was of less concern than were formal considerations.[22] In sum, it would appear that the precise order and evolution of the miracles was not as important as the total effect of archival completeness, with each scene becoming a separate document which displayed a different quality of the relic.

* * *

The painters of the True Cross cycle were faced with a twofold task. Aware that 'true history' required completeness of description and comprehensiveness of visual data, they knew also that a depicted miracle should appear to be simply found or discovered in nature, and therefore as irrefutably true as everyday life. Before examining more closely the manner in which the different artists responded to the challenge of depicting a miracle, we will look at the only painting of the cycle that was not intended to commemorate a supernatural event.

Lazzaro Bastiani and visual documentation

The *Donation of the Relic*, painted by Lazzaro Bastiani [Color Plate XVI], had somewhat different requirements from the other paintings. Here the aim was to establish the provenance and document the legitimate ownership of the relic, rather than to authenticate its miracle-working powers. The basic circumstances of the donation ceremony were available to Bastiani from the text of the *incunabulum*. It stated that Philippe de Mézières, the Grand Chancellor of Cyprus, after receiving the relic as a deathbed request from the Patriarch of Constantinople, had come to Venice,

> where having heard of the fame of the devoted and holy things that were carried out in the four *scuole* of Venice and especially in that of misser San Giovanni, he was moved by devotion of the glorious evangelist, as also by the good reputation of the most worthy guardian of the *scuola*, misser Andrea

> Vendramin, [and] decided to give the *scuola* an inestimable gift and precious gem: that is, to present it with that particle of the most sacred wood of the cross...[23]

According to the *incunabulum*, the donation had taken place in 1368 [*sic*] in the Church of San Giovanni Evangelista:

> Where the venerable Franciscan priest, Master Lodovico, professor of holy theology, with his chancellor, was present, having sung first the mass of the most sacred cross; [Mézières] gave the particle of the most sacred wood of the cross to misser Andrea Vendramin, Guardian, in the name of the scuola, being present here an innumerable multitude of persons among whom was misser Helia Giustiniani, misser Marco Moresini, misser Francesco Giustiniani, and many others, in addition to the witnesses [*testimoni*] of the said donation, who had come to see such a treasure...[24]

This passage was only a starting-point for Bastiani. Its brevity and lack of visual detail remind us of the unequal and yet reciprocal relationship between a written narrative and the image that illustrates it. In this case the text required the artist only to set the scene in the church adjacent to the Scuola, to feature Mézières and Vendramin and two clerics, and to include three named witnesses and a large number of spectators. Beyond that, Bastiani was left to his own resources to fill a large canvas with particulars sufficient to convince any sceptical viewer that such an event had indeed taken place. It was for him to determine – with advice, to be sure, from the Banca of the Scuola di San Giovanni – the exact number, nature and placement of the figures, as well as their costumes, attitudes and gestures. He had to decide, in addition, the parameters and realization of a setting that had been designated only as 'the Church of San Giovanni Evangelista'.

Bastiani chose to expand the text by providing the broadest possible scenographic frame for the event. In addition to the nave of the church he included the facade, a wide classicizing portico, the courtyards to the front and the side, and the meeting-house of the Scuola.[25] He centralized not only the architecture, but the full cast of characters as well. The effect of an 'innumerable multitude of persons' was achieved by massing groups of toga-clad gentlemen in the front plane to the left and to the right, framing the activities of the day without participating in them. It is in the deepest background of the painting, at the high altar of the Church of San Giovanni Evangelista, that the narrative core of the story unfolds [Plate 81]. Two men stand facing each other, observed at close hand by two rows of witnesses. The Guardian Grande Andrea Vendramin – probably the figure on the left – accepts from Mézières a simple wooden crucifix, much larger in scale than the tiny fragment that was later to be enshrined at the expense of the Scuola in a silver gilt and crystal reliquary and called *la santissima croce nostra* [Plate 20]. The exaggeration was justifiable; for if the painting was to function as a document of the donation, the relic had to be clearly visible.

Although the main protagonists of the narrative may appear to our eyes to be swallowed up and even overwhelmed by the architectural structure, they are well-anchored and are given compositional primacy through their placement on the vertical axis just below the vanishing-point of the perspective system. They form part of a nucleus that Rudolf Arnheim would call the 'dynamic center' of the composition.[26] They could not have been placed in a more geometrically potent, albeit embedded, position. The painting documents formally an occasion that was public and corporate in nature, and the complete ritual circumambient and membership of the Scuola were necessary to portray it in its fullness. Bastiani's densely described environment confirmed to any doubting viewer that it was, indeed, the Scuola di San Giovanni that had taken rightful possession of the relic back in 1369. The donation was thus not subsumed; it was simply properly framed.

Bastiani's conception – more descriptive than the *incunabulum* – became part of an expanded historiographical tradition that was to be drawn upon by later historians of the Scuola. In fact, the revised and updated text published by the

81. Lazzaro Bastiani, detail of the *Donation of the Relic* (Color Plate XVI)

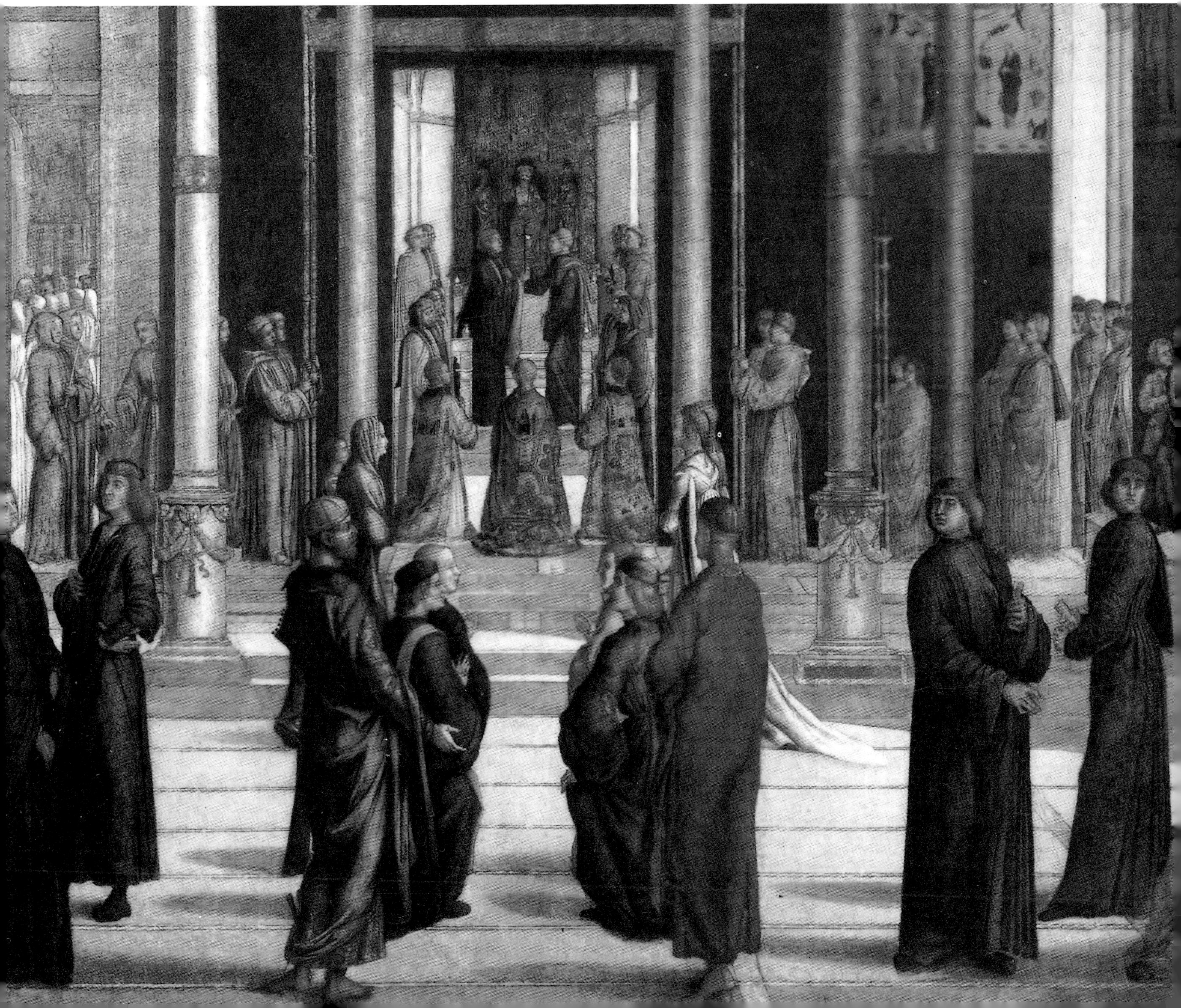

Scuola in 1590 – *Miracoli della Croce* – included a somewhat more detailed version of the Donation that probably depended upon the painting. It recounted that there was present 'a copious multitude of people of both sexes', and that Mézières had 'taken off his mantle with his own hands, with head bared, and had kneeled. . ., the mass having been sung before the altar. . .' The witnesses, we are now told, were 'Cittadini Nobeli Venitiani',[27] an observation that may reflect the heightened interest of late sixteenth-century Venetians in visible evidence of social rank. All of this was to be found in Bastiani's painted record.

More than any other *istoria* in the cycle, Bastiani's canvas represents a formally staged event, but it does not signal the abandonment of the eyewitness style. While that sense of happenstance which gave a depicted occurrence an artless – and thus truthful – appearance to the Venetian viewer is not completely missing, it is provided here more by a plethora of circumstantial detail than by the deliberate suppression of compositional hierarchy such as we will observe in some of the other paintings. This must have been a considered choice on the part of Bastiani, which was determined by the specific nature of the event portrayed. For his canvas was intended to carry the formalized authority of a notarized document, attesting solemnly and legibly to the act of donation, as well as to the witnesses and to the location. Unlike the miracles that follow, here the central episode was quite deliberately no 'accident'.

Miraculous processes

The task of the other artists who were commissioned to paint the miracles of the True Cross was a peculiar one. Two basic particularities come to mind. First, these were events that lacked, for the most part, a heroic protagonist. While paintings of miracles are typically intended to honor a holy figure – the Madonna or a saint – through whom divine power is expressed, here the vehicle of grace was simply a cross: a sign of Christ's power, to be sure, but an inanimate object. Furthermore, as we have seen, the circumstances of corporate patronage in Venice discouraged the singling out of any contemporary individual in relation to its faceless workings. Supporting casts were large, but Andrea Vendramin – dead for more than a century – is, in fact, one of the few individuals whom we can identify with real certainty in any of the paintings.[28] Deprived of a primary actor who would normally serve as a visual anchor in the ordering of a narrative composition, the artists were faced with a problem that required considerable ingenuity to resolve: the need to provide narrative structure and relevance without trivializing a known sacred event and without giving undue prominence to single individuals.

The second particularity is a question of selection. A miracle involved a process of transformation: from sick to healed, from imperiled to rescued, from possessed to exorcised. Its full representation required sequentiality. But just as the painters of the True Cross cycle ignored the chronological order of the miracles from painting to painting in the cycle as a whole, so too they rejected the strategy of simultaneous narrative, with two or more episodes included within the picture space of each individual scene, which would have provided temporal flow. The artists had to choose from amongst several possible moments the most salient – that is, the most convincing and the most relevant –

to depict, and represent through it a complete miraculous sequence on a single canvas.

In fact, we should allow that the beholder's share in these matters would have been more accessible to the Quattrocento viewer than to us. For the process of cause and effect in regard to miraculous transformations was probably well enough known to members of a religious confraternity to be taken for granted. Written accounts of miracles from this period typically follow a standard pattern which emphasizes the interplay of the human and divine protagonists: 1. dangerous situation; 2. prayer or vow offered by the participant; 3. divine intervention; 4. rescue or cure; 5. thanks for grace received, again offered by the participant.[29] Visually offered any part of this sequence, the pious viewer would have been expected to determine the rest from oral or written accounts or from his own experience of such situations. Thus, the paintings assumed a familiarity with miraculous processes and took on an emblematic quality that transcended their duty to narrate fully, and corresponded, rather, to their documentary function.

The narrative mode of Gentile Bellini

Aside from the *Donation* of Lazzaro Bastiani, the only paintings to be organized according to an obvious centralizing principle were the three painted by Gentile

82. Gentile Bellini, detail of the *Healing of Pietro de' Ludovici* (Color Plate XVII)

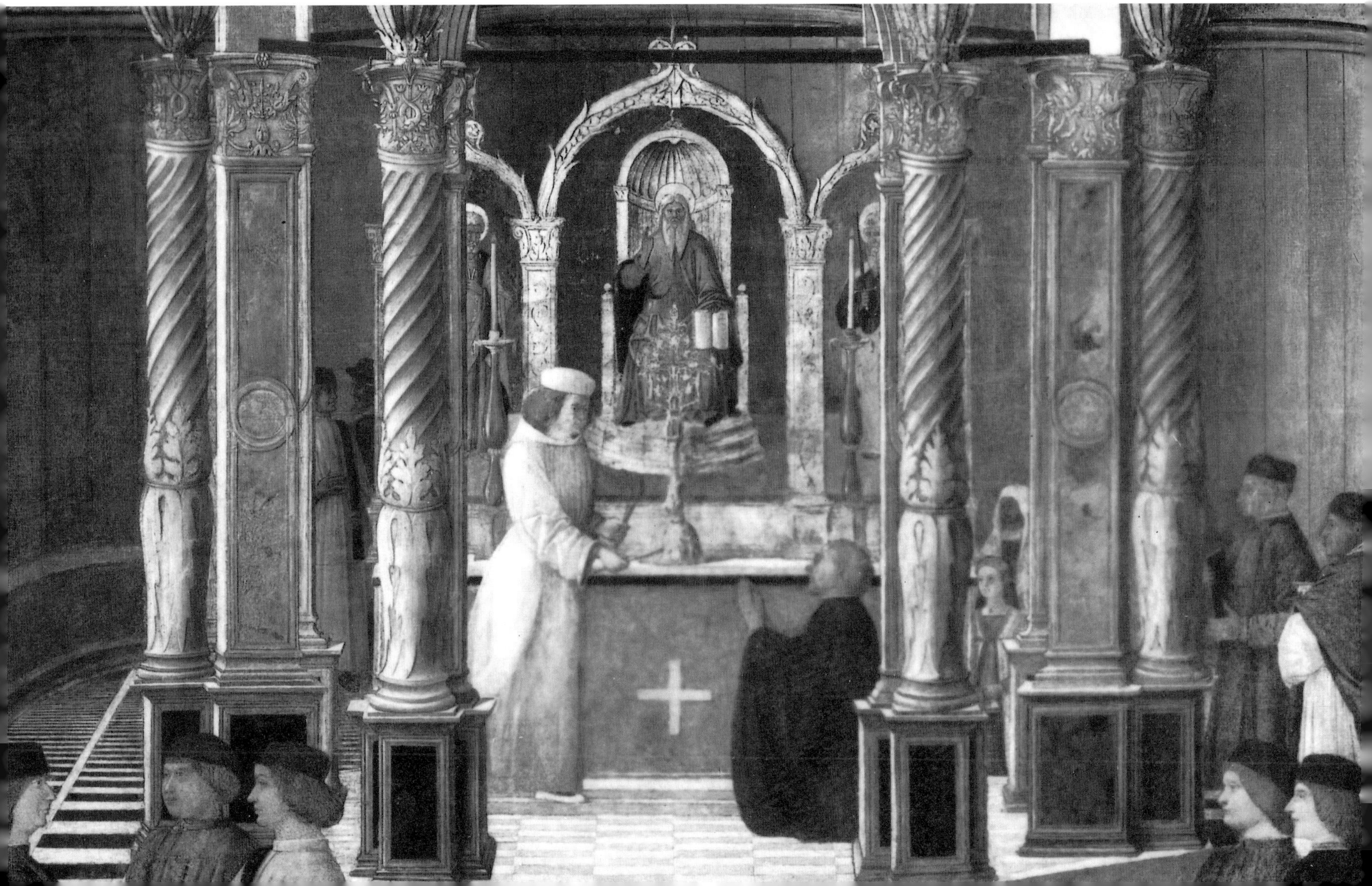

Bellini. The similarity between the *Donation* and the works by Bellini was probably no coincidence, for Bastiani's painting here bears the imprint of the Bellini workshop, as founded by Jacopo and continued by his sons. But in each of Gentile's paintings, a different result was obtained.

Let us first consider his *Healing of Pietro de' Ludovici* [Color Plate xvii]. De' Ludovici was a member of the Scuola who had suffered for months from a recurrent 'quartan fever' [malaria]. He was finally cured after taking to his bed with a candle with which he had touched the miraculous relic. The chosen moment that Gentile deemed most worthy to record was not the bedtime prodigy but the public occasion: de' Ludovici's vow in the church. The afflicted man kneels in the background partly hidden by the splendid *ciborium* that rises into a gold mosaic-lined apse above him [Plate 82].[30] His posture of supplication has a long history in votive paintings and would have been familiar to the contemporary viewer. But the more active agent of the narrative is his white-robed confraternity brother. Extending to him a candle, he condenses in this single gesture the whole miraculous process of grace sought and grace received. A small group of witnesses endow the event with authority and a certain solemnity: two women barely visible behind de' Ludovici, and to the right a cleric and a man in a toga. In the front plane, several groups of men stand around, unaware of the small drama unfolding in the apse. Some converse, others exchange papers, and one dispenses alms to an old woman, reflecting the charitable activities of the Scuola.

We see here a private act of devotion which had, in fact, few witnesses, with a number of bystanders who were preoccupied with their own affairs. Their apparent unawareness and even indifference allow de' Ludovici's activity at the altar to appear spontaneous – as if inserted, even though centralized, in the flow of everyday life – and thus to underline its genuineness. Unlike the *Donation*, it is not an orchestrated event that was meant to look staged. It is a simple human occasion which might have happened to any *confratello* of piety and good reputation.

In his *Procession in the Piazza San Marco* [Color Plate xviii], the artist grasped the opportunity to portray not only the physical center of religious and political ritual in the city, but also the feast-day of St. Mark, a time-hallowed celebration that was held every year on 25 April.[31] Within this context that was so central to Venetian civic and spiritual concerns, he had to document an event of particular significance only to the Scuola di San Giovanni: the miraculous healing of the son of Jacopo de' Salis, a Brescian merchant 'of good reputation and condition'.

The text of the *incunabulum* emphasized the circumstances of de' Salis's devotion more than the miracle itself. During a visit to Venice on the vigil of St. Mark, we are told, de' Salis had received distressing news. Back in Brescia, his small son had suffered a skull fracture and was not expected to live. Finding himself on the following day in the Piazza San Marco and watching the great annual procession in honor of the city's patron saint, de' Salis recalled that the True Cross of the Scuola di San Giovanni was famed for its prodigious miracles. As it was carried past, 'he bent over and threw himself on his knees, praying piously to the almighty God that through that *sanctissima croce* he would deign to work a miracle for his son and free him from so much pain and peril.' As it happened, when de' Salis returned home to Brescia, the doctors informed him that the child had been found to be perfectly healed 'without a blemish' on the very day after the Venetian procession. The merchant revealed the good news to

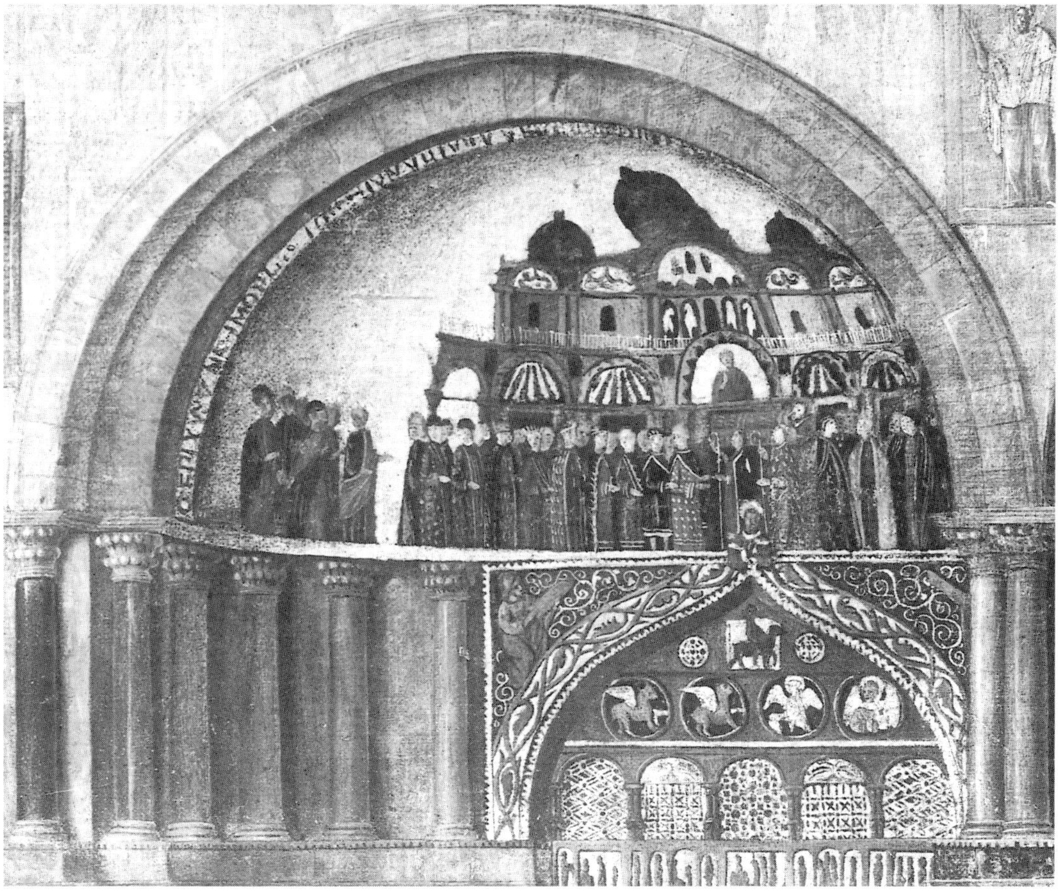

83. Gentile Bellini, detail of the *Procession in the Piazza San Marco* (Color Plate XVIII)

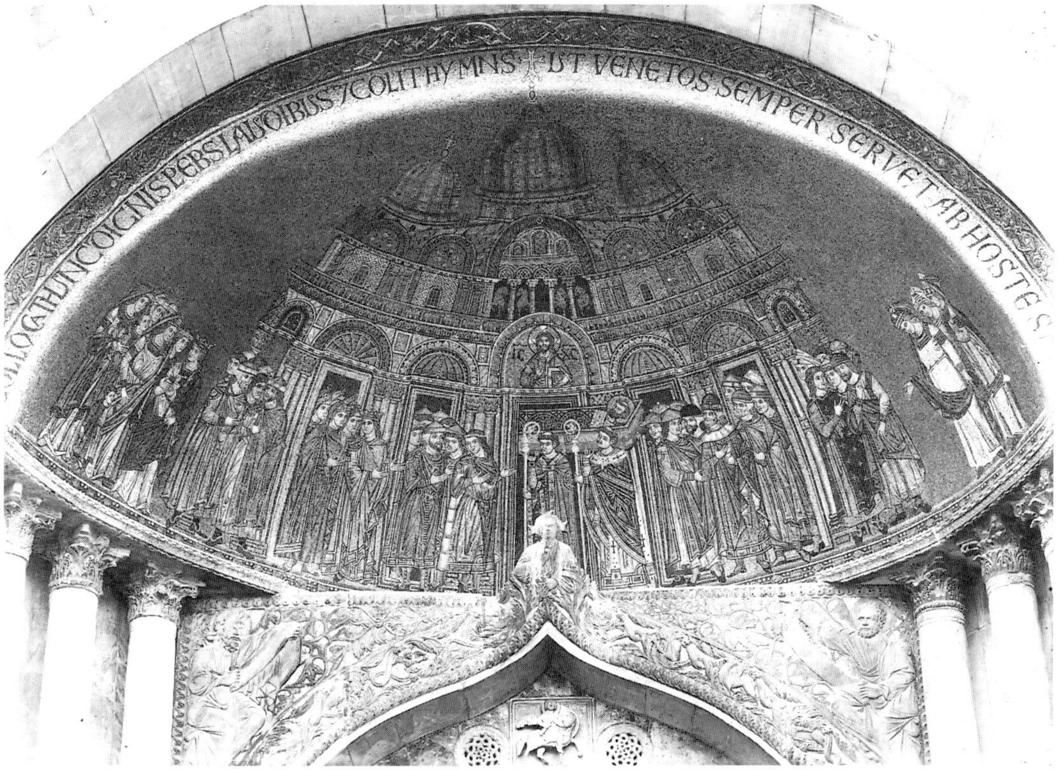

84. *Reception of the Relics of St. Mark*, mosaic (Venice, Basilica of San Marco, Porta di Sant'Alippio)

the Guardian Grande of San Giovanni and vowed to bring his son to the Scuola to pay due reverence to the Cross.

Unlike a typical *ex voto*, the painting displays neither the injury of the son nor his grace received, but only the devotional gesture of the father, made in the full ceremonial context of Venetian piety and flanked by the white-robed members of the Scuola di San Giovanni. Passing directly in front of us, they hold aloft their renowned relic of the True Cross, encased in a special reliquary cross of crystal and gilt silver resting on a gilded platform. Four *confratelli* support a *baldacchino* above it, flanked by others who carry twelve heavy *doppieri* (processional candles); together they provide an honorable frame for the relic. The choir of the Scuola leads the group, passing off the left side of the canvas, while other *confratelli* file in from the right and follow the relic, each carrying a candle.

The Scuola di San Giovanni, its members identifiable by the red insignia on the front of their robes, holds the central position in the long procession. In the background on the left side of the piazza, the other four Scuole Grandi already appear to have completed their marching and are waiting, *doppieri* held at attention, in neatly formed ranks. Above their heads a profusion of oriental carpets, each with its own distinct pattern, hangs from the windows of the Procuratie Vecchie, and in most of the arched openings women appear – two among them veiled in the Arabic manner – and observe the scene below [Color Plate XIX]. The feminine presence was an essential element of Venetian pageantry and confirmed the festive character of the day.

Scattered across the piazza is a demographic cross-section of Venice: ladies in low-cut gowns, a young woman holding two children and receiving alms from an old one clad in black, another carrying water, friars, Venetian gentlemen and citizens, priests, children, a dwarf, German merchants, a Moor, turbanned Turks, Greeks in black-brimmed hats, and young men clad in the parti-colored hose of the Compagnia della Calza. On the right, the procession continues, the participants bedecked in every hue of the Venetian spectrum of fabrics: *scarlatto*, *cremisino*, *rosato*, *pavonazzo*, *turchino*, *auro*, and of course *nero*.[32]

But dominating the scene is the golden Basilica of San Marco. Seemingly no particular was so minor as to escape Gentile's microscopic attention. Across the lower tier of the church in four portal lunettes we can read the same pictorial narrative – the *translatio* of St. Mark – that Martino da Canal had recommended to his readers two centuries earlier as evidence of his account of this signal event. Before his eyes the episodes had unfolded through the medium of brilliantly colored mosaic *tesserae* embedded in a gold background.

Gentile's representation of the Sant'Alippio portal on the far left may be compared to the original mosaic, the only *istoria* of the facade that remains today [Plates 83 and 84]. Considering the great difference in scale, the resemblance is striking and confirms for us the artist's dedication to topographical precision.[33] Gentile's fidelity to a monument that was so well-known to his viewers functioned in itself as implicit testimony to his accurate rendering of the pious event for which it formed a backdrop. In addition, in the composition of the mosaic lunette, we see in embryo his great painted *Procession* of 1496. Like a mirror within a mirror, a broad frieze of figures – men and women of every rank and station – extends across the lower edge of the curving surface; and in the middle two tonsured priests with croziers hold aloft the body of St. Mark, just as the lay brothers of San Giovanni display the miraculous crucifix of their

XVII (facing). Gentile Bellini, *Healing of Pietro de' Ludovici* (Venice, Accademia)

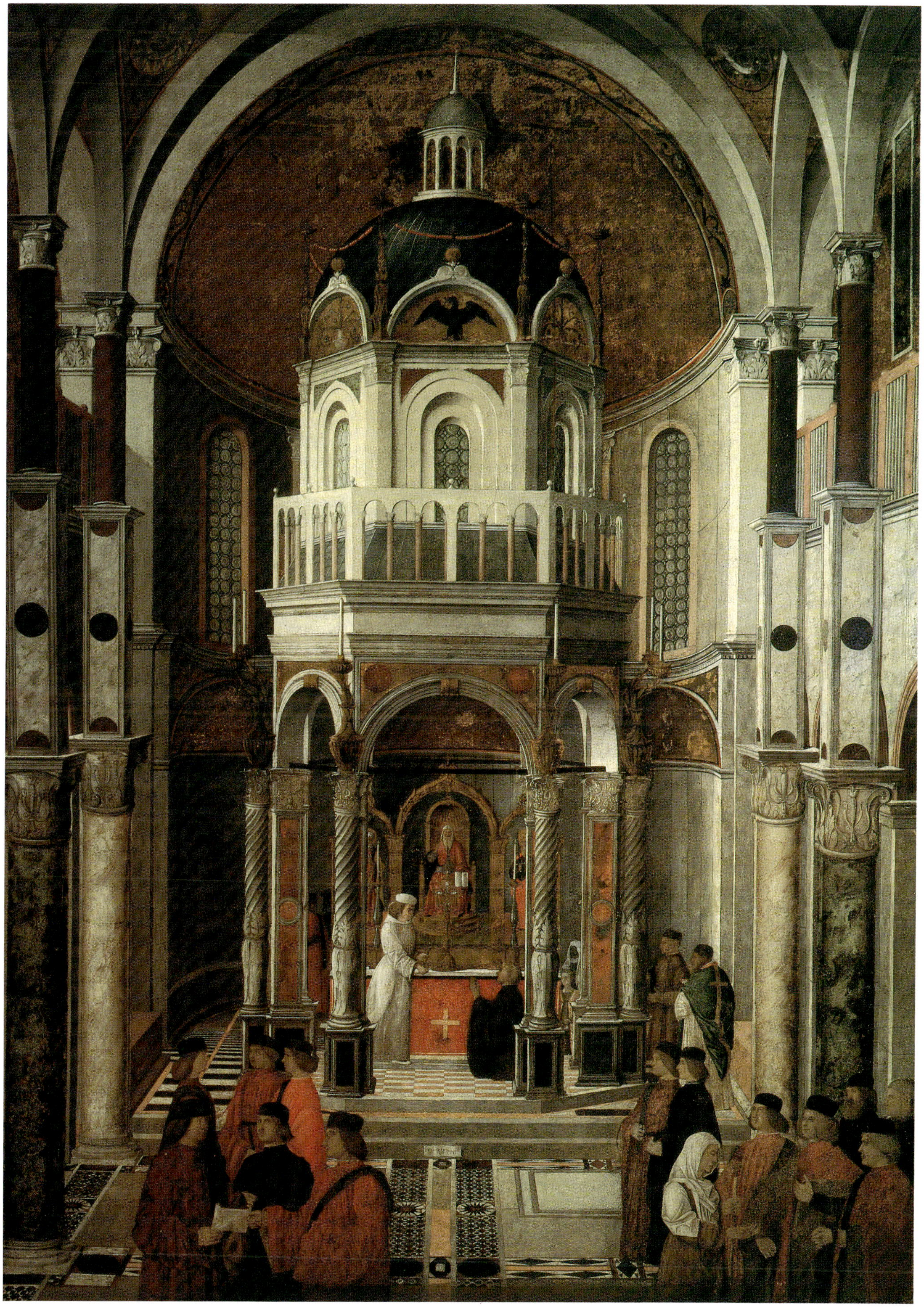

confraternity from whose charisma the community also benefits. Behind the row of observers and witnesses of the *translatio*, we see again the Basilica, but in its earlier state, with its facade as yet devoid of the mosaic decoration that Gentile will record in the painting.

The uninitiated viewer may be forgiven for overlooking Jacopo de' Salis, but Gentile distinguished him quite sufficiently for the eyes of a Scuola member of the time. Clothed in a red toga, normally reserved for Venetian patricians and secretaries, the Brescian merchant is the only figure amongst the multitude in the painting who kneels. Furthermore, he is bareheaded like the marching *confratello* in the front plane, who may well have been the Guardian Grande in 1496, when the painting was completed. The artist has created a gap in the procession of marchers to allow us to view de' Salis fully. For the Venetian patron, this 'votive moment' was the symbolic core of the narrative. But it was the civic context of the miracle that was of direct visual interest to him, and not the psychological state of the father or the physical appearance of the child. Thus de' Salis is neither an active participant in the procession nor a passive bystander. He fulfilled his role simply by being there and doing the right thing. For his gesture of devotion was as unexceptional as the parade itself, an event that was only one manifest display of reverence among so many others in the annual ritual cycle in which the Scuola participated.

As for the procession, Gentile had put the Scuola di San Giovanni into a privileged place that is underlined by its formal prominence in the painting, defining, as it were, the front plane. And yet here, communal harmony is maintained. For the magnificent canopy which the *confratelli* hold above their relic bears mute testimony to the Venetian consensus, with the tiny coats-

XVIII. Gentile Bellini, *Procession in the Piazza San Marco* (Venice, Accademia)

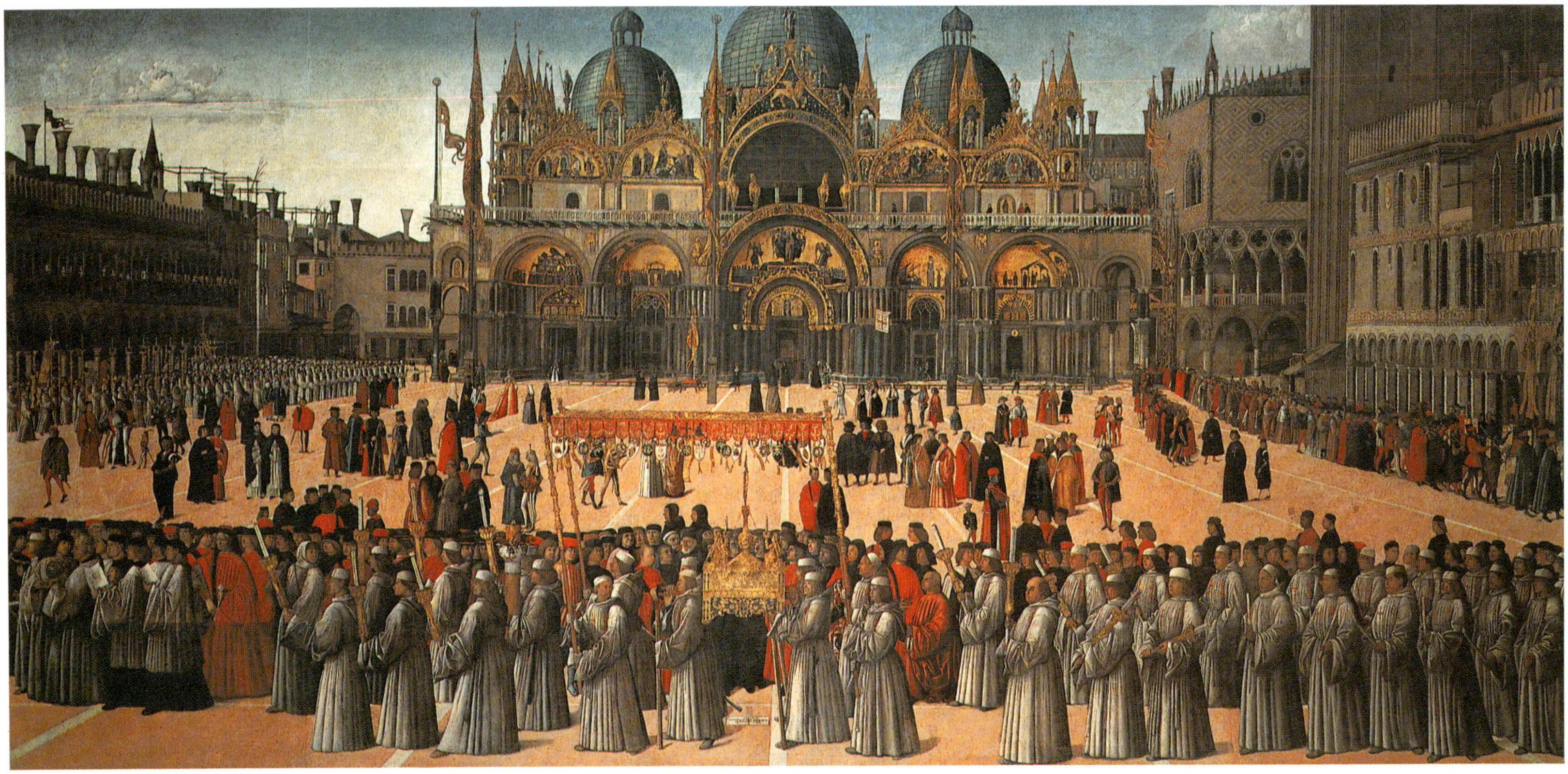

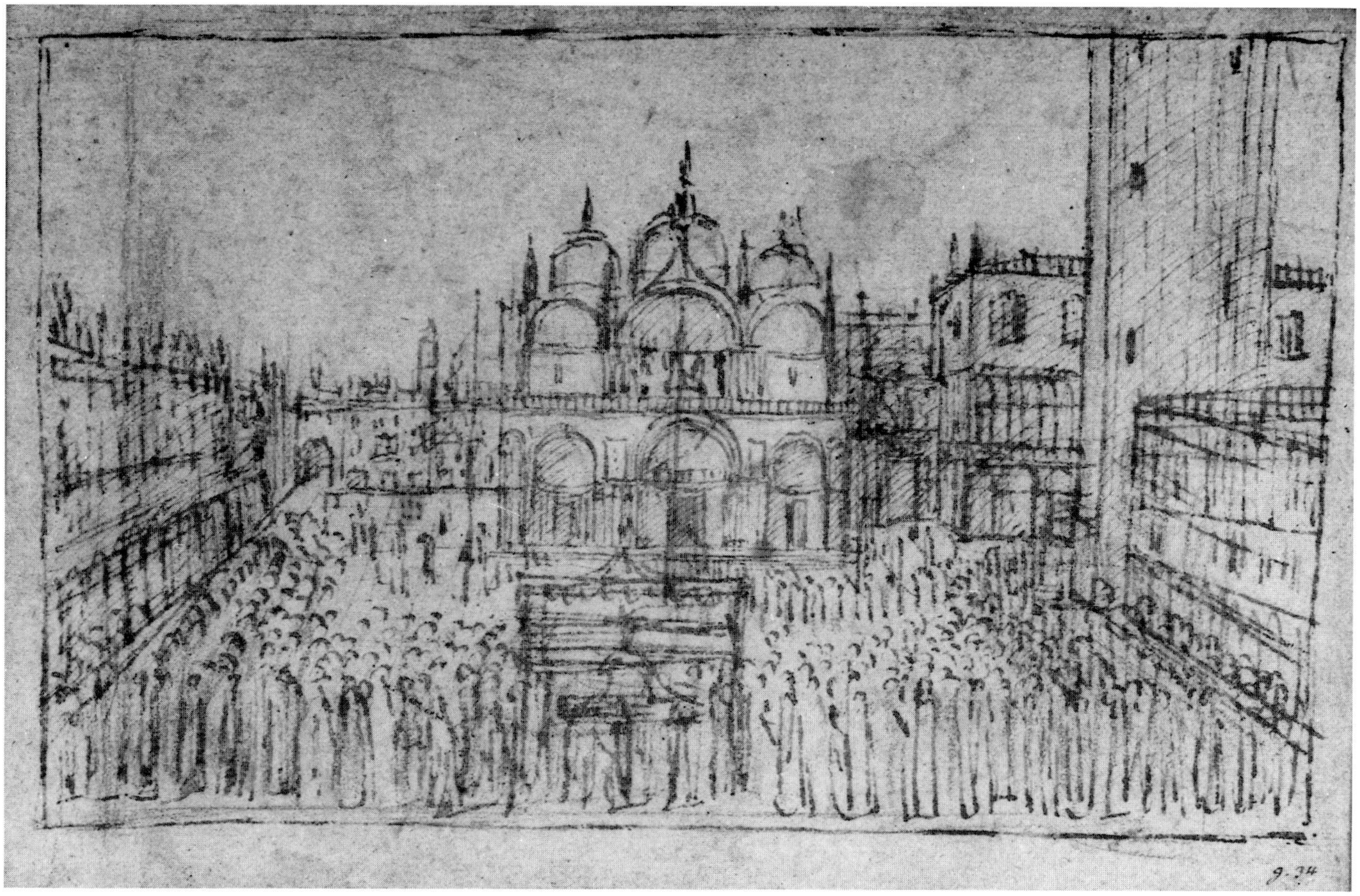

85. Gentile Bellini, preparatory drawing for the *Procession* (London, British Museum, 1933-8-3-12)

of-arms of each of the Scuole Grandi of the city hanging from its scalloped border. All the Scuole Grandi, with San Giovanni in the foremost position, thus become the *de facto* heart of the procession, while the supposed 'processional center' with the Doge as its nucleus is pushed to the periphery.[34] If we look closely at the spectators just behind the canopy, we may observe an extraordinarily intense concentration on the Cross that reinforces its spiritual as well as physical centrality in the composition.

At the same time, Gentile underlines the impression of happenstance by giving careful attention to the surrounding ambient. Our eye is not allowed to linger long on the foreground group, for it is pulled back ineluctably to the meticulously rendered Basilica behind. By its massive centrality the building organizes the random groups of figures in front of it and forms a strong vertical axis that leads the eye back to the holy relic in the foreground. A comparison of the painting with what appears to be a preparatory drawing indicates a progressive flattening of spatial depth [Plate 85].[35] In the sketch, Gentile is clearly attempting to come to terms with the wide format. With a high horizon line at about the level of the lower cornice of the Basilica, it offers a birds-eye view that takes in much of the piazza in front. The orthogonals on the left side are thrown up on a steep angle, pushing the background deep into space. There is no single vanishing-point, but rather two general vanishing areas, one just to the left of the Basilica and the other beneath its south dome.

In the finished painting, Gentile has settled on a single, lower vanishing-point in the archway of the central door of the Basilica. The panoramic advantages of an elevated vantage-point are retained, while accommodated to a direct frontal view of marching figures in the front plane. The side orthogonals become less steep and more horizontal, thus flattening the space. The spatial extension is also suppressed by cropping the buildings on the left. In this manner Gentile was able to create an expansive stage that would extend beyond the picture space and would imply a multitude of participants, even beyond the several hundred depicted.

In both the *Procession* and the *Healing*, Gentile began with the construction of the physical environment, working out the relationships between buildings and notionally filling the space with figures. Only as a second step did he attempt to impose the strict geometry of linear perspective upon the setting and then to work out the precise arrangement of the figures. The artist worked hard to get just the right viewpoint, whence he could capture an ambient into which he was able to fit the necessary participants – actors and patrons – so as to appear 'gratuitously' placed. The setting is thus not simply recorded through control of the viewpoint; it is, in fact, essentially manipulated. By controlling the spatial depth in the *Procession*, the artist makes it more present to us, and in fact makes us part of the scene as well.[36]

Yet Gentile Bellini would have us believe that the order which we observe here was not imposed by him. It was an order found – and in which a miraculous event was simply captured with all the unchallengeable certainty of a notarial act. And in fact, the miraculous event was all the more credible precisely because it could be apprehended visually within the context of public ceremonial life, irrefutably true because irrefutably normal and even a bit untidy.

Like Bastiani's *Donation*, Gentile Bellini's *Miracle at the Bridge of San Lorenzo* is a special case within the context of the cycle [Color Plate XX]. It is manifestly staged and artificial. Here the miracle does not go unnoticed within the context of daily life. Rather, it is highlighted by donor-type figures who kneel in rigid profile in the front plane on a kind of temporary wooden platform thrown across the canal [Color Plate XL]. Employing a centralized compositional scheme to the extent allowable by the asymmetrical character of Venetian architecture, it even features an identifiable hero: the Guardian Grande Andrea Vendramin. According to the *incunabulum*, the Cross had been jostled from its standard by the great crush of people on the bridge. It had fallen and hovered just above the waters of the canal, moving this way and that, thus eluding the attempts of many persons to retrieve it. Finally, Vendramin, 'with great devotion threw himself into the water' and was allowed to grasp the Cross and return it to safety [Plate 86].

With a true 'heroic focus', the painting is something of an anomaly in a compositional sense within the True Cross cycle; what are we to make of it? Upon closer examination we may note that Vendramin, holding aloft the Cross, functions as a formal pivot for three other areas of interest. Two of these are found in the figures kneeling on each side of the platform. Those in the group to the right – men in togas – are disproportionately large in scale relative to the other occupants of the front plane, a disjunction that violates the normal rules of linear perspective construction. On the left, the old woman and the child on the platform are visually joined to the row of women who stand in profile behind them, who can be identified as Caterina Cornaro and her maids of honor.[37] The The third area is found just above the center of the bridge at the vanishing-point of the linear perspective system. There we see a break in the line of the white-robed *confratelli*, a stratagem used by Gentile in the *Procession* to highlight the

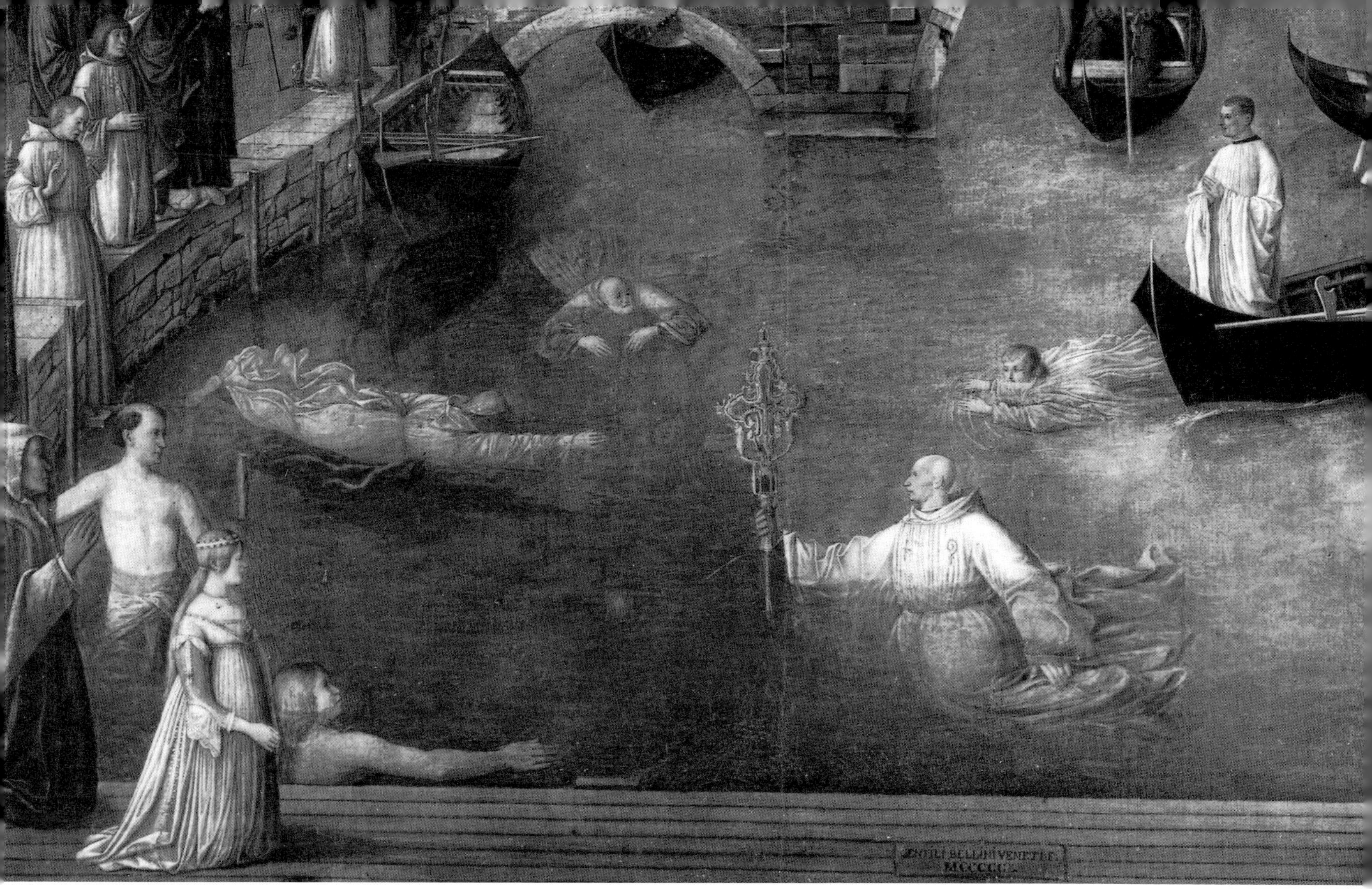

kneeling Jacopo de' Salis. Three men stand there – almost certainly patricians who had a special interest in the scene depicted – one in red senatorial toga, one in black and the other in the gold brocade robe of a *cavaliere*.

86. Gentile Bellini, detail of the *Miracle at the Bridge of San Lorenzo* (Color Plate xx)

This is a painting, one feels, in which a 'star group' with a personal stake in the miracle have been allowed to intrude upon the painting to a quite extraordinary degree. There have been several attempts to identify the donor group in the right foreground, none of them wholly convincing: Gentile Bellini with male members of his family, or members of the Cornaro family, or members of the Vendramin family whose ancestor was commemorated in the painting.[38] In any of these cases we would be witnessing a most unusual occasion where the normal boundaries between corporate and private patronage were transgressed. Another suggestion can be offered that would be more consonant with the institutional structure of the Scuola. If we accept the credible identification of Gentile Bellini as the fourth kneeling figure from the left, we might see the others as the four officers of the Banca in the year 1500. To the right would stand the *degani* – the remainder of the Banca – a group that no one as yet has sought to identify.

The unusual requirements of the painting put a special burden on the artist.

Gentile was torn between conflicting needs to maintain the credibility of the miracle with a faithful rendering of the topgraphy of the site, and to give special prominence to the group of donor figures – whoever they may have been – in the front plane. He chose to separate them definitively from the narrated action by the use of the platform. Deliberately placed, it is a disjunctive element to us, but one that would have appeared less inappropriate to its intended Venetian viewers. For temporary plank bridges were often built across the Grand Canal, and probably other waterways too, when the ceremonial occasion called for them. Thus, its provisional appearance would have preserved the integrity of the miraculous event more than a permanent, albeit picturesque, bridge such as that invented by Carpaccio for the *Leavetaking of the Betrothed Pair* in the Saint Ursula cycle [Plate 110]. Gentile's patrons are thus present at the miracle, but they are kept out of the 'found reality'. It is as if they were themselves looking at the painting.

The copious style of Mansueti

Giovanni Mansueti's inventorial approach and taste for clutter and detail may be observed at their most exuberant in his paintings for the Scuola di San Giovanni. The occasion depicted in the *Miracle at the Bridge of San Lio* is the funeral of a member of the confraternity [Color Plate XXI]. In contrast to the pious and celebrated Andrea Vendramin, this man is nameless and remembered only for his sad and dissolute life. This negative script made the positive one of Vendramin all the more powerful. The anonymous man was, so the *incunabulum* informs us, 'always found in taverns and dishonorable places'. During his lifetime, moreover, he had frequently expressed disbelief in the efficacy of the relic of the True Cross and refused to accompany it in funeral processions. After his death, his impiety was repaid. According to custom, the members of the Scuola dutifully formed a procession, with the True Cross carried in the lead, to bear the body of their dead *confratello* – lacking in honor and devotion though he

87. Mansueti, *Miracle at the Bridge of San Lio* (Color Plate XXI)

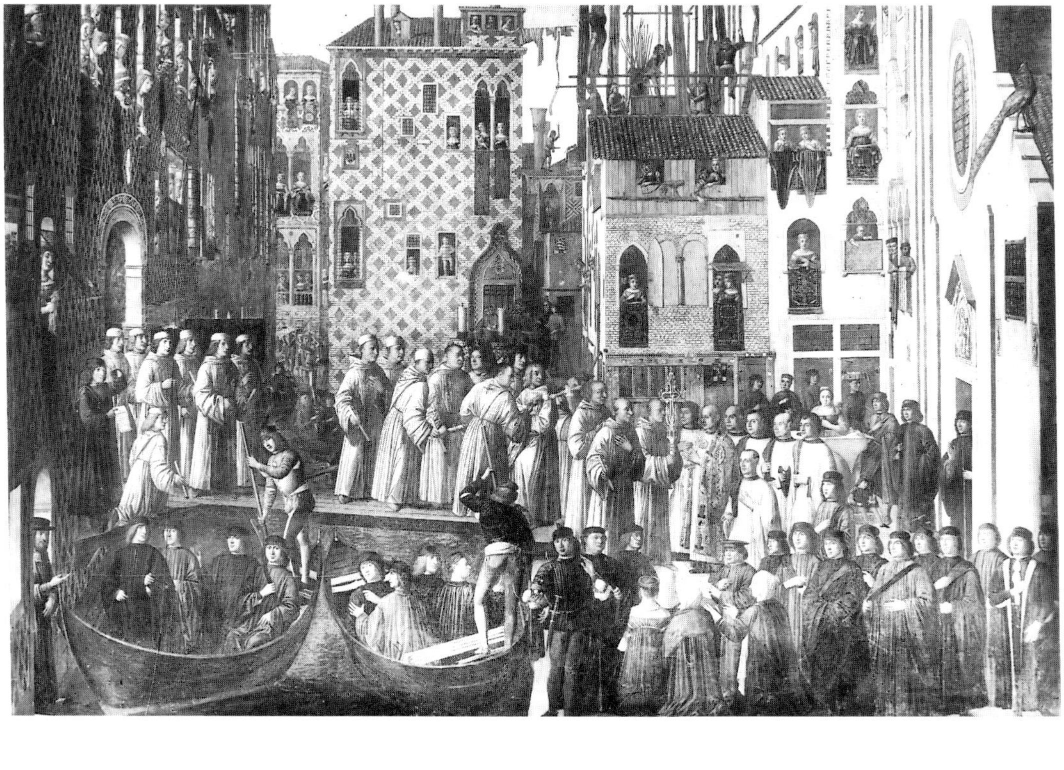

may have been – toward its burial place. When they attempted to carry the Cross over the bridge in front of the church of San Lio where the ceremony was to take place, it suddenly became as heavy as lead and defied attempts to carry it further. Finally, a priest was summoned from the church to bring out another crucifix. The True Cross was removed from its standard and carried into the church, and the procession resumed with the substitute.

In the center of Mansueti's painting, we see the brothers about to raise the simple replacement cross, but with straining gestures that seem to refer to the miracle itself. Just to the right, three others advance solemnly toward the church with the clearly recognizable reliquary of the True Cross, now detached from its standard. Although the attentive viewer can distinguish the two crosses once he is aware of the storyline, Mansueti was less concerned with narrative clarity than with the opportunity to pack the scene with as many participants as the space would hold. Even more than Gentile Bellini or Bastiani, he was reluctant to leave out any possible descriptive detail, and for him it was the human presence that was the most compelling. The enclosed space of the *campo* is made even more airless by the ranks of the confraternity and by the assembled citizenry. Even the windows are called into play, each framing a child or a woman – further witnesses to the shame of the miscreant dishonored by the painting (Plate 87).[39]

In constructing the scene, Mansueti was faced with the formal problem of including both the church and the bridge that flanked a rather wide *campo*. A preliminary drawing survives which was probably made by Gentile Bellini for Mansueti's use [Plate 88],[40] and which may help us to understand the evolution of the design. The drawing corresponds rather closely to the physical layout of the site as Barbari recorded it in his *View of Venice* of 1500 [Plate 89]. We see there an L-shaped space that is made up of two parts: a large square with a well in front of the church on the right; and a long arm extending to the left and terminating in a short bridge that leads to a tunnel-like portal. Proceeding from drawing to painting, Mansueti has contracted the space drastically. He has eliminated buildings that formed the left arm of the *campo* and replaced them with an extended bridge that takes up half the front plane. The *campo* and buildings immediately to the left of the church are carefully reproduced – even to the *altana* and drying laundry high on a rooftop – but the buildings in the background are pulled forward and the spatial recession is strongly suppressed.

Although the development of the composition would appear to be similar to that of Gentile in the *Procession*, the procedure is actually quite different. The sketch is unified by a single vanishing-point in the right half of the painting, focusing on the second story of the lower building in the back plane. In the painting, Mansueti retains a vanishing-area in approximately the same location, but he adds another one to the left in a roughly corresponding position. He was forced to do this if he wished to retain the two most important architectural components of the setting, iconographically speaking – the church and the bridge – in the form of high structures on each side of the scene, and to maintain a wide pictorial stage between them. By masking most of the ground orthogonals, he was able to maintain the credible look of the space. In the painting, the linear perspective construction becomes virtually irrelevant and the semblance of three-dimensional space is achieved more through the technique – archaic by that time – of overlapping layers of figures and objects.

Mansueti faced a different problem with the domestic setting of the *Healing*

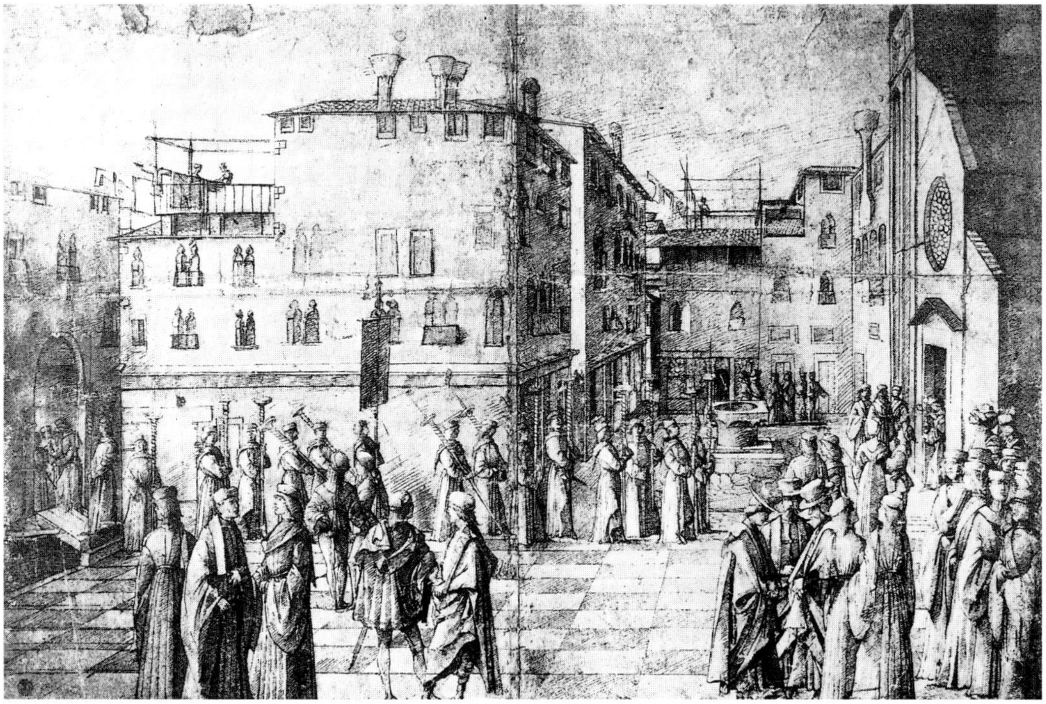

88. Gentile Bellini, preparatory drawing for the *Miracle at the Bridge of San Lio* (Florence, Uffizi, no. 1293)

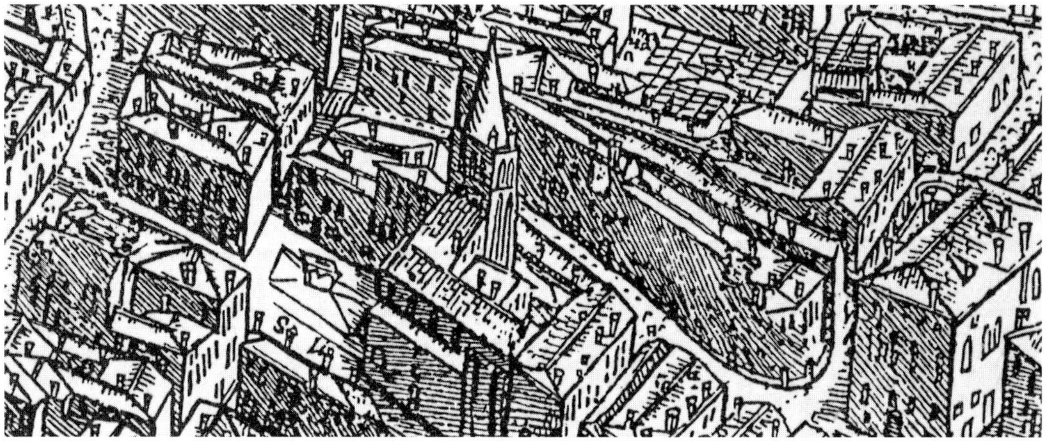

89. Jacopo dei Barbari, detail from the *View of Venice*, 1500, with the Campo San Lio at the lower left (Venice, Museo Correr)

90 (facing). Mansueti, *Healing of the Daughter of Ser Benvegnudo of San Polo* (Venice, Accademia)

of the Daughter of Ser Benvegnudo of San Polo [Plate 90]. The miracle had taken place in 1414 and was probably the occasion that had called forth the first campaign of *istorie* documented in the Scuola.[41] The *incunabulum* recounted at some length a chain of events that featured the three-year-old daughter of a Scuola member, Ser Nicolo di Benvegnudo. Blind since birth and afflicted with tremors, she was healed in her crib when her father touched her head with three candles with which he had touched the relic of the True Cross in the *albergo* of the Scuola. Although no witnesses are mentioned in the text, other than the child's mother, Mansueti has created a most festive and public event in a private home.[42] We do not know if he was asked to represent a particular dwelling or if he was allowed instead to exercise his own imagination. The structure is not as

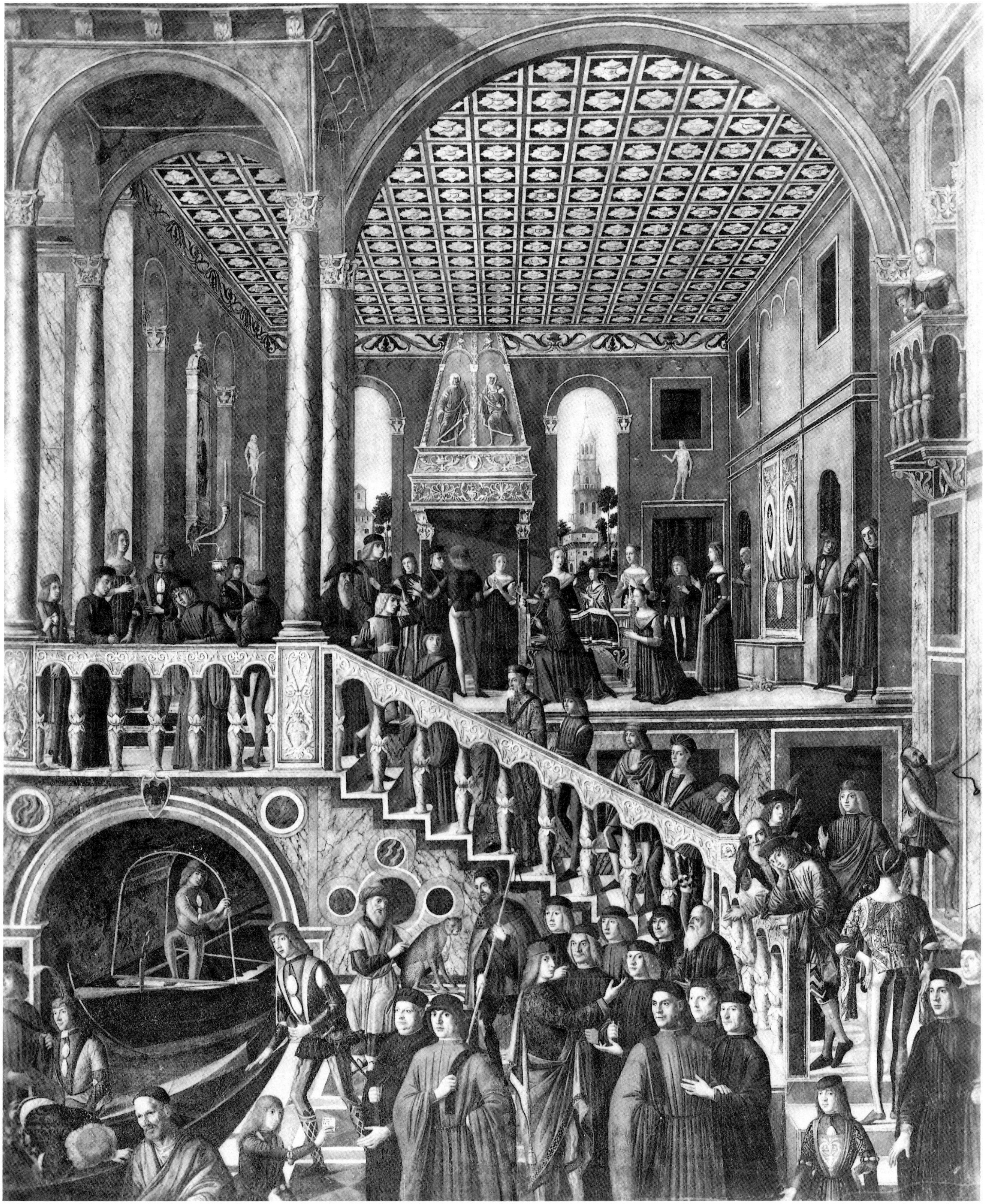

whimsical as it might appear at first glance. By simply removing the enclosing wall or balustrade from the *piano nobile*, the artist has portrayed a typical interior *cortile* of a Venetian palace. It is strikingly close to Ca' Dario, even to the motifs on the walls.

Mansueti returns here to standard one-point perspective to draw our eye to the miracle, with the vanishing-point just to the left of the genuflecting Nicolo di Benvegnudo. To his right we see the mother also kneeling, and behind, the child sitting up in her crib [Color Plate XXIII]. Discouraging the normal tendency of the viewer to confine his attention to the crowd of figures in the courtyard in the lower part of the front plane, the perspective construction is the only formal device to call attention to the narrative core of the work. And yet, as in the *Miracle at San Lio*, the resultant effect is more that of layered space, with one stratum stacked in front of the other, rather than of deep spatial recession. Although the architectonic structure – steps leading across the painting to a portico on one side – recalls the arrangement of the narrative tableau, the impression is not one of procession and resolution.[43]

For Mansueti, profuse description was essential to narration, but his compositions are by no means static. Figures move in and out of the scenes, gesture vigorously, and address each other and even the viewer directly with their glances. In both of these paintings he attempted to capture a process condensed in the moment just after the miraculous transformation: when the cross was replaced in the *Miracle at San Lio*, and when the child sat up in her crib in the *Healing*. The result is a certain confusion, and yet once the *istoria* is known it makes perfect sense. One suspects that part of the original attraction of his paintings was the visual exercise and delight in locating the narrative core of the scene. It is not an exercise that a modern connoisseur of art might wish to be forced to engage in. But if the painting was the record of a pious event, the viewer in the Scuola of the early Cinquecento would have accepted the challenge. Reverent and perceptive eyes would have sought out its pious core. It is against this background that we can appreciate the achievement of Carpaccio.

The singular vision of Carpaccio

Let us now turn to the *Exorcism* or *Healing of the Possessed Man* [Color Plate XXII]. The *incunabulum* defined the locale of this miracle only as the '*patriarchato*'. This would have been the palace of Francesco Querini, the Patriarch of Grado, at San Silvestro on the Grand Canal. Not surprisingly, Carpaccio rejected an interior view and set out to represent what Sanudo had called 'of all the world the richest part' – the Rialto.[44] If the buildings around the Piazza San Marco formed the religious and political core of the city, then the Rialto area was the economic heart which made possible the Venetian ideal of prosperity, tranquillity and justice. Grasping the opportunity to organize his scene around one of the major *loci* of Venetian life, Carpaccio laid out before us the Rialto Bridge and the business center of the city that clustered around it.

On the left, high buildings press up close to the narrow *riva* – the bank of the canal – which is filled with the bustle of commercial life. Venetians of various ages, dressed in red and black togas, are massed in the immediate foreground, many gazing out at the viewer. Two gentlemen stand out from the rest, splendidly clad in brocade robes and wearing the tall brimmed hats of

XIX (facing). Gentile Bellini, detail from the *Procession in the Piazza San Marco* (Color Plate XVIII)

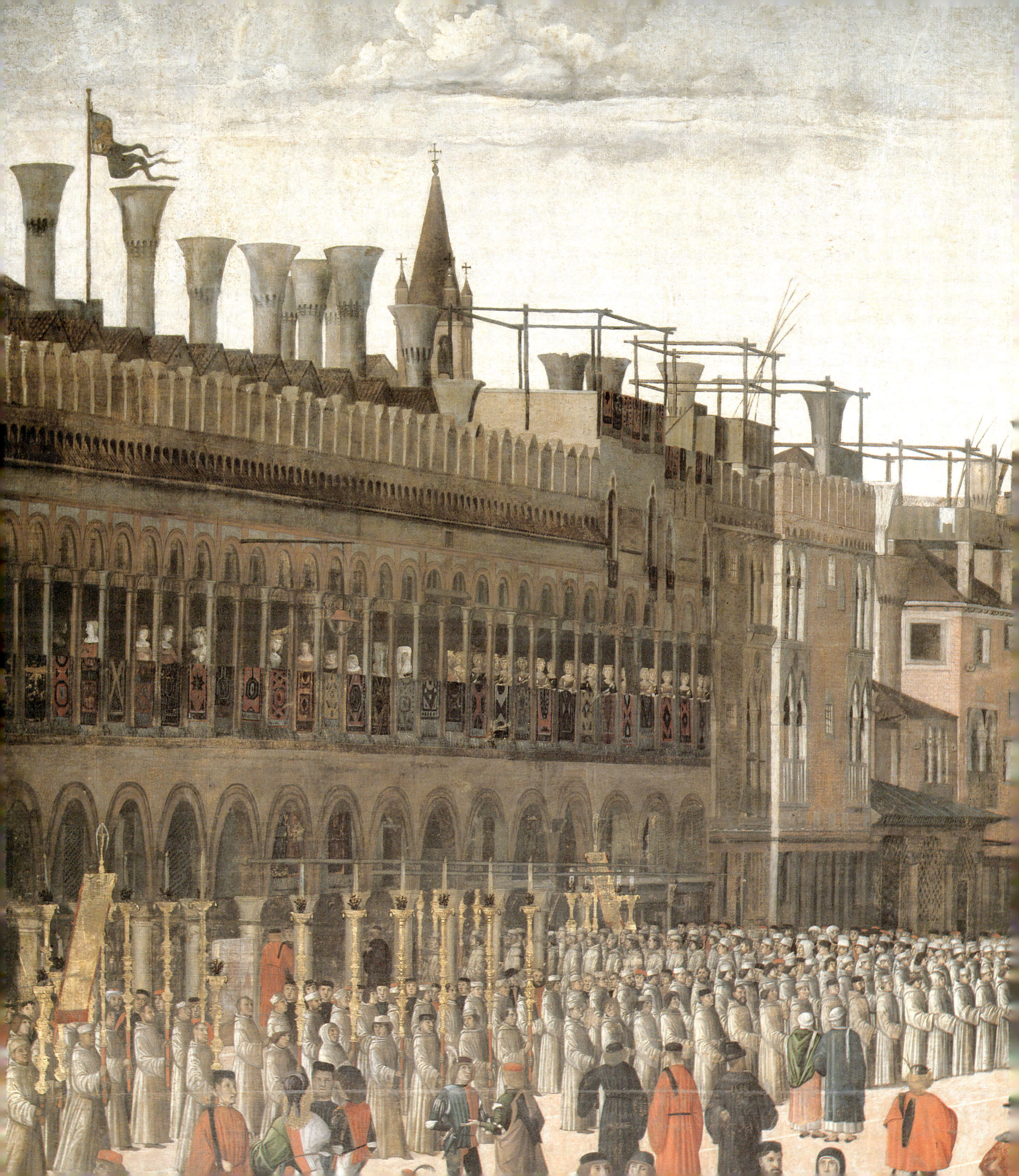

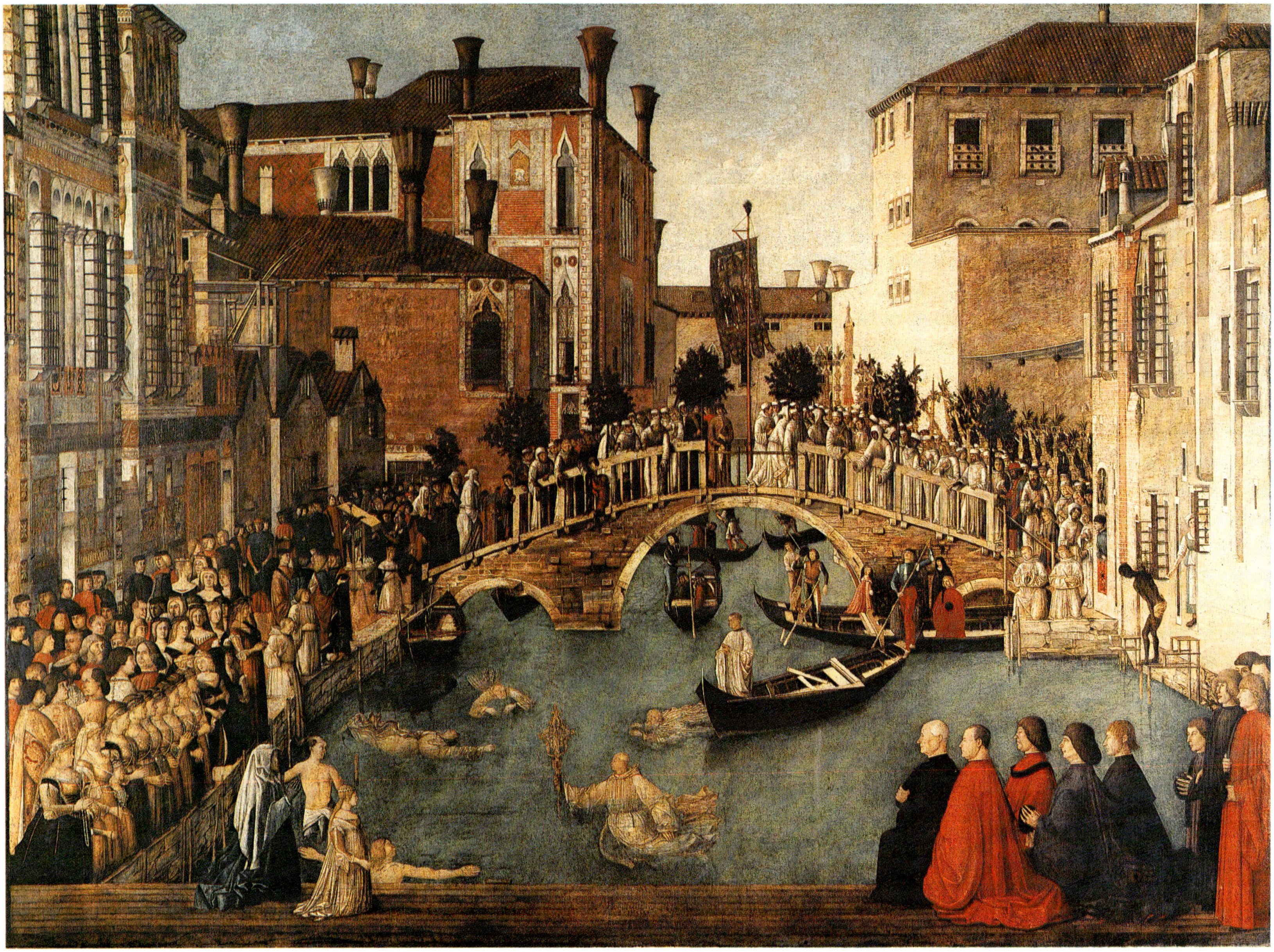

xx. Gentile Bellini, *Miracle at the Bridge of San Lorenzo* (Venice, Accademia)

Armenians or Greeks.[45] Three members of the Compagnia della Calza face away from us, themselves observing the scene.[46] The ubiquitous turbanned figures of Turks and Arabs are discernible in the distance in front of the open marble-columned loggia where the merchants customarily met.[47] Across a wooden bridge, which collapsed only a few years after Carpaccio made the painting,[48] the brothers of the Scuola di San Giovanni file in solemn procession, their red insignia just visible on their white hooded robes and their processional standard raised high. The Grand Canal spreads out to the right in a pool of dark green, dotted with rocking gondolas rowed by young men – one in the foreground a black African[49] – and filled with a variety of persons, and even a Maltese dog. The varying postures of the gondoliers give a sense of movement and transience; the passengers, a feeling of the immediacy of daily life.

In the left foreground is an architecturally distinctive two-storied portico, richly decorated with gilded profile portrait medallions of a Roman cast, but unabashedly non-classical in its detailing and capitals. It is here that the narrative moment is concentrated [Plate 91]. The patriarch emerges from a door at the left, followed by priests and men in togas and holding in both hands the heavy gilded reliquary of the True Cross of San Giovanni. He holds it above the head of a young man whose body is contorted and yet whose gaze is fixed upon the Cross. Unlike the other artists, Carpaccio chooses to capture the very act of healing – not the prayers of supplication and not the aftermath. No fantastic demon in the form of a basilisk – standard in exorcism iconography, and a major protagonist of Carpaccio's own *Miracle of St. Tryphon* in the Scuola di San Giorgio degli Schiavoni [Plate 112] – emerges from the mouth of the afflicted one. The wondrous exorcism is presented just as we would see it: dramatic and full of tension, but also in completely naturalistic terms.

Pushing the event to one side, Carpaccio removes it from the objective center of the painting and separates it from the life of the canal and the *fondamenta*. And yet he summons up a cast of supporting actors to draw our attention to it and endow it with a subjective centrality of its own. The white-robed brothers, both old and young, lean forward in attitudes of awe and devotion, focusing the viewer's attention on the act of healing. Two fall to their knees and others

XXI. Mansueti, *Miracle at the Bridge of San Lio* (Venice, Accademia)

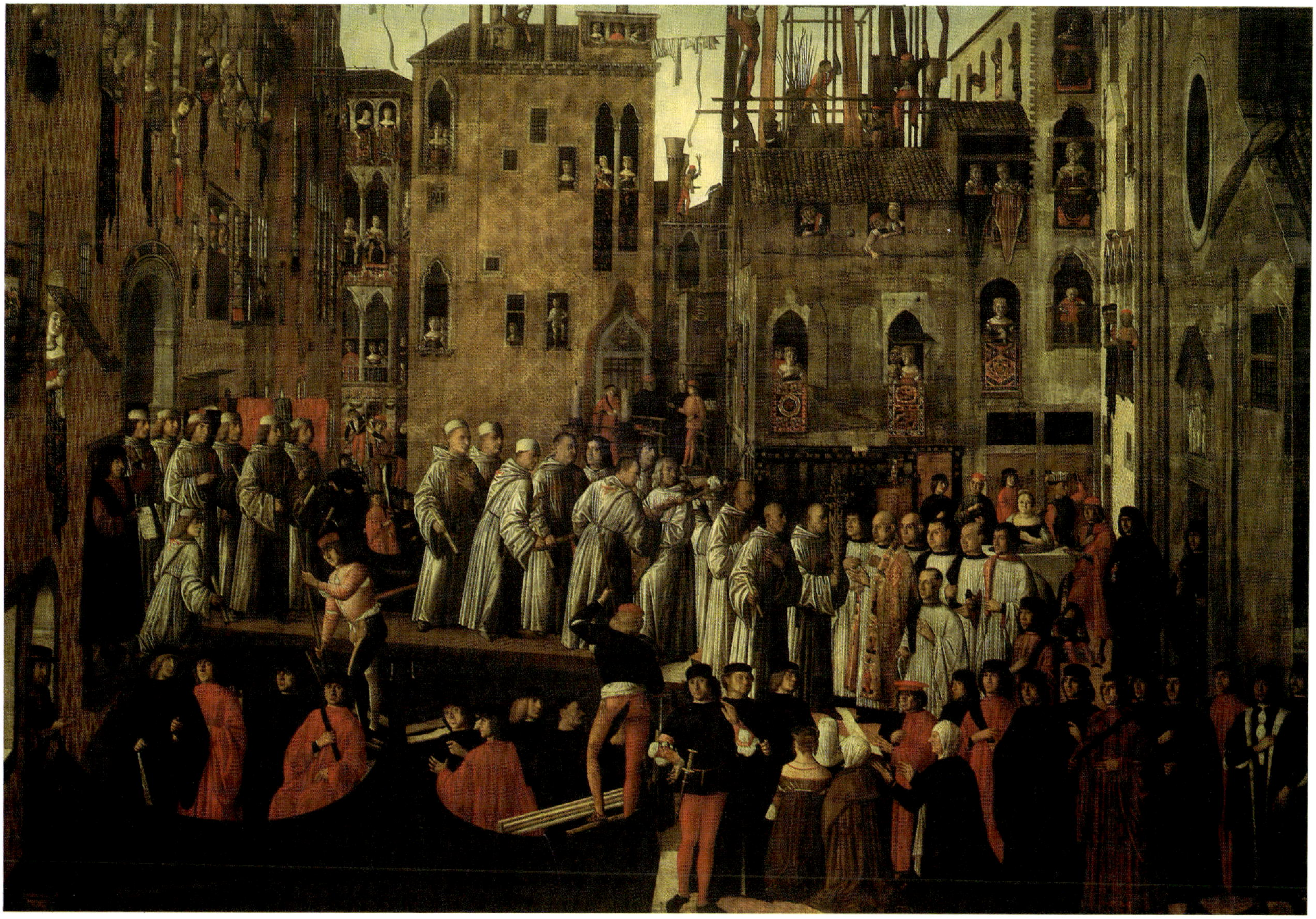

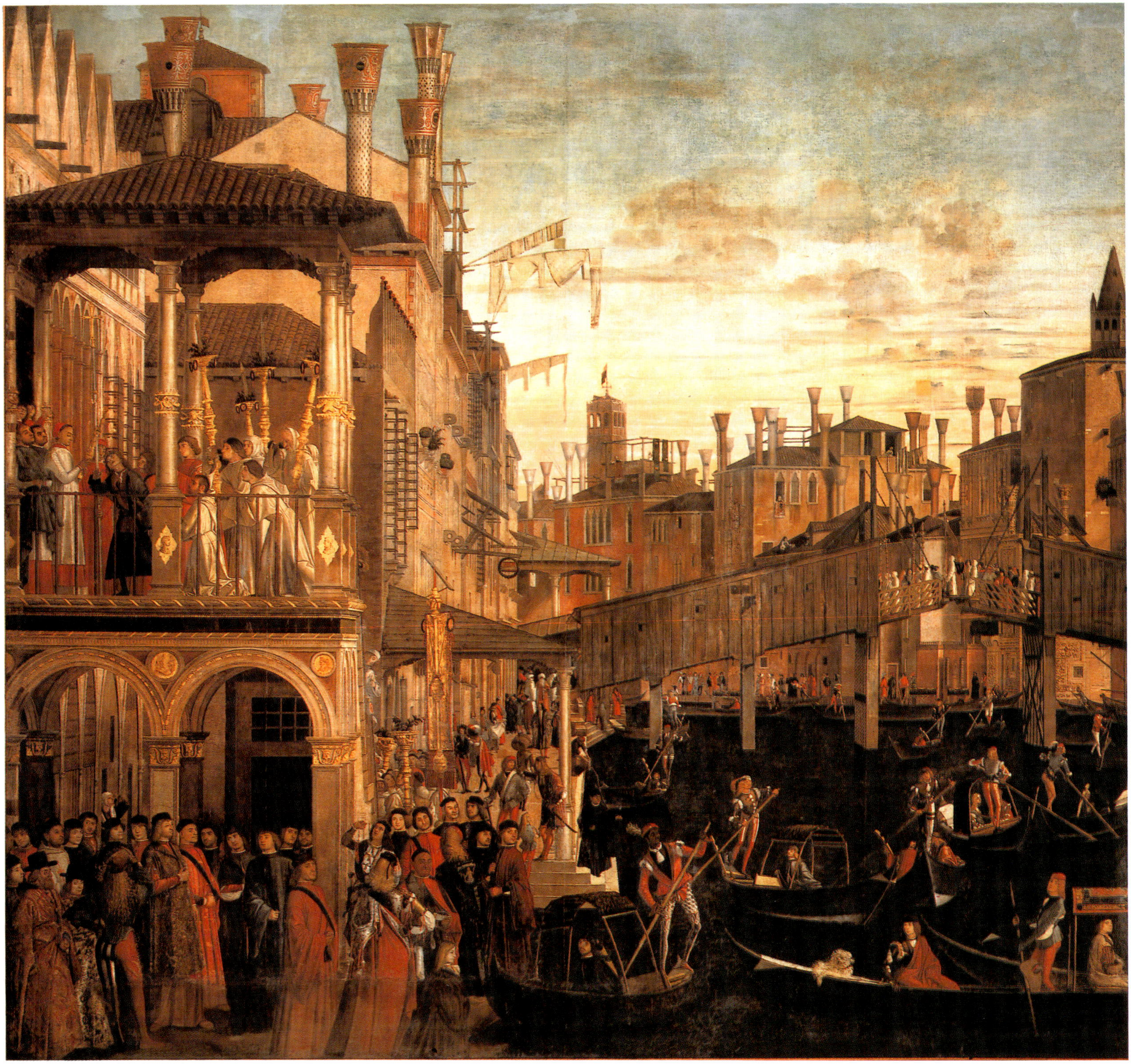

XXII. Carpaccio, *Healing of the Possessed Man* (*Exorcism*) (Venice, Accademia)

support *doppieri* – the double candlesticks which signal this a festive occasion. One clasps his hand to his head at the prodigy before him. Another stands behind the patriarch and the possessed man, holding the tall standard of a processional cross between them. On the ground below, two figures are aware of the unusual happenings above their heads: an old woman framed by the portico on the extreme left holds her hand above her forehead and looks upward, and likewise, a young man just to the right of the portico raises his arm in a gesture of surprise.

A similar stategy was used by Carpaccio in *St. Augustine in his Study*, in which he represented a scene from an apocryphal account of the life of St. Jerome. [Color Plate XIII]. Augustine recalled that he had just sat down at his desk to write Jerome a letter, when 'suddenly an indescribable light, not seen in our times, and hardly to be described in our poor language, entered the cell in which I was, with an ineffable and unknown fragrance, of all odors, at the hour of compline'.[50] Through that manifestation of unearthly light, Augustine wrote, he learned that Jerome had just died. In the painting, while Augustine sits with pen raised and looks toward the window, the small dog who draws back in surprise – the sole supporting actor – provides the real cue that we are viewing something more exceptional than simply a scholar going about his daily tasks by the light of a window.[51]

91. Carpaccio, detail from the *Healing of the Possessed Man* (Color Plate XXII)

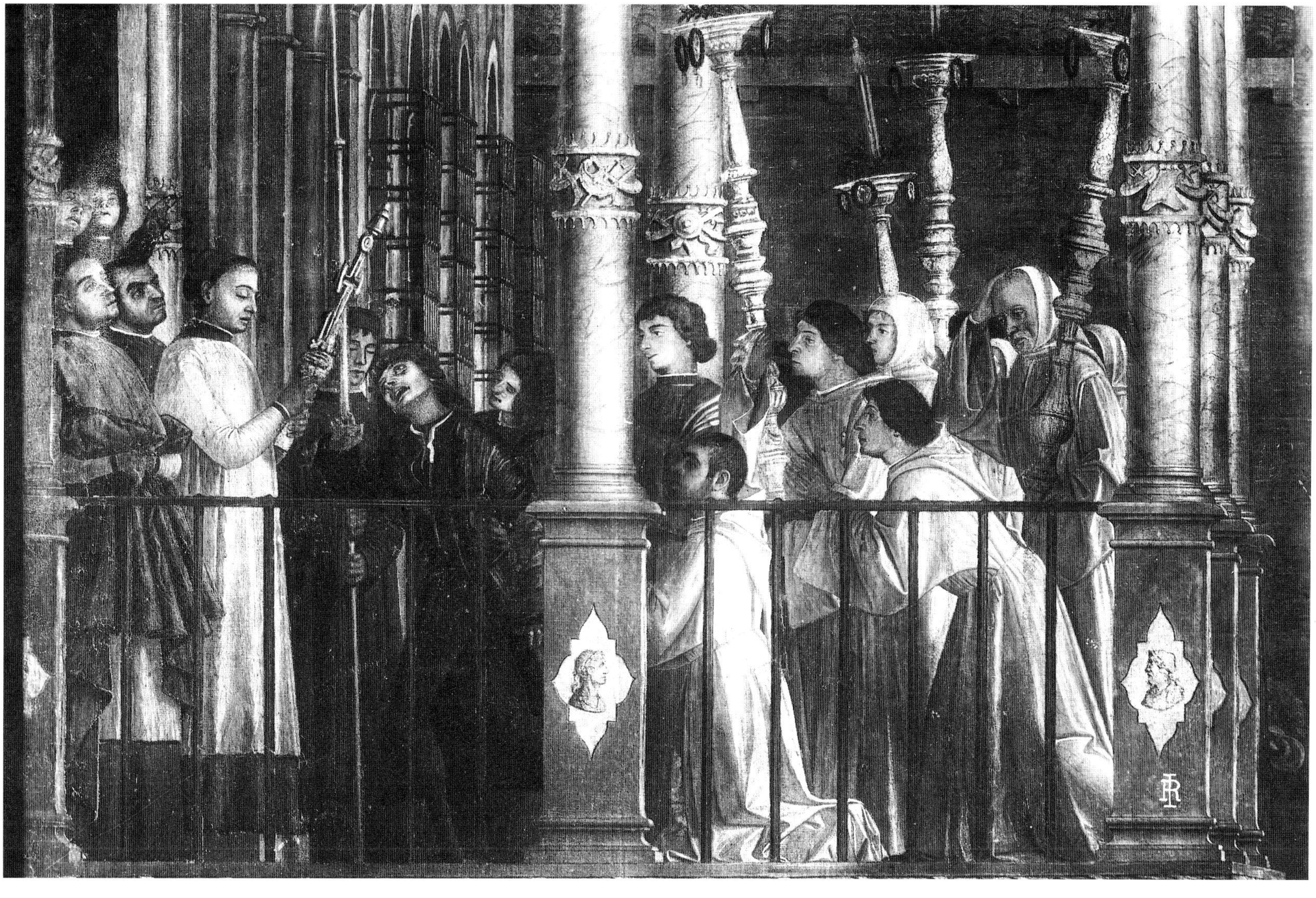

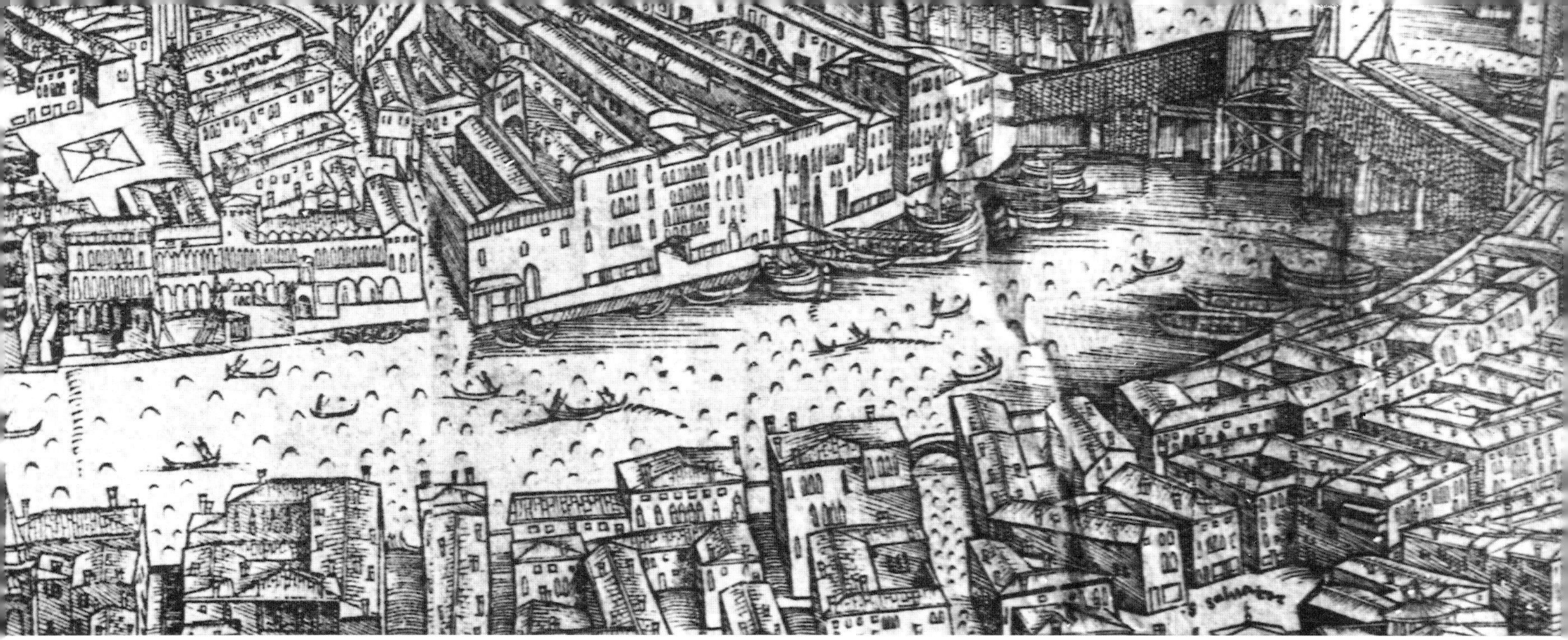

92. Jacopo dei Barbari, detail of the Rialto area from the *View of Venice*, 1500, with the palace of the Patriarch at the middle left (Venice, Museo Correr)

Returning to the *Exorcism*, we may observe that the ambient, on the whole, remains undisturbed: the distinguished assembly in the lower arcade of the portico gaze solemnly out at the viewer and the rest of the citizenry go about their affairs. Just as with Gentile Bellini, no detail, however minor, eludes Carpaccio's brush. The painted polychrome facades of the buildings, the decorated surfaces of the chimney-pots, a man repairing roof tiles, the shop sign of a well-known inn – the *Sturion* [Sturgeon] – the laundry hanging out to dry as in Mansueti's *San Lio*, and even a woman beating a carpet high on an *altana*, are all essential parts of the picture and necessary to confirm the historical authenticity of the event.

The two-tiered arrangement of the portico, which allows the inclusion of the group of portrait figures in the lower section, is probably also grounded in reality and not simply an invention of the artist to display the narrative action. For the Barbari *View* shows a general scheme and implantation which is similar to Carpaccio's representation [Plate 92]. Although it is difficult to discern with certainty the exact organization of the facade of the Patriarch's palace on the map, one can make out the zig-zag shaped cresting; the loggia that covers the foremost end of the Riva del Vin just behind it in the painting, as well as the small *rio* that separates them; and, most importantly, a structure that resembles the two-storied portico painted by Carpaccio. An open loggia on the canal facade, while unique in Veneto-Byzantine buildings, would probably have had a ceremonial function in the Patriarch's residence.[52] Carpaccio undoubtedly embellished considerably what was originally a simple structure. What is also apparent, if the Barbari plan is correct, is a suppression of spatial extension of the left foreground. The palace facade that extends well to the right of the portico on the Barbari plan has been strongly foreshortened in the painting, and flattened in a manner that recalls Gentile's procedure in the *Procession*.

In a sense, Carpaccio's composition appears the least contrived of all, and yet, to use a term of the later Renaissance, it must have required the most artifice. His lighter touch is evident in the carefully counterbalanced arrangement of the component parts of the composition. Depriving himself of a solid visual anchor in his perspective construction and choice of viewing-point, which hovers between the two levels of the portico in front, he offers a view wherein the permanent structures of wood and stone seem as transitory as the human protagonists. Here the vanishing-point for the buildings of the left foreground is located just below the formal center of the work, beneath the right bay of the loggia and behind the Rialto Bridge. On this unstable fulcrum the artist balances the deeper space on the right, with its single band of buildings and bridge poised between sky and water, against the physical mass of buildings and figures on the left that push against the picture surface. The curving canal affords no single focal point for the buildings on the right, and as they recede into the distance like stage flats, they provide with their horizontal emphasis a strong stabilizing element for the scene as a whole.

Unlike Gentile Bellini, Carpaccio selected the most dramatic moment to depict and rejected a centralized frontal view of the architectural setting to contain it. As a result, it was necessary to enlist the human agents, at home in their environment, to help stabilize and balance the composition. Let us see how this works. Gentile, along with the other artists, usually wished the primary narrative moment to be embedded and even subdued in a richly described environment; it was a mode of dramatic restraint. Carpaccio, by contrast, allows the miraculous exorcism its due dramatic force, but he offsets this in the most natural way with the competing activity and interest of life on the canal. The seemingly loose arrangement of gondolas and their passengers provides the diversity and visual excitement necessary to counterweight the compacted action of the exorcism on the left. The bright dots of color and flashes of white against the dark green water of the canal produce a staccato effect that draws the eye away from the miracle, and gives it the feel of authenticity by denying it a privileged position. Thus the composition is counterbalanced not only in its architectural massing, but also in the competing activities of the human protagonists both within and outside the central drama.

By rejecting the firmly centered and almost planar implantations of the other artists and by making the human figure an integral part of the scheme, Carpaccio represented the reciprocal relationship between man and his made environment that captured the essence of the physical city. In so doing he conveyed at the same time a sense of the momentary quality and ephemeral nature of both.

Compared with Gentile Bellini and Mansueti, Carpaccio struck a finer balance. While Gentile Bellini subordinated the figures to the constructed physical setting, Mansueti took considerable liberties with the spatial construction in order to adapt the stage to accommodate the copious cast of characters. But Carpaccio dealt with men and the physical environment in a 'polyphonic' manner. Playing one against the other responsively during the design process, he did not allow visual circumstance and description to overwhelm the narrative event and deny it its due weight. Carpaccio's near contemporaries recognized that his achievement was due little to an 'innocent eye' and even less to chance. In his treatise on perspective, Daniele Barbaro praised Carpaccio for his equivalence to Giovanni Bellini, 'in many of his perspective operations worthy by common judgment of eternal fame...' Both artists, he wrote, sought to perfect their use of perspective, not only to please their teacher, 'but to be better able to form their intentions truly in the eyes of the beholder'.[53]

In each of the works we have seen, the narrative core is anchored to a lesser or greater degree in the substance of normal and ongoing daily affairs. It is this quality that has caused art historians to view the religious *istorie* of Venetian artists from Jacopo Bellini through to Carpaccio as pious pretexts for profane interests, and as examples of secularizing tendencies within the society at large. And yet, if we look again at these triumphantly sumptuous canvases, however full of decorative dazzle, pomp, circumstance, ceremonial display and even trivia, we are forced to concede just how very serious they are. The *sanctissima croce* was to them no frivolous toy; it was an instrument of genuine power and sacredness. It imbued the area around it with a divine charisma – that is, in this case, the Rialto, the Piazza San Marco, the *campi* and *rii* of the city and, not least, the environs of the confraternity.[54]

The Cross, moreover, was an instrument controlled by the Scuola. During the later fifteenth century a tendency developed to withhold the relic from frequent public display in processions. At issue was the element of privileged access. Just as class lines were hardening, and entry to the Ducal Chancery as well as Scuola office was becoming more restrictive, so too the control of the holy object became increasingly a matter of concern to the group.[55] Even when their impact is maximized by rarity, rituals and processions are ephemeral things. To keep them present in the minds of spectators, reminders are necessary. The cycle of *istorie* in the *albergo* thus provided not only a suitable frame or setting for the relic, but also made visible in the most permanent manner its constant relationship to the men of the Scuola and the essential place of these men as guardians of virtue and guarantors of holiness in the society as a whole.

10

History As Ceremonial

The pre-eminence of ceremonial activities in the Venetian visual world is amply attested to by the processions depicted in the True Cross paintings, as well as by the attention given to them away from Venice by those professional eyewitnesses, the *viaggiatori*. Indeed, throughout Europe during this period, the 'ritual moment' was often the focus of any public occasion: the entry to the city, the civic or religious procession, the formal reception at court, the presentation of gifts [Color Plate XXIV]. All of these ritualistic forms were emblematic. They provided fixed points of reference for more extended activities. Renaissance artists thus tended to represent larger historical events in terms of the formalized ceremonial connected to them.[1] The meeting of heads of state – the local prince entertaining a visiting duke, for example – could be epitomized by the artist through the depiction of the formal entry of the duke into the city.[2]

Likewise, the Pope's consignment of *trionfi* to the Doge in the paintings of the Great Council Hall of Venice created a succession of repetitive ritual presentations, each of which symbolized certain abstract rights or privileges and, at the same time, implied a wider chain of events. In *The Pope Welcomes the Doge to Rome*, depicted in the Correr manuscript (as well as in the Great Council Hall), the Doge stands alone, while the Pope confers upon him the ceremonial banners and trumpets carried by the reception committee [Plate 93].[3] In a concrete narrative sense, this single action stands for the trip to Rome from

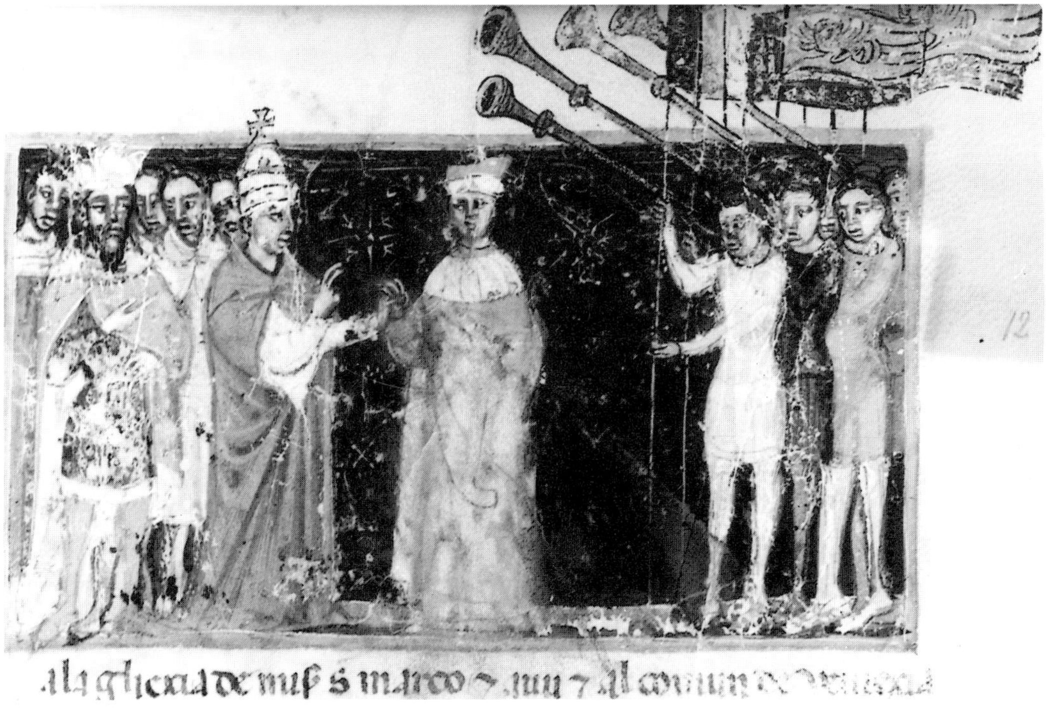

93. Venetian school, *The Pope Welcomes the Doge to Rome*, miniature (Venice, Museo Correr: Cod. Correr I, 383 [=1497])

Ancona, the entry to the city wherein the Doge is given a king's *adventus*, and the procession to the Lateran palace that followed. In a symbolic sense, these *trionfi* stand for the Doge's royal dignity and Venice's sovereignty.

The eyewitness painters with whom we are dealing were also prone to take such options, and in a far more elaborate form than we see in the Correr manuscript. They have rightly been called *pittori di cerimonia* – painters of ceremony. Their preference for emphasizing the ceremonial component of any given event is easy to take for granted. In some instances, they must simply have recorded what they saw. But the practice had further implications. If we examine it more closely, we discern three progressive levels of realization in Venetian artists' depictions of the ritual event during this period. The first level is the recording or representation of real ceremonies and rituals, whether or not actually observed by the artist, as in the True Cross cycle. Out of these potentially direct experiences, the painters developed compositional strategies that became what we might call 'ceremonial paradigms'. The second level is the application of these paradigms to a wholly invented visual narrative in a fictive setting, as in Carpaccio's *Life of St. Ursula*. And the third is their employment to construct narrative scenes that refer to no overt ceremonial or ritual action at all, as in a number of Carpaccio's paintings for the other *scuole piccole* and in Gentile Bellini's *St. Mark Preaching in Alexandria*.

THE RITUAL MOMENT

In order to understand the reportage of public ceremonial observances, it is necessary to stand back for a moment and consider their function in the life of a Renaissance city. Every community had a cycle of recurring feasts, as well as special occasions like princely entries. By virtue of its singular physical environment, public ceremonial in Venice had taken on an exceptional splendor. No traveler's diary was complete without an awe-struck account of one or more civic ceremonies. Praising Venice for its 'magnificent and pompous celebration of the feasts', the German priest, Felix Fabri, reflected a common view of the city's readiness to rise to the festive occasion, whether sacred or secular. He cited the great religious feast-days of St. Mark, the Sensa and Corpus Christi as the most impressive, but noted that likewise,

> on the entries of princes and ambassadors one sees marvels; and if the fleet arrives or the captain of the army, or [for] announcement of peace or of a desired alliance signed, they proclaim days of amusement, with incessant pealing of the bells and bonfires on their towers in the evening. By day they go in boats to the sea playing music and shooting fireworks, and set fire to the worn-out sails; such are the enjoyments of the solemnities. At these the Venetian matrons appear dressed with so much pomp and with so much style, that you would not believe them to be Christian ladies, but Trojan matrons, even hand-maidens of Helen and of Venus.[5]

As Fabri implied, civic festivity was an integral part of the elaborate diplomatic etiquette of the time. To the visitor of rank, it was a visible sign of the city's honor and piety, as well as of its prosperity. Upon his arrival at Fusina in 1495, the embarkation point for the city from the mainland, the French ambassador Philippe de Commynes had been greeted by twenty-five patricians, 'well and richly dressed', he noted approvingly, 'in beautiful fabrics of silk and scarlet'. Conducted by them along the Grand Canal, he observed: 'It is the most triumphant city that I have ever seen, and that gives most honor to ambassadors and foreigners, and which is the most wisely governed, and where the service of God is most solemnly made...'[6]

Venetian ceremonial thus addressed two audiences: the citizen and the stranger. Upon occasion these audiences could be very large indeed, with the spectators in the area of the Piazza San Marco alone equalling the population of a good-sized city of the period. Sanudo described the huge crowd which had turned out for the Palm Sunday procession in 1495 to celebrate the formation of the Holy League opposing Charles VIII of France:

> In the piazza there was a very great quantity of people, so that one could not pass nor get around; for everything was full. There seemed to be 68,000 in the piazza, on the palace [and] the balconies, and in the church.[7]

By the end of the fifteenth century in Venice, such spectacles had come to play an indispensable role in the presentation of the city to its inhabitants and to others. They were in no way marginal to civic life in the way parades are today. As Edward Muir has shown, the official fête was a major vehicle for reaffirming and propagating the myth of Venice and for adapting it to the needs of each generation. Because ephemeral, spectacle was a responsive genre, capable of addressing the historical necessity. As Muir put it, 'The significant demanded ritual.'[8]

Diagrams of society

According to recent studies, one aim of group public rituals of this sort is to eliminate ambiguities within the social order by giving visible structure, and thus legitimacy, to certain interpretations of civic reality.[9] It has often been pointed out that a Venetian procession created a diagram of society – immediately graspable at a glance. By showing how things were, or at least how they were meant to be, such processions conveyed a potent message of order and stability. The eyes of Renaissance people were well attuned to interpret visible marks of social rank. In 1502, Angelo Gabrieli, a Venetian patrician, recorded the triumphal progress through northern Italy of Anne of Foix, the bride of Ladislaw, King of Hungary. As the bride entered Padua on her way to Venice, Gabrieli observed:

> It was beautiful to see the respective orders. There were about six hundred French nobles with necklaces of gold, and some Hungarian captains with superb horses, with manes [cut] Spartan style, and with battle armor. The Paduan youth were radiant, crowned with laurel wreaths [and] dressed in silk with gold and silver embroidery. And with this march, it became crowded with the great number of peasants who filled the roads, up to three miles from Padua, where the Podestà with every class of citizens stood waiting the arrival of the Queen.[10]

In Venice itself, the various orders would also have their respective places in any ceremonial event. A series of woodcuts from the middle of the sixteenth century shows the prescribed sequence of the ducal segment for the Palm Sunday procession [Plates 95–8].[11] Marchers were ranked in a hierarchy

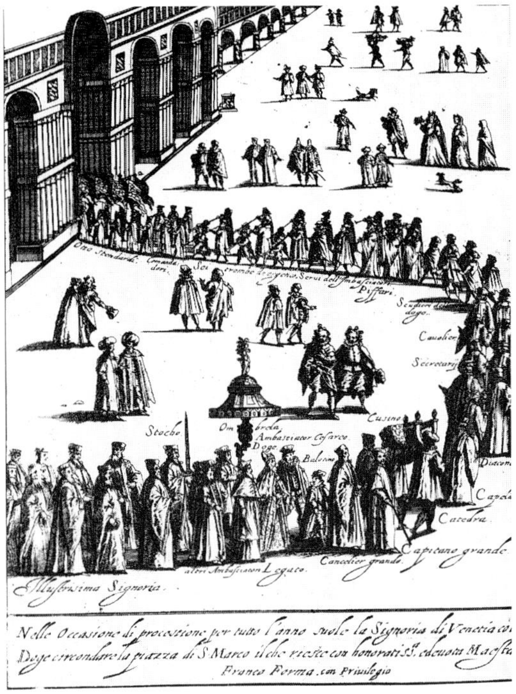

94. Giacomo Franco, *Ducal Procession with Ambassadors* (Venice, Museo Correr)

XXIII (facing). Mansueti, detail from the *Healing of the Daughter of Ser Nicolò Benvegnudo of San Polo* (Plate 90)

according to office and class. Beginning with the musicians, the non-noble functionaries of the Chancery, and the clergy, the line continued with the Patriarch, the citizen secretaries and the bearers of ducal insignia. It culminated in the Doge, who led off the foreign ambassadors and the fully patrician segment, with senators and magistrates. The ladies of the city were displayed in the windows above as spectators and ornaments of the event. In a real, living procession, the political, social and religious establishment at any given time was laid out as if on a map.

Modifications appropriate to the occasion could personalize the procession, but the principles remained the same. On the feast-day of St. Mark, depicted by Gentile Bellini in the *Procession in the Piazza San Marco*, the ducal segment duplicated that for Palm Sunday [Color Plate XXV], but the Scuole Grandi led off the entire parade. Or alternatively, in a print by Giacomo Franco, recording ambassadorial processions 'per tutto l'anno', one sees the servants of the ambassadors replacing the Chancery officials and the Patriarch, who are not essential to this particular occasion [Plate 94].[12]

That the display of such distinctions was important in the period of the eyewitness painters, even to Venetians who were placed well below the top of the hierarchy, is indicated by the disputes over processional order which erupted among groups like the Scuole Grandi, who prided themselves on their good citizenship. In 1451 two *scuole* in procession came to blows over the right of way in the Campo San Salvador, initiating a free-for-all that continued along the Spezieria into the Piazza San Marco, 'with the scandal of many'. The Council of Ten took quick action, making firm orders of precedence that were duly recorded in the Mariegola of the Scuola Grande di San Marco:

> Scuole going or returning from the processions cannot go against another one or interfere with it, crossing the road. And the one that enters first in a *calle* will be allowed to pass and the other will wait until it has passed. And thus also it will be observed in the Piazza under penalty of expulsion from the Scuola and whatever would be determined by the Council of Ten.[13]

Further measures prescribing appropriate deportment were taken again in 1513, following brawls that had erupted before the Good Friday procession in the Piazza San Marco. Here the issue was the position of the various confraternities within the parade.[14] Such disruptions do not necessarily indicate impiety or a deep-seated dissatisfaction with the order of things in Venetian society. Rather they reveal an acute awareness by the Scuola members of the importance of such ceremonies and of a preferred placement in them.

To some, then, the public procession offered an opportunity to reaffirm their group identity and status by marching in the white robes of a confraternity or in a red senatorial toga. To others, particularly the women, it was a time to display one's family wealth – and that of the polity – by dressing up. For clothing was also an instrument of statecraft, and sumptuary laws were frequently suspended in order to display the wealth of the Venetian state and to pay sufficient honor to visiting dignitaries.[15]

As central events of the annual ritual calendar, recurring processions thus displayed and reinforced the social hierarchy, with all its distinctions and differences of rank, role and class. Furthermore, by suggesting broad participation in the affairs of the city, they also provided the means for cohesion within that very unequal society.[16]

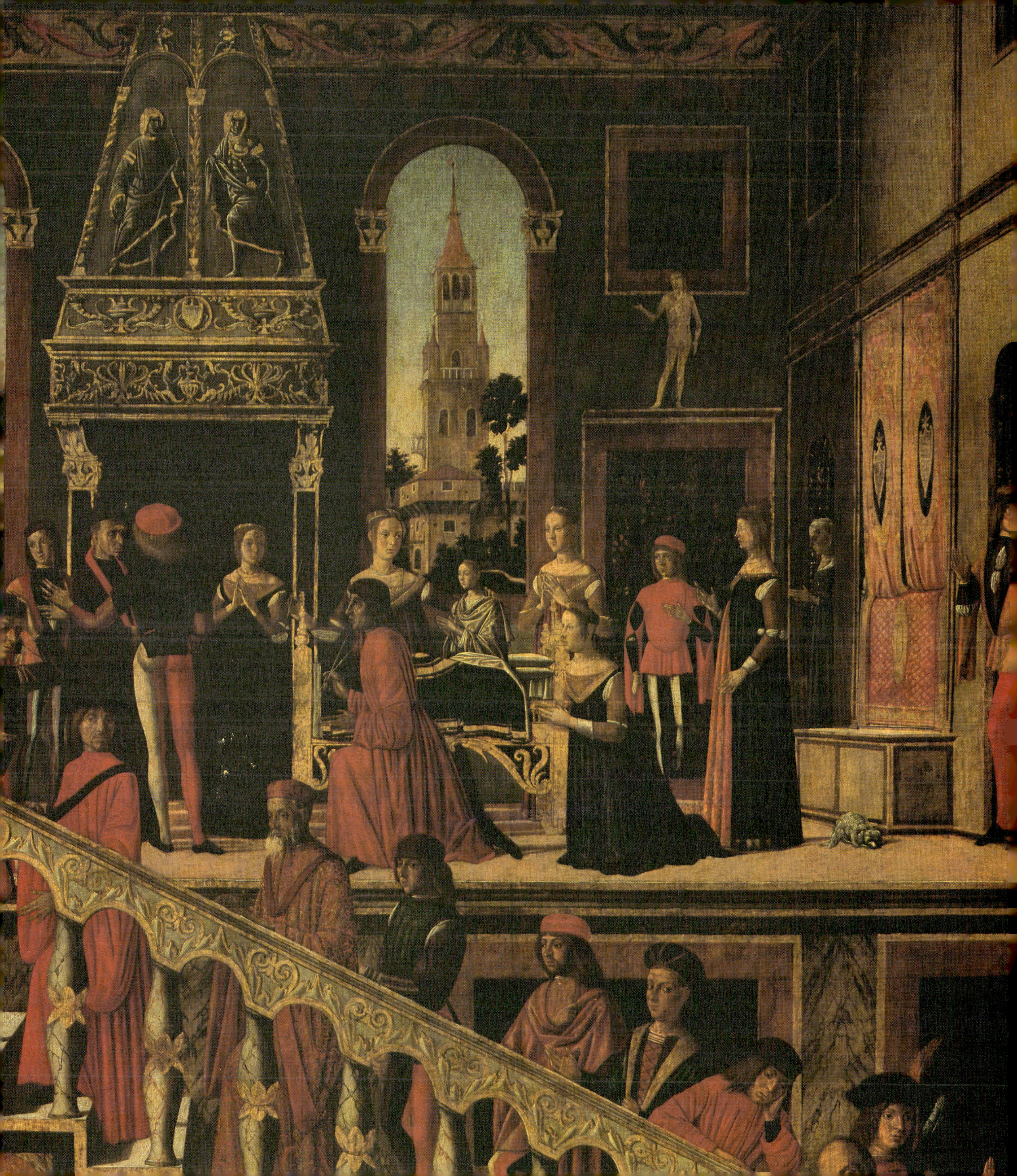

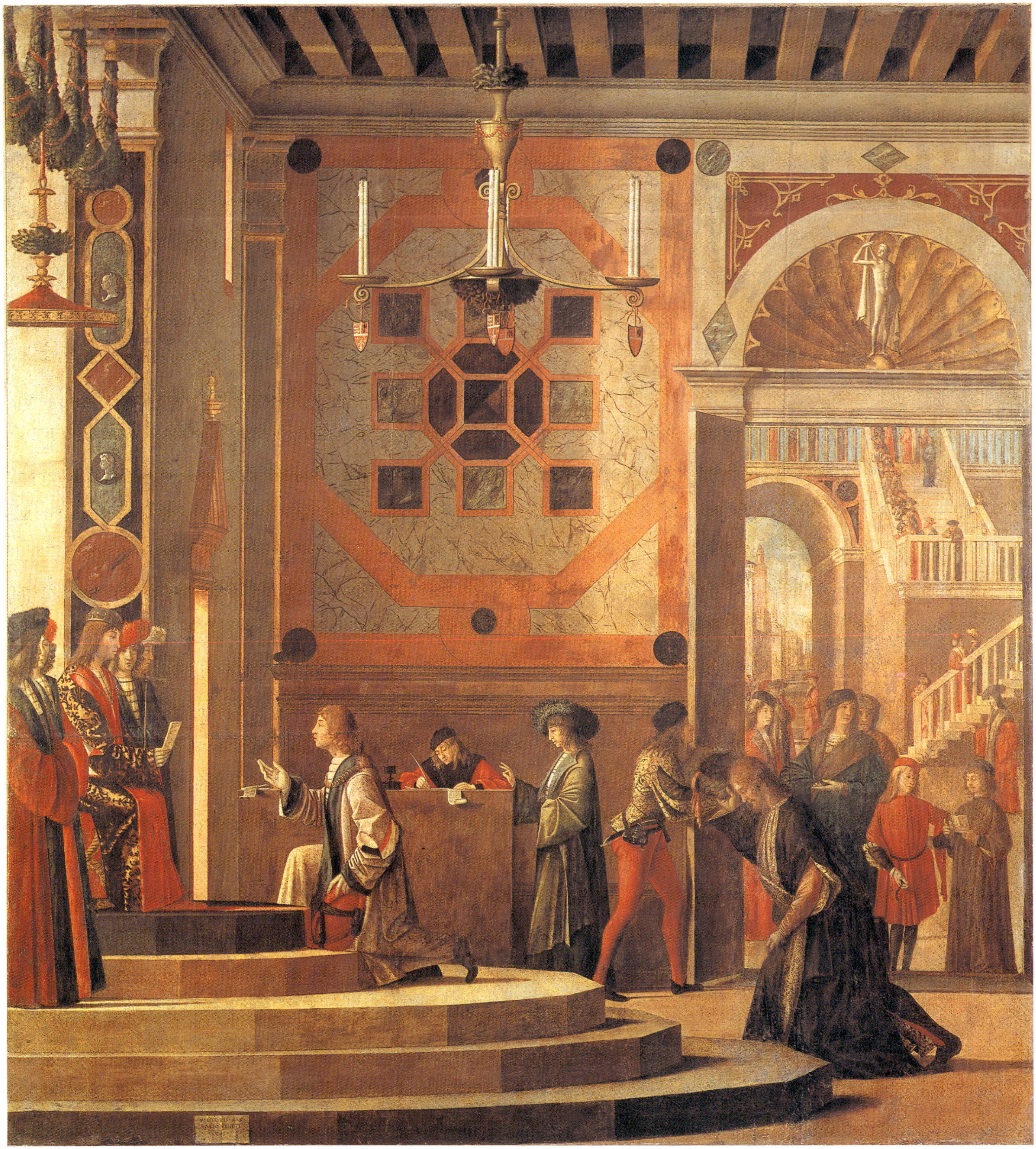

XXIV. Carpaccio, *Departure of the Ambassadors* (Venice, Accademia)

Recording the spectacle

By the early sixteenth century, civic ritual was becoming a professional matter and a corps of ceremonial specialists was in the making. They would be drawn from the secretarial order of *cittadini* who staffed the Ducal Chancery, and who were involved in the patronage of narrative painting – as well as in the stage-production of their own ceremonial devices – as officers of the Scuole Grandi. A typical example was Gasparo de la Vedoa, a member of the Ducal Chancery who had held office as Vicario in the Scuola Grande di San Marco in 1499. As a secretary to the Council of Ten in 1513, he was empowered with the weighty responsibility of censoring for their political content the *tableaux vivants* of the Scuole Grandi and the clergy in a procession celebrating a peace treaty with France. These were the dark years following the War of the League of Cambrai. Scrutiny of the festival devices was necessary, Sanudo wrote, 'so that they would not be offensive to any king or potentate of the world'.[17]

It is not surprising that measures were taken to record such deeply satisfying but ephemeral events, so that protocol could be standardized and experiences could be replicated. In 1593, a Chancery secretary was ordered to compile an official *Libro Cerimoniale*. Some of the entries gave prescriptions for recurrent observances, such as the colors to be worn by members of the Signoria on major holy days[18] or the proper formalities for the reception of cardinals.[19] Other entries described a wide variety of specific events: the *adventus* of the Emperor Frederick III in 1468; the proclamation of a league with the Duke of Milan and the Republic of Florence in 1474; the propitiatory procession ordered in 1579 to bring an end to two months of continuous rain.[20] The purpose of these accounts was more than anecdotal, for they were to serve as an ongoing reference for similar observances.[21] The power of ritual lies in its repetition.

Most of these ceremonies were products of their own time and were eventually forgotten, but we still get a sense of that festive city of the late Quattrocento, which had astounded Fabri and was so assiduously recorded by Sanudo, in the visual records of the eyewitness painters.

Extenders of time

It may be argued that their paintings were more than mere records. In his *Procession* Gentile Bellini depicted a celebration that he had personally witnessed on numerous occasions over the course of a long lifetime. Indeed, as a member of a Scuola Grande himself, he would have participated year after year in the St. Mark's Day procession, an annual event that ensured the patron saint's continuing attention to the city.[22] If familiar to the viewer, any ritual action transcends the particular occasion, for it recalls like actions of past, present and future. Seen in this light, then, the St. Mark's Day procession could act as an extender of time. And Gentile's reference in that procession to a unique – indeed extraordinary – narrative event such as a miraculous healing, situated that event within a normative or universalizing context.

All similar occasions that the viewer had seen or was yet to see gave resonance to the artist's allusion to this single miracle. They were given resonance back in return when the viewer returned to the next St. Mark's Day procession with an image of the painting in his mind. That the kneeling supplicant was not given

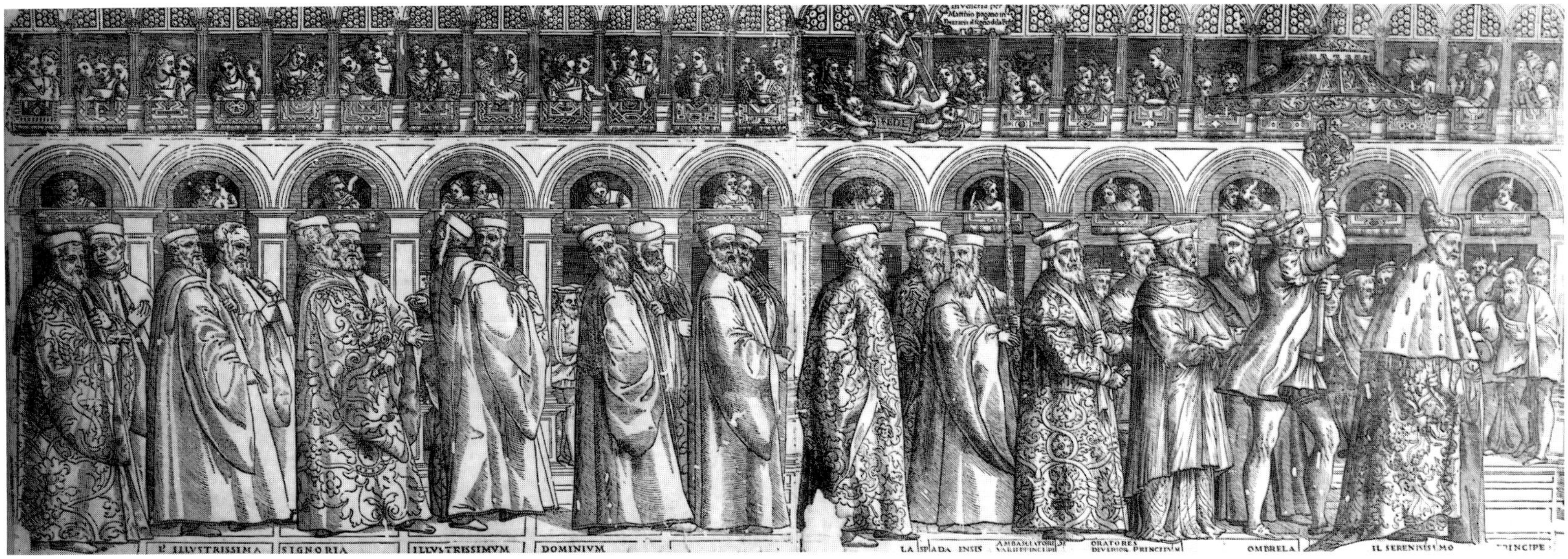

95. Matteo Pagan, *Procession of the Doge*, Segment 1, woodcut (Venice, Museo Correr)

much prominence in the composition as a whole was not really important. He was there more as an emblem. What was truly significant was that here a ritual occasion had created an opportunity in which the holy could happen, and this occasion with its stylized order and movement imparted a sense of timelessness and continuity that stretched beyond the single event depicted.

A recurrent procession therefore provided a base-line for all similar observances. It was a 'mental anchor'. Its reassuring predictability allowed any departure from the norm to become notable and noted. The gold cloth hung on the columns of the Basilica of the Palm Sunday procession of 1495 was thus proclaimed by Sanudo: 'a new thing and never done before'.[23] For the artist, a procession could function, furthermore, as a 'visual anchor' in a narrative painting. The procession was a 'given'; it was part of the furniture of the occasion. As such, it became a vehicle of familiar order. This aspect allowed the artist to give structure to a narrative situation without it looking contrived.

For example, in Gentile Bellini's *Procession*, the Scuole Grandi of the city led off the St. Mark's Day parade, just as they always did. The processional movement was orderly, just as it was supposed to be; it provided the structure

97. Matteo Pagan, *Procession of the Doge*, Segment 3, woodcut (Venice, Museo Correr)

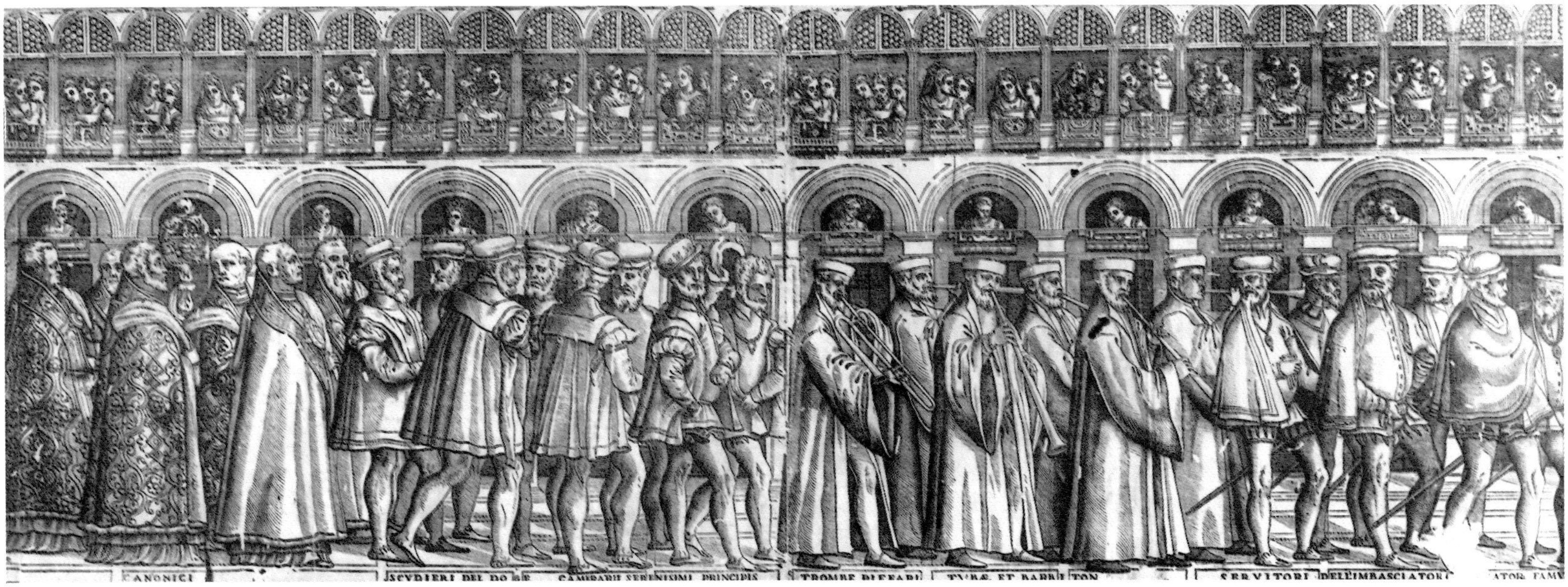

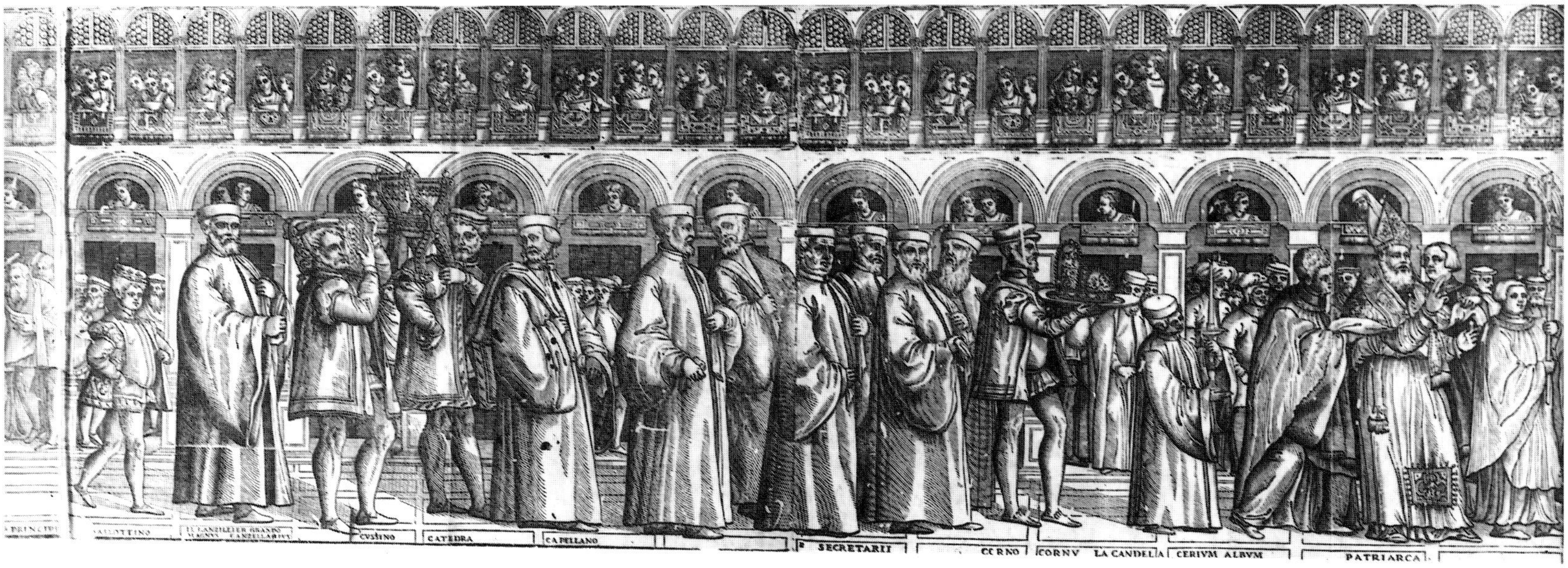

96. Matteo Pagan, *Procession of the Doge*, Segment 2, woodcut (Venice, Museo Correr)

for the composition as a whole. The most significant variables would have stood out immediately to the practised eye: the precise position of the Scuola di San Giovanni, directly preceding the ducal segment; the kneeling supplicant, bareheaded and clad in red, visible through a break in the line of marchers; and probably other features (unknown to us) that were 'a new thing and never done before'. The familiarity of the event allowed Gentile to make an unobtrusive but immediately recognizable reference to the miracle. He could thus retain the unpremeditated quality that made an *istoria* look credible and truthful to a Venetian viewer.

Forming the Paradigm

Let us consider further the representation of a procession. It posed certain problems for the artist. We need to remember that processions do not just go sideways and that they could just as well be depicted from several other vantage-points. The frontal view was already a well-established model in manu-

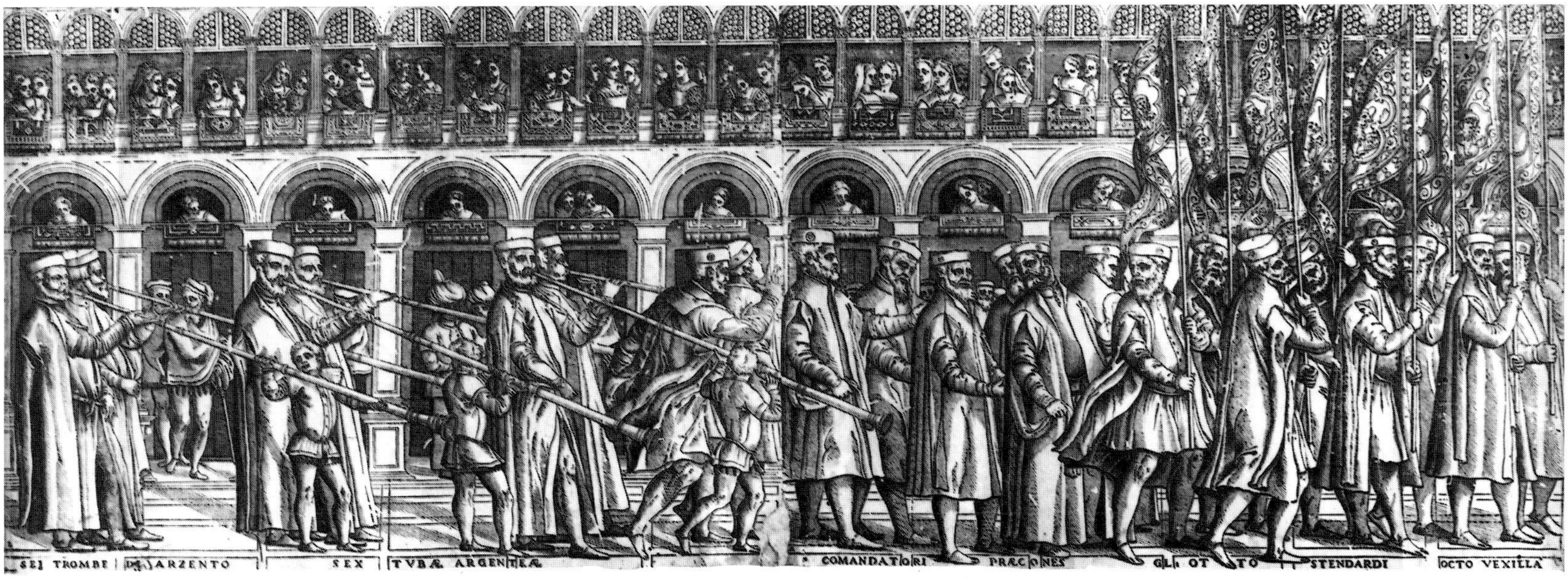

98. Matteo Pagan, *Procession of the Doge*, Segment 4, woodcut (Venice, Museo Correr)

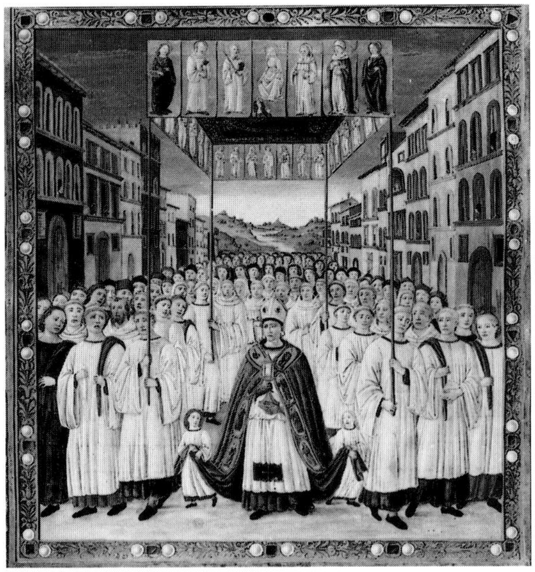

99. Attavante degli Attavanti, *Corpus Christi Procession in Florence* (Florence, Biblioteca Laurenziana, Chorale 4, c. 7v)

script illumination, as we see from numerous illustrations of Petrarch's *Trionfi.*[24] Such views, however, represent the event more as an arrival than as an ongoing process. The Florentine artist Attavante degli Attavanti uses a similar format in his miniature of a Corpus Christi procession [Plate 99]. Here the marchers come directly toward the viewer, an arrangement that has certain disadvantages. While it gives the impression of mass, the articulation and sequence of the different parts of the procession are obscured. Furthermore, it makes it difficult to convey the semblance of movement and once again becomes more of a portrait than a process.

Jacopo Bellini also experimented with the frontal procession in his *Funeral of the Virgin* [Plate 100]. Attempting to combine sequence with forward motion through a diagonal path of movement, he succeeded only in producing a forced effect. With the low viewing-point, the recessive tendency was too compelling. The viewer's eye was drawn irresistibly away from the marchers and toward the city gate where the focal point of the composition was located.

An unknown Venetian artist in the circle of Lazzaro Bastiani also attempted to represent the diplomatic entry of a prince or other dignitary from a frontal view-point, but again the effect is less than impressive [Plate 101]. The painting is located in the Museo Correr, and its precise subject is unknown; we will call it simply the Correr *Arrival.*[25] The location is the Piazzetta, with the two columns in the background marking the official entry portal to the city. Here the artist has raised the viewing-point so that the ground plane is more visible. In the central field, the Doge, flanked by two visiting dignitaries wearing shorter robes and the golden chains of knighthood, approaches the entrance to the Ducal Palace. These figures are followed by a double row of about thirty patricians, a typical Venetian reception committee for visitors of high rank.[26] The setting has breadth and depth and a clear spatial structure, but the processional escort straggles into the distance in compliance with the rules of linear perspective, and virtually gets lost in the ambient. Indeed, what is meant to be a spectacle is not very spectacular.

100. Jacopo Bellini, *Funeral of the Virgin* (Paris, Louvre Album, fol. 11)

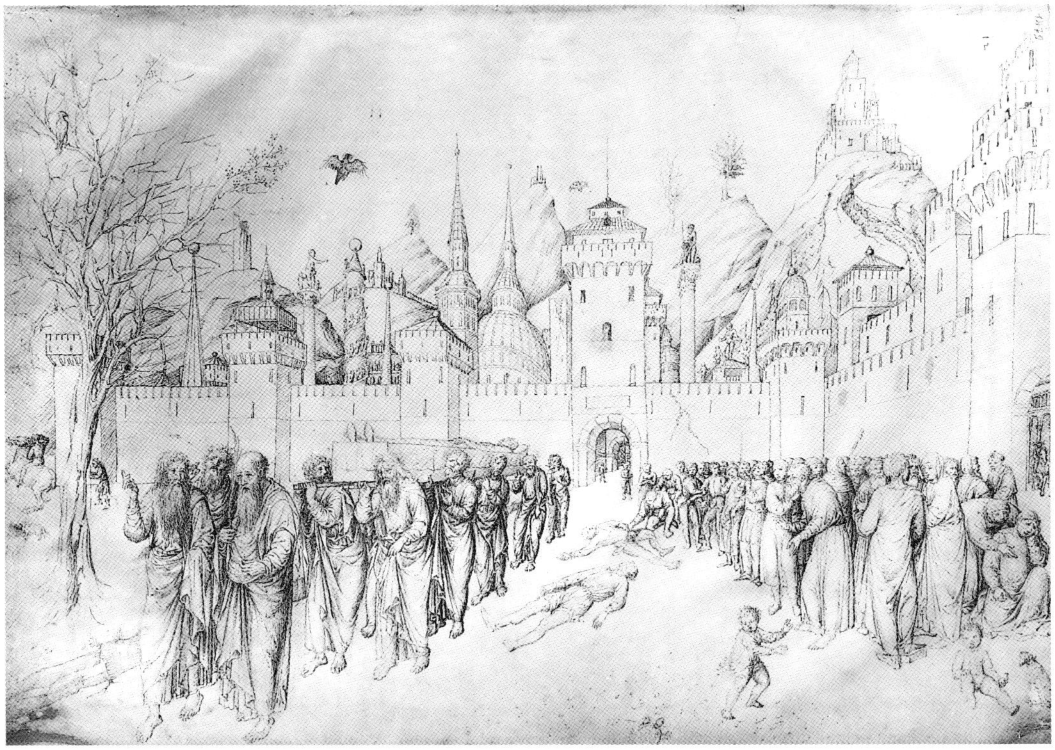

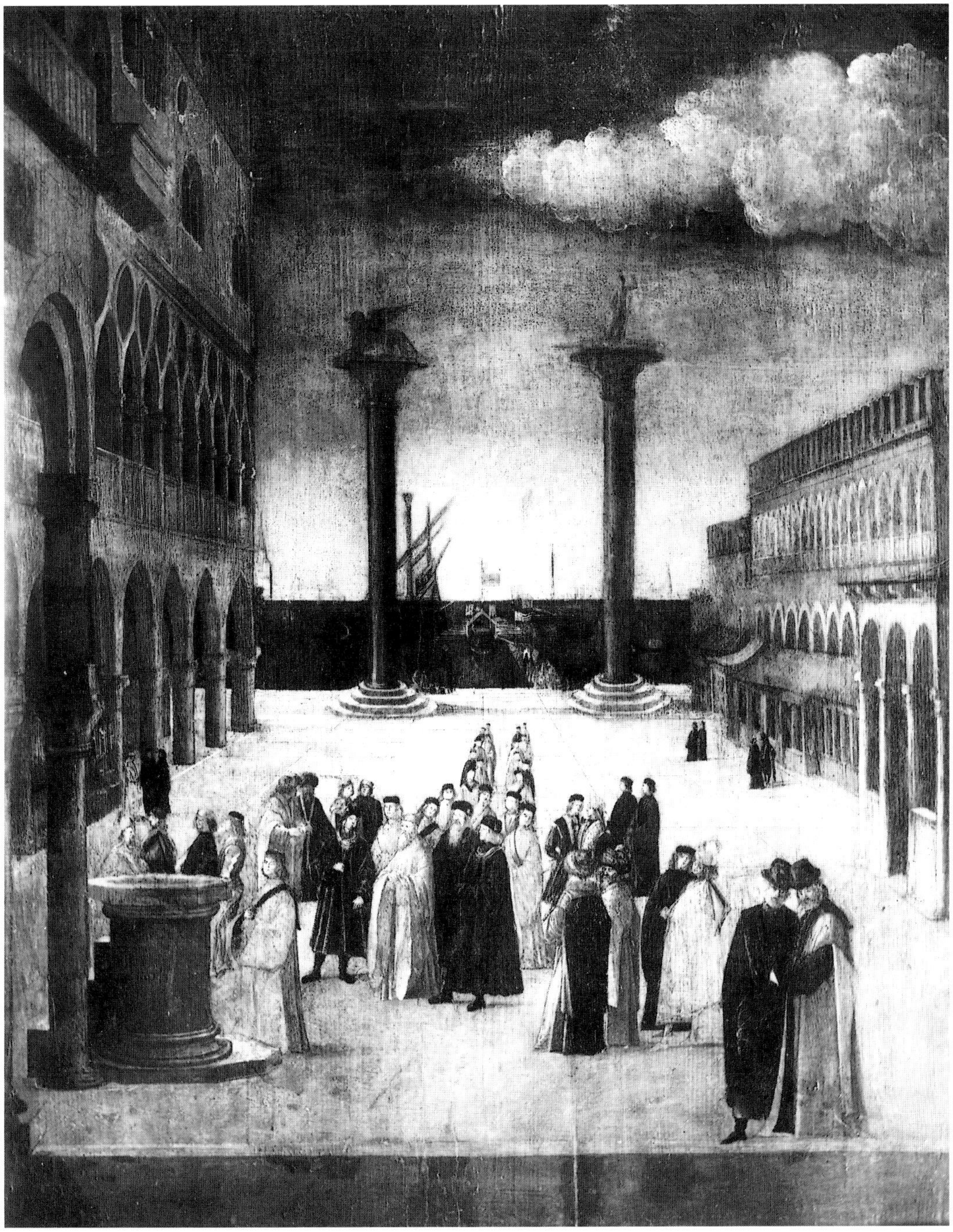

101. Circle of Lazzaro Bastiani, *Arrival of a Dignitary* (Venice, Museo Correr)

The Correr *Arrival* is instructive in its shortcomings, for it throws into sharp relief the problem faced by a painter of ceremonial: that of organizing large numbers of celebrants and spectators within the picture space in a readable, rational and hopefully splendid manner. Another option was that used by an engraver of a later date to record the procession celebrating the Holy League of 1571. Here a high birds-eye viewpoint allows the massed grandeur of community participation to be displayed on the ground plane like a map [Plate

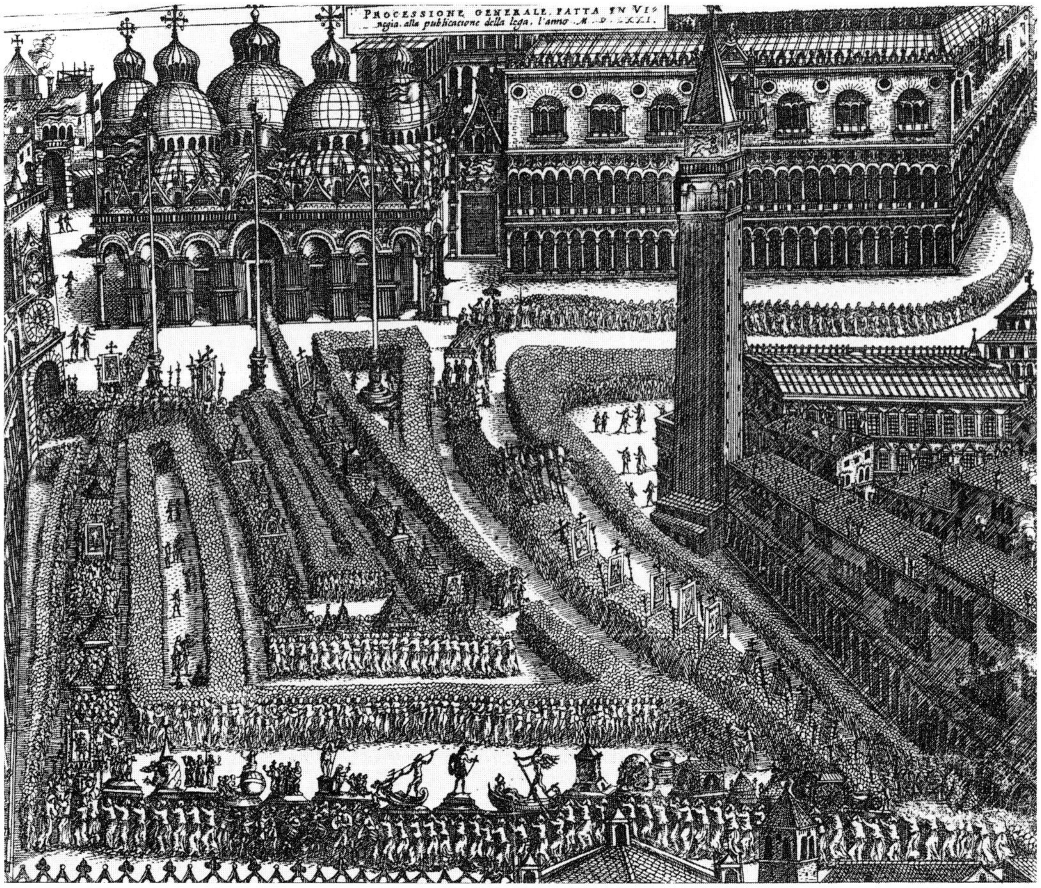

102. *Procession for the Holy League of 1571*, engraving (Venice, Museo Correr, Cod. Cicogna 760)

102]. The artist maintained the celebratory aspect, but the separate participants are not recognizable. He could not, moreover, avoid the heavy-handed look of contrivance.

These were not feasible solutions for the eyewitness painters. They wanted both an expansive picture space and also prominence for the individual figures. For them, the time-honored paradigm of the 'narrative frieze' provided the answer. The model was, of course an ancient one, used since late antiquity on the walls of churches throughout Italy. It was also prevalent in the Quattrocento in every genre of art, from cassone panels, tapestries and book illustration to the great narrative frescoes of Piero della Francesca and Ghirlandaio.[27] It appeared as well on the canvases of Mantegna, with his frieze-like representation of the Roman triumph.[28]

We do not know enough about the compositions of the frescoes of the Great Council Hall even to speculate as to their specific influence, but the narrative frieze was embedded deeply in the Venetian visual consciousness in the mosaics of the Basilica of San Marco. These would have provided venerable and compelling paradigms for narrative representation, which were ever-present and ever-available for any Venetian. Every time an artist walked through the Piazza San Marco, he could have followed the sequence of those late-thirteenth-century *istorie* across the facade of the Basilica depicting the translation of the relics of Saint Mark: the collecting of the relics in Alexandria; the voyage by ship to Venice; a cortege of marching figures carrying the relics through the city; and finally the reception of the relics in the Church of San Marco in the portal on the left [Color Plate XII].[29]

These lunettes include the two primary ceremonial forms that Venetian artists would most often be called upon to paint: the procession and the reception. The mosaic series points to the appositeness of the frieze form for narrative sequences, with the eye deliberately kept on the surface and led from one episode to the next. As Gentile Bellini studied them for inclusion in the *Procession*, they may well have served as the conceptual models for his own painting. But of course he went far beyond a simple narrative frieze and incorporated the procession within an expansive and convincingly three-dimensional urban view.[30] The painting itself became a paradigmatic statement of a Venetian procession: St. Mark's in the background, and a great line of figures strung across the piazza in front. Cesare Vecellio's *Ducal Procession* of 1586 shows how little the paradigm had changed by the end of the century [Plate 103].

Yet while Gentile Bellini recorded, invented and manipulated ceremonial observances, for the most part he resisted the dynamic principles that underlay a living procession. He captured the grand scheme of the marching groups in his *Procession*, but he did not set them convincingly into motion. What is absent is the ineluctable sense that further movement is about to happen.

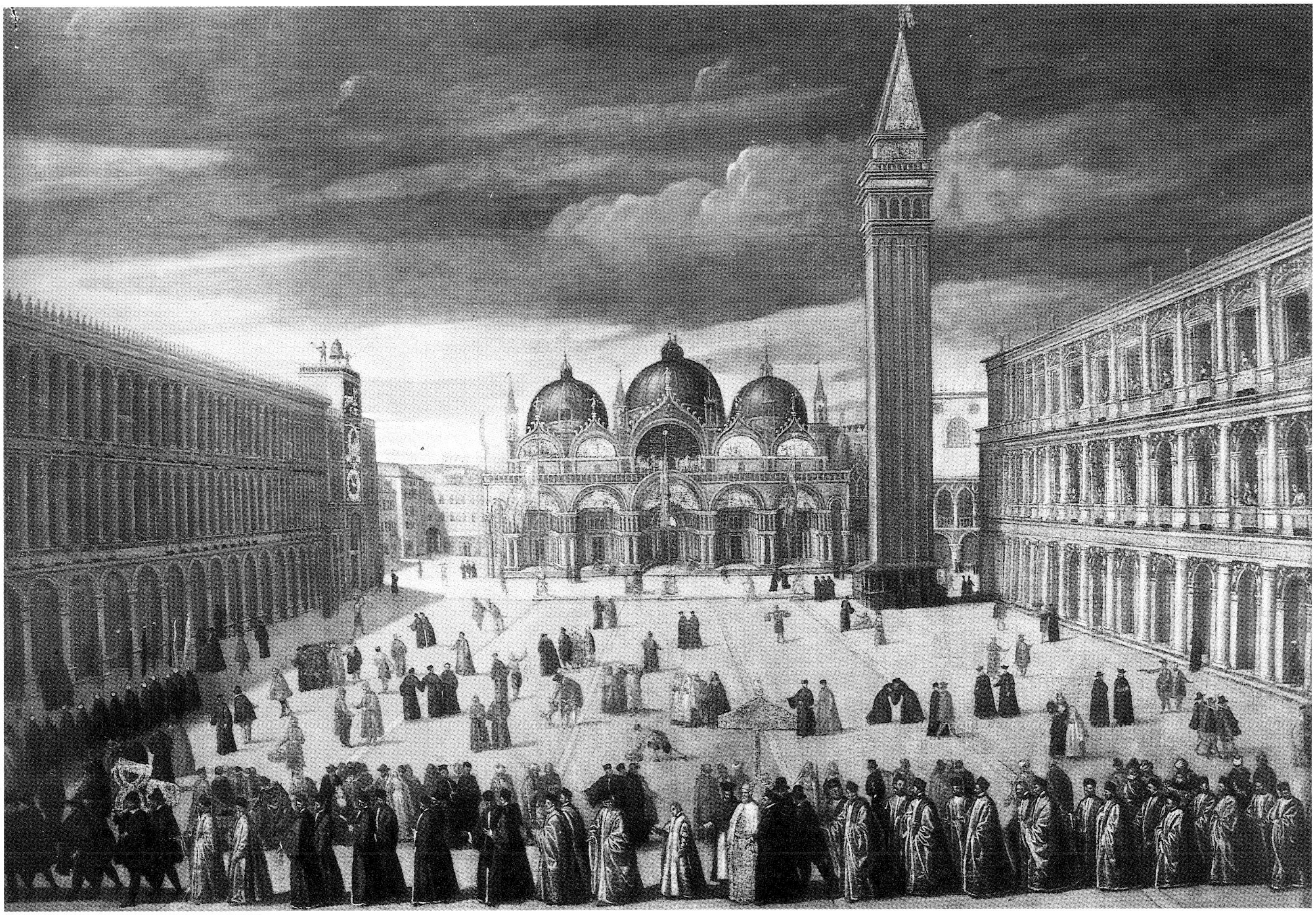

103. Cesare Vecellio, *Ducal Procession*, 1586 (Venice, Museo Correr)

The challenge of representing temporal process was a major preoccupation for artists of this period, engaging talents as diverse as those of Leonardo da Vinci and Michelangelo. Leonardo sacrificed color and blurred the edges of solid forms with his *sfumato* technique to achieve a sense of flux and transience in his paintings, while Michelangelo simply reduced his settings to a minimum and, without distraction, animated the human body with powerful and expressive gestures.[31]

While such initiatives were soon translated into Venetian terms by Giorgione and Titian, Venetian artists working in the eyewitness style remained unmoved by such solutions. For they were unwilling to sacrifice *copia*. The richly circumstantial rendering of the visible world had literally rendered immobile the participants in Gentile's procession. To find a different approach to movement, one that was based upon the flow and the actual rhythm of the ceremonial moment, we must move on to Carpaccio.

Applying the paradigm

It has often been observed that the ceremonial entry played a major role in Carpaccio's conception of the *Life of St. Ursula*.[32] Indeed, he presented the story in terms of a series of arrivals and departures with varying degrees of ritualized formality [Color Plates xxiv and xxvi–xxviii]. Ambassadors come and go: they arrive at one court, then depart with deferential gestures and arrive again with full protocol at another. Ursula and Etherius solemnly take leave of their parents; an angel arrives in Ursula's room; the affianced pair arrive in Rome with an entourage of eleven thousand virgins; they arrive again in Cologne; and then Ursula departs on a bier in her funeral procession. But the ceremonial element vanishes on the altar *pala* where the saint leaves the narrative and becomes an icon, borne slowly heavenward on a rising cloud [Plate 30].

Carpaccio's solutions seem so natural that one may question whether he could have presented the legend in any other way than as a series of greetings and farewells. In fact, if we look back for a moment at the fresco cycle of the life of Saint Ursula in nearby Treviso, painted more than a century earlier by Tomaso da Modena, we see a quite different emphasis.[33] Even allowing for the passage of time and the difference in style, the changes are striking. The first two scenes in the Treviso cycle – the *Dispatch of the Ambassadors* and the *Audience of the Ambassadors* – depict colloquies rather than receptions or dismissals [Plates 104 and 105]. Several elements from both compositions reappear in Carpaccio's *Reception of the Ambassadors*, suggesting that he was aware of the earlier works. But his conception is dissimilar in three significant ways: in tone or mood, in the distinction between public and private space, and in the feeling for process and movement. Let us examine them in turn.

First, in Tomaso's frescoes we are brought into an intimate, humanly warm and ceremonious, but not ceremonial, world. The gestures, while sometimes rhetorical and courtly, are animated and spontaneous. Even in court scenes there is little pomp, and the characters do not project the self-awareness and dignity of Carpaccio's. They are not creatures of public space and thus 'on view' to the spectator. The difference in tone of the two works represents more than a shift from an informal Trecento realism to something more stylized, if more accurately drafted, in the late Quattrocento. For if we compare Carpaccio's

xxv (facing). Gentile Bellini, detail from the *Procession in the Piazza San Marco* (Color Plate xviii)

xxvi (p. 180 above). Carpaccio, detail from the *Return of the Ambassadors* (Plate 107)

xxvii (p. 180 below). Carpaccio, *Reception of the Ambassadors* (Venice, Accademia)

xxviii (p. 181). Carpaccio, detail from the *Leavetaking of the Betrothed Pair* (Plate 110)

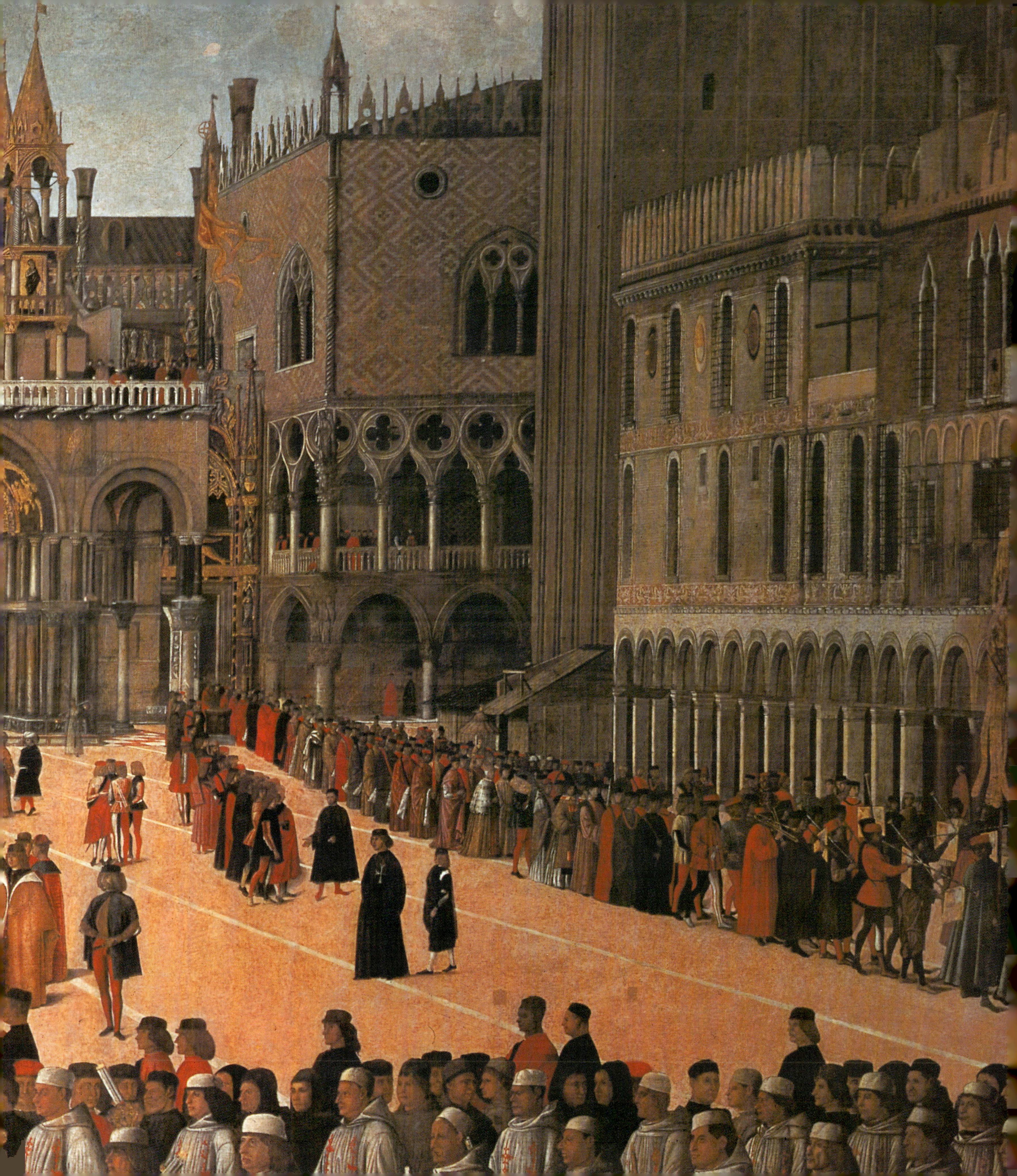

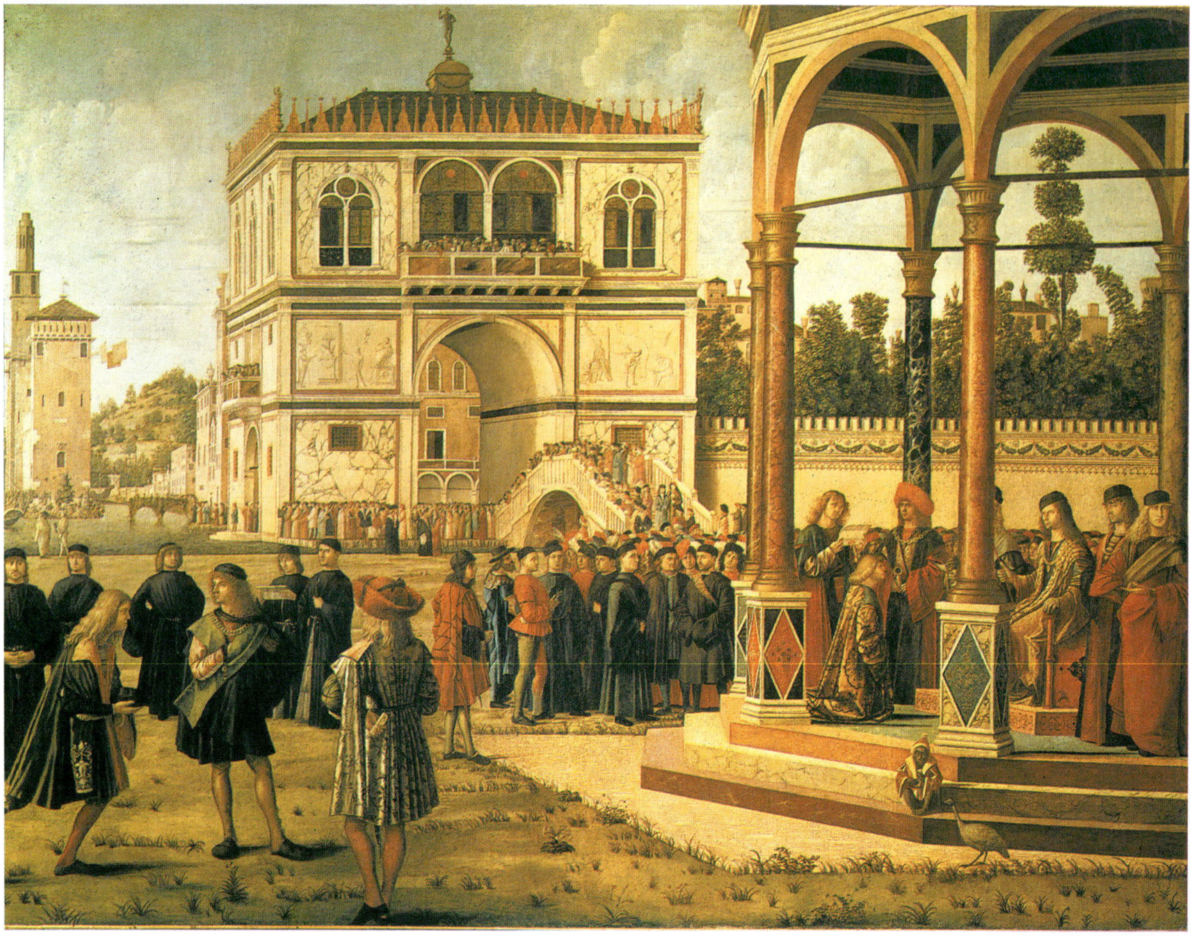

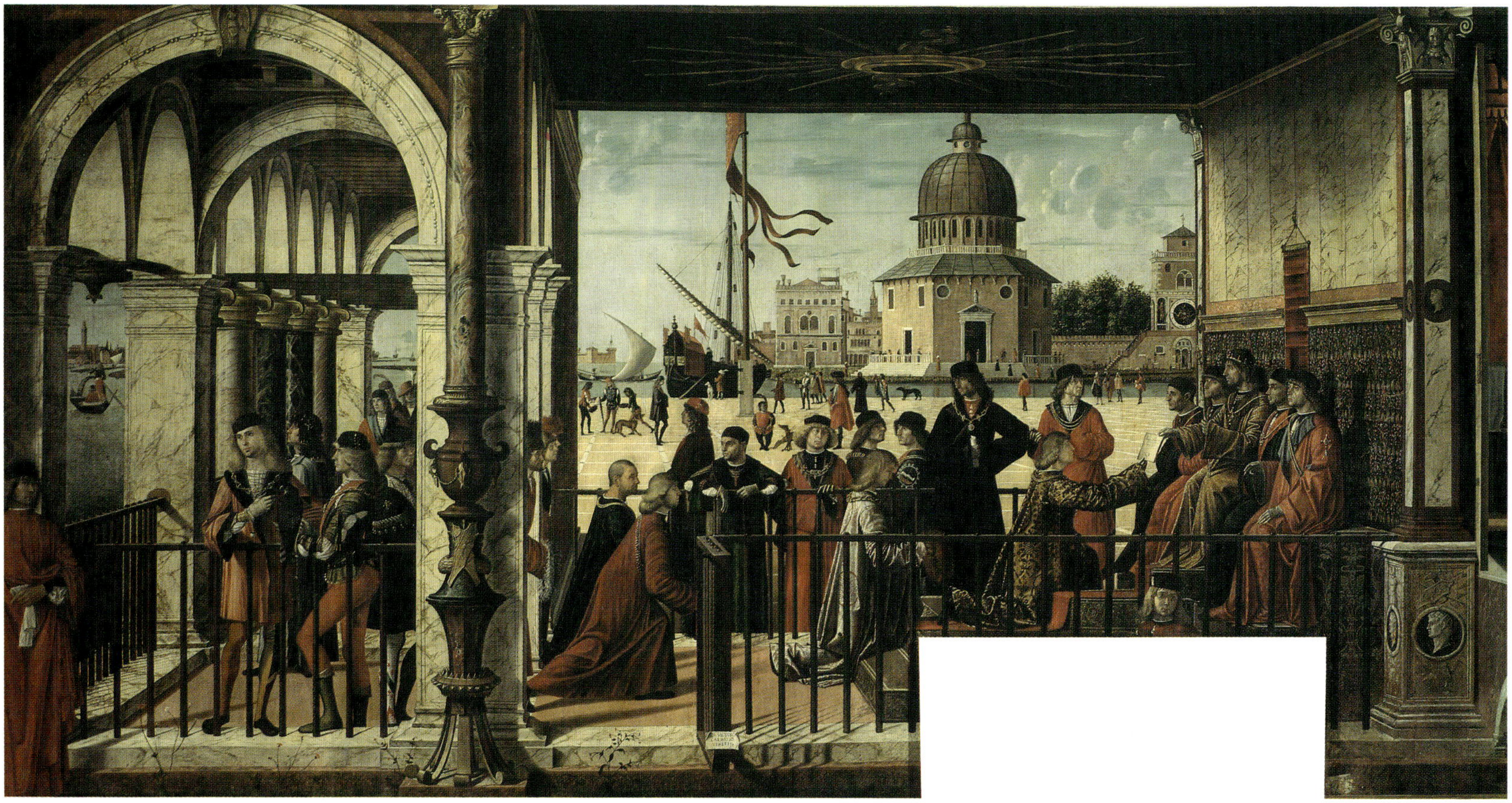

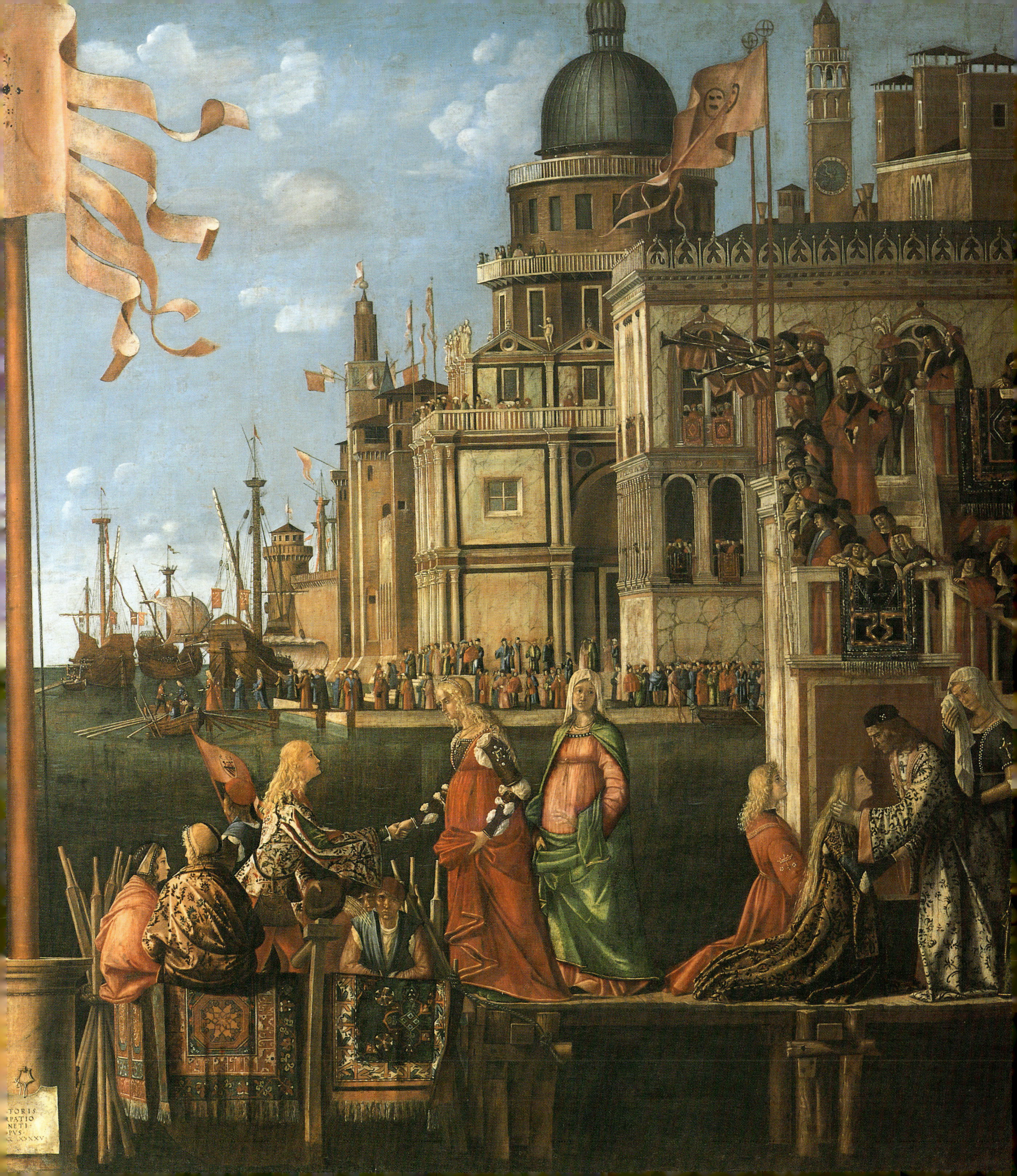
TORIS
RPATIO
NETI
PVS
XXXV

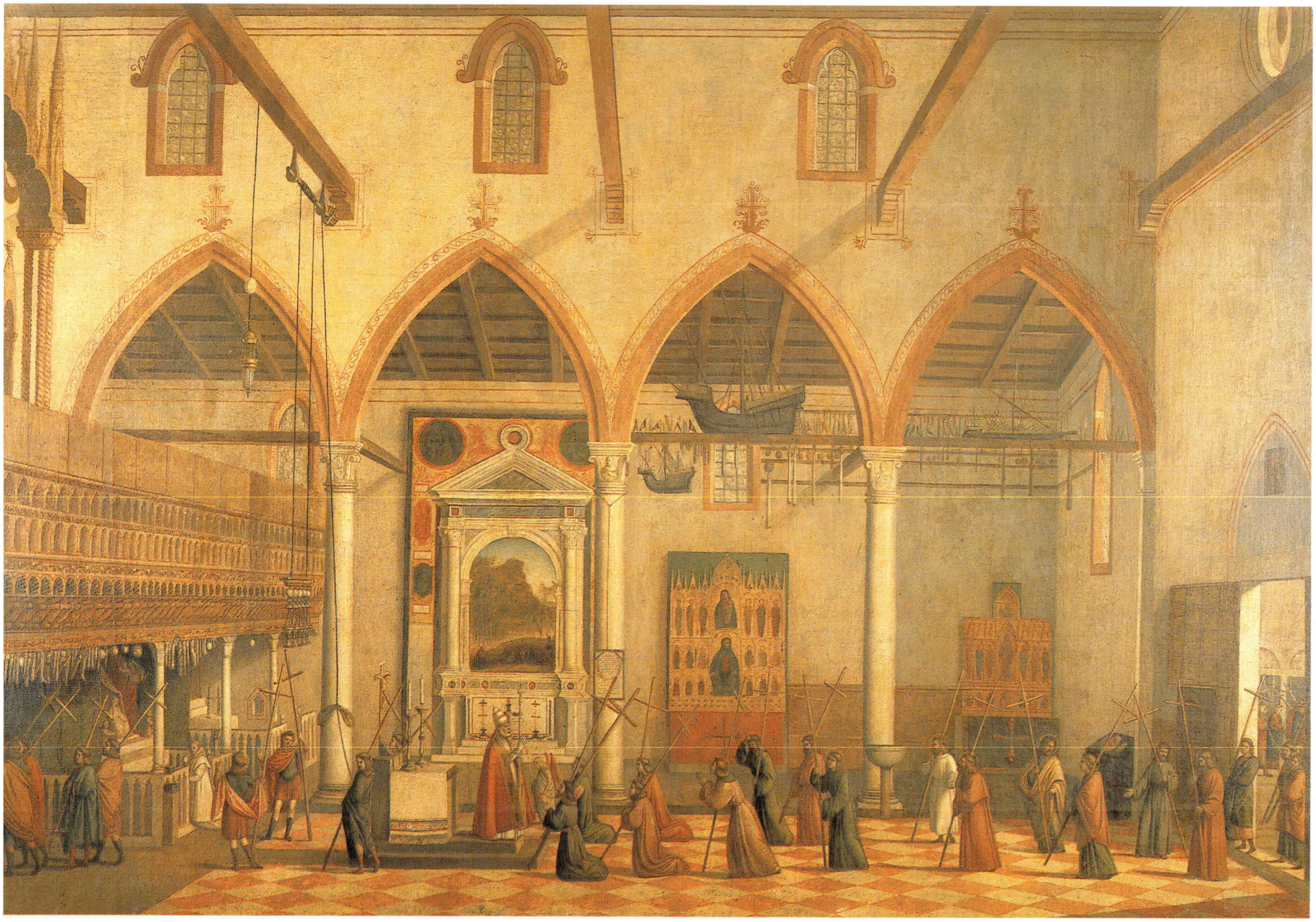

XXIX. Carpaccio, *Apparition of the Ten Thousand Martyrs* (Venice, Accademia)

Reception of the Ambassadors with a similar scene in the Correr manuscript [Plate 106], we find in both a similar decorous quality that is lacking in Tomaso da Modena. In the two Venetian representations, there is a 'ritual moment': an ambassador kneels before the King, who acknowledges him directly with gesture and glance. In Tomaso's painting, the ambassadors seem to speak to each other, while the King is engrossed in reading the letter. Even in the simple and rather crudely painted Correr miniature, one can already observe that feeling for civic ritual, rooted in a Byzantine past, which became a characteristic feature of public art and public life in Venice.

Secondly, and by extension, for Tomaso all the characters are participants, and none just a witness. Unlike Carpaccio, he includes no large audience within the picture space. When we speak of ceremonial, we are speaking of people in groups; and observers as well as actors are essential to the occasion. Such spectators were already present at the reception of St. Mark's relics in the mosaic

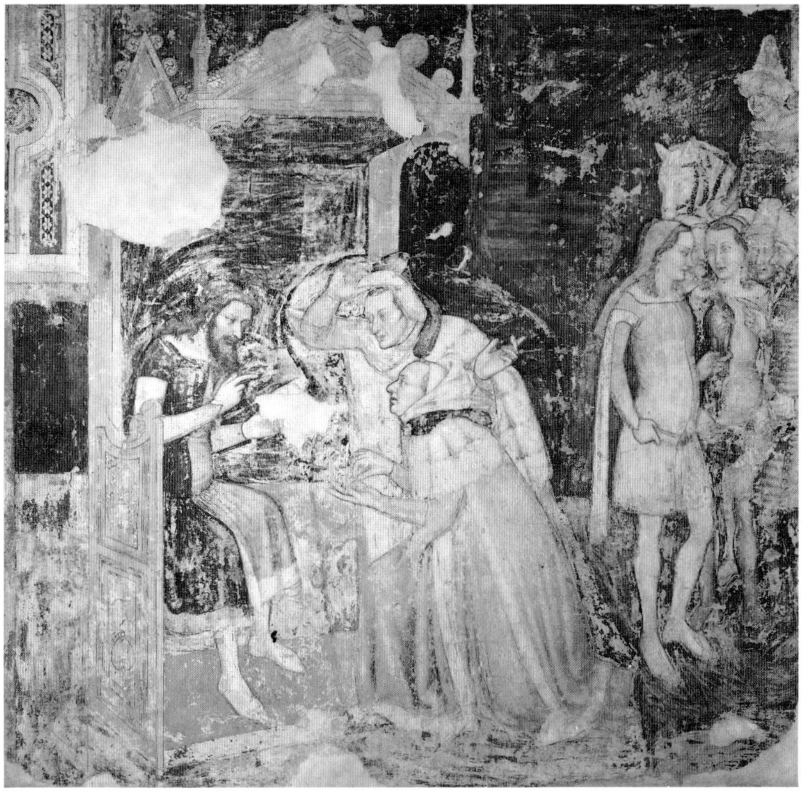

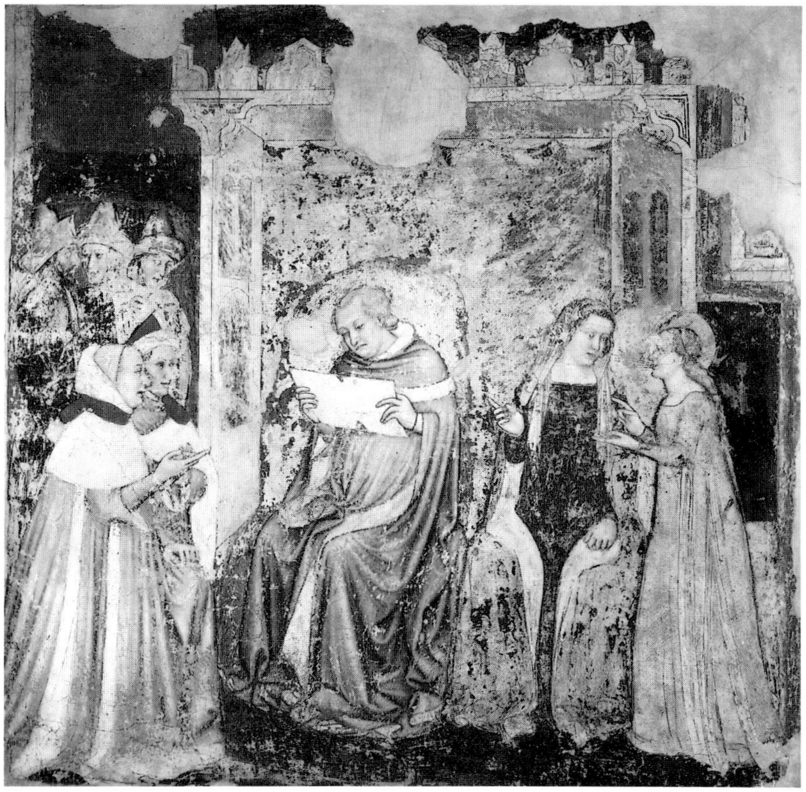

above the Porta di Sant'Alippio of the Basilica; and they bore witness as well to his miraculous apparition in the south transept [Plate 84 and Color Plate IV].

By Carpaccio's time the crowds had grown, with the spectators threatening to overwhelm the *istoria* itself. Some are clearly portraits of the patrons, but most are anonymous, simply those who observe. In Gentile Bellini's *Procession* they form a solid band behind the confraternity members who march across the front plane. They pack the *fondamenta* in the *Miracle at the Bridge of San Lorenzo*. In Mansueti's several works for the Scuole Grandi they appear in windows and gondolas, on rooftops, balconies and staircases; they seem to occupy every available space.

More than any other artist of the day, it was Carpaccio who discovered new ways to organize great numbers of people on canvas. Old but revered models

104 (left). Tomaso da Modena, *Dispatch of the Ambassadors*, detached fresco (Treviso, Museo Civico)

105. Tomaso da Modena, *Audience of the Ambassadors*, detached fresco (Treviso, Museo Civico)

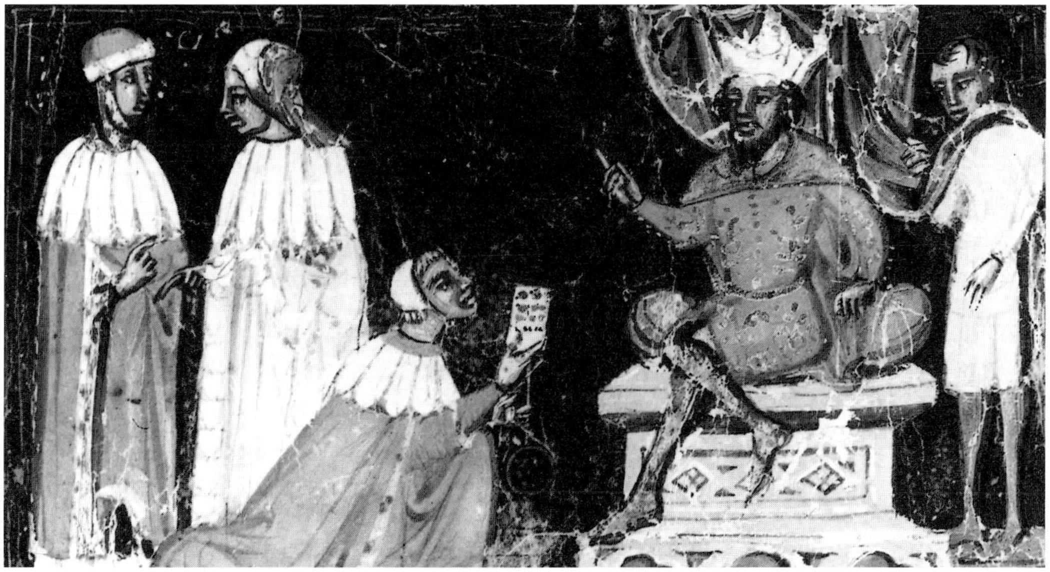

106. Venetian school, *Venetian Ambassadors before the Emperor*, miniature (Venice, Museo Correr, Cod. Correr I, 383 [=1497])

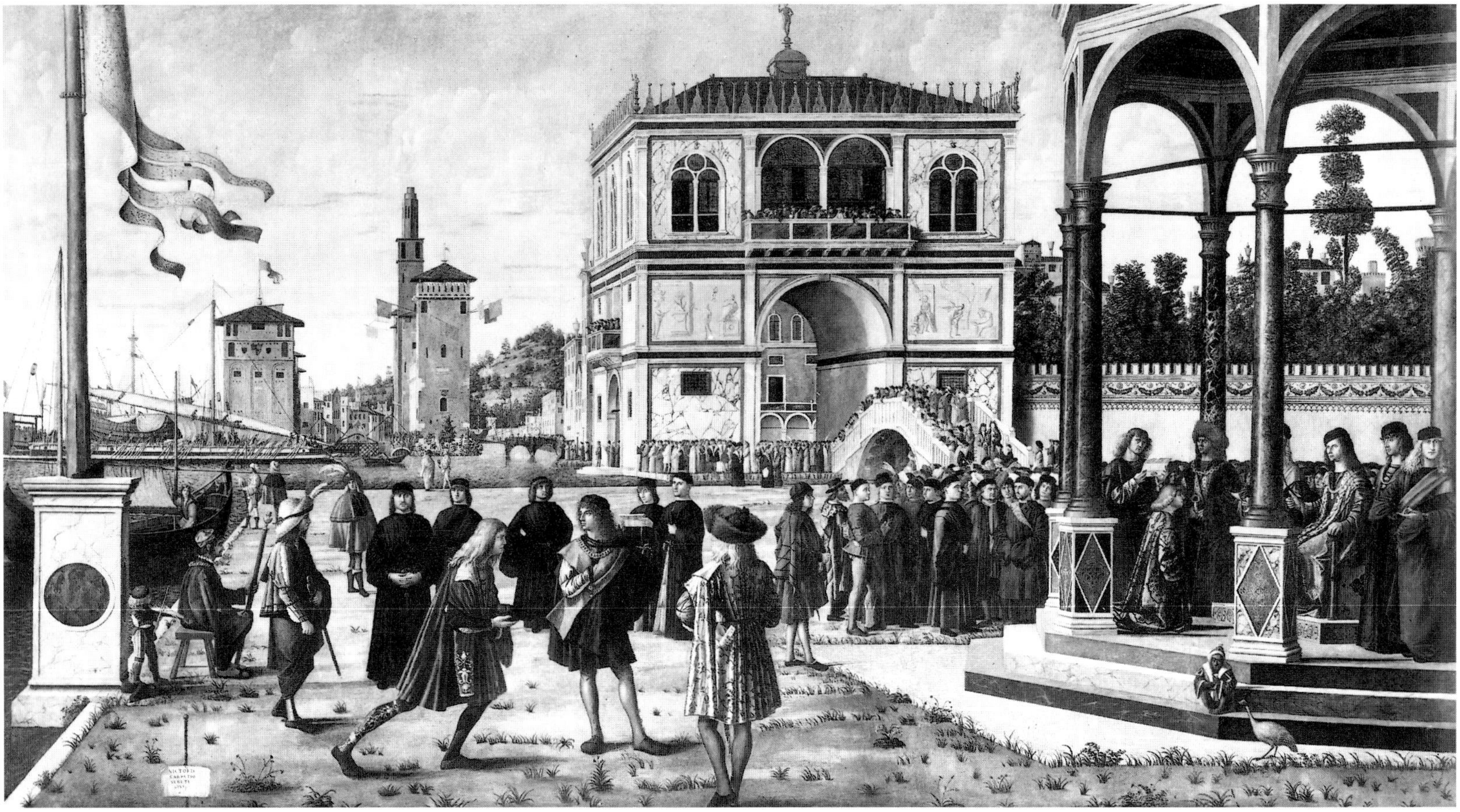

107. Carpaccio, *Return of the Ambassadors* (Venice, Accademia)

like the Basilica mosaics were insufficient to that particular task, and he looked beyond them to the living festivals of his time. He observed how processions and ceremonies were made up of groups rather than of individuals and how they could be disposed to achieve the variety and animation so earnestly sought by Mansueti, while maintaining the decorum and order of Gentile Bellini.[34]

The cycle of Saint Ursula is a primer in crowd control. To begin with, in the first scene, the *Reception of the Ambassadors*, the spectators are few [Color Plate XXVI]. Viewing the action from behind a railing, they close off the narrative stage from the deep background and invite the viewer's attention to complete the scene. They are mirrors of ourselves, reflecting back upon us our demeanor and attitudes as we pause before the panel. The loggia is effectively closed to them by the enclosure, but accessible to us through the open gateway. Carpaccio thus heightens the visual paradox, creating a physical boundary between actor and observer within his world of paint, and yet opening a gate of unobstructed access to the drama from the world of the viewer.[35]

In the *Return of the Ambassadors*, black-robed Venetians, reminiscent of the observers of the *Reception*, line up to view the returning emissaries [Color Plate XXVII and Plate 107]. But the audience expands. A larger group bunches together to the left of the *tempietto* and others mass on balconies and bridges. Pausing to watch and observe, they reflect a society of orderly spectators. It is the seemingly insignificant detail, like the small boy playing a stringed instrument at the far left, that gives the scene animation and spontaneity. Participation is heightened by small oases of non-participation: a monkey sits on the steps to the right and observes a guinea hen. The banner on the flagpole, an essential element in most of the scenes, is whipped by the wind and directs the narrative movement toward the right.

A small forest of flags held aloft by youths in Venetian attire draws us into the *Arrival in Rome* [Plate 108]. Carpaccio combines here both procession and reception in a single scene. The company of virgins trudge in on the left forming an extended arc; mitred bishops move slowly in on the right. In the central space, isolated by open areas of grass, are massed bishops and cardinals, representing the hierarchy of the church. Curving around to echo the shape of the circular bastions of the Castel Sant'Angelo in the background, they form a backdrop for the narrative core of the *istoria*: the Pope and the kneeling figures of Ursula, Etherius and others of their entourage. The lateral disposition of the figures on the front plane stabilizes the composition and counterweights the processions that trail into the distance on each side. Carpaccio thus avoids the inconsequential effect of the procession in the Correr *Arrival*, as well as the packed confusion of Tomaso da Modena's rendering of the same event [Plate 109].

The most grandly conceived panel of the cycle, and indeed one of the most impressive works of the entire period, is the *Leavetaking of the Betrothed Pair* [Color Plate XXVIII and Plate 110]. Measuring some eighteen feet in width, it encompasses a vast panorama extending from grim medieval buildings to sumptuous Renaissance structures: two worlds separated by water, but connected in the front plane by the *déroulement* of the legend along a narrow wharf. Again, spectators are part of the spectacle. They play trumpets, display banderoles, climb staircases, press against balustrades, line the docksides, record, point, watch and wait. Here we come to the third area of departure from the works of Tomaso da Modena, which, for all their vivacity, do not convey a sense of pro-

108 (left). Carpaccio, *Arrival in Rome* (Venice, Accademia)

109. Tomaso da Modena, *Arrival in Rome*, detached fresco (Treviso, Museo Civico)

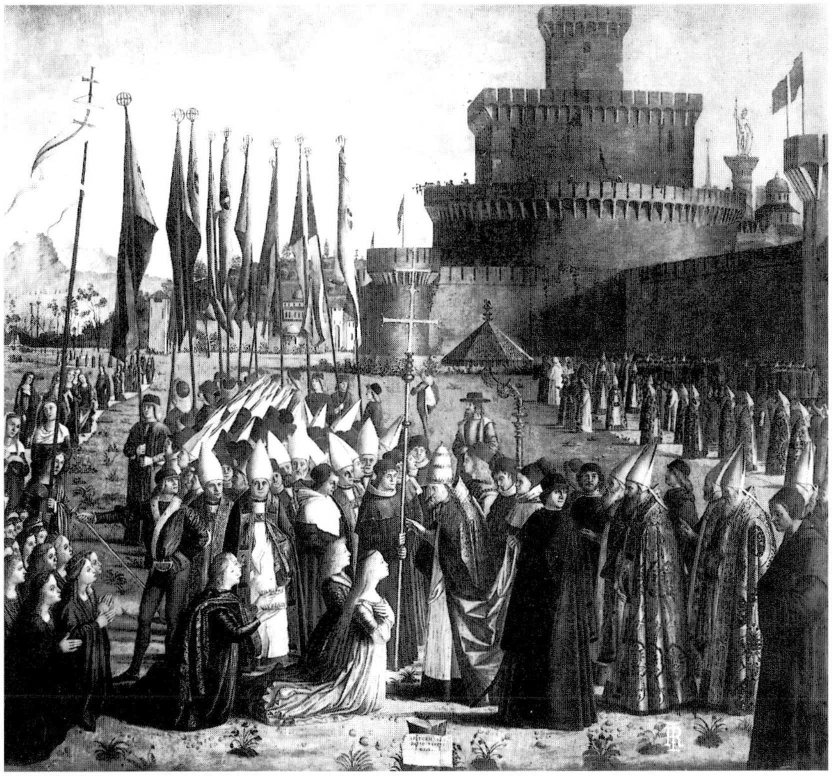

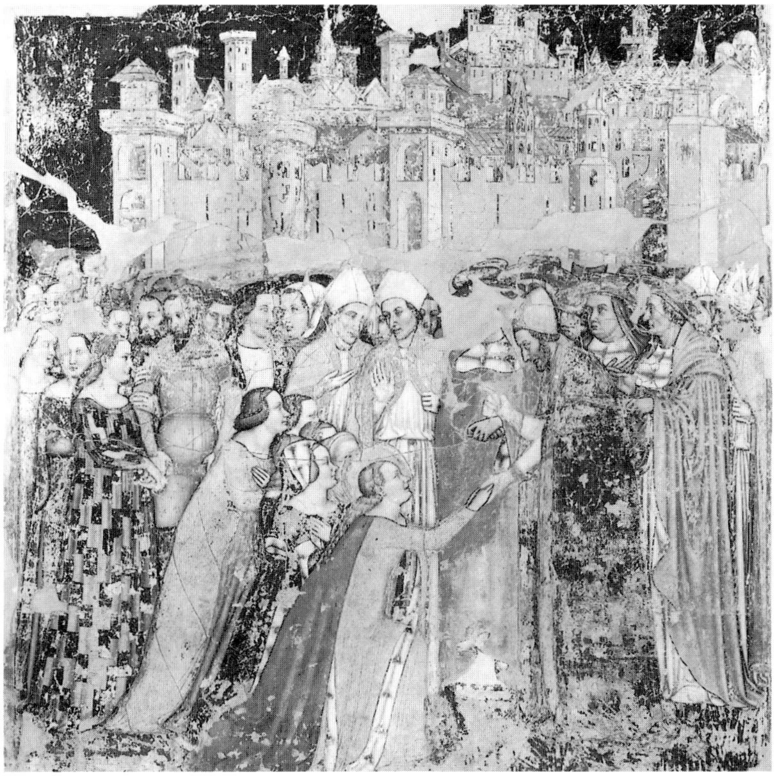

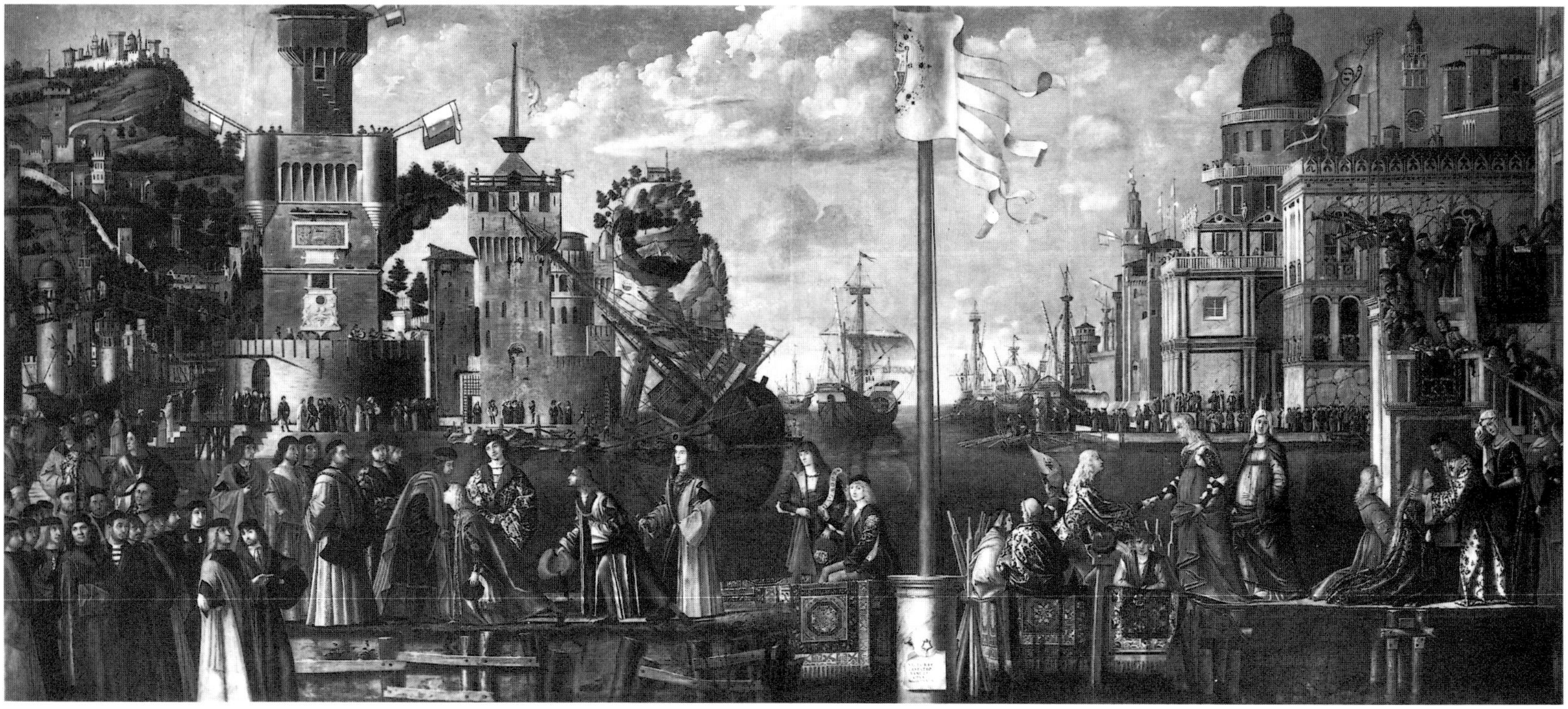

110. Carpaccio, *Leavetaking of the Betrothed Pair*, 1495 (Venice, Accademia)

cess. For him, the ambassadors are already at court; Ursula is already in Rome. There is no sense of a developing drama.

As in the *Reception of the Ambassadors*, the controlling logic of Carpaccio's *Leavetaking* was posited in the linear development of the foreground. In the *Reception*, the ambassadors enter the throne room from an antechamber on the left; two begin to drop to their knees; one is poised kneeling on the steps; and yet another, with a rising gesture, approaches the King at the right. As others have observed, the effect is one of unfolding: a sequence of gestures of a single movement as if recorded in a strip of movie frames. In the *Leavetaking*, the action develops in a similar way, but in counterpoint. On the left, Etherius kneels to kiss his father's breast. Behind him his companion rises from a similar posture. To the right, Etherius has turned, rising himself from bended knee as he takes Ursula's hand. Further yet to the right, both kneel, and then Ursula and her father embrace in a pose mirroring the paternal farewell to Etherius with which the sequence had begun.

Carpaccio had an acute sense of interval, of gesture, of cadence, and of the rhythmic placement of solids and voids. Unlike most of his contemporaries, he knew what to leave out. Thus the caesurae between his figures play a role fully as important as the figures themselves in conveying the impression of a ceremony that is under way at that very moment. A simple diplomatic ritual, instantly read and comprehended through a chain of familiar gestures, became the reference point to clarify and organize a confusion of competing events and objects.

In Carpaccio's *Apparition of the Ten Thousand Martyrs* we receive a similar impression of sequential development, of ongoing movement and of a vision in progress [Color Plate XXIX and Plate 111]. In this painting, Carpaccio – perhaps with the help of his workshop – gave form to a vision experienced in 1511 by a certain Francesco Ottobon, the prior of the monastery of Sant' Antonio di Castello in Venice. Ottobon fell asleep after praying for divine intervention against the plague on behalf of the monastery. In a vivid dream he saw himself inside the monastery church, kneeling in prayer before the altar of St. Anthony Abbot. He left a manuscript record of his experience which was later transcribed by Flaminio Corner, the eighteenth-century ecclesiastical historian:

> What now happened was that it seemed that a great noise was heard at the main portal of the church, and immediately thereafter a voice saying: open the doors! This said, the main doors were thrown open, and at once a great multitude was observed covering up the main space in great numbers and densely filling in the surrounding areas, who were led by one of great age: quick in pace, reverent in form, bearded, and decorous in his whole aspect, with sandals, in a purple dalmatic, with a sleeved tunic, pallium, mitre, and a pontifical sceptre in view. Everyone followed [him] into the church, two by two, resounding sweetly in hymns and songs.

111. Carpaccio, detail from the *Apparition of the Ten Thousand Martyrs* (Color Plate XXIX)

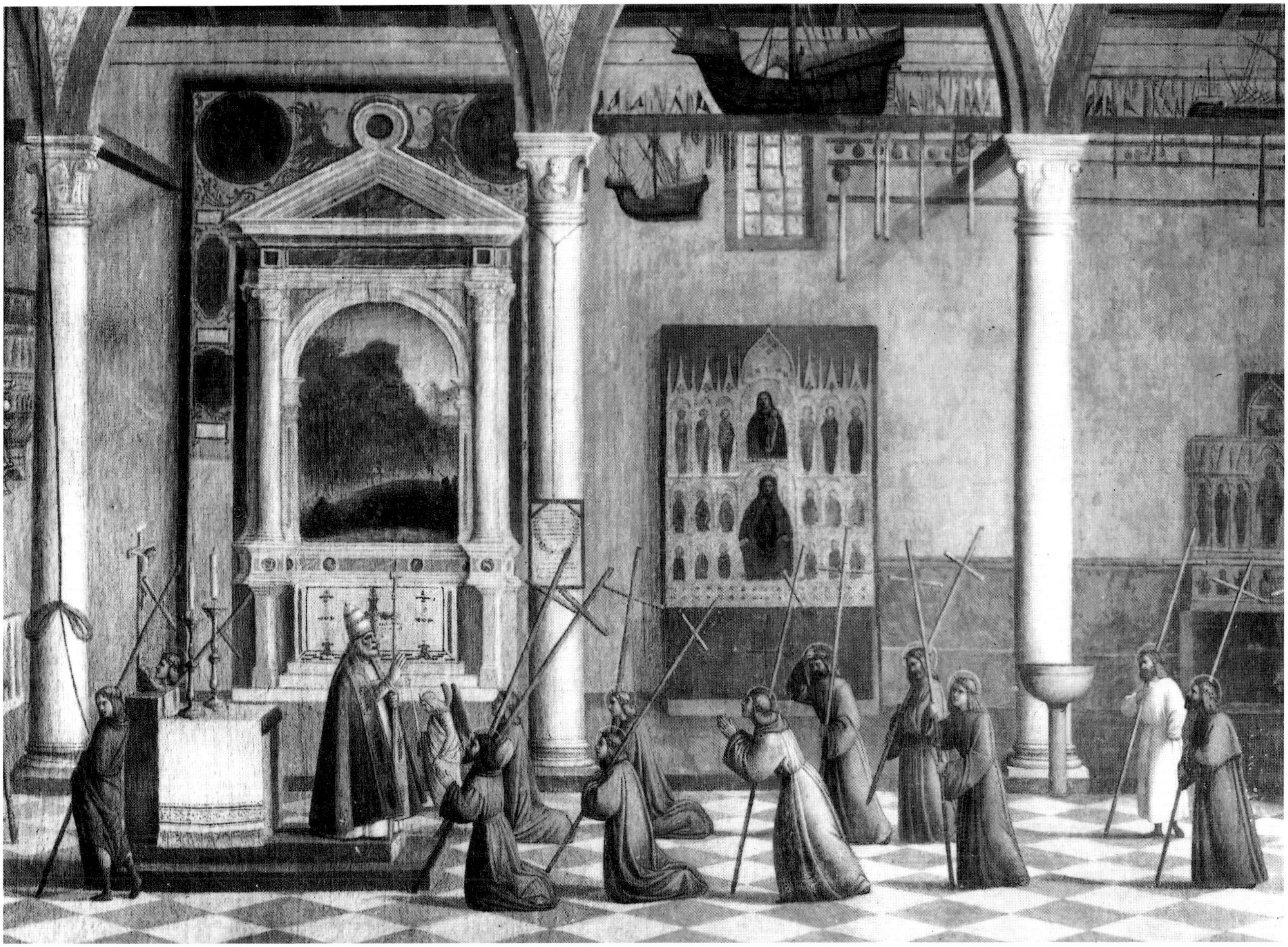

[I was] astounded by this sight, marvelous to say. Here everyone was crowned in the same way; each bearing a cross, for a short time they could be observed separately, in age, in form, and in dress. In the center of the church, everyone knelt down. I believe that the man to whom they dutifully genuflected was [St.] Peter, whose octave it was that day; he gave a solemn pontifical benediction. Soon all of them vanished from view. When they had withdrawn, a voice seemed to be heard coming from the statue of Saint Anthony: Do not doubt, remain constant, and I decree that by the intercession of all of these you will be saved from the imminent peril.[36]

Ottobon recognized the assemblage as the Ten Thousand Martyrs, a group of Christian soldiers who, according to legend, had been crucified on Mount Ararat in the early Middle Ages.[37] Upon awakening, he called together his canons and told them of the miraculous apparition. He later concluded that his vision must have been true, for none of the brothers subsequently contracted the plague. In pious gratitude, the prior asked his nephew, Ettore Ottobon, to erect an *ex voto* altar in the church.[38] A *scrivan* in the Salt Office, Ettore typified those *cittadini originari* who became significant patrons of the arts by virtue of their membership in Venetian *scuole*. He was already active in the Scuola Grande di San Marco and eventually served two terms as its Guardian Grande.[39] He would have had first-hand knowledge of the local artists, for in 1514 it was his responsibility to make salary disbursements to the painters who were working on the history paintings in the Great Council Hall.[40]

Following his uncle's instructions, Ettore commissioned a handsome marble altar that was consecrated in 1512 and completed in 1515 with a *pala* painted by Carpaccio, the *Crucifixion of the Ten Thousand Martyrs*.[41] The *Apparition* was probably executed around the same time. The work not only represents the vision itself but also records the marble altar that had been commissioned by Ettore Ottobon as a consequence of that vision.[42]

Carpaccio approached the problem with his characteristic careful attention to detail that implied a directly observed event. The irregular placement of the altars lining the wall of the church, the untidy assemblage of *ex votos* – ship models on the rafters above and the profusion of wax objects hanging from the old fashioned wooden *barco* in the choir – are recorded with notarial conscientiousness. The figures are divided into three groupings. On the right, the martyrs enter the door in an almost casual manner. As they proceed along the nave, two figures halt and lean on their crosses, providing a caesura to this phase of the procession. The attention of those in the central group is focused on the figure of the blessing Pope. Here the marchers strain forward; they begin to fall to their knees; finally they kneel before him. The single indication that the event has a supernatural quality is the small angel who kneels with them directly under the raised hand of the Pope. We then observe that these figures are about to stand and move on because of the third grouping over at the left. They pause and wait or simply walk right out of the picture frame beneath the wooden choir.

It is significant that Ottobon reported his vision as we see it here: the procession moving laterally as seen from the side by a third party. Encompassing both Ottobon himself kneeling on the left and the marchers to the right, it is the view of an *outside* witness. He did not, as one might expect, experience a frontal view of the martyrs marching toward him down the nave. In a reverse play of art back into ritual, the prior's own theatrical perception of the event seems to have been determined by images of processions with witnesses like those painted earlier by Carpaccio, or by *ex voto* paintings where it is essential to include the principal figure who is praying for and receiving an act of divine grace.

For his portrayal of motion, Carpaccio drew upon two aspects of ceremonial as he had seen it performed: the rhythm and interval of ritual and the postures of ceremonial gesture – genuflection, bowing, rising, a measured pace, a raised hand. Perhaps his most powerful model for sequential movement was the gesture of kneeling to show reverence or respect. It was a form used in both religious and diplomatic ritual as the paradigmatic statement of homage.[43] Thus a key element in his strategy was the inclined figure, whether kneeling or walking, with the axis tilted slightly forward instead of upright. Somewhat off-balance, it declares by its precarious stance its transitional state. It appears in the *Apparition* as well as in most of the scenes of the St. Ursula cycle, and shows up again and again in his drawings.

By grounding his *Life of St. Ursula* in a number of ceremonial paradigms, Carpaccio may seem to have sacrificed much of the look of the 'slice of life' that had been traditional in the Venetian *istoria* and was an essential quality of the True Cross paintings. His departure from this mode in the case of his paintings of saints' lives needs to be accounted for. We might first conclude that the 'truth' of the legend of St. Ursula, like the truth of the lives of all saints of the distant past, was a matter of pious, even 'mythic', certitude. It was not an incident of Venetian history. The artist's aim was thus didactic and inspirational rather than documentary, and credibility was not really an issue.

But there is more to the matter than that. The attractiveness of ritual elements in painting is their unambiguous certainty, and their appearance in the painted *istoria* may simply stand for yet another form of persuasion. As a recent study observes, ritual action presents its material authoritatively, as if axiomatic. Its conventional form renders it unverifiable and separate from the usual standards of truth and falsity. Thus ritual is frequently intended to express invisible and ineffable things – ideals like the perfect order and harmonious social structure of Venice – and to make them tangible and present.[44] The great St. Mark's Day procession does take place year after year, reifying and confirming those ideals. When Gentile Bellini painted such a ceremony, he confirmed them yet again and placed his *istoria* within a timeless – even sacrosanct – context.

With Carpaccio, the transition between living ceremonial and the painted image took place at one step beyond reportage and emerged only in an unseen world of the saints that was by necessity invented by the artist. Ritual gestures of homage and respect at Ursula's court are instantly readable for what they are: reassuringly familiar and thus prompting no challenge. If 'the significant demanded ritual', then to posit the pious legend within a ritualized context was, indeed, to endow it with the unimpeachable certainty and time-extending charisma of Venetian ceremonial life.

Transference of the paradigm

In his subsequent commissions for Venetian *scuole*, Carpaccio went on to make a number of paintings that did not record rituals or ceremonials *per se*, but which were influenced by their formal principles of rhythm, gesture and spacing. His *Disputation of St. Stephen* [Color Plate xv] for example, shows a number of formal analogies to the *Reception of the Ambassadors*: the lateral arrangement of figures in a portico in the foreground; a view through it to an expansive architectural panorama behind; the spectators who look out at the viewer from behind the narrative action; the gestural movement up toward Stephen who himself gesticulates in grand oratorical style. And yet all of this is without any specific activity that can be identified as a ritual.

A similar effect is obtained in the *Miracle of St. Tryphon* [Plate 112]. The formula worked out for the *Return of the Ambassadors* is here reconstituted to provide the rationale for a saintly miracle: movement from left to right across the front plane; the reception of this movement in a portico; an audience in the rear who fill balconies of high buildings across a grassy plain.

Carpaccio took a different tack in *St. Jerome and the Lion* [Color Plate xxx]. The sudden arrival of a lion on the monastery grounds has sent the monks flying with centrifugal force in all directions. Like the ambassadors in the *Reception* of the Ursula cycle, they spin out a whole sequence of moments of the same action. The same feeling for interval that inspired the distribution of figures across the platform in the *Leavetaking* of St. Ursula is also present here. Fleeing figures in a much smaller scale carry the movement deep into the background.

Carpaccio's unique sense of pattern, rhythm and figural movement is given sharper definition when we compare this canvas with two other renderings of the same subject. In Lazzaro Bastiani's predella in the Brera, Jerome and the lion are relegated to the background. The monks flee but in a disorganized and

112. Carpaccio, *Miracle of St. Tryphon* (Venice, Scuola di San Giorgio degli Schiavoni)

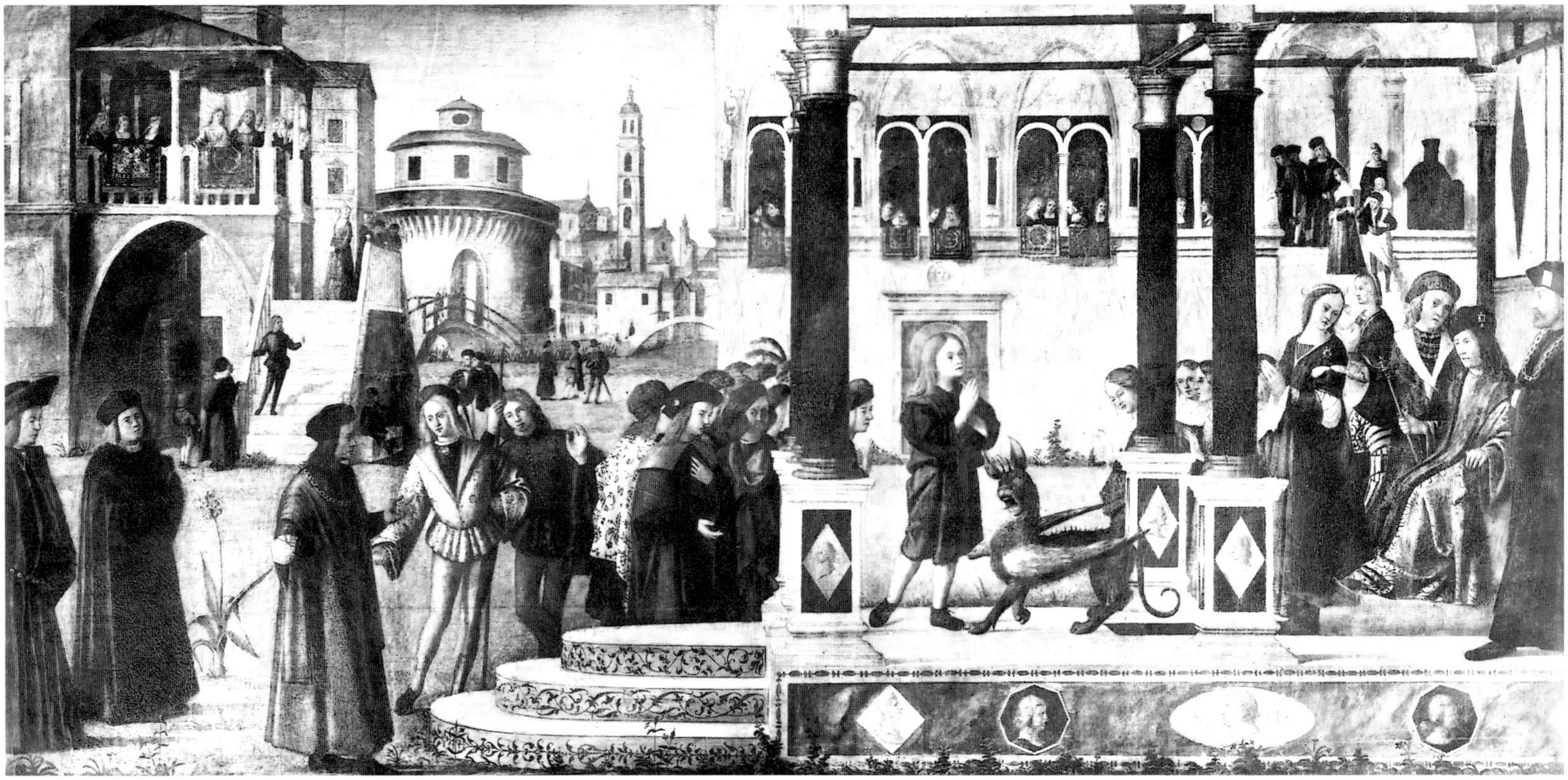

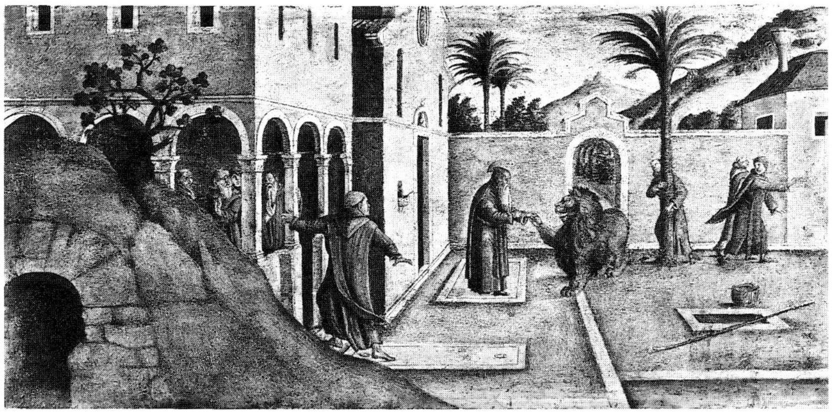

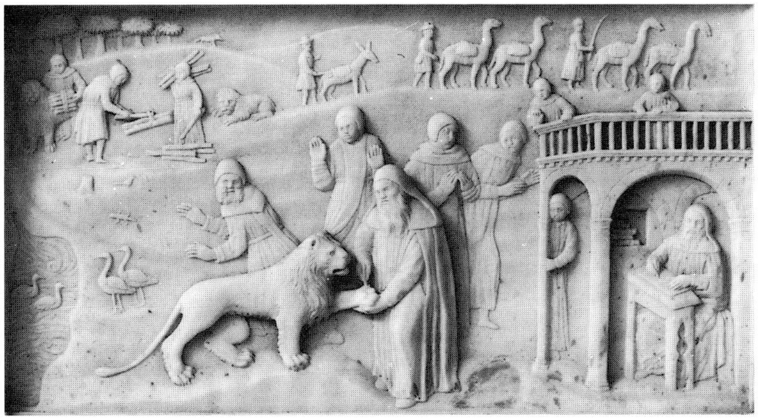

113 (left). Lazzaro Bastiani, *St. Jerome and the Lion* (Milan, Brera)

114. Anonymous, *St. Jerome and the Lion*, marble relief (Venice, S. Francesco della Vigna, Giustiniani Chapel)

unintegrated manner [Plate 113].[45] On a marble relief in the Giustiniani Chapel of San Francesco della Vigna, made around the first decade of the sixteenth century by an anonymous sculptor, Jerome and the lion resume their prominence in the front plane. The postures and gestures of the fleeing monks are not dissimilar from those of Carpaccio's work and may even have been based upon it [Plate 114]. But again, they lack the choreographed effect of concerted movement which at once both unifies and disperses the figures.

Carpaccio was not the only artist to situate himself between an eyewitness style and the use of a ceremonial paradigm in order to breathe life into his *istorie* of the lives of the saints. Gentile Bellini also turned the processional model to other uses. In his contract for *St. Mark Preaching in Alexandria* [Color Plate XXXIV], the *Procession in the Piazza San Marco* was specifically cited as the standard which he promised to surpass.[46] Indeed, the old paradigm held. Only here, instead of a procession, we have an audience of spectators stretching out in front of the saint in perfect – but now quite still – ceremonial order.

It has been observed that the ritualization of human activity is a defense against chaos, making life more predictable and more manageable. When we view these paintings within their larger social context, we witness the creative use of ceremonial paradigms to cast human relationships in a wide range of narrative situations within a hierarchical, cohesive and ordered structure.[47] It may thus be argued that the Venetian *pittori di ceremonia* were doing more than simply recording the ritual life of their time. They were constructing history itself and life as it should be in culturally resonant terms that were immediately graspable by their patrons.

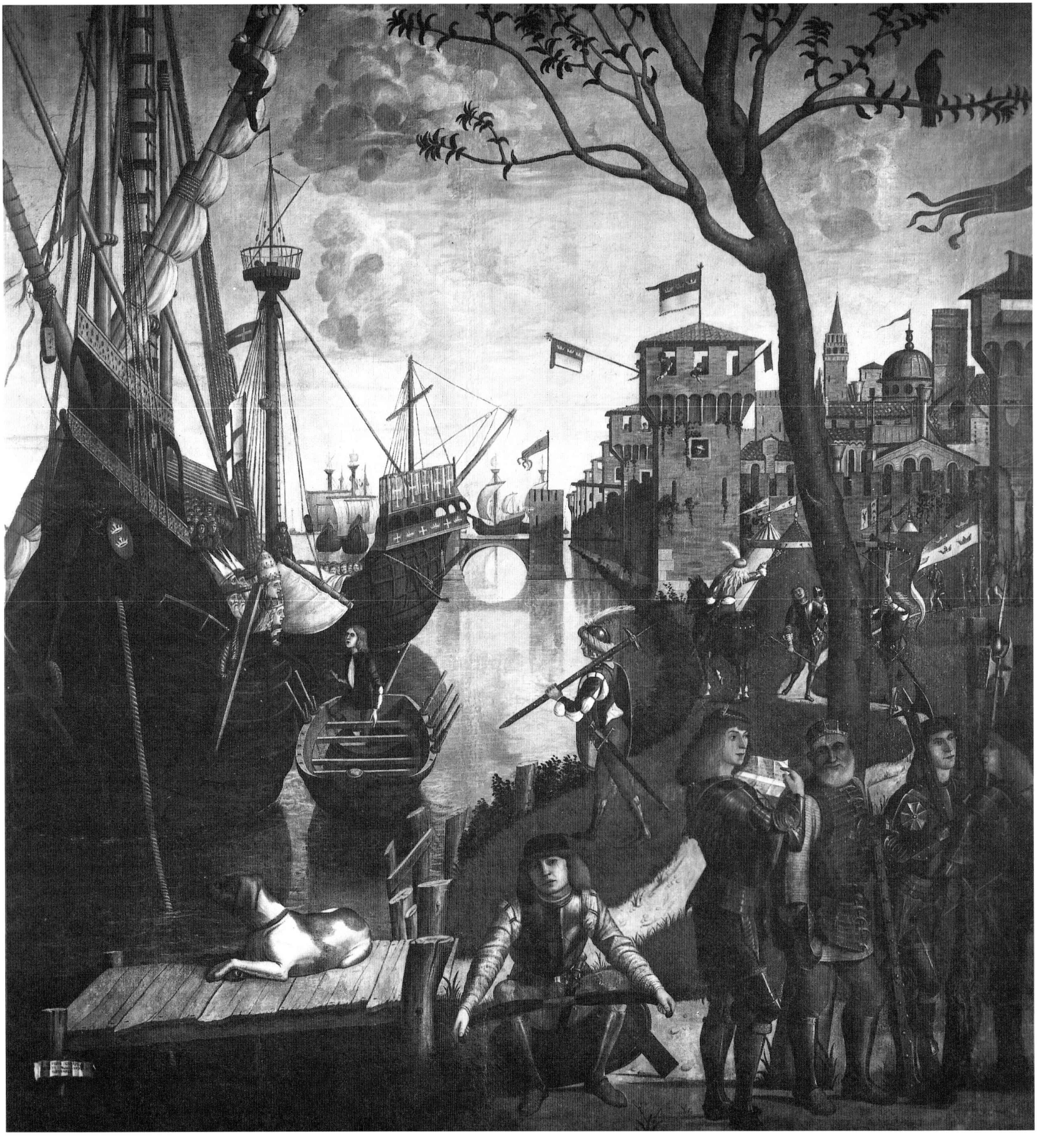

11

From Istoria To Fantasia

In his guide to Venice of 1490, Sabellico referred his readers to the 'most noble hall' of the Scuola Grande della Carità: 'Here one sees panels of famous painters, placed all around, not so much for religion as for adornment.'[1] The works to which he referred have disappeared for the most part, but one is reminded of the decorative qualities of the paintings of the other *scuole* that we have already seen. An art that reproduced the physical face of Venice, as in the True Cross cycle, or that replicated the ceremonial rhythms of Venetian life, as in the *Life of St. Ursula*, could well lay claim to purposes of ornament as well as veneration, even though the one function would not necessarily preclude the other.

The painters of the eyewitness school did not achieve their ornamental effects from gold and precious materials, in the manner of the International Gothic artists of the early Quattrocento who preceded them. Nor did they find them in the sensuousness of nature and of the human body, in the manner of Giorgione and Titian who followed. It was in their scenographic approach to the narrative ambient that they most successfully realized the classical aim of the artist to produce delight to the eye as well as enrichment to the soul. Apart from the True Cross cycle, this task involved the fabrication of imagined environments. It is to these that we shall now turn.

Fabricating Ursula's world

We will begin with Carpaccio and the *Life of St. Ursula*. Painted in the 1490s, it is the earliest surviving cycle of the eyewitness school which features a wholly invented ambient. Carpaccio's method of constructing its physical settings from bits and pieces of various monuments has often been discussed. To Anton Maria Zanetti, the eighteenth-century compiler of Venetian paintings, the artist showed here the richness of his imaginative powers in his *invenzione fondata sulla verità*: invention founded on truth[2]. But on what truth? Indeed, Carpaccio's paintings are so detailed and particularized that each structure seems as if it *must* exist somewhere. Demanding identification, his architectural inventions have sent one scholar after another in search of his various sources. The quest has generally been pursued from two directions: study of the parts, including architectural structures and details, as well as decorative motifs; and of the whole, the way in which these parts were put together in a composition.

Remaining in the world of St. Ursula, let us consider briefly the question of the parts. In this case we can be certain that Carpaccio had never visited the places that he depicted. It was thus his burden – and his opportunity – to invent

115 (facing). Carpaccio, *Arrival in Cologne* (Venice, Accademia)

a series of settings that would appear as if they came from the brush of an eye-witness. At least four different sources for them have been suggested.

First, Carpaccio frequently drew upon actual architecture in or around Venice as a starting-point for his inventive solutions. The *Arrival in Cologne* of 1490 was the first canvas completed for the St. Ursula cycle, and Carpaccio's earliest signed and dated painting [Plate 115]. The town of Cologne is shown as a city enclosed by crenellated walls that are punctuated by towers with projecting parapets. Venice, the 'city without walls', had remained safe and secure for centuries without such fortifications, but Carpaccio might have taken parts of the Arsenal as possible models and worked them up into a city wall.[3] And yet no part of Carpaccio's Cologne exactly replicates any structure of the Arsenal as we know it today. Indeed, the long stretch of wall next to the water's edge is just as strongly reminiscent of many cities of the Dalmatian coast. A similar corner tower still supports the wall of a fortress in Trau [Trogir], and old prints of Zara [Zadar] show a crenellated wall reinforced by square towers and bordered by the sea. These structures could have served as his models as well.

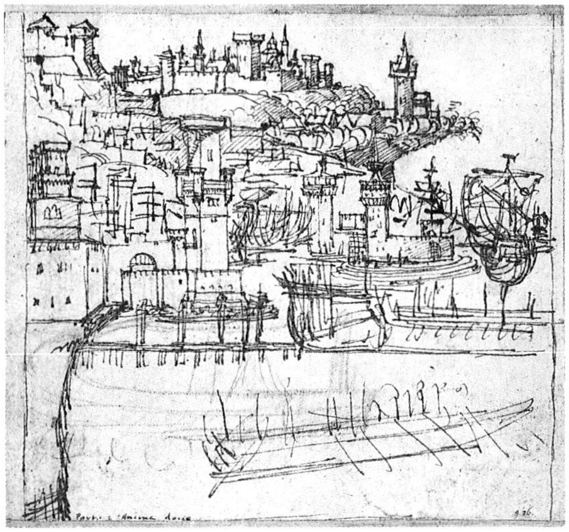

116. Carpaccio, Drawing of a harbor (London, British Museum, n. 1897–4-10-1)

In the *Leavetaking*, completed five years later, Carpaccio was moved to invent the Christian kingdom of Brittany on the model of contemporary Venice [Color Plate XXVIII]. On the right hand side of the painting, one sees roof-lines edged with cresting as on the Ducal Palace and the Ca d'Oro; walls reveted with white Istrian marble and decorated with roundels of *verde antico* and red porphyry as on the recently completed Ca' Dario and Pietro Lombardo's Santa Maria dei Miracoli; and the round-topped *bifora* windows of Mauro Codussi's Palazzo Corner-Spinelli.

Second, it has often been observed that Carpaccio was heavily indebted to book illustration. Close scrutiny by Molmenti and Ludwig of a preparatory drawing for the left background of the *Leavetaking* [Plate 116] yielded identifications of the Tower of the Cavaliers at Rhodes and the Tower of San Marco at Candia, both remodelled by the artist's pen. Others have observed in the drawing fragments of the ports of Modon and Corfu as well.[4] These elements, further altered when the composition as a whole was pulled together, served to define pagan England in the finished painting as a pile-up of late-medieval fortress architecture, in telling contrast to the shining kingdom across the waters.

Most scholars now feel that, whether or not Carpaccio had travelled to the Aegean island settings where the monuments stood, he obtained these architectural components from the engravings of Erhard Reeuwich in Breydenbach's *Opusculum Sanctarum Peregrinationum in Terram Sanctam*, published in Mainz in 1486.[5] Other motifs were deftly lifted from the book to reappear in glowing color in his paintings of the Holy Land for the *scuole piccole*.[6] Likewise, one can match up strikingly accurate details of Jewish ritual and costume, such as the vestments of the high priest in the *Marriage of the Virgin* that must have been drawn from woodcut illustrations in printed Bibles [Color Plate X].[7]

The third element that some have found in Carpaccio's aggregations of Venetian architectural forms is the apparatus of religious drama – the *sacra rappresentazione*: open-air porticoes [*loggie*], little architectural compartments placed side by side [*mansionarie*], small outdoor stages [*palchi*], and tiny temples [*edicole*].[8] The hypothesis is attractive at first glance, particularly when one notes the presence of members of Compagnie della Calza, known for their production of theatrical events, in most of the outdoor scenes. Likewise, for all their pious intent, there is a wit behind Carpaccio's works – consider the monkey dressed in senatorial robes who sits on the steps of the *loggia* in the *Return of the Ambassadors* – that speaks of a world of make-believe and impersonation. But it is difficult to sustain the nature of such a connection without any sure visual documents of theatrical productions from the period. One may always question the direction of influence and the priority of one form over the other.

Finally, we have intarsia panels. Carpaccio has been suggested as the designer of architectural perspectives in the marquetry of the sacristy of San Marco,[9] and indeed some elements common in intarsia work appear in his paintings: certain complex geometric forms like the *mazzocchio* (a multi-faceted ring), stacked polygonal platforms, columns, towers, the coiling ribbon, the armillary sphere. Carpaccio's free hand and manifest delight in painting these objects in his narrative scenes attest to his thorough grounding in perspective construction.[10]

The way in which these parts, gleaned from many sources, were put together in a composition brings us to the question of the whole. Not to belabor the matter, here again we are offered a choice. Intarsia reappears. Indeed, the correspondences between the panels in the sacristy of San Marco and several compositions in the St. Ursula circle are striking.[11] Theater sets are again proposed. But again they are problematic, for lack of surviving visual evidence.[12]

Carpaccio's visual archive could also have been well-stocked with elements and compositional structures from paintings made in Venice and elsewhere. Indeed, it is the site of his artistic formation in general that has drawn the most interest and sparked the most lively debate. Proposals for his training and influences, when taken together, constitute an ambitious itinerary. He has been hypothetically placed in his early years as close to Venice as Padua, Verona, Vicenza and Ferrara, and as far away as Rome, Urbino, Dalmatia and the Orient.[13] All seem possible, and yet much of the formal influence from these places that resounds in Carpaccio's paintings could have come to him at secondhand had he simply remained in Venice.

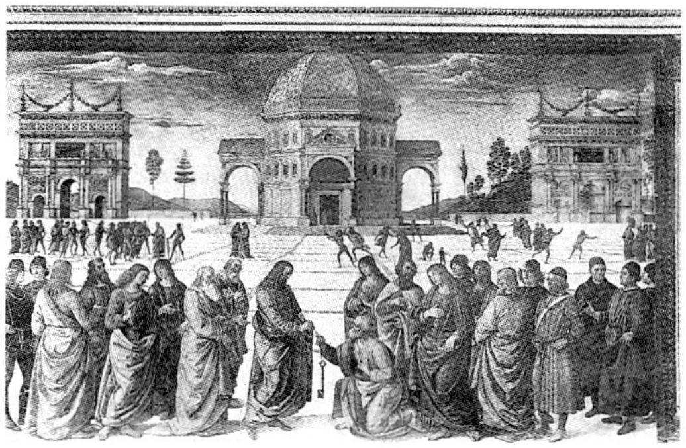
117. Perugino, *Consignment of the Keys*, fresco (Vatican, Sistine Chapel)

Let us look at just one compositional solution: the perspective view with a portico in front and a domed central-plan building in the background in the *Reception of the Ambassadors* [Color Plate XXVI]. Many viewers have found it unconceivable that Carpaccio could have created the spatial conception and distribution of the figures and architecture, with a high horizon line and ample middle ground, without direct knowledge of Perugino's *Consignment of the Keys* (1481) in the Sistine Chapel [Plate 117]. And yet Perugino can be documented in Venice by 1494 (some say earlier). He thus could have brought with him drawings, or even just ideas, that inspired Carpaccio to emulation without a trip to Rome.[14]

Likewise, Carpaccio's *Reception*, along with other paintings in the cycle and several of his later *istorie*, has often been linked to three famous perspective panels, now in Berlin, Baltimore and Urbino. The obscurity of the origins of these panels, with equally sensible cases made for both Urbino and Florence, should remind us just how portable such ideas could be.[15] Closer to home one sees Carpaccio surely drawing on the tradition of Jacopo Bellini, both directly and by way of Gentile Bellini, in his scenographic approach and emphasis on perspective views and his ability to recombine motifs with seemingly endless fecundity.

What is certain is that Carpaccio's sources were numerous and drawn from a wide range of material. This was not an art of the pattern book. With persistence we could undoubtedly add to the list. But that is not really the issue. The very elusiveness of Carpaccio's specific models may be the telling point. No single one of these motifs was ever adopted wholesale and untransformed. No known Venetian building was transplanted intact into any of the St. Ursula paintings. Carpaccio's constant aim appears to have been, above all, the creation of a particularized and unique setting, based upon the most distinctive models familiar to him.

VERSIONS OF THE EAST

The construction of Ursula's world had set one kind of challenge: the ambient was in the distant north, seldom frequented by Venetians and less accountable to the personal experience of the viewers. Just as Carpaccio was completing the St. Ursula cycle, the attention of other painters of the eyewitness school began to turn toward the lands of early Christianity, that eastern world of traditional and now growing concern. The task of representing a living oriental world – even though the events depicted were at least as ancient as the deeds of St. Ursula and her companions – posed different problems. For it was a world once embraced by Venetians which was now fast becoming distant to them.

Nonetheless, the Orient was still familiar territory to many Venetians of that time. To Josafat Barbaro, diplomat and practised eyewitness, it had been Venetian merchants and mariners who opened up the world of the east to the men of the west:

> In our time those that have seene some parte [of the earth] most commonly are merchauntmen or maryners, in which two exercises from the beginneng vnto this daie my Lordes and fathers the Venetians have beene and are so excellent that I believe they may verylie be called the principall. For syns the decaie of the Romaine estate (that sometime ruled over all) this inferior worlde hath been so divided by diversitie of languages customes, and religion, that the greatest parte of this little that is enhabited shulde have been unknowen, if the Venetian merchandise and marinership had not discovered it.[16]

But in the 1490s, this once open world seemed to be closing inexorably against the Venetians. With the rise of the Ottoman empire, the east had come to wear an alien and impenetrable face.[17] Increasing anxiety over the *stato da mar* may have been responsible in part for inducing Venetian artists to try to capture visually an oriental world previously frequented by mariners, merchants, diplomats and *viaggiatori*. This concern is revealed artistically in a precise and differentiated way in the paintings of the *scuole*. As shown by Julian Raby, orientalism in Venetian painting prior to 1495 was confined to Ottoman figures, populating western settings as '*membra disjecta*'.[18] For Gentile Bellini's one-year sojourn in Constantinople had produced no known immediate results in regard to the creation of a credible oriental ambient for the *istoria*. His influence seems to have been limited to a few authentic figure-studies of Ottoman Turks which artists could fit into their paintings, along with those members of Turkish embassies and trading delegations whom they might have observed personally in the streets of Venice. But there was, as Raby put it, no attempt to place these Ottomans into a 'corporate picture of the Ottoman world'.[19]

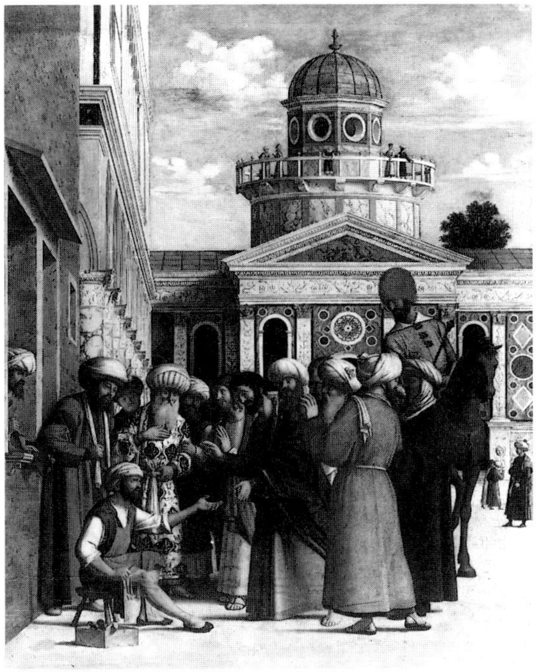

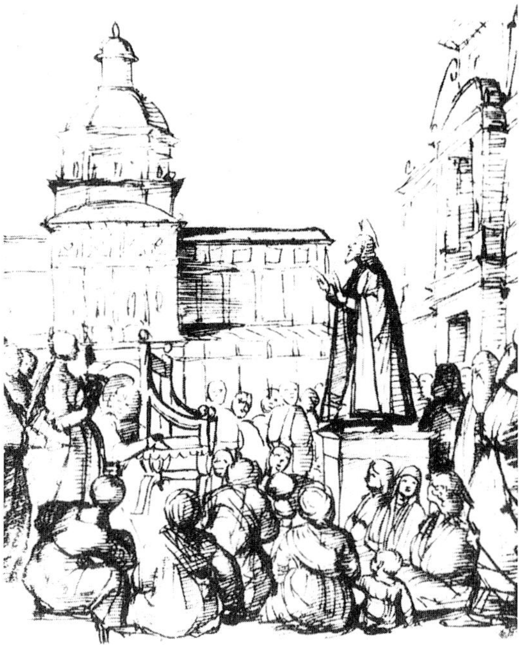

118 (far left). Cima da Conegliano, *St. Mark Healing Anianas* (Berlin-Dahlem, Staatliche Museen)

119 (left). Lattanzio da Rimini, *St. Mark Preaching*, drawing (formerly in Chatsworth, Devonshire Collection)

Although Carpaccio is probably the painter who most quickly comes to mind in relation to orientalism in Venetian art, it was first in the paintings of the Guild of the Silk-weavers (c. 1495–9) that a more thorough-going oriental mode began to develop. It is to them that we will now turn. In these scenes, the emphasis has shifted appropriately from the Ottoman Turks to the Mamluks of Syria and Egypt, where the events in the life of St. Mark actually took place. The change can be discerned most readily in the headgear. Instead of the relatively compact turban wound horizontally around the *taj*, or ribbed red cap, of the Ottomans, the figures in the surviving paintings of this cycle by Cima da Conegliano and Mansueti feature a whole range of hats worn only by the Mamluks: the great horned turban, sometimes called a waterwheel, worn by sultans and amirs; the tall domed hats and the red tufted bonnets of the military class; and most common of all, the cloth turbans wrapped vertically, without the *taj* [Plates 118–20].[20]

Raby proposed a single painting, the anonymous *Reception of an Ambassador* in the Louvre, as the vehicle of transmission of these motifs. It depicts the audience of a western delegation or embassy – almost certainly Venetian – with a Mamluk dignitary sitting in state and in full regalia on a platform on a street in Damascus [Color Plate XXXI and Plate 121].[21] In Raby's view, this painting represents more faithfully than did any of the other orientalizing paintings of the period, the costume, heraldry and architecture of the Mamluk world in its last days, before the Ottoman conquest of 1517.

What we have come to know of Venetian attitudes should caution us from concluding that the *Reception* was only a pretext for the artist to paint oriental genre. The patron, who was surely one of the more prominently situated members of the Venetian group, would have meant it to document incontrovertibly his presence at a specific place within a specific diplomatic context. Wishing to testify to an actual occurrence, the painter took pains to describe

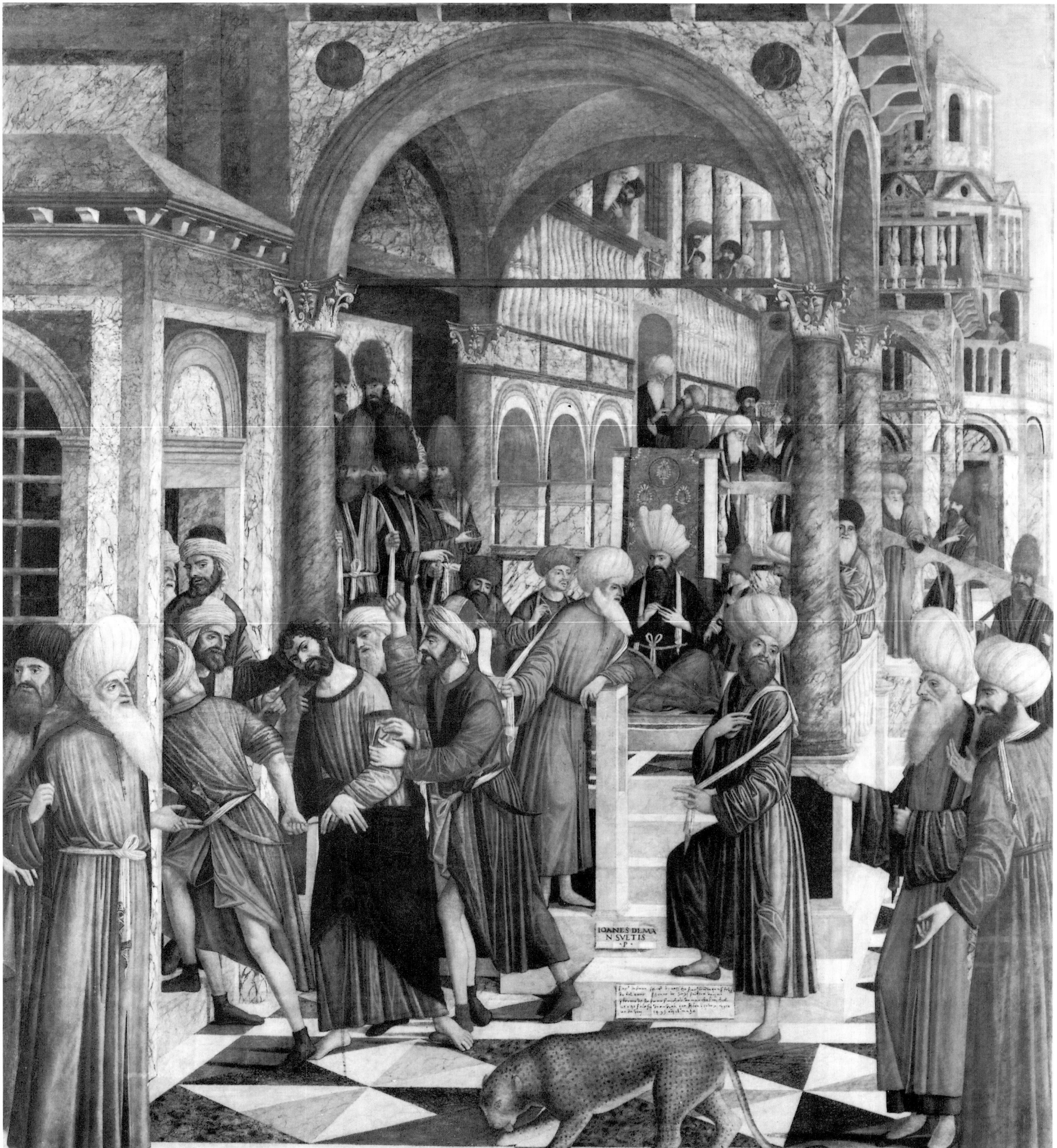
IOANES DI MA
N SVETIS
·P·

the ambient in detail. Its topographical accuracy confirms that he must have seen Damascus at first hand.[22] A date in the 1490s for the painting's execution would not be untenable, and would allow for it to have served the painters of the *Life of St. Mark* in the chapel of the Guild of the Silk-weavers as a primary source for the costume and custom of the oriental world.[23]

But considering the desire of Venetian artists of this period to reproduce historically convincing settings, it is significant, even allowing for the change of venue from Damascus to Alexandria, that Cima da Conegliano and Mansueti ignored completely the authentic middle-eastern architecture displayed in the *Reception*. In his *St. Mark Healing Anianas*, now in Berlin, Cima contrived a classically inspired architectural setting with reminiscences of the decorative surface treatments of Carpaccio in the St. Ursula cycle [Plate 118]. In the background, a cupola resting on a round drum rises above a building featuring a carved frieze in the manner of Pietro Lombardo and a pediment which contains a sculpted relief of a marine goddess.[24] A similar domed building dominates the background of Lattanzio da Rimini's drawing of St. Mark preaching, which probably reflects the composition of the next episode in the cycle [Plate 119].

In contrast to Cima's clarity – albeit a clarity enriched with color and pattern –

120 (facing). Mansueti, *Arrest of St. Mark* (Vaduz, Collection of the Prince of Liechtenstein)

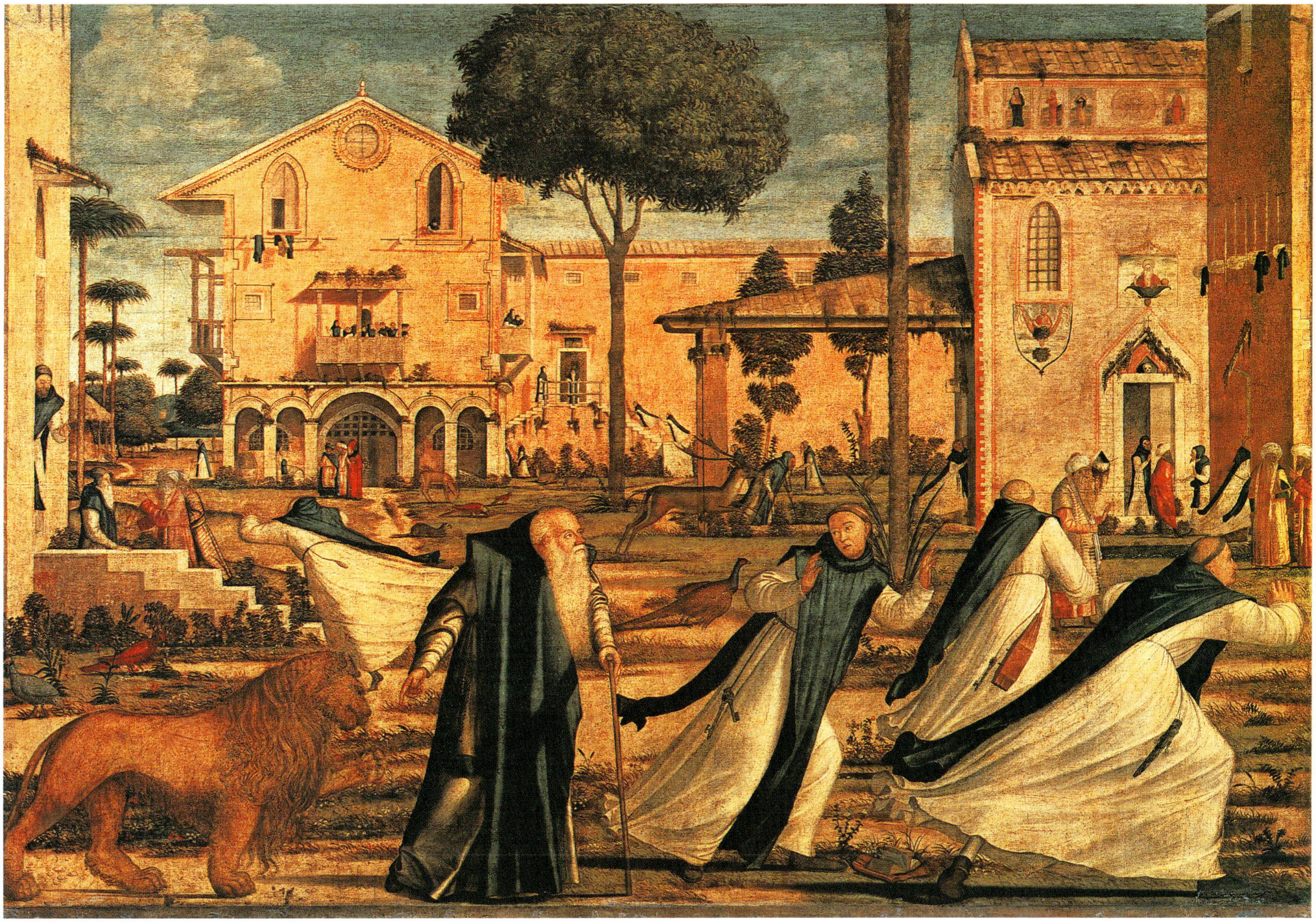

XXX. Carpaccio, *St. Jerome and the Lion* (Venice, Scuola di San Giorgio degli Schiavoni)

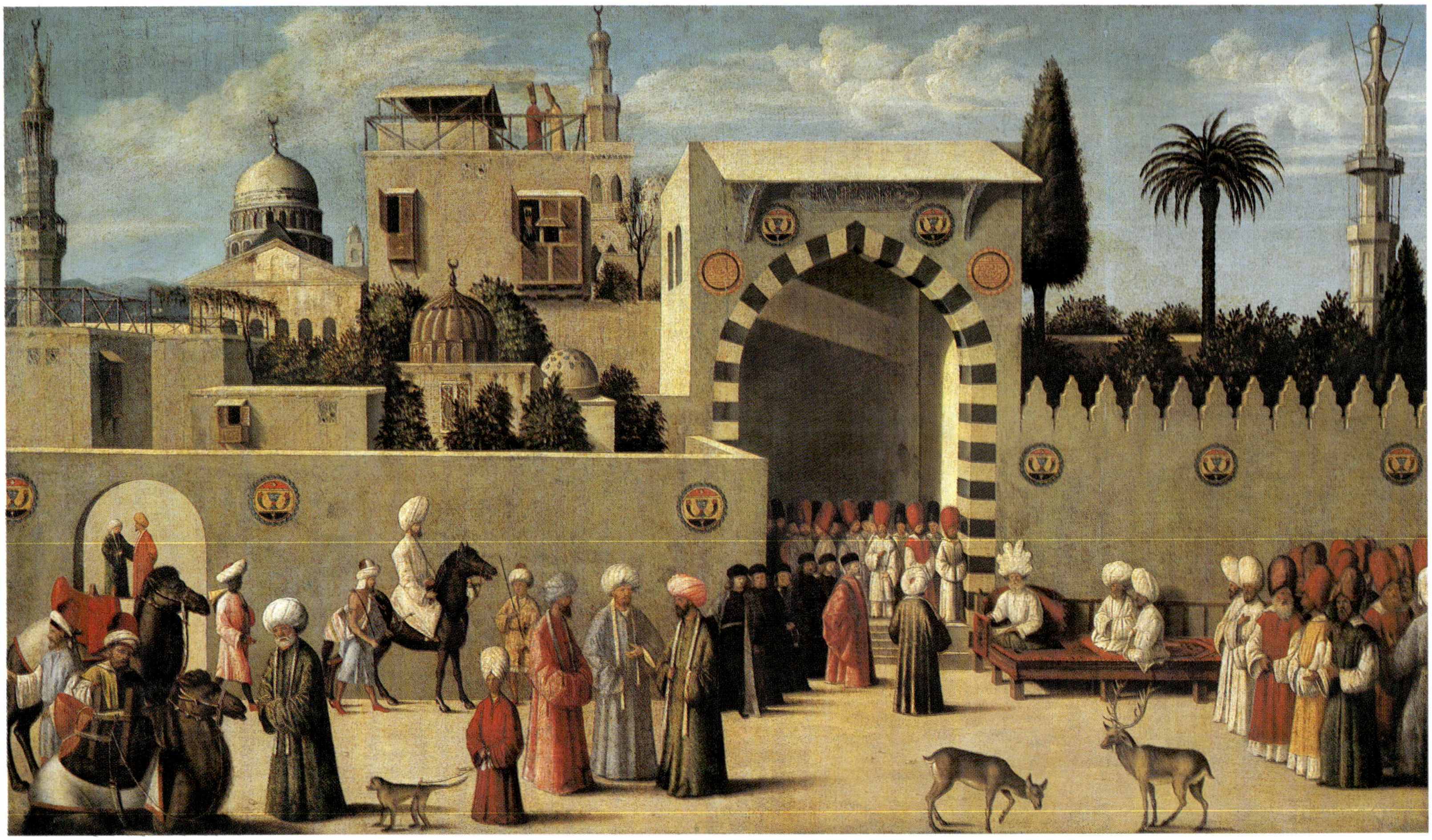

XXXI. Venetian artist, *Reception of an Ambassador in Damascus* (Paris, Louvre)

Mansueti opted, typically, for complexity bordering on confusion in his *Arrest of St. Mark* (now in Liechtenstein) [Plate 120]. Arcades and arches take the place of walls; mural surfaces are perforated with balustrades and extended with open loggias, balconies and porches. Mark is pulled into his prison chamber across a brightly patterned marble floor, while within a vaulted portico an official wearing a great water-wheel turban sits on a platform before a brocade cloth of state. He is surrounded by scribes recording his pronouncements on long scrolls. For all his visual loquaciousness, Mansueti achieves a credible quotation of life at a Muslim court. The scene could as well have been taken from the descriptive pages of a Venetian diplomatic report or even from an Islamic miniature. To Mansueti the essence of an Alexandrian setting was to be found in authentic-looking bearded figures wearing Mamluk headgear and costume, and in the additional touch of official reality of the seated scribes. These figures moved within a totally fanciful architecture that was based more on Venetian forms than on any other.

Another sure denotation of the world of St. Mark was the Mamluk coat-of-arms, so prominently displayed on the walls in the Louvre *Reception*. Just visible on a shield above the portal behind the Sultan's head [Plate 120], it was to be included in a round *tondo* form closer to its model – albeit with various changes – in Mansueti's three paintings for the Scuola di San Marco.[25]

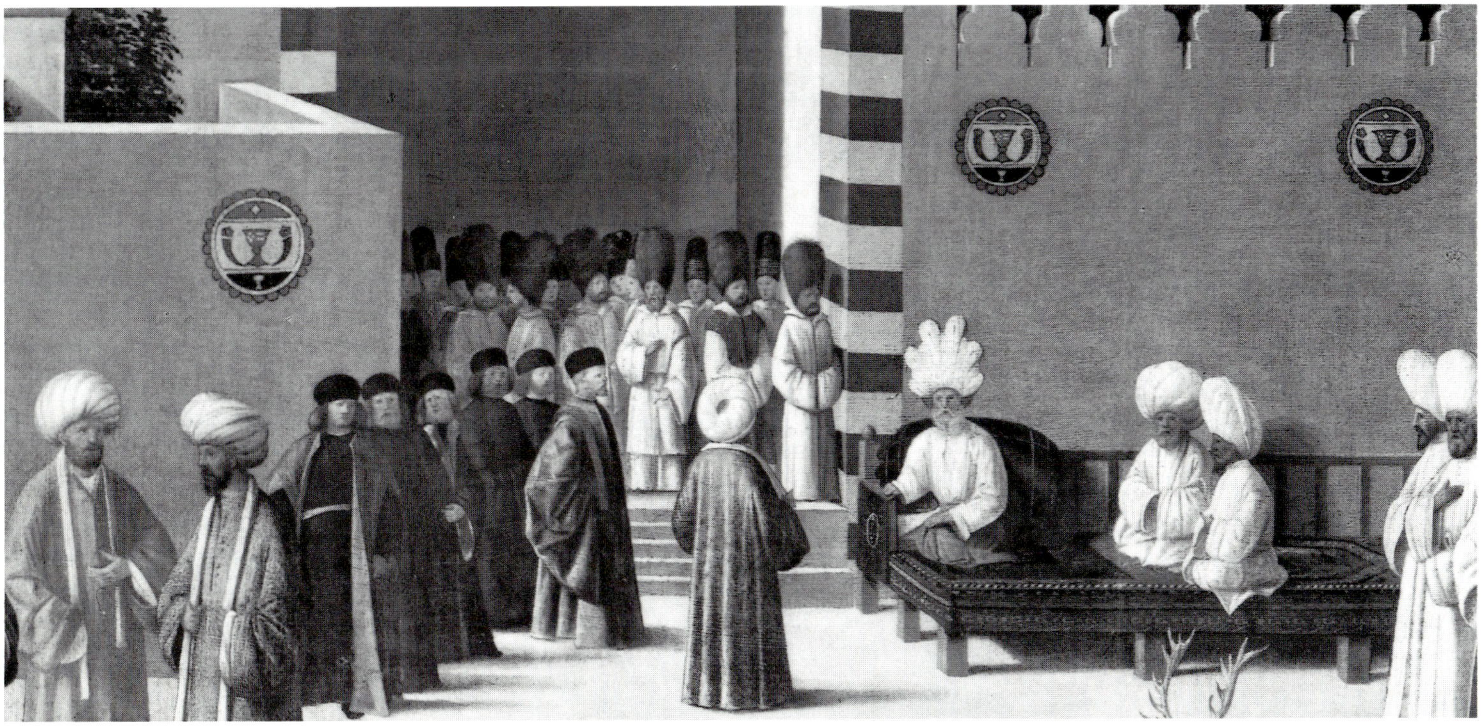

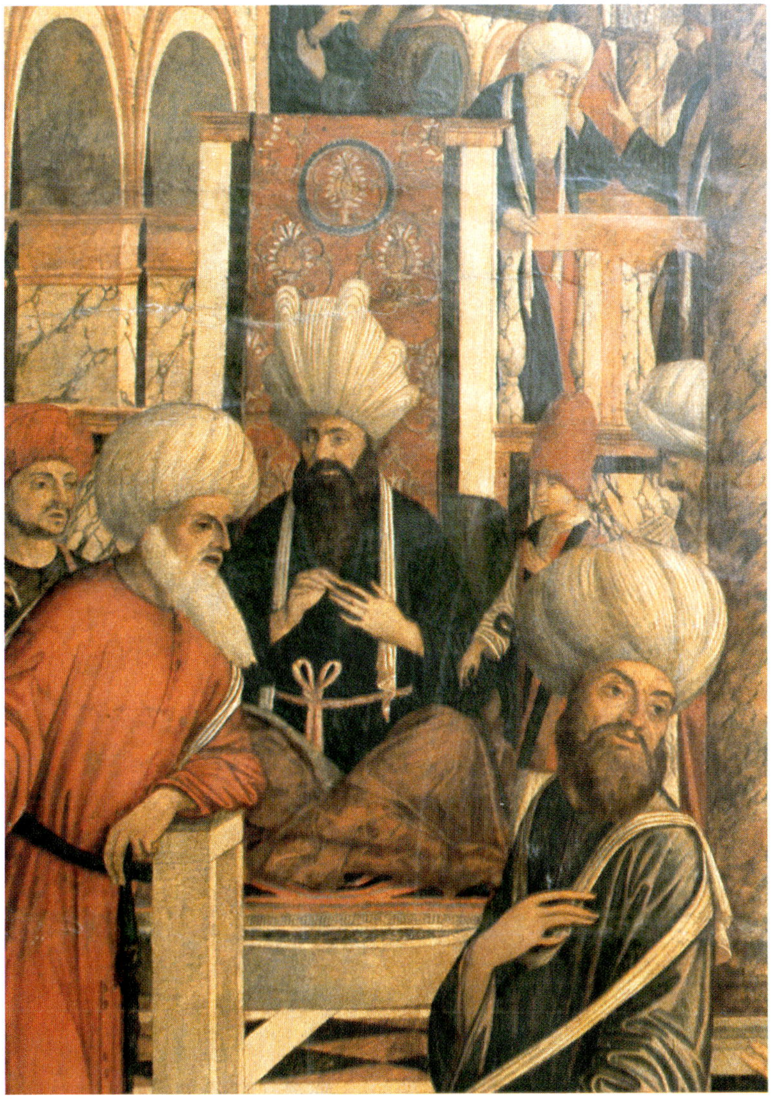

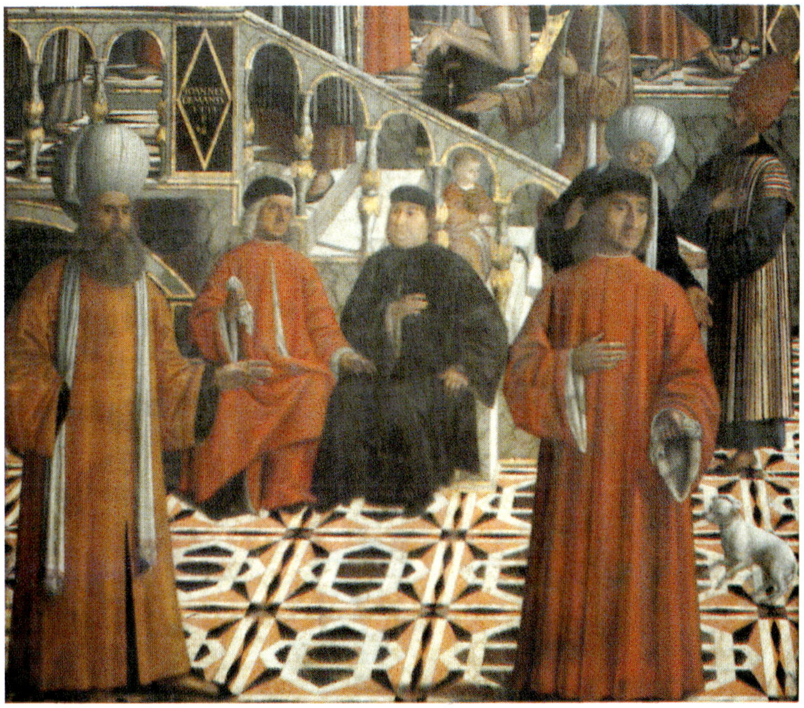

XXXIII. Mansueti, detail from *St. Mark Baptizing Anianas* (Plate 122)

121 (top). Venetian school, detail from the *Reception of an Ambassador in Damascus* (Color Plate XXXI)

XXXII (left). Mansueti, detail from the *Arrest of St. Mark* (Plate 120)

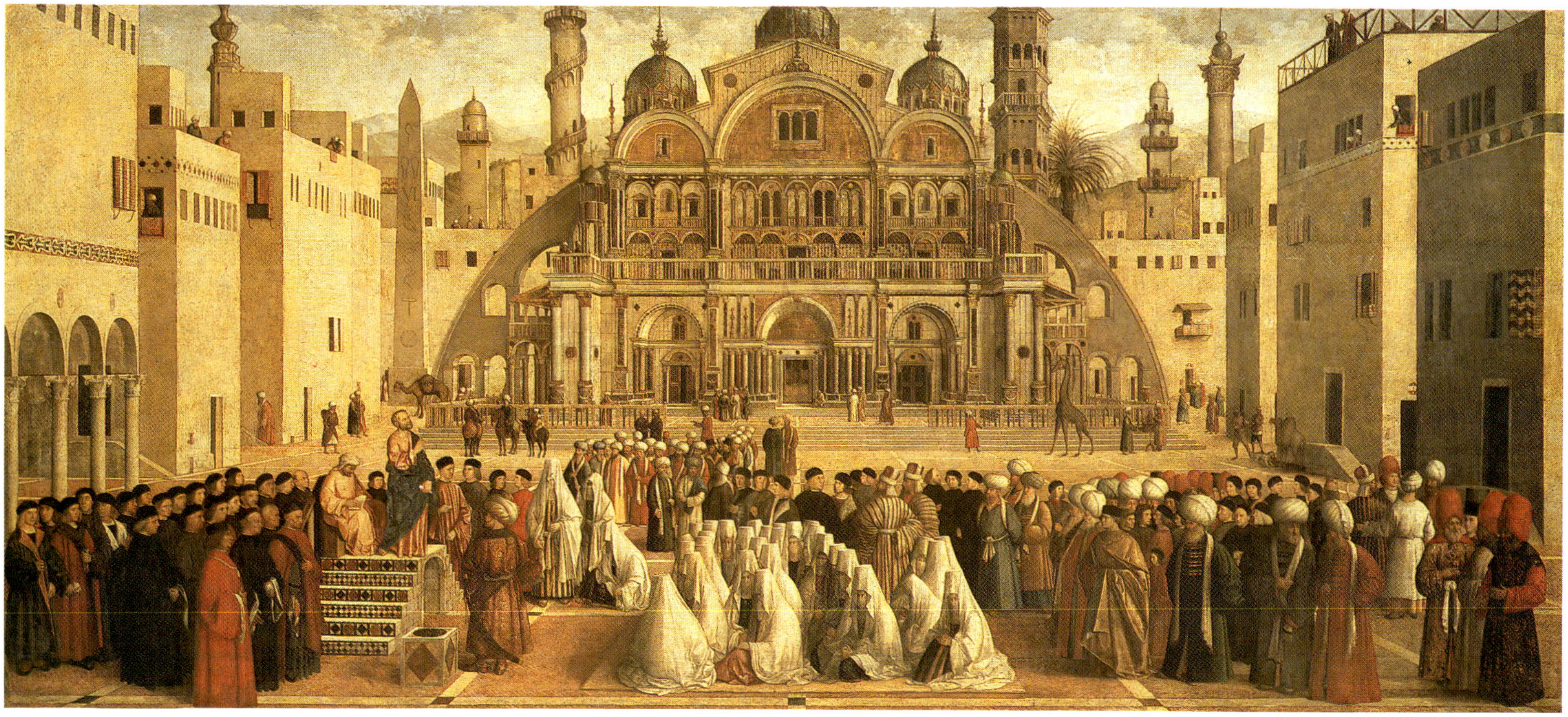

xxxiv. Gentile Bellini, *St. Mark Preaching in Alexandria* (Milan, Brera)

xxxv. Gentile Bellini, detail from *St. Mark Preaching in Alexandria* (Color Plate xxxiv)

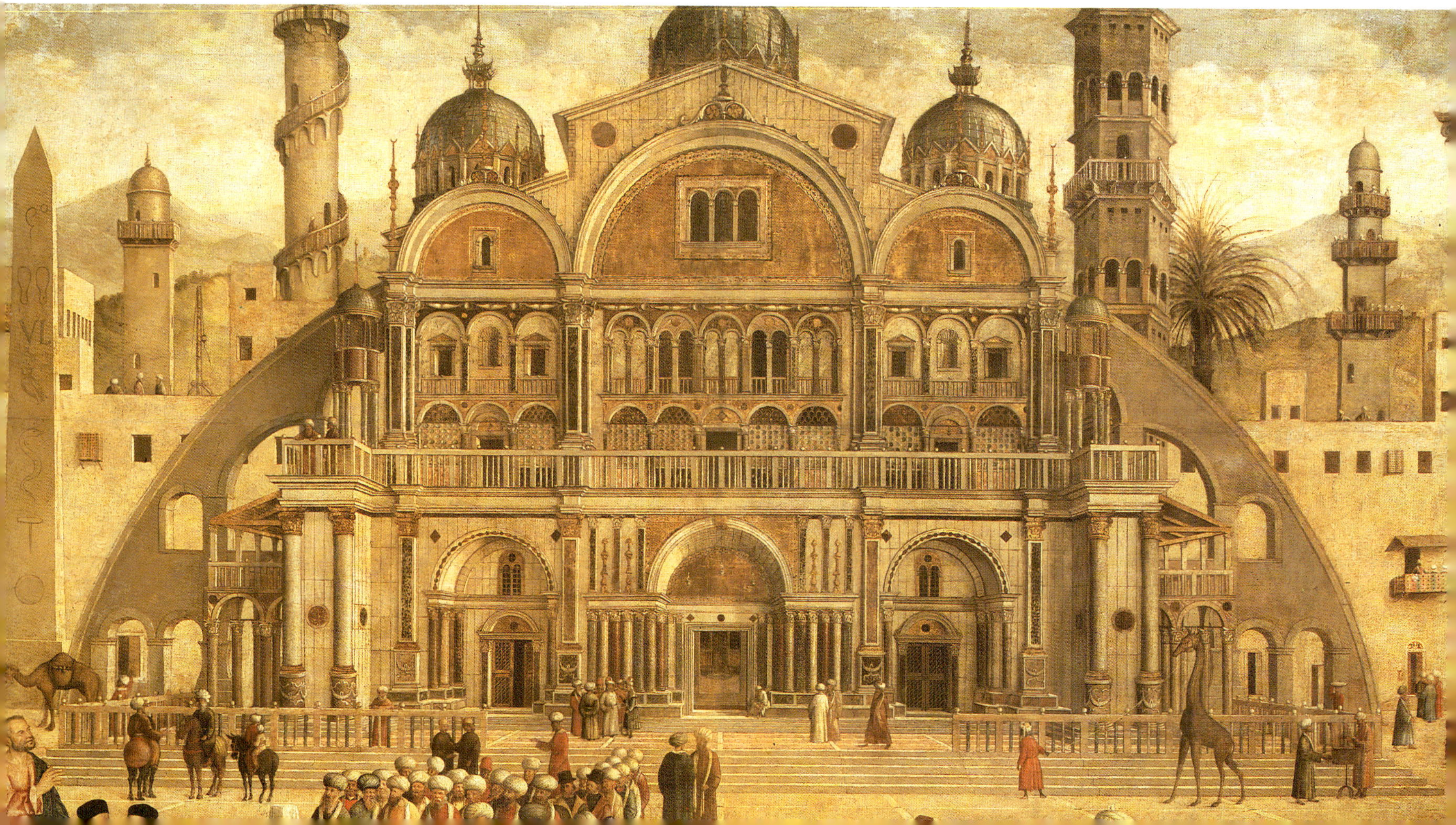

Mansueti continued to use the architectural structures and decorative elements developed for the Silk-weavers' commission in his subsequent works, adding or subtracting elements to suit the format and the needs of the narrative. Each subsequent scenographic apparatus involved the selection and re-organization of elements in those that had been painted earlier. Let us see how this worked. The *Healing of the Daughter of Benvegnudo* (c. 1506) in the True Cross cycle was probably his next narrative painting [Plate 90]. Even though it was set in Venice rather than the Holy Land, he did not hesitate to adapt features taken from the *Arrest of St. Mark* of the Silk-weavers – veined marble with colored inlays, red trimmed arches, a balcony with turned balusters viewed from the side – to a Venetian *palazzo*. But for the ceiling he added a splendid compartmented *soffitto alla veneziana*.

The *soffitto* must have been well-received, for it was co-opted back into an Alexandrian ambient in *St. Mark Baptizing Anianas* for the Scuola di San Marco [Plate 122 and Color Plate XXXIII]. Here Mansueti was faced with the difficult problem of composing a narrative scene in a narrow vertical format. He solved it by throwing a balcony across the upper zone of the painting. Featuring curved protruding platforms enclosed by a railing with widely spaced balusters, similar to the staircase in *Benvegnudo's Daughter*, the second storey was again completed with a gilded *soffitto*. For the lower zone, Mansueti adapted the groin-vaulted open portico from the earlier *Arrest of St. Mark*, and replaced some of the marble roundels in the spandrels with Mamluk emblems.

The curved balcony motif of *Benvegnudo's Daughter* reappeared above the centralized arcade of *St. Mark Healing Anianas* [Plate 76], but was rejected in Mansueti's final painting for the San Marco cycle, the *Episodes in the Life of St. Mark* [Plate 123]. In the latter work, he reshaped his favored open arcades and porticoes and returned to some of the features of Cima's painting of *St. Mark Healing*: straight balconies with straight balusters, domed buildings with white-framed *oculi*, and even a classical pediment. For the first time he picked up the authentic projecting window embrasures of the Louvre *Reception*.

Once he had hit upon his orientalizing paradigm, Mansueti was remarkably consistent, disregarding completely the grand open scheme of Gentile Bellini in *St. Mark Preaching in Alexandria*, along with its bits of authentic scenography, and the innovative assemblages of Carpaccio. As in the True Cross cycle, Mansueti approached the problem of constructing a setting like a stage designer. The repetitive galleries, balustrades and balconies are used more as scaffolds on which to organize and present the greatest possible number of actors and spectators than as self-contained and distinctive environments within which ongoing movement and action would be played out.[26] It is for this reason that these settings, for all their decorative and structural exuberance, would be truly tedious without the enlivening presence of the actors. In Gentile Bellini's last painting, we see a very different vision.

* * *

Although *St. Mark Preaching in Alexandria* [Color Plate XXXIV] was completed after Gentile's death by his brother Giovanni, radiographs made prior to a recent restoration confirm that Gentile Bellini was responsible for the overall composition and massing of figures and architecture.[27] He had completed the entire background, including the great Basilica structure, the wall and the monuments behind it, as well as the figures in Mamluk costume, and had at least roughed in nearly all the Venetian bystanders.

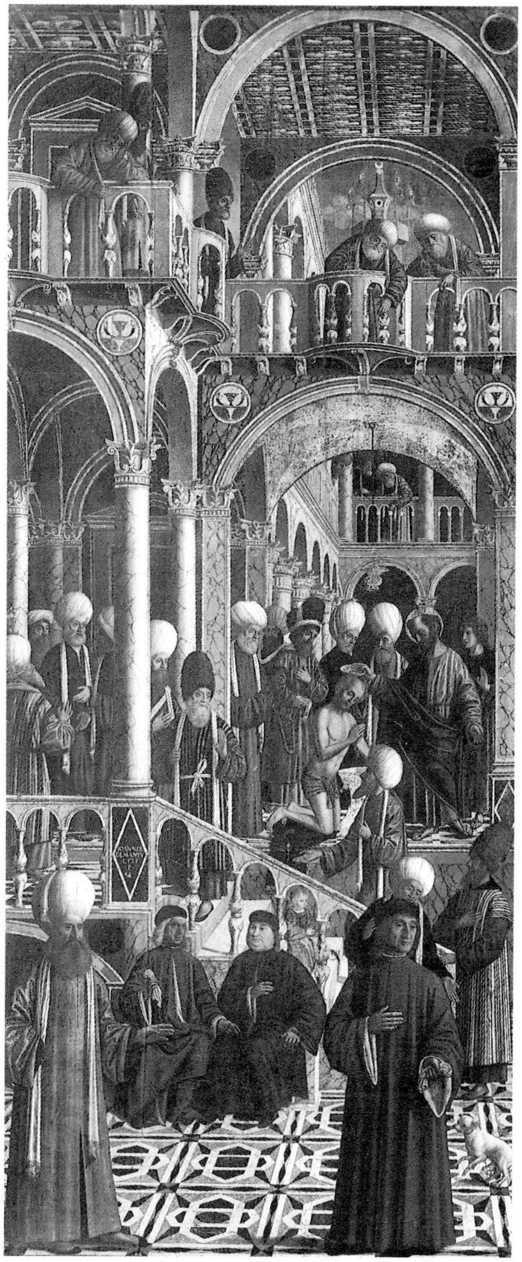

122. Mansueti, *St. Mark Baptizing Anianas* (Milan, Brera)

123 (pp. 204–5). Mansueti, *Episodes in the Life of St. Mark* (Venice, Ospedale Civile)

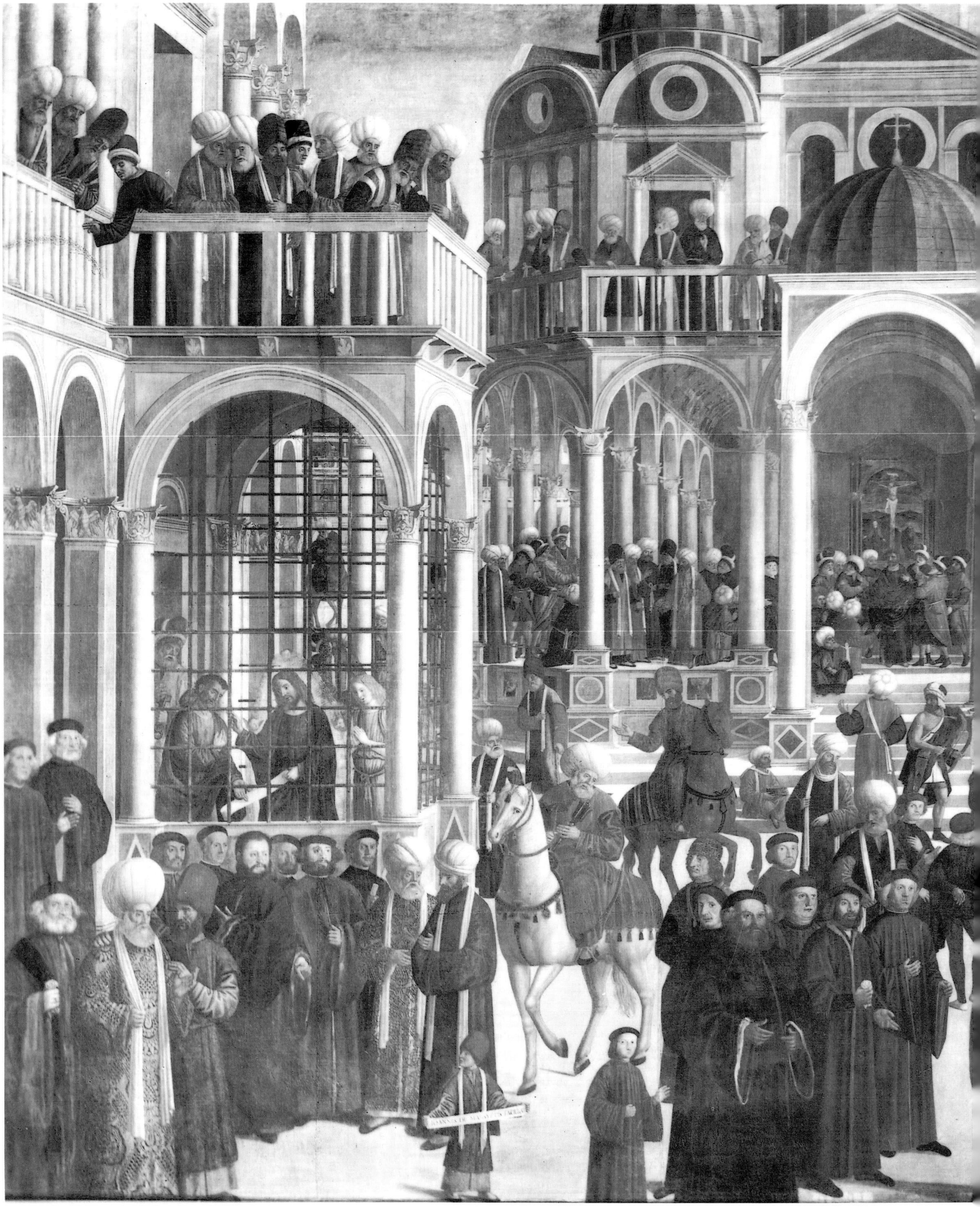

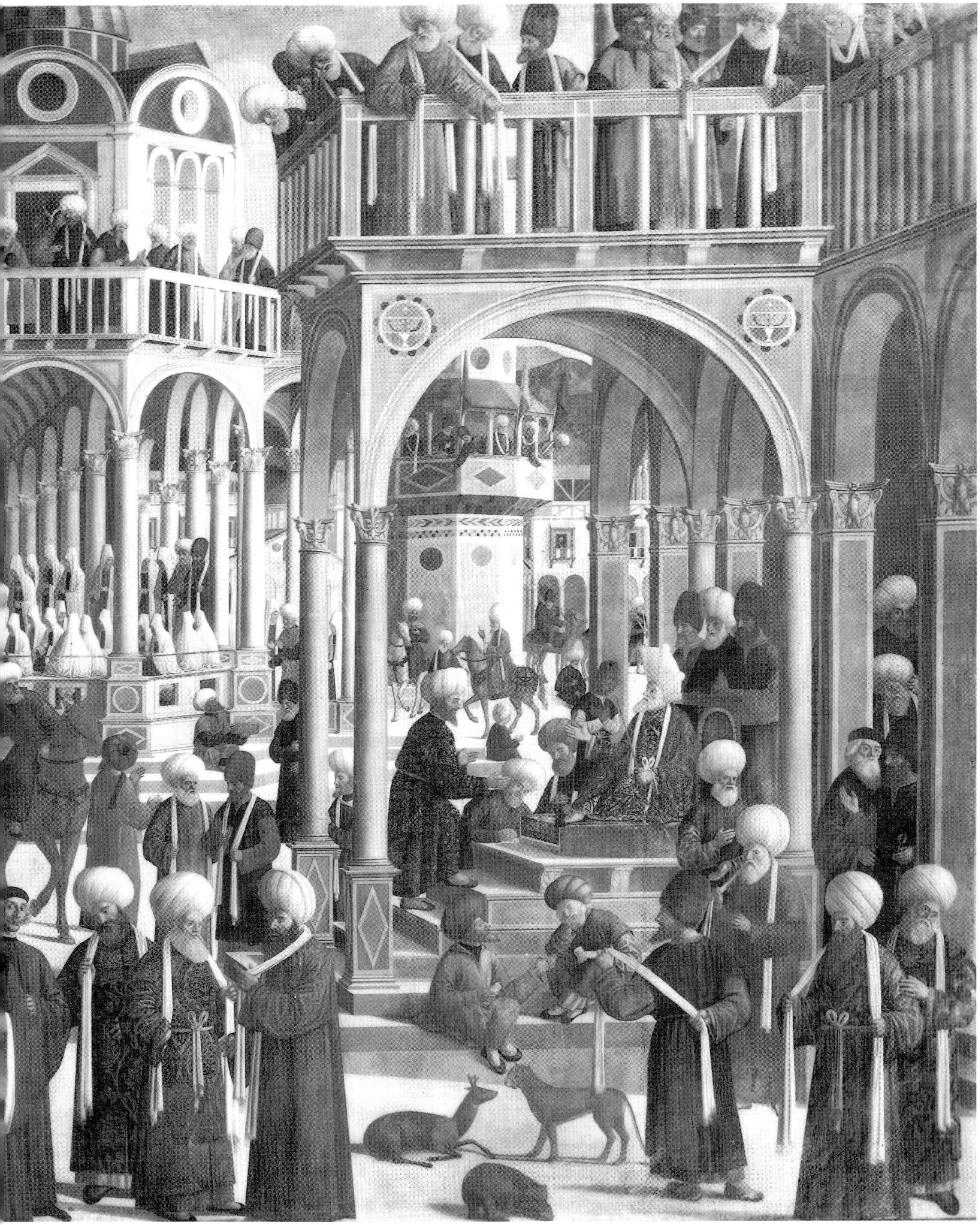

Giovanni's interventions were confined to the figures in the foreground and the buildings at the sides. As well as overpainting the entire figure of St. Mark and his scribe, he also painted in many of the faces of the *confratelli*. Since portraits were usually the last part of an *istoria* to be painted, Giovanni's work on them may have been a question more of completion than correction.[28] But he made two significant changes that we should regard as critiques on the narrative mode of his brother. He added the large cube in front of Mark's platform, thus providing a stronger focus – perhaps deliberately abjured by Gentile – to the narrative core of the painting. He also simplified the buildings on the sides, perhaps for the same reason. In the initial rendering, Gentile had painted six buildings on each side. Giovanni reduced them to just four on the left and three on the right, consolidating the roof lines, and decreasing the number of arches in the arcade on the left. He thus reduced the distracting complexities that would pull the viewer's attention away from the main subject.

There is no evidence that either brother had ever set foot in Alexandria, the site of St. Mark's ministry and martyrdom and the setting for most of the paintings of the San Marco cycle.[29] The painting, with its largely invented topography, itself tends to support this conclusion. Given the probability that Gentile was charged with inventing an oriental world that he had never seen, how, then, did he go about his task? For costumes, motifs and architectural details, he could have drawn upon a number of sources: his own experience of twenty-five years earlier in Constantinople; the sketchbooks of other artists who had travelled to Egypt and Syria; the Louvre *Reception*; and woodcuts like those of Reeuwich which were so useful to Carpaccio. He would also have seen examples of Mamluk dress right on the streets of Venice.[30]

Aside from visual sources, Gentile may even have had access to the verbal and written accounts of Venetian diplomats and *viaggiatori*. But such reports often read like medieval *mirabilia*, taking note only of the major monuments and fixing on details rather than topographical relationships. Zaccaria Pagani, a Bellunese noble in the service of the Venetian ambassador, presented a dreary picture of Alexandria in 1512:

> . . . nine-tenths of it are in ruins. I have never seen such decadence; the devastation of Candia does not approach this . . . A great part of the city is constructed over underground passages; one sees two mountains commonly called, 'mountains of rubbish'. The prison in which St. Catherine was shut up still exists. I wished to enter there for devotion. Close nearby stand two great columns on which the wheel was placed, instrument of the martyrdom of the saint. One sees also in the middle of a street, called the Street of St. Mark, a stone similar to a millstone on which the evangelist had been beheaded. One notices still two obelisks like those of St. Peter's in Rome; one is standing and the other fallen to the ground . . . Beyond the walls, one sees a great column where Pompey, who had taken refuge in Egypt after fleeing from Rome, was decapitated. The bazaars that we call at home *botteghe di merci* are very numerous . . . . The entry [to the port] is defended by the Pharos, a castle armed with artillery . . .[31]

Besides three Christian churches that he listed without description – Santa Saba, San Marco and San Michele – Pagani mentioned no other landmarks. His brevity is typical, and it is probable that Gentile would have had to piece together his environment from such a list, without any clear conception of how the monuments were placed in relation to each other.

To understand how he might have proceeded, it will be helpful to return once again to the Louvre *Reception* [Color Plate XXXI]. It should first be pointed out that the painting is not the equivalent of a photograph: a view recorded directly by the artist. Jean Sauvaget, the scholar who originally identified the depicted city as Damascus, described it as an amalgam that has been pieced together from three separate constituent parts: 1. the architectural backdrop, composed of known monuments like the Great Umayyad Mosque, with its high dome resting upon two superimposed polygonal drums, and the three distinctive minarets flanking its courtyard; 2. the formal audience in front of the pointed *iwan* arch, which forms the narrative core of the painting; 3. the collection of men and animals who fill the left foreground. Along with the Mamluk blason repeated along the wall, these genre elements provided what Sauvaget called a note of '*couleur locale*', and could have been assembled from separate sketches.[32]

In his *St. Mark Preaching in Alexandria*, Gentile followed very much the same procedure. We have seen how the *Procession in the Piazza San Marco* was the intended measure and model for the work, informing its general composition, architectural and figural massing and perspective construction.[33] In a similar manner, *St. Mark Preaching* is dominated and organized by an impressive structure in the background [Color Plate XXXV]. It is a curious building, composed of three naves, each topped with a blue dome, and flanked by large curving buttresses pierced with arches. Its resemblance to the Basilica of San Marco in Venice, the Scuola di San Marco and even the Hagia Sophia has been noted by observers from Ridolfi to the present.[34] We might further observe that the impulse to render a Basilica of San Marco that was stripped of its gothic pinnacles and ogee arches may have had its genesis in Gentile's redaction of the lunette mosaic or the Porta di Sant'Alippio for the *Procession* [Plate 81]. There he did the work of a miniaturist, recapturing the clean lines of the old thirteenth-century facade of the Basilica as it was shown above the door. It was a natural prototype for Gentile's rendering in the *Preaching* of another archaic building that was associated with the saint.[35] We will return further on to the question of its precise identification.

The narrative core of the work is centered on St. Mark, standing in the front plane on a small stepped platform and raising one hand in the oratorical gesture of preaching, while holding a scroll in the other. He speaks, and behind him a scribe records his words. A commanding turbanned figure in front of him, the only Ottoman in the painting, is balanced by Gentile Bellini himself to the left, distinguished by a red senatorial toga and the gold chain that had been given to him by the Sultan Mehmed II.[36]

Given the force of tradition in Venetian art and the concept of the *istoria* as visual testimony, Gentile would have been well aware of the paradigmatic weight of the mosaics that depicted Mark's life in the Basilica. And yet as we have already observed in relation to the Alexander legend, the constituents of historical proof had changed significantly since the twelfth and thirteenth centuries, along with expectations for a credible *istoria*. The twelfth-century mosaic of St. Mark preaching in the Cappella di San Pietro in the presbytery [Plate 124] was thus originally intended as an ideogram of one of the evangelist's characteristic activities rather than as a naturalistically convincing representation of 'how it really was'.

But, in fact, the Mark of the Scuola painting, whether painted by Gentile or

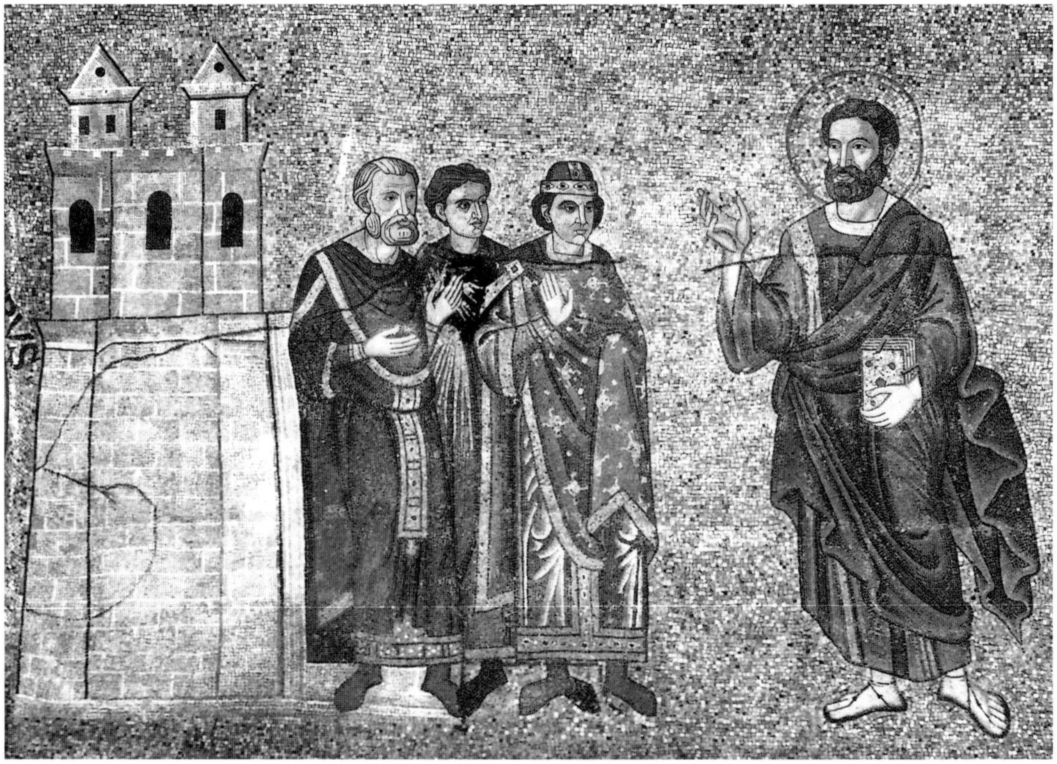

124. *St. Mark Preaching*, mosaic (Venice, Basilica of San Marco, Cappella di San Pietro)

by Giovanni Bellini, is similar indeed to the Mark of the mosaic. Both depict him with the same bearded visage, classical robes, stance and gestures, with one hand raised to speak and the other holding written material. In the painting as well as the mosaic, Mark preaches to a mixed group, each wearing distinctive dress. It was only here, in the core event of the historical narrative, that Gentile would repair to the venerable mosaic image and allow it its exemplary due.

For Sauvaget's *couleur locale*, Gentile added the camels, the giraffe and the palm tree, assorted minarets, and clusters of onlookers in Mamluk dress. To Giovanni Bellini we may owe the plain-walled stucco buildings flanking the square; unlike the Basilica that dominates the background, these are simply generic types, characteristic of any Islamic city.

To place St. Mark and his audience, as well as the great imaginary Basilica, firmly in Alexandria, Gentile had to do more than people the scene with actors in Mamluk dress.[37] It was also necessary to add known physical symbols of the city to fix its identity visually. Here he established a specific landscape that localized the action, in the same manner in which the Great Umayyid Mosque and minarets had located the Louvre *Reception* in Damascus. The Column of Diocletian, visible behind the wall to the right of the Basilica, was known in Alexandria from the days of the Crusaders onward as Pompey's Pillar. It marked the site of the ancient Serapeum, a pagan temple which had been destroyed by Christians in 391 AD. Its inclusion in the painting made a telling iconographical connection with St. Mark, who had been martyred precisely because he had preached against the worship of Serapis. The leftmost tower could have represented the Pharos, the famous lighthouse that guarded the harbor of Alexandria. These were celebrated monuments, of which Gentile would have been well

125 (facing). Gentile Bellini, detail from *St. Mark Preaching in Alexandria* (Color Plate XXXIV)

aware from numerous written accounts, and for which he may have had models of similar structures in his sketchbook from his stay in Constantinople twenty-five years earlier.[38]

The obelisk in front of the wall to the left of the Basilica corresponded to one that had stood in front of the Caesareum of Alexandria since the Emperor Augustus had brought it from the temple of Amon at Heliopolis [Plate 125].[39] Charles Dempsey's magistral deciphering of its inscriptions has allowed him to offer a convincing identification of the basilican structure and to give precision to the meaning of the painting as a whole. Basing his interpretation upon hieroglyphs in the *Hypnerotomachia Poliphili* published in Venice in 1499, and on inscriptions on known obelisks, he has suggested the following passage as a fair rendering of its message: 'Serapis subjectis suis vovit libens: ex ignorantia invidiaque in vita ventura fortuna sua decrescet' [Serapis willingly vowed to his subjects: his fortunes would decline in the life to come out of ignorance and envy]. Serapis thus prophesied the coming of Christianity and the fall of his own pagan cult, a vow that would be fulfilled with St. Mark's mission to Alexandria.[40] The painting, therefore, did more than simply record one of Mark's activities in the city. It also commemorated the establishment of the Church in Alexandria.

Following this line of argument, the analogies between the building in the background and San Marco in Venice were no coincidence. Gentile's Basilica here was the temple of Serapis, modelled on San Marco in Venice, and soon to be replaced by (or transformed into) a church of Christian worship. The inclusion of contemporary Venetians and Mamluks referred to the present and to the hope of reconverting these latter-day pagans of Islam back again to Christianity.

Dempsey points out that the *Hypnerotomachia Poliphili* was taken seriously at the time as an authoritative and genuine source. The ancient language of hieroglyphs was seen as a means to express ideas 'non in verbis sed in rebus'. Their inclusion in the painting brings Gentile into the humanist ambient and reveals one of those rare instances in the paintings of the eyewitness school where the influence of a learned advisor can be regarded as certain.[41]

In sum, the believability of an Alexandrian landscape, distant in time and space, was achieved in an anecdotal way. To locate the action in a particular city, it was only necessary to add certain identifying monuments or insignia as attributes. These could be a collection of known landmarks like Gentile's obelisk and array of towers in *St. Mark Preaching* or even the Mamluk blason in Mansueti's works. Fantasy was made factual by the insertion of authentic elements into a larger exotic setting that was defined as much by its 'non-westernness' as by its authentic 'easternness'.

Carpaccio's orient

Carpaccio's oriental phase began around the same time in the Scuola di San Giorgio degli Schiavoni. Most visitors to Venice have visited the ground-floor oratory where Carpaccio's paintings now hang [Plate 1]. No longer in their original location, probably on the upper floor of the building, the canvases still bring back some of the intended effect of a cycle of *istorie* that was painted *atorno atorno* a meeting-hall: a darkened room, lined with wood panelling two-thirds of

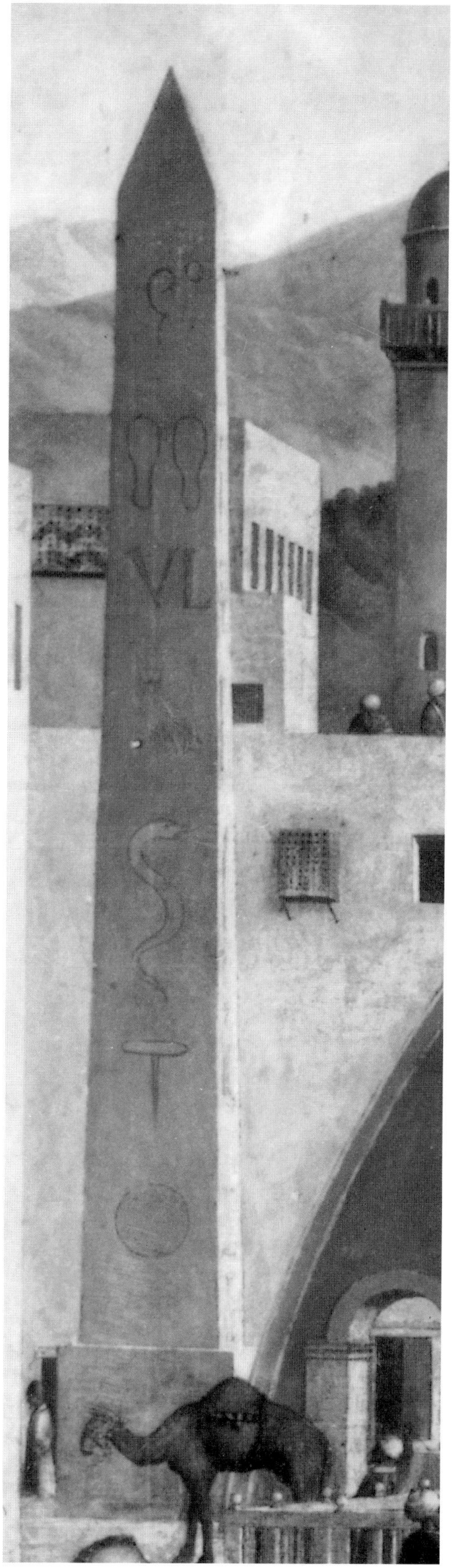

the way up, and above it a succession of brilliantly colored canvases, 'running long or short as suits their subjects', as Ruskin once put it. At the outset, it is their decorative properties which capture our attention, as they did Ruskin's. To him the overall effect had been that of 'an Eastern carpet, or old-fashioned English sampler, of more than usually broken and sudden variegation; nay suggestive here and there of a wayward patchwork, verging into grotesqueness, or even, with some touch of fantasy in masque, into harlequinade'.[42] Modern scholars tend to be less poetic, but they have equal difficulty in fixing the elusive character – and even more, the basis – of Carpaccio's orientalism. Often they appear to be speaking of two different artists.

On the one hand we have the Carpaccio of the 'innocent eye', as characterized by David Marshall:

> The fantasy and Oriental exoticism which are sometimes detected in these works is the consequence not so much of Eastern influences, or of a fantastic imagination, as of sometimes rather naive juxtapositions of motifs derived from disparate sources. Carpaccio was essentially a literal-minded artist, and when he confined himself to a unified setting that he knew well, like that in the Accademia *Miracle of the Reliquary of the True Cross*, this is apparent; but when confronted with the task of recreating a country he had probably never seen, his prosaic method of juxtaposing appropriate motifs created an impression of Oriental fantasy that was never intended.[43]

On the other hand, we have the imaginative Carpaccio of Gian Lorenzo Mellini, who contrasts the artist's approach with the documentary manner of Gentile Bellini as 'a visionary alternative, in which existing [things] are extended, integrated, and surpassed'.[44]

What is thus seen as a pedestrian dependence on concrete models to one becomes a means of transcendence to another. If we can come to terms with the causes for such conflicting interpretations, we may approach a better understanding of Carpaccio's art. Let us look again at some of the paintings in question.

Carpaccio presented the heroic *istoria* of St. George and the Dragon, taken from the *Golden Legend*, in three episodes for the Scuola di San Giorgio degli Schiavoni. In the first canvas we see the *Battle*, set in the countryside just outside Silena, a town in the province of Libya [Color Plates XXXVI–XXXVII]. Locked in combat before a large lake, the opposing forms of St. George and the dragon unite two sides of a panoramic landscape. It has been noted that the city gateway of the town of Silena on the left is adapted from the Bab al-Futuh in Cairo, and that the church high on the hill above the princess on the right is a fair copy of the church of St. Cyriacus in Ancona.[45] The townscape is further distinguished by an obelisk, an equestrian monument on a high pedestal, a row of date palms and several towers of distinctive appearance. It is more than just a generic middle-eastern town: it is a town that we would recognize again if we came upon it by chance. And this is the first point: each scene in this small cycle is highly particularized and different from the others. It is a lesson that Mansueti never learned.

A look at the design process of the *Triumph of St. George* will help to make the second point. Here we are brought inside the city walls to an open square that is dominated by a great domed building and surrounded by towers and minarets of various shapes [Plate 126 and Color Plate XXXVIII]. A preparatory

XXXVI (facing above). Carpaccio, detail from *St. George Fighting the Dragon* (Color Plate XXXVII)

XXXVII (facing centre). Carpaccio, *St. George Fighting the Dragon* (Venice, Scuola di San Giorgio degli Schiavoni)

XXXVIII (facing below). Carpaccio, *Triumph of St. George* (Venice, Scuola di San Giorgio degli Schiavoni)

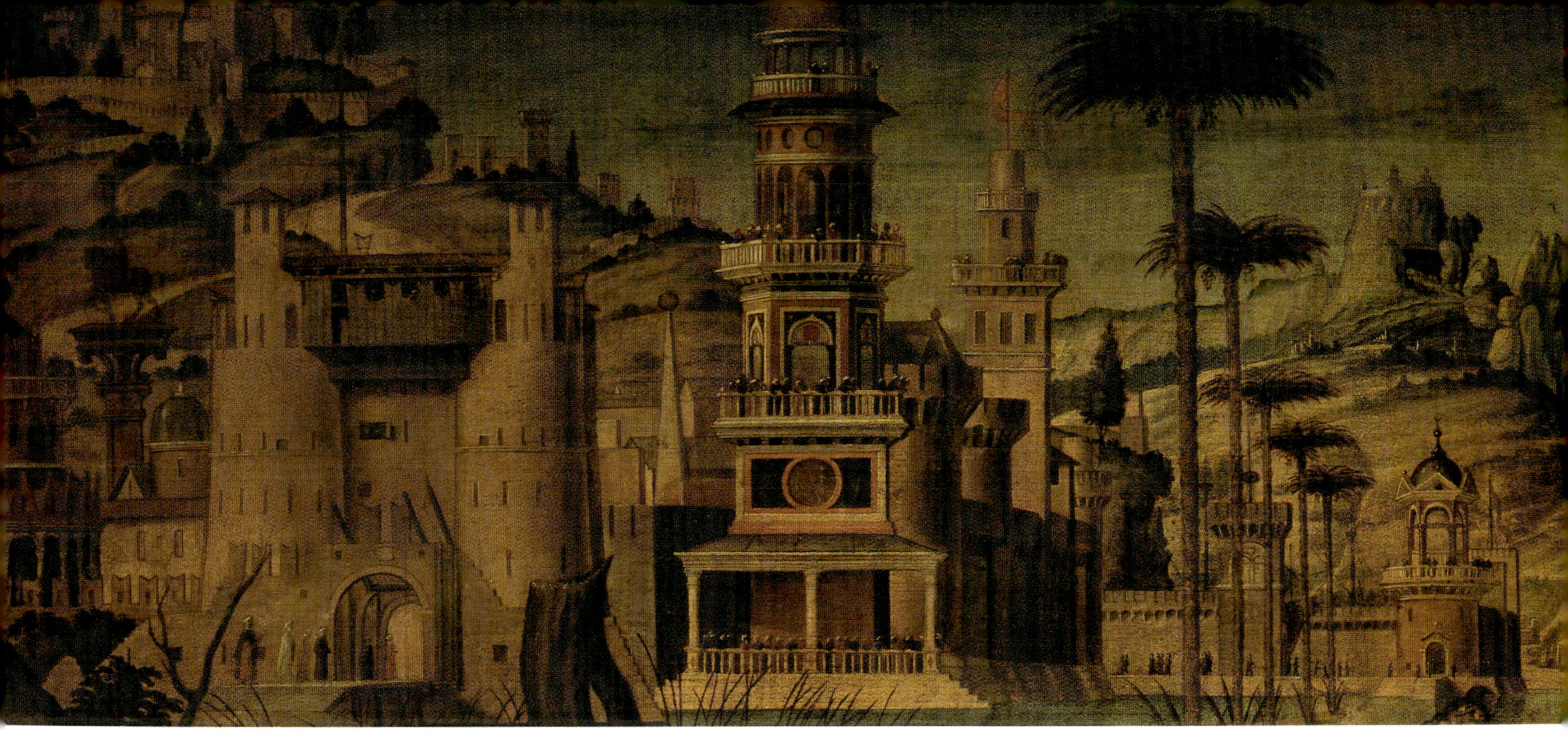

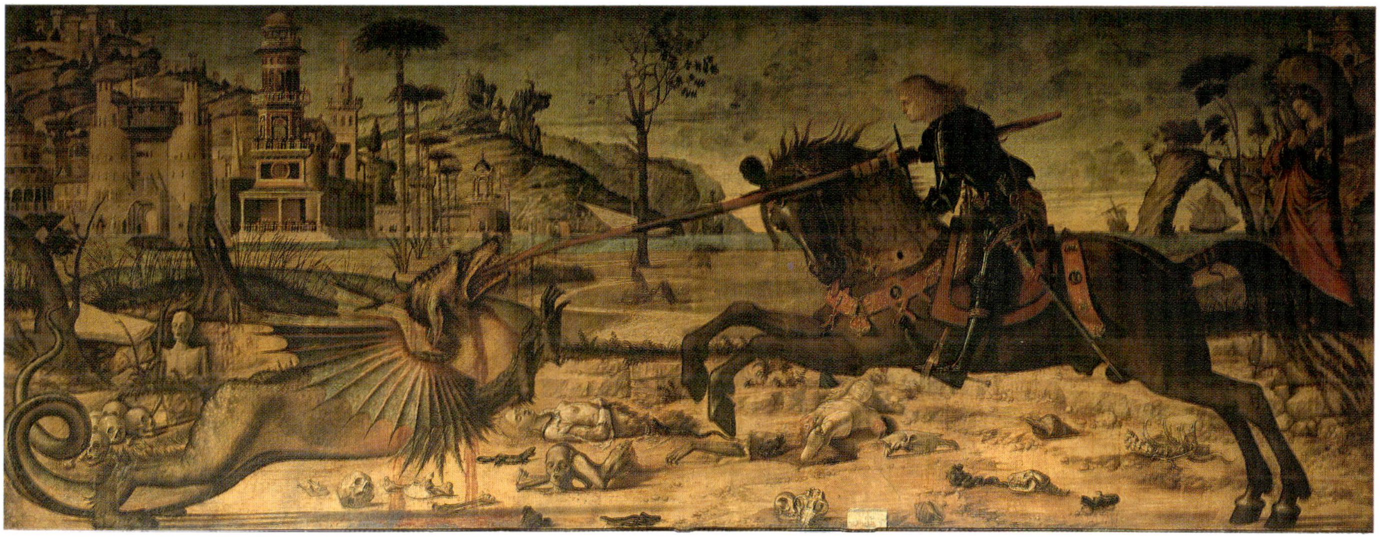

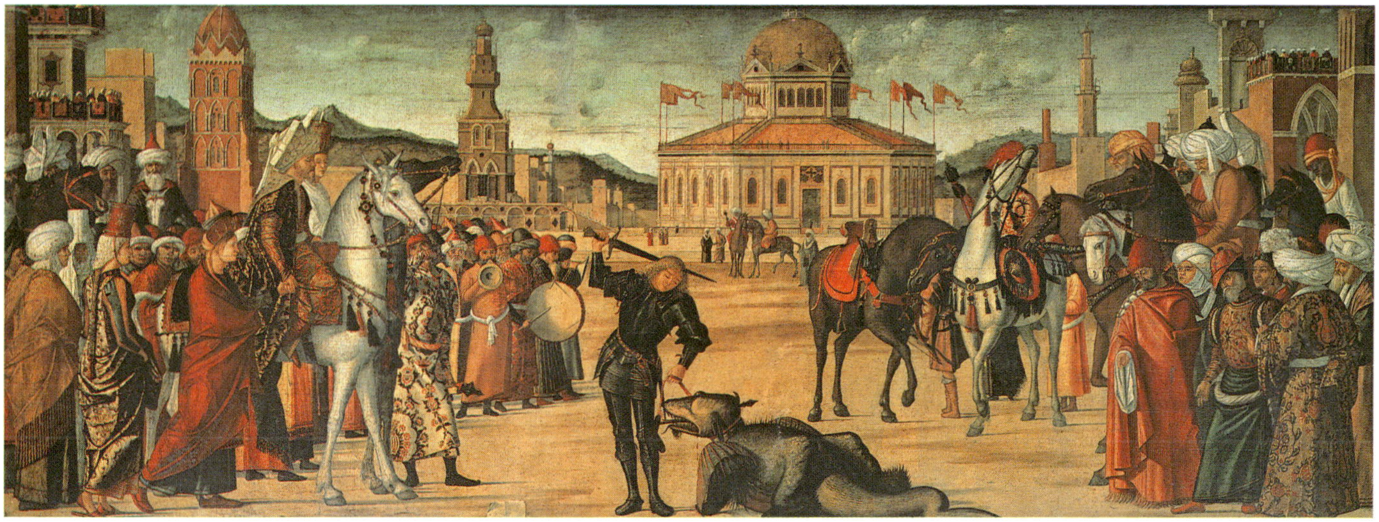

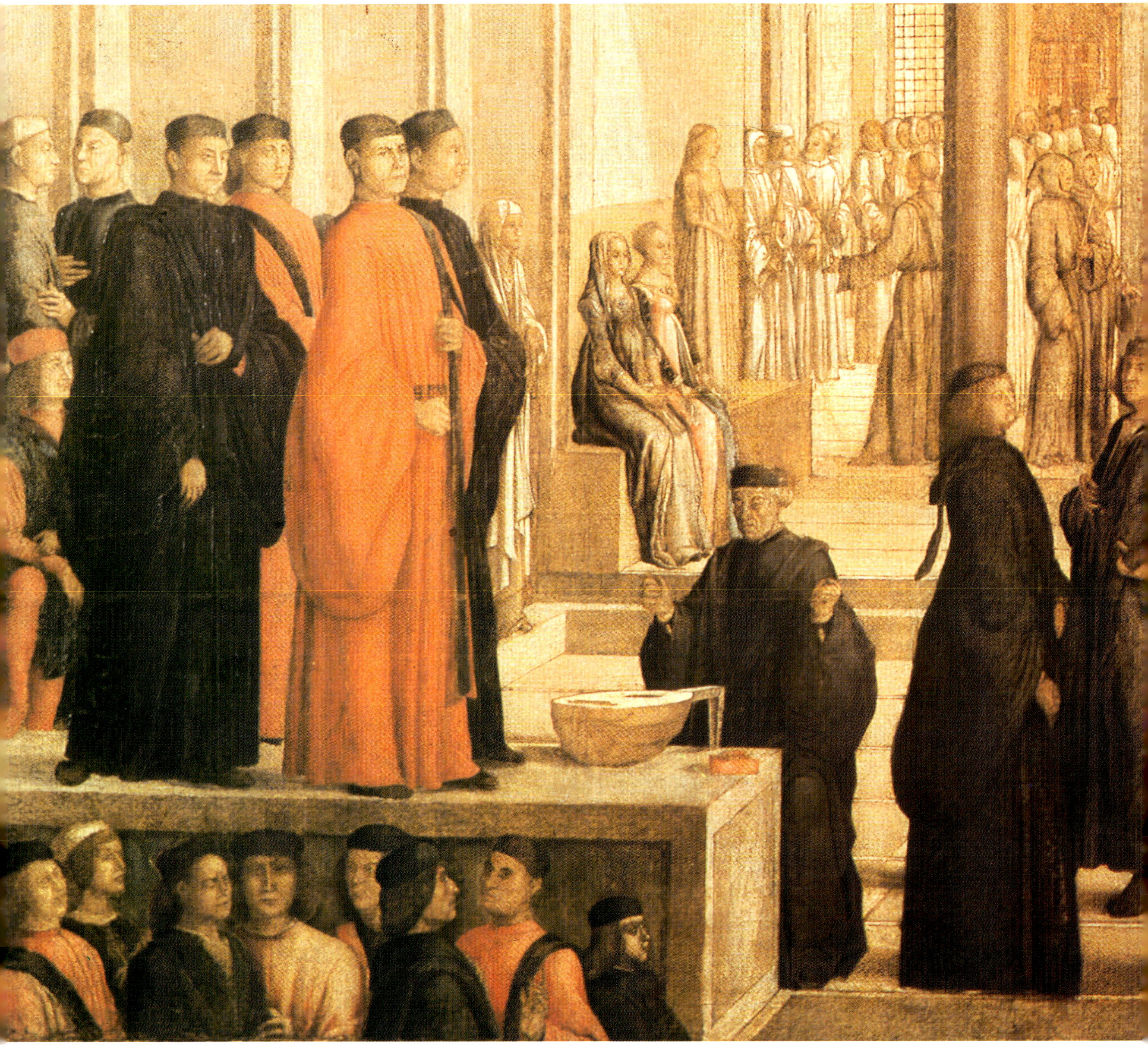

drawing shows an earlier conception [Plate 127]. Here Carpaccio had anchored the central vertical axis with a building adapted from the Dome of the Rock in Jerusalem. In the background to the left rises a tower with many arches and a ribbed cupola that imitates Reeuwich's engraving of the Holy Sepulchre in Breydenbach's *Peregrinationes* [Plate 130].[46] The figures are clustered into several groups within the front plane and middle ground.

In the finished painting, Carpaccio proceeds to adjust the relative positions and sizes of the actors and architectural structures for greater compositional integration and unity. The figures maintain their relative groupings, but close ranks to form a great arc around St. George and the dragon in the foreground which will balance the townscape in the rear. The princess and her father on horseback are enlarged and shifted in toward the center from the left. And in an inspired decision, Carpaccio increases lateral movement and adds dynamic

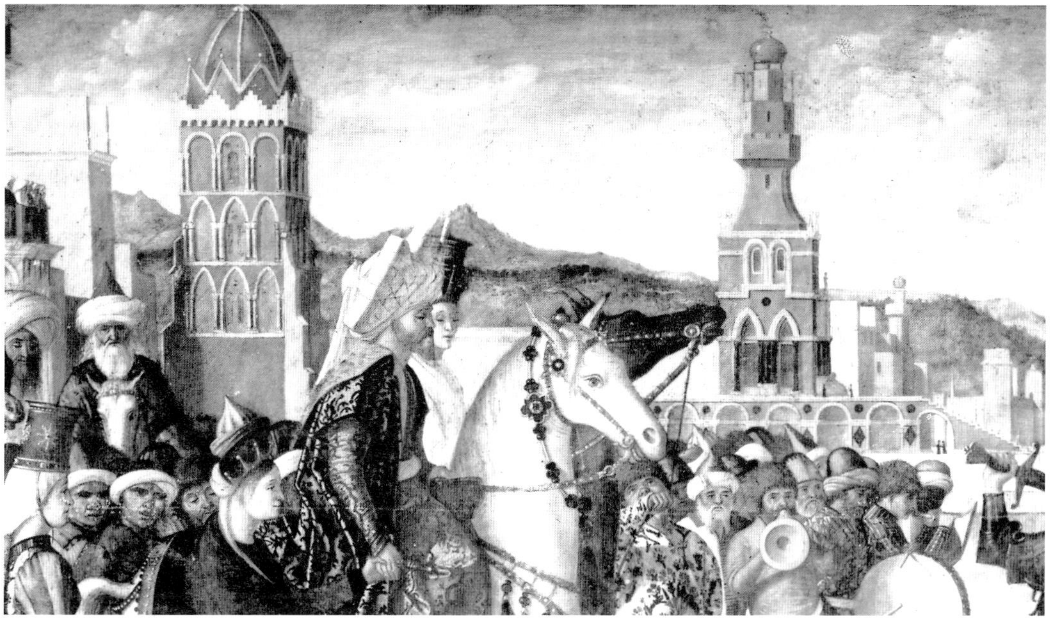

126. Carpaccio, detail from the *Triumph of St. George* (Color Plate XXXVIII)

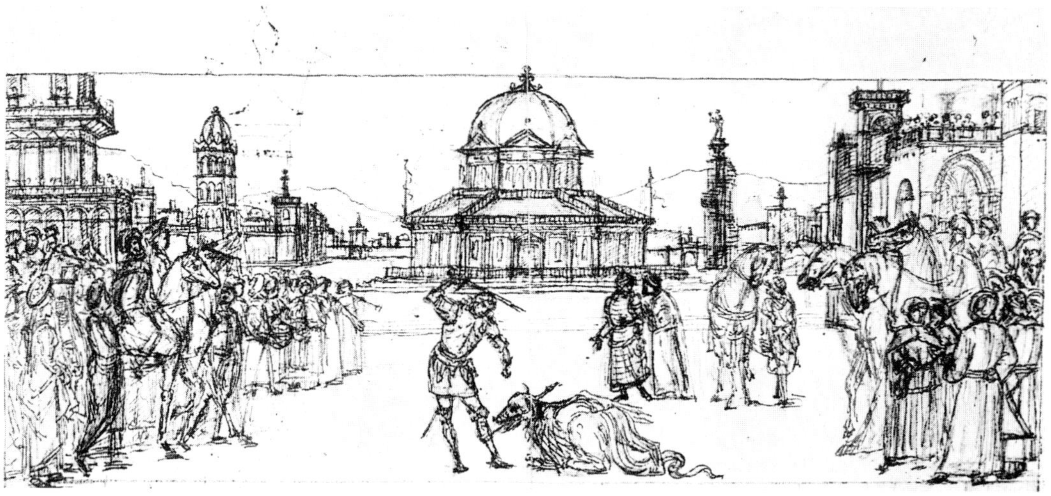

127. Carpaccio, preparatory drawing for the *Triumph of St. George* (Florence, Uffizi)

XXXIX (facing). Lazzaro Bastiani, detail from the *Donation of the Relic* (Color Plate XVI)

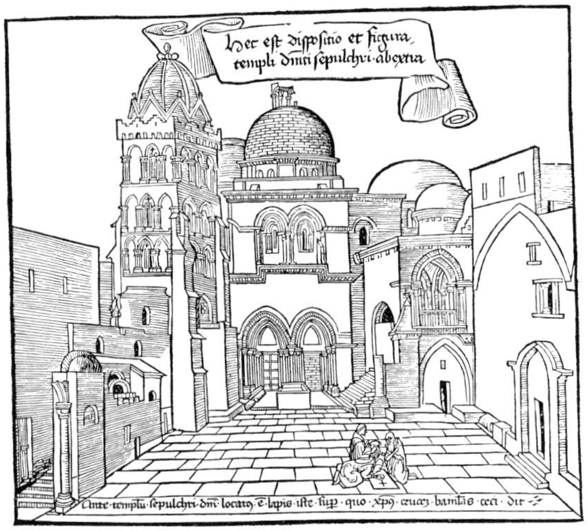

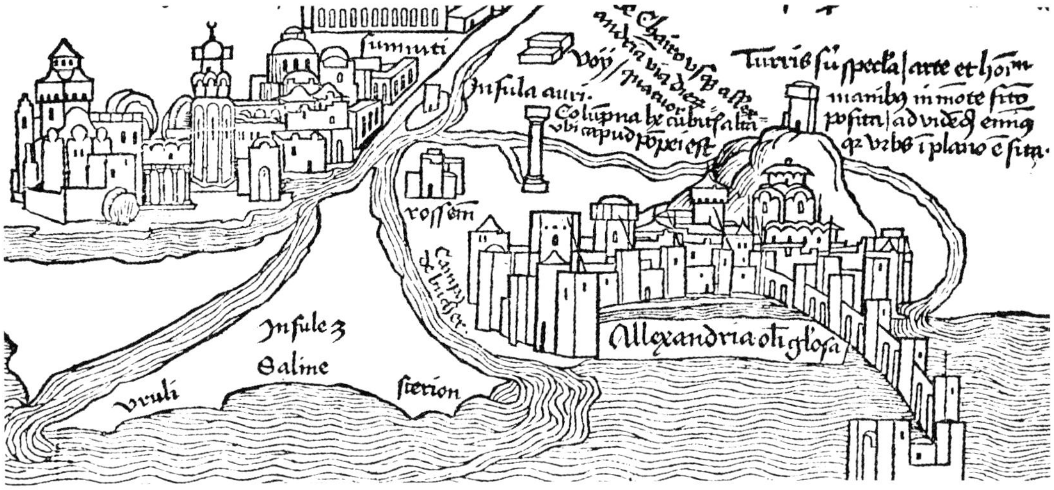

128 (right). Erhard Reeuwich, *View of Alexandria* (detail from woodcut in Breydenbach, 1486)

130 (above). Erhard Reeuwich, *Holy Sepulchre in Jerusalem* (woodcut in Breydenbach, 1486)

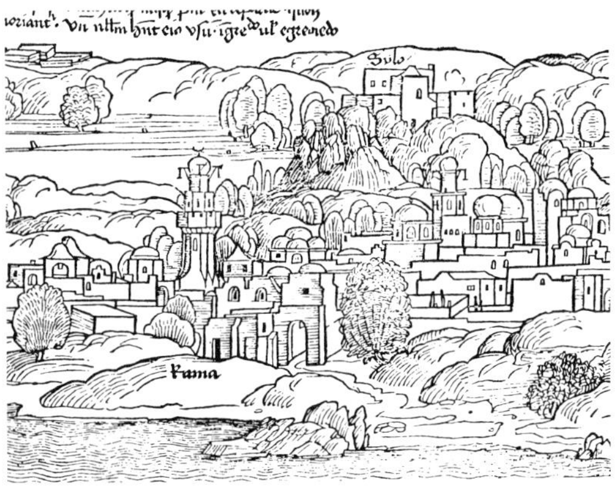

129. Erhard Reeuwich, *View of Rama* (detail from woodcut in Breydenbach, 1486)

tension to the composition by inserting the bridling horse on the right. The artist further reinforces this effect by shifting the centralized building to the right as well, reducing the size of its dome in proportion to the walls, and making the banners on top whip in the wind.

There is now a large area in the left background to fill, and he again repairs to outside sources. By placing the minaret of the mosque at Rama atop the facade of the Holy Sepulchre – both recorded by Reeuwich [Plates 129 and 130] – and positioning them on a broad platform with niches on the sides, he produces a satisfying visual anchor behind the group of musicians in the central plane. Along with an enlarged tower of the Holy Sepulchre that has been pushed further to the left, the new hybrid structure also serves to frame the stately progress of the princess and her father. The essential lesson here is the way in which Carpaccio never stopped with an architectural quotation. Only by the continued manipulation and responsive adjustment of figures and architecture was he able to achieve an extensive and believable oriental ambient.

In the third and final painting of the cycle, *St. George Baptizing the Pagans*, the story reaches its happy conclusion [Plate 131]. Carpaccio returns here to the formula of procession and arrival used so often in the St. Ursula cycle, and again he shows us a different view of the town of Silena. The unity of the three canvases is sustained and any sense of disjunction overcome by the consistent horizon line and even more by the common palette: the full spectrum of warm tones from red to yellow bathed in a golden light.

As we have already seen in the True Cross cycle, a primary difference between Carpaccio and his contemporaries was his ability to integrate protagonists and setting, while allowing each element its full particularity. Gentile Bellini's great Temple of Serapis in *St. Mark Preaching* is pure artifact. It surely creates a setting distinct from any other – and is thus intrinsically interesting and plausible because so particular – but it is a setting that needs no *istoria* to justify its existence. The human protagonists come to an environment that exists already and will continue to exist after they leave the scene. Mansueti's generic orientalizing constructions, on the other hand, can *only* be justified by the *istoria* which they display. With Carpaccio, however, the built environment is more than a function of the narrative as with Mansueti, and more than a panorama of intrinsic interest in itself as with Gentile Bellini, although it is both of these.

And Carpaccio's deliberate elusiveness – that reluctance to accept unchanged any reference to a 'real situation' that was observed by Mellini – is founded on this understanding of the organic integrity of the picture space.

But one may argue that the comparison is unfair. For in the San Marco paintings, Gentile Bellini and Mansueti were both burdened with the task of incorporating a large and extraneous group of confraternity brothers within the composition. Although few of Carpaccio's paintings of the Orient contain many such portraits, the *Disputation of St. Stephen* is a notable exception [Color Plate XV]. A key element of the artist's strategy here is the portico. Within it the narrative core of the story is posited, with Stephen arguing the Christian case with the Jewish elders. It is only through its columns that we can see the city, its peculiar monuments rendered with Carpaccio's characteristic attention to detail. And between these two zones the brothers are placed in a space of their own. The intervening columns not only bind background to foreground, but also help to differentiate and anchor this long line of patrons within the composition as a whole.

The background of the scene looks familiar, and if we refer back to *St. George Fighting the Dragon* [Color Plate XXXVI], we find that salient parts of the city of Silena are extracted from that painting only to be recycled into this town near Jerusalem. And yet there are significant changes. The tower and city wall on the right have as many differences as they have similarities. The obelisk becomes a pyramid, and the equestrian monument is placed on an elaborate new base. If we return once again to Jacopo Bellini and his drawing-books, we find similar phenomena. Atop a Roman tombstone, probably copied for its inscrip-

131. Carpaccio, *St. George Baptizing the Pagans* (Venice, Scuola di San Giorgio degli Schiavoni)

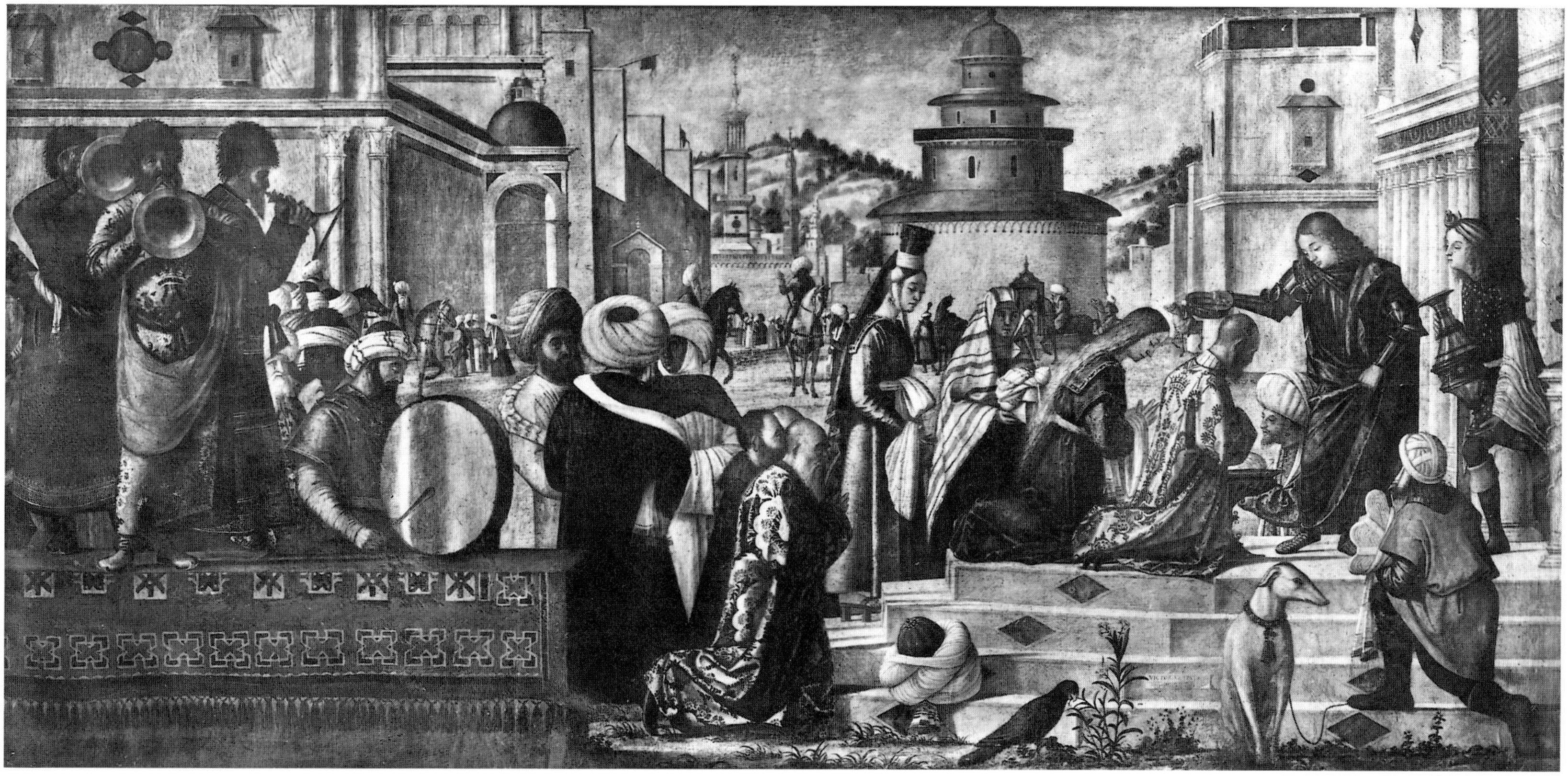

tion, he unabashedly placed the figure of Perseus, holding the head of Medusa and surrounded by winged *putti* [Plate 132]. Here, too, highly specific motifs were recombined with total confidence into a credible object which could never have existed.[47]

There is a peculiar tension between the very particularity of Carpaccio's monuments – with their false promise of an actual observed locality – and their integration into larger fictive schemes, that intrigues and compels us to try to find the sources of his motifs and then to condemn him for his prosaic mind when we do. But those monuments and motifs taken from life, if always somewhat transformed to something more than mere replicas, are precisely what ground his oriental *istorie* in an alternative world that we feel could exist and perhaps should exist.

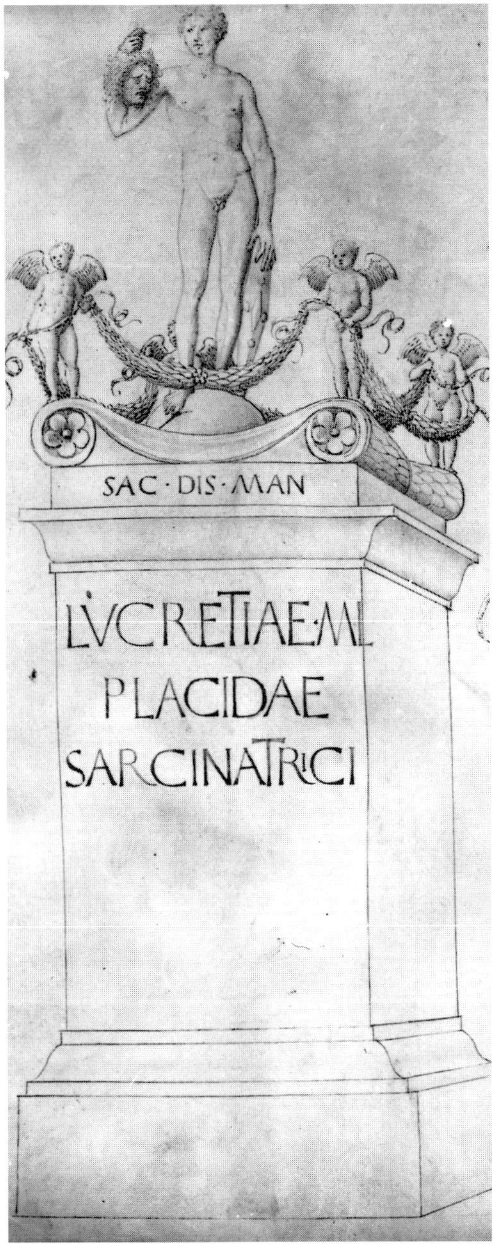

132. Jacopo Bellini, detail from a drawing of Roman monuments (Paris, Louvre Album, fol. 45)

Fantasia and the artist's share

With these scenes set in lands outside Venice, the eyewitness painters seem to have moved away from the primarily documentary – and hence, didactic – functions of the *istoria*, toward those of aesthetic enjoyment, at least in the halls of the *scuole*. The development was accompanied by a growing awareness, apparent in Venetian documents and correspondence of this period, of the artist's share in the composition of pictorial narrative. His self-proclaimed role was shifting subtly from that of recorder toward that of creator.

We see this in 1495 in the intention of the Scuola Grande di San Giovanni Evangelista to decorate their Sala Capitolare with 'qualche bella istoria'.[48] The works seem never to have been painted, but there is clearly a mandate for paintings that were pleasing to the eye, as well as (one hopes) edifying to the mind and inspiring to the soul. We see it again in 1502 when Giovanni Bellini balked at the demand of Isabella d'Este that he should paint a Nativity scene that included John the Baptist. He advised her that the Baptist was out of place in that *istoria* and that he would paint instead the infant Christ with the Baptist 'and something in the background with other fantasies which would be much better'.[49] He was standing firm in his insistence on his own share of the invention of the work.

Although the term *fantasia* had made sporadic appearances in Quattrocento discourses on art from the time of Cennino Cennini, and was a central theme in the writings of Filarete, Giovanni's use of the word may be the earliest that survives in the sources ascribed to Venetian artists.[50] It also entered the vocabulary of the eyewitness school. In 1505, Gentile Bellini offered to paint a second canvas for the Scuola di San Marco, to join *St. Mark Preaching in Alexandria*, and promised that it would be 'una bela fantasia'.[51] In the next year his brother Giovanni again resisted Isabella's attempts to bind him to a strict program. Pietro Bembo advised the Marchesa on that occasion:

> But the invention, which you tell me I am to find for his drawing, must be adapted to the *fantasia* of the painter. He does not like to be given many written details which cramp his style; his way of working, as he says, is always to wander at will in his pictures, so that they can give satisfaction to himself as well as to the beholder.[52]

Filarete had defined *fantasia* in his treatise as an imaginative process which complements and extends rational thought. While he seems to have drawn his ideas from Greek texts and was a great admirer of the Byzantine architecture of Venice,[53] it seems more likely that the Bellini brothers got their vocabulary, and the conception of artistic prerogatives implied by it, from more recent sources. Admittedly Venetian artists could have picked up such notions in their correspondence with the courts, but one thinks immediately of Leonardo da Vinci, who visited Venice in 1500.[54]

Leonardo was the first theorist after Filarete to deal with *fantasia* in a serious way. As Martin Kemp has shown, imaginative fantasy was embedded in (and not at odds with) Leonardo's commitment to objective, scientific observation: 'In terms of the medieval psychology of the inner senses which he adopted and adapted, this is the realm of *fantasia* – active, combinatory imagination – which continually recombines sensory impressions, visualizing new compounds in unending abundance'.[55] The visions of a cosmic nature in flux produced by Leonardo's own *fantasia* may seem far from the earnestly inventorial or topographical works of the eyewitness painters, but his conception of the artistic imagination was particularly compatible – at least on the surface – with Venetian expectations for the *istoria*. For his ultimate aim was to produce a work that obeyed natural truth and the laws of nature.[56] To him nature was a process, but to the eyewitness artists it was still an entity that could be fixed and captured through careful empirical observation of its outer surfaces.

Kemp noted that Leonardo's concept of *fantasia* in his writing of the 1490s was often linked with the verb *fingere* and the production of *fintioni*. Since Latin antiquity, the term *fingere* had generally been applied only to the sculptor, in the sense of a modeller in wax or clay; to the poet, as one who gives verbal form to mental images; and to the art of the theatre, in its simulation of reality.[57] Alberti had extended it in a limited way to the painter in his vernacular translation of *De pictura*,[58] but it seems to have been Leonardo who first called the painter a *fintore*. He employed the term frequently in his notes for a treatise on painting, as a way of establishing equivalence between painter and poet:

> The poet says that his science is invention and measure; and this is the simple body of poetry, invention of material and measure in verses...; to which the painter responds that he has the same obligations in the science of painting, that is invention and measure; invention in the material, which he must feign [*fingere*], and measure in the things painted, so that they would not be disproportionate.[59]

We are returned once more to Venice, this time to Carpaccio. Some years ago Michelangelo Muraro called attention to the way in which the artist signed a number of his works using various forms of the Latin verb *fingere*, rather than the usual *facere* or *pingere*: *fingebat*, *ficti*, or – as we see in the *Disputation of St. Stephen* – *finxit*.[60] Carpaccio's employment of the term as an inscription in a painting to denote the nature of his share in its making seems to be a unique case in Renaissance art, without precedent or following.[61]

We know little of the circumstances of Leonardo's sojourn in Venice in 1500, but it is suggestive that Carpaccio's first use of the verb was in 1502 on the *Funeral of Saint Jerome*: VICTOR CARPATIUS FINGEBAT MDII. One can hardly doubt that he wished to make a point: that it is the business of the artist not only to imitate that which he sees, but also to invent that which he has never seen.[62] Carpaccio's receptivity to humanist influence is seen also in the evolution of his signature. The good Venetian name *Scarpazza* was rendered in dialect as *Scarpazo* on his earliest signed work. Throughout the period of the St. Ursula cycle it appeared as *Carpatio*. In the paintings of the Scuola di San Giorgio Schiavoni it became a fully Latinized *Carpathius*.[63]

Carpaccio was clearly conscious of the role of the painter as a creator of 'visionary alternatives'. If we compare the integrity and visual plenitude of his painted fictive worlds with the stage-sets of Mansueti and the montages of Gentile Bellini, we may come close to understanding how well Carpaccio fulfilled his special vision.

12

Witnesses

In 1557, about three decades after the demise of the eyewitness style, Ludovico Dolce published his treatise on painting; not surprisingly, he had his own views on the painted *istorie* in the Great Council Hall of the Ducal Palace:

> And since the truth ought not to be hushed up, I should not refrain from saying that, as regards the *historia*, the man who painted in the Sala. . . next to Titian's battle picture, the history of the excommunication of the Emperor Federico Barbarossa by Pope Alexander, and included in his invention a representation of Rome, exceeded the bounds of propriety in a serious way – in my opinion – when he put in so many Venetian senators and showed them standing there and looking on without any real motivation. For the fact is that there is no likelihood that all of them should have happened to be there simultaneously in quite this way, nor do they have anything to do with the subject.[1]

Dolce's disapproval could just as well have been directed to many paintings of the *scuole*, particularly those of the Scuole Grandi; for if we were asked to name one of their most striking features, it would be the inclusion of a great number of contemporary – and indeed, to us, anonymous – persons who do not participate in the essential narrative. Neat ranks of toga-clad Venetian citizens listen to St. Mark preaching in Alexandria, gaze out at us impassively as he is arrested while performing the mass, and stand witness to his death. They fill the *cortile* of Ser Nicolo di Benvegnudo while on the *piano nobile* his daughter is miraculously healed, and form a stolid company across the front plane of the Campo San Lio when the relic of the True Cross refuses to enter the church. They listen to St. Stephen disputing, and are present when St. Ursula and her betrothed bid farewell to their parents and undertake their pilgrimage toward martyrdom.

Even when the ritual occasion called for an audience, these bystanders seem superfluous. Their attention often appears to be focused less on the ceremony or the supernatural event than on the imaginary viewer standing before the canvas. In Bastiani's *Donation*, two claques of such spectators were grouped in front of the low walls in the foreground. They were so offensive to later tastes that they were simply painted out, being uncovered only in recent years. [Color Plate XXXIX].[2]

Now we must grant that group portraiture in history paintings was not unique to Venice. Numerous contemporary examples in other places can be cited.[3] But the phenomenon became so prevalent there that John Pope-Hennessey, crediting Pisanello with its introduction, was once moved to write:

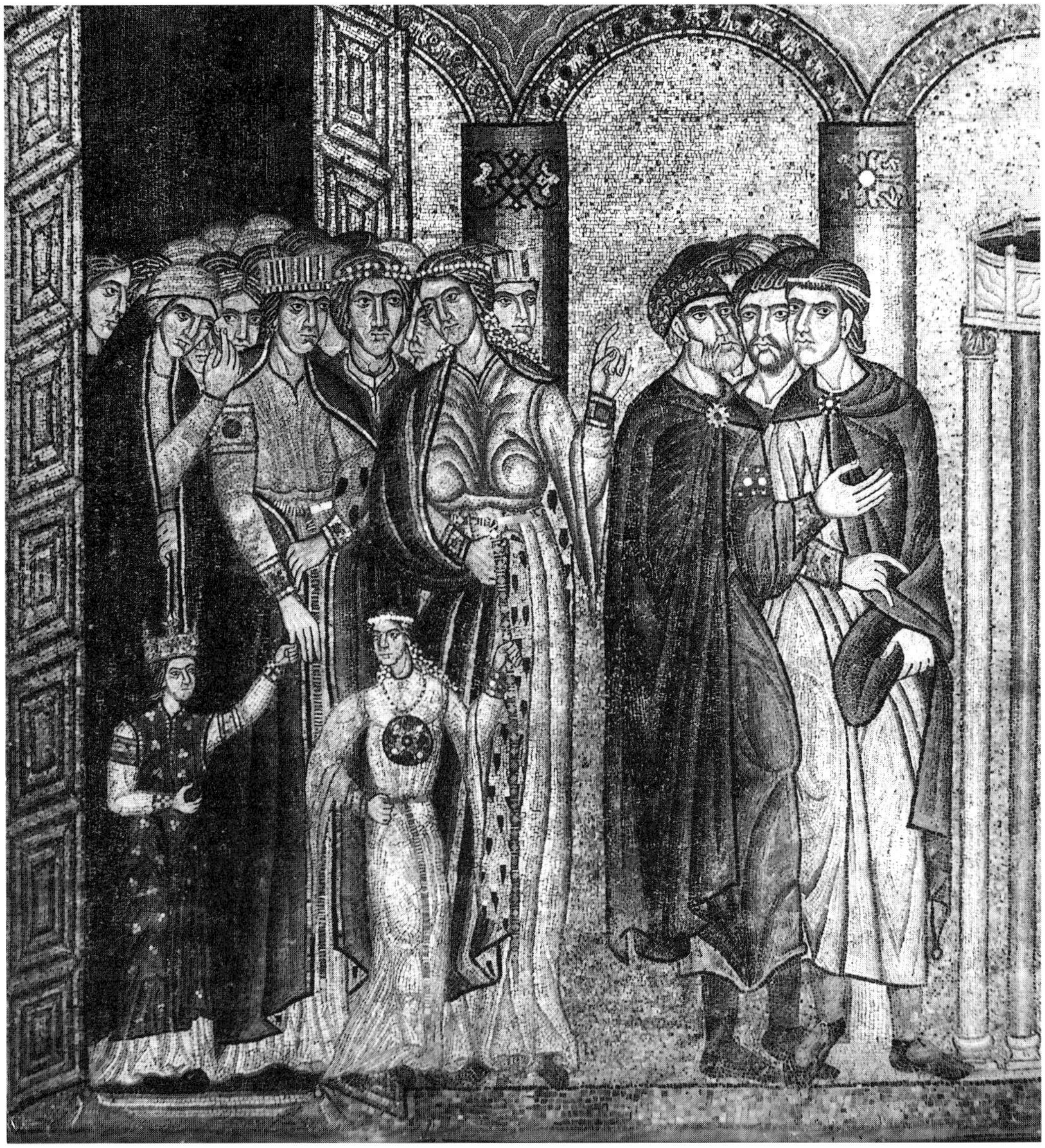

133. Detail from the *Apparition of St. Mark's Relics* (Color Plate IV)

'In North Italy the collective portrait made its appearance rather later than in Florence, and like all late infections, it struck with special violence.'[4] In fact, the tradition may well have begun as early as the thirteenth century in Venice in the Basilica of San Marco. Otto Demus called attention to possible portraits in the mosaics of the south transept depicting the *Prayer* and the *Apparition of St. Mark's Relics*. He proposed that the features of the current Doge, Ranieri Zen (1253–68), were used to represent the Doge of the historical narrative, Vitale Falier (1084–96) [Plate 133]. The other protagonists in the scenes – the Patriarch, the noble ladies, the children and others – were all to be identified as Zen's contemporaries who stood in, so to speak, for their forebears of two centuries earlier.

Likewise, in the *Reception of the Relics*, the surviving facade mosaic of the Porta di Sant'Alippio, Demus saw an event of the ninth century given a thirteenth-century aspect. In his view, Doge Lorenzo Tiepolo (1268–75), dressed in the ducal regalia of his time, was portrayed with members of his family against the back-drop of a fair rendering of the Basilica as it actually looked during his reign [Plate 134].[5] Demus understood such anachronisms in terms of a 'two-fold historicity' and defined the scenes as 'a self-representation of Venetian society', engaged in collective prayer and celebration.[6]

According to tradition, contemporary figures were also depicted in the Great Council Hall paintings of the early fifteenth century. Sansovino wrote that Pisanello's fresco of *Otto before the Emperor* was painted 'with diverse portraits, among which was that of Andrea Vendramin, who was the most beautiful youth in Venice in those times'.[7] This was the same Vendramin who became Doge in 1476. Furthermore, we have circumstantial reports in addition to Dolce's, that such portraits were an integral part of the campaign of renewal begun by Gentile Bellini in 1474 in the Great Council Hall.[9] There the practice was to honor distinguished persons in various fields of endeavors. As Sansovino observed of the *Consignment of the Umbrella*, the Pope, the Emperor and the Doge arrived at the port of Ancona and were

> followed by a company of personages, all exceptional in Greek and Latin letters and renowned in erudition. And these were John Argyropoulos, Theodore Gaza, Manuel Chrysoloras, Demetrius Chalcondyles, and Georgius Trapezuntios [George of Trebizond], all dressed in the Greek manner with hats on their heads, almost in the Albanese fashion.[8]

While Dolce later criticized such intrusions, he also granted that the commemoration of distinguished individuals in this manner could even 'save' a bad

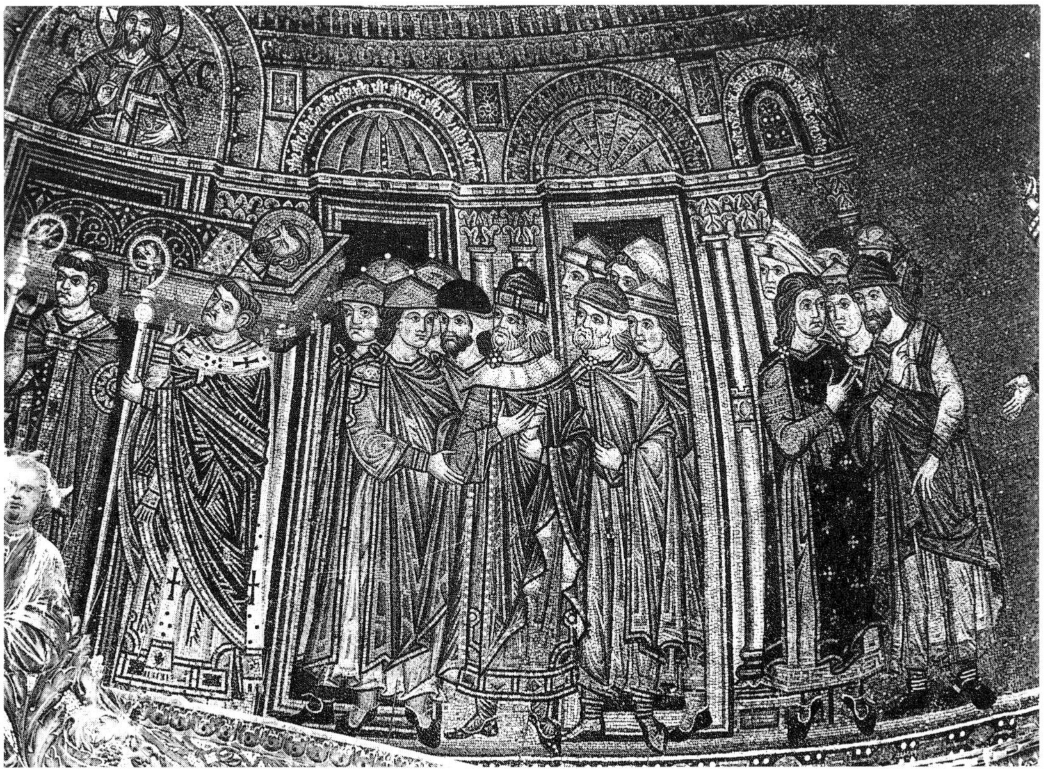

134. Detail from the *Reception of the Relics of St. Mark* (Plate 84)

painting and bring honor to the artist himself:

> One thing is sure: This invention of his deserves praise – if on no other grounds – for the nobility of those exceptional lords who appear in it; the fact is, indeed, that representations are very often revered because of the people they include in portrait form, even if they are the work of poor masters.[9]

In spite of the documentary status of the *istoria* in Venice, which might seem to have demanded a greater attention to historical consistency, such portrayals remained tenacious components of Venetian painting long after Dolce had called attention to them. These anachronisms cannot be viewed simply as products of artistic license, foisted by mediocre artists on undiscriminating patrons. They were clearly of sufficient importance to both artist and patron to remain a conspicuous element of the narrative canon. Let us therefore delimit the phenomenon more carefully.

135. Carpaccio, detail from the *Arrival in Rome* (Plate 108)

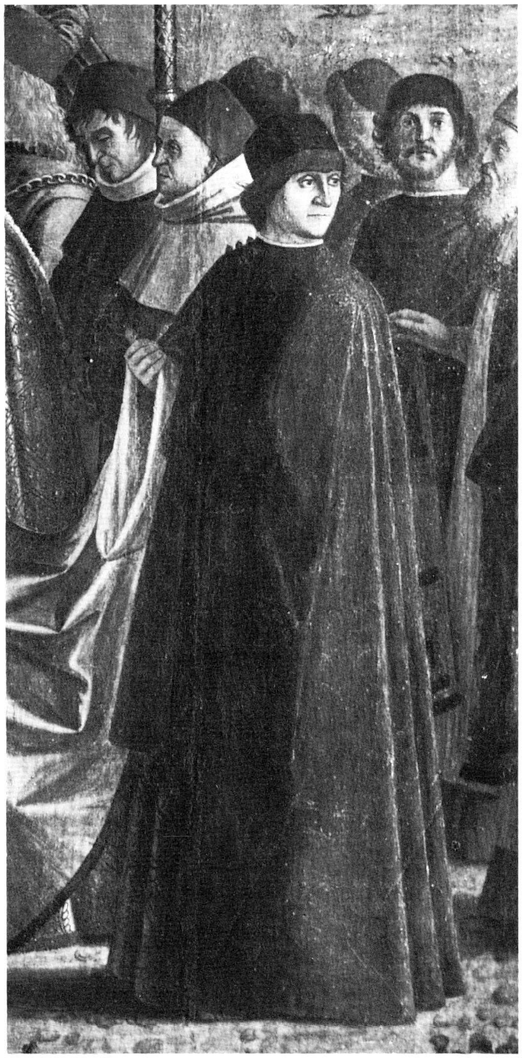

Honorable proxies

Contemporary figures could appear in history paintings in two basic ways. First, as in the mosaics of San Marco, the living individual could impersonate the historical protagonist of a given event. All but one of the occurences depicted in the *Miracles of the True Cross* had taken place at least fifty years before the commencement of the cycle in the 1490s. Thus, any living member of the Scuola di San Giovanni portrayed as one of the *confratelli* marching in processions, or otherwise actively participating in any of the *istorie*, would probably fall into this category. In these cases, the artist was able to give contemporary relevance and convincing particularity to the scene while bestowing honor on those patrons who had very likely underwritten its expense.[10]

But some of these proxy figures may not have been patrons at all. We see one probable example in the *Miracle at the Bridge of San Lorenzo*. Doge Andrea Vendramin, whose features seem to have been used to portray his grandfather of the same name, had died in 1478, more than two decades before the work was painted.[11] Compelling arguments have been offered, furthermore, that Carpaccio used prominent figures as major protagonists in his lives of the saints in at least two instances. The great Venetian humanist Ermolao Barbaro was placed in the front plane, holding back the mantle of the pope, in St. Ursula's *Arrival in Rome* [Plate 135];[12] and Cardinal Bessarion, another notable humanist, probably served as a model for the saint in *St. Augustine in his Study* [Color Plate XIII][13].

Venice, admittedly, had no monopoly on such portrayals. Nor did history-painting. The notion would have been familiar to any observer of medieval sacred dramas, in which living actors played historical roles. The custom had been extended easily into painting with the rise of naturalistic narrative depiction. In the more permanent medium of the painted *istoria*, these portrait figures could have satisfied several demands at once: they served as *exempla*; they gave the 'sitters' a degree of immortality; and they brought honor to a *scuola* by their presence.

Contemporary witnesses

The second type of portrait placed a contemporary person in the painted history in his or her own right, rather than as proxy for a historical figure. An adaptation of the donor portrait, common enough on altarpieces since the late thirteenth century, it seemed to express a more passive role. The person portrayed did not actually participate in the narrative in any active sense. His degree of integration into the scene and interaction with the holy figures or sacred event could range from total detachment to a more responsive presence, as a non-participating but attentive observer.

These figures are often described as witnesses to the *istoria*. Their distribution was uneven in the paintings of the Venetian confraternities. Appearing to some degree in nearly all the painted histories of the Scuole Grandi and the Scuola di Sant'Orsola, they are evident in only a few of Carpaccio's paintings for the other *scuole*. With a few exceptions, all of these persons remain unidentified today.[14] Who, then, was portrayed in the *istoria*? Documentation is almost totally lacking on this issue, but what fragmentary evidence we have may allow us to make a few suggestions. We would expect that, unlike the figures honored in the paintings of the Great Council Hall, most of the *scuola* portraits found their way into paintings as a direct consequence of personal gestures of financial support, either by acting officers or by individual contributors from within the *scuola* or even, in some cases, from outside.[15]

It is also reasonable to suppose that those who held office on successive *banche* during the course of a decoration campaign would have had a fair chance to be portrayed in the paintings along with those who had made special contributions. A document of 1508, recording a special subscription to complete the decoration of the *albergo* of the Scuola Grande di San Marco, is revealing. A pledge was signed by thirty-two members, each in his own hand,

> whom the divine Majesty would condescend by his innate mercy and clemency to prosper in this world and to allow eternal life in the other; and to inspire our other brothers to offer their help in this, such a pious and good work.[16]

Beginning with Tomaso Sabadini, the Guardian Grande, who promised twenty-five ducats, other officers of the Banca along with ordinary members offered contributions in lesser amounts ranging from one to fifteen ducats. A similar collection was taken in 1518 to finance a new ceiling in the Chapter Hall and two canvases in the *albergo*.[17] Again we would expect that the contributors to these appeals were the brothers who found their way onto those canvases. Allowing that portrayal in a narrative painting was probably linked to financial support for the artistic project, let us turn to the significance of such portraits within the *istoria* itself.

The testimonial function

Several distinct and often overlapping functions can be claimed for these figures. Most potent was the testimonial function. When Bernardo Giustiniani concluded his history of Venice with *De Divi Marci Evangelistae Vita, Translatione e Sepulturae Loco*, he sought to attest to his readers the truth of the miracle of the *inventio* of St. Mark. For his witnesses, he turned to the city itself:

> I do not disavow that it is prudent to hold suspect these things which are seen to happen contrary to the laws of nature, unless they are sanctioned by the strongest and most certain testimony and reason. . . . Therefore, let us see by whose testimony we are supported, and whether it should be held of little account. Let us begin with the people.[18]

He stressed that many eyes had witnessed the supernatural event. In consequence, he explained, annual ceremonies had been ordered that were repeated year after year in confirmation of it. It was the presence of the populace, and the ritual re-enactment, visible to later generations, that provided the telling evidence:

> Therefore, indeed, these things having been witnessed by the whole people, not by words but by deeds, confirmed through such a sequence of generations, does this not prove it?

Deceit in this case was clearly impossible, he concluded, given the known piety and character of the Venetians: 'a great and religious people'.[19]

Giustiniani wrote in the 1480s, during the period of ritual elaboration of the legend of their relic of the True Cross by the Scuola Grande di San Giovanni, and only a few years before the first painting commissions. His mode of proof, involving reliable witnesses to the event and the continuing confirmation by generations of good citizens, seems particularly apposite to the painted *Miracles of the True Cross*. As we examine these *istorie*, we see the impassive faces of those Scuola members in one scene after another – grave and serious men, who silently bear witness to a series of miraculous events whose validity they guarantee by their attendance. And here we must recall the presumptive role of the *cittadino* in Venetian society as the carrier of traditional values and the exemplar of moral virtue. Giustiniani could have wished for no more reliable witnesses than those men of 'discretion' who became members of the Scuole Grandi and were praised by outsiders like Jacopo d'Albizotto Guidi for their respectability:

> They will not take anyone who uses taverns
> or keeps concubines or plays at dice
> or is said to have other vices.
> But merchants, artisans, and not soldiers,
> and other people of discretion,
> and mariners who have manned well
> Galleys or ships of other types,
> who do not wish to sail, but to remain
> in this land in their homes.[20]

Furthermore, in order for the Scuola member or any contemporary person to function convincingly as a witness or guarantor of the holy scene, he had to remain distinct from the narrative participants. If he were engrossed in their activities or focused too intently on the miraculous happening, he would simply become part of the story and lose his semblance of impartiality. Thus the white-robed *confratelli* who march across the Piazza San Marco in Gentile's *Procession* are not witnesses, but the bank of stolid men behind them are. As such, they also act as intermediaries between us and the event, taking our place as observers within the picture space.

Alberti had already commented on the magnetic pull of a familiar person in a 'historia': 'the face that is known draws the eyes of all spectators, so great is the power and attraction of something taken from Nature.'[21] Consequently, the contemporary person of good reputation depicted in the history painting could also function to a certain degree as a trusted commentator, for he attested to its validity by his very presence. As George Hanfmann said of the introduction of spectators into Greek narrative reliefs, they acted as a 'responsive framework and commentary on the story, somewhat after the manner of the chorus in Greek drama'.[22] Not fully absorbed into the depicted scene, the recognizable portrait was like a notarized statement, or like the many sworn testimonies by witnesses to miracles that were compiled during canonization and beatification proceedings by ecclesiastical authorities.[23]

Corporate honor

In the paintings of lives of the saints, the testimonial role of the witness would have been less relevant than in those of the relatively recent miracles of the True Cross. These *vite* were pious legends. Whether apocryphal or not, they were based upon a long-standing hagiographical tradition. The primary function of the witness in these cases would have shifted from verification of the depicted event through a visible presence, to the display of one's own relation to what was irrefutably holy. Such a goal is operative in the typical donor portrait and is shared by the fourteen witnesses in the *Disputation of St. Stephen* [Color Plate xv]. There the figures are not attesting to the truth of the event – which no one must have doubted – as much as to their devotion to the saint. But this devotion is expressed in a collective manner and thus results in a special kind of donor portrait.[24]

We should not take the group presence for granted. It reflects more than simply the corporate financing of the *istoria* and its placement in a confraternity meeting-house. It also symbolizes in a quite explicit way the social experience and ideals of the confraternity brothers who are pictured there together. The same may be said of their contemporaries who were portrayed in a similar manner in other *istorie*. As we saw in an early chapter of this book, each of these men would have been cautioned from boyhood that he should not seek to stand out above his fellows within his estate. His commitment was henceforth to be to the community as a whole. That was the celebrated ideal of Venetian consensus, but such high aims did not always find spontaneous compliance. The Council of Ten had to reinforce them in the Scuole Grandi with a number of rules against self-aggrandisement. During the fifteenth century, for example, Guardiani Grandi were forbidden to include their own names on confraternity epitaphs or to sit on thrones in their meeting-halls.[25]

However, this suppression of individual *fama* does not mean that families could not be praised. It was just that it was best for them to be honored collectively. A characteristically Venetian type of encomium can be noted, which was conceptually the counterpart of the group portraiture in the history paintings of the Ducal Palace, with obvious implications for those of the *scuole*. Inserted into Pietro Barbaro's manuscript of 1538. 'Cronaca matrimoni', is a hand-written celebration of the patriciate of Venice entitled 'Cronaca in versi delle famiglie'. A few lines of its tortuous and virtually untranslatable verse reveal the general tenor of the piece:

And so I would like to recount
all the noble stock
which are descended
from good royal blood
. . . .
our most serene
most excellent Foscari
and all his stock
who wish to be astute,
to the house of the Falieri
Memi and Condulmeri
and then of the Corneri
Troni and Balori
with the Sanudi and Magrini
and also of Justigniani
and of noble Polani
Michieli and Zivrani;
Behind them with strength,
and oh with how much modesty,
go the Bragadini
and as well the Morosini
besides, Zentil chapelo,
the house of Cazaruolo
I do not wish to forget;
for wishing to do well
I shall speak of the Dolfini
Marsoli and Foscarini,
with so much good counsel do they go:
I am much amazed
at so many Contarini
Tiepoli and Quirini. . .[26]

Indeed, by the time he finished many stanzas later, the chronicler had forgotten few names, for the complete poem reads like the Libro d'Oro – the Golden Book of the Venetian nobility. These men of reputation were not treated in isolation. Taken together – and only together – they added up to the sum total of the collective virtue of the Venetian Republic.[27]

Such labored inventories can be seen as Venetian variants of the Renaissance tradition of *huomini illustri*, which dates back to the time of Dante and Giotto.[28] What they reveal is the determined effort of Venetian society to maintain a strong group identity. The communal ethic does not necessarily preclude individual achievement and distinction, but it does contain such achievement within the collective framework.[29] In a similar manner, the portrait of the *scuola* member in a history painting allowed him distinction, but only within the integrated group.

With the black toga prescribed for citizens and patricians alike, the levelling effect of the dress code was also, as we have seen, a matter of some pride to Venetians. As Sabellico pointed out, 'at first view, one does not see the difference between the orders.'[30] But distinctions were made. These were matters of office and occasion more than of class. A deliberation of the Great Council in 1485 required a number of patrician office-holders, as well as non-noble secretaries of the Ducal Chancery, to 'wear colors' when performing their public duties and when going through the city. This rule was deemed necessary 'to provide for the honor of this state'.[31] Like the secretaries, top magistrates customarily wore *scarlatto* or other shades of red; certain other officials wore *pavonazzo* [a dull red].

Special events, such as the reception of foreign ambassadors, funerals or feast-days, required adjustments of color and sleeve-length down the line. When the Doge wore gold, the senators wore the brilliant red *cremisino*. When he wore *cremisino*, the senators wore *scarlatto*, and when he wore *scarlatto*, which would only be in case of mourning, then the senators wore black.[32] Within the Scuole Grandi, the Guardian Grande was allowed to wear a toga of *cremisino* with sleeves *alla ducale* like a senator, and the Vicario was to be dressed in *pavonazzo* with sleeves *à comito*. The distinctions were granted, Sansovino later wrote, because the officers were serving 'as representatives of the Dominion in these roles'.[33] The transitory nature of such privileges and requirements underlined the assumption that a man should be publicly defined by his office and official role in society, and not by his individual wealth or position.

Social definition

Along with group identity, the definition of place within the social hierarchy was also an important aspect of collective portraiture. The aim of the *cittadino*, as we have seen, was not to contest his assigned position within the general order of society, but to consolidate it within the allowed parameters. As a result, he had to do more than simply emulate his patrician betters: he would also wish to establish visual ties with them. One vehicle for forging and displaying such links for all to see would be his close juxtaposition to members of the nobility within the painted urban landscapes of the *istorie*.

Gentile Bellini's *Miracle at the Bridge of San Lorenzo* shows a good example of such an enhancement of status by visual association. The presence of Caterina Cornaro, the deposed Queen of Cyprus, standing as an attentive witness with the ladies of her court to the pious actions of Doge Andrea Vendramin, not only gives honor to the miraculous relic and to the Scuola, but to all the individuals portrayed in the scene [Plate 136].[34] Of course, Caterina, in turn, would herself be honored by close proximity to the relic. The inclusion of noble members of the Compagnie della Calza in some of the *istorie* may have had a similar function.

We should thus expect that *nobili* would mingle with *cittadini* in many of the paintings of a Scuola Grande. But the dress codes allowed for so much overlap of color and type of costume among the two estates that any attempt to differentiate them on a purely visual basis without outside documentation would probably be neither fruitful nor conclusive. A distinguished figure wearing a red toga with a black stole could just as well be a *cittadino* secretary of the senate as a patrician member of that body. Their dignified behavior would have been studiously similar. One suspects that these men would have smiled at the characterization of them by one modern art historian as 'identical wooden effigies'.[35] It was just as they wished to be seen. Looking identical was no disgrace, and 'woodenness' to them was a virtue. They would have conformed rather well to the precepts of the merchant, Benedetto Cotrugli, who wrote *Il mercante perfetto*, a manual of etiquette, business practice and moral counsel for his contemporaries. He advised them to maintain their composure at all times, for '. . . all the speakers who wave the head, hands, or feet when they speak do it from weakness of the brain, and not for any other reason . . .'[36]

The inclusion of representatives of the *popolari* and *stranieri* in the paintings was also essential to the fullest self-definition of the donors. Indeed, the complete network of associations for a Renaissance Venetian was constituted from patronage chains that were linked vertically – both up and down – as well as horizontally between peers.[37] The *cittadino*'s place in the hierarchy was only secured by the presence of his inferiors and of those who did not share the privilege of citizenship with him. The old women receiving alms in the background

136. Gentile Bellini, detail from the *Miracle at the Bridge of San Lorenzo*, (Color Plate xx)

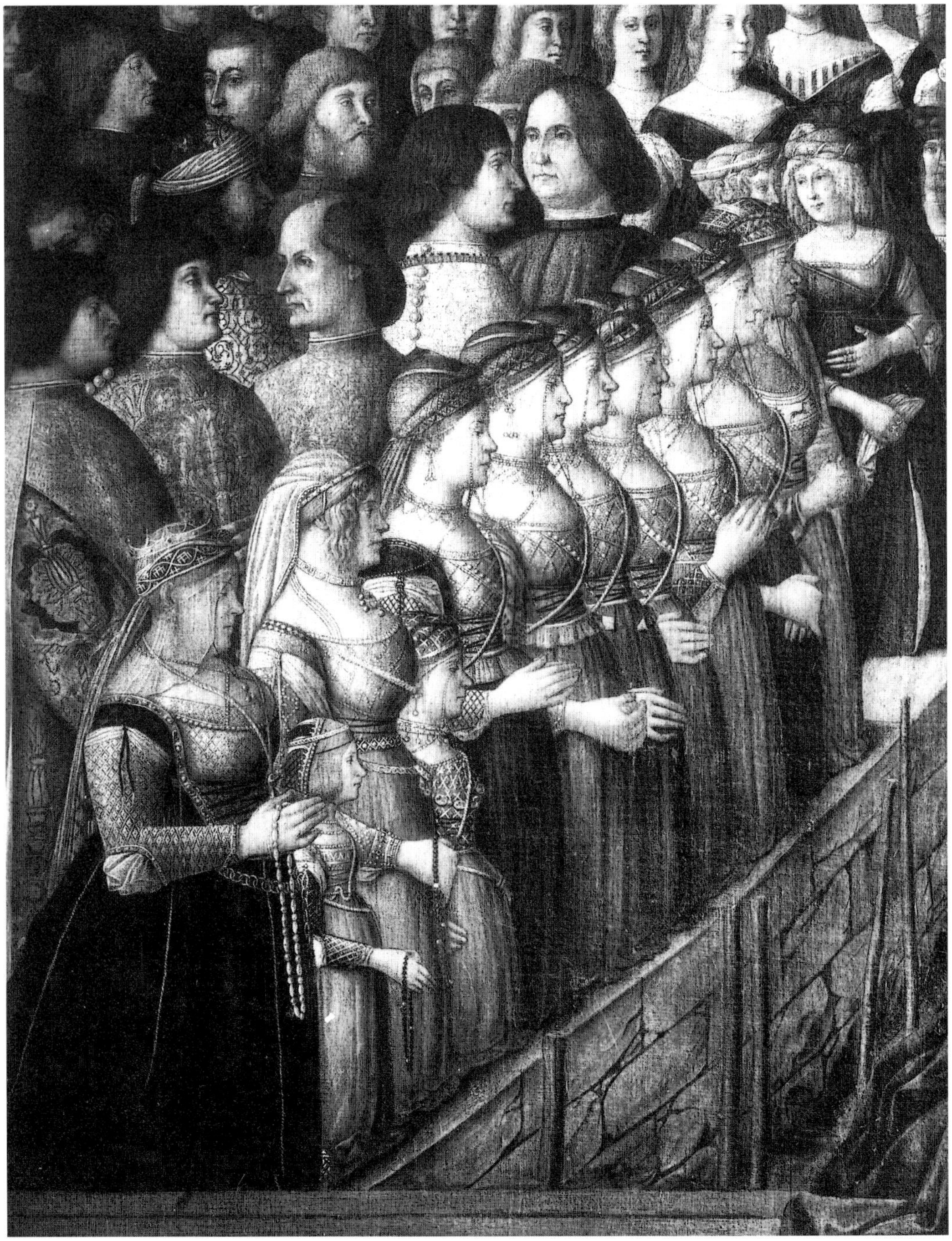

xl (facing). Gentile Bellini, detail from the *Miracle at the Bridge of San Lorenzo* (Color Plate xx)

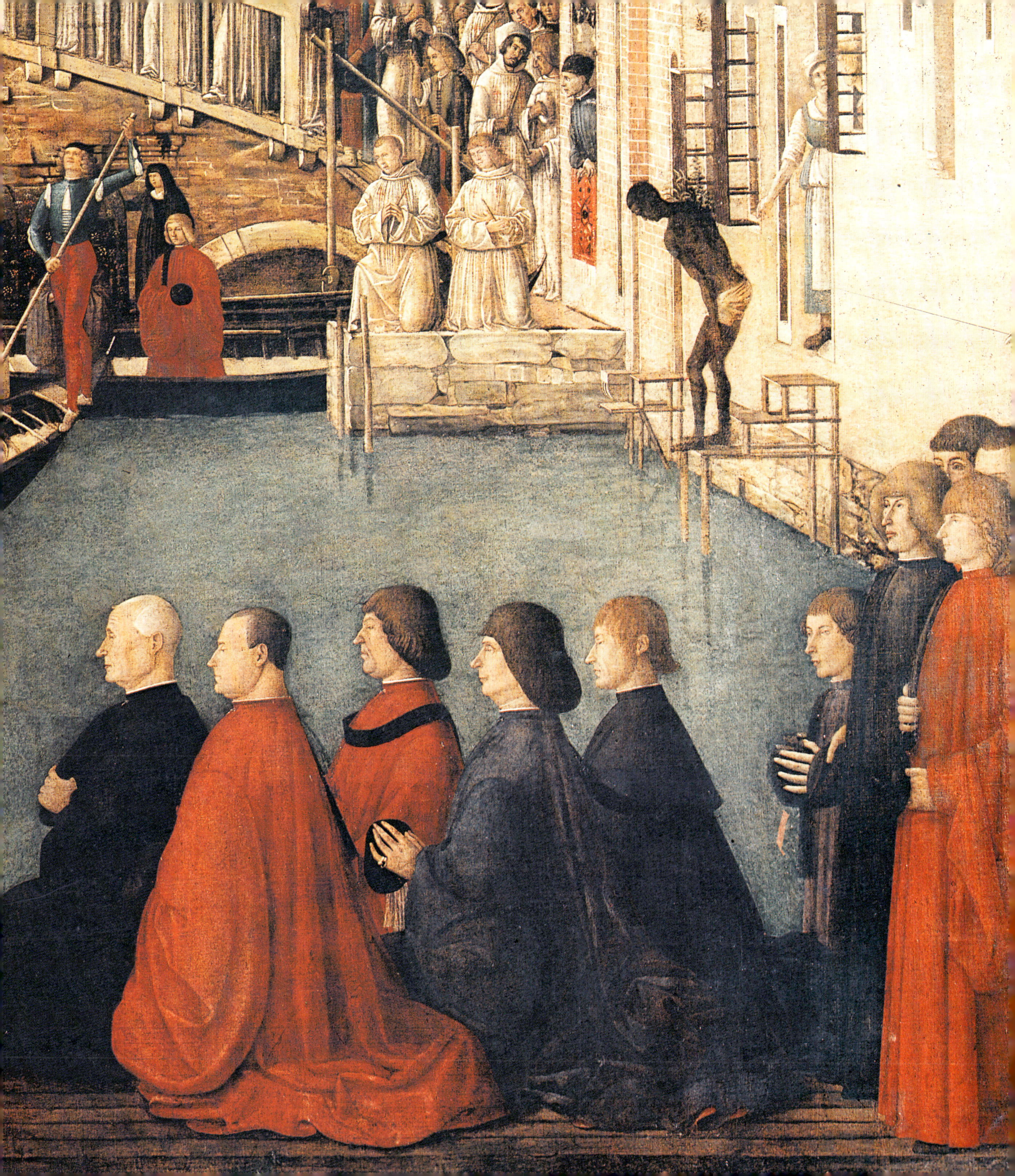

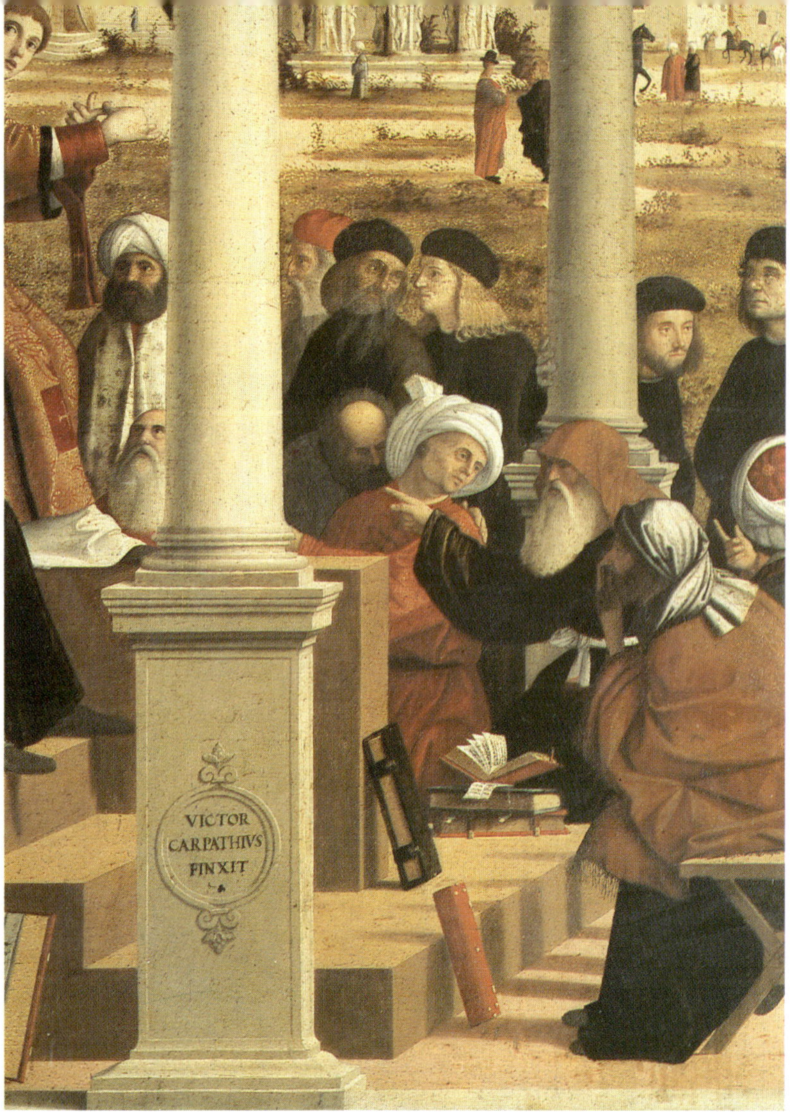
VICTOR
CARPATHIVS
FINXIT

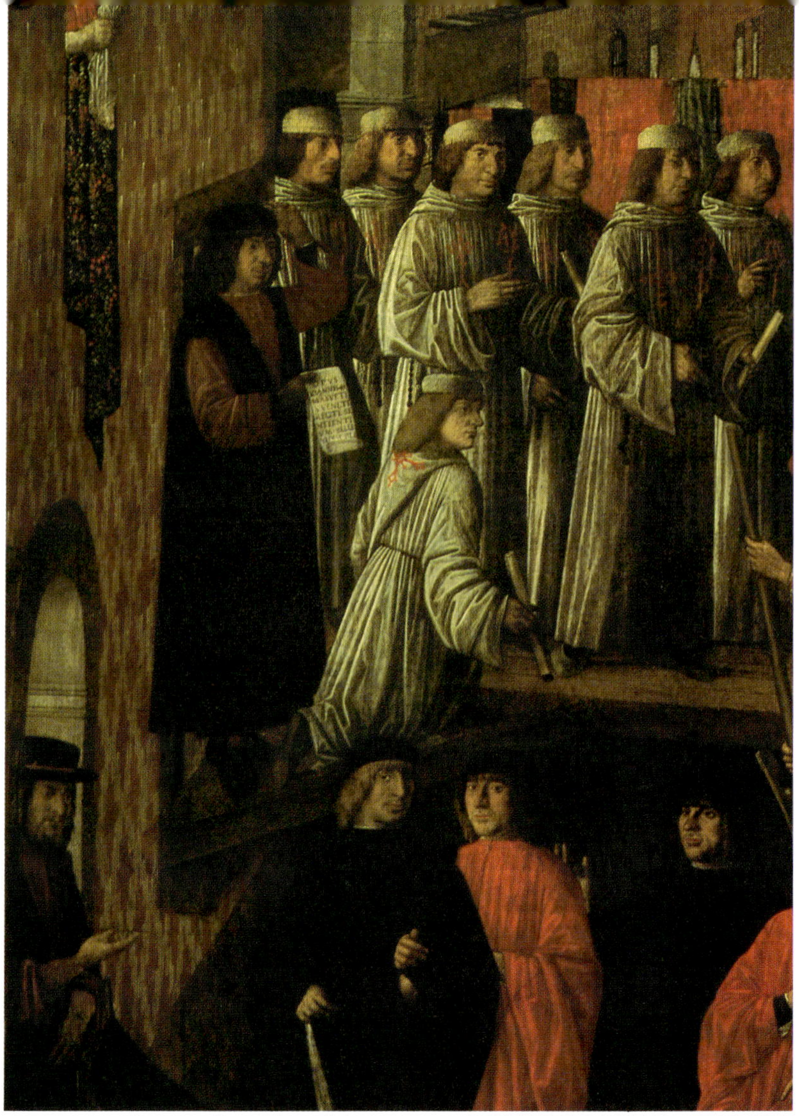

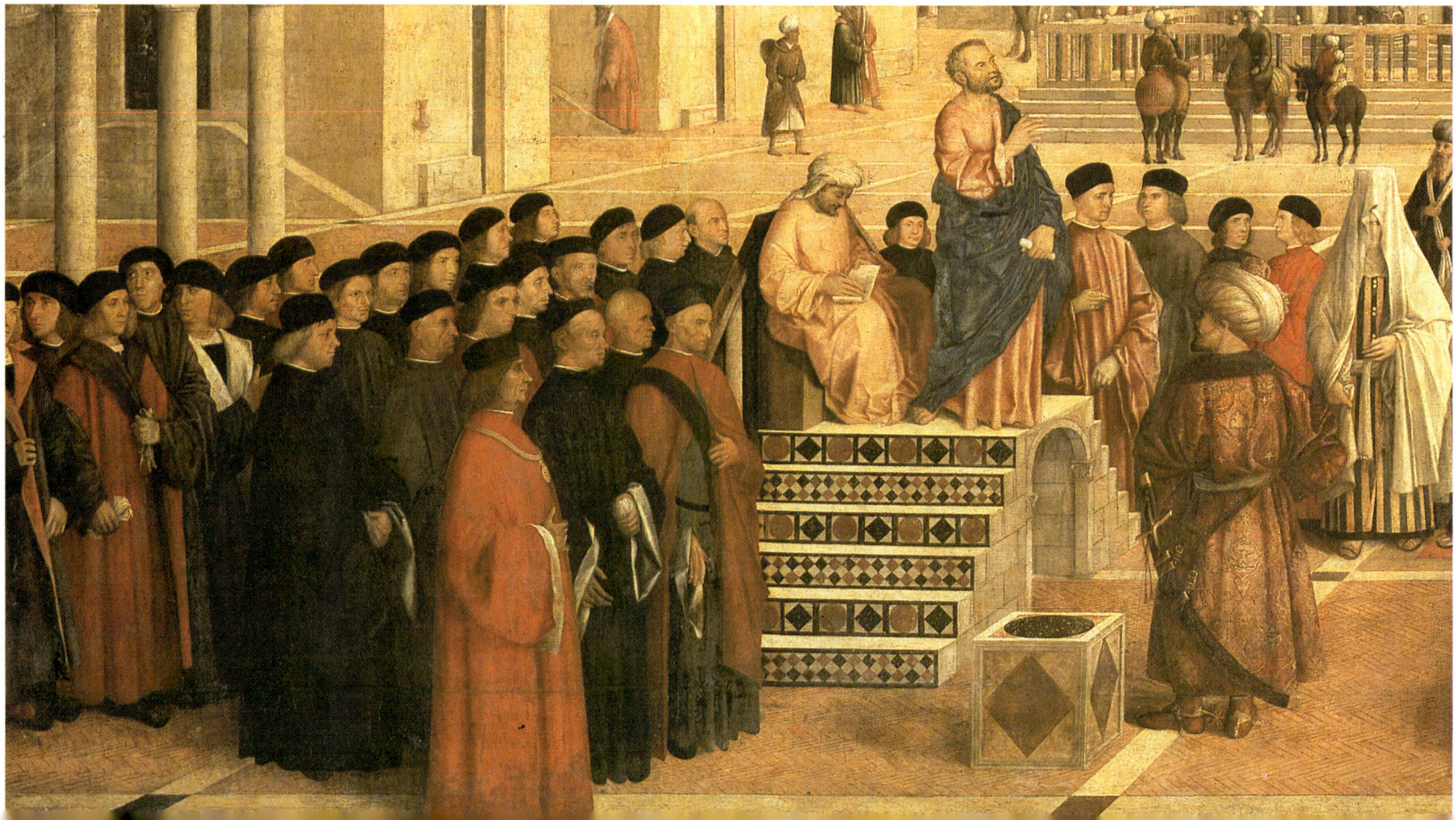

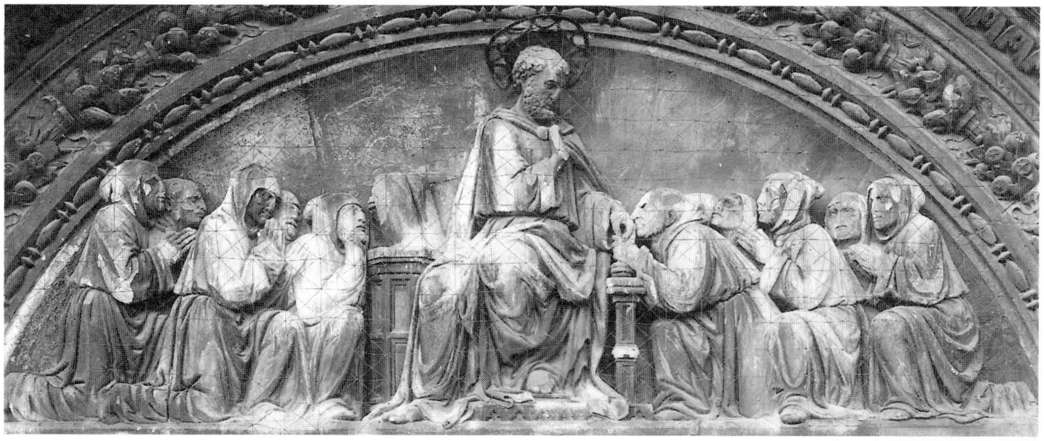

137 (below). *Madonna della Misericordia*, facade relief, Scuola dei Calegheri (Venice, Campo San Tomà)

138 (left). Bartolomeo Bon (?), *St. Mark Blessing the Confratelli*, tympanum relief (Venice, Scuola di San Marco)

of Gentile's *Procession* and in the foreground of his *Healing of Pietro de' Ludovici* thus portrayed Venice as a place where charity was given, and brought honor to the members of a Scuola Grande as agents of such charity. The black house-servant about to dive into the canal of San Lorenzo; the galley slave painted by Mansueti into the courtyard of Ser Nicolò di Benvegnudo of San Polo; the Greeks in their brimmed hats, the monks in their distinctive habits, the Arabs in burnooses and Turks in turbans: these too defined the Venetian polity and were thus gathered into the *istoria*.

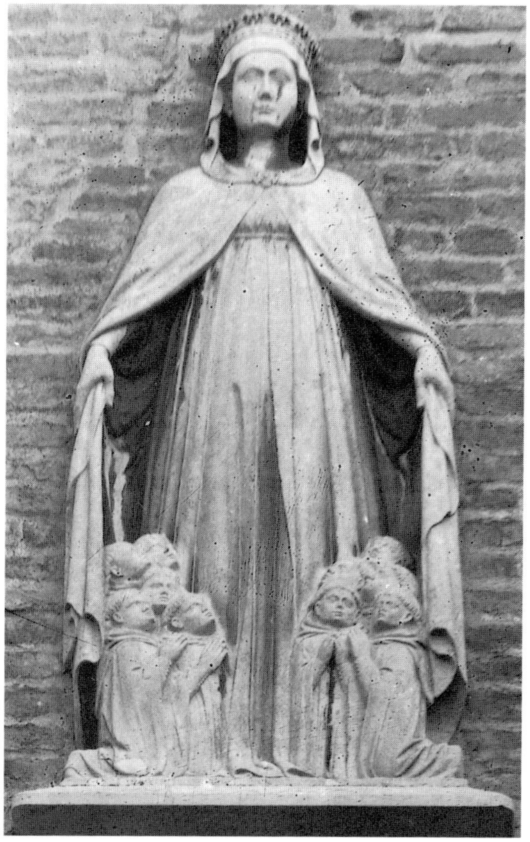

Corporate devotion

At this point we come to an aspect that would co-inhere with all the other functions of the portrait in the paintings of the *scuole*: the expression of religious devotion. Pictorially, it was grounded in three general traditions. In the first, the confraternity as a group was depicted in a direct relationship to their holy patron or to a cult object which they venerated. Examples of such images are the manuscript illuminations in the Trecento *Mariegole* of the confraternities, which depict the flagellant brothers grouped around a patron saint, placing themselves under his protection; or sculptural reliefs of similar themes such as the Madonna della Misericordia, which one still encounters on many Venetian walls [Plates 137 and 138]. While some of the faces in these early representations may, in fact, be portraits, the emphasis is on group solidarity and collective dependence upon direct divine patronage and care.

The second strand of influence comes from the single donor portrait tradition. Although examples are known from the fourteenth century, it was not as well-established in Venice as it was elsewhere in Italy until the 1470s. Probably for the same reasons that underlay the suppression of individual glorification, we can find only a few scattered instances of full-sized donor figures in larger scenes before that period.[38] However, few of the figures in the *scuole* paintings, with the exception of some of the main actors in the miracle scenes of the True Cross cycle, are shown in the attitude of prayer or veneration that is typical of the donor portrait. They are simply there, and their reverence is implied only by their presence.

These figures recall a third tradition which was particularly relevant to the True Cross canvases: the *ex voto* painting. Both types of image were born of

XLI (facing above left). Carpaccio, detail from the *Disputation of St. Stephen* (Color Plate XV)

XLII (facing above right). Mansueti, detail from the *Miracle at the Bridge of San Lio* (Color Plate XXI)

XLIII (facing below). Gentile Bellini, detail from *St. Mark Preaching in Alexandria* (Color Plate XXXIV)

similar impulses: to make visible man's links with the divine and thus to allow him to share in some of its qualities. Aside from its often amateurish execution and ingenuous quality, the *ex voto* – like the donor portrait – differed from the *istoria* most significantly in its personal rather than collective orientation. In the *ex voto*, group consensus and corporate piety were not at issue as they were in the True Cross paintings, but rather an individual response to grace received.[39]

Personal devotion

And finally, let us consider the artist himself. The self-portrait, painted by the hand of the master into an *istoria*, was common enough at this time, if we are to accept Vasari as a reliable witness. However, many of these portrayals cannot be securely verified in the absence of corroborating images. Carpaccio unfortunately falls into this category. In his *Vite* of 1568, Vasari wrote that he was placing Carpaccio at the head of a list of twenty-five Venetian painters (including Mansueti and Benedetto Diana), for one reason only: that he possessed a portrait of the artist.[40] Vasari's woodcut of a bearded man in profile has since served scholars as the basis for a number of tentative identifications of self-portraits in his history paintings and elsewhere [Plate 139].[41] In 1789, for example, Luigi Lanzi identified a painting in a private collection in Venice as a self-portrait of Carpaccio [Plate 140]. Bearing a Greek inscription and a date of 1522, however, it was attributed by Molmenti and Ludwig to an artist named Vittore Greco. They also doubted its resemblance to Carpaccio.[42] Perhaps Lanzi's judgment should not be dismissed too quickly, for the face of whoever was portrayed by Greco seems already familiar to us from a number of Carpaccio's *istorie*.

So let us make a further suggestion, equally hypothetical (and unprovable), based on additional formal considerations. In the *Disputation of St. Stephen* we should look back through the portico from the column base where Carpaccio inscribed his authorship of the work: VICTOR CARPATHIVS FINXIT. Gazing out from behind the corresponding column in the layer of space allocated to the Venetian witnesses would appear to be the face in the Greco portrait. Wearing, like him, the Venetian *cappello*, he is the only member of the group who is physically isolated and does not touch one of his fellows [Color Plate

139 (right). *Portrait of Carpaccio*, woodcut (from Vasari, *Vite*, 1568)

140 (far right). Vittore Greco? *Portrait of a Man*, once in the Palazzo Giustiniani-Recanati on the Zattere in Venice (photograph taken from Ludwig, 1905)

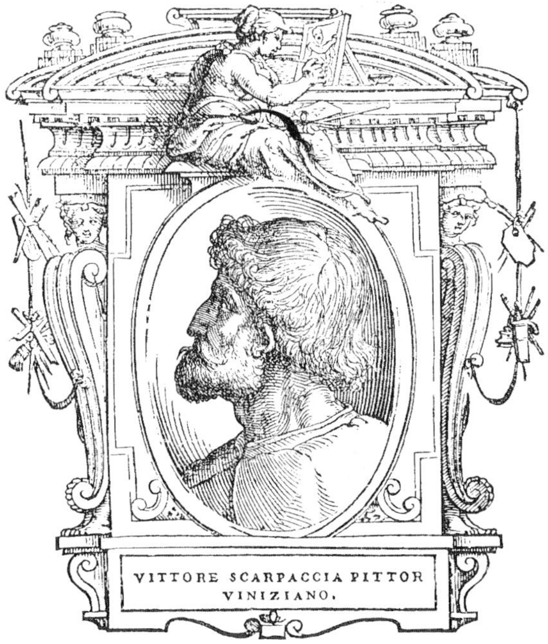

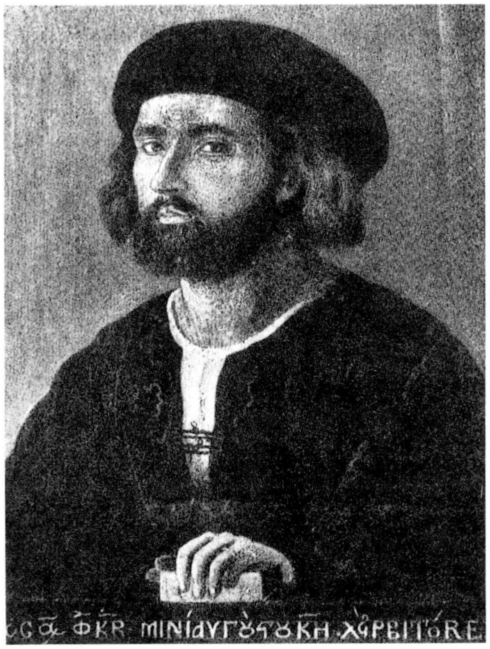

XLI]. The dress of the figure in the Greco portrait is more casual, but both share a beard and moustache with a similar cut, heavy-lidded eyes, hair at chin length and a mouth with slightly parted lips that is nearly identical. Although Carpaccio would probably have been well over fifty at the time, the painted image of a sitter is not a photograph and his youthful appearance would not necessarily be proof against such an identification. One suspects that the structural link established by the portico between Carpaccio's signature and his 'living image' is a conceit that would have intrigued the *fintore* of painted histories.

With Mansueti we are on firmer ground. True to his characteristic habit of piling detail upon detail, he went to special lengths to document his own self-portrayal. In the *Miracle at the Bridge of San Lio*, a figure in artisan dress stands to the left with one hand raised to his head and the other holding a *cartellino* [Color Plate XLII]. Documenting his artistic debt to his master and his orthodoxy of religious faith, he also appears to add his personal testimony of belief in the miracle that he depicted: 'Work of Giovanni Mansueti, Venetian, disciple of Bellini, believing rightly'.[43]

It is probable that Gentile Bellini included himself, as well, in at least two of the paintings that he made for the Scuole Grandi: the *Procession in the Piazza San Marco*, and *St. Mark Preaching in Alexandria*.[44] In the latter work, he stands in the front plane, resplendent in a red toga and wearing the gold necklace that he had received with a knighthood from the Sultan Mehmed II [Color Plate XLIII]. Next to him are three other figures, and behind them are two rows of six men each, all wearing togas. To the rear are two more. Distinguished from this block of men is a group of five on the far left who wear the collared robes customarily worn by Venetian merchants outside Venice, and a bald man on the right with the turned-down hood of a priest.

In this group portrait, Gentile made transparently clear to his contemporaries his pre-eminent status in Venetian society, his rank in the confraternity and his devotion to the cult of St. Mark. Gentile was Vicario of the Scuola in 1504, the year in which the painting was begun, and the layout suggests that he portrayed here the complete administrative hierarchy of the confraternity. The block of eighteen men in togas form a visible diagram of the *banca* of a Scuola Grande: four officers, twelve *degani*, and two *masseri*. The artist gave himself a position of prominence, closest to the viewer.[45] But the place of honor closest to the saint must have been reserved for the Guardian Grande, Marco Pellegrino, the only other figure in the group wearing a red toga.[46] Named as an executor by Gentile in his will, it was he who saw the painting through to completion by Giovanni Bellini.[47]

Gentile's personal motivation in placing himself in the forefront of his own *istoria* was born from the complex mixture of piety and pride that inspired every man of that period. At least two of his paintings for the Scuola di San Giovanni originally bore inscriptions that made plain not only his devotion but also his knightly status. Placing his own image discreetly amongst the spectators (perhaps, with his brother Giovanni, flanking Giovanni Dario) in the *Procession in the Piazza San Marco* [Plate 34], he added a *cartello* with the message: 'A Work of Gentile Bellini, Venetian, Knight, Inflamed by Love for the Cross.'[48] A similar inscription was recorded by earlier observers on the *Miracle at the Bridge of San Lorenzo*. It should not stretch credibility too far to suggest that the sentiment would have served as well for all the other figures whom he and his contemporaries portrayed from life in the painted histories of the *scuole*.

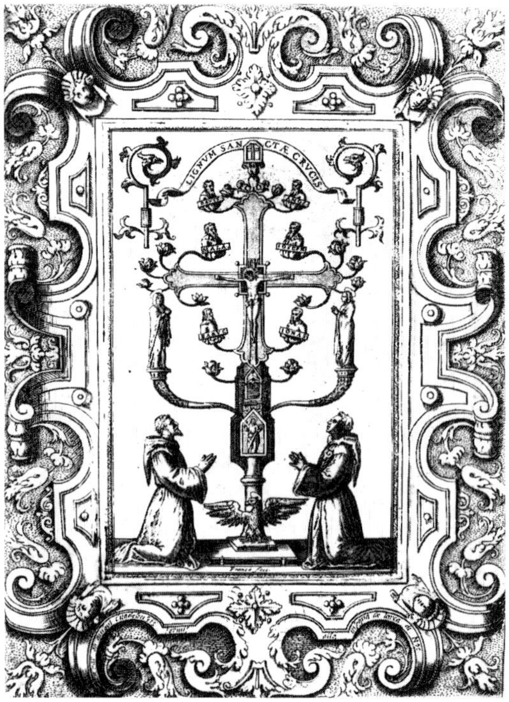

141. Frontispiece of *Miracoli della Croce Santissima*, Venice, 1590

The members of the Scuola di San Giovanni, by so visibly bearing testimony and demonstrating their devotion for the holy relic, helped to sanctify the urban space of Venice that they called *la terra sancta nostra*. Likewise, the *confratelli* of other *scuole*, portrayed in their corporate identities, could re-establish a Christian presence in the alternative worlds of Alexandria and Jerusalem, once pagan and now home of the infidel. For one of the most potent roles of the witnesses in all of these scenes was to re-appropriate the past for the benefit of the present. Through them, familiar in face and in dress, against backgrounds made up of real or imagined contemporary architecture, the dead and gone was made relevant to the here and now.[49] Their anachronistic presences were thus not naive intrusions, but necessary to actualize fully the sacred narratives in the minds of pious observers.

In fact, the stolid, unshaken countenances of these so-called 'non-participants' help to reveal the meaning of the pictures themselves. The *way* in which the 'non-participants' are present at the scene – solemn, devout, trustworthy – shows us how the events portrayed were viewed in the time in which they were painted. The *istorie* were not just stories about miracles or tales of the saints. They were also about the human response of a particular group of people in a particular time and a particular place – that is, the *scuola* itself – to holy events. In a sense, they are the *real* participants of the *istoria*. Thus it is not correct either to call the portraits 'intrusions' that are simply jammed into the narrative fabric of the *istoria*, or to view the stories as mere narrative vehicles whose real purpose is to carry the weight of a group portrait. In those paintings where such witnesses were included, both the story and the portraits were necessary constituent parts, with the portrayals of contemporary people just as essential as the painted architecture and events – whether miraculous or ordinary – that went on around them. For the *scuola* members wished to capture not only their times but also themselves in these paintings, as silent, reverent and dependable witnesses to their own devotion and even to the truth of the events recorded.

Such a desire was felt especially by the officers of Venetian *scuole*, whose position in that society depended increasingly on their ability to present themselves as honorable men, the most trustworthy element in a Republic at risk, and thus the most reliable witnesses of all to the events that showed the continuing favor of God on their city. The words of the *Miracoli della Croce Santissima*, printed by the Scuola di San Giovanni in 1590 [Plate 141] from the version published about a century before, sum up the self-images of these men:

> From the Santissima Croce that is found in the Scuola, already established for many years. . . were seen before, and are seen to shine forth yet, stupendous and glorious miracles. . . the ancient custodians and protectors of this venerable Fraternity with many most noble paintings, made with important expense, have tried to conserve to men such a pious, holy and religious meditation. . .[50]

In these solemn words we have the self-portrait of an age, the 'text' followed by those consummate eyewitnesses: Gentile Bellini, Carpaccio and their lesser colleagues who painted their contemporaries into the histories of their time.

EPILOGUE

By the time the last painting of Giovanni Mansueti was hung, apparently reluctantly, in the *albergo* of the Scuola di San Marco around 1530, the eyewitness style seemed already to be slipping out of fashion. Following the artist's death, his daughter Cecilia was forced to bring suit against the confraternity to obtain payment for the work. She complained at that time to the Auditori Vecchi, a court of appeal, that the Scuola officers

> ...had the effrontery to tell the [magistrates] that my late father wanted to make the painting and in case they did not want it, to keep it for him as a kindness; and they have made a comedy among themselves against his work, having my father's labors thrown to the winds, neither paying the money nor coming to see the work, although he portrayed those of the scuola and many other things...[1]

Three decades later, Giorgio Vasari entered the *albergo* of the Scuola Grande di San Giovanni Evangelista and tried to make sense of the great canvases that surrounded him. To Vasari these paintings were not so much documents of historical truth as they were appropriate vehicles to demonstrate once more his own skills as a master story-teller in the ekphrastic mode. For Vasari, as it had been for Alberti, narration was the constant and ultimate goal of the artist. When he discussed any painting that was more than a devotional image, he invariably sought out the story in it, which he then recounted with observations on the artist's ability to achieve psychological expression in the figures and skilful imitation of material things.[2]

Not surprisingly, Venetian paintings often left Vasari puzzled. He tried to come to terms with the canvases of the True Cross cycle, but with bizarre results. By the time he visited the Scuola, memories regarding the specific subjects of each canvas must have dimmed. He focused immediately upon the only painting that clearly depicted a miracle: Gentile Bellini's *Miracle at the Bridge of San Lorenzo* [Color Plate xx]. As Andrea Vendramin swims across the central foreground and holds aloft the precious reliquary, spectators lining the banks frame the action and focus attention upon him. The primary narrative episode – and this is exceptional in the True Cross cycle – can be grasped immediately by any viewer with the vaguest knowledge of such an event. This was an *istoria* that Vasari could recount with confidence. His description indicates that he understood it to be the only one in the room, with all the other canvases referring to it. Gentile's *Procession in the Piazza San Marco* and Carpaccio's *Healing* with its view of the Grand Canal were simply two episodes in the *istoria* of the miracle at San Lorenzo:

The said Cross was thrown, I know not by what chance, from the Ponte della Paglia into the Canal, and, by reason of the reverence that many bore to the piece of the Cross of Christ that it contained, they threw themselves into the water to recover it; but it was the will of God that no one should be worthy to succeed in grasping it save the Prior of that Scuola.

Gentile, therefore, representing this story, drew in perspective, along the Grand Canal, many houses, the Ponte della Paglia, the Piazza di S. Marco, and a long procession of men and women walking behind the clergy; also many who have leapt into the water, others in the act of leaping, many half immersed and others in other very beautiful actions and attitudes; and finally he painted the said Prior recovering the Cross. Truly great were the labour and diligence of Gentile in this work, considering the infinite number of people, the many portraits from life, the diminution of the figures in the distance, and particularly the portraits of almost all the men who then belonged to that Scuola, or rather, Confraternity. Last comes the picture of the replacing of the said Cross, wrought with many beautiful conceptions.[3]

To Vasari, the entire cycle of some nine canvases was reducible to the miracle at the Bridge of San Lorenzo. Beginning there with the central and initial episode, he then constructed his own narrative that proceeded logically around the room. What he saw as the 'replacing of the said Cross', was in reality Lazzaro Bastiani's *Donation*.

Vasari's eye, or that of most central Italian observers, would by this time have been attuned to Albertian principles which strove to guarantee narrative relevance in the painted *istoria*. Measured against such standards, the painters of the True Cross cycle would indeed be found wanting on all counts. They aimed for monumental size more than dramatic focus; their copiousness frequently tipped over into verbosity and confusion; the compositional system, while constructed according to the rules of linear perspective, ignored the hierarchy of narrative action; and the figures were often superabundant.

The eyewitness painters were to be judged less sympathetically by their fellow Venetians than they were by Vasari. We have already heard from Ludovico Dolce on the impropriety of the numerous portraits in the *istorie* of the Great Council Hall. He also remarked that these works had been painted

by various artists who were more or less skilful, although the style of the times was rough, and not yet capable of producing pictorial excellence. Subsequently [the Council] called on Titian to do two canvases there. And would to God that his brush had done the painting in its entirety; for then perhaps this same Hall today would be one of the most beautiful and respected sights to be found in Italy.[4]

Sansovino was even less charitable, accusing Gentile Bellini of being unable to improve the earlier frescoes of the Great Council Hall and thus simply repainting them through envy.[5]

We must allow that the art of Carpaccio and Gentile Bellini was the product of a very different cultural and aesthetic environment from that of Vasari, Dolce and Sansovino. What had looked unaffected and true at the beginning of the sixteenth century would later simply look rough: hence the dismissive treatment received by Mansueti's daughter even as early as the 1520s, when the cultural situation of Venice was quite different from that of thirty years before.

As we observed in Chapter 6, the chronicle – the verbal counterpart of the eyewitness paintings – was fast being replaced by the humanist *historia* as the dominant mode of Venetian history-writing. The latinization of writing found its counterpart in the romanization of painting, with new standards of narrative relevance for both. Thus, the 'aesthetic of credibility' in historical writing and painting was shifting from descriptive abundance and the look of gratuitousness to a more edited account of human action with the suppression of superfluous detail. Even in Carpaccio's work we have already noted a similar development toward a more rhetorical manner.

The deaths of Mansueti and Carpaccio in the 1520s ended an era. Although they both had lived long enough to establish workshops and to train a new generation of painters who could have continued to provide *istorie* in the eyewitness mode, such was not to be. The argument that an artistic style has its own internal dynamic – simply running its course and wearing out over time – tends to be a circular one. It is based on a notion of progress which we should not take for granted in the case of Venice without further explanation. For we cannot ignore political events and their consequences. While interest in the east remained vigorous throughout the sixteenth century, it was no longer an east on which Venice could project its own image and thus 'appropriate' for itself. The fall of Cairo to the Ottoman Turks in 1517 effectively eliminated the Mamluks as a distinct Islamic alternative, and along with them the Mamluk pictorial mode in which the once Christian east had been presented in paintings of the *scuole*.[6]

While the notion of Venice's 'turning in on herself' in the 1520s may be true in regard to her withdrawal from the east, it is less so in terms of her relationship with the west. What happened was not so much a turning in as a turning around. Bessarion had called Venice the new Byzantium. There was little real hope of that any more. A determined and energetic Doge, Andrea Gritti, was elected in 1523. He threw the power of his office behind the increasingly expressed desire to make Venice the new Rome. The idea was not new, and indeed had been a standard component of Quattrocento panegyric.[7] But in the 1520s such urges would find broad patrician support, probably in response to Venice's shrinking hegemony in the political arena of the eastern Mediterranean. One form that it took was a drive for primacy in arts and letters. It was Gritti who persuaded the Procurators of San Marco to hire Adrian Willaerts as choirmaster for the Basilica in 1527. And for Gritti the Sack of Rome proved to be a most providential affair. With the infusion of Roman-trained architectural talents like Jacopo Sansovino, Sebastiano Serlio and Michele Sanmicheli, it finally gave Venice its Roman Renaissance. It even produced Pietro Aretino, who became the most outspoken apologist for the new style of Venetian art.[8]

With the 'cultural policy' of Gritti and the active presence of the Roman architects, the government center of the city that spread around San Marco and the Ducal Palace was renewed *all' antica*. The old Venetian pioneers of a romanizing architectural style – the Lombardi, Mauro Codussi and Bartolommeo Buon – had, in fact, never been to Rome, and their efforts to reproduce a Roman style in Venice had been based upon second-hand information.[9]

The *Sea Storm*, begun by Palma Vecchio and completed by Paris Bordone, and the *Presentation of the Ring*, with which Paris completed the *albergo* decoration of the Scuola di San Marco in 1534, could be regarded as the first tangible deposits of the changing aesthetic sensibility in the halls of the *scuole* [Plates 142 and 143]. The *Sea Storm* depicts a miracle of the fourteenth century, in which

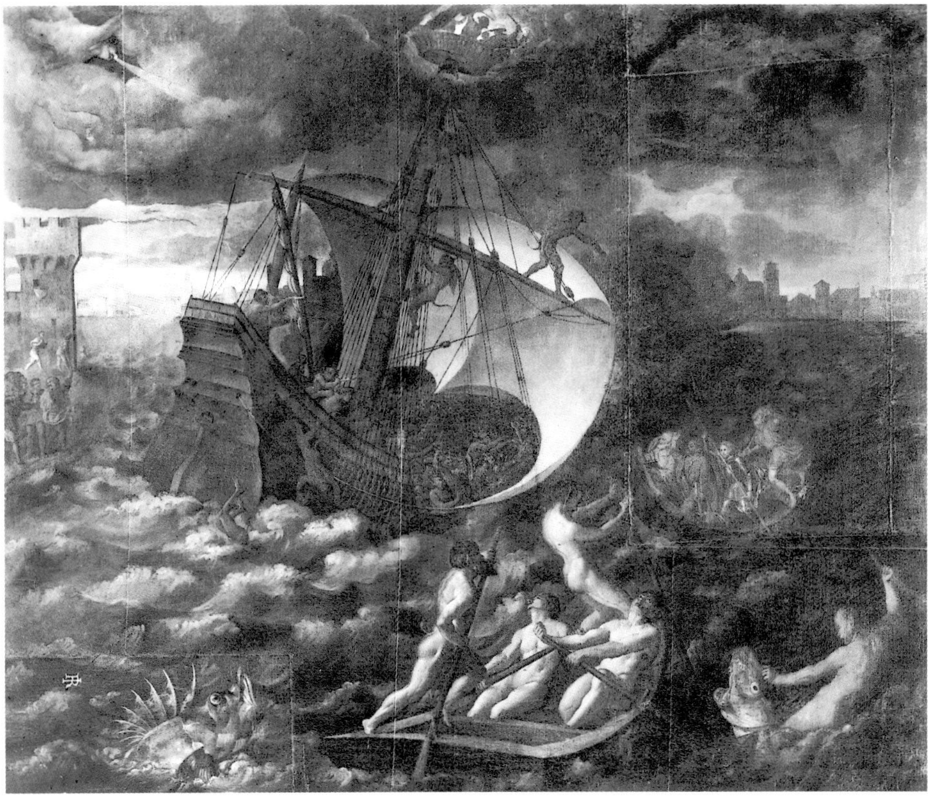

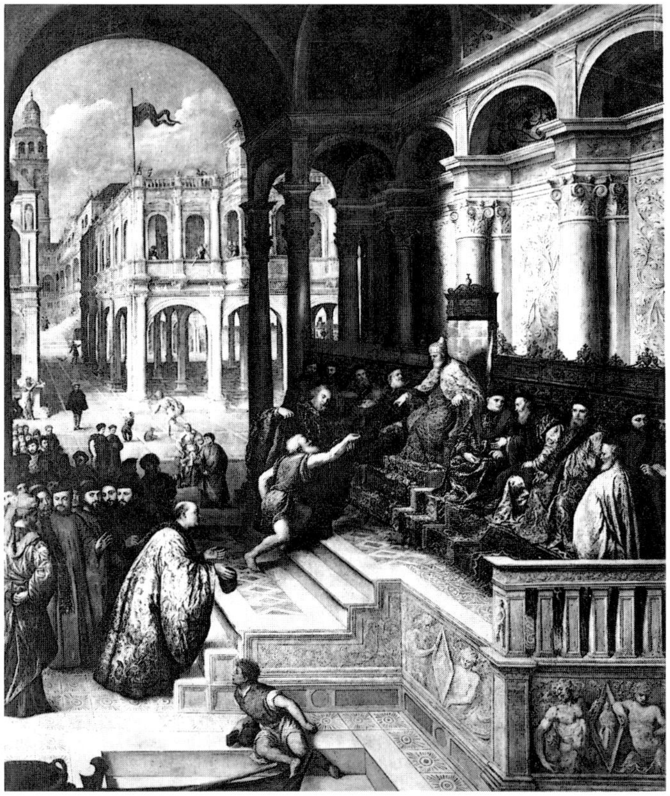

142. Palma Vecchio and Paris Bordone, *Miracle of St. Mark in a Storm at Sea* (*Sea Storm*) (Venice, Ospedale Civile)

143 (right). Paris Bordone, *Presentation of the Ring to the Doge* (Venice, Accademia)

St. Mark saves the city from destruction during a violent storm provoked by devilish forces.[10] Although the work has suffered extensive repainting (the sea monster is a later addition, probably of the eighteenth century), and its precise dating is uncertain, we can still make some general observations about it. A ship full of devils, tossed on the turbulent sea, takes up the middle field. In front is a rowboat in which four devils – powerful nude figures – strain to keep their craft afloat. To the left is the fortress on the Lido which guards the entrance to the lagoon. In the distance on the right is Venice itself. More dramatic than any of the canvases that we have observed in the Venetian *scuole* to date, it reveals a new taste for excitement and high drama in religious art. It was a mode that developed initially in Rome and appeared in Venice first on the canvases of Titian.

But some of the traditional sensibility remains. The heroic protagonists – St. Mark, accompanied by an old Venetian fisherman and by St. George and St. Nicholas, also protectors of the city – are inserted in the middle field to the right of the galley. Like Jacopo de' Salis in Gentile Bellini's *Procession*, they might pass unnoticed by those not already familiar with the story. If the great battle scenes of the Great Council campaign of 1474 had survived, we might see similar accommodations between the orderly eyewitness mode and an inherently unruly event.

In the *Presentation of the Ring*, Paris Bordone depicted the sequel to the *Sea Storm*.[11] The fisherman has returned safely to Venice and upon Mark's instruction reports to the Doge and his procurators that the city has been saved through the interventions of its patron saints. He shows them a ring, normally kept in the treasury of San Marco but removed by Mark's divine power, as a sign of the truth of his story. Although vertical in format, the composition was derived from Carpaccio's wide narrative tableaux and retained certain elements of the eyewitness style: the description of fabrics and stuffs; genre elements like the dwarf and monkey in the background; and the familiar company of confraternity witnesses. But along with a more continuous and integrated progression into the depth of space, there is a new aristocratic tone; a restraint in detail and elimination of distractions; and a clear subordination of parts to the whole for a more dramatic narrative focus. The scene is set in Venice, and yet the precise location (unlike those of the True Cross cycle) is difficult to determine. It could just as well be Rome.

What we are witnessing is the breakthrough of *romanitas* in style, narrative mode and even architecture in Venetian *scuola* painting, in more than just an anecdotal way. In the earlier works, distant places – Brittany, Alexandria and Jerusalem – had been recast in the image of Venice. Now Venice was to be remade in the image of Rome.

By the time we come to the *istorie* of Tintoretto in the Chapter Hall of the Scuola di San Marco at mid-century we find little of the circumstantiality of the earlier works. Big figures, dramatic actions and great sweeping brushstrokes have replaced the collective casts, the solemn ceremonious movements and the earnestly rendered details of the eyewitness artists. In the *Miracle of the Slave*, we have no doubt that what we are witnessing is a supernatural event. It is a miracle that looks miraculous. The story is set in Lyon; that city too is given a Roman facade [Plate 144].

This changing aspect of the city and its vision of itself would also be reflected over the next decade on the canvases executed by Titian and lesser artists for the

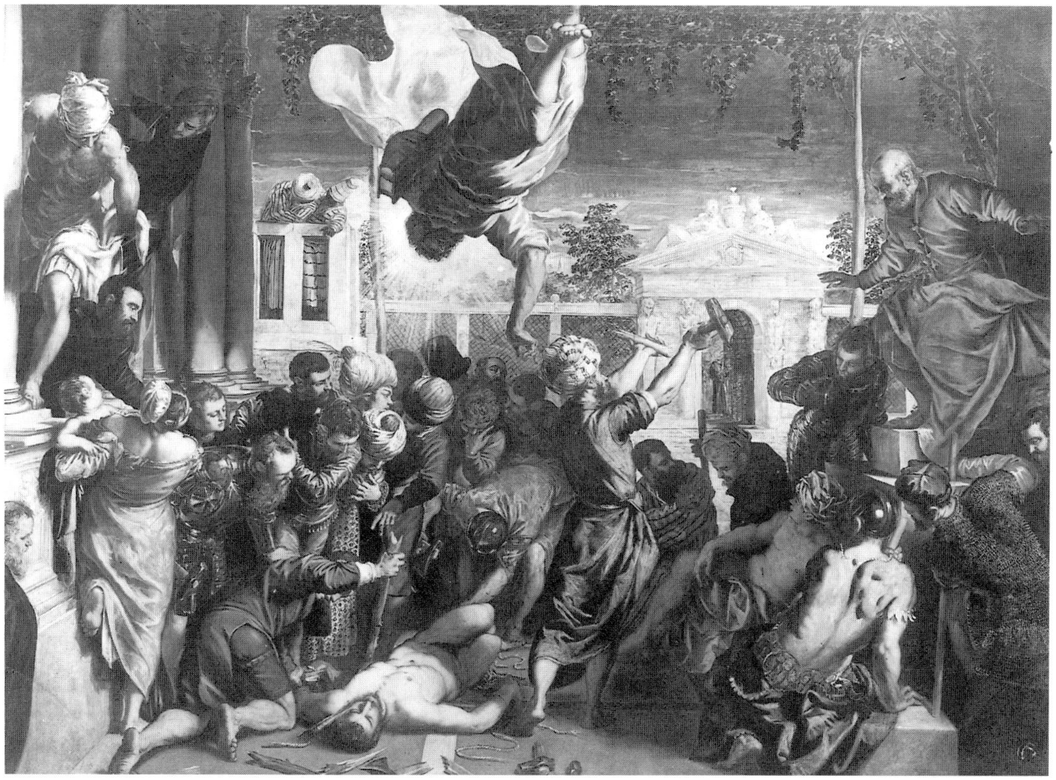

144. Tintoretto, *Miracle of the Slave* (Venice, Accademia)

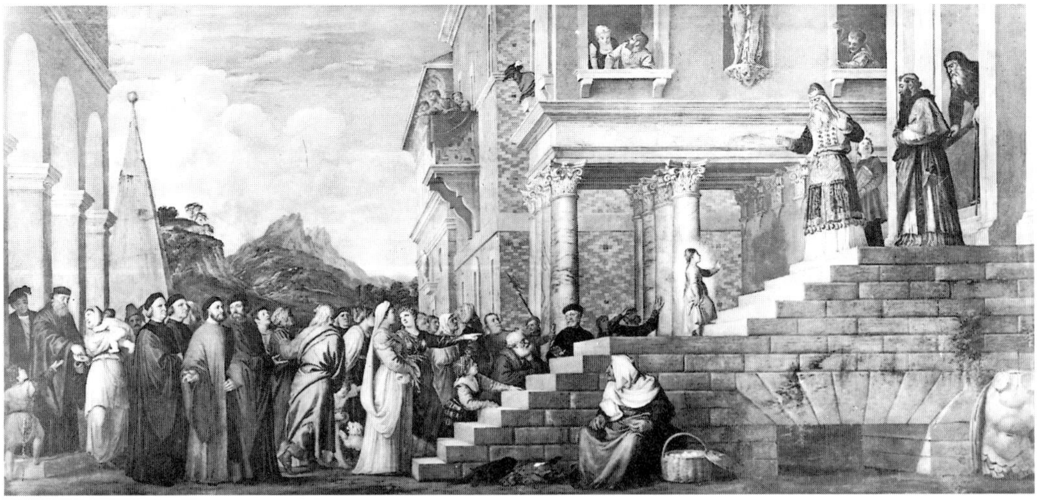

145. Titian, *Presentation of the Virgin* (Venice, Accademia)

albergo of the Scuola Grande di S. M. della Carità. Titian's *Presentation of the Virgin* cast elements of the Ducal Palace of Venice in an idiom of Roman antique grandeur [Plate 145].[12] And yet even there, the tenacious appeal of the eyewitness style was not altogether forgotten. As David Rosand points out, Titian returned once again to Carpaccio's narrative tableau format and demonstrated 'the still vital potential of the native tradition'.[13] But the scene is no longer one that began with an eyewitness. Despite the virtuoso quality of its naturalistically rendered details, the *Presentation* began with the mind – the *idea* – rather than with the eye. Titian did not (as Carpaccio and Gentile Bellini would have done) diligently record the 'real world' so that he could present it as if from the brush of an eyewitness. A *fantasia* from the beginning, the painting is a richly symbolic allegory that is cast in the pictorial language of the real world. At the moment when the Virgin becomes a source of radiant light within the painting, the real world has become supernatural and transcendent. It is a transcendence that the eyewitness painters never aimed to achieve.

* * *

In the course of this book we have come a long way from Ruskin's 'magic mirror'. For between the actuality of life in Venice around 1500 – the processions, the healings, the exorcisms, the challenges from both east and west, the crowded streets, the busy canals – and the painted microcosms of that world which line the walls of museums today, there existed an 'aesthetic space'.[14] This aesthetic space was a space in the minds of the artists and their patrons. It was filled with assumptions about the *istoria*, with artistic practices and stylistic trends, with concerns about honor and piety, and with a host of related ideological and cultural tendencies that no modern viewer can claim to share. It was a space richer, more varied, and frequently filled with more anxious cares and marked by deeper seriousness, than an uninformed modern viewer can imagine. The 'innocent eye' that Ruskin liked to see behind the art of Vittore Carpaccio was more acute and discriminating than he thought. For it guided the artist's hand in a delicate task of mediation. The result is *la vera historia*. It is not what Venetians saw, but what they wished to see.

APPENDIX

Giovanni Dario: Secretary of the Senate and Guardian Grande of the Scuola Grande di San Giovanni Evangelista

Giovanni Dario has played a large role in this book as a leading figure in the Scuola Grande di San Giovanni Evangelista. In his monograph on Dario, the renowned Venetian secretary who negotiated a peace treaty with the Sultan Mehmed II in 1479, Franz Babinger did not touch upon his membership in the Scuola. The purpose of this Appendix is to bring together the two Darios – government functionary and confraternity officer – and to establish that they are one and the same person.

1. Giovanni Dario: confratello and Guardian Grande

A certain *Zuan Dario*, the only person with that surname, is listed as member of the Scuola di San Giovanni during the period 1478–1501. Reg. 12, the Mariegola for the relevant period, was begun in 1478. All the men enrolled in the Scuola as of that year were entered into the register. It was then kept up to date, with new admissions added yearly through to 1501. The members 'ala disciplina' are listed alphabetically by first name. Dario's entry appears under the letter 'Z':

1480 rec. zuan Dario secretario s. postolo 149. . . 12 Maggio passò da questa vita.

The entry indicates that a Zuan Dario, secretary, residing in the parish of Santi Apostoli, joined the Scuola in 1480. He died on 12 May in 149– [the ink is smeared, obliterating the last numeral].

There is a certain amount of confusion in the records as to Dario's exact number of terms as Guardian Grande.

Reg. 6 gives Zuane Dario four terms which seems unlikely: 1480 (listed with Silvestro Sandeli), 1481, 1488 and 1492. Probably begun in the early 15th century, this register contains a membership roll, with death dates noted into the 1470s. A list of Guardiani Grandi is included, which was kept up to date until the 17th century (1301–1642).

In Reg. 73, Registro di Banchi (1465–1690), Dario is credited with a more plausible two terms: 1480 and 1492. This register is more detailed than Reg. 6, listing the full *banca* for each year. The relevant entries here also appear to have been written in the 15th century.

Cf. two later compilations in the Biblioteca Correr. MCV, Gradenigo 194: 1480, 1488, 1492; and MCV, Cicogna 3063: 1480, 1491 ('Gio. Dario Segretario, per la seconda volta'). The latter reference has numerous errors and should not be trusted. A possible explanation for the discrepancies of dating in the 1480's would be Dario's frequent trips abroad, when his terms in office might have been interrupted. In any event, his Guardianship in 1492 is documented in both of the original registers of the Scuola cited above (Reg. 6 and 73), and is corroborated by a further citation in Reg. 13.

The designation of *segretario* (*secretario*) was not common in the 15th century. It was generally earned only on diplomatic missions abroad (Neff, 1981, p. 40). The usual designation for a member of the Chancery was *nodaro*. In Reg. 12, the membership roster of the Scuola covering the relevant period, only two members are listed as *secretario*: Zuan Dedo, the Grand Chancellor, and Zuan Dario.

From the above evidence, we can conclude that a secretary named Zuan Dario was a member of the Scuola during that period. Since he is the only person with that name on the rolls, he must be the same man who served as Guardian Grande in 1492.

2. Giovanni Dario: Secretary of the Senate and Venetian plenipotentiary

The will of Babinger's Dario was opened on 13 May 1494, 'viso cadavere', as Babinger put it. He concluded that Dario must have died that day (Babinger, 1961, p. 103). As we have seen, in the Scuola register a notice is written next to Dario's name: '149. . . 12 Maggio passò da questa vita'. The corroboration is strong, but not as firm as we might like. However, there are further data to strengthen it.

First, Babinger's Dario had a close relationship with one of the ranking officers of the Scuola. Dario made three wills: in 1489, 1492 and 1493. The first two were drawn up by Lodovico Zamberti, a notary at the Avogaria di Comun, who held Scuola office as Guardian da Matin in 1494 and Vicario in 1498. He also presided at the opening of Dario's third will after his death in 1494 (ibid.).

Second, the nephew of Babinger's Dario joined the Scuola in 1491 under the special concession of extra members granted for works in the *albergo* (Cat. XV, doc. 2): ASV, San Giovanni, Reg. 12. He was the son of Dario's sister and was originally named Francesco Pantaleo. He adopted the Dario surname, however, and lived in the Ca' Dario with his uncle. Francesco's entry into the confraternity for such a purpose at that time again puts Babinger's Dario within the immediate ambient of the Scuola during the relevant period.

Third, a register compiled of members of the Ducal Chancery in the 15th century lists only one Zuane Dario (BMV, Cod. It. VII, 1667 (=8959), 'Tabelle nominative e cronologiche dei segretari della Cancelleria Ducale'). We may thus reject the possibility that there may have been two homonym secretaries living during that period.

Finally, in his last will of 1493, Babinger's Giovanni Dario made the Scuola di San Giovanni the heir of all his possessions in case his line died out (ASV, Notarile, Testamenti, Giacomo Grassolario, B. 1183, no. 248 (1 Oct. 1493)). He was clearly a member of the Scuola.

It seems, therefore, beyond reasonable doubt that we are dealing with a single person.

NOTES

Abbreviations

ASV	Archivio di Stato, Venice
ASV, S. Giov.	ASV, Scuola Grande di San Giovanni Evangelista
ASV, San Marco	ASV, Scuola Grande di San Marco
BMV	Biblioteca Nazionale Marciana, Venice
MCV	Biblioteca del Museo Civico Correr, Venice
MCV, Inc. H222 bis	*Questi sono i miracoli delasantissima croce dela scola de misier san zuane evangelista.* N.p., n.d.
RIS, o. s.	*Rerum Italicarum Scriptores*, ed. L. A. Muratori, 25 volumes, Milan, 1723–51 [old series]
RIS. n. s.	*Rerum Italicarum Scriptores*, ed. G. Carducci et al. 32 volumes in 119, Città di Castello and other locations, 1900–75 [new series]
Sanudo, *Diarii*	Marin Sanudo, *I Diarii*, ed. R. Fulin et al, 58 volumes, Venice, 1879–1903
Sanudo, *Vite*, 1900 edn	Marin Sanudo, *Le Vite dei Dogi*, ed. G. Monticolo and G. Carducci, In RIS, n.s., 22:4, Città di Castello and Bologna, 1900–1902
Sanudo, *Vitae*, 1733 edn	Marin Sanudo, *Vitae Ducum Venetorum*, ed. L. Muratori. In *RIS*, o. s., 22, Milan, 1733.

Chapter 1

1. Ruskin, 1894, pp. 192–93.
2. Zampetti, 1966b, pp. 84–85.
3. Lauts, 1962, p. 27.
4. See Barthes, 1975, pp. 237–72; Terence Hawkes, *Structuralism & Semiotics*, Berkeley, 1977, pp. 1–56; and White, 1981, pp. 1–24.
5. See the inscriptions in Cat. XV.2, 5 and 7.
6. Ludovico Zamberti, cited by Monticolo in Sanudo, *Vite*, 1900 edn, pp. 370–71. See also Chapter 6, n. 32 below.
7. See Turner, 1981, pp. 137–64.
8. Molmenti and Ludwig, 1907, p. 34.
9. In *The Cicerone: or, Art Guide to Painting in Italy*, freely translated in summary form by Mrs. A. Clough, London, 1873, p. 81.
10. See Rosand, 1982, pp. 91–101.
11. The basic divisions are drawn from literary analysis; see Robert Scholes and Robert Kellogg, *The Nature of Narrative*, London, 1966. As nonverbal media, images obviously require their own approach. Within recent years, three international symposia have been devoted to problems of pictorial narrative representation. The papers are published in 'Narration in Ancient Art: A Symposium', *American Journal of Archaeology* 61 (1957) : pp. 43–91; *Texte et image: Actes du Colloque international de Chantilly (13 au 15 octobre 1981)*, Centre de recherches de l'université de Paris X, Paris, 1984; and 'Pictorial Narrative in Antiquity and the Middle Ages', ed. Herbert Kessler and Marianna Shreve Simpson, *Studies in the History of Art* 16 (1985). Also important is Marilyn Lavin's forthcoming book on the ordering and arrangement of the narrative scenes in Italian fresco cycles in churches from the early Middle Ages through the Renaissance. See also Brilliant, 1984; and Winter, 1981, pp. 2–38.
12. The categories are defined in detail in Kurt Weitzmann, *Illustrations in Roll and Codex. A Study of the Origin and Method to Text Illustration*, Princeton, 1947 (1970 edn), pp. 12–36. Cf. Winter, 1985, pp. 11–12.

Chapter 2

1. Casola, 1907 edn, p. 147. But cf. Fabri, 1896 edn, I, p. 109, for the confusion of a Corpus Christi Procession out-of-doors: 'There is nothing but a confused crowding, running and pushing multitude.'
2. Philippe de Commynes, 1893 edn, p. 406.
3. Guylforde, 1851 edn, p. 8.
4. The painting was originally made for the Palazzo dei Camerlenghi at the Rialto. See Lauts, 1962, p. 249; and Martineau and Hope, 1983, p. 166. For the predestination (*praedestinatio*), see Chapter 3, n. 11 below.
5. For an extensive analysis, with earlier bibliography, see Grubb, 1986, pp. 43–94. See also Muir, 1981, pp. 13–61.
6. See the references in Chapter 1, n. 4 above.
7. For the eastern front during this period, see Babinger, 1978; Lucchetta, 1980a; Cozzi and Knapton, 1986; and *Venezia e i Turchi. Scontri e confronti di due civiltà*, Milan, 1985. For the situation in Italy, see Cozzi and Knapton, 1986; and Mallett, 1981, pp. 267–88.
8. Malipiero, 1843 edn, I, p. 58. One must be cautious about Malipiero. The autograph manuscript no longer exists, and the printed edition was taken from a redaction of the late 16th century in which Malipiero's observations, composed chronologically, were reordered according to themes. For a caveat regarding the diarist's accuracy, see Finlay, 1980, pp. 7–8. But even if he does not always get the facts straight, Malipiero's observations are still useful as an indication of Venetian responses and attitudes toward contemporary events. His feelings are often corroborated in the proceedings of state councils. For a Venetian chronology of dealings with the Turks, 1450–1502, see Sanudo, *Diarii*, 4, cols. 324–28.
9. Malipiero, 1843 edn, I, p. 107.
10. See Chapter 3 below.
11. Sanudo, 1980 edn, pp. 34–35.
12. See Babinger, 1978, pp. 369–76.
13. Malipiero, 1843 edn, I, pp. 176–79.
14. Lucchetta, 1980, pp. 410–11. Cf. J. Wansbrough, 'A Mamluk Ambassador to Venice in 912–1507', *Bulletin of the School of Oriental and African Studies*, University of London 26 (1963) : pp.521–24.
15. Tenenti, 1973, p. 28.
16. Mallett and Hale, 1983, pp. 1–5, 50–55 and 199–210. See also Cozzi and Knapton, 1986, for the entire period.
17. Ibid., pp. 55–59. For a contemporary view, see Sanudo, *Spedizione*, 1883 edn.
18. Mallett and Hale, 1983, pp. 59–64.
19. Priuli, 1912–41 edn, pt. 3.1, p. 112.
20. Ibid., p. 113.
21. Ibid., p. 180.
22. Mallett and Hale, 1983, pp. 221ff.
23. For Venetian awareness of the city's phy-

sical vulnerability, see Pavan, 1981, pp. 467–93. Cf. Finlay, 1980, pp. 27–37.
24. King, 1986, pp. 92–205.
25. Ibid.; and idem, 'Caldeira and the Barbaros on marriage and the family: humanistic reflections of Venetian realities', *Journal of Medieval and Renaissance Studies*, 6 (1976) : pp. 46–49.
26. Cited in *Viaggi in Persia*, 1973 edn, p. 231.
27. For the Serrata, see Cracco, 1967, pp. 106–34; idem, 1986, pp. 109ff; Lane, 1971, pp. 237–73; and Ruggiero, 1980, pp. 56–64. Cf. Chojnacki, 1973, pp. 47–90.
28. For citizenship in Venice, see Pullan, 1971, pp. 99–108; and Cozzi and Knapton, 1986, pp. 133–40. Cf. S. Ell, 'Citizenship and Immigration in Venice, 1305 to 1500', Ph.D. dissertation, University of Chicago, 1976.
29. Sanudo, 1980 edn, p. 22.
30. Any such percentage is, of course, only an educated guess. The statistics cited here are taken from Daniele Beltrami, *Storia della popolazione di Venezia dalle fine del secolo XVI alla caduta della Repubblica*, Padua, 1954, pp. 193–213 and Table 14. Sanudo (1980 edn, pp. 22 and 146) had put the population in 1493 at 150,000, and the number of adult male patricians at 2600. Lane (1973, pp. 19–20) suggested c.120,000 as a more realistic total c.1500 and put the nobility at 6 percent of the population in the mid-16th century. D. Herlihy ('Mapping Households in Medieval Italy', *Catholic Historical Review* 58 (1972) : pp. 5–6) estimated Venice's population in 1509 at c.102,000. In any event, the relative proportion of nobles and *cittadini* within the whole society was small.
31. Pullan, 1971, pp. 105–6.
32. Sanudo, 1980 edn, p. 22. The sleeve, *a comedo*, is full, but gathered at the wrist.
33. BMV, Cod. It. VII 165 (=8867), 'Memorie della famiglia Freschi'. The handwriting dates to the very late 15th or early 16th century. The miniatures are not dated, but the costumes shown in them correspond quite closely to those in paintings of the time. For the Freschi family, see Neff, 1981, pp. 33–63.
34. Sabellico, 1772 edn, col. 8.
35. See Lowry, pp. 184–87, on the surprising degree of social fluidity in Venetian education. Lowry found that schooling equivalent to that offered to the children of the patriciate, and sometimes in company with them, was available to male children of the laboring classes.
36. Pullan, 1971, pp. 102–5. Cf. King, 1986, pp. 76–91; and Finlay, 1980, pp. 37–58.
37. Neff, 1981, pp. 33–63. See also Trebbi, 1980, pp. 65–125; and Paola de Peppo, 'Memorie di veneti cittadini': Alvise Dardani, Cancellier Grande', *Studi Veneziani*, n.s. 8 (1984) : pp. 413–53.
38. Pullan, 1971, p. 103, citing Gasparo Contarini, *The Commonwealth and Government of Venice*, trans. L. Lewkenor, London 1599, pp. 142–44 (Latin version: *De magistratibus et republica Venetorum libri quinque*, Basel, 1547).
39. See n. 79 below.
40. Pullan, 1971, pp. 107–8, citing Contarini (as in n. 38).
41. For Italian confraternities in general, the fundamental but outdated work is Monti, 1927. Cf. Weissman, 1982.
42. For a good summary, see Henderson, 1978, pp. 47–60. See also Alberigo, 1960, pp. 156–244.
43. For Venetian confraternities, see Pullan, 1971, passim; idem, 1981, pp. 9–26; and G. Scarabello, 'Caratteri e funzioni socio-politiche dell' associazionismo a Venezia sotto la repubblica', in Gramigna and Perissa, 1981, pp. 5–24.
44. For their unusual independence from ecclesiastical authorities, see Pullan, 1971, pp. 43–50. For the suspicion with which they were often viewed in Florence, see Weissman, 1982, pp. 116–18 and 163–94. Cf. Trexler, 1980, particularly pp. 252–56, 382–87 and 403–18.
45. See Trexler, 1980, Part I; and Sbriziolo, 1967–68, pp. 405–42; idem, 1967, pp. 167–97 and 502–42; and idem, 1970, pp. 715–63.
46. ASV, Scuole piccole, Reg. 597, ff. 3–3v, cap. xii: 'Ancora volemo che se alguna persona de la nostra scuola per si fesse o consentisse per altri alguna cossa la qual fosse inzuria, dano o despresio de Miser lo Doxe de Veniesia o del so conseio over de questa benedeta citade la qua sie eleta da Dio pare onipotente per recovramentò e sostegnimento de tutti li triboladi descazado e fedel de la santa mare gliesia, che quela persona sia lo piu tosto che se pora apalentada e denuntiada per misser lo gastaldo eli suo compagni a misser lo doze e alo so conseio e sia fuora dela scuola perpetualmente.' Cf. Molmenti-Ludwig, 1907, p. 63.
47. Jacopo d'Albizotto Guidi counted more than 200 in 1442 (Sem. Pat. Venice, Cod. 950, f. 31). Sanudo observed 210 *scuole piccole*, in addition to the 5 Scuole Grandi, who participated in the funeral procession of Cardinal Zen in 1501 (*Diarii*, 4, col. 63). In 1732 there were 347 officially recognized lay-religious associations (Pullan, 1971, p. 34).
48. BMV, God. Ital. VII 2398 (=10527), 'Memorie d'arte, religione e di beneficenza'. p. xvii: 'Per lo più accanto alle nostre chiese, anzi ad esse addossate stanno una ò più Scuole di devozione, le quali invasero l'area libera, che la chiesa vetusta circondava; curiosa appendice, come se la vastità del tempio non fosse dessa sufficiente alle preghiere ed alle pie pratiche dei buoni fideli.'
49. According to Sbriziolo, 1970, p. 737, the first references to the Scuole dei Battuti as *scolae magnae* in official documents appeared on 17 April 1467 in the deliberations of the Council of Ten: ASV, Consiglio dei Dieci, Parti Miste, Reg. 17, f. 20v. The four Scuole dei Battuti who were given the status of Scuola Grande at that time dated back at least to the beginning of the fourteenth century and were dedicated to Santa Maria della Carità, San Giovanni Evangelista, Santa Maria Valverde della Misericordia and San Marco. In 1489, the Scuola di San Rocco was given full Scuola Grande status, and a sixth, the Scuola di San Teodoro, was added in 1552. See Pullan, 1971, pp. 33–38; and Maschio, 1981, pp. 193–206.
50. Pullan, 1971, pp. 86–89.
51. See Sbriziolo, 1967–68.
52. ASV, S, Giov., Reg. 13.
53. For the *nazionali*, see Sbriziolo, 1967–68, pp. 405–42. The standard work on the *arti* is G. Monticolo and E. Besta, *I capitolari delle arti veneziane*, Rome, 1894–1914. See also C. Levi, *Notizie storiche di alcune antiche scuole di arti e mestieri scomparse o ancora esistenti a Venezia*, Venice, 1985; R. MacKenney, 'Arti e stato a Venezia tra tardo medio evo e '600', *Studi Veneziani*, n.s., 5 (1981) : pp. 127–43; and idem, 'Guilds and Guildsmen in Sixteenth-Century Venice', *Bulletin for the Society of Renaissance Studies* 2 (1984).
54. That the admission of both sexes was standard in the *scuole comuni* is indicated by the permission of the Council of Ten to establish the Scuola di S. Ludovico in 1401 on the condition that it accept both men and women 'in huiusmodi scolis similibus' (Sbriziolo, 1967–68, p. 423, citing ASV, Consiglio dei Dieci, Parti Miste, Reg. 8, f. 76). However, the role of women was probably very restricted.
55. This assumption is based upon a random selection of Mariegole. See, for example, the patrician gift made to the Scuola di Santa Marina (MCV, Mariegola IV, 68, f. 47): 'la cassa sopra laltar amezo de la pala doro, la qual fece far la magnifica madona Antonia dona del magnifico miss. Marin da cha di garzoni come nobel fradelo, e sorela de la dita schola.'
56. Pullan, 1971, pp. 34–40; and Sbriziolo, 1970; but see also Sbriziolo, 1967–68, p. 431, where she notes that the Scuola dei Fiorentini practiced flagellation, an activity that seems to have been carried out inside the meeting-house.
57. Sem. Pat. Venice, Cod. 950, ff. 32–32v (cited in n. 47 above). For further information on Guidi and some excerpts transcribed from his poem, see Rossi, 1893, pp. 397–451. A *doppiere* is a large two-branched candlestick carried by Scuola members in processions. See Fogolari, 1924–25, pp. 775–94.
58. Wurthmann, 1975, pp. 107–11.
59. For this concept, see Trexler, 1980, pp. 16–17 and passim.
60. Ruggiero, 1980, pp. 82–94. His conclusions are corroborated by G. Scarabello, 'Devianza sessuale ed interventi di giustizia a Venezia nella prima metà del XVI secolo', in *Tiziano e Venezia*, Vicenza, 1980, p. 78.
61. Wurthmann, 1975, pp. 191–236. See also Pullan, 1971, pp. 112–15; and Sohm, 1982, pp. 6–11.
62. See the references in n. 61. Sohm, 1982, pp. 13–19, argues that the *banche* were dominated by a few families, year after year. One may interpret the statistics differently. My own survey of the four top office-holders in the Scuole di San Giovanni and San Marco for the years 1490–1510 and 1498–1525 respectively, revealed 116 surnames for 180 office-holders (ASV, S. Marco, Reg. 6 bis

and ASV, S. Giov., Reg. 73).
63. Wurthmann, 1975, pp. 207–36.
64. They were probably advanced in age. Two-thirds of the four top officers of the Scuola di San Giovanni (1490–1510) and the Scuola Grandi di San Marco (1498–1525) died within a decade of their term of office. (ASV, S. Giov., Reg. 12, 13 and 73; and ASV, S. Marco, Reg. 4 and 17). Cf. Pullan, 1971, p. 116.
65. Pullan, 1971, pp. 109–11.
66. Tucci, 1973, pp. 360–61.
67. See, for example, Chapter 4, n. 45 below.
68. Venetian patrician wills often specified such a turnout.
69. See Sbriziolo, 1970, pp. 726–29 and 735–36; and Pullan, 1971, pp. 72–74.
70. Sbriziolo, 1970, p. 725 n. 3; and Pullan, 1971, pp. 38–40 and 50–52. It is unclear whether all members were obliged to go through this probationary period, or if the *disciplinati* constituted a permanent cadre in a Scuola dei Battuti. It is possible that some combination of the two options was followed, with some members moving from *disciplinati* to regular membership and others never practising the discipline. Felix Fabri (1843 edn, pp. 428–29) described such a procession in 1484.
71. For example, the 1501 Mariegola of the Scuola di San Giovanni which contains the full membership roll, is divided into four categories: priests, nobles, physicians and surgeons, and 'fradeli a la disciplina' (ASV, S. Giov, Reg. 13). All of the officers of the Scuola are listed in the latter group.
72. Pullan, 1971, pp. 75–76.
73. Cozzi, 1973, pp. 295–300; and Finlay, 1980, pp. 197–201.
74. Morosini, 1969 edn, particularly pp. 81–85 and 134–37. For an analysis of Morosini's writings, see Cozzi, 1970a, pp. 405–58. See also Labalme, 1969, pp. 263–87; and King, 1986, pp. 140–50.
75. Cited by Finlay, 1980, p. 75.
76. Gilbert, 1980, pp. 21–24.
77. Bistort, 1912, p. 352. See also Cozzi, 1980, pp. 52–55; and Newett, 1907, pp. 245–78.
78. Finlay, 1980, pp. 75–81.
79. Pullan, 1971, p. 108.
80. ASV, Consiglio dei Dieci, Parti Miste, Reg. 19, f. 99v (4 March 1478).
81. ASV, Maggior Consiglio, Deliberazioni, Stella, Reg. 24 (1480–1502), f. 64v (new numeration).
82. ASV, Consiglio dei Dieci, Parti Miste, Reg. 31, ff. 62v–63 (31 Aug. 1506): '. . .che la dignita del nostro mazor conseio non fosse ne potesse esser contaminata, maculata, over altramente quovismodo denigrada . . .' See also Sanudo, *Diarii*, 6, col 406.
83. MCV, Cod. Correr 1391, 'Matrimonario Veneto', covers the period c. 1190–1620, but most of the entries date to 1350–1550. It is divided into two sections: I. 'Gentildonne Patrizie Viniziane maritate in Gentilhuominj Popolari Viniziani' (167 entries); II. 'Gentildonne Popolari Viniziane maritate in Gentilhuominj Patrizie Viniziani' (936 entries).
84. ASV, Consiglio dei Dieci, Comune, Reg. 2, f. 16v (26 April 1526). Particular attention was paid at this time to the status of the wife, that is, to her father's quality and condition.
85. The provisions were duplicated first in 1538 for prospective candidates to the Chancery. By 1569 they were extended to the *cittadino* order as a whole (Trebbi, 1980, pp. 70–71).
86. For the different experience of Florence, see Trexler, 1980, pp. 17–19.
87. Tucci, 1973, pp. 370–71. See also Cozzi and Knapton, 1986, pp. 117–31.
88. Ibid., citing Donado da Lezze, *Historia Turchesa (1300–1514)*, 1909 edn, p. 229. For another view, cf. Gabriele Vendramin's advice to his nephews in Pouncey, 1938–39, pp. 191–93.
89. Cited by Tenenti, 1973, pp. 21–22, who also interprets the passage in terms of the increased status accrued to the ownership of land, and not simply of territorial conquest. Cf. King, 1986, pp. 132–40.
90. For the situation in general, see Trebbi, 1980, pp. 65–125. For the galleys, see the observations of Newett in Casola, 1907 edn, pp. 106–8; and Ugo Tucci, 'I servizi marittimi veneziani per il pellegrinaggio in Terrasanta nel Medioevo', *Studi Veneziani*, n.s., 10 (1985) : pp. 43–66.
91. On the education of Venetian secretaries see, in particular, Trebbi, 1980, pp. 66–67 and 80–81; and King, 1986, pp. 76–91. Cf. Logan, 1972, Chapters 4 and 5; J. B. Ross, 'Venetian Scholars and Teachers, 14th to Early 16th Century: a Survey and a Study of Giovanni Battista Egnazio', *Renaissance Quarterly* 29 (1976) : pp. 521–66; and Gilbert, 1979, pp. 13–26. On distinctions between patricians and commoners in humanist circles, see King, 1986, p. 238. See also Chapter 6 below.
92. As Francesco Sansovino wrote in 1565, the secretary 'should have ears and mind, but no tongue outside the councils' (*L'avvocato e il segretario*, ed. P. Calamandrei, Florence, 1942, p. 152).
93. Trebbi, 1980, pp. 75ff. For the extension of the *cittadino originario* requirement to hold lower bureaucratic positions, see Neff, 1981, n. 5. For earlier patrician dominance in Venetian intellectual life, and the relationship between secretaries and their noble employers, see King, 1975, pp. 295–312.
94. BMV, Cod. It. VII, 166 (7307); and ASV, Consiglio dei Dieci, Parti Miste, Reg. 30, f. 87 (16 Sept. 1504). Cf. ASV, San Marco, Reg. 8, 'Summario Generale di tutte le leggi, ordini constitutioni & terminationi,' ff. 1–2. This was a tightening-up of an earlier rule that simply required notaries of the Chancery to obtain permission first before taking Scuola office: ASV, Consiglio dei Dieci, Parti Miste, Reg. 18, f. 70v (23 May 1474).

Some Chancery employees who held office in the Scuola di San Marco after 1504 were Andrea della Scala, Vicario in 1508; Vettor Ziliol, Vicario in 1509 and Guardian Grande in 1515 and 1524; Giacomo Dardani fu Alvise, Vicario in 1511 and Guardian Grande in 1523; and Alvise Bon Rizzo, Vicario in 1525 (ASV, S. Marco, Reg. 17). Cf. Pullan, 1971, pp. 109–11.
95. This statement is based upon a study of the *banche* of the Scuola di San Giovanni (1490–1510) and the Scuola di San Marco (1498–1525). In San Giovanni, the secretarial group supplied 33 per cent of the Guardiani Grandi and constituted 21 per cent of those who held the four top offices. In San Marco the figures for those offices were, respectively, 35 per cent and 21 per cent (ASV, San Giovanni, Reg[i]. 6, 12, 13, and 73; ASV, San Marco, Reg[i]. 4, 6bis, and 17; MCV, Cod. Gradenigo-Dolfin 83, 192, and 194; MCV, Cod. Cicogna 2156, 3063/IV (fasc. 10), and MCV, Cons. IXD1, Tassini, 'Cittadini veneziani', vols. I-V). Cf. Pullan, 1971, pp. 109–11, who notes that the higher men rose in the social hierarchy, the less likely they were to describe themselves by occupation.
96. See Brown, 1987: in press.
97. Ibid., n. 43.
98. ASV, S. M. della Carità, Reg. 253, f. 84. From Sohm, 1982, doc. 142.
99. ASV, S. M. della Carità, B. 2, perg. n. 107. From Sohm, 1982, doc. 144.
100. See Richard Goldthwaite, *The Building of Renaissance Florence. An Economic and Social History*, Baltimore and London, 1980, pp. 12–13. For family chapels in the Frari, see Goffen, 1986, particularly pp. 38–39. Although Goffen hypothesizes a missing fresco cycle depicting the Life of the Virgin in the sacristy chapel, built by the Pesaro family, there are insufficient remains to draw any firm conclusions. It is safe to say that nothing on the order of the frescoes in the Sassetti Chapel of Santa Trinità in Florence would have lined the walls.
101. Cited by Finlay, 1980, p. 35.

Chapter 3

1. Sanudo, 1980 edn, p. 62.
2. Sanudo (ibid., p. 146) stated that 2600 patricians were qualified to sit in the Great Council in 1493. He observed that attendance was ordinarily between 1400 to 1500, but when a Procurator was to be elected, it might rise to 1800 or more. It could be much less (see Cat. XIII, doc. lb).
3. Ibid., p. 34.
4. For the significance of the 1177 event, see the fine summary in Muir, 1981, pp. 103–34.
5. For the campaign of 1474, see Chapter 4 and Cat. XIII.
6. Sanudo, 1980 edn, p. 24. For the mosaics, see the magisterial study of Demus, 1984. For the church see idem, 1960; and Sinding-Larsen, 1974, pp. 179–217.
7. Demus, 1984, I, pp. 54–83. See also Muir, 1981, pp. 78–92.
8. An episode that Demus, 1955, pp. 112–13, called 'l'ideale punto centrale e di cristallizzazione

nella elaborazione della storia patria veneziana, anzi addirittura delle visione veneziana del mondo in generale'.

9. For the Fourth Crusade see Donald Queller, *The Fourth Crusade*, Leicester, 1978; and Angeliki Laiou, 'Observations on the Results of the Fourth Crusade: Greeks and Latins in Port and Market', *Medievalia et Humanistica* 12(1984) : pp. 47–60. For Venetian views of the affair, see Carile, 1969. For 13th-century Venice, see Angeliki Laiou, 'Venice as a Centre of Trade and of Artistic Production in the Thirteenth Century', in *Il medio oriente e l'occidente nell'arte del XIII secolo*, ed. Hans Belting, Bologna, 1983, with further references.

10. For the 13th-century mosaic program, see Demus, 1984, II, pp. 185–91.

11. Ibid., p. 187. See also Silvio Tramontin, 'San Marco', in S. Tramontin et al., *Culto dei Santi a Venezia*, Venice 1965, pp. 43–73; and idem, 'Realtà e leggenda nei racconti marciani veneti', *Studi Veneziani* 12(1970) : pp. 35–58.

12. Demus, 1984, II, pp. 187 and 192–206.

13. Ibid., pp. 27–44.

14. Cat. II, doc. 1. Cf. docs. 10–11.

15. Cat. II, docs. 2, 6, 8, 9.

16. For the yearly masses, see Muir, 1981, pp. 98–99. A law passed in the Great Council on 25 Oct. 1457 required the Doge to hear mass in the chapel every Tuesday (MCV, Cod. Donà dalle Rose, 68, f. 435, cited by Sinding-Larsen, 1974, p. 209). Sansovino, 1663, I, p. 321, reported that the Doge had been required to go there daily, but he wrote long after the 13th-century chapel had been razed. For the papal indulgence, see Cat. II, doc. 5. For the signing of contracts, see Lorenzi, 1868, no. 97.

17. 'Historia de discordia...,' in Sanudo, *Vite*, 1900 edn, pp. 370–411). An early attempt to compile all the accounts of the event was made by Angelo Zon in a signed article, 'Memorie intorno alla venuta di Papa Alessandro III in Venezia all'anno 1177 e ai diversi suoi documenti', in Cicogna, 1824–27, IV, pp. 574–93. See also Muir, 1981, pp. 103–19.

18. MCV, Cod. Correr I, 383 (= 1497): 'Il libro della leggenda degli Apostoli Pietro e Paolo, di S. Albano e della venuta a Venezia di Papa Alexandro III'. For the dating, see Cat. II.

19. Taken from Bonincontro da Bovi, 'Historia de discordia', in Sanudo, *Vite*, 1900 edn, pp. 374–410.

20. G. Soranzo, *La guerra tra Venezia e la S. Sede per il dominio di Ferrara*, Città di Castello, 1916. For this period see also Cracco, 1986, pp. 115–128. For the devastating effect of an interdict on a community, see R. Trexler, *The Spiritual Power. Republican Florence under Interdict*, Leiden, 1974.

21. Sanudo, *Vitae*, 1733 edn, col. 598 (*Vita* of Giovanni Soranzo). But cf. Sansovino, 1581, cc. 237–237v for a different explanation of the nickname.

22. The Venetian use of legend and painted *istorie* to reinforce claims of sovereignty is analogous to papal employment of the Donation of Constantine, portrayed in mosaic in the portico of the Lateran Basilica in the 12th century. See Walter, 1970, pp. 169ff.

23. See Monticolo in Sanudo, *Vite*, 1900 edn, pp. 404–6.

24. See Muir, 1981, pp. 119–25; and Padoan Urban, 1968, pp. 291–353.

25. For the notion of narrative scripts for real-life activities, see Turner, 1981. For the use of the *trionfi* in processions, see Muir, 1981, pp. 185–211; Pertusi, 1965, pp. 56ff; and Fasoli, 1973, pp. 261–95.

26. See Cat. IV.

27. 'Venetiane pacis inter ecclesiam et imperium Castellani Bassianensis', in Sanudo, *Vite*, 1900 edn, pp. 485–519.

28. See n. 16 above.

29. For Venice of the mid-Trecento, see Cracco, 1967; idem, 1986, Chapter IV; and two useful collections of essays: *La civiltà veneziana del Trecento*, Florence, 1956; and *Storia della cultura veneta. 2. Il Trecento*, ed. G. Arnaldi, Vicenza, 1976. Two important narrative programs of mosaic decoration were executed in San Marco during this period: scenes from the life of John the Baptist in the Baptistery (1330–40s) and scenes from the life of St. Isidore and the translation of his relics (1348–55). See Muraro, 1970, pp. 123–24.

30. Favaro, 1975, pp. 15–28. Cf. Muraro, 1961, pp. 263–74.

31. Datable to the 1350s and c. 1360–65, respectively. See Flores d'Arcais, 1974, pp. 27–30, 64–65 and 69–70.

32. For Guariento, see ibid., pp. 39–41 and 72–73; Sinding-Larsen, 1974, pp. 45–56 and 65–66; and Cat. IV. For the drawing, see references in Cat. IV.2.

33. Vasari, *Vite*, 1966 edn, p. 431. Degenhart and Schmitt, 1980, II-1, pp. 117–24, also suggest Lorenzo Veneziano and Nicoletto Semitecolo. Cf. Cat. IV.

34. Cat. IV, doc. 3.

35. For this period, see Cozzi and Knapton, 1986, Chapter 1; and Reinhold Mueller, 'Effetti della Guerra di Chioggia (1378–1381) sulla vita economica e sociale di Venezia', *Ateneo Veneto*,, n.s. 19 (1981): pp. 29–41.

36. Cat. IV, docs. 4 and 5.

37. Cat. IV, doc. 6.

38. Lorenzi, 1868, no. 148(a).

39. For this period see Cozzi and Knapton, 1986; Mallett and Hale, 1984, passim; and Lane, 1973, pp. 189–201.

40. Cat. IV, doc. 10.

41. See Pesaro, 1978, pp. 44–57, who proposes the participation of Jacobello del Fiore in the campaign. Pignatti, 1971, p. 112, suggests several other possibilities as well: Michelino da Besozzo, Michele di Matteo and Giambono. Noting that Jacobello was on the payroll of the Signoria at the time, Christiansen, 1987, pp. 166–67, adds Niccolò di Pietro, Zanino di Pietro and Michelino da Besozzo as other candidates for the campaign.

42. Sanudo, *Vitae*, 1733 edn, col. 968. This occasion should not be confused with the first meeting of the Great Council in the room, which was on 30 July 1419 (see n. 38 above). For the *Commemoriali*, see Cat. IV, doc. 8.

43. Cat. IV, doc. 9.

44. Schlosser, 1895, p. 215; see also G. T. Van Ysselsteyn, *Tapestry. The Most Expensive Industry of the XVth and XVIth Centuries*, The Hague, Brussels, 1969. Cf. Chapter 7, n. 53 below.

45. See ibid., pp. 183–225; and Mommsen, 1952, pp. 113–16. For a 16th-century notice of tapestries in the Doge's apartments depicting the Trojan origins of Venetians see Muir, 1981, p. 67.

46. *The Anonimo*, 1969 edn, p. 37. Cf. Mommsen, 1952, pp. 95–116.

47. For the general problem, see Belting, 1985, pp. 151–68, particularly pp. 157–60; and Wieruszowski, 1944, pp. 14–33. For the Sienese programs, see Southard, 1974.

48. Usually the first room to be decorated in the meeting-house of a *scuola*. See Sohm, 1982, pp. 36 and 62–79.

49. See Chapter 2, n. 49 above.

50. ASV, Consiglio dei Dieci, Parti Miste, Reg. 8, f. 71v (26 Oct. 1401).

51. See Chapter 2, n. 79 above.

52. See Sbriziolo, 1970, pp. 715–63.

53. For a detailed survey, see Wurthmann, 1975.

54. The sources date the donation, made on 23 December, to various years: MCV, Inc. H222 bis = 1368; *Miracoli della Croce*, 1590 = 1369; and Bibliothèque Arsenal, Paris, MS 499, ff. 141v–142, cited by Jorga, 1896, p. 403 = 1370. The weight of evidence falls in favor of the 1369 dating cited in the 1590 booklet.

55. Cat. VI, doc. 1.

56. ASV, S. Giov., Reg. 1 ff. 21v–23v.

57. They seem to have existed still in the 1480s. See Cat. VI, doc. 2. For other early cycles, see Cats. I, III and V.

58. Cat. VII, doc. 1.

59. The artist served as a Degano for the *sestiere* of San Marco in 1441 and 1454. See ASV, S. Giov., Reg. 72, cited in Paoletti, 1894, p. 6.

60. Cat. VIII, doc. 1.

61. Ibid., doc. 2.

62. Angelo Decembrio in his *De Politia Litteraria*, Pars LXVIII, f. 162v (from Baxandall, 1963, pp. 314–15). For the competition of 1441, see ibid.; Venturi, 1896, pp. 46–47; and references in Chapter 7 n. 48.

63. Ulisse de' Aleotti, 'Ulixis pro Iacopo Belino Pictore', printed in Ricci, 1908, I, p. 52.

64. Cat. XV, doc. 1.

65. Ridolfi, 1914 edn, I, p. 53.

66. Cat. X, docs, 2–4.

67. Cat. X, doc. 5.

68. Ricci, 1908, I, pp. 58–59.

69. Cat. X, doc. 6.

70. Cf. Meyer zur Capellen, 1985, pp. 12ff and 51ff; Tietze, 1939, pp. 34ff; and Gibbons, 1965, pp. 146–55. For arguments on Gentile's age, see Gibbons, 1963, pp. 54–8. Cf. Cat. XV.

71. Cat. X, docs. 7–10.

72. See Cat. XI. For the membership of the Scuola, see Lowry, 1981, pp. 193–218. However, his assumption that a Chapter General membership of 30 denotes a small total membership is unwarranted. By my own count, the Marigola of 1504 listed 131 regular members, 12 priests and 27 nobles for that year, a substantial number for a *scuola piccola*. Even in the Scuole Grandi a Chapter General generally numbered only 30–50 men (see Chapter 2, n. 61 above).
73. Cf. Goffen, 1986, pp. 19 and 174 n. 19, who postulates narrative frescoes in the nave of the Frari.

Chapter 4

1. Cat. XIII, doc. la-b.
2. Ibid. The amount is not stated, but when Giovanni Bellini was appointed to work with his brother in the Great Council Hall, he too was promised the next vacant *sansaria*. Until it became available, he was given an allowance of 80 ducats per year (Lorenzi, 1868, no. 195). See also Cat XIII, doc. 24, stating that Titian had been receiving 118–120 ducats per year from his *sansaria* between 1523 and 1537. For more information on *sansarie* see Hope, 1980; and H. Simonsfeld, *Der Fondaco dei Tedeschi in Venedig*, Stuttgart, 1877, II, pp. 23–28.
3. Paoletti, 1894, p. 11. Cf. Meyer zur Capellen, 1985, pp. 12–13 and 24, who makes a good case for specialization within the family workshop, with Gentile getting the large format paintings on canvas and the portraits, and Giovanni the smaller devotional works.
4. That is: 'our faithful citizen'. Likewise, Carpaccio was addressed as 'Prudens fidelis civis noster Victor Scarpatius pictor solertissimus', in a painting commission given to him by the Council of Ten on 18 Aug. 1502: Molmenti and Ludwig, 1907, p. 239. No other artist of the period is thus designated in the documents compiled by Lorenzi in his *Monumenti* (1868). Official documents were often signed 'fidelis civis vester'.
5. For the Emperor's visit, see Lorenzi, 1868, pp. 83–84, no. 186, wherein a banquet in the Great Council Hall on 9 Feb. 1468 m.v. [=1469] is described; and Malipiero, 1843 edn, I, p. 237, who noted his entry to the city on 1 Feb. 1468 m.v. [=1469]. See also Ghinzoni, 1889, pp. 133–53.
6. For Gentile's early work, see Meyer zur Capellen, 1985, pp. 39–54. For the notarial act of 28 Aug. 1501, testifying to his knighthood, see Meyer zur Capellen, 1985, doc. 55, pp. 116–17. For Mantegna's desire to procure the same title during the Emperor's visit, see Lightbown, 1986, p. 120.
7. Meyer zur Capellen, 1985, p. 14.
8. Cat. XII. The same subject was later painted by Pinturicchio in the Piccolomini Library in the Duomo of Siena.
9. Ibid., doc. 1.
10. Cited by Ghinzoni, 1889, p. 139.
11. For arguments on dating, see Cat. XII. See also Malipiero, 1843 edn, II, pp. 659–60.
12. See, for example, Lorenzi, 1868, pp. 83–84, no. 186.
13. Malipiero, 1843 edn, II, p. 663. See also Babinger, 1978, p. 336.
14. Malipiero, 1843 edn, I, p. 338. Cf. Mallett, 1981, pp. 267–88.
15. For the events of 1313, see Chapter 3, nn. 20–21 above. The Republic may also have been moved to emulate decorative programs recently completed in rival states: eg., the Sala del Pisanello in Mantua and the Salone dei Mesi in the Palazzo Schifanoia in Ferrara.
16. Malipiero, 1843 edn, I, p. 122.
17. Ibid.
18. BMV, Cod. It. VII, 157 (=7771), f. 88, transcribed by Meyer zur Capellen, 1985, p. 109, doc. 14a. See also a similar passage in BMV, Cod. It. VII 125 (=7460), f. 372v, a 16th-century copy of Sanudo's notes, originally taken from the Cronaca of Pietro Dolfin.
19. Malipiero, 1843 edn, I, p. 123.
20. See Meyer zur Capellen, 1985, pp. 55–67 and 176ff.
21. Ridolfi, 1914 edn, I p. 56, n. 3.
22. Cat. XIII, doc. 2. Cf. docs. 3a–3b.
23. As in n. 76 below.
24. It was discovered in Smyrna in the 18th century by an agent of the French King Louis XV (Tietze and Tietze-Conrat, 1944, p. 107).
25. Donado da Lezze, 1909 edn, pp. 119–21; now in Meyer zur Capellen, 1985, doc. 14g, pp. 109–10.
26. For Sanudo's comment see BMV, Cod. It. VII 125 (=7460), f. 372v: '. . . e dal Signor turco chel fu fo ben visto, et fatto cavalier, et si feze dipinzer alchune cosse maxime una veniexia'.

For Gentile's sojourn in Constantinople see Meyer zur Capellen, 1985, pp. 17–21 and Chapter V; Villa, 1985, pp. 160–71; Thuasne, 1888; and Raby, 1980, pp. 67ff.
27. Raby, 1980, pp. 21 and 111, doc. 21. See also Franz Babinger, 'Ein vorgeblicher Gnadenbrief Mehmeds II für Gentile Bellini (15 Jänner 1481)', *Italia Medioevale e Umanistica* 5 (1962): pp. 85–101.
28. Meyer zur Capellen, 1985, p. 130, Cat. A 10 c. See also Thuasne, 1888, p. 49 n. 2; Bernardo Giustiniani, *Historie Cronologiche dell' origine degl'Ordini Militari*, II, Venice, 1692, pp. 856–60; and Francesco Sansovino, *Origine de' cavalieri*, Venice, 1566, pp. 8–8b.
29. Meyer zur Capellen, 1985, p. 21.
30. Cat. XIII.10.
31. Foresti, 1486, f. 293r. Luca Pacioli, *Summa de Arithmetice Geometria Proportioni e Proportionalità*, Venice, 1494, p. 2, praised both Gentile and his brother Giovanni in the art of *perspectiva*.
32. Cat. XIII, doc. 7. Although Vivarini seemed to be offering his services *gratis*, this was not actually the case. In 1495 he was receiving a salary of 60 ducats per year, the same as Giovanni Bellini (ibid., doc. 11). Bellini's compensation would have been in addition to his *sansaria*. See ibid., doc. 14a, (31 May 1513), which refers to his 'Sansaria in Fontego di todeschi'.

It was apparently not unusual for an artist to allow his fee to be determined by the generosity of a distinguished patron. When Carpaccio offered a painting of Jerusalem to Francesco Gonzaga, the Marquis of Mantua, in 1511, he wrote: 'Del pretio non dico nè son per dirlo, salvo che el remeto alla S.V. all qual humilmente me ricomando'. See Cat. XIII, doc. 13.
33. Cat. XIII, doc. 11.
34. See Chapter 3 n. 1 above.
35. See Johannes Wilde, 'The Hall of the Great Council of Florence', *Journal of the Warburg and Courtauld Institutes* 7(1944) : pp. 65–81; and Felix Gilbert, 'The Venetian Constitution in Florentine Political Thought', in *Florentine Studies*, ed. Nicolai Rubinstein, London, 1968, pp. 463–500.
36. ASV, Scuole piccole, Reg. 597, f. 1: 'Cum co sia cosa che la scritura santa dise che le bon e aliegra cosa habitar insembre et esser unidi in lo amor de dio.' Molmenti and Ludwig, 1907, offer partial translations and transcriptions (and sometimes paraphrases that are presented as quotations) of some passages in the Mariegola. They should be checked against the original text.
37. Cat. XIV, doc. 1.
38. See Chapter 12, n. 18 below.
39. See Cat. XI and Chapter 3 above.
40. See Cat. X and Chapter 3 above.
41. See Cat. XIV.
42. A convincing case for a birthdate around 1465 was made by Terisio Pignatti, 'Proposte per la data di nascita di Vittore Carpaccio e per la identificazione della Scuola di Sant' Orsola', *Venezia e l'Europa, Atti del XVIII Congresso internazionale di Storia dell' Arte, 1955*, Venice, 1956, pp. 224–26.
43. Voragine, 1941, pp. 627–30.
44. See particularly Bardon, 1983, pp. 43–79. This material is elaborated in idem, 1985, pp. 21–50. Cf. Guy de Tervarent, *La Legende de Sainte Ursule dans La Litterature e l'Art du Moyen Age*, 2 vols., Paris, 1931.
45. ASV, Scuole piccole, Reg, 597, f. 8 (1370) : 'E questo si e fato a bone fin e per acressimento dela dita scuola perche molte persone intrava in la dita scuola alla condition di nobeli per esser asenti dali offitij dela scuola no temando la spexa de un ducato e cosi le done. E per questo muode la scuola vien amancar de boni homeni da far officiali.'
46. Ibid., f. 11. No similar surname appears on Sanudo's (1980 edn, p. 68) list of noble families in 1493.
47. For the tomb, see Renosto, 1963, pp. 37–50. Cf. Molmenti and Ludwig, 1907, pp. 74–78.
48. Ibid., Reg. 599, 'Missa desumpta ex Missali antiquissimo in Carta Pergamena anni 1499 impresso Venetij per Georgius Arrivabene. . . . Deus gloria virginum: et amator earum: qui Beate Ursule in palma martyrij contulisti undecim millium virginum comitatum: concede nobis: earum multiplici interventu petitionum efficaciam: fidei

constantiam: et operis puritate[m].'
49. ASV, Scuole piccole, Reg. 597, ff. 1v–2.
50. Sanudo, 1980 edn, p. 50. The two extant manuscripts that include this part of the work are not autograph. They date from 1587. See ibid., pp. xix-xx and Caracciolo Aricò, 1979, pp. 419–37.
51. Molmenti and Ludwig, 1907, p. 60.
52. Cat. XIV, docs. 3 and 4.
53. Text in V. Rossi, 'Da un Rimatrice e di un Rimatore italiano del XV secolo', *Giornale storico della letteratura italiana* 15 (1890): p. 183. The translation used here is taken from Molmenti and Ludwig, 1907, p. 45. Cf. Simona Varzaru, 'Tre fonti letterarie riguardanti l'opera di Vittore Carpaccio', *Revue Roumaine d'Histoire de l'Art*, ser. beaux-arts, 15 (1978) : pp. 117–20.
54. See Brown, 1987: in press.
55. Sanudo, 1980 edn, pp. 48–53.
56. Ibid., pp. 50–52. See also Sheard, 1977, pp. 219–68.
57. Cat. VI, doc. 2.
58. MCV, Inc. H222 bis. See Brown, 1982, pp. 5–8.
59. Sabellico, 1772 edn, col. 7.
60. Cat. XV, doc. 2.
61. Ibid., docs. 3 and 4a–b.
62. Ibid., passim.
63. For Bastiani, see Molmenti and Ludwig, 1907, pp. 1–15, although their suggestion that he was the master of Carpaccio is not convincing. For a more recent view, see Collobi, 1939–40, pp. 33–53.
64. ASV, Scuola Grande de Santa Maria della Misericordia, B. 23 (Commissaria, Bartolomeo Gruato), letter dated 18 Apr. 1473, no foliation): Paoletti, 1894, pp. 12–13.
65. Cat. XV.5.
66. For the most complete discussion of Mansueti's work presently available, see Miller, 1978, pp. 77–115.
67. But cf. Chapter 11, n. 21 below. For a summary of his career, see Paolucci, 1966, pp. 3–20. See also Ludwig, 1905, p. 59.
68. Cat. XIII, doc. 10.
69. Cat. XIII, docs. 14a–b, 15, 16, 19c, 20.
70. Cat. XV.3.
71. For Gentile's professional activity in the 1490s, see Luzio, 1888, p. 276.
72. Dario's life was researched by Babinger, 1961, who did not, however, pick up his activity in the Scuola di San Giovanni (nor did Sgarbi, 1984). An 18th-century manuscript (MCV, Cod. Gradenigo 83, II, f. 201) does identify Babinger's Dario as Guardian Grande of the Scuola di San Giovanni in 1480 and 1492. But homonyms are the bane of Venetian historians, and it is necessary to establish more firmly that we are dealing with the same person. For evidence and arguments, see the Appendix.
73. Babinger, 1961, pp. 84–85; idem, 1978; and Malipiero, 1843 edn, I, pp. 121–22. For Dario's knighthood, see *Cronaca di Anomino Veronese, 1446–1488*, ed. G. Soranzo, in *R. Deputazione Veneta di Storia Patria*, ser. III, *Cronache e Diarii*, IV, Venice, 1915, p. 346; and Sanudo, *Vitae*, 1733 edn, col. 1210.

On 21 June 1479, as a reward for Dario's successful dealings with the Sultan, the Senate voted to give him some lands in Crete or elsewhere that would bring in rents of 100 ducats per year and to allow him to keep the *eques* (presumably the knighthood) and the gowns of gold given him by the Sultan (ASV, Senato, Terra, Reg. 8, f. 51v [21 June 1479]).

The outcome was reported by Sanudo in BMV, Cod. It. VII, 801 (=7152), f. 74v, his autograph manuscript for the *Vite dei dogi*. After a legal review by the Raxon Vecchie, the Collegio voted 101–40–4, 'che le possession non sia preso, le veste sì'. A new redaction is currently being prepared by A. Carraciolo Aricò (Marin Sanudo il giovane, *Le vite dei dogi, 1474–1494*, 1ª parte, forthcoming), who was kind enough to share this information with me. For the land that Dario was given instead,see n. 74 below.
74. Malipiero, 1843 edn, I, p. 136: [1484] 'A Zuane Dario secretario, de nazion Cretense, è stà donà una possession a Noenta de Padoana, comprà per 1,500 ducati, e 600 ducati de contadi all'officio del sal, per el maridar d'una fiola; perchè la Terra se chiama molto ben satisfatta de lui, havendo concluso la pase co 'l Turco'. This gift is probably different from that denied him in 1479 (See n. 73 above). Cf. Babinger, 1961, pp. 85–86, who puts the dowry at 1000 ducats. In 1483, Sanudo (*Itinerario*, 1847 edn, p. 115) reported seeing Dario's country house at Noventa Padovana.
75. Babinger, 1978, pp. 377–78.
76. ASV, Senato, Terra, Reg. 8, f. 59 (new numeration) '. . . Qui vehementer instat habere unum sculptorem et funditorem eris, sicuti etiam hoc desiderium suum declararunt orator suus, qui hinc discessit, et fidelissimus secretarius noster Joannes Darius. Et quia in simili re, adeo optata ab eo, oratio sibi satisfaciendum est'. See also ASV, Collegio, Notatorio, 1474–79, f. 107 (3 Sept. 1479), for the order to the Galley captain to provide passage for Gentile and two associates and also for 'duos socios magistri Barthei fusoris Metalli. . .'
77. Babinger, 1961, p. 89.
78. Dispatch of Bartolomeo Minio, Provveditor e Capitanio [military governor] at Napoli di Romania [Nauplia], 14 August 1480: 'adi XII data de qui è zonta la gallia Cocha che primo era Salomona, parti da Costantinopoli adi 3 detto, la qual conduce il Magnifico Sjnabej protogero de la Grecia, deputado per il Signor Turcho a la partition de i confinj ed i luogj de la Vostra Signoria, et con esso è venuto ser Zuan Dario; il qual Sjnabej per quanto me ha notificato ser Zuan Dario lè homo de gran reputation apresso il Signor Turcho. . .' From MCV, Cod. Cicogna, no. 2653, f. 18v. Cf C. Sathas, *Documents Inedits relatifs à l'Histoire de la Grèce*, 6, Paris, 1885, p. 141. See also ibid., p. 219, for a notice of Dario's departure from Constantinople on 3 Aug. 1480 in the Annali veneti of Stefano Magno (MCV, Cod. Cicogna, no. 3532). Sinabei was an agent of the Sultan. Dario was to travel with him to determine disputed borders and boundaries in Albania, Schiavonia and Greece.
79. On 28 April 1480, Dario had been given 300 ducats for travel expenses and 50 ducats for an interpreter (ASV, Senato, Terra, Reg. 8, f. 94).
80. Cited in Babinger, 1961, p. 72 without the source.
81. Ibid. For Dario's early years see F. Babinger, 'Veneto-kretische Geistesstrebungen um die Mitte des XV. Jahrhunderts', *Byzantinische Zeitschrift* 57 (1964) : pp. 62–77. For his further non-diplomatic exploits in the east, see Phyllis Lehmann, 'Theodosius or Justinian? A Renaissance drawing of a Byzantine Rider', *Art Bulletin* 41 (1959) : pp. 39–57; and Raby, 1980, pp. 242–46.
82. For the palace, see Sgarbi, 1984; and McAndrew, 1980, pp. 215–21. For the dates of the paintings, see *Miracoli della Croce* (1590). For Dario's death, see Babinger, 1961, p. 103. For his wills, see ASV, Notarile, Testamenti, Lodovico Zamberti, B. 1066, no. 71 (30 Apr. 1489), and no. 80 (1 Mar. 1492); and Giacomo Grassolario, B. 1183, no. 248 (1 Oct. 1493). In his last will he made the Scuola di San Giovanni a residual heir in case his line died out without issue.
83. See Chapter 12, n. 54 below.
84. Lieberman, 1982, Pl. 16, with text. Sgarbi, 1984, p. 33, even suggested Dario as Carpaccio's advisor in matters of diplomatic ritual and protocol for the St. Ursula cycle.
85. Cat. XIX, doc. 1.
86. Sohm, 1982, pp. 102–103, and docs. 60, 63, 70, and 72.
87. For example, 1487 (ASV, San Marco, Reg. 52 and 16bis, f. 10); 1488 (Reg. 52, fasc. 3, f. 7); 1490 (Reg. 46, fasc. 1); 1491 (Reg. 16bis, f. 20); and 1495 (Reg. 16bis, ff. 35v–36).
88. Ibid., Reg. 16bis, ff. 35v–36v: Sohm, 1982, doc. 69.
89. Sohm, 1982, pp. 30 and 243.
90. Cat. xix, doc. 1.
91. The Arte dei pittori in Venice was firm on such matters. In 1436 an older rule forbidding any master from taking a commission belonging to another artist was re-affirmed: 'Che alcuno de l'arte nostra di depenzare non ardischa nè prosuma nè se intrometta de tuor et far alcun lavorerio che altri maestri havessero tolto a far sopra de si.' From Favaro, 1975, p. 74.
92. See Sohm, 1982, pp. 30–31.
93. Vatican Cod. lat. 4033, f. 86. From Mercati, 1939, p. 39. See also Fletcher, 1981b, pp. 453–67.
94. Vatican Cod. lat. 4033, f. 86 (as in n. 93).
95. MCV, Mariegola 48, Arte de tesitori de pani de seda. It covers the period c.1483–1652 but does not mention any paintings.
96. Cat. XVI.
97. See Humfrey, 1983.
98. Cat. XIII, doc. 11.
99. See Raby, 1982, and Chapter 11 below.
100. Cat. XVII.

101. Mariegola, 'La Fraternitade overo Scuola in honore de missier san zorzi et missier san trifon', Capitolo XLV.
102. Perocco, 1975, p. 24. See also Fedalto, 1980, pp. 521–24.
103. Cat. XVII, doc. 3b.
104. Ibid., passim.
105. Cat. XVII.5.
106. Perocco, 1975, p. 5.
107. Pallucchini and Perocco, 1961, p. 71.
108. Cat. XVIII. See also Fedalto, 1980, pp. 521–24.
109. Ibid., doc. 1.
110. BMV, Cod. It. VII, 737 (=8666), Mariegola, Scuola degli Albanesi, Cap. [*Capitolo* = Chapter] 132 (24 Feb. 1502 m.v.)
111. Ibid., Cap. 143 (25 Feb 1507 m.v.).
112. Cat. XVIII.
113. Documents in Molmenti and Ludwig, 1907, pp. 239–40. The total payment was 50 ducats.
114. Cat. XIII, docs. 12 and 14b.
115. Ludwig, 1905, p. 59.
116. ASV, Magistrato al Sal, Notatorio 6, c. 95. From Molmenti and Ludwig, 1907, p. 240.
117. Cat. XXII, doc. 1.
118. Ibid., doc. 2.
119. A suggestion by Molmenti and Ludwig, 1907, p. 180, that has been repeated by most later writers.
120. Cat. XIX, doc. 2.
121. ASV, S. M. della Carità, Reg. 253, f. 68v: 'Onde che nuj jnsperadi piuj presto da madona santa Maria madre nostra de charita che de niuna ochaxion voler far depenzer uno telaro e quello meter in faza de lalbergo sopra la porta, et far la instoria a laude de nostra dona como la fo oferta al tenpio che segondo el desegnio sera nobellissima cosa etc'. From Rosand, 1982, p. 232, Doc. 13.
122. Ibid.
123. Brown, 1987: in press.
124. Molmenti and Ludwig, 1907, p. 173.
125. Ibid., pp. 90–91 and docs. 13–17.
126. Cat. XIX.2. For the subject matter, see G. Pavanello, 'San Marco nella Leggenda e nella Storia', *Rivista di Venezia*, 7 (1928): pp. 293–324. A 15th-century Latin manuscript stressing the miraculous aspects of Mark's story may have been relevant for the cycle: MCV, Cod. Cicogna 2987–88, 'Miscellanea antica', fasc. 17: 'Passio et translatio quedamque miraculagliossimi Marci evangelista'. Possibly more directly influential would have been Bernardo Giustiniani's (1772 edn) life of Mark: *De Divi Marci Evangelistae vita, translatione, et sepulturae loco*, appended to his history of Venice and published posthumously in 1493.
127. About 9 per cent of the members of the Scuola di San Giovanni [1478–1515] and 17 per cent of San Marco [1480–1525], of those who listed occupations. The study was based on ASV, San Giovanni, Reg. 6, 12 and 13; and San Marco Reg. 4, 6bis and 17. Pullan, 1971, pp. 96–97, found the same nautical advantage in favor of San Marco in a comparison with San Rocco.
128. For Barbaro, see ASV, Notarile, Testamenti, Francesco Malipede, Reg. 718, no. 128 (6 Dec. 1492). For the other two, see ASV, San Marco, Reg. 4, f. 1v. For Contarini's donation of the True Cross, see ASV, San Marco, Reg. 75, ff. 15–17. For recent scholarship on *viaggiatori*, with further references, see Tucci, 1980, pp. 317–53.
129. See Preto, 1975. Cf. Chapter 2, nn. 12 and 14.
130. Cat. XIX, doc. 3.
131. Ibid., doc. 4.
132. Ibid., doc. 8; cf. doc. 7.
133. For Vittore Belliniano, see Ludwig, 1905, pp. 72–79.
134. Mansueti died between 6 Sept 1526 and 26 March 1527 (Ludwig, 1905, pp. 66–67). Cf. Cat. XIX and the Epilogue.
135. Cat. XIX, doc. 14.
136. Ibid., doc. 15.
137. Cat. XIX.6.
138. Rosand, 1982, p. 100.
139. Ibid., pp. 90–91.
140. See Brown, 1987: in press.
141. In Sansovino, 1604, p. 20v.

Chapter 5

1. Chapters 5 and 6 recast the arguments first presented in my 'Painting and History in Renaissance Venice', *Art History* 7 (1984) : pp. 263–94. Generally speaking, Chapter 5 is a condensation and Chapter 6 an elaboration of the themes first discussed there.
2. Cat. VI, doc. 2.
3. Martin da Canal, 1972 edn, pp. 156–57.
4. Ibid., pp. 20–21: 'Et se aucun vodra savoir la verite tot ensi com je le vos ai conte, veigne veoir la bele yglise de monsignor saint Marc en Venise et regarde tres devant la bele yglise que est escrit tote ceste estoire tot enci com je la vos ai contee...'
5. Limentani, 1966, p. 1181. The mosaics appear to have been completed in the late 1260s: Demus, 1984, II, p. 205. Canal's words were later echoed, after a fashion, by Marcantonio Sabellico in his own description of the *translatio*: 'la qual cossa quasi non se poria credere ali scriptori se questo al presente non se vedesse figurata in Istoria con mirabel arte nela giesia de S. Marco'. (*Croniche che tractano de la origine de veneti...volgarizatte per Matheo Vesconte de Sancto Canciano*, Venice, n.d. [probably c. 1506 or shortly thereafter], p. xviii).
6. Martin da Canal, 1972 edn, p. 155.
7. As lucidly demonstrated by Herbert Kessler, 'Pictorial Narrative and Church Mission in Sixth-Century Gaul', *Studies in the History of Art* 16 (1986) : pp. 75–91. Cf. Andrei Corneia, 'On "Fiction" and "Authenticity" in Byzantine Pre-iconoclastic painting', *Revue Roumaine d'Histoire de l'Art*, ser. Beaux-Arts, 17 (1980): pp. 3–11.

A recognition of the power of history paintings with cautions on their use is shown by Walter, 1970, p. 157, who quotes Agobardus, an 11th-century bishop of Lyons [*Liber de imaginibus sanctorum*, *Patrologia Latina*, 104: Col. 225]: 'Sed causa historiae ad recordandum non ad colendum; ut verbo gratia gesta synodalia...iusta morem bellorum tum externorum cum civilium ad memoriam rei gestam, sicut in multis locis videmus'. Cf. Wolters, 1983, p. 166, citing a letter from a German bishop warning Pope Hadrian IV of the dangers inherent in history-painting: 'a pictura cepit, ad scripturam pictura processit, scripturam in auctoritatem prodire conatur'.
8. Carile, 1970, pp. 85–87. Cf. Pertusi, 1970, pp. 269–331.
9. Fasoli, 1958, pp. 463–66.
10. See Pertusi, 1970, pp. 272ff; and King, 1986, Chapters 2 and 3. For a brief summary of the sacral nature of Venetian government see Finlay, 1980, pp. 27–27; and also the rich study of Sinding-Larsen, 1974.
11. Priuli, *Diarii*, *RIS*, n.s., 24:3:4, p. 384.
12. See Pavan, 1981
13. Sansovino, 1604 edn, p. 1.
14. Fasoli, 1958, pp. 447–79
15. See Chapter 3 above, and Cats. II, IV, XIII.
16. In his *Vite*, 1900 edn, p. 296: 'Et per verifichatiom [sic] di tal historia a Siena nela capella dil suo palazo si trova ditta historia depinta, perchè ditto papa fu senese; etiam è dipenta ne la nostra sala dil Mazòr Conseglio, che si la non fusse sta vera, li nostri Venitiani non la arîano fata mai dipenzer.' For Spinello's fresco, commissioned on 18 June 1407, see Southard, 1974, pp. 377–91, with full bibliography.
17. The Greek humanist Manuel Chrysoloras expressed similar thoughts on viewing antique narrative reliefs in Rome in 1411: 'Erodoto e gli altri storici han fatto gran cosa con le loro opere; ma solo nelle immagini è possible vedere ogni cosa come se fosse in quel tempo stesso in cui accade [...], e perciò è, questa [fatta con le immagini che vediamo a Roma], una storia assolutamente e semplicemente esatta; o meglio, se così posso dire, non è storia, ma osservazione diretta e personale [*autopsia*] e viva presenza [*parousia*] di tutto ciò che accadde allora' (Migne, *Patrologia Graeca*, 156, cols. 24–29, cited in Italian by Salvatore Settis, 'Continuità, distanza, conoscenza. Tre usi dell'antico', in *Memoria dell'antico nell'arte italiana*, ed. S. Settis, III. *Dalla tradizione all'archeologia*, Turin, 1986). Cf. Wolters, 1983, p. 165.
18. In Monticolo's commentary to Sanudo, *Vite*, 1900 edn, pp. 340–41. For the new paintings and inscriptions, see Cat. XIII.
19. Sansovino, 1663, I, pp. 341–343. Monticolo (in Sanudo, *Vite*, 1900 edn, p. 340) rejects Petrarch's authorship on the basis of the Latin style. See also Wickhoff, 1883, p. 25, n. 83: 'scheint eine schöne Erfindung des venezianischen Local-patriotismus'.
20. Sansovino, 1581, cc. 198v–199.
21. Bardi, 1587b, p. 60, See also Francesco Patrizi, *Della historia diece dialoghi ne' quali si ragiona di tutte le cose appartenenti all'historia, et allo scriverla, et all' osservarla*, Venice, 1560.

For the persistence of this tradition well into the 17th century, see Wolters, 1983, pp. 39–43 and 161–81. Angelo Zon in his examination of the Alexander legend in Cicogna, 1824–27, IV, p. 583, also made special note of the Venetian respect for the documentary aspect of paintings. In a special section entitled 'pitture antiche' he asserted: 'Anche queste formano un argomento validissimo pei Veneziani al quale in ogni tempo essi diedero un gravissimo peso.'
22. Rona Goffen, 'Icon and Vision: Giovanni Bellini's Half-Length Madonnas', *Art Bulletin* 57 (1975) : pp. 503ff. See also Rosand's (1982, pp. 1–46, esp. pp. 1–14) perceptive analysis of Venetian artistic conservatism.
23. Cat. III, doc. 1.
24. Cat. IX, doc. 1.
25. See Cat. IX.
26. Bardi, 1587, p. 64: 'che dovendosi ridipingere si fatta Historia, vi si ritornassero le medesime cose di prima'. Bardi was a Camaldolese friar who had come to Venice from S. Maria degli Angeli in Florence and died in Venice in 1594. See Wolters, 1966, pp. 217ff. and Cicogna, 1824–27, IV, p. 584.
Similarly, the Procurators of the Basilica di San Marco had ordered a restoration of the mosaics in 1556, specifying that it should follow faithfully 'li effetti delle figure, lettere et parole': cited by Silvio Tramontin, 'I santi dei mosaici marciani', in *Culto dei Santi a Venezia*, ed. S. Tramontin et al, Venice, 1965, p. 136.
27. Tietze-Conrat, 1940, pp. 15–16.
28. See Cat. II.
29. Vasari, *Vite*, 1966 edn, p. 433.
30. For further examples, see Brown, 1984, pp. 273–77.
31. See also Wolters, 1984, pp. 180–81, who equates the practice with that of the historian who includes pieces of text from older sources as part of his argumentation. Cf. Richard Krautheimer, 'Introduction to an Iconography of Mediaeval Architecture', *Journal of the Warburg and Courtauld Institutes* 5 (1942) : pp. 1–33, for an analogous phenomenon.

Chapter 6

1. In Escher, 1919, p. 107.
2. See Chapter 5, n. 1 above.
3. This conclusion is drawn from Cochrane, 1981, pp. 59–133, particularly pp. 106–18. Other exceptions were the cities of Emilia: Piacenza, Modena, and Parma. See also Louis Green, *Chronicle into History*, Cambridge, 1972; and Denys Hay, *Annalists and Historians*, London, 1977.
4. Carile, 1970, pp. 81–82. Cf. M. Thiriet, 'Les Chroniques Vénitiennes de la Marcienne et leur importance pour l'histoire de la Romanie Greco-Vénitienne', *Mélanges d'Archéologie et d'Histoire* (École Francaise de Rome) 66 (1954) : pp. 241–92.
5. Cochrane, 1981, pp. 72–74. In Florence, of course, the *ricordanza*, which focused on personal and business affairs, was the common diaristic element of family life.
6. King, 1986, Chapter 1.
7. For the painting, see Cat. XVII.5. On the Greeks, see Pertusi, 1980, pp. 177–264; and Fedalto, 1980, pp. 499–514. Cf. Geanakoplos, 1962; and idem, 1966, pp. 112–38.
8. On the library, see Lotte Labowsky, 'Il Cardinale Bessarione e gli inizi della Biblioteca Marciana', in *Venezia e l'Oriente fra tardo medioevo e rinascimento*, ed. Agostino Pertusi, Florence, 1965, pp. 159–82; Martin Lowry, 'Two Great Venetian Libraries in the Age of Aldus Manutius', *Bulletin of the John Rylands Library*, 57:1 (1974) : pp. 128–66; and idem, 1979, pp. 229–31.
9. King, 1986, p. 187 and passim. Cf. Branca, 1980, pp. 123–27.
10. King, 1986, p. 233.
11. Carile, 1970, pp. 81–87 and 118–20; and Cochrane, 1981, pp. 62–63. See also Baron, 1968, pp. 172–73.
12. The Freschi chronicle (BMV, Cod. It. VII, 165 [= 8867]) must be one of the earliest to survive. It recounts the family history in public terms: the offices held and government assigments carried out by the sons of the family, and the wedding celebrations of the daughters. See also Cochrane, 1981, p. 70; and Baron, 1968, pp. 172–73.
13. Carile, 1970, pp. 105–10.
14. Monticolo in Sanudo, *Vite*, 1900 edn, p. 416.
15. See Cat. II.
16. Ibid., doc. 3.
17. Monticolo (in Sanudo, *Vite*, 1900 edn, p. 416) writes of the contemporaneous production of the chapel paintings and Bonincontro's legend: 'Per queste somiglianze intrinseche è molto probabile che la rappresentazione figurata e la rappresentazione letteraria del medesimo avvenimento, l'una eseguita per ordine del Governo, l'altra da un funzionario della corte ducale, sieno state fatte nel medesimo tempo a reciproca illustrazione e compimento e che questo tempo sia stato l'anno 1320.'
Another possible example of pictorial imagery influencing the historical text may be seen in Sanudo's account of the Battle of Canale Orfano of c. 808 in his *Vite dei Dogi*. Monticolo could find no written precedent for Sanudo's description of the event 'con artellarie', and suggested his dependence upon the painting of the scene in the loggia of the Rialto (Cats. III and IX), which may well have included artillery. Ibid., p. 108, n. 8.
18. Ibid., pp. 406–9.
19. Ibid., pp. 511–12.
20. Carile, 1970, pp. 98–109. Cf. King, 1986, pp. 208–17; Similar changes can be seen in Trecento literature throughout Italy. See Belting, 1985, p. 160.
21. Carile, 1970, pp. 109–10.
22. See Cozzi, 1970b, pp. 333–58; and two important studies that focus on Florentine historiography: Mark Phillips, 'Machiavelli, Guicciardini, and the Tradition of Vernacular Historiography in Florence', *American Historical Review* 84 (1979) : pp. 86–105; and idem, 'Barefoot Boy Makes Good: A Study of Machiavelli's Historiography', *Speculum* 59 (1984) : pp. 585–605.
23. Cozzi, 1970b, p. 348.
24. Ibid., p. 347.
25. Giustiniani, 1772 edn. See Labalme, 1969, pp. 256–96.
26. Cozzi, 1963–64, pp. 218–22. For Barbaro's response, see Cochrane, 1981, p. 84. See also King, 1986, passim.
27. Cozzi, 1963–64, p. 221.
28. King, 1986, p. 236. Cf. Branca, 1980, pp. 123–75.
29. King, 1986, pp. 236–51. Cf. Lowry, 1979.
30. For Ziliol's history, see BMV, Cod. It. VII 328 (=8513). For Scuola membership see ASV, San Marco, Reg. 17. Cf. the histories of other *cittadini*: MCV, Cod. Cicogna 2813, Antonio de Corradi, 'Cronaca Veneta' (1445); and BMV, Cod. It. VII 127 (=8034), Giangiacomo Caroldo, 'Historia Veneta in volgare' (early 16th century).
31. See Felix Gilbert, 'The Last Will of a Venetian Grand Chancellor', in *Philosophy and Humanism*, ed. E. P. Mahoney, Leiden, 1976, pp. 502–17. Stella left several history books (including Livy, Valla and Pliny) to his nephew, Zuan Antonio Dario. He was the son of Stella's sister who had married Francesco Dario, the nephew of Giovanni Dario (ibid., p. 510).
32. BMV, Cod. It. VII 1809: cited by Monticolo in Sanudo, *Vite*, 1900 edn, pp. 370–71.
33. In the *parte* of nomination he was thus described by the Council of Ten: 'predito de singular litteratura latina e greca et de stilo de dir tal che per sententia de tuti i docti in Italia nè fuora el non ha paragon . . .' (ASV, Consiglio dei Dieci, Parti Miste, Reg. 39 (1515–1516), Pt. II, f. 39. From Cozzi, 1963–64, p. 225).
34. R. Sabbadini, *Il metodo degli umanisti*, Florence, 1922, pp. 79–80. Cf. Peter Burke, *The Renaissance Sense of the Past*, London, 1969; D. Wilcox, *The Development of Florentine Humanist Historiography in the 15th Century*, Cambridge, Mass., 1969; Nancy Struever, *The Language of History in the Renaissance*, Princeton, 1970; and E. B. Fryde, *Humanism and Renaissance Historiography*, London, 1983.
35. Cited by Cochrane, 1981, pp. 11–16.
36. For their relationship to the paintings of the eyewitness artists in the Venetian *scuole*, see Sarah Wilk, 'Titian's Padua Experience and Its Influence on His Style', *Art Bulletin* 65 (1983) : pp. 51–61.
37. Carpaccio also employed the simultaneous narrative mode in the *Leavetaking*, which included 4 episodes, with Ursula and her fiance boarding a ship in the background. But there is no sense of cause-and-effect.
38. For attributions, a probable dating to c. 1509 and its poor condition, see Davies, 1986, pp. 65–67. Cf. Robertson, 1968, pp. 125–27: c. 1500–5. There is also a smaller painting of the same subject in the Lee Collection of the Courtaul Institute Galleries (no. 32). Its attribution and dating have received a similar assessment to the

other work: probably produced in Giovanni Bellini's workshop from his drawings, but with the aid of different assistants (*General Catalogue to the Courtauld Institute Galleries*, London, 1977, p. 44). Robertson, 1968, p. 127, suggests the authorship of Andrea Previtali, who did not actually work in Giovanni's shop.
39. Lowry, 1979, pp. 135–38.
40. MCV, Mariegola no. 9, Arte dei Casaruoli, f. 21, Cap. 59: 'Fo provisto che in la nostra mariegola over capitolario era sta canzellardo escrito de piu forte littera marchadantescha et pessima da lezer: la qual cosa e contra a quelo capitolo che dixe debia essere scrita de bona littera grossa e formada azio che cadaun possa lezer...'
41. MCV, Mariegola no. 113, Scuola di S. Girolamo, Cap. 7 (28 April 1504): 'Le gran manchamento de gastaldi e suo officiali de le scuole nostre de veniexia, abiando belle mariegole de gran valor e scrite de belle lettere de forma. Lassino scriver si brutamente in le suo mariegole lettere de diverse man corente e de piu forte e inbruta i a questo modo le suo mariegole. Landera parte per lavegnir che algun gastaldo over suo compagni scrivera over fara scriver suxo le suo mariegole de altra lettera cha de forma sia altuto cazado de la scuola azo che tanto fallo non se cometa per lavegnir. etc.'

Chapter 7

1. Erwin Panofsky, 1971, I p. 346.
2. Joost-Gaugier, 1975, pp. 1–28; idem, 1977b, pp. 95–112 and 291–313; idem, 1980, p. viii. Cf. the concurring opinion of Collins, 1982, pp. 300–3: and the dissenting one of Moffitt, 1982, pp. 3–24.
3. Degenhart and Schmitt, 1984, pp. 19–21.
4. See Pesaro, 1978, pp. 44–57; and Christiansen, 1987, pp. 166. ff.
5. For a summary of arguments about Jacopo's presence in Florence during the period 1423–25, with a negative verdict, see Joost-Gaugier, 1974, pp. 24–36. But cf. Christiansen, 1987, p. 168; and Fletcher, 1981b, p. 462.
6. Joost-Gaugier, 1974, p. 37, nn. 64–65.
7. Christiansen, 1982, p. 16.
8. Luciano Anelli, 'Ricognizione sulla presenza bresciana di Gentile da Fabriano dal 1414 al 1419', *Arte Lombarda*, n.s., 76/77 (1986): pp. 31–54. See also V. Terraroli, 'Scoperto nel sottotetto un ciclo di affreschi: Gentile da Fabriano?', *Il Giornale dell'Arte*, 30 (January 1986); and Christiansen, 1987, pp. 167–68.
9. Sanudo, *Itinerario*, 1847 edn, p. 71.
10. Christiansen, 1982, pp. 63–65.
11. Ibid., pp. 111–13; and idem, 1987, pp. 168 ff.
12. Datable to 1448–49, according to Paccagnini, 1972, pp. 45 ff, with photographs. For the program, see Joanna Woods-Marsden, 'French Chivalric Myth and Mantuan Political Reality in the *Sala del Pisanello*', *Art History* 8 (1985): pp. 397–412.
13. For the Paduan cycles see Margaret Plant, 'Portraits and Politics in Late Trecento Padua: Altichiero's Frescoes in the S. Felice Chapel, S. Antonio', *Art Bulletin* 63 (1981): pp. 406–25, with earlier bibliography.
14. See Cat. IV, doc. 10.
15. Cat. IV.22. See M. Krasceninnikova, 'Catalogo dei disegni del Pisanello nel Codice Vallardi del Louvre', *L'Arte* 23 (1920) : p. 10; and Fossi Todorow, 1966, pp. 67–68.
16. Degenhart, 1941, pp. 28–30, also observed this. Cf. Wickhoff, 1883, pp. 21–22.
17. Alberti, 1972 edn, p. 3. For an argument on the priority of the Italian edition, see M. Simonelli, 'On Alberti's Treatises of Art and their Chronological Relationship', *Yearbook of Italian Studies* (1971) : pp. 75–102.
18. Alberti, 1972 edn, Books One and Two. See Baxandall, 1971.
19. Alberti, 1972 edn, pp. 73–87.
20. Translation from Baxandall, 1965, pp. 200–1. Cf. Grayson's translation in Alberti, 1972 edn, p. 79.
21. As suggested by Pope-Hennessey, 1950, p. 17.
22. For a summary of attribution and dating problems see Hartt, 1959, pp. 225–36. For further arguments and a study of the patronage situation, see Muraro, 1961, pp. 263–74.
23. Hartt, 1959, pp. 225–34, makes a convincing case for Castagno and sums up the literature to date on other attributions. Uccello and Mantegna have also been suggested, but neither seem as tenable. See Lightbown, 1986, pp. 93–94, who rejects Mantegna's participation. A. Chastel, 'La Mosaique à Venise et à Florence au XVe siècle', *Arte veneta* 8 (1954): p. 122, suggested that Castagno also designed the architecture for the *Visitation*. See also Pincus, 1976. pp. 93–95.
24. As argued by Ettore Merkel, 'Un problema di metodo: la 'Dormitio Virginis' dei Mascoli', *Arte Veneta* 27 (1973): pp. 65–80.
25. See Robert Scheller, *A Survey of Medieval Model Books*, Haarlem, 1963, pp. 212–15; and Degenhart and Schmitt, 1984, p. 11, who concur that many of the drawings are 'complete and finished works of art in themselves'. For a recently discovered painting whose design is credibly attributed to Jacopo, which may give some idea of his approach to color as well, see Colin Eisler, 'Saints Anthony Abbot and Bernardino of Siena: designed by Jacopo and painted by Gentile Bellini', *Arte Veneta*, 39 (1985): pp. 32–40.
26. Degenhart and Schmitt, 1984, pp. 11–27. Cf. Marcel Rothlisberger. 'Notes on the Drawing Books of Jacopo Bellini', *Burlington Magazine* 98 (1956) : pp. 358–63; idem, 'Studi su Jacopo Bellini', *Saggi e memorie di storia dell'arte* 2 (1958–59): pp. 43–89; and Ames-Lewis, 1981, pp. 125–28.
27. This drawing is also discussed in detail by Joost-Gaugier, 1977b, pp. 4–5, who cites it as an example of Trecentesque space construction.
28. Joost-Gaugier's interpretation of this phenomenon as a secularization of religious iconography is unconvincing (ibid., pp. 16–26). Her suggestion that descriptive qualities of the drawings are similar to the Tuscan *novella* and that they indicate a common technique of conceptualization may be true, but I see little actual relationship between the two. As Joost-Gaugier herself points out, the theme or plot remains of primary importance in the *novella*, while it seems to be of secondary concern to Jacopo.
29. See Berlin-Dahlem, 1978, p. 469; and Pallucchini, 1962, pp. 29ff and 102.
30. Uccello was in Venice c. 1425–30, working on mosaics in San Marco (Pope-Hennessey, 1950, pp. 156–57; and Joost Gaugier, 1977b, p. 313, n. 48). Masolino passed through Venice in 1425–27, on his way to Hungary (Ugo Procacci, 'Sulla cronologia delle opere di Masaccio e di Masolino tra ill 1425 e il 1428', *Rivista d'arte* 28 [1953]: pp. 42–43; and Joost-Gaugier, 1977b, pp. 101–4). Fra Filippo Lippi worked in Padua in 1434 (Meiss, 1956, p. 62). Donatello worked on the high altar of the Santo in Padua c. 1444–54 (Pope-Hennessey, 1986, pp. 259–62).
31. See Pope-Hennessey, 1950, pp. 10–31 and 45–47; and Borsook, 1980, pp. 67–74.
32. Pope-Hennessey, 1950, pp. 259–62; and H. Janson, *The Sculpture of Donatello*, Princeton, 1957, pp. 185–86.
33. Joost-Gaugier, 1974, p. 21.
34. Degenhart and Schmitt, 1984, p. 14.
35. Ibid., p. 15; and Joost-Gaugier, 1977b, pp. 299–300, who sees this as a 'casual attitude towards Alberti's insistence on methodology', and concludes that it indicates Jacopo's lack of scientific rigor.
36. Baxandall, 1971, pp. 133–34: '[Mantegna's] engravings are the proper visual appendix to De pictura II, and penetrated to the painters – the *Lamentation* even to Raphael and Rembrandt – as a book never could'.
37. Painted after 1453 and destroyed by bombing in 1944. See Lightbown, 1986, pp. 47–57 and 387–400.
38. Ibid., pp. 86–88 and 413–15.
39. Meiss, 1956, p. 65.
40. Ibid., pp. 58–69; Robertson, 1968, pp. 8–9 and 56–58; Castelfranchi Vegas, 1983, passim; and Shigetoshi Osano, 'Rogier van der Weyden e l'Italia: problemi, riflessioni e ipotesi', *Antichita viva* 20, no. 4 (1981): pp. 14–21; and no.5 (1981): pp. 5–14.
41. Meiss, 1956, p. 65. A major primary source for Netherlandish paintings in collections in Venice and the Veneto is Marcantonio Michiel, published in English as *The Anonimo*, 1969 edn. For Michiel, see Fletcher, 1981a; and idem, 1981b. See also Lorne Campbell, 'Notes on Netherlandish Pictures in the Veneto in the fifteenth and sixteenth Centuries', *Burlington Magazine* 123 (1981): pp. 467–77; and Castelfranchi Vegas, 1983.
42. Meiss, 1956, p. 68.
43. Baxandall, 1971, p. 133–39. On Gentile da Fabriano's 'ekphrastic mode', see Russell Panc-

zenko, 'Gentile da Fabriano and Classical Antiquity', *Artibus et historiae* 2 (1980): pp. 25–27.
44 Baxandall, 1971, p. 11.
45. Ibid., pp. 88–91.
46. Ibid., p. 94.
47. Ibid., pp. 92–96.
48. N. Gramaccini, 'Wie Jacopo Bellini Pisanello besiegte. Der Ferrareser Wettbewerb von 1441', *Idea, Jahrbuch der Hamburger Kunsthalle* 1 (1982): pp. 27–53; cf. Joost-Gaugier, 1974, p. 21; and Christiansen, 1987, pp. 170–72.
49. Baxandall, 1963, p. 314.
50. Ibid., pp. 316–17. For the Italian taste for Northern tapestries, see Aby Warburg, 'Flandrische Kunst und florentinische Fruhrenaissance (1902)', in his *Gesammelte Schriften*, ed. Gertrud Bing, Leipzig and Berlin, 1932.
51. Baxandall, 1963, pp. 318–19.
52. Panofsky, 1971, p. 3.

Chapter 8

1. Ridolfi, 1914 edn, I, p. 50.
2. Valcanover, 1981, p. 103.
3. For the tradition of *viaggiatore* accounts in general, see Tucci, 1980, pp. 317–53; and Lucchetta, 1980b, pp. 433–89.
4. The English translation was made in the 1540s by William Thomas, Clerk of the Council to Edward VI of England, and is found in *Travels to Tana and Persia*, 1873 edn, pp. 3–4.

For Barbaro, see Amat di S. Filippo, 1882, pp. 44–45; N. di Lenna, 'Giosafat Barbaro (1413–1494) e suoi viaggi nella regione russa (1436–1451) e nella Persia (1474–1478)', *Nuovo Archivio Veneto*, n.s. 28 (1914); and Donazzolo, 1927, pp. 30–32.
5. *Travels to Tana and Persia*, 1873 edn, pp. 90 and 31, respectively.
6. Ibid., p. 171. For Contarini, see Amat di S. Filippo, 1882, pp. 164–65; N. di Lenna, *Ambrogio Contarini, politico e viaggiatore veneziano del secolo XV*, Padua, 1921; and Donazzolo, 1927, pp. 51–52. Unlike Barbaro, Contarini saw his account published during his lifetime: *Questo è el Viazo de misier Ambrosio Contarin ambasador de la illustrissima Signoria de Venesia al signor Uxuncassam re de Persia*, Venice, 1487.
7. Cited in G. Berchet, *La Repubblica di Venezia e la Persia*, Turin, 1865, pp. 150–51.
8. 'The Travels of a Merchant in Persia', in *Travels to Tana and Persia*, 1873 edn, p. 143.
9. Ibid., pp. 146–47.
10. Pagani, 1884 edn, p. 188.
11. *Viaggio del magnifico messer Piero Querino* in Ramusio, 1563, III, pp. 203D–E.
12. *Viaggio di Nicolo di Conte Venetiano*, in Ramusio, 1559 edn., I, p. 341C. Dei Conti, a Venetian *cittadino* who spoke both Arabic and Persian, travelled in India, the Middle East and south-east Asia in 1428–53 and wrote a detailed account of the geography, plants, animals, and the religious, social and funerary practices of those regions. His *relazione* is probably the most important of the asiatic *viaggi* of the 15th century: Amat di S. Filippo, 1882, pp. 132–36.
13. *Travels to Tana and Persia*, p. 81.
14. For a typical mercantile manual whose contents ranged from weights and measures and the proper appearance of sugar ('biancho e secho') to medical recipes, prayers and a passage from a *romanzo* of Tristan, see *Zibaldone da Canal*, ed. A. Stussi, Venice, 1967. On the taste for quantification, see Tucci, 1980, pp. 317–23; and M. Cortelazzo, 'La cultura mercantile e marinesca', in *Storia della cultura veneta dalle origine al Trecento*, I, ed, G. Folena, Vicenza, 1976, pp. 671ff. See also J. Burckhardt's insights on Venice as the birthplace of statistical science in *The Civilization of the Renaissance in Italy*, trans, S.G.C. Middlemore, New York, 1958, I, pp. 90–91; and Smith's (1987, pp. 27–32) analysis of the perceptual habits of Cyriacus of Ancona in an important article that appeared when this book was already in press.
15. Cozzi, 1963–64, pp. 227 and 234.
16. Barthes, 1975, p. 265, saw such a tendency as the product of modern mass culture. But clearly, the taste for the look of artlessness or an apparent lack of guile is not the sole property of the modern *bourgeoisie*.
17. Again, parallels for the concern for careful and elaborate detail in pictorial representations of historical events are found in other periods and places. Demus, 1984, I, p. 71, observed that the need for a convincing representation of the *translatio* 'led to the adoption of a certain objective realism in the rendering of naval matters, the material for which Venice could provide better than any other place'.

Winter, 1981, p. 18, noted a similar quality in neo-Assyrian historical reliefs: 'Because the scenes appear so real – even to appropriate landscape elements and dress – the denoted images function to naturalize the underlying rhetoric; the very realness 'innocents the semantic artifice of connotation,' allowing the message to be bought without defensive armor, since the message is seemingly founded in nature.' Indeed, Brilliant, 1984, pp. 100–1, found that the exact description and detailed rendering of costume, weapons, ethnographic and topographical elements on Trajan's column actually had the effect of convincing modern scholars of the historicity of the representions. See also F. Bäuml, 'Varieties and Consequences of Medieval Literacy and Illiteracy', *Speculum* 55 (1980): pp. 262–64; Frank Kermode, *The Genesis of Secrecy. On the Interpretation of Narrative*, Cambridge, Mass., 1979, p. 118; and J. Culler, *Structuralist Poetics: Structuralism, Linguistics, and the Study of Literature*, Ithaca, 1975, pp. 140–60 and 192ff.

Chapter 9

1. MCV, Inc. H222 bis: 'Fra laltre degne Reliquie che alpresente si atrovano in venetia veramente La croce de lascola de misier San Joane evangelista e la piu degna & piu excellente che sia ne laqual certissima & indubitamente si crede eser del Legno de lacroce dove pendete il nostro salvator per nui salvar & questo si prova per molti miracoli intravenuti in diversi tempi iqual qui sotto sarano notati ordinata mente...'
2. Cf. R. Trexler, 1973, pp. 125–44, especially p. 128.
3. Ibid., p. 127.
4. Cat. XV, doc. 2.
5. Trexler, 1973, p. 130.
6. Cf. ibid., pp. 126–33.
7. See Cat. XV.
8. For the *pala* see ibid., doc. 1. For the securing of the reliquary in a locked *capitelo*, see ASV, San Giovanni, Reg. 140, f. 165v (20 Jan. 1457 m.v.).
9. As in the present oratory of the Scuola di San Giorgio degli Schiavoni, dating to the mid-16th century. See Plate 1.
10. Schulz, 1966, pp. 89–96.
11. Schulz, 1978, pp. 425–74, particularly pp. 464–67. For the interest in geography, see also idem, 1970; and E. Bevilacqua, 'Geografi e consmografi', *Storia della cultura veneta*, ed. G. Arnaldi and M. Pastore Stocchi, 3/II, pp. 355–74. For city views in paintings, see Gibbons, 1977, pp. 174–84.
12. Schulz, 1978, p. 468.
13. Cf. Puppi, 1978, pp. 73–78; and Chiara Frugoni, *Una lontana città. Sentimenti e immagini nel Medioevo*, Turin, 1983.
14. For a comparison of the two writers, see Cozzi, 1970b, pp. 333–58.
15. Sanudo, 1980 edn, p. 23. See also Caracciolo Aricò, 1979, pp. 419–37; and Sheard, 1977, pp. 219–68.
16. See Cat. XV.9.
17. It deceived Vasari, who thought that the entire cycle pertained to a single miracle. See Epilogue, n. 3 below.
18. The only natural source of light in the room came from three windows on the south wall.
19. The light source in the Saint Ursula cycle, for example, is located at the altar (east) end of the room for all the paintings on the side walls, and on the south for the paintings on the end walls.
20. For the *Donation*, the viewer faces east, with the sun coming from the south. His orientation is the same for the *Healing of Pietro dei Ludovici* which is set in the Church of San Giovanni Evangelista, but here the sun comes from the west. He faces north for *San Lorenzo* and *San Lio*, with the sun in each case coming from the west. For the *Procession* and the *Exorcism* he faces the north-east; in the first instance the sun is in the west, and in the second it is in the east. We do not know the topographical orientations of the *Healing of the Daughter of Benvegnudo* or the *Healing of Finetti's Son*, but in the latter instance the sun is directly overhead, indicating midday.
21. Luzio, 1888, p. 276. See also H. Tietze and E. Tietze-Conrat, 'The artist of the 1486 View of Venice', *Gazette des Beaux Arts*, ser. 6, 23 (1943): p. 88.
22. In his 'Twisted Tales; or, Story, Study, and

Symphony', in *On Narrative*, ed. W. Mitchell, Chicago and London, 1981, p. 105.
23. MCV, Inc. H222 bis: 'Dove havendo udito per fama Lecose devote & sancte che si adoperavano nelle quatro scole di venetia & maxime in quella de misier sancto Ioanne conmosso si per devotione del glorioso evangelista come etiam perla bona fama del dignissimo guardiano de lascola misier Andrea vendramino si delibero di dotar la predicta scola de uno inextimabel dono & pretiosa gema cioe di apresentarli quella particula del sacratissimo legno de lacroce...'
24. Ibid.: 'Dove essendo presente el venerabel religioso maistro Lodovico fra menor professor de la sacra theologia con el suo cancellario cantata prima la missa de la sacratissima croce dono ladicta particula del sanctissimo legno de la croce a misier Andrea vendramino vardiano per nome de la scola essendo qui presente inumerabil moltitudine di persone tra lequale infu misier helia zustignan misier marco moresini misier franzesco zustignan & molti altri itestemoni de dicta donatione iquali erano venuti per vedere tanto thesoro...'

Cornaro, 1749, 6, p. 338, identified the priest as 'Ludovicus Donatus Ordinis minoram, postea S.R.E. tit. S. Marci Presbyter Cardinalis ab Urbano VI, electus anno 1738' [sic = 1378].
25. Bastiani's composition appears to correspond fairly closely to the architectural layout at that time. For a reconstruction, see Pazzi, 1985, pp. 15–22. A *portego* was built in front of the church entrance in 1458: ASV, S. Giov., Reg. 72, f. 230. An entry dated 30 Nov. 1499 states that brothers of the Scuola were buried under the *portego* (ibid., f. 197).
26. In Chapter II of his stimulating book on visual composition, *The Power of the Center*, Berkeley and Los Angeles, 1982. Cf. Sixten Ringbom 'Some pictorial conventions for the recounting of thoughts and experiences in late medieval art', in *Medieval Iconography & Narrative*, ed. G. Andersen, Odense, 1980, pp. 38–69.
27. *Miracoli della Croce*, 1590, ff. A3 verso and 2B recto: '& presente copiosa moltitudine de populo dell'uno, & l'altro sesso.... El Nobel homo & Insigne M. Philippo di Masseri Cavallier ...de man propria spogliato del palio, del capo nudo, & ingenocchiado...cantata prima la Messa avanti l'altare...'
28. Cat. XV.2.
29. For a contemporary Venetian example see MCV, Cod. Gradenigo Dolfin 56, 'Memorie lasciate da' Francesco Amadi della sua famiglia', with descriptions of miracles ascribed to the Madonna of S. M. dei Miracoli between 1480 and 1493.
30. Preliminary sketches for the painting survive. See Baumeister, 1934, who argues that the painting was changed from a horizontal to a vertical format during the development of the design. Since its placement between two windows requires the vertical shape, it may originally have been intended for a different location in the room. This initial uncertainty implies, furthermore, that the cycle may well have been worked out in its entirety before any of the paintings were begun.
31. A number of modern references to this painting incorrectly cite the occasion as the Feast of Corpus Christi. For further discussion, see Meyer zur Capellen, 1985, pp. 71–73.
32. Most of our knowledge about the terms used to designate colors of Renaissance dress is based upon guesswork and visual observation of paintings. For a good recent work on the meaning of costume and color during this period, see Herald, 1981. The following data is taken from the Glossary (pp. 209–31). *Scarlatta* was originally a type of woollen cloth and not a color, but eventually it came to designate the color scarlet. *Cremisino* or *chermisino* was a dark purplish-red color that was derived, like *rosato* – a pinkish red – from an insect dye. *Pavonazzo* was a brownish red, although literally translated the word means 'peacock-colored'. *Turchino* was probably a turquoise blue.
33. For Gentile's simplification of the mosaics, see Demus, 1984, II, pp. 193–94.
34. Muir, 1981, pp. 189–90, who defined the ducal group as the core of a civic procession in Venice, symbolizing the Venetian conception of sovereignty: 'in effect, the ducal procession was the constitution'. For the St. Mark's Day procession see ibid., pp. 85–86 and 198–211; and Sansovino, 1663, II, pp. 505–8. Cf. Chapter 10 below; and Tenenti, 1980, p. 24, who stresses that class distinctions are projected, rather than erased, at public spectacles.
35. See Tietze and Tietze-Conrat, 1944, p. 70, no. 270.
36. Pomponius Gauricus (*De Sculptura*, ed. and trans. Andre Chastel and Robert Klein, Geneva, 1969, p. 185) recommended the birds-eye view to artists to obtain greater legibility of a narrative scene. See also Robert Klein, 'Pomponius Gauricus on Perspective', *Art Bulletin* 44 (1961): p. 214.
37. See Meyer zur Capellen, 1985, pp. 78–79.
38. See Cat. XV.2.
39. See Weissmann, 1982, pp. 77–78, for the way in which a bad member reflects on a group and how narrative and ritual are necessary to repair its honor.
40. See Tietze and Tietze-Conrat, 1944, p. 69, no. 265, who ascribe it to Gentile, but who also list other attributions.
41. See Cat. VI.
42. The subject matter of this painting was misunderstood by later critics. See Cat. XV.6.
43. For this compositional type, see Rosand, 1982, p. 39–43; and Chapter 11 below.
44. Sanudo, 1980 edn, p. 27. Calling the Piazza San Marco the most privileged space of the city for public ceremonial display, Tenenti (1980, p. 25) defined the Rialto area as its second gravitational center.
45. Armenian: Herald, 1981, p. 199; Greek: Raby, 1982, p. 88 n. 15; Cretan: P. Humfrey, 'Two fragments from a Theseus cassone by Cima', *Burlington Magazine* 123 (1981): pp. 477–78.
46. The fundamental study on these groups of Venetian youth is that of Venturi, 1908 and 1909. For a recent re-examination, see Muraro, 1981, pp. 315–41.
47. For the loggia, see Cessi, 1934, pp. 60–70 and 317–19.
48. In a perilous condition since Carpaccio's time, the bridge finally collapsed in 1524 (ibid., pp. 170–77). For Carpaccio's treatment of the setting, cf. Magagnato, 1964, pp. 228–38; and idem, 1963, pp. 70–81.
49. See R. Smith, 'In Search of Carpaccio's African Gondolier', *Italian Studies* 34 (1979): pp. 45–59.
50. *Hieronymus. Vita et transitus*, Venice, 1485, fols. 22r-v, as translated by Roberts, 1959, p. 292.
51. A similar strategy was employed by Carpaccio in the *Dream of St. Ursula*, where the small dog at the foot of Ursula's bed appears to be awakened at the appearance of the angel.
52. Cf. P. Maretto, *L'edilizia gotica veneziana*, 2nd edn, Venice, 1978, p. 62.
53. BMV, Cod. It. IV, 39 (=5446), fol. 2r, Daniele Barbaro, 'Pratica della prospettiva', cited by Davis, 1980, p. 184, n. 4. The translation is mine.
54. Cf. Donald Weinstein, 'Critical Issues in the Study of Civic Religion in Renaissance Florence', in *The Pursuit of Holiness in Late Medieval and Renaissance Thought*, ed. C. Trinkaus and H. Oberman, Leiden, 1974, pp. 267–68.
55. See Brown, 1987: in press. Cf. Trexler, 1973, p. 131, in relation to the Florentine experience: 'Indiscriminate and repeated unveiling of social and divine power by random individuals decreased the devotion of the people and therewith the social efficacy of the object.'

Chapter 10

1. A short *précis* of this chapter was presented in the session on Art and Ritual at the 26th International Congress of the History of Art, 10–15 August 1986, Washington D.C. Entitled 'The Ritual Conception of History in Venetian Renaissance Art', the paper will be published in *World of Art: Themes of Unity in Diversity. Acts of the XXVIth International Congress of the History of Art*, ed. Irving Lavin (Pennsylvania State University Press, forthcoming).

The word 'ritual' will be used in this chapter in a general way to describe stylized, formalized and repetitive actions within either secular or sacred contexts. By 'ceremony' or 'ceremonial', I will be referring to sequences of ritual acts or gestures that are performed in public. See also Muir, 1981, p. 48n, where the meaning is more exclusively political. Cf. Trexler, 1980, pp. xxiv–xxv; and E. H. Gombrich, 'Ritualized gesture and expression in art', *Royal Society of London, Philosophical Transactions*, ser. B., biological sciences, 251 (1966): pp. 393–401.

2. Cf. Anne Hedeman, 'Restructuring the Narrative: The Function of Ceremonial in Charles V's *Grandes Croniques de France*', in *Studies in the History of Art*, 16 (1985) : pp. 171–81.
3. MCV, Cod. Correr I, 383 (=1497). See Chapter 3 above and Cat. II.
4. Valcanover, 1981, p. 98.
5. Fabri, 1843 edn, IV, p. 433.
6. Philippe de Commynes, 1843 edn, II, pp. 405–6.
7. Marin Sanudo, *Spedizione*, 1873 edn, p. 300.
8. Muir, 1981, p. 231: the standard work on Venetian public ceremonial. See also Wolters, 1983, pp. 45–55 and 223–29; and M. T. Muraro, 1981, pp. 315–41. Still useful is Molmenti, 1928.

For civic ceremonial outside Venice, see Jacques Heers, *Fêtes, jeux et joutes dans les sociétés d'Occident à la fin du moyen-age*, Montreal, 1971; Trexler, 1980, Parts III and IV; Roy Strong, *Art and Power. Renaissance Festivals, 1450–1650*, Suffolk, 1984; and Robert Scheller, 'Gallia cisalpina: Louis XII and Italy 1499–1508', *Simiolus* 15 (1985): pp. 5–60.
9. See Moore and Myerhoff, 1977, pp. 3–6; Lecoq, 1976, pp. 83–100; Trexler, 1973, pp. 125–44; and Tenenti, 1980, pp. 21–26.
10. Gabrieli, 1837 edn, pp. 25–27: 'Bello era il vedere le rispettive ordinanze. V'erano seicento circa Nobili francesi con collane d'oro, ed alcuni Capitani ungheresi con superbi cavalli, colla capigliatura alla spartana, e con armatura di battaglia. Brillavano coronati d'alloro i giovani padovani, vestiti di seta con ricami d'oro e d'argento. E con questa marcia affollatosi da per tutto immenso numero di villici, che ingombravano le strade, si giunse a tre miglia da Padova, dove il Podestà con ogni classe di cittadini stavasi aspettando l'arrivo della Regina.'
11. Signed by Matthio Pagan and dated to c. 1555–60 by David Rosand and Michelangelo Muraro, *Titian and the Venetian Woodcut*, Washington, D.C., 1976, pp. 281–88.
12. From Giacomo Franco, *Habiti*, Venice, 1610. See Lina Padoan Urban, 'Apparati scenografici nelle feste veneziane cinquecentesche', *Arte Veneta* 23 (1969) : pp. 8–10; idem, 1980, pp. 156–57.
13. ASV, San Marco, Reg. 8, f. 1 (19 May 1451): 'Scole andando ò tornando dalle Processioni non possino andar una contra l'altra ò interromperla attraversando la Strada. E quella prima entrarà in una Cale sia lassada passar e l'altri aspetti fin che sarà passada. E cosi si osservi in Piazza sotto pena di privation delle Scole, et altra ad Arbitrò del Cons. X'. Cf. ASV, Compilazione Leggi, Reg. 344, f. 118; and Consiglio dei Dieci, Parti Miste, Reg. 14, f. 47.
14. ASV, San Marco, Reg. 8, f. 2; San Giovanni, Reg. 140, ff. 201–203v; and Compilazione Leggi, Filza I, B. 344, f. 170. Cf. Muir, 1981, pp. 200–2.
15. See Newett, 1907; Bistort, 1912, pp. 34–38; and Diane Owen Hughes, 'Sumptury Law and Social Relations in Renaissance Italy', in *Disputes and Settlements*, ed. John Bossy, Cambridge, England, 1984, pp. 90–91.
16. Muir, 1981, pp. 192–8.
17. Sanudo, *Diarii*, XVI, col. 287. For de la Vedoa's position in the Scuola, see ASV, San Marco, Reg. 6bis.
18. ASV, Collegio, Ceremoniale, I, ff. 16v–17
19. Ibid., f. 13.
20. Ibid., f. 77.
21. Muir, 1981, pp. 187–9 and 232–3.
22. Ibid., pp. 78–92. Cf. Trexler, 1980, pp. 215–78.
23. Sanudo, *Spedizione*, 1873 edn, p. 300: 'Ancora fo messo panni d'oro a le colonnele di la Chiesia da una banda a l'altra sopra la piazza, cossa nuova et *numquam* più fatta.'
24. See W. Weisbach, *Trionfi*, Berlin, 1919; and Dorothy Shorr, 'Some Notes on the Iconography of Petrarch's Triumph of Fame', *Art Bulletin* 20 (1938): pp. 100–7.
25. Museo Correr, inv. Cl. I, 1428. Oil on a wood panel, 104.7 x 81.8 cm. The Doge in the painting was credibly identified as Agostino Barbarigo by Della Rovere, 1902, pp. 33–36; his attribution of the work to Carpaccio, however, is unconvincing. Other attributions were made by Molmenti and Ludwig, 1907, p. 15 (studio of Lazzaro Bastiani); Claude Phillips, 'Some Figures by Giorgione (?)', *Burlington Magazine* 14 (1909): pp. 331–37 (Gentile Bellini's studio with the four figures on the far right painted by the young Giorgione); and Lionello Puppi, in *Architettura e Utopia nella Venezia del Cinquecento*, Milan, 1980, p. 94 (circle of Bastiani). Bastiani's studio or circle (or even his own hand) is the most likely possibility.
26. See ASV, Collegio, Ceremoniale 1; and Muir, 1981, pp. 231–37, for princely entries. Della Rovere, 1902, attempted to identify the visitors as the Duke of Ferrara, Ercole D'Este, and his son Alfonso. Malipiero, 1843 edn, I, p. 684, described such an entry on 17 Feb. 1488. Cf. Venturi, 1909, pp. 72–74. Ercole's entry was also described by a Ferrarese diarist, Bernardino Zambotti (*Diario Ferrarese* in *RIS*, n. s., 24:7, p. 193).
27. See Rosand, 1982, pp. 39–43.
28. See Andrew Martindale, *The Triumphs of Caesar*, London, 1979, and Lightbown, 1986, pp. 140–53.
29. See Chapter 3 above.
30. Damisch, 1984, pp. 137–43, observed a tension in Carpaccio's paintings between narrative demands and the geometrical thrust into deep space.
31. On Leonardo's influence on Venetian artists see David Rosand, 'Giorgione e il concetto della creazione artistica', in *Giorgione: Atti del Convegno Internazionale di Studio per il 5° Centenario della Nascita*, Castelfranco Veneto, 1979, pp. 135–39.
32. Most recently by Bardon, 1985, pp. 71ff.
33. For Tomaso, see Luigi Menegazzi, *Tomaso da Modena*, Treviso, 1979, with an extensive and up-to-date bibliography.
34. For Rembrandt's use of drawings by Gentile Bellini and Carpaccio as models for organizing large groups of figures, see Kenneth Clark, *Rembrandt and the Italian Renaissance*, New York, 1966, pp. 163–66.
35. Cf. Rosand, 1982, pp. 41–42; and Muraro, 1971, pp. 7–19.

The effect of the action taking place between the depicted spectator and the real-life viewer is suggestively close to two tournament scenes in the National Gallery in London (inv. nos. 1211 and 1212). They may originally have been part of a *cassone*. Ascribed by the Gallery to Domenico Morone, they are attributed (to my mind, correctly) by several Italian scholars to Carpaccio. For arguments and further references, see Davies, 1986, pp. 381–82. The formal correspondences between the London panels and the backgrounds of the canvases of the St. Ursula cycle suggest that Carpaccio's earliest experience with pictorial narrative was predominantly with small works like these, and that his stylistic development in the 1490s centered on expanding a '*cassone* aesthetic' into monumental mural-painting.
36. Cornaro, 1749, 4, pp. 301–3. Cf. idem, 1758, p. 69.
37. According to legend, 10,000 soldiers who were crucified with their leader on Mount Ararat. Purported relics of the group were brought to Western Europe during the Crusades. See *Acta Sanctorum*, June IV (1707), pp. 175–88.
38. Corner, 1749, 4, p. 303. The altar bore an inscription (transcribed in Cicogna, 1824–27, 1, pp. 162–63, with further information).
39. He served as *degano* in 1504 and Guardian Grande in 1521 and 1527 (ASV, Scuola Grande di San Marco, Reg. 4, f. 43, Reg. 6bis, and Reg. 17). For more information on the Ottobon family, see BMV, Cod. It. VII, 341 (=8623), ff. 11v–12v. Ettore was not, as Lauts, 1962, pp. 250–51, and others have written, a Cardinal.
40. Lorenzi, 1868, no. 342.
41. The work suffered excessive overpainting in the 19th century. See Moschini Marconi, 1955, no. 106; and Lauts, 1962, pp. 250–51.
42. Moschini Marconi, 1955, no. 107, who states that the *pala* on the Ottobon altar depicted in the painting was originally Carpaccio's own *Crucifixion of the Ten Thousand Martyrs*, but is now overpainted with a *Prayer in the Garden*. Any such under-painting is not presently visible to the naked eye. In fact, Terisio Pignatti, *The Golden Century of Venetian Painting* Los Angeles, 1979, p. 44, suggests (more credibly) that the *Prayer* was depicted in the *Apparition* from the beginning, and represents a work that was temporarily placed in the altar between 1512 and 1515. He judges the *Apparition* to be a late autograph work of Carpaccio himself (an opinion with which I concur), but cf. the list of attributions in Lauts, 1962, p. 263, which range from full authorship by Carpaccio to none at all. I am grateful for the insights of Leslie Reinhardt, who wrote a paper on this work in my graduate seminar at Princeton University in Spring 1984.
43. A suggestion that Carpaccio's rhythmic placement of figures was derived from musical

modes and from the reflections of forms on water was made by Guido Luzzatto, 'Le temps et le mouvement dans la peinture de Carpaccio', in *Venezia e l'Europa, Atti del XVIII Congresso internazionale di Storia dell' Arte, 1955*, Venice, 1956, pp. 220–21, Cf. Muraro, 1971, pp. 7–19; Damisch, 1984, pp. 137–43; and Baxandall, 1974, pp. 71–81.

44. Moore and Myerhoff, 1977, p. 18.

45. Brera, Milan, no. 221: one of three scenes from the Life of St. Jerome on a wood panel measuring 25 × 152 cm.

46. Cat, XIX, doc. 2b.

47. See, in particular, Moore and Myerhoff, 1977, pp. 3–24; Barbara Myerhoff, 'A Death in Due Time: Construction of Self and Culture in Ritual Drama', and Victor Turner, 'Liminality and Performative Genres', in *Rite, Drama, Festival, Spectacle*, ed. J. MacAloon, Philadelphia, 1984; Victor Turner, *The Ritual Process: Structure and Anti-Structure*, Chicago and London, 1969; and idem, *Dramas, Fields and Metaphors: Symbolic Action in Human Society*, Ithaca, 1984.

Chapter 11

1. Sabellico, *De Situ*, 1772 edn, col. 5, cf. Michiel, 1969 edn, p. 131.

2. Zanetti, 1771, p. 35.

3. As suggested by Bardon, 1985, pp. 57 and 140. See also pp. 58–60 for further examples of Venetianizing architecture in the cycle.

4. Molmenti and Ludwig, 1907, pp. 95–97; and Lauts, 1962, p. 23.

5. In addition to references cited in nn. 3 and 4 above, see Fletcher, 1973, p. 599; and Sgarbi, 1979, cat. no. 6, with further citations. For arguments regarding Carpaccio's possible travels in the east, see ibid., p. 58 n. 69.

6. Molmenti and Ludwig, 1907, pp. 134–35.

7. For example, the figure of the High Priest in the *Marriage of the Virgin* (Cat. XVIII.3) is an almost exact copy of the same figure in the Venetian Bible of Nicholas of Lyra of 1489. See John Shearman, 'The Expulsion of Heliodorus', in *Raffaello a Roma*, Rome 1986, p. 80. See also Bardon, 1985, pp. 60–70.

8. Proposed by Muraro, 1971, pp. 7–19. See also Zorzi, 1971, pp. 21–51; idem, 1977; Povoledo, 1972, pp. 75–86; M. T. Muraro, 1964; and Rosand, 1982, pp. 145–214.

9. Muraro, 1966, p. 21 and pl. CCLXV; and Zorzi, 1971, p. 41.

10. Davis, 1980, pp. 132–98. For Daniele Barbaro's notice of Carpaccio's and Giovanni Bellini's instruction in perspective by Hieronimo Malatini, see ibid., p. 184.

11. For examples, see Bardon, 1985, figs. 11, 12, 35 and 38. This study offers the most intensive formal analysis to date of the cycle as a whole. See, in particular, pp. 99–180. See also Maganato, 1964, pp. 228–38; and idem, 1963, pp. 70–81.

12. Muraro, 1971, pp. 7–19.

13. See Muraro, 1966, pp. 49–52; and Zampetti, 1963b, Introduction.

14. See Smyth, 1979, p. 231; and Cat. XV.3.

15. For the case for Florence, with a summary of earlier arguments, see Howard Saalman, 'The Baltimore and Urbino Panels: Cosimo Rosselli', *Burlington Magazine*, 110 (1968): pp. 376 ff. See also Susan McKillop, *Franciabigio*, Berkeley, 1974, pp. 213–14; and Damisch, 1984, pp. 137–44.

16. *Travels in Tana and Persia*, 1873 edn, p. 2.

17. See references in n. 41 below and Chapter 2, n. 7 above.

18. Raby, 1982, p. 21–22.

19. Ibid., pp. 35–43.

20. Ibid., pp. 55–65.

21. Louvre, Inv. 100, oil on canvas (175 × 201 cm). This work has puzzled art historians for nearly a century. In addition to Raby's study, for a summary of earlier scholarship, see Rouillard, 1973, pp. 297–304. Once attributed to Gentile Bellini, among others, the painting has most recently been ascribed to Benedetto Diana. See Conti, 1977, pp. 58–61. The Louvre recently changed its attribution from 'School of Gentile Bellini', to simply 'Venetian School, first half 16th century'. For an unconvincing suggestion that the painting may not represent a contemporary event at all but one that was historically distant or even legendary, see Meyer zur Capellen, 1985, p. 93. He sees the work as a copy of a lost original by Gentile. In fact, the planar mode of composition is quite different from Gentile's surviving *istorie*.

22. See particularly Sauvaget, 1945–46, pp. 5–12.

23. Raby, 1982, p. 73, who confirms the observations first made by Sauvaget, 1945–46. My only reservation to Raby's dating of the canvas is the fact that most of the Venetians depicted in it wear beards. An examination of dated portraits and *istorie* of this period indicates that beards became generally popular in Venice only toward the second decade of the 16th century. Perhaps the fashion was popular at an earlier time with Venetians abroad.

24. For the cycle of the Silk-weavers, see Cat. XVI.

25. See Raby, 1982, pp. 43–53, who traces the evolution of the motif in the Venetian paintings. See also O. Kurz, 'Mamluk Heraldry and *Interpretatio Christiana*', *Studies in Memory of Gaston Wiet*, Jerusalem, 1977, pp. 297–307; and W. Leaf, 'Not trousers but trumpets: A further look at Saracenic Heraldry', *Palestine Exploration Quarterly* (1982): pp. 47–51.

26. Sanudo's simile in the entry on Doge Sebastiano Ziani in his *Vitae*, 1733 edn, col. 506, is suggestive of Mansueti's fictive architecture: 'Questo Doge fece fare attorno la Piazza di San Marco case con colonne alle finestre, dove si andava attorno, come a un Teatro...' Cf. ibid., col. 519.

27. See Cat. XIX.2. Drawings showing the areas that were overpainted, and that distinguished Gentile's from Giovanni's contributions, were made in 1979 by a restorer, Maria Marcella Sorteni. They were displayed in the Brera in 1984, and my conclusions are based upon them. They are as yet unpublished, and as of January 1987 the painting was not yet back on public display. See also the letter of Carlo Bertelli in *Giornale dell'Arte*, IV, no. 40 (Dec. 1986): p. 38.

28. For example, see Cat. XIX, doc. 12, which shows that Mansueti's *Episodes in the Life of St. Mark* was all but complete at his death, except for some portrait heads.

29. A conclusion of Lehmann, 1977, p. 21, n. 3, but cf. Meyer zur Capellen, 1985, p. 93. For the possible travels of Venetian painters in the east, see Raby, 1982, particularly pp. 63–65; and idem, 1980, pp. 121ff.

30. Cf. Raby, 1982, p. 66–72.

31. Pagani, 1884 edn, pp. 173–74.

32. Sauvaget, 1945–46, pp. 5–12.

33. Ibid. See also Cat. XIX, doc. 2.

34. Lehmann, 1977, pp. 7–8. Cf. Collins, 1970, p. 63; and Smith, 1987, pp. 16–32.

35. R. Gallo, 'Il Portico della Carta del Palazzo Ducale', *Rivista di Venezia* 12 (1933): p. 296, asserted that Gentile's painting showed the early state of the Venetian Basilica before the addition of its marble and mosaic decorations, and called it 'un felice anachronismo'. However, there is no reason to think that Gentile was trying to reconstruct the Venetian church as such – that is, in its own identity – for it is structurally quite different from the painting. Furthermore, Gentile's church has crescents atop slim pinnacles flanking the attic lunettes, difficult to explain in terms of a Christian church.

36. See Chapter 4 above.

37. Mayer, 1952, pp. 81–82, identified them as such. The only exception is the imposing figure in the turban, standing in front of St. Mark.

38. For the monuments, see Lehmann, 1977, pp. 8–9; and Collins, 1960, pp. 63–66. For the artistic consequences of Gentile's sojourn in the east, see Meyer zur Capellen, 1985, pp. 97–101.

39. Lehman, 1977, p. 9.

40. Dempsey, forthcoming. I am most grateful to Professor Dempsey for making the typescript available to me. His article was originally given as a lecture and will be published without footnotes.

Dempsey identified the characters from top to bottom as follows: 1. crooklike form and circle: shepherd's staff (attribute of Serapis) and sun (godhood) = Serapis; 2. soles of two sandals = subjects; 3. Roman letters, V. L.: *votum libens* or *vovit libens* = willing vow; 4. owl = death or ignorance; 5. eel = hatred or envy; 6. awl: Tau cross = life to come; 7. Old moon in circle of new = declining fortune.

For Renaissance hieroglyphs see K. Giehlow, 'Die Hieroglyphenkunde des Humanismus in der Allegorie der Renaissance', *Jahrbuch der kunsthistorisches Sammlungen des Allerhöchesten Kaiserhauses, Wien* 32 (1915): pp. 1–229; E. Iversen, *The Myth of Egypt and its Hieroglyphs in European Tradition*, Copenhagen, 1961, Chapter 3; and R.

Wittkower, 'Hieroglyphics in the Early Renaissance', in *Developments in the Early Renaissance*, ed. B. Levy, Albany, 1972, pp. 58–97.
41. Dempsey, forthcoming. For notions of conversion, see Dionisotti, 1966, pp. 478–9; R. Schwoebel, 'Coexistence, conversion and the Crusade against the Turks', *Studies in the Renaissance* 12 (1965): pp. 164–87; and Giampolo Tognetti, 'Venezia e le profezie sulla conversione dei Turchi', in *Venezia e i Turchi. Scontri e confronti di due civilta*, Milan, 1985, pp. 86–90. Preto, 1975, p. 259, holds that none of the Venetian poetic texts and laments from 1453 right up to 1571 calls for a Crusade. Cf. A. Medin, *La storia della Repubblica di Venezia nella poesia*, Milan, 1904, pp. 199–228.
42. Ruskin, 1894, pp. 164–65.
43. Marshall, 1984, pp. 619–20.
44. In *La Pinacoteca di Brera*, ed. G. Nannicini, Milan, 1970, pp. 102–3. On Carpaccio's orientalism, see also Raby, 1982, pp. 66–76; and Zampetti, 1966, pp. 511–26.
45. For the Bab al-Futuh, see Molmenti and Ludwig, 1907, p. 133. For a photograph of the actual gate, see Raby, 1982, p. 77, whose doubts seem unjustified, given Carpaccio's habit of altering such quotations. For St. Cyriacus, see Fiocco, 1930, p. 74; and Cat. XVII.6. The church reappeared again (with a crescent) in Belliniano's *Martyrdom of St. Mark* (Cat. XX.5). It was probably also painted into the fresco on which Carpaccio was working in the Great Council Hall at that time, the *Consignment of the Umbrella* (Cat. XIII.19), for it was present in Gamberato's painting of the late 16th century which replaced it. See Chapter 5 above.
46. Cf. Ames-Lewis, 1981, pp. 143–44. See also Gilles de la Tourette, 1924, p. 140, who shows that Carpaccio's rendering of the Dome of the Rock is closer to the original structure than Reeuwich's engraving; and Molmenti and Ludwig, 1907, p. 134.
47. Cf. Bernhard Degenhart and Annegrit Schmitt, 'Ein Musterblatt des Jacopo Bellini mit Zeichnungen nach der Antike', in *Festschrift Leopold Dussler*, Munich, 1972, pp. 139–68. I am presently preparing an article on Jacopo's relation to the antique, to be published in *ROME: Tradition, Renewal and Innovation*, a collection of papers presented at the Canadian International Art History Conference held in Rome, June 1987, in honor of Richard Krautheimer and Leonard Boyle.
48. Cat. XV, doc. 6a–b.
49. Speaking through Isabella's agent, Michele Vianello (3 Nov. 1502): '. . .lo faria lavoro dove sie el puto, eziam el San Zoan batista et qualche luntani et altra fantaxia che molto staria meglio . . .' see Braghirolli, 1877, p. 380 (Eng. trans. Chambers, 1971, pp. 128–29). Cf. the letter of Lorenzo da Pavia (10 Sept. 1502), stating that Giovanni 'dice che lui farà il quadro e farà una fantasia a suo modo' (Braghirolli, 1877, p. 379).
50. See other citations in Kemp, 1977, pp. 373–75.
51. Cat. XIX, doc. 3.
52. See G. Gaye, *Carteggio inedito d'artisti* 2, Florence, 1840, pp. 71–73 (Engl. trans. Chambers, 1971, pp. 131–32).
53. Kemp, 1977, pp. 369–73.
54. Kenneth Clark, *Leonardo da Vinci*, Cambridge, 1967, pp. 101–3.
55. Kemp, 1981, p. 160. See also Kemp, 1977, pp. 375–81.
56. Kemp, 1977, pp. 379–80.
57. Ibid., p. 381; and Lecoq, 1975, pp. 226–30.
58. Lecoq, 1975, p. 238.
59. Cited in ibid., p. 233. Cf. Rensselaer W. Lee, '"Ut Pictura Poesis," The Humanistic Theory on Painting', *Art Bulletin* 22 (1940): pp. 197–269.
60. Muraro, 1966, pp. 75–78.
61. Lecoq, 1975, p. 225. Isabella d'Este used the term in her correspondence to Michele Vianello about the painting that she sought from Giovanni Bellini (28 June 1501): 'Se Zoanne Bellino fa tanto male voluntieri quella historia, como ne haveti scripto, siamo contente remetterne al judicio suo, pur chel dipinga qualche historia o fabula antiqua, aut de sua inventione ne finga una che representi cosa antiqua, et de bello significato. . .' From Braghirolli, 1877, p. 377.
62. Lecoq, 1975, p. 242, sees these two activities of the painter as incompatible. For Carpaccio's humanist culture, see Perocco, 1960, p. 12; and Wazbinski, 1968, pp. 21–29.
63. For his signatures, see Cancogni, 1967, p. 84.

Chapter 12

1. Roskill, 1968, p. 125.
2. Moschini, 1960, pp. 353–54.
3. For example in the Old and New Testament scenes on the walls of the Sistine Chapel; and in Ghirlandaio's cycles in Florence: the Sassetti Chapel in S. Trinità and the Tornabuoni Chapel in S. M. Novella. On the phenomenon in general, see Aby Warburg, 'Bildniskunst und florentinisches Bürgertum. Domenico Ghirlandaio in Santa Trinita: Die Bildnisse des Lorenzo de' Medici und seiner Angehörigen' (1902), in *Gesammelte Schriften*, ed. Gertrud Bing, I, Leipzig-Berlin, 1932; Jacob Burckhardt, 'Das Porträt', in *Beiträge zur Kunstgeschichte von Italien* ed. H. Trog, Stuttgart and Berlin, 1911, pp. 171–83 and 230–37; H. Keller, 'Die Entstehung des Bildnesses am Ende des Hochmittelalters', *Romisches Jahrbuch für Kunstgeschichte*, 3 (1939): pp. 298–341; and Pope-Hennessey, 1966, pp. 9–23 and 257–300.
4. Pope-Hennessey, 1966, p. 19.
5. Demus, 1984, 2/I, pp. 201–3. See also idem, 'Das älteste venezianische Gesellschaftsbild', *Jahrbuch der österreichischen Byzantinischen Gesellschaft*, 1 (1951): pp. 89–101.
6. Demus, 1984, 2/I, pp. 28–31.
7. Sansovino, 1663, I, p. 325
8. Ibid.
9. Roskill, 1968, p. 127.
10. For portraits in the paintings of the Scuole Grandi, see also Wolters, 1983, pp. 153–59.
11. Collins, 1982c, p. 206 n. 2.
12. See Cat. XIV.6.
13. See Cat. XVII.6.
14. For possible identifications of figures in Gentile Bellini's *Miracle at San Lorenzo*, see Cat. XV.2. None of Molmenti and Ludwig's (1907, pp. 75–78) identifications of portraits in Carpaccio's cycle of St. Ursula have been substantiated. In the Albanesi cycle, there are three portraits in the *Funeral of the Virgin*. In the San Giorgio cycle, there may be one or two portraits in the *Calling of Matthew*, and possibly some in the *Miracle of San Trifone*.
15. See Fletcher, 1986, pp. 427–28 for indications that noblemen were specially recruited into the Scuola di Sant'Orsola at a higher entry fee to help finance Carpaccio's paintings. She also alludes to evidence (soon to be published) that the portrait figures in the Great Council Hall were 'often quite literally lifted out and repeated in [the] Scuola paintings'.
16. ASV, San Marco, Reg. 77, filza 3, f. 13: 'Iqual la divina Maiesta se degni per sua innata misericordia et clementia. In questo mondo prosperarlj et in laltro prestarli Vita eterna: et inspirar ali altri nostri fradeli a porger el suo aiuto a questa tal pia et bona opera'. (Cat. XIX, doc. 7).
17. Ibid., Reg. 17, f. 78 (Cat. XIX, doc. 9).
18. Giustiniani, 1772 edn, col. 188.
19. Ibid., col. 189. Cf. Chapter 5, above.
20. Sem. Pat. Venice, Cod. 950.
21. Alberti, 1972 edn, p. 101 [Book 3, para. 56].
22. G. Hanfmann, 'Narration in Greek Art', *American Journal of Archeology*, 61 (1957): p. 74.
23. For the importance of witnesses to miracles, see André Vauchez, *La Sainteté en Occident aux Derniers Siècles du Moyen Age*, Rome, 1981, pp. 40–41 and passim; and Giorgio Cracco, 'Realismo e tensioni ideali nella cultura trevigiana del tardo medioevo', in *Tomaso da Modena e il suo tempo: Atti del convegno internazionale di studi per il 6° centenario della morte (Treviso 31 agosto – 3 settembre 1979)*, Treviso, 1980, pp. 119–32.
24. For a penetrating study of group portraits in Dutch painting, see Alois Riegl, 'Das Holländische Gruppenporträt', *Jahrbuch der kunsthistorischen Sammlungen des allerhöchsten Kaiserhauses*, 33 (1902): pp. 171–278. The section on Geertgen tot Sint Jans's *The Legend of the Relics of St. John the Baptist* deals with confraternity portraiture in a narrative painting and appears in English translation in W. Kleinbauer, *Modern Perspectives in Western Art History*, New York, 1971, pp. 124–38.
25. For epitaphs, see MCV, Cod. Gradenigo 194, 'Scole Grandi' (23 May 1443). For thrones, see ASV, Consiglio dei Dieci, Parte Misti, Reg. 13, f. 13 (12 May 1445).
26. ASV, Avogaria di commun, Reg. 106/1, Petri Barbaro, 'Liber nuptiarum nobilitatis venetae ab anno MCCCC usque ad annum

MDXXXVIII cum additamentis usque ad a MDLX', ff. 2r–3r: 'E si vorio narare/ Le nobel stirpe tute/ El qual son descendute/ da bon sangue reale/. . . . El nostro serenissimo/ Foscari ecelentissimo/ E la sua stirpe per tuto/ chi vol eser astuto/ al cha di Falieri/ Memi e Condulmeri/ Et poi deli Corneri/ Troni e Balori/ con le Sanudi e magrini/ dito di Justigniani/ e di nobil Polani/ Michieli e Zivrani/ Driedolli con forza/ O quanta modesta/ Vanno i Bragadini/ ancor i Morosinj/ a qual Zentil chapelo/ la cha de Caz a ruolo/ non mi voglio dimentizare/ per vole bon fare/ diro delli Dolfini/ Marsoli e Foscarini/ vano su qual conseglio/ molto mi maraveglio/ de tanti Contarini/ Tiepoli e Quirini/. . . .'

Despite its title, the volume also includes several chronicles, passages of poetry and other items.

27. A similar listing that enumerated a long list of individuals instead of families appeared in a small book entitled *Triumpho e gloria di Venitiani de tuti quelli sono stati homini valorosi e reputati in la republica veneta*, Venice, 1502. A third Venetian example of the genre is Pietro Contarini, *De voluptate Argoa*, Venice, 1542, discussed by B. Nardi, 'La Scuola di Rialto e l'umanesimo veneziano', in *Umanesimo europeo e umanesimo veneziano*, ed. V. Branca, Venice, 1963, pp. 127–31.

28. See Mommsen, 1952, pp. 95–116.

29. Cf. Girolamo Bardi's (1587a, ff. 2v–3r) program for the repainting of the Great Council Hall following the fire of 1577, wherein he stresses the importance that no individual Venetian be unduly praised above his fellows.

30. Sabellico, 1772 edn., col. 8.

31. ASV, Maggior Consiglio, Deliberazioni, Stella, Reg. 24 (1480–1502), f. 64v (new num.). Cf. Chapter 2, n. 81.

32. Verbal communication from Stella Mary Newton, Courtauld Institute, London. See also Gilbert, 1980, pp. 12–13, who notes that the colorfulness of dress was frequently seen by outsiders as a further sign of the 'miraculous character' and harmonious unity of Venetian society. For prescriptions of dress for officials during Holy Week, see ASV, Collegio Cerimoniale, Reg. 1, f. 16v. Details of male dress and deviations from the norm were carefully enumerated by Sanudo. Two examples out of many are found in his *Diarii*, XXVII, p. 444; and LVI, pp. 198–202 and 376 (my thanks to Christine Junkerman for these references).

33. Sansovino, 1663, I, p. 282.

34. The heavy-set woman on the *fondamenta* has been identified convincingly as Caterina Cornaro by, among others, Billanovich, 1973, p. 373. Cf. Cat. XV.2.

35. Frederick Hartt, *History of Italian Renaissance Art*, 2nd edn, Englewood Cliffs, N.J., 1979, p. 410.

36. Cotrugli, 1573, c. 31b. Cf. Tucci, 1973, pp. 346–78.

37. For patronage networks, see Trexler, 1980, particularly Chapter 4.

38. See Susan Moulton, 'Titian and the Evolution of Donor Portraiture in Venice', Ph.D. dissertation, Stanford University, 1977, pp. 23–27; and Meyer zur Capellen, 1985, pp. 55–62.

39. For ex votos, see L. Kriss-Rettenbeck, *Ex Voto, Zeichen Bild und Abbild im christlichen Votivbrauchtum*, Zurich, 1972, p. 155; G. Bronzini, '"Ex Voto" e cultura religiosa popolare problemi d'interpretazione', *Rivista di storia e letteratura religiosa* 15 (1979): pp. 8–11; and A. Vecchi, 'Per la lettura delle tavolette votive', *Studia patavina* 21 (1974): pp. 602–21.

40. Vasari, 1966 edn, p. 617.

41. See Cancogni and Perocco, 1967, p. 83.

42. The portrait (wood panel, 21 × 27 cm), was seen by Lanzi in the Palazzo Giustiniani-Recanati on the Zattere in Venice (*Storia pittorica dell'Italia dal Risorgimento delle belle arti fin presso la fine del XVIII secolo*, Bassano, 1789, X, p. 834). His notice was repeated by L. Federici, *Memorie Trevigiane*, 1803, I, p. 238. Cf. the rejection by Momenti and Ludwig, 1907, pp. 30–31. For further information on Vittore Greco, see Ludwig, 1905, pp. 108–12. I have been unable to locate the present where-abouts of the painting.

43. Zanotto, 1833–34, fasc. 55. See also Moschini Marconi, 1955, p. 134; and Foscari, 1933, p. 247.

44. Foscari, 1933, p. 248. For the suggestion that Gentile portrayed himself along with his family in the *Miracle at the Bridge of San Lorenzo*, see Cat. XV.2.

45. Proposing that Gentile meant this painting to be a testament to himself, Sohm (1982, pp. 247–48) observed that the figure of the artist was equal to one-half the width of the squares in the pavement and to one-half the radius of the circle created by the church's buttresses. In so doing, Gentile made his own figure the 'proportional measure which governs this geometrically lucid composition'. Cf. Fiocco, 1938, pp. 3–16.

46. ASV, San Marco, Reg. 4, f. 90 and Reg. 17. Cf. Cat. XV.2 for the possible depiction of a *banca* in Gentile's *Miracle at the Bridge of San Lorenzo*.

47. Giovanni requested that he deal only with Pellegrino in this matter see Cat. XIX, doc. 5.

48. Probably the figure to the left of the white-haired man in a red toga (possibly Giovanni Dario: see Chapter 4, n. 73 above), who was flanked on the left, according to some suggestions, by Giovanni Bellini. See Foscari, 1933, pp. 274–62. For the inscription, see Cat. XV.5.

49. I am grateful for Richard Brilliant's observations on this issue. Cf. Rosand, 1982, pp. 118–24, 167–74 and 182–90.

50. *Miracoli della Croce*, 1590.

Epilogue

1. Cat. XIX, doc. 12.
2. Alpers, 1960, pp. 190–215.
3. Vasari, 1568, De Vere edn, III, pp. 174–75. Cf. 1966 edn, p. 429.
4. Roskill, 1968, pp. 116–17.
5. Sansovino, 1663, I, p. 325.
6. See Raby, 1982, pp. 82–83. Cf. J. Shearman, *Mannerism*, Harmondsworth, 1967, p. 40, who cautions against trying to make direct links between shifts in aesthetic taste and concrete political and economic events.
7. See Barbara Marx, 'Venezia – altera Roma? Ipotesi sull' umanesimo italiano', *Quaderni del Centro tedesco di Studi veneziani* 10 (1978): pp. 3–18; and D. Chambers, *The Imperial Age of Venice, 1380–1580*, London, 1970, pp. 12–30. Cf. Tafuri, 1982.
8. For this period, see Tafuri, 1984.
9. Deborah Howard, *Jacopo Sansovino*, New Haven, 1975, pp. 1–7; and idem, 1980, pp. 136–59.
10. Catalogue XIX.6.
11. Catalogue XIX.7.
12. Rosand, 1982, pp. 85–144.
13. Ibid., p. 133.
14. The concept is developed by Winter, 1981.

CATALOGUE

Early Venetian Cycles of Narrative Paintings

The catalogue is intended to provide a chronology of all cycles of large-scale narrative paintings documented in Venice prior to 1534. That date marks the conclusion of the campaign in the *albergo* of the Scuola Grande di San Marco, and with it, the virtual disappearance of the 'eyewitness' style as it is defined in this book. For this reason, the cycles will be listed in order of the earliest known date relating to each and will not be separated into categories of extant and lost works, as is more customary in *catalogues raisonnés* of individual artists.

By its very nature, this catalogue will be incomplete. A number of early cycles of narrative painting must have vanished without a trace. Others have been alluded to in the sources, but have left too little concrete evidence of their actual existence to warrant inclusion in the list. New documents will surely be discovered in the archives. Some forms of pictorial narrative have been intentionally omitted: for example, mosaics, tapestries, manuscript illumination and small-scale paintings on predella and furniture panels.

In a practical sense, the catalogue was constructed as an adjunct to the main text of the book. It was intended to disencumber the latter of information regarding each cycle's composition, documentation and bibliography. The reader should thus be able to find the basic facts on each cycle and a summary of pertinent scholarship in systematic order, complete and in one place. Furthermore, the catalogue is meant to augment and not to supplant more comprehensive catalogues in which the cycles appear. Most important are Jan Lauts, *Carpaccio*, London, 1962; Manlio Cancogni (ed.), *L'opera completa del Carpaccio*, Milan, 1967; and Terisio Pignatti, *Le scuole di Venezia*, Milan, 1981. Bibliographical entries will thus emphasize primary sources and only the major works of secondary literature of prior years, along with more recent scholarship. The condition of paintings will be commented on only if new information has become available.

An abbreviation system has been adopted to avoid needless repetitions. Within each catalogue entry, documents referred to are understood to be within the same entry unless otherwise specified. For example, in Catalogue XV, document 1 is referred to simply as doc. 1. Elsewhere (in the main text or in another catalogue entry) it will be cited as cat. XV, doc. 1. Paintings are denoted by a decimal system. Painting no. 1 from the same catalogue entry is cited as cat. XV.1.

Many of the documents are printed elsewhere. If the text given here is taken from another printed source, that source will be preceded by the word 'from'. If the text given here is taken directly from the original document but is also printed elsewhere, the other printed source will be preceded by the word 'cf.'

Reconstruction drawings are included in five catalogue entries. It should be stressed that they are based upon incomplete data. Most of the rooms have undergone structural changes over the years, including alterations in ceiling height and the addition or subtraction of doors and windows. Even when still intact, they no longer contain original decorative elements such as wood paneling, moldings and benches. These features, when included in the drawings, are conjectural. The reconstructions should thus be regarded as hypothetical (rather than definitive) reflections of the original schemes.

The Venetian year (*more veneto* = m.v.) began on March 1. All dates given here are modern style unless otherwise noted.

I. Scuola della SS. Annunziata

Scenes from the Life of Christ and the Life of the Virgin (lost) 1314

HISTORY: Founded as a *scuola di devozione* in 1314, the Scuola della SS. Annunziata moved into its own meeting-house in 1360 on the Rio dei Servi, directly opposite the Cappella dei Lucchesi and facing the Church of S. M. dei Servi (Zorzi, 1984, p. 367). First noted in the sources by Boschini in 1664 (doc. 1), its cycle of 14 paintings in tempera carried the date 1314.

The building suffered a fire in 1769 and was restored only in 1791, but Zanetti reported seeing the panels in 1771 in the sacristy of the nearby church. Including them in the section on the oldest paintings known to him in Venice, he confirmed the date of 1314 and added that they had been recently retouched with oil and varnish. They had, he observed, originally been painted 'con la solita antica maniera...' (Zanetti, 1771, p. 5).

The paintings were in the sacristy of the *scuola* in 1797 when another writer characterized their style as 'della maniera prima Greca' (*Pittura veneziana*, 1797, II, p. 103). By 1815 the panels had disappeared (Moschini, 1815, II, p. 7), and in 1862 the Scuola building was demolished (Zorzi, 1984, p. 367).

DOCUMENTS AND SOURCES:

1. 1664. Boschini describes the decorations of the Scuola: 'Nella detta Scuola, per l'antichità delle Pitture, benchè non siano di molto rarità, essendo state fatte dell'anno 1314, sono degne di ammirazione, e sono à tempera, non si vede però il nome dell' Autore; contengono molti delli detti quadri, la vita di Christo et altri la vita di Maria Vergine: e sono in tutti al numero di 14.'

Boschini, 1664, pp. 470–71.

LITERATURE: Boschini, 1664, pp. 470–71; Boschini, 1674, Cannaregio, p. 51; Zanetti, 1771, p. 5; *Della pittura veneziana*, 1797, II, p. 103; Moschini, 1815, II, p. 7; Cicogna, 1824–27, I, p. 98; Sagredo, 1852, p. 30; Testi, 1909, I, p. 152; Zorzi, 1984, pp. 367–68.

II. Church of San Nicolò, Ducal Palace

Story of Alexander III (lost) c. 1319–31

HISTORY: According to tradition, the Church di S. Nicolò (variously called *Ecclesia* or *Capella*) was built by Doge Pietro Ziani (1205–29) in fulfillment of a vow made by his predecessor Doge Enrico Dandolo during the siege of Constantinople of 1204 (docs. 7, 10, 11). Destroyed in the 16th century, the church seems to have been located in the area just north of the present Scala dei Censori in the east wing of the Ducal Palace. The approximate site is marked by a marble plaque, once attached next to its portal and now affixed to the wall on the loggia level of the Ducal Palace. Trincanato (1970, pp. 112 and 122) implied that the church was actually located in that place, but cf. Bassi (1962a, pp. 34–36), whose notion of a free-standing building is more plausible. An early document spoke of a cistern outside its entrance, which seems to place it at ground level (Lorenzi, 1868, no. 145).

The 13th-century Church of S. Nicolò should not be confused with the private chapel of the Doge which burned in 1483 (see Lorenzi, 1868, p. 92; and Sabellico, 1772 edn, col. 19). The latter chapel was located on the second floor of the east wing of the Doge's palace adjacent to San Marco. When it was restored in 1505–23, it was also given the name of S. Nicolò (Pincus, 1976, p. 22 n. 27; cf. Sinding-Larsen, 1974, p. 209, who treats the two churches as one).

There are conflicting reports of painted *istorie* commissioned by Doge Pietro Ziani for the first church of S. Nicolò (docs. 7, 10, 11), but the first certain notices of its decoration date to 1319 when the Great Council appropriated funds to paint it with scenes from the story of Pope Alexander III. The walls are described at that time as 'tota nuda picturis' (doc. 1). The story celebrates the mediating role of Doge Sebastiano Ziani (father of Pietro Ziani) in bringing about a peace treaty in 1177 between the Pope and Emperor Frederick II Barbarossa. Although the event was recorded in earlier sources, it was first brought together in a coherent narrative form c. 1320 by Bonincontro da Bovi, a notary in the Ducal Chancery (*Historia de discordia*..., publ. in Sanudo, *Vite*, 1900 edn, pp. 370–411).

The chapel was enlarged in 1322–23, probably incorporating the narthex into the body of the church (Lorenzi, 1868, nos. 47 and 49; see Bassi, 1962a, p. 36). Payments for work in the church totalling 30 lire di grossi (300 ducats) are documented between 1323–29, at which time the paintings were probably completed (docs. 2 and 3). A Master Paolo, probably Paolo da Venezia, was paid for an altarpiece for the chapel in 1347 (doc. 4; cf. Muraro, 1970, p. 125). In 1362 Urban V granted a special indulgence to those who prayed there for the souls of poor prisoners in the nearby prisons of the Ducal Palace (doc. 5). By 1400 the wall paintings were in poor condition, and funds were appropriated for their restoration (doc. 6). The staircase that was constructed in 1415 for a more impressive entry to the newly completed Great Council Hall had its lower terminus at the entry portal to the church (Lorenzi, 1868, no. 145). The Trecento paintings may well have survived into the 16th century, for Sanudo described the chapel in 1523 as 'dipenta et istoriada' (doc. 8). In 1525, after the completion of the new Doge's chapel which was given the same name, the first church of San Nicolò was destroyed (doc. 9).

The only other room of the palace for which painted decoration is reliably cited for this early period is that of the Senate (Sala dei Pregadi). Describing it in 1525, Sanudo claimed that it dated back to the time of Doge Piero Gradenigo (1298–1311). It was painted with trees of three sizes, representing the three ages of man (Sanudo, *Diarii*, 39, coll. 27–28; see also Wolters, 1983, pp. 16–17).

DOCUMENTS AND SOURCES:

1. 11 Dec. 1319. Paintings are commissioned for the chapel. 'Quia ecclesia beati Nicolai de Palacio est tota nuda picturis: capta fuit pars quod denarii qui provenient de bonis condam cuius de ca'Cuppo mentecapi quibus comune debet succedere, debeant expendi et poni in laborerio picturarum dicte ecclesie, pingendo in ea hystoriam pape quando fuit Veneciis cum domino Imperatore et alia que videbuntur...'

ASV, Maggior Consiglio, Deliberazioni, vol. Fronesis 1318–25, c. 28v; and ibid., vol. Neptunus, no. 1056, f. 106v. Cf. Sanudo, *Vite*, 1900 edn, p. 416 and Lorenzi, 1868, doc. 36.

2. 3 Feb. 1328 m.v. (=1329). The final payment is made for works in the chapel. 'Intrante dedimus nos Procuratores ecclesie sancti Marci libras 5 soldos 4 grossorum completos de ratione Palatij pro complemento et integra satifacione librarum 30 grossorum, quas accepimus mutuo de ratione ecclesie Sancti Marci pro laborerio ecclesie sancti Nicolai de Palatio...'

ASV, Procuratia de Supra, B. 77, processo 180, fasc. I (17th-century copy of a 'quaderno delle spese del Palazzo', now lost). Cf. Lorenzi, 1868, no. 68; for earlier payments see ibid., nos. 50, 52, 57, 58, 61 and 63.

3. 15 Dec. 1331. The paintings serve as a model for a new literary rendition of the story of Alexander III. 'Quod fiat gratiam Magistro Castellano, qui compilavit metrice librum de istoria quondam domini pape Alexandri et Imperatoris Frederici, de guerra et pace habita inter eos et postmodum Venetiam confirmata, secundum quod depicta est in Sancto Nicolao de palacio et cronicam, ad honorem domini ducis et Comunis Veneciarum cum magno studio et labore...'

ASV, Cassiere della Bolla Ducale, Grazie del Maggior Consiglio, Reg. 4 (no. antico 2), 21 Aug. 1331–17 June 1332, f. 12 (new num.). vol. IV. Cf. Cecchetti, 1886, p. 331, n. 2. The passage refers to a Latin *poemetto* written by Castellano da Bassano, entitled 'Venetiane pacis inter ecclesiam et imperium Castellani Bassianensis', (publ. in Sanudo, *Vite*, 1900 edn, pp. 485–519). The author was paid 1000 *salmas* of grain for his efforts.

4. 20 Jan. 1346 m.v.(=1347). An altarpiece is completed for the chapel. 'Dedimus ducatos 20 auri magistro Paulo pentore Sancti Lucae, pro pentura unius Anchone facte in ecclesia Sancti Nicolai de Palacio.'

ASV, Procuratia de Supra, B. 77, Processo 180, fasc. I. Cf. Lorenzi, 1868, no. 92 (with an incorrect date).

5. 1362–70: Pope Urban V grants an indulgence to all who visit the chapel and give alms for the prisoners. It is recorded on a marble plaque near the door to the chapel (now near the entrance to the Scala dei Censori on the east loggia floor). A photograph of the plaque, showing the full text, is in Bassi and Trincanato, 1966, fig. 15. Cf. doc. 8.

6. 22 July 1400. The paintings, now in poor condition, are to be restored. 'Cum picture Ecclesiae sive Capele sancti Nicolai de Palatio propter vetustatem delete sint et de necessitate sint ipsam Ecclesiam reparare, considerato loco notabili et excellenti ubi sita est dicta Ecclesia: Vadit pars, quod possit accipi de pecunia nostri comunis tantum quantum erit necesse pro repingendo et reaptando in dicta Ecclesia ubi et sicut de illis istorijs que videbuntur dominio.'

ASV, Maggior Consiglio, Deliberazioni, vol. Leona 1384–1415, c. 106v. Cf. Lorenzi, 1868, doc. 127.

7. c. 1490s: Sanudo writes in the *Vita di Doge Pietro Ziani*: 'Sotto questo Doge fu edificata nel Palazzo Ducale la Capella di San Niccolò, e fatta dipignervi attorno la storia di suo padre.'

Sanudo, *Vitae*, 1733 edn. col. 538. He may well have been referring to the program of 1319, still visible and painted in an archaic style, while assigning to it an earlier (and, to him, logical) date.

8. 6 Dec. 1523. Sanudo reports that mass is celebrated in the newly completed chapel of S. Nicolò with the Doge in attendance, and that the old church with the same name will now be torn down: 'sichè la chiexia di san Nicolò vechia se ruinerà, ch'è assà bella, dipenta et istoriada, et con musaici, et a la porta uno epitaphio in marmoro di una bolla papal fata al tempo di missier Lorenzo Celsi doxe, per Papa...'

Sanudo, *Diarii*, 35, cols. 254–55.

9. 8 Oct. 1525. Sanudo records the destruction of the church: 'In questa matina fo principiato a butar zoso la sala di Pregadi qual fu fatta al tempo del Doxe messer Piero Gradenigo, che'e sta un gran peccato et poteva ancora disfar (?) assa' tempo remediata alquanto et si ando' ruinando assai et la chiesola di San Nicolò e tutto, e non compete.'

Sanudo, *Diarii*, 40, col. 15.

10. 1573. Paulo Rannusio repeats the tradition that the church had been built by Doge Pietro Ziani (1205–29), but claims that it was painted with scenes of the Fourth Crusade: 'Sed Zianus qui pia liberalitate Sacellum Divo Nicolao erexerat, in eiusdem quoque; parietibus, bellum Constantinopolitanum rubrica depictum, quod Sacello adhuc integro Maiores nostri viderunt, à posteris spectari voluit: ut quam Aedem Dandulus difficillimo bello, pro Reipublicae amplitudine vovisset in eadem quoque ipsius studio, et cura, ad totius posteritatis memoriam, & non dubium gloriosae victoriae testimonium, totius belli series spectaretur.'

Rannusio, 1604, p. 279 (Autograph MS = BMV, Cod. Lat. X, 79 [=3077], dated 1573). See also Carile, 1969, p. 76.

11. 1581. Sansovino follows Rannusio's notice: 'Il Principe in tanto fece la cappella di San Nicolò in Palazzo, in escutione, come si dice, d'un voto fatto dal Doge Henrico, overo, come altri dicono, per sua commodità. Nella quale fu dipinto l'acquisto di Constantinopoli di verde chiaro & scuro.'

Sansovino, 1581, p. 233. Cf. ibid., c. 120, where he confuses the church with the Doge's chapel adjacent to San Marco, restored by Doge Loredan (as in doc. 8 above).

ORIGINAL ARRANGEMENT: Nothing certain is known about the appearance of these paintings, which must have been frescoes, but they may well be reflected in eleven miniatures in a 14th century manuscript in the Museo Correr entitled 'Il libro della leggenda degli Apostoli Pietro e Paolo, di S. Albano e della venuta a Venezia di Papa Alexandro III' [MCV, Cod. Correr I, 383 (=1497)]. Subtitled 'Historia di Alessandro III,' the text of the relevant section of the manuscript is published in *Archivio Veneto*, 13 (1877): pp. 361–69.

Scholars have proposed various dates and pictorial sources for the miniatures. Current opinion is divided between the dates of c. 1340 and c. 1370 (arguments summarized in Brown, 1984, pp. 293–94, nn. 46–47). Stylistically, a date of execution c. 1370 as suggested by Levi d'Ancona (1967, pp.36 ff.) and others is most credible, but her suggestion that the miniatures reflect the frescoes painted in the Great Council Hall campaign of 1365 (see Cat. IV below), is unconvincing. Although Wolter's (1966, pp. 277–78; and idem, 1983, p. 164, n. 11) proposal for an earlier date of execution should be rejected, he is probably right when he suggests connections between the miniatures and the frescoes of the Church of S. Nicolò (as do Huse, 1972, pp. 56–57; and Pignatti, 1972, pp. 91–92). For similarities between several of the miniatures and those in Guido delle Colonne's 'Historia destructionis Troiae' (Milan, Biblioteca Ambrosiana, Cod. H. 86 sup.), see Degenhart and Schmitt, 1980, II–1, pp. 91–104, and II–3, Cat. 643.

Indeed, both the text and miniatures of the Correr manuscript correspond far more closely to the main episodes of Bonincontro da Bovi's Latin prose version of c. 1320 than to those that made up the fresco cycle of 1356 (cf. ibid.). The pre-Venetian part of the story, dealt with in summary fashion by Bonincontro, was only fully developed with specifically named battles in the poem written by Castellano da Bassano in 1331 (doc. 2 above). Castellano's verses, in fact, provided the models for the inscriptions of the 1365 cycle and for its greatly expanded number of scenes (see Monticolo's notes in Sanudo, *Vite*, 1900 edn, pp. 342–59 and p. 417). While the Correr manuscript excludes virtually all the events that took place prior to the Pope's escape to Venice, the 1365 cycle devoted no fewer than 11 scenes out of 28 to this phase of the legend.

Miniatures in MCV, Cod. Correr I, 383 (=1497), 'Historia di Alessandro III' that may reflect the fresco cycle of the Church of S. Nicolò:

1. A Venetian citizen informs Doge Sebastiano Ziani of the presence of Pope Alexander III in Venice.
2. Doge Ziani kneels before the Pope in front of the Church of S. M. della Carità. [Color Plate v]
3. The Pope presents the white candle to the Doge.
4. The Venetian ambassadors plead the case of the Pope before the Emperor Frederick II Barbarossa. [Plate 106]
5. The Pope presents the sword to the Doge. [Color Plate vi]
6. The Battle of Salvore, between the naval forces of the Venetians and the Emperor.
7. The Pope presents the ring to the Doge. [Color Plate vii]
8. Otto, having been captured by the Venetians, is sent back to treat for peace with his father, the Emperor.
9. The Pope and the Emperor make peace in front of the Basilica of San Marco. [Color Plate viii]
10. The Pope presents the Doge with the umbrella in Ancona. [Plate 40]
11. The Pope, the Doge and the Emperor are welcomed to Rome, and the Doge receives the trumpets and the ceremonial banners. [Plate 93]

LITERATURE: Sansovino, 1663, I, p. 321, and II, p. 562; Zanotto, 1858, pp. 28–30 and 52; Wickhoff, 1883, pp. 3–4 and 23 n. 75; Testi, 1909, I, pp. 156–57; Bassi, 1962a, pp. 34–36; Pallucchini, 1964, pp. 40 and 220; Wolters, 1966, pp. 277; Trincanato, 1970, pp. 111–18; Huse, 1972, pp. 56–57; Pignatti, 1972, pp. 91–94; Wolters, 1983, p. 164; Brown, 1984, pp. 267ff.

III. Loggia at the Rialto

Battle of Canale Orfano and Rout of Pepin (lost) After 1325

HISTORY: Passing through Venice in the 1440–50s, the Florentine historian Flavio Biondo observed some history paintings surrounding a *mappamondo* in the portico of the *telaruoli* (linen merchants) at the Rialto (doc. 1). They depicted one of the 'foundation myths' of the Venetian Republic: the Venetian defence of the bridge in 807 from attack by French forces commanded by Pepin, son of Charlemagne. The event also involved a naval battle in the straits of Canale Orfano. According to tradition, the Venetian victory marked the establishment of the ducal seat on the islands of the Rialto, which would lead to the development there of the urban center of Venice (Sanudo, *Vite*, 1900 edn, pp. 108–9).

The paintings would not have been all of 200 years old, as Biondo had thought, for the portico that he saw was built only in 1322–25 (Cessi, 1934, pp. 38–39). But they may well have dated to the years immediately following its construction. The Senate ordered the scenes to be copied before the structure was destroyed in 1459, so that they could be repainted on a new loggia that was to be built in the same location (Cat. IX, doc. 1).

Given the coincidence of dates, it is possible that the following passage from Sansovino (1581, c. 134v) also refers to the Trecento paintings in the loggia: 'Scrive Pietro Guilombardo che visse l'anno 1330 in certi suoi memoriali, che il palazzo del comune in Rialto, era presso alla Beccaria, dove soleva esser la merceria, & che fu cominciato del 1322. & finito del 1324, & che fu dipinto per tutto, & che nel mese di Gennaio, vide scoprir le dette pitture.'

DOCUMENTS AND SOURCES:

1. 1440–50s. Flavio Biondo writes: 'Cerniturque in Rivialti mercatorum porticu pictura insignis, ante ducentesimum annum facta, equites ostendens in eo ponte praelium committentes.'

Biondo, 1531, p. 167. Cf. Sanudo, *Vite*, 1900 edn, p. 108 n. 8.

LITERATURE: Cecchetti, 1885, pp. 29–30; Cessi, 1934, pp. 64–70; Schulz, 1978, p. 450. See also Cat. IX.

IV. Great Council Hall, Ducal Palace

Story of Alexander III (lost) c. 1365–1419

Plates 18, 19, 55, 56

HISTORY: In December 1340 the decision was made to construct a new Great Council Hall (Lorenzi, 1868, nos. 79–80). The *serrata* of 1297, while closing the Great Council to new families, had had the effect of enlarging it as well, for all the male members of patrician families were now eligible to enter it upon reaching the prescribed age. The Council, which had numbered only 317 in 1264, grew to 900 in 1310 and reached 1017 by 1340. Thus the hall which had been completed in 1309 to accommodate the initial expansion in membership was no longer adequate (Wickhoff, 1883, pp. 4–5).

With delays from the Black Death of 1348–49, the basic structure was probably completed shortly after 25 Dec. 1362 (ibid.; and Lorenzi, 1868, no. 103). In its finished state c. 1419, it had a ship's-keel ceiling of wood (cf. Palazzo della Ragione, Padua) which remained until the fire of 1577 (ibid., no. 842). There were two doors, one at each end of the east wall. Illumination was provided by a balcony opening (made in 1400–4) and six large *trifore*, four in the south wall and two in the west wall. The north wall was unbroken by doors and windows in the lower zone. There were also 13 small windows in three walls of the clerestory zone: 5 ogival-shaped in the north wall and the remainder circular, 3 and 5 respectively, in the west and south walls (now concealed by the dropped ceiling). The surviving *trifore* retain the original form, but without the gothic tracery (Howard, 1980, p. 83).

The painting of the walls with frescoes must have begun around 1365. The final program consisted of three basic elements: 1. the *Paradise* on the east wall, painted by Guariento; 2. a row of Doges' portraits in lunettes above a cornice around the upper zone of the walls (Lorenzetti, 1933, pp. 387–98; and Romanelli, 1982, pp. 125–45); 3. the *Story of Alexander III* in 22 scenes beneath the portraits. The *Paradise* is dated by its inscription to 1365–68 (doc. 1), with Guariento documented in Venice in March 1366 (Flores d'Arcais, 1974, p. 82). By December 1366, at least part of the Doges' portraits were completed, for that of Doge Marin Falier, executed for treason, was ordered to be painted over at that time as a *damnatio memoriae* (Lorenzi, 1868, no. 104). Guariento was back in Padua by December 1367 (Flores d'Arcais, 1974, p. 82). By 22 Sept. 1370 he had died, when a dispute over payment between his heirs and the Signoria of Venice was resolved (doc. 2).

Aside from the *Battle of Spoleto*, assigned to Guariento by Sansovino (doc. 11), the extent of the painter's further activity in the room can only be hypothesized. Wickhoff (1883, pp. 17–19) assumed that the frescoes on the east and south walls of the Great Council Hall were completed by 1382, when measures were taken to preserve 'so much solemn work' from destruction (doc. 3). He proposed that Guariento would have been reponsible for the entire south wall, and, giving credence to Vasari's (1568, 1966 edn, p. 431) claim that Antonio Veneziano painted in the room, suggested that the latter was entrusted with the shorter west wall. Degenhart and Schmitt (1980, II-1, pp. 117–24, and II-3, Cats. 647–649), proposing that three surviving drawings can be identified as details of the Trecento composition, suggested the participation of Nicoletto Semitecolo and Lorenzo Veneziano.

In 1400–04 the balcony, designed by Piero Paolo dalle Masegne, was added to the south wall (Lorenzi, 1868, no. 126). The painting campaign was again under way in 1409, with the work lasting c. 6–10 years (docs. 5–8). It was during this period that Gentile da Fabriano and Pisanello would have painted in the room (Paccagnani, 1971, pp. 128–40; and Christiansen, 1982, pp. 138–39). Venetian artists may have worked there as well. The fact that only painters from outside Venice are mentioned in the sources suggests that local artists were simply not as newsworthy (cf. Pesaro, 1978, pp. 44–56; and Christiansen, 1987, pp. 166–68). The ceiling was also finished during this period. Sansovino wrote that during the term of Doge Michele Steno (1400–13) the wooden ceiling (*cielo*) was divided into squares, covered with gold and adorned with stars (doc. 11).

A new staircase followed in 1415 (doc. 6).

Finally, in 1419, the Great Council met in the new hall for the first time (Lorenzi, 1868, no. 148[a]), but already in 1422 the frescoes were in need of restoration and a conservator was appointed (doc. 7). The room was officially inaugurated on 23 April 1423, when Francesco Foscari made his first public appearance as Doge (Sanudo, *Vite*, 1733 edn, col. 968).

Although Michele da Savonarola saw the room in the 1440's and praised it with superlatives (doc. 11), the frescoes continued to decay. By the 1450s Gentile da Fabriano's *Battle of Salvore* was in a ruined condition (doc. 12). It was with his fresco that Gentile Bellini began the new restoration campaign of 1474 (see Cat. XIII, doc. 3a).

DOCUMENTS AND SOURCES:

1. 1365–68. An inscription on Guariento's Paradiso dates it to the dogate of Marco Cornaro: MARCUS CORNARIUS DUX ET MILES FECIT FIERI HOC OPUS.

Flores d' Arcais, 1974, p. 73.

2. 22 Sept. 1370: A lawsuit is resolved between the heirs of Guariento and the Venetian government over payment to two of his assistants, Vittore dall'Oro and Pietro Fisica. The document states that Guariento was employed for two years at a cost of 300 ducats per annum.

ASV, Cassiere della Bolla Ducale, Grazie del Maggior Consiglio, Reg. 15?, no. antico 13, c. 117. From Cecchetti, 1885, pp. 78–80, who summarizes the case. The relevent *registro* is presently missing from the shelf in the Archivio.

3. 10 July 1382. Funds are appropriated and the Procurators of San Marco are ordered to take steps to preserve the works already painted in the Great Council Hall: '. . . quod faciant haberi curam et diligentiam bonam Sallae Nove Maioris Consilij et locorum spectantium ad dictam Sallam, Ne tam solennissimum opus devastetur in picturis vel aliis rebus. . .'

ASV, Maggior Consiglio, Deliberazioni, Novella 1330–84, Reg. 19, c. 189v (new num.). Cf. Lorenzi, no. 107.

4. 25 May 1409. Many of the paintings are already damaged and need restoration: 'Quia Sala nostri Maioris Consilij superior multum destruitur in picturis. . . .' An appropriation is made of a maximum of 200 ducats: '. . . quod dictas picturas faciant reaptari. . .'

ASV, Maggior Consiglio, Deliberazioni, Leona, 1384–1415, c. 186v (new num.). Cf. Lorenzi, no. 137.

5. 19 April 1411. A further appropriation of 20 lire de grossi (200 ducats) is made for the restoration of the paintings.

ASV, Maggior Consiglio, Deliberazioni, Leona, 1384–1415, c. 210v (new num.). Cf. Lorenzi, no. 140. Cecchetti, 1885, p. 78, states incorrectly that this sum is for the restoration of paintings in the Church of S. Nicolò.

6. 21 Sept. 1415: The decoration of the Great Council Hall must now be nearing completion for it is already a special attraction for important visitors: 'Et hoc patet quum omnes dominj ac notabiles persone proficiscentes ad terram nostram desiderant illam summe videre propter ipsius maxime pulcritudinis famam et pro tam excellenti opere quod fit modo.'

ASV, Maggior Consiglio, Deliberazioni, Ursa, 1415–1451, c. 13 (new num.). Cf. Lorenzi, no. 145.

7. 9 July 1422. The paintings in the hall are already deteriorating, and 'unum sufficientem et aptum magistrum pictorem' is to be appointed at a salary of 100 ducates per year to keep them in good repair: '. . . pro laudabili et perpetua fama tanti solenissimi operis, et pro honore nostris dominij et civitatis nostre . . .'

ASV, Senato, Misti, 1422, reg. 54, c. 39. From Lorenzi, no. 148.

8. 1425 m.v. By public decree, the inscriptions accompanying the paintings are copied into the Commemoriali: 'Verba descripta in capitellis picturarum historie depicte in sala magna maioris consilii.'

ASV, Commemoriai, Reg. 11 (1418–27). cc. 111v–113v (new num.). Cf. Sanudo, *Vite*, 1900 edn, pp. 340–59; and Lorenzi, 1868, doc. 153. See below.

9. c. 1445: Michele da Savonarola describes the hall: 'Guarientus autem magnificum, stupendum, superbumque nimis serenissimi dominii Veneti pretorium, quod Sala Maior nominatur, digitis propriis miro cum artificio depinxit, illudque mirum, in modum ornavit. Cuius intuitus tanta cum aviditate expectatur, ut cum adest solempnis Ascensionis dies, quo omnibus ingressus licet, nulla supersit diei hora, qua locus innumerabili diversarum patriarum hominum copia non repleatur, tantusque est earum admirandarum figurarum iucundus aspectus, et tanti depicti conflictus admiranda res, ut nemo exitam querat.'

Savonarola, 1902 edn, p. 44.

10. 1456: Bartolomeo Facio records two paintings in the room by Gentile da Fabriano and Pisanello.

Gentile da Fabriano: 'Pinxit et Venetiis in palatio terrestre proelium contra Federici Imperatoris filium a venetis pro summo Pontifice susceptum gestumque. quod tamen parietis vitio pene totum excidit.'

Pisanello: 'Pinxit venetiis in palatio Federicum Barbarussam Romanorum Imperatorem et eiusdem filium supplicem, magnumque ibidem comitem coetum germani corporis cultu. orisque habitu sacerdotem digitis os distorquentem. et ob id ridentes pueros tanta suavitate. ut ascipientes ad hilaritatem excitent.'

Bartolomeo Facio, *De viris illustribus*, Florence 1745 edn. For Engl. transl. see Baxandall, 1964, pp. 101 and 105.

11. 1581. Sansovino writes: 'Di quindi scendendo si penetra nella Sala del Gran Consiglio, cominciata dopò l' anno 1309. & finita l'anno 1423. Fu la prima volta dipinta à verde di chiaro, e di scuro; e la seconda fu rifatta di diversi colori, & il primo, che vi colorisse fu il Guariento, il quale, l'anno 1365. vi fece il Paradiso in testa della Sala. Vi laborò anco alcuni altri quadri, fra quali vno fu quello della guerra di Spoleti vltimamente ricoperto da Titiano. Et l'an. poi 1400. vi si fece il cielo compartito à quadretti d'oro, ripieni di stelle, ch'era la insegna del Doge Steno.'

Sansovino, 1581, c. 123v. Further references to the cycle of 1365 are found in the passage that followed (See IV.13 and IV.16).

Sansovino's confusing statement regarding two painting campaigns, the first in chiaroscuro and the second in color, has brought forth various interpretations: that the room was painted first by other artists in green *chiaroscuro*, to be followed by Guariento who painted in color (Ridolfi, 1914 edn, I, p. 32; and Cavalcaselle , 1887, pp. 192 ff); that Guariento painted both phases himself, first in *chiaroscuro* fresco and later with color *a secco* to cover it (Moschetti, 1904, p. 396); or that Guariento painted only the *Paradise* in color, with the *istorie* on the side walls painted in *chiaroscuro*. (Flores d'Arcais, 1974, p. 73). But Wolters (1983, p. 17), proposing that Sansovino was referring to two entirely different rooms, offers the most potentially satisfactory solution: that the earlier Great Council Hall of 1309 was painted in *chiaroscuro*, with the new hall of 1340 painted in color by Guariento. However, no frescoes are documented in the earlier hall.

ORIGINAL ARRANGEMENT: The wall measurements of the Great Council Hall of 1365, rebuilt on the same plan after the fire of 1577, were virtually the same as those of the existing room today (in meters): 52.7L × 24.65W × 11.5H. The wall openings would have been the same, with the exception of the north wall which did not originally have doors and windows (see Cat. XIII for their construction).

The subject matter and arrangement of the narrative frescoes of the 1365 campaign must be deduced from the inscriptions recorded in the Commemoriali in 1425 (doc. 8) and from Sansovino's later description of the 1474 cycle. There is an apparent discrepancy between the two which up to this time has not been satisfactorily explained. The correct interpretation of the word *capitello* is crucial for a reconstruction of the cycle.

One key seems to be offered in the passage of the Commemoriali which begins the description of the north wall: 'In primo angulo qui firmat versus curias Palatii scriptum est ita in uno capitello sive columna, videlicet . . .' (Sanudo, *Vite*, 1900 edn, p. 350). From this we learn that a *capitello* was some kind of column with writing inside it and that here it was in a corner (cf. Pignatti, 1972, p. 279, who suggested that the scenes might have been framed by small gothic arches on slender columns, but did not deal with the inscriptions). The word implies an inscription field in a vertical shape. Such a field was used by Tomaso da Modena in frescoes for the chapterhouse of S. Nicolò in nearby Treviso, completed in 1352. A row of Dominican saints in their studies was painted around the upper zone of the chapter-house, and each was preceded by a white column-like vertical strip, on which was written in dark letters his name and details of his scholarly and religious achievements. The highly abbreviated Latin script was written in short horizontal lines down the length of the field, like a newspaper column. If the *capitelli* were vertical columns, they could have framed the Council Hall frescoes in a similar manner. As 'chapter headings' or post-scripts, they would have enriched the narrative and provided continuity between the scenes.

Although the Commemoriali placed most of the inscriptions inside these *capitelli*, it located several others in painting fields outside them. There were 28 *capitelli* in all: 11 on the south wall, 4 on the west and 13 on the north. Sansovino, however, listed quite distinctly only 22 scenes. The sources offer no evidence that the number of scenes was reduced in the repainting of the cycle begun in 1474, for the earlier frescoes seem to have been replaced on a one-to-one basis (but cf. Wolters, cited below). We must also bear in mind that the entry in the Commemoriali appears to record an earlier written record and is not based entirely on direct visual observation of the existing frescoes (Monticolo, in Sanudo, *Vite*, 1900 edn, p. 342 n. 1).

The larger number of *capitelli* in relation to narrative scenes on the south and west walls could be accounted for by the door and window openings which could have been flanked by *capitelli*. This reading is not without its problems, but it comes closer to the actual language of the Commemoriali than other solutions. Cf., for example, Wickhoff (1883, pp. 13–15) who understood *capitelli* to denote small compartments (presumably horizontal in shape) for inscriptions that were painted in frieze-form within the larger fields; and Wolters (1983, p. 168) who took a *capitello* to be an entire painting field. He proposed that the 11 *capitelli* on the six available spaces of the south wall could be accounted for by two registers of narrative scenes, with the exception of the first scene which took up an entire field. But the text of the Commemoriali does not support such a reconstruction. It should be pointed out that additional subsidiary episodes may have been painted in the fields above the windows on the south wall, and that Sansovino did not designate them separately. Perugino's contract in 1494 (Cat. XIII, doc. 10) suggests that this was the case. In any event, the narrative sequence began at the east end of the south wall and continued clockwise around the room.

The Great Council Hall in 1425:

EAST WALL:
Guariento
Paradise, flanked by the *Angel Gabriel and Virgin Annunciate* fresco, about 800 × 2465 cm Plate 18
Inscriptions: see doc. 1; and a second inscription, below the throne (now illegible): "L'Amor che mosse già l'eterno Padre / Per Figlia haver de sua deità trina / Costei che fu del Suo figliuol poi madre / De l'universo qui la fa Regina" (Sansovino, 1581, c. 124)

Guariento's fresco was discovered in 1903 when Tintoretto's canvas was removed for repairs to the wall. The fresco was detached at that time and cut into pieces. Most of these were preserved and are now installed in the Ducal Palace in a room to the east of the Great Council Hall (Moschetti, 1904, pp. 394–97).

There was a door at each end of the wall. Sansovino (1581, c. 124) also reported a fresco of the Holy Hermits, Anthony and Paul, painted in the lunette above the door on the right (south) end, but it is not known when this was painted (it was there in 1524: Lorenzi, doc. 386). Ridolfi (1648, p. 17) claimed that it too was painted by Guariento.

LIT.: Zanotto, 1853, p. 64; A. Schiavon, 'Guariento, pittore padovano del sec. XIV', *Archivio Veneto*, 35, 1888, pp. 317ff; F. Saxl, 'Petrarch in Venice' (1935), in *Lectures*, London, 1957, I, pp. 139ff.; Muraro, 1960, pp. 51–52; Sinding Larsen, 1974, pp. 45–56; Schulz, 1980, p. 120; Sinding-Larsen, 1980, pp. 40–49; Wolters, 1983, 290–92; Goffen, 1986, pp. 143–44.

The Story of Alexander III
In the list that follows, the subjects of the scenes are drawn from Sansovino's account and matched to the inscriptions of the Commemoriali (doc. 8; cf. Monticolo in Sanudo, *Vite*, 1900 edn, pp. 340–59, whose own correspondences between the two texts are similar to those offered here). In some cases, the precise order of *capitello* and painted narrative scene is not clear. To avoid confusion, the *capitelli* are listed *beneath* the related pictorial representation, although they may well have preceded it in the actual frescoes.

SOUTH WALL (toward the lagoon and the Isola di San Giorgio):

1. *Coronation of Frederick Barbarossa by Pope Hadrian IV in St. Peter's in 1162.*

Capitello 1 (*in angulo*): 'Anno Domini Mclxij Fredericus barbarossa coronatur imperator Romanorum in eclesia sancti Petri a papa Adriano IIII natione anglico.'

2. *Attack by armed Romans on the Emperor's troops near the Castel Sant' Angelo.*

Capitello 2: no inscription.

After the *capitello*, in two spaces beneath the attack at Rome, are two inscriptions above the lower border (*frisium*). In the first space: 'Cum imperator ad pratum Neronis ubi stabat exivisset, Romani armata manu familiam eius in porta Sancti Angeli crudeliter invaserunt usque ad tentorium imperatoris.' In the second: 'Clamore invalesente inflamati theotonici Romanos turpiter reppulerunt, adeo quod prostratis multis et captivatis, vix ad preces papae captivi sunt restituti.'

Related drawing?: Anon, London, British Museum, Sloane Coll. 5226. 57r [Plate 19]
LIT.: Wolters, 1983, p. 169; and references in IV.16.

Capitello 3: no inscription.

3. *Acknowledgement of Victor IV, the schismatic Pope, by Barbarossa in Pavia.*

Capitello 4: 'Vicit quatuor scismaticos, Victorem scilicet Pasqualem Calixtum Inocentium quorum tres fecit presbiteros cardinales, quarto autem magnam dignitatem contulit et honorem.'

Capitello 5: 'Tres cardinales predicti, velut colubri in gremio nutriti,-seminaverunt discordiam et ingentia scandala inter papam et Imperatorem; tandem excomunicati mala morte perierunt.'

4. *The excommunication of Barbarossa by Alexander III.*

Capitello 6: 'Orta gravi discordia papa processit spiritualiter et temporaliter contra Imperatorem.'

Capitello 7: 'Imperator indignatus statuit ne ulla tellus vel princeps sustineat papam.'

Guariento

5. *Battle of Spoleto.* The city, faithful to Pope Alexander III, is destroyed by the Emperor.

Capitello 8: 'Urbs Spoletana que sola pape favebat, obsessa et victa ab Imperator deletur'.

Capitello 9: 'Papa non confidens de viribus Urbis, metu Imperatoris clam et habitu incognito ivit ad regem Francie.'

LIT.: Sansovino (doc. 13); see also Muraro, 1960, p. 52; and Flores d'Arcais, 1974, pp. 39–41 and 72–73).

6. *Alexander III with the King of France, who has decided to support him and is making preparations for his defense.*

Capitello 10: 'Fredericus Imperator intelligens papam esse et publice tenere curiam in regno Francie, indignatus contra regem Francorum, misit ad eum per epistolas et legatos ut pontificem sibi mittat vel eum pellat e regno, alioquim se paret ad arma.'

On a letter held by the Chancellor of the King: 'Fredericus divina favente clementia Romanorum Imperator semper augustus.'

In a space beneath the Pope and the King: 'Inclitus rex elegit potius bellum pro defensione pape. Ergo utrinque arma parantur, Congregat Imperator Boemos, Dacos, Gotosque et omnes Alemanie populos cum magna parte Italie. Regi Francie favent Anglici, Britani, Flandrenses, Burgondienses et Vascones.'

7. *The Pope flees incognito to Venice.*

Capitello 11: 'Papa nolens esse causa cedis tot milium christianorum, more humilis Sacerdotis incognitus se transtulit ad liberam Venetiarum urbem anno Domini Mclxxvij.'

WEST WALL (toward the Piazzetta):

8. *Doge Sebastiano Ziani greets Pope Alexander III at S. M. della Carità in Venice.*

Capitello 1 (*in angulo*): 'Prima nocte declinavit apud canonicos Sancti Salvatoris qui duxerunt eum ad monasterium sancte Marie de caritate. Ibique in forma incognita, humiliter serviebat: et postquam fuit cognitus' ipsam eclesiam cum maxima venia dedicavit.

On four lines in the painting field outside the *capitello*: 'Quidam peregrinus nutu dei ex voto venerat Venetias, qui dum visitaret eclesiam suprascriptam sancte Marie de caritate, cognovit papam. Notificat Illustri domino Sebastiano Ziani tunc inclito Venetiarum duci qualiter summus pontifex est in tali eclexia.'

On another four lines outside the *capitello*: 'Dux, Consiliarii, nobiles et tota Venetiarum civitas, similiter patriarcha Gradensis et episcopus Castellanus cum toto clero perveniunt cum crucibus ad dominum papam dubitantem de tanto concursu. Devotissimus dux genibus flexis dedit oscula ad beatissimos pedes presentans clamidem, mitram et ornamenta pedum et confortans ut metu deposito assumat animum et pontificalia ornamenta, quia est in urbe tutissima, libera ac potenti.'

Capitello 2: 'Papa amplius se celare non valens ac considerans fervorem fidei et promptitudinem devotionis Venetorum suam benedictionem contulit domino duci et toti patrie.'

Between the two trifore, a relief sculpture of the Lion of St. Mark (see Cat. XIII).

9. *The Presentation of the white candle to the Doge.*

Capitello 3 (already illegible in 1425): 'Dux universo populo comitante ad altare ecclesie sancti Marci papam cum cantibus et devotione perducit, ubi personam facultatem Magnitudinem civitatis et totam comunitatem in protectionem suam et ecclesie contra quoslibet offert ei.'

Capitello 4 (also illegible in 1425): 'Papa presentat duci cereum album quo ipse et ducantes post eum perpetuo in suis processionibus uterentur.'

Painted by Guariento, according to Muraro, 1960, p. 52; and Flores d'Arcais, 1974, p. 78).

NORTH WALL (toward the courtyard of the Ducal Palace):

10. *The departure of the Venetian ambassadors to the court of the Emperor.*

Capitello 1 (*in angulo*): 'Pro pace tractanda mittuntur ad Imperatorem tunc in Apulia residentem solemnes Ambassiatores, cum literis ducalibus quas papa mandat per ducem muniri bulla plumbea cum figura sancti Marci atque ducis.'

11. *The ambassadors plead the Pope's case before the Emperor.*

Capitello 2: 'Imperator primo Ambassiatores letanter recepit, sed audito quod venerant ad tractandum pacem, rigide respondit quod papam fugitivum sibi tradant, et nolint facere guerram alienam suam nec sustinere quem totus mundus sequitur, alioquin parent se ad bellum.'

On the opened ducal letters in the hand of the chancellor of the Emperor: 'Serenissimo et excellentissimo domino Frederico divina favente clementia Romanorum Imperatori semper augusto Sebastianus Ziani dei gratia dux Venetiarum.'

12. *The consignment of the sword to the Doge.*

Capitello 3: 'Legati referunt pape et duci rigidum imperatoris responsum Papa plurimum expavit. Sed benignissimus dux ipsum hortatur dicens quod ob reverentiam fidei catolice et sancte matris ecclesie viriliter defendetur.'

Capitello 4: 'Inclito duce et Venetis paratis cum triginta galeis armatis ex devotione absque stipendio, Papa eos hortatur quod viriliter vadant ad pugnandum pro fide deditque ensem duci et successoribus suis in signum perpetue iusticie, et indulsit omnibus ad pugnam euntibus plenissimam veniam.'

Gentile da Fabriano

13. *Battle of Salvore.* The Venetian navy, commanded by Doge Ziani, overcomes the imperial forces led by Otto, son of the Emperor, off the coast of Istria.

Capitello 5: 'Annuntiato quod hostes cum LXXV galeis, quarum est capitaneus Otto filius Imperatoris, iam pervenerat ad pontam Salbloie in finibus Istrie, strenuus dux dat prudentissimum et cautum ordinem, ad pugnam dicens: sequimini, me quia primus experiar hunc ensem in hostes.'

After the *capitello*, four lines written beneath the sea battle and above the picture border: 'Pugnant viriliter partes, tandem clarissimus dux et probissimi Veneti Deo assistente obtinent victoriam, et triunphum capto Ottone filio imperatoris, et omnibus galeis imperialibus devictis et positis in conflictum, de quibus Lx capte fuerunt, reliquis consumptis unda vel igne, exceptis paucis que rapuerunt fugam.'

Attrib. Facio (doc. 10); and Sansovino (1581, c. 1245): 'Il quadro del conflitto navale, fu ricoperto da Gentile da Fabriano Pittore di tanta riputatione, che havendo di provisione un ducato il giorno, vestiva à maniche aperte.' See Christiansen, 1982, pp. 10–11 and 138–139.

14. *The presentation of the ring to the Doge.*

Capitello 6: 'Papa ducem cum tanta victoria redeuntem letanter suscepit dicens: bene venerit verus dominus salsi maris. ac donans sibi anulum, cum quo tunc et singulis annis mare sponsatur in signum veri perpetuique dominii.'

Between the 6th and 7th *capitello*, under the feet of the Pope, in two lines: 'Dux autem magno pro munere summo pontifici Ottonem Imperatoris filium consignavit.'

15. *Otto is released to treat for peace with Barbarossa.*

Capitello 7: 'Otto Imperatoris filius divina inspiratione offert se procuraturum bonam pacem inter papam et ducem ex una parte et Imperatorem ex altera. Idcirco permittitur abire sub fide.'

Related drawing: Pisanello, Paris, Louvre, Codex Vallardi, N. 2432r [Plate 56]

Pisanello

16. *Otto before the Emperor*

Capitello 8: 'Imperator viso filio valde letatur, sed pacem omnino recusat; longa disceptatione habita inter eos, tandem considerata filiali constantia dat pater filio potestatem tractande pacis.'

Attrib. Facio (doc. 12). Cf. Sansovino (1581, c. 124): 'Conciosia che il quadro dove Othone liberato dalla Repub. s'appresentana [sic] al Padre, essendo prima stato dipinto dal Pisanello, con diversi ritratti, fra quali era quello d'Andrea Vendramino, che fu il più bel giovane di Venetia à suoi tempi, fu ricoperto da Luigi Vivarino.'

Related drawing: Veronese school, copy after Pisanello, London, British Museum, Sloane 5226, 57v [Plate 55].

LIT.: Degenhart, 1941, pp. 28–30; Paccagnini, 1972, pp. 128–40; Degenhart and Schmitt, 1980, pp. 120ff.

17. *The Emperor humbles himself before the Pope at the entrance to the Basilica of San Marco.*

Capitello 9: 'Imperator Ottoque accesserunt Venetias cum galeis pro conclusione pacis. Filius applicuit in vigilia Ascensionis dominice. Pater vero mane sequenti, die Ascensionis firmata fuit pax.'

After the 9th *capitello*, on five lines beneath the feet of the pope, and above the border of the painting: 'Stans enim papa ad introitum eclesie beati Marci tetigit pede colla flexa Imperatoris dicens illud davidicum: Super aspidem et basiliscum ambulabo, et conculcabo ora leonis et draconis, cui imperator: non tibi sed Petro. Replicat papa: et michi et Petro.'

18. *Mass is celebrated in San Marco.*

Capitello 10: 'Pape in eclesia sancti Marci missam celebravit. Indulsitque perpetuo singulis annis veniam plenissimam pene et culpe a vespere vigile Ascensionis usque ad vesper ipsius Ascensionis; per Octavam autem remittitur septima pars scelerum.'

On an apostolic bull, held by the Pope: 'Alexander episcopus servus servorum Dei universis Christi fidelibus presentes literas inspecturis salutem et apostolicam benedictionem.'

On three lines under the feet of the Pope and above the border of the painting: 'Summus pontifex egit gratias duci et Venetis de tot benefitiis perpetuo memorandis. Post hec parate sunt Venetiis decem galee, cum quibus Imperator et dux sociant papam ad suam Romanam sedem.'

19. *The consignment of the umbrella to the Doge in Ancona.*

Capitello 11: 'Dum applicarent ad civitaten Anchone occurrerunt eisdem Anchonitani cum duabus umbrellis, una pro papa, altera pro Imperatore, papa mandat ut tercia umbrella portetur pro duce, conferens ipsam sibi et successoribus perpetuo deferendam.'

20. *The entry into Rome of the Pope, the Doge and the Emperor.*

Capitello 12: 'Deinde papa imperator et dux Romam solemnissimo proficiscuntur equitatu, quibus applicantibus occurrunt in maxima devotione et leticia primo cardinales cum toto clero, secundo principes et nobiles Romani. Tercio universa turba.'

21. *The presentation of the eight standards and the trumpets to the Doge.*

After the 12th *capitello*, under the feet of the Pope, above the border of the painting: 'Romani obtulerunt pape octo pulcerima vexilla sirica varii coloris ac totidem tubas argenteas, que quidem vexilla et tubas papa duci donavit, quibus ipse successoresque perpetuis temporibus et solemnitatibus uterentur.'

22. *The presentation of the sedia* (ceremonial throne) *to the Doge in the Lateran Palace.*

Capitello 13: 'Ascenderunt Papa, Imperator et dux in palatium Lateranense, ubi papa in propria sede resedit. Et cum ibi non forent nisi duo troni, unus pro papa, alter pro Imperatore, papa fecit alterum tronum donari duci Venetiarum pro se, et successoribus suis.

LITERATURE: Sansovino 1581, cc. 123v–124; idem, 1663, pp. 324–25; Ridolfi, 1914 edn, pp. 32–33, 40–41; Zanotto, 1858, I, pp. 58–73; Wickhoff, 1883, pp. 17–26; Cecchetti, 1885, pp. 78–80; Berchet, 1899/1900, ii, pp. 949–61; Escher, 1919, pp. 87–125; Bassi and Trincanato, 1960; Bassi, 1962b, pp. 41–46; Bassi, 1964, pp. 181–87; Levi d'Ancona, 1967, pp. 34–44; Trincanato, 1970, pp. 111 ff; Arslan, 1971, pp. 141–54; *Il Palazzo Ducale*, 1971; Pignatti, 1972, pp. 95–112; Huse, 1972, pp. 56–71; Sinding-Larsen, 1974, pp. 45–56 and 65–66; Pincus, 1976, pp. 34–40; Pesaro, 1978, pp. 44–57; Degenhart and Schmitt, 1980, II-1, pp. 117–24, and II-3, cats. 647–649; Howard, 1980, pp. 79–85; Christiansen, 1982, pp. 138–39; Wolters, 1983, pp. 166–69; Brown, 1984, pp. 266–77; Christiansen, 1987, pp. 166–68; and U. Franzoi, T. Pignatti and W. Wolters eds., *Il Palazzo Ducale*, Treviso, 1988 (in press and not seen).

V. Oratorio del Volto Santo (Scuola dei Lucchesi)

Nicoletto Semitecolo

Story of the Volto Santo (lost) 1370

HISTORY: According to early Venetian accounts, about 400 families immigrated to Venice from Lucca between 1309–1317 in response to political upheavals in their own city. Chroniclers (with some exaggeration) credited the new community of Lucchesi with the introduction of silk manufacturing to Venice. In 1360 these immigrants and their descendents, many of them wealthy, founded a confraternity dedicated to the Volto Santo, a highly venerated relic in Lucca. In 1376 they consecrated an oratory adjacent to S. M. dei Servi. It is unclear whether they built the chapel themselves or simply took over a pre-existing building (sometimes called the Cappella del Centurione: Zorzi, 1984, p. 239).

The hall was dominated by a handsome Trecento painted wood altar, recorded by Grevembroch (MCV, Cod. Gradenigo-Dolfin, 208, I, c. 40). Without specifying the medium or number of scenes, Sansovino reported that it was also decorated with the history of the Volto Santo, painted by Nicoletto Semitecolo in 1370 (doc. 2; cf. doc. 1). The paintings were destroyed before 1674, when Boschini observed that 'diverse' paintings of the Volto Santo at the Scuola dei Lucchesi had been painted by Pietro Ricchi to replace those of Nicoletto Semitecolo which had been ruined by age.

The building still stands (2372 S. Fosca) and is now used as an oratory for the Istituto Canal-Marcovich. Paoletti (1893–97, p. 66 n. 2) reported seeing vault frescoes in the late 19th century, so badly overpainted and retouched that their original appearance was virtually effaced. He doubted that they were by Semitecolo.

DOCUMENTS AND SOURCES:

1. 1370. An inscription in the 'Cappella del

Centurione, detta de Lucchesi', at the Church of the Servites: MCCC°LXX . X . DECEMBRIO . NICOLO SEMITECOLO . FECIT HOC OPUS.

Recorded by Cicogna, 1824–27, I, p. 97.

2. 1581. Sansovino writes of the newly prosperous Lucchesi immigrants of the later 14th century: 'I predetti adunque, edificato con X. case per dare a i poveri, il predetto Oratorio, fecero anco un salone per condurvi il Rettore co suoi compagni per governo della fraterna. Et lo fornirono d'argentarie, di paramenti, & d'altre cose necessarie al culto divino. & vi spesero intorno a 22. mila ducati. . . . Et fu dipinta la Historia del Volto Santo, nella fraterna, da Nicoletto Semitecolo l'anno 1370.' According to an inscription on a pilaster, the building was consecrated in 1376.

Sansovino, 1581, c. 58v–59.

LITERATURE: Sansovino, 1663, I, pp. 161–62; Boschini, 1664, p. 467; Boschini, 1674, Cannaregio, p. 48; Cornaro, 1749, 2, pp. 55–57; Cicogna, 1824–27, I, p. 97; Sagredo, 1852, p. 22; Paoletti, 1893–97, p. 66 n. 1; Testi, 1909, I, pp. 152 and 316–17; Muraro, 1960, pp. 56–58; Gramigna and Perissa, 1981, pp. 119–20; Zorzi, 1984, pp. 239–40.

VI. Scuola di San Giovanni Evangelista, Albergo

The Miracles of the True Cross (lost) — After 1414

HISTORY: Founded in 1261 as a flagellant confraternity, the Scuola di San Giovanni Evangelista first met in the Church of San Aponal in the *sestiere* of San Polo. It moved to the nearby Church of San Giovanni Evangelista in 1307, where the members established an altar. In 1340 it obtained the *piano nobile* of a hospice for the aged adjacent to the church maintained by the Badoer family. The group occupied the entire building in July 1414, promising to build a new hospice elsewhere (Sohm, 1982, pp. 72–76). A cycle of miracle paintings was planned in November. The artists, number and media of these works are unknown. In 1416 a new altar of wood with a *pala* was commissioned for the Sala Capitolare (chapter hall), often referred to simply as the Sala, on the *piano nobile* (ibid., doc. 174, p. 316). The major part of the building campaign was probably completed by around 1421 (ibid., p. 76).

Paintings of miracles were mentioned in the Scuola as late as 1484 (doc. 2), although there is no evidence that they were those commissioned in this campaign.

DOCUMENTS AND SOURCES:

1. 4 November 1414: A Chapter General of 40 members votes: 'chel fose li miracolli che per lo tempo pasado e fato la nostra chroxie santa in storiado per muodo che sia noticia de piui devotion de nostri fradelli.' The campaign might have been prompted by the healing in 1414 of the daughter of a member of the Scuola, Ser Nicolo Benvegnudo of San Polo (see MCV, Inc. H222 bis). A new *mazza* (processional standard) for the Cross is also commissioned at this time.

   ASV, S. Giov, Reg. 71, f. 188. Cf. Bernasconi, 1981, p. 202, n. 27. See also ASV, S. Giov., Reg. 2, f. 56; Reg. 38, f. 56; and Reg. 140, f. 70v.

2. 25 March 1484: In a document deeding some land to the Scuola, reference is made to the miracle at the Bridge of San Lorenzo (see Cat. XV.2), adding 'et pene alia inumerabilia miracula publica documenta, et antiqua pittura et historie fraternitatis predicte testantur. Que omnia ad memoriam revocantes et praeterea mentes tenentes qui quicquid hominis et dignitatis quicquid bonorum et facultatum nobis a Domino è collatum.'

   ASV, S. Giov., Reg. 89, ff. 86–86v.

ORIGINAL ARRANGEMENT: Urbani de Gheltof (1895, pp. 9–10) and Wurthmann (1975, p. 142) place the cycle in the *albergo* without giving evidence, but this seems probable, for a separate decoration campaign for the Sala Capitolare was begun in 1421 (see Cat. VII below).

LITERATURE: Cornaro, 1749, 6, pp. 328–77; Cicogna, 1885; Paoletti, 1893, p. 3 n. 3; Urbani de Gheltof, 1895; Lorenzetti, 1929; Wurthmann, 1975, p. 142; Gramigna and Perissa, 1981, pp. 84–89; Bernasconi, 1981, p. 200; Pignatti, 1981, pp. 48–49; Sohm, 1982, pp. 72–76 and 314–15; Zorzi, 1984, pp. 379–82; Pazzi, 1985. See also Cats. VII and XV below.

VII. Scuola di San Giovanni Evangelista, Sala Capitolare

Jacopo Bellini (in part)

Scenes from the Old and New Testaments (lost) — 1421–c.1460s

HISTORY: In 1421 the Scuola Grande di San Giovanni Evangelista voted to continue its decoration campaign (as in Cat. VI) with a narrative cycle of the Old and New Testaments. The paintings were to be placed *atorno atorno* (all the way around) the Sala Capitolare, the large hall used for assemblies of the entire membership (doc. 1). Completion of the altar commissioned for the room in 1416 was also urged at this time. In 1422 a new ceiling was planned at the cost of 500 ducats (Sohm, 1982, p. 76). It was replaced by another one in 1441, in emulation of a 'sofitado meravioso' just completed in the Scuola Grande di San Marco (Paoletti, 1929, p. 16).

Although Sansovino records the existence of the narrative cycle in 1581, and states that Jacopo Bellini was responsible for 'la seconda parte', further documentation on its artists and dates of execution has not been found in Scuola records. The cycle was replaced at the end of the 16th century by a new one depicting events from the life of San Giovanni Evangelista, painted by Domenico Tintoretto, Sante Peranda and Andrea Vicentino (Urbani de Ghelthof, 1895, p. 19; Mason Rinaldi, 1978, pp. 293–301).

DOCUMENTS AND SOURCES:

1. 10 April 1421. By a 48–8 vote, 'iera deliberado de far instoriar la Sala de la nostra chaxa atorno atorno del testamento vechio e nuovo.'

   ASV, S. Giov., Reg. 72, f. 100v. Cf. Reg. 140, ff. 75v–76; Reg. 32, f. 187).

2. 31 Jan. 1465. Jacopo Bellini receives a final payment of 8 ducats for unspecified work 'per resto d'ogni raxon fin questo dì.'

   ASV, S. Giov., Reg. 72, f. 269. This entry may or may not refer to the cycle in the Sala.

3. 1581. Sansovino indicates that the cam-

paign had been completed as planned and implies that it had been carried out in two phases: 'Vi sono medesimamente pitture diverse, della historia del testamento vecchio, & nuovo, con la Passione di Christo, non punto volgari, & la seconda parte di questa opera fu di mano di Iacomo Bellino, che fece anco la seconda parte della Natività.'

Sansovino, 1581, c. 100v.

4. 1648. Relying on accounts of old painters, Ridolfi lists an altarpiece and 17 narrative scenes painted by Jacopo Bellini that were formerly in the Scuola. They are listed below. Ridolfi concludes his account: 'Tali furono le opere da Iacopo dipinte in quella Sala servendogli i figliuoli d'alcuno aiuto; ma già non hebbe parte alcuna ne' quadri de' miracoli della Croce, come vuole il Vasari, che furono dipinti nell'altra Sala per altre mani e da Gentile.'

Ridolfi, 1914 edn, I, pp. 53–54 (Engl. trans. in Molmenti and Ludwig, 1907, p. 3–4).

ORIGINAL ARRANGEMENT: The Sala Capitolare measured (in meters) 27.5 L × 13 W × 7 H in the middle of the 15th century. Later construction added 7m to the length and 4m to the height (Massari, 1971, pp. 48–50). Neither the original disposition of the early paintings in the room nor their subsequent fate is documented. Two areas of controversy concerning them should be noted: the possible survival of some of the works and the relative share of Jacopo Bellini in the execution of the cycle.

In the 19th century, the Venetian artist Natale Schiavone (together with Francesco Cavella) owned eight tempera paintings on canvas depicting scenes from the life of the Virgin, and claimed that they were part of the original cycle of the Scuola di San Giovanni Evangelista. Four of these works are known to survive today: *Annunciation* and *Birth of the Virgin*, Galleria Sabauda, Turin (112 × 152 cm each); and *Marriage of the Virgin* and *Epiphany*, Stanley Moss Coll., New York (111 × 151 cm each). Collins (1982, pp. 466–72) presented an argument in support of Schiavone's claim for an Evangelista provenance. Accepting Longhi's (1946) attribution to Jacopo's sons Gentile and Giovanni, and a dating in the early 1460s, he also offered a reconstruction of their original placement in the Scuola.

His proposal fails to address several key issues. First, we should remember that the New Testament scenes constituted only part – perhaps only one-half – of the full cycle. In his arrangement of the paintings, Collins places nine on each of the long walls of the room (ignoring the fact that Ridolfi listed only 17 paintings). Acknowledging that the horizontal spacing is purely conjectural, he still does not attempt to provide for the inclusion of Old Testament scenes or the Passion of Christ mentioned by Sansovino. Even so, his proposal does not rise or fall on this issue. For 17 canvases of the same dimensions as the paintings in question could easily have been accommodated on one wall, if they were arranged to form a continuous band with only a molding between them, as is typical in the surviving narrative cycles of a later period. There would even have been 2 meters to spare for a doorway. Sansovino must have seen the works in a similar configuration.

But secondly, a more serious problem arises when we compare the surviving paintings to Ridolfi's rather detailed descriptions of the works originally in the Scuola. The Turin *Birth of the Virgin* lacks a writing Joseph: 'In nobile stanza nel primo quadro veniva Maria bambina lavata dall'ostretrici, S. Anna nel letto, e S. Gioachino stavasi scrivendo.' No crowd of exulting angels celebrate the Turin *Annunciation*: 'L'haveva dipoi il saggio Artefice figurata, come fù annunciata da Gabriele, e fattovi sopra numerosa schiera d'Angeletti festeggianti.' Only the Moss *Marriage of the Virgin* fits Ridolfi's specifications without serious discrepancies: 'vedevasi sposata à Gioseppe per mano del sommo Sacerdote, accompagnata da molte Citelle: v'erano giovani ancora con le verghe in mano à canto al Santo Gioseppe.'

Ridolfi did not list the *Epiphany* at all. Collins dismisses the omission as a possible oversight by the critic due to the poor condition of the paintings and the possible vagueness of verbal accounts. Adding that Ridolfi did cite a *Nativity*, he implies (but does not claim) that this might be the Moss *Epiphany*. Ridolfi's description of the *Nativity*, however, again includes celestial elements that are missing in the *Epiphany* and the correspondence of the two works is doubtful: 'E come poi sotto ad humile capanna adorava il nato bambino, & in un raggio di gloria fece le militie de' Beati cantori con brevi in mano, ne' quali era scritto il Gloria in excelsis Deo, ch'era il tenore della loro celeste canzone. Stavasi in un lato Gioseppe, e i due vili animali refocillavano col fiato il lor nato Signore.' In fact, Ridolfi's description conforms rather well to an *Adoration* in Jacopo Bellini's Louvre drawing-book (fol. 31) [Plate 61]. Thus, unless we dismiss Ridolfi's unusually detailed account as a well- embroidered fabrication, we must allow that Collins's reconstruction has such serious drawbacks as to be considered unproven (see also the forceful rejection of the proposal by Meyer zur Capellen, 1985, Cats. C18 and C28).

Although Paoletti (1984, p. 9) proposed that Jacopo Bellini himself began the project in 1421 and was responsible for painting both cycles, this seems unlikely. Aside from Sansovino's reference to his participation only in 'la seconda parte' of the work, the young artist was probably working outside Venice during much of the 1420s (Degenhart and Schmitt, 1984, p. 14; but cf. Testi, II, p. 144; and Joost-Gaugier, 1974, p. 21). Indeed, it is suggestive that Michele Giambono was enrolled as a member of the Scuola in 1422 (ASV, S. Giov., Reg. 72, f. 36), a privilege that was often granted to artists when they began an important commission for a confraternity.

Only on 3 March 1437 was Jacopo himself inscribed as a member, an event that may well have marked his own entry into the decoration campaign (ibid., f. 43v). It is certainly possible that his sons would eventually assist him with it, as Ridolfi later observed. Jacopo served as a *degano* in the Scuola for the *sestiere* of San Marco in 1441 and 1454 (ibid., ff. 57 and 93), and on 25 Feb. 1453, his daughter Nicolosia was given a dowry subvention of 20 ducats for her marriage to artist Andrea Mantegna (ibid., f. 199). Although a payment of 8 ducats made to Jacopo in 1465 (doc. 2) has been understood by some to provide a *terminus ante quem* for the paintings in the Sala Capitolare, it is also possible that it refers to an altar commissioned in 1457 for the *albergo* (see Cat. XV below).

PAINTINGS CITED BY RIDOLFI:

Jacopo Bellini (with sons Gentile and Giovanni)

1. Birth of the Virgin
2. Presentation of the Virgin
3. Betrothal of the Virgin
4. Annunciation
5. Visitation
6. Nativity
7. Presentation of Christ in the Temple
8. Flight into Egypt
9. Domestic scene in Egypt with the Virgin sewing and Joseph working as a Carpenter
10. Return of the Holy Family to Judea
11. Christ among the Doctors
12. Leavetaking of Christ from the Virgin
13. John telling the Virgin of Christ's Arrest
14. Christ carrying the Cross to Calvary
15. Crucifixion
16. Resurrection of Christ, who appears to

the Virgin
17. Assumption of the Virgin
18. Altarpiece

PAINTINGS CITED BY SANSOVINO:
19. Old Testament scenes of an unknown number
20. Passion of Christ

LITERATURE: Sansovino, 1581, c. 100v; Sansovino, 1663, I, p. 284; Ridolfi, 1914 edn, I, pp. 53–54; Paoletti, 1894, I, pp. 6–9; Urbani de Gheltof 1895, pp. 9–10; Testi, 1909, II, pp. 143–44, 163 and 257; Molmenti and Ludwig, 1907, pp. 3–4; Crowe and Cavalcaselle, 1912, p. 112; Collins, 1970, pp. 162–63 and 175–76; Wurthmann, 1975, p. 143; Collins, 1982, pp. 466–72; Meyer zur Capellen, 1985, cats. C18 and C28, pp. 156 and 160). See also Cats. VI and XV.

VIII. Scuola di San Marco, Albergo

Jacopo Bellini

Paintings of unknown subjects (lost) — After 1444

HISTORY: Founded in 1260 as a flagellant confraternity, the Scuola di San Marco first met at the Church of S. Croce di Luprio. In 1437 it leased land from the Dominican friars at the convent of SS. Giovanni e Paolo and began construction of a new meeting-house. The building was completed with great speed, with the Scuola moving in on 25 April 1438: appropriately, the feast-day of St. Mark, patron both of the Scuola and of the Republic itself. Decoration of the meeting-house began immediately with ornate ceilings in the chapter hall and the *albergo*, and proceeded with a painting cycle in the latter room in 1444. Pictorial decoration of the chapter hall was under way by 1463 (see Cat. X), but was still unfinished when the building was destroyed by fire on 1 April 1485. For the decoration and structure of the first meeting-house at SS. Giovanni e Paolo, see Sohm, 1982, pp. 80–97. For the second meeting-house, built after the fire of 1485, see Cat. XIX below.

DOCUMENTS AND SOURCES:
1. 4 October 1444. The Chapter votes 'di far istoriar el nostro albergo dela schola de misser san marcho per lo mior modo li parera, ttuttj fono di questo pare.' The vote was 39–0.
   ASV, Scuola Grande di San Marco, Reg. 16bis, Pt. 2, f. 12. Wurthmann (1975, p. 147) states without substantiation that stories from the Bible or the Life of St. Mark were proposed. Cf. Humfrey, 1985a, p. 237.
2. 15 July 1492: Gentile Bellini offers to make paintings for the rebuilt *albergo* in honor of his father Jacopo, 'dele chui opere avanti lincendio del bruxar de essa schuola in esso Albergo faceva...'
   ASV, San Marco, Reg. 135, no fol. no. Full text in Paoletti, 1894, p. 17. See also Cat. XIX, doc. 1.

LITERATURE: Wurthmann, 1975, pp. 146–47; Puppi and Olivato Puppi, 1977, pp. 196 and 259ff.; Pignatti, 1981, p. 132; Sohm, 1982, pp. 79–97. See also Cats. X and XIX.

IX. Loggia at the Rialto

Battle of Canale Orfano and Rout of Pepin (lost) — About 1459

HISTORY: When the old portico of the *telaruoli* at the Rialto was torn down in 1459, the history paintings on the wall were carefully copied so that they could be painted again on a new loggia for the use of merchants and nobles (doc. 1; cf. Cat. III). Only a few weeks later the Senate changed its plans and called for a different type of structure, replacing a solid back wall with one pierced with windows (ASV, Senato, Terra, Reg. 4, ff. 113v–114: 17 July 1459). Cessi assumed that the painting program was dropped at this time, but Sanudo's entry in the *Vite dei Dogi* and Sansovino's citation of Pietro Dolfin indicate that the scenes were in fact repainted, possibly in another location at the Rialto (docs. 2 and 3). There is no record of the artist, although we may assume that the paintings were frescoes, given their outdoor location. In 1514 the area was swept by a great fire, 'che in poche hore brusò et devorò quasi tuta l'isola di Rialto' (Cessi, doc. 10, p. 322; and Sanudo, *Diarii*, XVII, cols. 458 ff.), and the works were probably destroyed at that time (Cessi, 1934, pp. 86–87).

DOCUMENTS AND SOURCES:
1. 31 May 1459: The Senate orders the old portico housing the *botteghe* of the *telaruoli* that backs on the *pescheria* (fish market) to be torn down. A new larger loggia for the use of merchants and nobles is to be built and repainted with the history paintings that were on the walls of the earlier building: '...prepositum est fieri quedam logia in Rivoalto pro comoditate nobilium civium et mercatorem nostrorum...Quod in muro novo construendo ponantur et pingantur istorie depicte in veteri muro pro ipsius istorie memoria antiquitatis construenda, que antequam ipse murus, in quo picte sunt, diruatur, excipi et accopiari debeant, ut in muro novo ipsemet instaurari et depingi possent: Et similiter reficiatur descriptio Orbis sive Mapamundus qui in medio ipsarum picturarum extare consueverat...'
   ASV, Senato, Terra (1456–61), Reg. 4, c. 109 (new num.). Cf. Cessi, 1934, doc. VI, pp. 317–18; cf. Lorenzi, 1868, no. 183, pp. 81–82).
2. c. 1490s. Sanudo writes in the *Vite dei Dogi* for the year 1459: 'Adi 31 mazo fo preso sgrandir il portego di San Marco e fo refata la storia di Canal orfono et il Mapamondo.'
   BMV, Cod. It. VII 125 (=7460), f. 337v (a late 16th-century copy of Sanudo's manuscript). Cf. Sanudo, *Vitae*, 1733 edn, col. 1167.
3. 1581. Sansovino also indicates that the paintings were actually redone: 'Vi furono anco rifatti i portichi sotto il Doge Foscari, alle spese di Scipion Bono. Et l'anno 1459. sotto Pasqual Malipiero, furono slargati, col rimuovere i telaruoli, & vi fu rifatta, cosi scrive Pietro Delfino, la historia del Canale orfano, (che'era la battaglia, che si hebbe con Pipino, ma in qual parte di Rialto dipinta non lo so) & il Mappamondo. Ultimamente arso Rialto l'anno 1513, fu restaurato di nuovo con le volte di sopra l'anno 1520. sotto il Principe Loredano.'
   Sansovino, 1581, cc. 133v–134.

LITERATURE: Lorenzi, 1868, pp. 81–82, no. 183 (A-B); Monticolo in Sanudo, *Vite*, 1900 edn, p. 108 n. 8; Cessi, 1934, pp. 66–70. See also Cat. III.

X. Scuola Grande di San Marco, Sala Capitolare

Scenes from the Old Testament and the Passion of Christ (lost) c. 1463–85

HISTORY: Soon after beginning the decoration of the *albergo* in its newly completed meeting-house (see Cat. VIII), the Scuola di San Marco commissioned an altar (1445) for the Sala Capitolare (doc. 1 below). By 1463 the confraternity had begun a series of commissions for a cycle of *istorie* in the Sala. Contracts for at least 9 paintings were made with artists over the next 20 years, and the pictorial decoration was probably nearing completion when the building was destroyed by fire on 31 March 1485 (Paoletti, 1929, pp. 122–32; Wurthmann, 1975, pp. 152–57; Pignatti, 1981, p. 132). Sabellico (*De situ*, 1772 edn, col. 13) described the room at that point as 'greatly adorned with gold and noble paintings'.

DOCUMENTS AND SOURCES:

1. 21 Sept. 1445. The Chapter votes 20–19 to have an altar made for the Sala.
   ASV, S. Marco, Reg. 16bis, Pt. 2, f. 12. Cf. Sohm, 1982, doc. 14; see also doc. 3 below.
2. 17 March 1463. The Chapter votes 46–5 to continue the decoration of the Sala already begun, and to commission two or three more paintings of unspecified subjects: '... nui possano dar afar do over tre di queste istorie che achadera luno opiuj maistri quel parera de nuj eser piuj sofezedi...' That commissions for *istorie* had already been made is indicated by a marginal note; 'che poter seguir afar instoriar la sala...'
   ASV, S. Marco, Reg. 16bis, f. 30. See also Sohm, 1982, doc. 17.
3. 13 Apr. 1466. An inventory is made of Scuola possessions. It lists two canvases by Jacopo Bellini: 'Al altar de misier san marcho suxo la salla ne son do teleri compidi per maistro Iacomo belin pentor 1ª palla de l'altar con Misier san Marcho dorado. 1ª cortina azura de tella con san Marco in mezo con 1ª vida d'oro atorno.'
   Also listed are two *teleri* by the hand of *maistro squarzon* [Squarcione], which appear to have been at the head and the foot of the staircase. The subject of one of the canvases painted by Squarcione was the Passion.
   MCV, Mariegola no. 19, f. 9. Cf. Testi, 1909, II, p. 255; and Paoletti, 1894, pp. 9–10.
4. 6 July 1466. The Chapter declares that two *teleri* have already been completed for some time 'a chavo' (at the north or altar end) of the Sala, but that no others have followed. It votes 38–8 to commission three to five more.
   ASV, San Marco, 16bis, Pt. 2, f. 34. Cf. full text in Paoletti, 1894, p. 10.
5. 17 July 1466. Jacopo Bellini is commissioned to paint two *teleri* for a sum of 375 gold ducats: '...de far in la testa de la Schuola varda suxo el champo tuta quela faza nela qual ne entra una pasion de X° in chroxe richa de figure et altro che stia benisimo. Item uno teler dal chanto sopra la porta de lalbergo che prinzipia a mezo el volto e compie fina ala fenestra conzonzerse con l'altro quaro suxo el qual quaro farà la Instoria de Jeruxalem chon X° ej ladronj e sa et qual lavor sia fato si belo e ben fato melio che maj lavor labia fato.'
   ASV, San Marco, 16bis, Pt. 2, f. 35. Cf. full text in Molmenti, 1892, pp. 126–27.
6. 15 Dec. 1466. Gentile Bellini is commissioned to paint two *teleri* with scenes from the life of Moses, for which he will be paid 150 ducats each: 'de far suso uno historia chome faraon esci fuora dela zità chon el so ezerzito e chome el se somerse et in laltro chome el so populo se somerse e chome laltro populo de moise fuzi nel deserto...' He is obligated '...far mior e maior opera over tanta chome quela de so padre mistro Jacomo belin....'
   ASV, San Marco, Reg. 16bis, Part 2, f. 36. Cf. full text in Meyer zur Capellen, 1985, doc. 6, pp. 106–7; and Molmenti, 1892, pp. 128–29).
7. 10 Jan. 1467. Andrea da Murano and Bartolommeo Vivarini are commissioned to paint scenes from the life of Abraham in two fields: 'de depenzer uno teler in do pezi suso j qual de depenzer la jstoria de bramo in zoe una per pezo le qual istorie de esser bone e bele e ben fate chomprexe de tuto chome se rechiede ale dite jstorie e depente de bonj cholorj finj oro azuro oltramarin marizi lacha e verdi e altrj cholorj achadera ale sopra schrite istorie che tutj sia in perfezion...' They are to be paid the same fee that Jacopo Bellini received for some unspecified works of the same size.
   ASV, San Marco, Reg. 16bis, Pt. 2, f. 36. Cf. full text in Paoletti, 1894, p. 10, who transcribed 'buram' for the word that I read as 'bramo', and suggested that the subject of the work related to Burano. His reading has been followed by later scholars. I would interpret the word *bramo* to mean Abramo.
8. 7 Jan. 1469 [= 1470]. By his own request, Lazaro Sebastian [Lazzaro Bastiani] is commissioned by a 12–1 vote of the Banca to paint scenes from the life of David on a canvas in two fields: 'sopra et proximo al volto de la scalla ne li qual el debi depenzer l'instoria de David.' He is to be paid at the same rate by size as Jacopo Bellini, and must submit a drawing of the painting for approval by the Banca before proceeding. Only three of the paintings commissioned since 1463 have been started by this time.
   ASV, San Marco, Reg. 16bis, Pt. 2, f. 38. Cf. full text in Molmenti, 1892, p. 130.
9. 24 Apr. 1470. Giovanni Bellini is commissioned to paint a two-part canvas with scenes from the life of Noah: '...fo deliberato de dar el teller in cavo de la schuola primo verso l'altar grando de campi 2 a ser Zuan bellim nel qual die far el deluvio et larcha de noe...' His pay will be the same as that of his father, Jacopo Bellini.
   ASV, San Marco, Reg. 16bis, Pt. 2, f. 38. Cf. full text in Molmenti, 1892, pp. 129–30.

10a. 15 Aug. 1482. The Guardian is authorized to complete the decoration of the room with the remaining *istorie*.
   ASV, San Marco, Reg. 16bis, Pt. 1, f. 4v.

10b. 23 Feb. 1483. The Chapter orders the Guardian Grande to take steps to assure the completion of all paintings not yet finished. Giovanni Bellini's painting (doc. 9) is perhaps not even begun, for Bartolomeo Montagna is commissioned to paint two *teleri* with scenes from Genesis at a total price of 200 ducats. One subject, the Flood, was previously assigned to Giovanni.
   'Consit chel fosse prexo adi 15 Agosto 1482 de far far e conpir do telerj a Maistro bortolameo montagna depentor e per suo marzede aver dovesse duc. 200...con queste condizion che su luno dovesse far el deluvio con altre zircostanzie de penture che sia al preposito e su l'altro far la creazion del mondo overamente vertir in sul genesis de farli far qualche altra chossa degna e congrua segondo li sara ordenado...'
   ASV, San Marco, Reg. 16bis, Pt. 1, f. 6v. Cf. full text in Paoletti, 1894, pp. 11–12. See also Sohm, 1982, docs. 30 and 32.

ORIGINAL ARRANGEMENT: There is insufficient evidence to propose a reconstruction of the decoration of the Sala, but the documents allow us to make a few observations. The room measured about 44 × 15 meters (Sohm, 1982, p. 89). The altar was placed at the north end of the room and had a *pala* depicting St. Mark, probably with a gold leaf background, painted by Jacopo Bellini.

The same artist also painted the saint on a blue canvas *cortina* (*pala* cover?) with a gold vine leaf border and two *istorie* of unspecified subjects nearby.

Jacopo Bellini's *Passion of Christ* covered the entire south wall at the opposite (facade) end of the room between the windows. Functioning as a prologue to the *Passion* would have been his *Story of Jerusalem* (Road to Calvary), immediately adjacent on the east wall, and extending northward down the wall to the staircase opening. From the available wall space, we may estimate that each work could have measured up to c. 8 meters in width.

Bastiani's *Story of David* would have been on the east wall, adjacent to the *Story of Jerusalem*. It was to be placed above and next to the stairway portal, probably extending toward the north wall. The scenes from Genesis, first commissioned from Giovanni Bellini as a single canvas and then from Montagna as two works, were to hang at the north end of the room right next to the high altar.

The locations of the other canvases were not specified, but they were probably intended to hang between the windows on the west wall (canal side). The disposition of these windows was not discussed by Sohm, but since the early building followed the dimensions of S. M. della Misericordia (Sohm, 1982, p. 89), it may be hypothesized that it also had just four windows in that wall, leaving ample space for *istorie*. Sohm points out that the superimposed orders of pilasters of the post-1485 meeting-house – with their ten closely spaced windows along the canal side to the west – were new in Venice at this later time (ibid., p. 139).

THE SALA CAPITOLARE BEFORE THE FIRE OF 1485:

Jacopo Bellini
1–2. Two canvases of unknown subjects at the altar.
3. *Passion of Christ on the Cross*
4. *Story of Jerusalem with Christ and the Thieves*

The subject of X.4 must have been a Road to Calvary (and not Christ Driving the Money-changers from the Temple, as Wurthmann, 1975, p. 153, suggested). Although it is generally believed that Jacopo's drawings in the Louvre and British Museum albums never found realization in actual paintings, it is suggestive that two consecutive drawings in the Louvre album [fols. 19 and 18] depict these subjects in panoramic scale and composition that match up rather well to the terms of the contract (Plates 21 and 22). This correspondence extends even to the respective titles of the drawings listed in the 15th-century index to the album: 'una passion di Xpo con i ladronj' and 'come Xpo viene messo fuora d'Ierusalem' (Degenhart and Schmitt, 1984, fol. 93).

Gentile Bellini
5. *Life of Moses*: Exodus and Crossing of the Red Sea
6. *Life of Moses*: Israelites in the Desert.
LIT.: Meyer zur Capellen, 1985, cat, B12, pp. 145–46.

Andrea da Murano and Bartolommeo Vivarini
7. *Life of Abraham*, in two fields

Lazzaro Bastiani
8. *Life of David*, in two fields

Bartolomeo Montagna (and Benedetto Diana?)
9. *Life of Noah: the Flood*
10. *Creation of the World* (or a similar subject from Genesis)

Sansovino, 1581, c. 102, wrote that Montagna had begun a painting of Noah's ark, but that Benedetto Diana was completing it when the fire of 1485 destroyed all the contents of the Scuola. Borenius suggested that a drawing of the *Drunkenness of Noah* by Montagna in the Pierpont Morgan Library, N. 1, 56, may be a preparatory sketch for his painting (but cf. Puppi, 1962, II, pp. 31, 42, 76, and 149; and Gilbert, 1967, pp. 185–86).
LIT.: T. Borenius, *I pittori di Vicenza*, Vicenza, 1912, I, p. 7 n. 3.

LITERATURE: Sansovino, 1663, I. pp. 286–87; Molmenti, 1892, pp. 109–36; Paoletti, 1894, pp. 9–12; Testi, 1909, II, p. 255; Paoletti, 1929, pp. 80–82 and 122–32; Wurthmann, 1975, pp. 153–54; Sohm, 1982, pp. 259–63; Meyer zur Capellen, 1985, pp. 145–46. See also Cats. VIII and XIX.

XI. Scuola di San Girolamo

Life of St. Jerome

c.1464–1480s
Plate 23

HISTORY: Founded in 1377, the Scuola di San Girolamo was a typical *scuola di devozione*, drawing its members from both sexes and from most trades and occupations in Venetian society. According to a Mariegola begun in 1504, the primary requirement for membership was a good reputation (doc. 1). The confraternity's meeting-house, now virtually destroyed, was part of the complex of the church of the same name in Cannaregio, in the area near the ghetto. No information regarding its building construction has survived, nor has any documentation concerning the execution of the painting cycle. Although Vasari cited a painting with 'figure piccole, molto lodate', by Giovanni Bellini in the Scuola in his 1550 and 1568 editions of the *Vite* (1966 edn, p. 434), he did not name the subject nor did he describe it as part of a larger cycle. Ridolfi (1648) was the first writer to account for all five canvases that made up the full cycle.

As Humfrey (1985b, pp. 43–44) observes, the chronology appears to be relatively straightforward. The campaign would have begun with the altarpiece (painted by Antonio Vivarini, in Humfrey's view, and not by his son Alvise as the sources imply). It would have been followed by the two canvases by Giovanni Bellini, of which XI.2 was signed and dated 1464 (Martinióni, in Sansovino, 1663, I, p. 176). Then came two works by Bastiani (ascribed to Carpaccio in the early sources), generally dated on the basis of style (credibly so, although a later dating is possible) to the 1470's. Alvise Vivarini's painting (XI.1), known to us only through an engraving, probably completed the cycle in the late 1470s or early 1480s.

In 1771, Zanetti (pp. 37–38 and 48) observed the 'miseri avanzi' of Bellini's paintings, comparing them unfavorably to those of Bastiani (attributed by him to Carpaccio) which were in good condition. Vivarini's was damaged, but still beautiful (ibid., p. 13). Zanetti also spoke of other works by Vivarini in the Scuola (without naming any) which had been dispersed by that time. Bellini's works were no longer mentioned in 1797 (*Pittura veneziana*, II, p. 98). Only Bastiani's works had survived from the cycle when the Scuola was suppressed in 1810. Sent to Vienna in 1838, they were returned to Venice in 1919 and were taken into the Accademia (Moschini Marconi, 1955, p. 52).

DOCUMENTS AND SOURCES:

1. 1504. 'Inventario de tute cosse esser ne la scuola de misser San Jeronimo o nele man deledone i munege dela contrada de san marcuola' [excerpts]:

> Una caxa de muro apresso la giesia de san Jeronimo in la qual havemo la nostra scuola, con una cortexella apresso la ditta scuola.
> La istoria de san ieronimo in giesia [added in different ink:] in teler.
> Una istoria de san ieronimo dentro da la scuola.
> Item uno san ieronimo intaiado e uno san zuane batista e uno santo augustino metudi uno da un ladi e uno da laltro astar suso a laltar da basso in la scuola nostra.
> Item uno teler suso laltar nostro de sora in la chaxa con san ieronimo de pento con san zuane batista da uno ladi da laltro santo augusti.

MCV, Mariegola 113, Scuola di San Girolamo. The singular form of the word *istoria* is sometimes used to refer to an entire cycle and may do so here.

ORIGINAL ARRANGEMENT: Humfrey's analysis is plausible, and it may be summarized as follows. He calculated from a later plan that the meeting-house was a single room. Enclosed by the church on three sides, it measured c. 2.8 × 7 m. An entry door in the center of the fourth wall would have been flanked by a window on each side which provided all the light for the room. The *istorie* were arranged on the other three walls in chronological order according to Jerome's life. Vivarini's *St. Jerome leading the Lion* covered the short wall to the left. Directly ahead, on the long wall facing the entrance, was the altar. It was flanked on the left by Bellini's two canvases, whose horizontal dimensions, taken together, equalled Bastiani's *Last Communion* which was situated to the right. The adjacent short wall on the right would have been covered with Bastiani's *Funeral of St. Jerome*. An ornamental frieze, painted in grisaille, filled the space between the tops of the canvases and the ceiling. In the center of the ceiling was a roundel of God the Father, painted by Alvise Vivarini (credibly dated by Schulz, 1968, pp. 85–86, to the 1490s; cf. Pallucchini, 1962, p. 106: 1470s).

ORIGINAL CYCLE:

Alvise Vivarini
1. *St. Jerome Leading the Lion into the Monastery* (lost)
Ridolfi described monks fleeing in fear and a church situated across a river. According to Boschini, the church was in the distance.
Cf. the engraving of Seroux d'Agincourt (illus. in Humphrey, 1985b, fig. 3); and Bastiani's predella panel of the same subject (Brera, no. 221).
LIT.: Ridolfi, 1914 edn, pp. 36–37; Pallucchini, 1962, p. 132; Steer, 1982, p. 198.

Giovanni Bellini
2. *St. Jerome Discoursing outside the Monastery* (lost)
Ridolfi described the saint sitting next to the wall of the convent with the brothers sitting around him. Above them in a loggia another brother hung out some laundry.
LIT.: Ridolfi, 1914 edn, p. 64; Zanetti, 1771, p. 48.

Giovanni Bellini
3. *St. Jerome in his Study* (lost)
According to Ridolfi, the saint was sitting at a writing desk in his study 'in the act of reading'. The brothers were around him, some studying and others conversing.
LIT.: See no. 2.

Lazzaro Bastiani
4. *Last Communion of St. Jerome*
Oil on canvas, 193 × 241 cm. Probably cut along 3 edges: top, bottom and left (according to Humfrey, 1985b, p. 46, n. 14)
Accademia, Inv. 1021
Restored in 1948–49.
Ascribed to Carpaccio in all the early sources, but convincingly assigned to Bastiani by Paoletti and Ludwig, 1900, pp. 3 ff.
LIT.: Ridolfi, 1914 edn, p. 45; Zanetti, 1771, pp. 37–38; Moschini Marconi, 1955, pp. 52–53; Nepi Scire and Valcanover, 1985, p. 84.

Lazzaro Bastiani
5. *Funeral of St. Jerome*
Oil on canvas, 211 × 264 cm Plate 23
Accademia, Inv. 1004
Restored in 1948–49
Cf. Bastiani's predella panel of the same subject (Brera, no. 221).
LIT.: see no. 4.

Alvise Vivarini (or Antonio?)
6. Altarpiece with five painted panels and a statue
Upper register: Angel Annunciate and Virgin Annunciate flanking the Dead Christ with Nicodemus and the Magdalen
Lower register: St. John the Baptist and St. Augustine flanking a carved figure of St. Jerome
LIT.: Zanetti, 1771, pp. 13–14; Pallucchini, 1962, p. 106; Steer, 1982, p. 175.

LITERATURE: Sansovino, 1663, I, p. 176; Boschini, 1664, pp. 462–64; idem, 1674, Cannaregio, p. 44; Zanetti, 1733, pp. 404–5; idem, 1771, pp. 37–38 and 48; Cicogna, 1824–27, VI, pp. 954–55; Paoletti and Ludwig, 1900, pp. 3ff; Moschini Marconi, 1955, pp. 52–53 (with earlier bibliography); Schulz, 1968, pp. 85–86; Pignatti, 1981, p. 226; Lowry, 1981, pp. 193–218; Steer, 1982, pp. 174–75; Zorzi, 1984, pp. 371–72; Humfrey, 1985b, pp. 41–46.

XII. Sala delle do nape, Ducal Palace

Meeting of Doge Cristoforo Moro and Pope Pius II in Ancona (lost) c. 1464–69

HISTORY: The Sala delle do nape was also called the Sala de l'Audientia. Its vernacular name seems to have been derived from two maps (*do nape* or *nappe*: observed in the room in 1442 by Jacopo d'Albizotto Guidi [Rossi, 1893, p. 415]). Gallo (1943, p. 51 n. 1) cited a tradition stating that these maps dated from the time of Doge Francesco Dandolo (d. 1339). Although Schulz (1978, p. 450, n. 85) points out that the word *nappe* [or *nape*] could also mean 'fireplaces', Sanudo's use of the word *mappe* (doc. 2b) seems to resolve the ambiguity. The room was located in the Doge's palace on the east side of the Ducal Palace complex.

In 1459, the Senate determined that the room was not properly decorated, considering the fact that the Collegio held audiences there: 'non solum personis privatis sed principibus, dominis, prelatis, oratoribus et aliis dignis et honorabilibus personis . . .' Funds were appropriated at that time for a new *soffito* (Lorenzi, 1868, no. 183).

No documents survive relating to commissions for the painting cycle, whose existence is known of only through notices of its destruction by fire in 1483 (doc. 2). It depicted Doge Cristoforo Moro's meeting in Ancona with Pope Pius II in 1464 to launch a crusade against the Turks. For Moro's reluctance to take part in the venture, see Malipiero, 1843 edn, I p. 32; and MCV, Cod. Cicogna 2853/II, 'Cronaca Agostini', ff. 5v–6. Santo Brasca saw the paintings in 1480, providing a *terminus ante quem* for their execution (doc. 1). But it is probable that they were made even before Moro died on 10 Nov. 1471, for he was an unpopular figure. Although a Doge was a symbolic personage and more than the sum of his personal characteristics, it is still improbable that Moro would have been honored after his death. Malipiero (II, p. 663) noted at the time: 'He has died with the worst reputation: sad, hypocritical, vindictive, duplicitous, and avaricious; and he has been badly regarded by the people. In his time the land has always had expense, war and tribulation.'

Gentile Bellini, at least 35 years old when the painting program was begun, is a likely candidate for its execution. His participation in it would help to explain his commission in 1474 to 'renew' the paintings in the Great Council Hall (Cat. XIII).

The fire of 1483 began in the Doge's private chapel adjacent to the apse of San Marco (see Cat. II above) and destroyed much of his palace. Reconstruction began the following year under the supervision of Antonio Rizzo (Lorenzo, 1868, no. 198). Construction continued on the east wing until c. 1550. The equivalent room in the rebuilt palace is called the Sala dello Scudo (Trincanato, 1970, p. 122).

DOCUMENTS AND SOURCES:

1. 1480. Santo Brasca, a Milanese pilgrim on his way to the Holy Land, first describes the Great Council Hall and then writes: 'Descendo per molti gradi glie la Sala de Laudientia: la quale e la piu bella de tuto el palazo . . . Quivi glie depinta historia de Papa Pio quando andoe in Anchona per lexpeditione contra el Turco. Quivi se da laudientia a gli ambasciatori: & a li altri homeni da bene.'

Santo Brasca, 1497, no pag.

2a. 14 Sept. 1483. Malipiero reports the fire: 'La note de 14 Settembrio, se ha impizà fuogho in palazzo del Dose, dalla parte de sora. Era stà lassà acceso el stopin del candeloto della capela de palazzo, dapuo' detta la messa, et era stà apuzà el dopier all'ancona; e la note, 'l fuogo ha dà su le tovaglie dell' altar, e s'impizò. I primi che s'acorse del fuogho, fo quei de casa de Anzolo Trivisan, per mezo 'l palazzo. Se ha brusà la capela, le camere, e la sala dorà delle do nape, dove era depenta l'andata in Ancona del Dose Moro, e 'l so retorno. Se ha anche brusà el Mapamondo con la Italia, fatta de man de Pre Antonio di Leonardi; che era opera singular.'

Malipiero, 1843 edn, II, p. 673. The maps to which he referred were not those in the Sala delle do nape, but in a nearby room. See Gallo, 1943, pp. 48–51.

2b. Sanudo describes the same event: 'Adi 14 septembrio a hore 5 de note se impio fuogo in questa citta nel palazo del doge et comenzo abrusar dala parte dove erra lacapella chel doxe ogni zorno udiva messa causato perche elzago lasso il stupin dilcandeloto acceso credendolo averlo ben stuado, da poi compita lamessa lamatina, ilqual candeloto cazete et impio fuogo e ando brusando siche ala ditta horra dete fuora. Brusoe la sala dele do nape dove si dava audientia el colegio se reduseva atorno di la qual erra depento la istoria quando el doxe domino Christoforo Moro ando in Ancona per andar contra turchi . . .'

BMV, Cod. It. cl. VII, cod. 801 [=7152], Cronaca Veneta (Vite dei Dogi), Part III. From Lorenzi, 1868, no. 198. See also Sanudo, 1829 edn, p. 103.

ORIGINAL ARRANGEMENT: Nothing is known of this cycle except for its subject matter. Sanudo's use of the word *atorno* in doc. 2b to describe its painted decorations suggests wall murals painted around the room on the order of the paintings in the *scuole* or in the Great Council Hall.

LITERATURE: Zanotto, 1858, I, pp. 87–99. Lorenzi, 1868, no. 183; Testi, 1909, I, pp. 102–3; R. Gallo, 'Le mappe geografiche del Palazzo Ducale di Venezia', *Archivio Veneto*, ser. 5, 32–33 (1943): pp. 47–49; Bassi, 1962b, pp. 51–52; Trincanato, 1970, p. 122; Moretti, 1982, pp. 252–53.

XIII. Great Council Hall, Ducal Palace

Story of Alexander III (lost) 1474–1564

Plates 25, 41, 42, 116

In 1474 a complete renewal of the painting cycle in the Great Council Hall was begun, with Gentile Bellini commissioned to begin replacing the damaged frescoes with paintings on canvas (docs. 1a–b). The structure of the hall had remained virtually unchanged since its completion c. 1419 (see Cat. IV above), with the exception of the opening of two doors at the west end of the north wall to lead to the newly constructed Palace of Justice, 1424–c.1440 (Bassi, 1962b, pp. 44–46). The large room adjacent to the Great Council Hall was designated in 1468 as the repository for Bessarion's library and was thus called Sala della Libreria, as well as Sala Nova, in documents of the time (Lorenzi, 1868, nos. 236 A–B–C).

The redecoration campaign of the Great Council Hall proceeded in two phases. The first involved the west and north walls of the room and began with Gentile Bellini's replacement of Gentile da Fabriano's *Battle of Salvore* (docs. 1 and 3a; see Cats. IV.20 and XIII.20). Giovanni Bellini joined the project in 1479, and Alvise Vivarini in 1488 (docs. 2 and 7). In 1494 Pietro Perugino was commissioned to paint the *Battle of Spoleto* on the south wall, but never took up the contract (doc. 10). In 1495, seven painters and two helpers were recorded on the payroll. Gentile Bellini is not among those listed (doc. 11). In 1507, Carpaccio, Vittore Belliniano and a certain Hieronimo were commissioned to assist Giovanni Bellini in completing the canvases left unfinished at the death of Vivarini (doc. 12). In 1513, Titian's offer to replace the *Battle of Spoleto* was accepted, but a dispute over his mode of payment followed over the next three years (docs. 14–16, 20). He was not to complete it until 25 years later. The first phase seems to have terminated with the completion of *The Emperor humbles himself before the Pope* (XIII.17) by Titian in 1523. It is probable that he was given this commission following Giovanni Bellini's death on 29 Nov. 1516 (Wethey, 1975, III, p. 233). Sansovino (1663 edn, I, p. 333) wrote that it was the first painting that Titian made in the room.

In 1524 the *Paradise* was cleaned and restored (Lorenzi, 1868, no. 386). In 1529–32, the two doors leading into the Sala della Libraria were enlarged when it was decided to use the room for purposes other than as the library. After this time it was often referred to in the documents as the Sala del Scrutinio, a name that it retains today (ibid., nos. 405–411, 414, 417, 418). The former Sala del Scrutinio had been located to the east of the Council Hall (see ibid., no. 223).

The second phase began in 1537–38, when Titian finally completed the *Battle of Spoleto* (doc. 24; see also Wethey, 1975, III, pp. 225–32). The replacement of the frescoes on the south wall continued for another 30-odd years and involved the participation of Antonio Pordenone, Jacopo Tintoretto, Paolo Veronese, and Orazio Vecellio (docs. 25–27; Sansovino, 1663, I, pp. 326–28; and Wolters, 1983, pp. 170–73).

In 1552 two windows with small balconies (*pergoli*) were opened in the north wall to provide better ventilation in the warm season. They were considerably smaller than the present windows and did not cut into the painting fields. The *parte* ordering their construction indicates that they should match the height of the doors opening into the Sala del Scrutinio, which extended up to the frieze bordering the lower edge of the paintings: 'non rompendo il muro alto di quanto è la ditta porta della sala nova, cioè, sino alli frisi solamento...' During the cold months, they were to be fully covered with the high-backed wood benches that lined the rest of the wall (Lorenzi, 1868, no. 590). Writing in 1581, Sansovino (1663 edn, p. 325) stated that the Doge's throne, then at the east end of the room beneath the *Paradise*, had formerly been 'nel mezzo, dove sono hora le due finestre che guardano in Corte'. I have not been able to ascertain just when the throne was moved.

On 20 Dec. 1577, the Great Council Hall and the adjacent Sala dello Scrutinio were gutted in a devastating fire, and all the canvases were destroyed (Lorenzi, 1868, no. 842). In 1578, fifteen architects were invited to submit plans for the reconstruction of the room. Following the proposal of the *proto*, Giovanni Antonio Rusconi, it was decided to rebuild the room, following its earlier plan in the essential details (ibid., nos. 849–856 and App. no. 25). The major change was the replacement of the original ship's-keel vaulted ceiling by a flat *soffitto* with carved wood compartments framing paintings of historical and allegorical subjects. The small windows in the clerestory zone were covered over and no longer supplied light to the room, but the *pergoli* in the north wall (along with the doors) were greatly enlarged, cutting significantly into the painting fields.

The *Story of Alexander III* was again repainted, but was greatly abridged (to twelve scenes) and its order reversed. Beginning with the episode of XIII.8 at the east end of the north wall, it now proceeded along that wall from right to left, with a final scene (the equivalent of XIII.22) at the north end of the west wall. The *Fourth Crusade* (1204) was painted in eight scenes. It ran from left to right along the south side of the room, again with the final episode on the west wall (see Bardi, 1587a; Schulz, 1968, pp. 107–11; Franzoi, 1982, pp. 222–61; Wolters, 1983, passim). A single episode from the *War of Chioggia* (1378–81) was painted between the windows on the west wall. The new *Paradise*, painted 1588–94 for the east wall by Jacopo Tintoretto with the help of his son Domenico, Palma il Giovane and numerous assistants, was to conceal Guariento's badly damaged fresco for nearly three centuries (Schulz, 1980, pp. 112–26).

The narrative cycle was painted over a period of nearly a century, and it is not intended in this catalogue entry to provide an exhaustive list of documents and sources pertaining to it. Full documentation will thus be cited only for the first phase of decoration, completed in 1523, with the remainder summarized.

DOCUMENTS AND SOURCES:

1a. 1 Sept. 1474. The Senate votes to commission Gentile Bellini to renew the paintings of the Great Council Hall: 'Havendo bisogno la Sala de gran Conseio per esser gran parte caduca et spegazada le figure de quella de esser reconzade et reparade per honor de la nostra Signoria: Et conzosia che maistro Zintil Bellin pentor egregio et optimo maistro se offerischa et sia contento esser obligato in vita soa reconzar tute dicte figure et penture. Et si al presente chome in futuram tegnirla ben in chonzo senza algun premio, ma che per sustentation sua et premio de tal sua fatica la nostra Signoria li conzieda la prima Sansaria de Fontego che vachera. Et per proveder ala reparation de dicta Sala qual e di principal ornamenti de questa nostra Cita. Et considerate le optime condition del dicto maistro Zintil Venetian nostro fidelissimo: Landara parte, che per auctorita de questo Conseio el sia deputa ala dicta opera del reconzar et reparar le figure et penture dela predicta et refar dove bisognera, et in ogni luogo dove li sera conmesso per i Provededori nostri del Sal, E che dicta Sansaria che prima vachera li sia data et conferita . El qual officio del Sal, per aspetar cussi a quelli, li habia a far la spexa di colori et altre cose necessarie in tal opera.
De parte....126 – De non...6 – Non sincere...2'

ASV, Senato Terra, 1473–1477, reg. 7, c. 50. Cf. Lorenzi, 1868, no. 188; also Meyer zur Capellen, 1985, p. 107.

1b. 21 Sept. 1474. The Great Council confirms the decision of the Senate by a vote of 319–29–21: 'Obtulit se fidelis civis noster venetus Gentilis Bellino pictor egregius instaurare et semper donec vixerit in concio: et bene pictas tenere figuras et picturas huius Sale Maioris Consilij que pro maiori parte sunt caduce, sine aliquo salario: Sed pro suo sustentamento humiliter petiit sibi aliqualiter provideri.... Vadit pars, quod auctoritate istius Consilij dictus Gentilis deputetur ad dictum opus instaurandarum renovandarumque prefate Sale figurarum et picturarum.'

ASV, Maggior Consiglio, Deliberazioni, vol. Regina 1455–79, Reg. 23, c. 144v (new num.). Cf. Lorenzi, 1868, no. 189; also Meyer zur Capellen, 1985, pp. 107–8 (both with an incorrect vote). See also BMV, Cod. Ital. cl. VII, 157 (=7771), Sanudo, 'Somarii di Storia Veneziana', f. 68.

2. 29 Aug. 1479: When Gentile is dispatched to Constantinople to work for Sultan Mehmed II, Giovanni Bellini is appointed by the Great Council to take over the work already begun in the hall. Like Gentile, he will receive the first vacant *sansaria* for compensation. Gentile, however, will retain his own and is expected to resume his labors upon his return to Venice. The vote of the Great Council is 350–11–4.
'Quoniam fidelis civis noster Gentilis Belinus pictor, qui instaurabat figuras, et picturas huius Sale Maioris Consilij, de mandato nostri Dominij proficiscitur Constantinopolim ad serviendum nostro Dominio: Et sit necessarium quia dicta Sala inter cetera huius civitatis nostre ornamenta, est de principalioribus, quod eius instauratio persequatur. Vadit pars, quod auctoritate hujus Consilij, fidelis civis noster Joannes Belinus pictor egregius, deputetur ad dictum opus instaurandum, renovandumque, et teneatur id instaurare atque renovare quando et ubi fuerit opus, ac sibi mandabitur per Provisores nostros Salis: qui sibi providere debeant expensis nostris de coloribus et alijs rebus eidem operi necessarijs. Verum quia omnis mercenarius dignus est mercede sua: Captum sit, quod in premium laborum suorum, prima Sansaria Fontici que vacabit, auctoritate istius Consilij sibi conferatur in vita sua. Quemadmodum factum fuit predicto Gentili: Et si quod Consilium est contra, sit suspensum pro hac vice tantum. Remaneat tamen predicto Gentili officum suum Sansarie, qui cum redierit Venetias sit etiam obligatus predictum opus prosequi.'

ASV, Maggior Consiglio, Deliberazioni, vol. Regina 1455–79, Reg. 23, f. 200 (new num.) Cf. Lorenzi, 1868, nos. 192 and 195; also Meyer zur Capellen, p. 110 (both with an incorrect vote).

3a. After 1479, Malipiero reports on the affair, indicating that the first work to be replaced was Gentile da Fabriano's fresco, the *Battle of Salvore* (Cat. IV. doc. 12): 'E stà principià a restaurar la depentura del conflitto dell'armada della Signoria con quella de Ferigo Barbarossa, in sala del Gran Conseio, perchè la era cascà dal muro, da humidità e da vechiezza. Quei che ha fatto l'opera è Zuane e Zentil Belino, fratelli; i quali ha habù in premio delle so fadighe, due sansarie in fontegho, e ha promesso che la durerà 200 anni: e fazzandosse tal opera, è stà levà l'arma del Dose Contarini, che difese la Terra in la guerra de Zenoesi, e se ha mormorà grandemente: e in Consegio de X è stà preso, che tutte le arme antighe che era in quella sala, avanti che se desse principio a renovar la depentura, sia retornae....'

Malipiero, 1843 edn, II, p. 663.

3b. After 1479. Sanudo records the same events, referring to new paintings in the plural (*quadri*) and comparing Gentile to Giovanni in a negative way: 'Sicché in ditta sala è quadri di tutti doi ma quelli di Zuane è piu belli.'

BMV, Cod. It. cl. VII, no. 125 (=7460), Sanudo, 'Cronica Sanuda,' f. 340v. Cf. Meyer zur Capellen, p. 108, with a good transcription of the full text, but an incorrect citation for the manuscript.

4. 1 July 1480. Giovanni Bellini will be given an allowance of 80 ducats per annum until a *sansaria* at the Fondaco dei Tedeschi becomes available: '...ut predictus Johannes habeat causam et modum se, et familiam alendi, atque libero animo pingendi...'

ASV, Collegio, Notatorio, 1474–1481, c. 127v. Cf. Lorenzi 1868, no. 195.

5. Oct. 1481. A certain Maestro Francesco di Giorgio is commissioned to paint in the hall: 'Marcado e convention fata per loffitio con maistro Francesco de Zorzi depentor de depenzer la Sala del gran conseio...C.[e] 7.'

ASV, Provveditori al Sal, B. 59 (Notatorio 1, 1482–95), c. 237v. Cf. Lorenzi, 1868, no. 196, who observed that this citation comes from the index to the Notatorio and that the page (c. 7) containing the main entry is unfortunately missing. This artist does not appear in any of the other documents checked.

6. 26 Feb. 1482 m.v. (=1483). Giovanni Bellini is to be called *pictor nostri Dominij* and will be exempted from office and other duties in the Scuola dei Pittori to allow him to devote himself to his work in the Great Council Hall: 'Ioannes Bellinus per egregium ingenium suum in arte picture, pictor nostri Dominij est appellatus, et ideo assumptus ad renovandam Salam Maioris Consilij: et a nostro Dominio publice premiatus, utque ad eam solam rem vacare possit liber ab omni alia cura: Per infrascriptos Dominos Consiliarios exemptus factus fuit ab omnibus officiis et beneficiis scollae seu fratalae pictorum: eo tamen faciente omnes angarias et factiones fratalae suae hoc est luminariae et aliarum angariarum sicuti caeteri scolae predictae faciunt: Et hoc nuntiari debeat officialibus Justitiae veteris ut hanc nostram deliberationem observent et faciant observari.'

ASV, Collegio, 1481–1489, Notatorio, c. 22. Cf. Lorenzi, 1868, no. 197.

7. 28 July 1488. Alvise Vivarini offers to paint in the Great Council Hall. 'Essendo io Alvise Vivarin da Muran fidelissimo servitor de la Vostra Serenita et di questo Illustrissimo Stado desideroso da bon tempo in qua demostrar qualche operation del exercitio mio dela pintura et far che la sublimita vostra per experientia vedi et congnosci chel continuo studio et diligentia per me adhibita non e reusita in vano, ma in honore, et laude di questa inclita cita. Come devoto, Me offerisco, senza algun premio ne pagamento de la faticha chio ponero cum la propria persona, de far sopra de me uno teller; zoe depenzerlo in la Salla de gran Conseio nel modo che lavorano al presente li do fradellj Bellinj....'

Vivarini's offer is accepted, and he is commissioned to replace a painting by Pisanello: 'preparari faciendo eidem tellarium in loco ubi extat pictura Pisani....'

ASV, Collegio, Notatorio 1481–1489, c.168v; and Provveditori al Sal, B. 59 (Notatorio 1, 1482–93), cc. 181–181v. Cf. Lorenzi, 1868, no. 221.

8. 1493. Sanudo writes: 'Qui è la salla del Mazor Conseio grandissima, et si rinova attorno di dipinture di mano delli più eccellenti, o di quelli nel numero di più degni pittori che hozzi sia nel mondo, e di gran fama: Gentil Belin et Zuan Belin fratelli, l'opere delli quali dimostra quanto sieno da esser esistimati...Et *continue* rinovano ditta salla, sora telleri la historia di Alessandro 3° Pontefice romano, et di Federico Barbarossa Imperator...'

Sanudo, 1980 edn, p. 34.

9. 24 Dec. 1493. Because of complaints over the high cost and slow progress of the painters in the Great Council Hall, Bortolomio Bon, *proto* for the Salt Office, is appointed to visit the room daily to verify that each is doing his job: '...la qual si vede per ditti depentori esser per tal modo diducta in longo che tardi e per vederse il fin di quella, corendovi i suoi de danari de mexe in mexe, con assai murmuration dila terra, et ogni di andarà impezo si altramente non si fa nova provixion...[Bon] habia et deba solicitar cum ogni diligentia ogni zorno ala Sala granda di Palazzo et veder si li depentori solicitano a lavorar et non li trovando lavorar per ogni volta li debano apontar per ordene di lofficio nostro, da esser sfalcadi i ponti cum il suo salario.'

ASV, Provveditori al Sal, B. 61 (Notatorio 3, 1493–1507), c. 11v. Cf. Lorenzi, 1868, no. 235; also Meyer zur Capellen, p. 115.

10. 9 Aug. 1494. Pietro Perugino is commissioned to paint one segment of wall between two windows on the south side of the hall: 'I Magnifici Signori missier Fantin Marcello et Compagni dignissimi Provedadori al Sal de comandamento dil Serenissimo Principe hano fato marchado et sono rimasti da cordo cum maistro Piero Peroxin depentor el qual ha tolto adepenzer nela Sala de gran Conseio uno Campo tra una fenestra et laltra in ver san Zorzi, tra el qual campo et el campo de la historia dila charitade e uno altro campo over quadro; il qual campo ha tolto a depenzer si e da una fenestra al altra, et sono tre volti compidi e mezo, nel qual die depenzer tanti doxi quanti achadera et quella historia quando il Papa scampo da Roma et la bataia seguida di soto, havendo a compir quella cossa achade in cima di le fenestre oltra la mitade. Item el ditto maistro Piero sara obligato far tuor in desegno lopera e al presente et quella dara ai prefati Magnifici Signori Provedadori, essendo obligado far essa historia più presto miorar che altramente de li altri lavori facti ne la dita Sala si come si convien a quello degno luogo. Dovendo far ditta opera più richa dela prima a tutte soe spexe de oro arzento azuro et colori et de tute quelle cosse apertien a larte del depentor. Et li Magnifici Signori Provedadori li farano far il teller de legnami et de telle da depenzer suxo, et i soleri et altri inzegni, azo depenzer si possi. Hara ditto maistro per suo pagamento del ditto lavor cun li muodi dichiaridi di sopra ducati quatrocento doro, zoe ducati 400, fazando da cima fino abasso sopra il bancho tuti quelli lavori meio parera star bene in menor fatura di quello e al presente. Il qual pagamento suo hara daloffìcio del Sal de tempo in tempo si come sara necessario et che esso maistro lavorera.'

ASV, Provveditori al Sal, B. 61 (Notatorio 3, 1493–1507), cc. 25v–26. Cf. Lorenzi, 1868, no. 237. Chastel, 1983, p. 261 uses an incomplete transcription and misleading translation.

11. 23 Dec. 1495. The painters working in the hall since 1489 are listed: 'Li infrascripti sono quelle che sono sta azonti dapoi la cassation de le spexe fo del 1489. . . .

Maistro Zuan Bellin depentor in gran Conseio comenza adi 25 mazo 1492 a ducati 5 al mexe al anno . . . . duc. 60

Maistro Alvixe Vivarin depentor in gran Conseio comenza a di 24 mazo 1492 a ducati 5 al mexe da esser scontadi del suo lavor per termination di Signori al anno . . . . duc. 60

Christofalo da Parma depentor ut supra comenza adi primo marzo 1489 a ducati 3 al mexe li fu cresudo adi 8 otubrio 1492 ducati 8 al ano . . . . duc. 44

Latantio da Rimano haveva ducati 40 al anno li fu cresudo adi 8 octubrio ducati 8 che sono al anno . . . . duc. 48

Marco Marcian depentor in Palazo el suo lintrar adi 10 zener 1492 chel fu tolto a ducati 24 al anno . . . . duc. 24

Vicenzo da Treviso fu tolto adi 14 Marzo 1495 a ducati 3 al mexe che son al anno . . . . duc. 36

Francesco Bissuol depentor comenza el suo
salario adi 5 novembrio 1492 a ducati 2 al mexe al anno . . . . duc. 24

Perin fante di depentori comenza adi 15 zener 1492 a ducati 6 al anno per un anno . . . . duc. 6

Matthio dicto Maxo fante di depentori comenza adi primo mazo 1492 al anno . . . . duc. 6

ASV, Consiglio dei Dieci, Parti Miste, 1493–1495, Reg. 26, cc. 199–200; and Provveditori al Sal, B. 6 (Collegio, 1482–1514, Reg. 4), c. 76v. Cf. Lorenzi, 1868, no. 239.

12. 28 Sept. 1507. Alvise Vivarini died, having been assigned three paintings. While the first canvas seems to have been close to completion, the second is only partly done and the third is not yet begun. The Council of Ten assigns Giovanni Bellini to supervise the execution of the remaining works. He will be assisted by Vittore Carpaccio [Vector dicto Scarpaza], Vittore Belliniano [Vector quondam Mathio], and a Hieronymo depentor.

'Essendo di non picol ornamento de la Salla nostra de gran Conseglio de ultimar tandem li tre quadri principiati de pictura videlicet quello de quondam Alvise Vivarin, et li altri do restano, uno de i qual non è anchor principiato: siche poi compir si possi el resto de dicta Salla, che non resti piuj impedita, come fin hora è stata; et che una volta tuta dicta Sala finita et expedita sia: come si convien al ornamento di quella, juxta li aricordi di Provededori nostri del Sal. Havendosi etiam per questo offerto el fidelissimo citadin nostro Zuan Bellin, per la obligation lui ha, de usar ogni solecita diligentia cum la solertia sua de imponer fin à simel opera de li prefati tre quadri: dummodo habia in adiuto suo li infrascripti nominati pictori: pero,

Landera parte: che apresso la persona del predicto Zuan Bellin, el qual havera cura de tal opera el sia azonto maistro Vector dicto Scarpàza cum salario de ducati 5 al mese: maistro Vector dicto Scarpaza cum salario de ducati 5 al mese: maistro Vector quondam Mathio cum ducati 4 al mese, et Hieronymo depentor cum ducati do al mese, i qual siano diligentj et solleciti in adiuto dil predicto ser Zuan Bellin, in depenzer di predicti quadri: siche bene et diligentemente cum quella piu presteza di tempo possibel sia, siano compiti. I salarij di qual tre maistri pictori soprascripti cum le spese di colori et altro occorrera pagar si debano di danarj de la cassa granda per lofficio nostro di Sal. Hoc per expressum declarato, quod dicti pictores provisionati teneatur et obbligati sint laborare de continuo et omni die, ut dicti tres quadri quantum celerrime perficiantur et sint ipsi provisionati at beneplacitum huius Consilij.

De parte. . .23 – De non. . .3 – Non sincere . . .0'

ASV, Consiglio dei Dieci, Parti Miste, 1506–1507, Reg. 31, c. 154v; and Provveditori al Sal, B. 6 (Collegio, 1482–1514, Reg. 4), cc. 183v–184. Cf. Molmenti and Ludwig, 1907, p. 30; and Lorenzi, 1868, no. 296. See also ibid. no. 305 (3 Aug. 1508), reporting the death of Hieronymo and appointing Ludovico de Zuane in his place. The former cannot be identified with Girolamo da Santa Croce, who died in 1556 (cf. notes of von Hadeln in Ridolfi, 1914 edn, I, pp. 80–81). But by 23 Sept. 1509, Ludovico de Zuane is not attending to his work and another Hieronymo depentor is hired to replace him (Lorenzi, no. 317).

13. 15 Aug. 1511. Carpaccio writes a letter to the Marquis of Mantua referring to his own ongoing work in the Great Council Hall. The painting to which he refers would be the *Consignment of the Umbrella* (XIII.19), set in Ancona: 'Primo signor mio illustre, io son quello pictore della nostra Illustrissima Signoria conducto per depingere in salla grande dove la Signoria Vostra se dignò a scender sopra il sollaro ad veder l'opera nostra che era la historia delAncona et il nome mio è dicto Victor Carpathio. . . .'

Archivio di Stato, Mantua, Carteggio di Venezia, E. XLV, N. 682. From Bertolotti, 1885, pp. 151–52; also Muraro, 1966, pp. 61–70 with an analysis. Eng. trans. in Chambers, 1971, pp. 122–24.

14a. 31 May 1513. Titian addresses the Council of Ten, proposing to paint scenes on the south side of the hall. He wishes to begin 'dal teller nel qual e quella bataglia da la banda verso de piaza ch e la piu difficile et che homo alcuno, fina questo di non ha voluto tuore tanta impresa' (the *Battle of Spoleto*). For payment he requests the next vacant *sansaria*, notwithstanding others who are waiting ahead of him, and cites the precedent of Giovanni Bellini. The offer is accepted by a vote of 10–6–0.

ASV, Consiglio dei Dieci, Parti Miste, Reg. 35, 1512–13, cc. 183v–84. See also ibid, filza 31, 1513:1; and ibid., Capi del Consiglio dei Dieci, Notatorio 4, 1513–19, c. 5. From Lorenzi, 1868, no. 337; see also ibid., no. 338 for a confirmation of the decision. See Hope, 1980, for a discussion of the affair.

14b. 29 May 1513. Sanudo records Titian's commission, revealing that Carpaccio also has been promised a *sansaria*: 'In questo conseio x semplice fu preso che Tiziano pytor debbi lavorar in sala dil gran consejo come li altri pytori, senza perho alcun salario, ma la expectativa solita darsi a quelli hanno pynto che stà Zentil et Zuan Belin et Vetor Scarpaza: hora mo sarà questo Tiziano.'

Sanudo, *Diarii*, 16, col. 316.

15. 20 March 1514. The Council of Ten revokes its decision to offer Titian the next vacant *sansaria* for painting in the hall, on the basis that it would not be fair to others who already hold a *spettativa* (*expectativa*) for the privilege. He will have to wait his turn with the others.

ASV, Consiglio dei Dieci, Parti Miste, Reg. 36, c. 124. Text in Lorenzi, 1868, no. 341. See also Hope, 1980, pp. 301–5.

16. 28 Nov. 1514. Titian appeals against the revocation, stating that he has already begun the work 'quale fino questo zorno saria a bon termene si non fusse sta la astutia et arte de alcuni che non voleno vedermi suo concorrente'. But he concedes that he will wait until the death of Giovanni Bellini to receive a *sansaria* and asks only that his two *zoveni* (*giovani* = assistants) be paid, along with the cost of materials. After two ballots (7–6–0 and 9–4–0), the Ten agree to Titian's stipulations. Repairs are made at this time to the roof of the former house of the Duke of Milan at San Samuele, where the *modelli* (probably presentation drawings with the compositions well worked out) for the paintings of the Great Council Hall are kept.

ASV, Consiglio dei Dieci, Parti Miste, Reg. 38, c. 11v; and Provveditori al Sal, B. 6 (Collegio, Reg. 4, 1482–1514), c. 274v. From Lorenzi, 1868, nos. 344 and 345. See Crowe and Cavalcaselle, 1877, I, p. 157; and Hope, 1980, pp. 301–5, for two views of the matter.

17. 27 Feb. 1515. Vittore Belliniano, who has worked with Giovanni Bellini in painting the hall, is paid 8 ducats.

ASV, Provveditori al Sal, B. 60 (Notatorio 2, 1491–1529), c. 176v. From Lorenzi, 1868, no. 347.

18. 27 Sept. 1515. The paintings, already deteriorating, are to be cleaned: 'cussi excellente opera si mal conditionata che in breve seria ruinata guasta et reduta ad nihilum. . . .' Luca dipintor [sic], son of the deceased Andrea Comandador who served the Great Council, is hired to do the job. He has worked for a long time in the room with both Gentile and Giovanni Bellini without salary or contract.

ASV, Consiglio dei Dieci, Parti Miste, Filza 36, 1515:2. From Lorenzi, 1868, no. 348. See also ibid., nos. 349 and 350.

19a. 29 Dec. 1515. Francesco Valier, Provveditore al Sal, complains of the huge sums already spent on the paintings, and a full investigation is ordered by the Ten: '. . . ne le Picture de i telleri del nostro Mazor Conseio sonno sta spesi tanti danari che non solum se haveria compido tuto el Palazo; Ma saria sta fatta tre volte tanta opera cum quello e sta exborsato, ultra che i pictori habino havuti Officij et diverse altre concessione de utilita conveniente. . . .'

ASV, Consiglio dei Dieci, Parti Miste, Reg. 39, f. 74 (new num.) Cf. Lorenzi, 1868, no. 352.

19b. 30 Dec. 1515. Valier reports that drawings have not yet been made for two of the canvases on which more than 700 ducats have already been spent. Other masters of painting are said to be available and willing to paint a canvas for only 250 ducats. The Senate votes (150–6–1) to dismiss all the painters then working in the room and to empower the Provveditore al Sal to choose the best among them to continue with the work at their own expense. The paintings would be paid for only after completion.

ASV, Senato Terra, 1515–16, Reg. 19, c. 61v. Text in Lorenzi, 1868, no. 353.

19c. Dec. 1515. Sanudo reports the affair, observing that it was all due to a misunderstanding and that the painters have explained everything to the Signoria: 'et nota fu uno parte non vera, perche i pittori chiariteno il tuto ala Signoria et fo per deliberazione del Collegio approva e fato con quel medemo pitor chiamato Tiziano uno novo mercato.'

Sanudo, *Diarii*, 21, col. 393.

20. 18 Jan. 1516. Titian responds to the criticisms of the past few weeks and proposes a new contract for the *Battle of Spoleto* on which he has been working for two years (XIII.5). In addition to 10 ducats for his colors, three *onze* of azure blue, and a salary of 4 ducats per month for one of his two *garzoni*, he requests 400 ducats for the painting upon completion. He states that this sum is only half that offered to Perugino, who 'had not wished to make it for 800 ducats'. The Collegio agrees to his demands, but cuts the payment for the painting to 300 ducats.

ASV, Collegio, Notatorio, 1515–20, c. 25v; and Provveditori al Sal, B. 60 (Notatorio 2, 1491–1529), c. 198. Text in Lorenzi, 1868, no. 354. Cf. Wethey, 1975, III, p. 228, for a different interpretation of the documents.

21. 5 Dec. 1516. Following the death of Giovanni Bellini, Titian is not allowed to move to the head of the list of those holding *expectative*. The vote by the Ten is 10–4–1.

ASV, Consiglio dei Dieci, Parti Miste, 1516–17, Reg. 40, c. 147. Text in Lorenzi, 1868, no. 356. See Hope, 1980, p. 303; and Wethey, 1975, III, p. 228.

22. 3 July 1518. Refering to a canvas not yet begun, the Council of Ten orders Titian to get to work within eight days or he must complete it at his own expense.

Provveditori al Sal (Notatorio 7, 1516–21), c. 90. From Lorenzi, 1868, no. 366. Wethey's assumption that this citation refers to *The Pope and Emperor Make Peace in front of San Marco* (XIII.17) is credible. He suggests that the work, assigned to Giovanni Bellini upon the death of Vivarini, had probably only been sketched out by the time Bellini himself died. Titian would have been given the commission at that time (Wethey, 1975, III, p. 233). This canvas would have been the last to be completed on the north wall, and it is likely that the *Battle of Spoleto* was regarded as a less urgent affair in terms of the total effect of the room.

23. 11 Aug. 1522. The painting (XIII.17) is still unfinished, and the Ten order Titian to complete it by June 1523 or else his *spettativa* will be revoked and he will have to return all funds paid to him thus far (300 ducats). A marginal note dated 20 July 1523, confirms Titian's completion of the painting.

ASV, Consiglio dei Dieci, Parti Miste, 1522, Reg. 45, f. 128; and Provveditore al Sal, B. 7 (Collegio, 1453–1531). Cf. Lorenzi, 1868, no. 373. It is probably at this time that Titian finally received his *sansaria* (see ibid., no. 591), but cf. doc. 24. See also Hope, 1980, p. 303; and Wethey, 1975, III, p. 233.

24. 23 June 1537. Titian is threatened with the loss of his *sansaria*. According to this *parte*, he received it upon the death of Giovanni Bellini without having to wait his turn, upon conditon that he paint 'el teler dela bataglia terrestre' (XIII.5). He has been receiving about 118–120 ducats from it annually, and since the painting is not yet complete, he must repay all the monies paid him to date.

ASV, Senato, Terra, Reg. 20 (1538), c. 158v (new num.). Cf. Lorenzi, 1868, no. 462. He must have completed the work by 28 Aug 1539, when the *sansaria* was again confirmed (ibid., no. 591).

25. 22 Nov. 1538. The Council of Ten affirms the decision of the Collegio to commission a painting for the space 'fra li colonnelli no. 6 & 7 della sala del magior conseglio a maistro Zuan Antonio da Pordenon. . .' Pordenone will be paid 200 ducats for the work.

ASV, Consiglio dei Dieci, Comuni, Reg. 12 (1537–38), ff. 195–195v (new num.). Cf. Lorenzi, 1868, no. 471.

26. 7 Jan. 1561 m.v. (=1562). It is decided to commission the three remaining *istorie*. One of these has already been allotted at a 'bon pretio', and the other two will be given to artists on the basis of low bid and good reputation. The first work should be finished in six months, and the paintings already completed, and now deteriorating through age, will be restored.

ASV, Consiglio dei Dieci, Comuni, Filza 83 (1561 Nov., Feb.). Cf. Lorenzi, 1868, no. 661.

27. 12 Aug. 1564. Orazio Vecellio, who has made one of the new paintings, is told that he must be satisfied with a payment of 100 ducats, the amount already paid for each of the other two works.

ASV, Capi dei Consiglio dei Dieci, Notatorio 25 (1564–65), c. 34v. Cf. Lorenzi, 1868, nos. 689 and 695.

ORIGINAL ARRANGEMENT: The canvases of the 1474 campaign seem to have replicated on a one-to-one basis the subject matter of the frescoes which they replaced. Benches would have lined the walls, as in the existing room, with the paintings installed above them and extending up to the cornice. Nearly all the fields must have been vertical in shape to accommodate the required number of scenes. Those of the north wall were probably more equal in size than those of today, since there was as yet no need to allow for smaller fields above the window openings. The entire wall surface up to the level of the cornice, including the area above the windows, was undoubtedly considered part of the pictorial field and was painted (see doc. 10). Since Sansovino makes no mention of inscriptions inside *capitelli* or similar framing devices, it is probable that they were dispensed with in the cycle of 1474. When he does give the location of an inscription, it invariably seems to be below the painting, as in XIII.1 where it is described as painted on field of gold.

THE CYCLE BEFORE THE FIRE OF 1577: The inscriptions given in this section were apparently composed by Sabellico (Monticolo in Sanudo, *Vite*, 1900 edn, pp. 342–43 n. 1) and are taken here from Sansovino's transcription (1581, cc. 125–30). Both Sansovino and Vasari (1966 edn, pp. 431–35) offer a number of descriptive details of the paintings.

EAST WALL:
Guariento
Paradise c. 1362–65
See Cat. IV.

SOUTH WALL:
Jacopo Tintoretto [attr. Sansovino]
1. *Coronation of Frederick Barbarossa by Pope Hadrian IV in St. Peter's in 1162.* 1562–64
In a field of gold below the painting: ADRIANVS PONT. MAX. FEDERICVM ENOBARVBM ROMANI IMP. INSIGNIBUS IN D. PETRI DECORAVIT. MCLXII.
LIT.: Pallucchini and Rossi, 1982, p. 265; Wolters, 1983, p. 171.

Orazio Vecellio [attr. Sansovino]
2. *Attack by armed Romans on the Emperor's troops near the Castel Sant' Angelo.* 1562–64
ROMANI FAMILIAM IMPERATORIS A PRATO NERONIS PROFECTI AD MOLEM ADRIANI AGGREDIVNTVR AD TENTORIVM VSQVE IMP.
LIT.: Wethey, 1975, III, p. 232.

Veronese [attr. Sansovino]
3. *Acknowledgement of Ottavian, the schismatic Pope, by Barbarossa in Pavia.* 1562–64
ALEXANDRVM III. PON. MAX. RITE CREATVM ET OCTAVIANVM VITIO FACTVM IMP. FEDERICVS TICINVM EVOCAVIT, ALEX. DICTO EIVS AVDIENS NON FVIT. ITAQ. FEDERICVS ID AEGRE FERENS, OCTAVIANVM QVI AD SE IIT PONT. DECLARAVIT, AC VENERATVS EST.
LIT.: Pignatti, 1976, p. 253; Wolters, 1983, p. 172.

Jacopo Tintoretto [attr. Sansovino]
4. *The excommunication of Barbarossa by Alexander III.* 1553
INSOLENTES FEDERICI CONATVS ALEX. PONT. ANATHEMATE ET BELLO INDICTO DEPRIMIT ET PROPVLSAT. FEDERICVS IMP. INIQVO EDICTO SVBDITOS SVOS AB ALEX. PONT. ALIENAT.
LIT.: Pallucchini and Rossi, 1982, p. 265; Wolters, 1983, p. 171.

Titian [documented]
5. *Battle of Spoleto, in which the city, faithful to Pope Alexander III, is destroyed by the Emperor.* 1513–38
[No inscription beneath it]
LIT.: Wethey, 1975, III, pp. 225–32, with earlier bibliography; Wolters, 1983, pp. 193–94.

Pordenone [documented]
6. *Alexander III with the King of France, who has decided to support him and is making preparations for his defense.* comm. 1538
PRAETVLIT REX INCLITVS BELLVM QVIETI, VT PONTIFICIS DIGNITATEM TVERETVR PARANTVR VTRINQVE ARMA, ADSVNT FEDERICO BOEMI, DACI, GETAE, GERMANI, & ITALI. REGI FRANCIAE FAVENT ANGLICI, BRITANNI, FLANDRENSES, BVRGVNDIENSES, ET VASCONES.
LIT.: Wethey, 1975, III, p. 226. Sansovino assigned no artist to this work.

Pordenone ?
7. *The Pope flees incognito to Venice.*
PONTIFEX NE TOT CHRISTIANORVM MILLIA SVA CAVSA HOSTILITER CONFLIGERENT, CELATA PERSONAE DIGNITATE, E MEDIO EXCESSIT, VENETIASQ. LIBERAM VRBEM SE CONTVLIT GREGARII SACERDOTIS HABITV, FVITQ. HIC SEPTVAGESIMVS SEPTIMVS SVPRA CENTESIMVM, AC MILLESIMVM EO QVI FVIT HVMANAE SALVTIS.

WEST WALL:
Giovanni Bellini [attr. Sansovino]
8. *Doge Sebastiano Ziani greets Pope Alexander III at S. M. della Carità in Venice.*
Written below (letters almost fallen off): PRIMA NOCTE DECLINAVIT APVD CANONICOS SANCTI SALVATORIS, QVI DVXERVNT EVM AD MONASTERIVM S. MARIAE CHARITATIS, IBIQVE IN FORMA...SERVIEBAT.

A small distance away: QVIDAM PEREGRINVS NVTV DEI, EX VOTO VENERAT VENETIAS, QVI DVM VISITARET ECCLESIAM SVPRASCRIPTAM S. MARIAE DE CARITATE, COGNOVIT PAPAM, NOTIFICAT ILLVSTRI SEBASTIANO ZIANI, TVNC INCLYTO VENETIARVM DVCI, QVALITER SVMMVS PONT, EST IN TALI ECCLESIA.

And nearby: DVX CONSILIARII, NOBILES, ET TOTA VENETIARVM CIVITAS, SIMILITER PATRIARCHA GRADENSIS, ET EPISCOPVS CASTELLANVS CVM TOTO CLERO PERVENIVNT CVM CRVCIBVS AD D. PAPAM DUBITANTEM DE TANTO CONCURSU. DEVOTTIS, DVX GENIBVS FLEXIS DEDIT OSCVLA AD BEATISS. PEDES PRAESENTANS CLAMIDEM, MITRAM ET ORNAMENTA, PEDVM, ET CONFORTANS VT METV DEPOSITO, ASSUMERET ANIMVM ET PONTIFICALIA ORNAMENTA, QVIA EST IN VRBE TVTISSIMA LIBERA ET POTENTE.
Possible related drawing: Devonshire Collection, Chatsworth, 738.
LIT.: Tietze and Tietze-Conrat, 1984, p. 69, no. 263; Huse, 1972, pp. 61–62; Ames-Lewis and Wright, 1983, p. 57.

Sansovino (1663, I, p. 329) writes that between the two large windows on this wall 'era scolpito un S. Marco con l'armi del Doge Vendramino [1476–78] da i lati, che toglievano in mezzo l'arme Contarina, d'Andrea ultimo Doge of quella famiglia [1368–82]'. The San Marco was almost certainly a sculpted relief of the Lion of San Marco and not an image of the saint himself. The Contarini arms may confirm the date *ad quem* for the first decoration campaign of the room, just as the Vendramin arms indicated the work of the second campaign in progress on this wall.

Gentile Bellini [attr. Vasari, Sansovino]
9. *The presentation of the white candle to the Doge.*

DVX, VNIVERSO POPVLO COMITANTE AD ALTARE ECCLESIAE SANCTI MARCI PALAM CVM CANTIBVS ET DEVOTIONE PERDVCIT, VBI PERSONAM, FACVLTATEM, MAGNITVDINEM CIVITATIS, ET TOTVM DOMINIVM IN PROTECTIONEM SVAM ET ECCLESIAE CONTRA QVOSLIBET OFFERT ETC.

The words continued 'dall'altro lato' (on the other side): PAPA PRAESTAT DVCI CEREVM ALBVM, QVO IPSE ET DVCANTES POST EVM, PERPETVO IN SVIS PROCESSIONIBVS VTERET.

According to Meyer zur Capellen, this was the first painting of the renewed cycle

to be completed.
LIT.: Meyer zur Capellen, 1985, p. 146; Huse, 1972, p. 62.

NORTH WALL:
Gentile Bellini [attr. Vasari: Gentile; Sansovino: Gentile, but names Giovanni in another passage]
10. *The departure of the Venetian ambassadors to the court of the Emperor.*
PRO PACE TRACTANDA MITTVNTVR AD IMPERATOREM TVM IN APVLIA RESIDENTEM, SOLENNES AMBASCIATORES CVM LITERIS DVCALIBVSQVAS PAPA MANDAT PER DVCEM MVNIRI BVLLA PLVMBEA CVM FIGVRA S. MARCI VTQUE DUCE.

Below the painting 'Gentilis patriae dedit havc monumenta belinus, othomano accitus, munere factus eques'.

According to the inscription, the work was completed (and possibly painted in its entirety) following Gentile's return from Constantinople in 1481. Huse doubts that Gentile could have painted scenes 10–14 by himself, since the True Cross paintings would have taken much of his time, but he ignores the possible contributions of the workshop.
LIT.: Meyer zur Capellen, 1985, p. 146; Huse, 1972, p. 62.

Gentile Bellini [attr. Vasari]
11. *The ambassadors plead the Pope's case before the Emperor.*
Written below: IMPERATOR PRIMO AMBASCIATORES LETANTVR RECEPIT, SED AVDITO, QVOD VENERANT AD TRACTANDVM PACEM RIGIDE RESPONDIT, QVOD PAPAM FVGITIVVM SIBI TRADANT, ET NOLINT FACERE GVERRAM ALIENAM SVAM, NEC SVSTINERE QVEM TOTVS MVNDVS SEQUITVR, ALIOQVIN PARARE SE AD BELLVM.

Followed by: LEGATI REFERVNT PAPAE ET DVCI RIGIDVM IMPERATORIS RESPONSVM. PAPA PLVRIMVM EXPAVIT, SED BENIGNISSIMVS DVX IPSVM HORTATVR DICENS, OB REVERENTIAM FIDEI CATHOLICE ET SANCTAE MATRIS ECCLESIAE VIRILITER DEFENDETVR.

Sansovino assigns no artist to this work.
LIT.: Meyer zur Capellen, 1985, pp. 146–47.

Gentile Bellini [attr. Vasari]
12. *The consignment of the sword to the Doge.*
Written below: HORTATVR ALEXANDER PONT. MAX. PRINCIPEM ET VENETOS, VT CVM XXX. TRIREMIBVS PVBLICE AD BELLVM INSTRVCTIS, PRO PIETATE ET RELIGIONE FORTETER IN HOSTEM MOVEANT, DATQVE INCLITO DVCI, ET SVCCESSORIBVS ENSEM PERPETVVM IVSTITIAE INSIGNE HABENDVM. CETERIS AD BELLVM EVNTIBVS PLENISSIMAM DAT VENIAM.

On the other side: POSTQVAM TREPIDE NVNCIATVM EST QVINQ. ET SEPTVAGINTA HOSTIVM TRIREMES OTHONIS IMP. FILII DVCTV ADVENTARE, TVM VENETVS DVX CIRCA SALBLOICVM HISTRIAE PROMONTORIVM, SVOS AD PVGNAM HORTATVS EDICIT, VT QVOM FERRVM A SE IN HOSTEM VIBRATVM VIDERINT, SVO EXEMPLO DIMICARENT.
Related drawing: British Museum, Nr. 1891-6-17-23 [Plate 25]
LIT.: Meyer zur Capellen, 1985, pp. 147–48; Tietze and Tietze-Conrat, 1944, no. 269, pp. 69–70.

Gentile and Giovanni Bellini [Vasari: Gentile; Sansovino: Giovanni]
13. *The Battle of Salvore.*
Written below: ATROX UTRINQVE PRAELIVM COMMITTITVR, DEMVM DVX FORTISSIMVS, DIVINA OPE, VENETAQVE VIRTVTE NIXVS, IMPERATORIA CLASSE DISIECTA, OTHONEM CVM TRIREMIBUS LX. CAPIT. RELIQVIS PRAETER PAVCAS QVAE CELERI FVGA ABIERANT, AVT IGNE ABSVMPTIS, AVT ALTO MARI DEPRESSIS.

Sansovino claimed that Giovanni had worked on the painting for 11 years. Wickhoff (1883, p. 29) rejected this citation, since the work was placed in the middle of a group of canvases otherwise painted by Gentile. Huse (1972, p. 62) followed Sansovino's view. In support of Gentile's share in the work, we might point out that this seems to have been the first work commissioned, and that presumably he had done considerable work on it during the five-year period before Giovanni was brought into the campaign. Malipiero's notice could be interpreted to mean joint execution by both artists (doc. 3a).
LIT.: Meyer zur Capellen, 1985, p. 148.

Gentile Bellini [attr. Vasari]
14. *The presentation of the ring to the Doge.*
COMPLECTITVR LAETABVNDVS PONTIFEX VENETVM DVCEM INCLITAM VICTORIAM REPORTANTEM, ET PELAGI DOMINVM SALVTAT. TRADIT ET ANVLVM QVO ILLE ET RELIQVI PRINCIPES, IN VERI PERPETVIQVE IMPERII ARGVMENTVM QVOTANNIS IPSVM SIBI MARE DESPONSARENT.
LIT.: Meyer zur Capellen, 1985, p. 148.

Alvise Vivarini [attr. Vasari]
15. Otto is released to treat for peace with Barbarossa.
OTHO IMPERATORIS FILIVS DIVINA MOTVS VOLVNTATE, SE FVTVRAE PACIS CVM FEDERICO PATRE ARBITRVM PONTIFICI ET VENETIS POLLICETVR ATQ. ITA FIDE AB EO ACCEPTA, CVSTODIA LIBERATVR.

One of the three works commissioned from Alvise Vivarini that were left unfinished after his death in 1503/5 (doc. 12); it must have been nearly complete. Sansovino assigned it to no artist.
LIT.: Steer, 1982, pp. 175–76; Meyer zur Capellen, 1985, p. 148 (who attaches the above inscription to the following scene).

Begun by Alvise Vivarini, finished by Giovanni Bellini [attr. Vasari and Sansovino]
16. *Otto before the Emperor.*
LAETATVR IMPERATVR VISO FILIO, CVIVS CONSTANTIA QUOD ALIOQVI ABHORRVERAT ANIMVS, TANDEM VICTVS, EI TRACTANDAE PACIS TRIBVIT POTESTATEM.
LIT.: See no. 15.

Titian [Vasari: begun by Giovanni Bellini, completed by Titian; Sansovino: Titian alone] c. 1518–23
17. *The Emperor humbles himself before the Pope at the entrance to the Basilica of San Marco.*
IMPERATOR OTHOQVE FILIVS, HIC PRIDIE FESTO, ILLE CHRISTIANAE ASCENSIONIS DIE, TRIREMIBVS VENETIAS ADVECTI, EODEM DIE CVM ROM. PON. VENETOQVE DVCE PACEM FIRMARVNT.

Originally intended for Alvise Vivarini, assigned to Giovanni Bellini after Vivarini's death, and finally painted by Titian. Sansovino wrote that it was the first painting that he made in the room.
LIT.: Wethey, 1975, III, p. 233; Steer, 1982, pp. 175–76.

Carpaccio [Vasari: Giovanni Bellini; Sansovino: Carpaccio]
18. *Mass is celebrated in San Marco.*
OPERATVS SACRIS IN DIVI MARCI AEDE ALEX. PONT. OMNIBVS DOMINICAE ASCENSIONIS DIE INTRA BINAS VESPERAS F...ADEVNTIBVS

PLENAM DELICTORVM VENIAM PERPETVO CONCESSIT, SEPTIMA PECCATORVM PARTE PER OCTAVAM FREQUENTATIBVS REMISSA.

See comments for no. 19.

Carpaccio [Vasari: Giovanni Bellini]

19. *The consignment of the umbrella to the Doge in Ancona.*

Sansovino reported that the inscription had fallen off.

See doc. 13, showing that Carpaccio was still working on this painting in 1511. Carpaccio's share in this work is unknown, for he was assigned to work as Giovanni Bellini's assistant (doc. 12). That his rate of pay, however, was equivalent to Giovanni's and was more than the other two assistants, suggests considerable independence.

Related drawings: Colville Collection, London; Crocker Art Gallery, Sacramento; and (?) British Museum, 1897–4–10–1 (Lauts, 1962, cat. drgs. nos. 26, 31, 34, 49) [Plates 41, 42, 116]

LIT.: Tietze and Tietze-Conrat, 1944, p. 155, no. 635; Lauts, 1962, p. 257; Huse, 1972, pp. 60–63; Muraro, 1977, pp. 55–56 and 76–77.

Giovanni Bellini [attr. Vasari]

20. *The entry to Rome of the Pope, the Doge and the Emperor.*

PROFICISCVNTVR HINC ROMAM CVM CELERI EQITATV ALEX. PONT. IMPERATOR ET DVX VENETVS, QVIBVS IBI APPROPINQVANTIBVS OMNES SVPREMI ORDINIS ANTISTITES CVM TOTO CLERO PRODEVNT OBVIAM, SEQVVTI PRIMORES CIVITATIS...TOTAQVE NOBILITAS, POSTREMO MVLTITVDO INGENS STVDIO EFFVSA, VENIENTES CVM MVLTA LAETITIA, ET VENERATIONE EXCIPIT.

Giovanni Bellini [attr. Ridolfi]

21. *The presentation of the eight standards and the trumpets to the Doge.*

OBTVLIT ROMANVS POPVLVS ALEXANDRO INGRESSO, OCTO VARII COLORIS VEXILLA TOTIDEMQVE ARGENTEAS TVBAS, QVAE DIGNITATIS ORNAMENTA VLTRO PONTIFEX VENETO DVCI DETVLIT. QVIBVS IPSE ET OMNIS DVCVM POSTERITAS, SOLEMNI POMPA VTERENTVR.

Giovanni Bellini [attr. Ridolfi]

22. *The presentation of the ceremonial throne to the Doge in the Lateran Palace.*

INVISIT ALEX. PONT. LATERANENSEM BASILICAM CVM IMPERATORE ET VENETO DVCE. HIC CVM FORTE SELLA ESSET VNA PONTIFICI ALTERA FEDERICO IMPERATORI STRATA, TERTIAM VENETO STERNI IVSSIT, DEDITQVE TAM ILLI AD CVRRVLIS SELLAE INSIGNE QVAM POSTERIS VENETORVM DVCIBVS PERPETVO HABENDVM.

LITERATURE: Pietro Contarini, *Argo Vulgar*, Venice, n.d. [1542]; Vasari, 1966 edn, pp. 430–37; Sansovino, 1581, cc. 123v–131v; Sansovino, 1663, I, pp. 325–36; Ridolfi, 1914 edn; Francesco Sansovino, *Lettera intorno al Palazzo Ducale e descrizione dei quadri nella Sala del Gran Consiglio esistenti prima dell'incendio del MDLXXVII*, Venice, 1829; Zanotto, 1858, III, pp. 3–21; Crowe and Cavalcaselle, 1877, pp. 153–69; Wickhoff, 1883, pp. 24–37; Paoletti, 1893, I, pp. 37–45, 151–57, 181–83, 221–22; Ludwig, 1905, pp. 24–25; Gronau, 1909, pp. 22–51; Escher, 1919, pp. 87–125; Tietze-Conrat, 1940, pp. 15–26; Gallo, 1949, pp. 31–32; Wolters, 1966, pp. 271–318; Padoan Urban, 1968, pp. 291–317; Robertson, 1968, pp. 81–83; Collins, 1970; *Il Palazzo Ducale*, 1971; Pignatti, 1972, pp. 118–34; Huse, 1972, pp. 56–71; Sinding-Larsen, 1974, pp. 179–217; Hope, 1980, pp. 302–5; Wolters, 1983, pp. 169–73; Brown, 1984, pp. 266–77; Meyer zur Capellen, 1985, pp. 21–24. See also Cat. IV.

XIV. Scuola di Sant' Orsola

Carpaccio

Life of St. Ursula c. 1490–1500

Color Plates XXIV, XXVI–XXIX; Plates 27–30, 47, 107, 108, 110, 115, 116, 135

HISTORY: The Scuola di Sant' Orsola was founded on 15 July 1300 and dedicated to SS. Dominic, Peter Martyr and Ursula. In 1306, the confraternity built a chapel in the cemetery adjacent to the south flank of SS. Giovanni e Paolo. Although the building was long thought by scholars to have been destroyed, excavations carried out in 1928 (but published only in 1963) identified the original structure as the present *canonica* attached to the right (south) apse of SS. Giovanni e Paolo. It has undergone extensive alterations over the years and only in the east end can the lines of the early building be discerned (Renosto, 1963, pp. 37–50).

Although some have suggested that the confraternity was a society of nobles, there is evidence that this was not the case during the period in which it employed Carpaccio. A list of the Banca for 1484 produces few potentially noble surnames and a number of a decidedly artisan character (e.g., Varoter, Casseler, Favro, Pelizaro: ASV, Proveddi-tori di Comun, Reg. U, f. 602). In 1488 the group voted to commission paintings of the life of St. Ursula (doc. 1). The new works may have replaced an earlier fresco decoration, traces of which were discovered on the north wall in the 1928 investigation (Renosto, 1963, p. 44).

Carpaccio's first canvas must have been the *Arrival in Cologne* (XIV.7), which bears the date 1490 and is the least stylistically evolved of the group. The remaining works would have been executed over the next decade (see below).

The canvases were still in place when the Scuola was suppressed in 1806. They were transferred to the Accademia Galleries in 1810, where they unfortunately suffered trimming to adapt them to the new location (Zorzi, 1984, p. 375). The earlier state of the canvases was recorded by engravings made by Giovanni Del Pian (now in the Biblioteca del Museo Correr).

DOCUMENTS AND SOURCES:

1. 16 Nov. 1488. At a full chapter meeting the members vote (19–13) to impose a special tax on officers of the Banca, with part of the funds to be spent on canvases depicting the life of St. Ursula. Other funding will be provided by *ponti* (fines) imposed on members for various infractions of the rules of the confraternity.

'...Item le stado provisto a più beneficio de dita schuola, che el gastaldo con isuoi compagni che serano de tempo in tempo da mo avanti siano hobligadi de dar ogni segonda domenega del mexe el di ordenado el gastaldo soldi [?]* ij et li compagni soldo [?] 1 per chadauno che serano soldi [?] xvj al mexe et questi tal danari siano messi con quelli dei ponti come e dito di sopra et i diti danari siano de la nostra scuola, tamen con questa condicion chel se habia aspender questi tal danari in questo modo. Prima che el se meta tanti in la scola quanti sera per el pan ela chandela che se darano a li x fratri che sono hobligadi adir le messe ut supra. El resto de i diti danari se debia spender in fabricha dela schuola o concier ho far far i teleri dela istoria de madona santa orssola per infina che isara compidi et da poi finidi i teleri i danari de dita chasseleta tutti vada in la nostra schuola come vano tute le altre intrade ma, ma domentre che non sarano fato e depenti i diti teleri questi tal danari non se possa spender in altro che per el pan et chandelle ut supra soto pena el gastaldo de pagar del suo tutto quello lavera spexo in altro che in li diti teleri ut supra, et azo che i diti danari se possono schuodere et azo nessun non se possa schusar de non pagar i suoi ponti, zoe de quelli che dira la bruta parola, over che non vegnera ai corpi et de altre hobligation, come apar per lordene nostro che chi non pagera et tasserasse haver ponti V . . .'

ASV, Scuole piccole e suffragi, Sant' Orsola a SS. Giovanni e Paolo [= ASV, Scuole piccole], Reg. 597, f. 11v.

*The sign used for the monetary denomination is a long s [*ʃ*] with a diagonal slash. The only Venetian coinage it seems likely to refer to is the *soldo*. Yet I have some reservations about this reading, since the sums thus implied are so small [124 *soldi* = 1 ducat].

2. 1492. The tomb of Marco Loredan (d. 1363) is removed from the interior wall of the chapel, presumably to make room for the paintings.

ASV, Barbaro, Genealogie patrizie: famiglia Loredan (see also Moschini Marconi, 1955, p. 98; and Gallo, 1963, p. 2).

3. 30 Nov. 1500. The Scuola requests a concession of land at the east end of the building from the Dominican brothers of SS. Giovanni e Paolo, to construct 'unam tribunam post dictam Ecclesiam S. Ursulae.'

ASV, SS. Giovanni e Paolo, B. 0/1, n. 317, c. 16 (cf. ibid., n. 311).

4. 4 Aug, 1504. Having received the necessary land, the Banca votes to enlarge the chapel with a new chancel on the east end to contain the high altar: 'M. Fantin Zaccaria el Dottor Guardian. . . avendo visto et saminado tutti li altri dessegni de fabrica de altri maistri, che se debba cosi concluder e dar zoso el partido dela Fabrica della Capella dell' Altar Grando di ditta Scola con Maistro Mattio Davala et Maistro Batto Tagiapiera.'

ASV, Scuole piccole, B. 601, f. 144; cf. B. 599.

5. 1493–1530. Sanudo mentions the cycle in his *Cronachetta* under the rubric, 'Queste sono cosse notabile in diverse chiese': '*Item*, la capella de Santa Orsola, le historie et figure che è atorno bellissime.'

Sanudo, 1980 edn, p. 50.

6. 21 July 1520. The first restoration of the paintings is documented, with the scuola paying L.5 s.10 'a uno depentor depense i theleri dela schuola in piui luogi dove j erano rotti.'

ASV, Scuole piccole, B. 602, Giornale 1516–28, f. 57. Another restoration is recorded on 13 June 1546: ibid., B. 602, Libro de rezever (1529–1560), f. 21v. Cf. Gallo, 1963, p. 6.

ORIGINAL ARRANGEMENT: The chapel of Carpaccio's time measured 16.3 × 7.7 meters. It had at least two doors: the main entrance on the west facade and a small door in the north wall leading to the *albergo* above the portico. The hall was illuminated by two windows flanking the altar on the east wall (Renosto, 1963, p. 57; Zampetti, 1963b, pp. 25–28). An apse was added to the building in 1504 (docs. 3 and 4) and a new floor installed which raised the pavement level by 40 cm. Major remodeling was undertaken in 1646–47 when the front portico was torn down, nine lunette windows were added in the chapel, and a square room was built around the apse with exit doors replacing the former windows (Sansovino, 1663, I, p. 72; Gallo, 1963, pp. 8–16). It was probably at this time that the floor was raised again, and a door was either added or enlarged in the south wall to give access to the cemetery, necessitating the cut in XIV.1.

The reconstruction in Fig. 1 follows the present order of the paintings in the Accademia Galleries, as first arranged in the late 1940s by Vittorio Moschini [Moschini Marconi, 1955, pp. xxviii]. For earlier reconstructions see Gallo, 1963, pp. 12–14. Even though the original arrangement cannot be established with absolute certainty, Moschini's reconstruction follows the sequence of events given in Voragine's *Golden Legend* (1969 edn, pp. 627–31), and appears to offer the most logical solution. With a single exception, it also follows the sequence recorded by Ridolfi in 1648 (1914 edn, pp. 46–47) and Boschini (1664, pp. 213–15), who wrote the earliest surviving descriptions of the cycle as a whole. Their citation of XIV.5 and XIV.6 in the reverse order to that given here is supported by Zorzi (1985, pp. 437–59), but as Pignatti (1981, p. 85) has suggested, the two canvases may well have been switched in the remodelling of the Scuola building undertaken in 1646–47.

The clockwise arrangement of the narrative sequence was confirmed in 1963, when a light source was ascertained at the east end of the room corresponding to that depicted in the paintings, as well as the existence of the door in the south wall in the same position as a cutout portion of canvas in XIV.1 (Zampetti, 1963b, pp. 25–28; Gallo, 1963, pp. 16–17).

The cycle is generally dated by scholars to 1490–1500, with some exceptions (summarized by Pignatti, 1981, pp. 74–88; cf. further arguments below). Sanudo's reference to the cycle in his *Cronachetta* (doc. 5), although cited by Nepi Scire and Valcanover (1985, p. 103) as evidence that the project must have been nearly complete by 1493, is inconclusive. As Caracciolo Aricò points out (in Sanudo, 1980 edn, pp. xix–xx)), it was only the first draft of the text that was completed

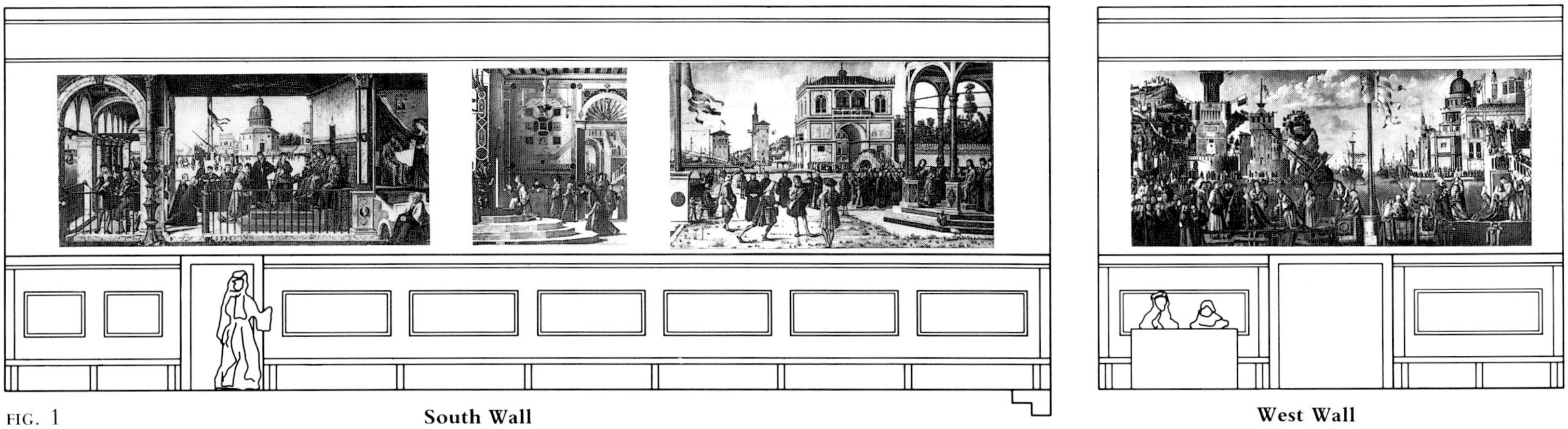

FIG. 1 **South Wall** **West Wall**

by 1493, for Sanudo continued to annotate it over the years up to 1530. The extant manuscripts of the relevant text date to 1587 and do not allow a precise dating of the individual entries.

The full cycle was restored in 1982–84 by Ottorino Nonfarmale. It had undergone (and suffered from) no less than nine earlier documented restorations (see Moschini Marconi, 1955, p. 99; and Gallo, 1963, p. 22 n. 37).

ORIGINAL CYCLE:
Now in Venice, Accademia Galleries

Carpaccio
SOUTH WALL:
1. *Reception of the Ambassadors*
Oil on canvas, 275 × 589 cm, cat. n. 572
Color Plate XXVI, Plate 104
(before restoration)
Inscription: OP. VICTORIS / CARPATIO / VENETI
Cut-out at lower edge: 53 × 132 cm

The restoration of 1983 revealed a missing part of the candelabra on the left side, and the head and bust of a boy just above the cut-out for the door which may have been painted over when the canvas was cut.

Proposed dates from c. 1494 (Muraro, 1966, p. xxx) to shortly before 1500 (Pignatti, 1981, p. 77). Although the composition is the most complex of the cycle (as Nepi Scire observes), its tighter handling suggests that it was the first canvas to be painted for the south wall, probably around 1495–96 or shortly thereafter. In his later work, Carpaccio developed toward a more comprehensive, less aggregative, conception of the spatial ambient (as in XIV.2 and 3).

2. *Departure of the Ambassadors*
Oil on canvas, 280 × 253 cm, cat. n. 573
Color Plate XXIV
Inscription: VICTORIS CAR/PACIO VENETI / OPUS˙

The painting is noticeably abraded in parts, with the face of the bowing figure on the right now simply a blur.

Proposed dates from c. 1494 (Muraro, 1966, p. xxxvi) to c. 1500 (Pignatti, 1981, p. 77). The later date is preferable. Both this work and XIV.3 reveal a sureness of touch that suggests their late execution, at the very end of the campaign.

3. *Return of the Ambassadors*
Oil on canvas, 297 × 527 cm, cat. n. 574
Color Plate XXVII, Plate 107
Inscription: VICTORIS / CARPATIO / VENETI / OPUS˙

The recent restoration revealed the work to be in the best state of conservation of the entire cycle. Although the cleaning removed much of the green tone from the grassy area of the ground plane, the result is still impressive in terms of overall chromatic effect. The work as a whole has a luminous quality, due in large part to the light tonality of the sky.

Proposed dates from c. 1494 (Muraro, 1966, p. xxxviii) to c. 1499 (Pignatti, 1981, p. 78). The later date is preferable, as stated above.

WEST WALL:
4. *Leavetaking of the Betrothed Pair* 1495
Oil on canvas, 280 × 611 cm, cat. n. 575
Color Plate XXVIII, Plates 110, 116
Inscription: VICTORIS / CARPATIO / VENETI˙/ OPUS˙/ MCCCCLXXXXV˙

Despite the recent restoration (1983–84), many of the colors have a sunken, pasty quality and the tonality of the work, particularly in the blues of the sky, is noticeably darker than that of XIV.3.

NORTH WALL:
5. *Dream of St. Ursula* 1495
Oil on canvas, 274 × 267 cm, cat. n. 578
Plate 28
Inscription (probably retouched):
VICTOR˙ CARP. F. / MCCCCLXXXXV

This work is the most damaged of the cycle. Trimmed at the top and on each side, it has been heavily retouched over the years. Much of the repainting was removed in the recent restoration (1984), and the colors are dull and rather murky. There is no reason to reject the date given in the inscription.
LIT.: Zorzi, 1985, pp. 448–59.

6. *Arrival in Rome*
Oil on canvas, 281 × 307 cm, cat. n. 577
Plates 108, 135
Inscription: VICTORIS / CAR / PATIO˙ VENETI / OPUS˙

Proposed dates from 1490–91 (Moschini Marconi, 1955, p. 102) to c. 1496 (Vertova, 1952, fig. II). Arguments that the work must have been painted after the death of Ermolao Barbaro because of his prior disgrace are inconclusive (Pignatti, 1981, p. 85), but the spatial handling, similar to that of the *Exorcism* (XV.4), suggests a date around 1494–95.
LIT.: Branca and Weiss, 1963, pp. 35–40; Zorzi, 1985, pp. 437–48.

7. *Arrival in Cologne* 1490
Oil on canvas, 280 × 255 cm, cat. n. 579
Plate 115
Inscription: OP. VICTORIS CHARPATIO / VENETI MCCCCLXXXX M. / SEPTEMBRIS

8. *Martyrdom of the Pilgrims and Funeral of St. Ursula* 1493
Oil on canvas, 271 × 561 cm, cat. n. 580
Plate 47
Inscription: VICTORIS CARPATIO / VENETI˙ OPUS / MCCCCLXXX / XIII

Radiographs (1984) show extensive repainting, particularly in the sky and on figures in the front plane.

EAST WALL (CHANCEL):
9. *Apotheosis of St. Ursula and her Companions* 1491
Oil on canvas, 481 × 336 cm, cat. n. 576
Plate 30
Inscription: OP. VICTORIS / CARPATIO / MCCCCLXXXXI

The dating of this work has been much discussed, since its style has been seen by some as more consonant with Carpaccio's works of the early 16th century than with those of the early 1490s. For a summary of the arguments, see Lauts (1962, p. 228

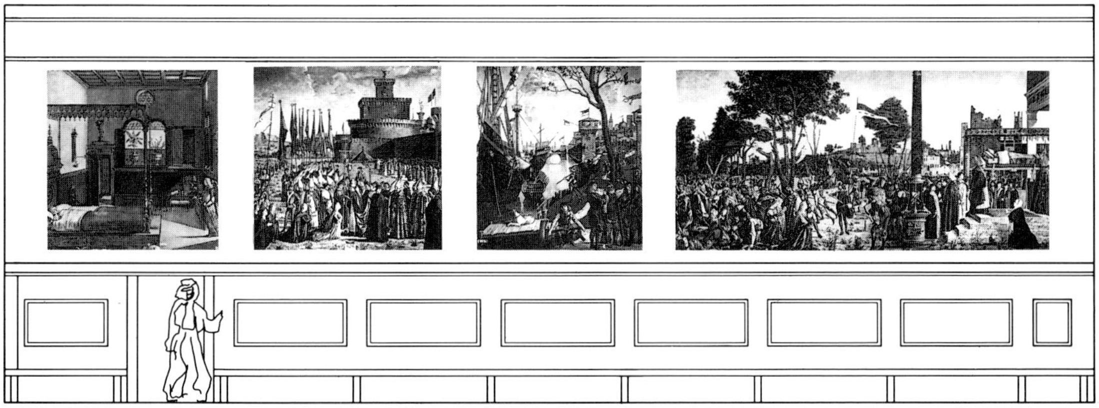

North Wall

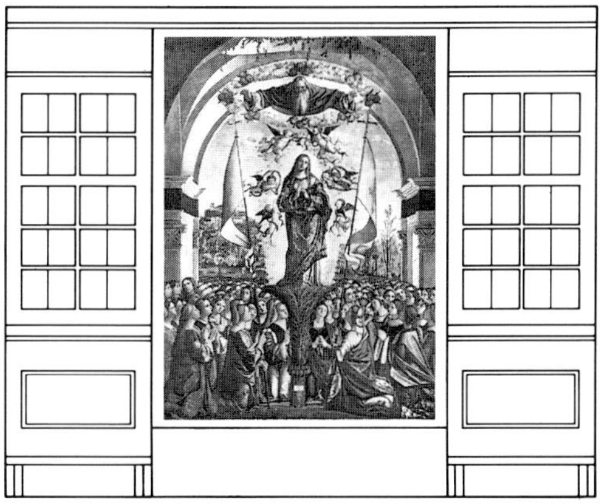

East Wall

[=1491]) and Pignatti (1981, p. 88 [= repainted c. 1510–20 by Carpaccio]). Radiographs made in 1982–83, however, seem to confirm the inscribed date. The underdrawing shows that no extensive changes were made in later repaintings; the clear remains of *spolveri* indicate that Carpaccio may well have entrusted much of the actual execution of the work to assistants (Nepi Scire and Valcanover, 1985, p. 103).

LITERATURE: Vasari, 1966 edn, p. 622; Sansovino, 1581, c. 23; idem, 1663, I, p. 65; Ridolfi, 1914 edn, I, pp. 45–47; Boschini, 1664, pp. 213–15; Boschini, 1674, Castello, pp. 52–53; Cornaro, 1749, 7, p. 235; Zanetti, 1771, pp. 35–36; Molmenti and Ludwig, 1907, pp. 56–110; Moschini Marconi, 1955, pp. 97–105; Lauts, 1962, pp. 227–30; Zampetti, 1963a, pp. 23–82; idem, 1963b, pp. 25–28; Renosto, 1963, pp. 37–50; Gallo, 1963, pp. 1–24; Muraro, 1966; Sgarbi, 1979, cat. nos. 2–11; Pignatti, 1981, pp. 74–88; Bardon, 1983, pp. 43–79; idem, 1985; Nepi Scire and Valcanover, 1985, pp. 103–6; Zorzi, 1985, pp. 437–59.

Measurements from Nepi Scire and Valcanover, 1985, pp. 103–6.

XV. Scuola Grande di San Giovanni Evangelista, Albergo

The Miracles of the True Cross c. 1494–1505/10

Color Plates II, III, XII, XVI–XXIII, XXV, XXXIX, XL

Plates 34, 80–88, 90, 91, 136

HISTORY: During the second half of the Quattrocento, the Scuola Grande di San Giovanni Evangelista engaged in a series of architectural and decoration campaigns, culminating in the 1490s with the True Cross cycle (for earlier programs see Cats. VI and VII above). Initially, attention was centered on the *albergo*, which presumably had received no decorative embellishment since the second decade of the century. In 1453, the room had just been 'rifatto a nuovo a spese dei confratelli' (ASV, S. Giov, Reg. 2, f. 18; and Paoletti, 1893, p. 57: inscription on outside wall). The basic forms of the *albergo* and *sala capitolare* on the *piano nobile*, with their ogival windows, were completed at this time (Pignatti, 1981, pp. 48–49). A commission for a new altar was authorized on 4 May 1457, with the Council of Ten allowing the Scuola to take in thirty extra members above quota, whose entry fees would be applied to the project (doc. 1). On 8 June 1460 a new ceiling was planned; it was completed only in 1467 (Sohm, 1982, p. 330).

In 1478–81 the ill-defined public space in front of the building – little more than an alleyway in comparison to the great *campo* stretching in front of the Scuola di San Marco – was given visual distinction with a new entry court created by a marble screen. Joining the meeting-house of the Scuola di San Giovanni to the homonym church, it is generally attributed to Pietro Lombardo (Lieberman, 1982, pl. 81; but cf. McAndrew, 1980, pp. 144–49). In the 1490s the ceiling of the *albergo* was again replaced (doc. 4a) and possibly raised, although the sources are unclear about this (cf. Bernasconi, 1981, p. 199). In 1493–95 the *sala capitolare* was raised by about 6 *piedi* (c. 2.1 meters) to match the height of the *albergo* (docs. 4a–b). During this period the cycle depicting the Miracles of the True Cross was begun (Bernasconi, 1981, pp. 198–202). In 1498 a new interior staircase was begun by Mauro Codussi (doc. 11). In 1512, soon after the paintings were completed, the building was further adorned with a new entrance portal (Puppi and Olivato Puppi, 1977, pp. 218–20; McAndrew, 1980, pp. 364–77).

A new *albergo* and *archivio* were added to the east in 1540–45, and the old *albergo* became simply the Sala della Croce, a name that had been attached to it occasionally even earlier (Schulz, 1966, pp. 89–96). In the 18th century, further remodelling was carried out by Giorgio Massari, particularly in the *sala capitolare* where a tribune was added at the west end and the ceiling raised again (Massari, 1970, pp. 48–50). The confraternity was suppressed in 1806, but in 1929 it was reformed as the Scuola Grande Arciconfraternita di S. Giovanni Evangelista and retook possession of the relic of the cross. The group presently meets in the Sala della Croce and maintains the building (restored in recent years by the Venice Committee). The canvases were taken into the Accademia as a group in 1820.

DOCUMENTS AND SOURCES:

1. 4 May 1457. An altar is commissioned for the newly remodelled *albergo*: '. . . sia de necessitade de far conpir, et far indorar, et adornar uno altar fato in lalbergo dela dita scuola et altre cosse, nel qual se tien quela sacratissima et gratiosissima nostra croxe, cum le altre reliquie.'

ASV, S. Giov., Reg. 72, f. 220; cf. Reg. 140, f. 162v.

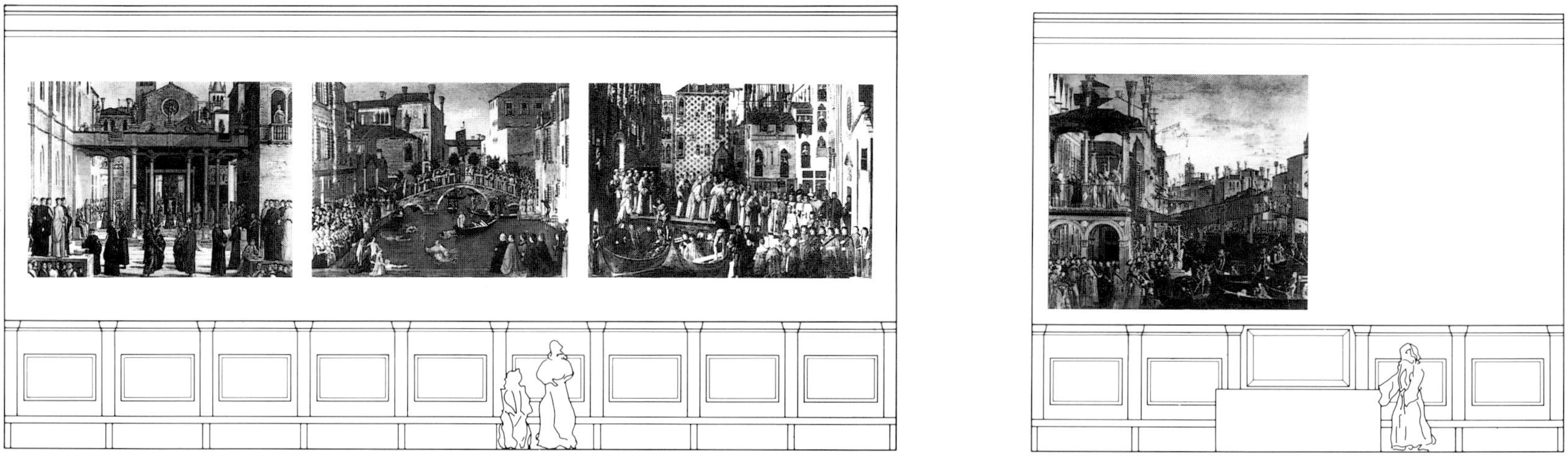

FIG. 2 North Wall East Wall

2. 26 Feb. 1490 m.v. [=1491]. The Scuola receives a concession from the Council of Ten to take in 25 additional members to finance improvements in the *albergo*: 'ut possint perfixere albergum suum, et alia pia opera facere hoc anno possint dicta scola, ultra numerum eis habemus concessum accipere homines vigintiquinque qui excomputent per mortem, et consumationem condensit hominem accipiendor.' No paintings are mentioned.

ASV, Consiglio dei Dieci, Parti Miste, Reg. 24 (1488–90), f. 205. Cf. ASV, S. Giov., Reg. 13, f. 138: 'Mccccl xxxx Adi xxvi Fevrer in tempo de messer francesco pin fo concesso xxv. per l'albergo.'

3. 19 Sept. 1492. The Council of Ten allows the Scuola to suspend its usual distribution of charity for one year to the amount of 200 ducats, and to use the money for the 'fabrica et alijs ornamentis'.

ASV, Consiglio dei Dieci, Parti Miste, Reg. 25, f. 124v.

4a. 22 Feb. 1492 m.v. [=1493]. The Scuola makes a new appeal, this time to take in 50 extra members to finance the raising of the ceiling of the *sala capitolare* to correspond to that of the *albergo*. It is not stated whether the *albergo* itself had been heightened when it received its new *soffito*.

'...cum sit che mediante la gratia de la vostra Serenita lhabino compido el sofitado de lalbergo dove tengono quella miracolosa et sanctissima croxe: lo qual e molto ben confito et satisfa molto a quelli, che concoreno a la devotion de la dicta religa: quali tuti confortano: che se alza anche la sala azioche luna parte corrisponda alaltra: et apreso la devotion sia anche per ornamento a questa gloriosa cita: concorrando continuamente ambassadorj, et molte persone egregie si forestiere como terriere, a la devotion de la dicta sancta religa pero desyderosi di satisfar al una parte, & al altra, hano deliberado de alzar la dicta sala, et equalizarla cum al dicto Albergo: ma obstandoli la Impotentia de la dicta Scuola per le gravissime spexe, che li occore per el gran numero di poverj, che li convien mantegnire, et de povere novizze, che ogni zorno maridano, recorreno a la gratia, et suffragio de la vostra Serenita supplicando se degni conciederli, che oltra persone circa oto [8], che son manendi in lanno presente possino acetare in la dicta Scuola persone 50 boni citadini, et grati a questo ex.mo conseio j qual se habino aconsumar per si medesimi, como la Vostra Serenita per la soa clementia ha concesso a le altre scuole in simeli besogni, et la elemosina che se recevera da li dicti 50 sia dedicada al alzar, et alafabrica, et ornamento de la dicta salla, et che non si possa spender in altro soto pena, alo vardian de ducati 200 di so proprij bene, et de privation de dicta scuola, recommandando se a la gratia de la Vostra Excellentissima Serenita.'

ASV, Consiglio dei Dieci, Parti Miste, Filza 6, f. 300. Cf. Bernasconi, 1981, p. 199.

4b. 27 Feb. 1492 m.v. [=1493]. The Council of Ten grants the request of the Scuola, but the language of the concession is more general concerning the use of the funds: '...non possint expende in alia re, quae in elevando et ornando scolam predictam...'

ASV, Consiglio dei Dieci, Parti Miste, Reg. 25 (1491–92), f. 159.

4c. 8 March 1493. In recording the members taken in under the special concession, the Scuola states that they are for the *albergo* without any mention of the *sala capitolare* – perhaps indicating that their entry fees were used for both rooms: 'Mccccl xxxxiii Adi viii marzo in tempo de messer zuan dario fo concesso L.ª [50] per lalbergo. j quali fo tolti parte in suo tempo e parte in tempo i suo successori ut infra.'

ASV, S. Giov., Reg. 13, f. 138. Names of members admitted under this exemption were listed under three separate years: 1493 = 31; 1495 = 2; 1498 = 7; for a total of 40. According to Bernasconi, 1981, p. 202, n. 26, the list includes only the names of members alive after 1501. All 50 names are listed in Reg. 12. Cf. Sohm, 1982, doc. 189.

5. 21 Aug. 1495. Having raised the ceiling of the *sala capitolare*, the Scuola now requests permission from the Council of Ten to take in 50 extra members to finance a new stone staircase, providing land can be obtained from the Zane family: '...che conzosia che per dicto Guardian e compagni al presente el se fazi alzar la Sala de dicta schola pie vj. circumcirca, la qual cossa corresponde a grandissimo ornamento di dicta Schuola chome manifestamente se vede: et à compida et total perfection de tal opera, el sia necessario far la schala de piera di fuoravia; chome sono rimaste dacordo con Missier Marin Zane & nevodi...'

ASV, Consiglio dei Dieci, Parti Miste, Reg. 26 (1493–95), f. 209 (new num.). Cf. Mason Rinaldi, 1978, p. 299.

6a. Before 12 Nov. 1495 (date effaced). Since the Scuola has been unable to reach an agreement with the Zane family for the extra land, it requests that funds obtained from 50 extra members under the concession of 21 Aug. be used to commission painted *istorie* to cover the wall space left empty by the raising of the ceiling of the Scuola: 'Et perche havemo alzado la dicta schuola pie sie et si reman el muro vuodo a torno a torno che despar molto forte se non se fa qualche bella istoria suxo j teleri, et chuvergar quel vuodo de la nostre depenture in suxo...Nui possano trar tanto che facemo queste belle istorie che sara a compimento fornida la sala piu nobile et piu bella se podesse dir et a laude de la sanctissima [croxe] et honor et laude de Vostra Illustrissima Signoria...'

ASV, Consiglio dei Dieci, Parti Miste, Filza 9, f. 198. Cf. Bernasconi, 1981, p. 198.

6b. 12 Nov. 1495. The petition 'volendo far alguna bella historia sopra et coprir dicto muro' is recorded and passed by the Council of Ten by a vote of 15–0–0.

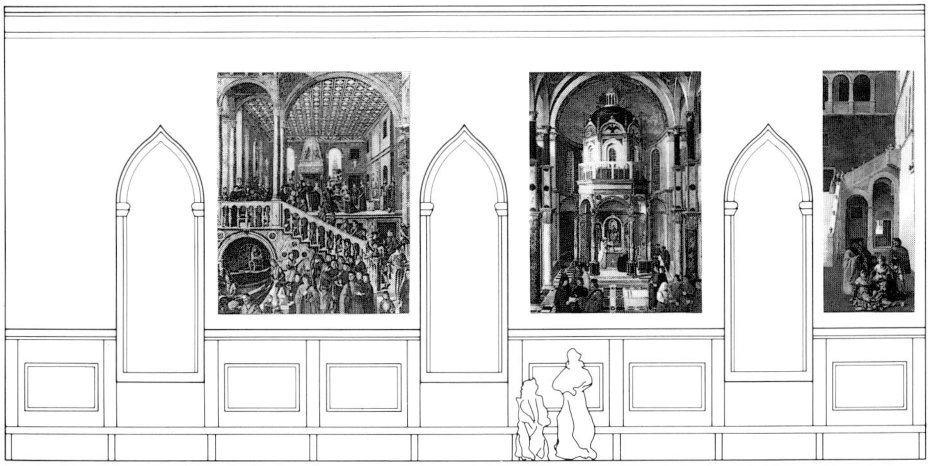

South Wall

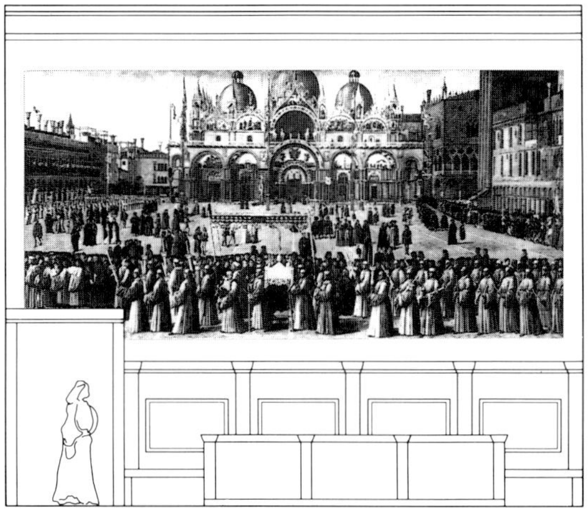

West Wall

ASV, Consiglio dei Dieci, Parti Miste, Reg. 26 (1493–95), f. 220 (new num.). Cf. Bernasconi, 1981, p. 198.

6c. 17 Jan 1495 m.v. [=1496]. The concession of the previous November for works in the *sala capitolare* is recorded: 'In tempo de misser francesco pin fo concessi L.[a] [50] per la fabrica de la sala e fo tolti come a par qui desotto.'

ASV, S. Giov., Reg. 13. Listed are 45 names. There is no evidence that any paintings were ever made for the *sala capitolare* during this period (see Bernasconi, 1981, pp. 198–202).

7. 19 Dec. 1498. The project for the staircase is revived, the Scuola having obtained the necessary land. There is no mention of the *istorie* once planned for the *sala capitolare*.

ASV, Consiglio dei Dieci, Parti Miste, Reg. 27 (1496–98), f. 206v. See Bernasconi, 1981, p. 202, n. 20, for additional archival references.

8a. 26 Nov. 1501. In the earliest specific reference to paintings in the *albergo*, the Scuola requests 50 extra members to continue the project already underway but not completed due to lack of funds.

'Suplicha el Vardian grando de la schuola di batudj de m. San Zuane evangelista e chum sit che per le tenue elemosine rezevono la schuola nostra et atento le graveze de tempj prexentj el non se possj proseguir le depenture principiade ne tellerj se fano per hornamento del albergo, ad honor et reverentia de quella Santissima chroxe et se dimanda de grazia che el sia concesso al ditto Vardian et chompagnj et suzessorj che i possino rezever in ditta sua schuolla hominj L.[a] [50] oltra el numero hordinario i qual rezevudj se habino ascontar overo consumar per se medemj chome a questa et altre Schuole in simel chasj de fabriche et hornamentj altre volte e sta chonzesso azo che la elemosina et oferta de quellj serano rezevudj se possj andar driedo a dittj telerj et hoc petunt de grazie specialj.'

ASV, Consiglio dei Dieci, Parti Miste, Filza 14, f. 279. See also ibid., Reg. 29, f. 10. Cf. Bernasconi, 1981, p. 201; and Mason Rinaldi, 1978, pp. 299–300.

8b. 22 Feb. 1501 m.v. [=1502]. The concession of the previous November for paintings in the *albergo* is recorded: 'Mcccccj de fevrer in tempo de misser Michiel Malombra fo concesso .50. per proseguir j telleri de lalbergo cum condiction chel se sconti X al anno come apar in catastico notado a carte 150.' The members were taken in as follows: 1501 = 1; 1502 = 14; 1503 = 4; 1504 = 2; 1505 = 9; 1506 = 6; for a total of 56.

ASV, S. Giov., Reg. 13, f. 141.

9. c. 1490–1506. An *incunabulum*, entitled *Questi sono imiracoli dela santissima croce delascola demisier san zuane evangelista* (n.d., n.p.), is published, describing the donation of the relic and nine miracles of the cross. No paintings are mentioned.

To my knowledge, the only extant copy of this pamphlet is in the Biblioteca Correr [MCV, Inc. H222 bis]. See Brown, 1982, pp. 5–8.

10. 16 Apr. 1544. Cut-outs must be made in the paintings on the east wall of the old *albergo* (now the Sala della Croce) to accommodate two doors leading to the new *albergo*.

ASV, S. Giov., Reg. 141, f. 135. Full text in Schulz, 1966, p. 93, doc. III.

11. 22 Dec. 1560. The Guardian Grande states that the paintings 'sono scuridi, et à penna si vedono, et questo per esser sporchi . . .' He announces that cleaning is underway and requests funds to complete the project.

ASV, S. Giov., Reg. 43, Mare Rosso, f. 113

12. 4 Jan. 1567. The Sala della Croce and the *albergo* are damaged by fire and repairs are necessary.

ASV, S. Giov., Reg. 142, f. 138. From Mason Rinaldi, 1978, p. 298.

13. 1581. Francesco Sansovino describes the cycle: 'Nell' albergosi veggono dipinte le historie de i miracoli della predetta Croce, di buona mano, & di diversi maestri. Conciosia che la prima tela a man destra fu di Benedetto Diana. La seconda di Gian Bellino, amendue lodatissimi & famosi maestri. La terza di Giovanni de Mansueti, & la tela alla sinistra dell' altare, di Vittorio Scarpaccia huomo di rara eccellenza. L'altra all'incontro fu di Giovanni Mariscalco. Et oltre all'altare, la prima tela dalla sinistra fu dipinta da Lazaro Sebastiani. La seconda da Gentil Bellino, & la terza da Giovanni de Mansueti. La palla dell'altare fu opera di Iacomo Bellino.'

Sansovino, 1581, cc. 100v–101.

14. 1590. The Scuola publishes a pamphlet entitled *Miracoli della Croce Santissima*, with accounts of the donation and ten miracles. Seven paintings are mentioned (see specific citations in list of paintings below).

ORIGINAL ARRANGEMENT: According to Bernasconi (1972, pp. 19–34), the basic shell of the old *albergo* (Sala della Croce) remains the same today (in meters): north wall = 14.15; south wall = 14.48; east wall = 8.40; west wall = 8.05. The walls themselves underwent several alterations. The west wall probably had only one door, located at the south end, in the first decade of the 16th century. In 1560 a second door was added at the other end of the wall. The north wall is unchanged, and, although a different window arrangement on the south wall is possible, it too is probably intact. The addition of two doors at the ends of the east wall in the 1540s, necessitating the cut at the bottom left corner of Carpaccio's painting (XV.4), is well documented (doc. 13). The other painting in question was, in all likelihood, Perugino's lost canvas (XV.3).

The reconstruction in Fig. 2 is based primarily upon two early accounts: Sansovino's description of the room written in or before 1581, and *Miracoli della Croce* (1590).

Sansovino cited eight narrative paintings, omitting Gentile Bellini's *Procession*, which was, however, already documented above the entrance door (west wall) in 1504 (Cat. XIX, doc. 2b). The only major discrepancy between his account and *Miracoli della Croce* is Sansovino's citation of a painting by Marescalco (Giovanni Buonconsiglio), which he appears to place on the east wall to the right of the altar, although his terminology is unclear. By contrast, *Miracoli della Croce* makes no reference to any painting by Mariscalco, but cites a work by 'un Perusino' (omitted by Sansovino), generally interpreted as Pietro Perugino (Pignatti 1981, p. 52). The room as presently constructed could easily have accommodated a tenth painting (of the size of XV.9) at the east end of the south wall. It is thus physically possible that both artists contributed to the cycle and that both of their paintings were damaged or destroyed in the fire of 1567 (see doc. 17). Two of the miracles listed in *Miracoli della Croce*, furthermore, cannot be specifically related to paintings.

However, it seems more likely that the two accounts referred to the same painting, and that Sansovino had simply misidentified a work by Perugino. Vasari last visited Venice in 1566, before the fire of 1567 and presumably when the cycle was still intact. In the 1568 edition of the *Vite*, he was not precise in his description of the cycle, citing eight or nine paintings in the *albergo*, (Vasari, 1966 edn, pp. 428–29); but in order to accommodate both Perugino and Mariscalco, there would have to have been ten. From all indications, therefore, the original program consisted of nine paintings in all (cf. Nepi Scire and Valcanover, 1985, p. 84). Bernasconi's reconstruction (1972), worked out independently, is the same as that proposed here.

The paintings were later rearranged, probably more than once. In 1674 Boschini recorded Diana's painting to the left of the altar and Carpaccio's to the right. The other paintings followed the reconstruction given here. When Zanetti (1771) described the Scuola he placed the three paintings originally on the north wall of the *albergo* in the *sala maggiore*.

The full cycle was restored 1958–60. See Moschini, 1960, pp. 353–61. For earlier restorations see Moschini Marconi, 1955, pp. 57–58.

A note on dating: As cited below, *Miracoli della Croce* (1590) dated four of the paintings to 1494. This date was generally accepted until Ballarin (1978, pp. 237–38) and Mason Rinaldi (1979, p. 299) called it into question, citing a document of 6 Nov. 1495 (doc. 6b above) calling for *qualche bella istoria*. To them, this seemed to indicate that the True Cross paintings were not yet begun as of that date. Their argument was accepted by Sgarbi (1979, cat. 12) and Pignatti (1981, p. 52). However, as Bernasconi (1981, pp. 198–99) has argued quite convincingly, the reference referred to paintings (probably never made) for the *sala capitolare* and not to those of the True Cross in the *albergo*. There is thus no compelling evidence to reject the dates cited in the 1590 booklet.

ORIGINAL CYCLE:
Now in Venice, Accademia Galleries

NORTH WALL:
Lazzaro Bastiani
1. *Donation of the Relic* 1494
Oil on canvas, 319 × 438 cm, cat. n. 561
Color Plates XVI, XXXIX; Plate 81

The paint surface is very abraded.

Miracoli della Croce (1590): '. . . fatta l'anno 1494 per man de M. Lazzaro Sebastiani, huomo all' hora in tal professione di gran fama.'

For the early appearance of the church and its portico see Pazzi, 1985, pp. 17ff; cf. Paoletti, 1893, I, p. 57.

LIT.: Ridolfi, 1914 edn., I, p. 49; Zanetti, 1771, p. 41; Collobi, 1939–40, p. 43; Moschini Marconi, 1955, pp. 56–58; Pignatti, 1981, p. 59 (with incorrect measurements); Nepi Scire and Valcanover, 1985, p. 84.

Gentile Bellini
2. *Miracle at the Bridge of San Lorenzo* 1500
Oil on canvas, 323 × 430 cm, cat. n. 568
Color Plates III, XX, XL; Plates 86, 136
Inscription: GENTILI BELLINI VENETI F. / MCCCCC

The inscription was probably repainted. Ridolfi recorded it as: 'Gentilis Bellinus Eques pio sanctissimae crucis affectu lubens fecit. MCCCCC.', while Zanetti reported only: Gentilis Bellini / MCCCCC.

Miracoli della Croce (1590): 'un quadro fatto l'anno 1500. per man de M. Zentil Bellini all'hora Pittor famosissimo.'

Various proposals have been made regarding the foreground figures, none of them convincing. Gibbons (1963, pp. 54–58) proposed that the group of five men kneeling in the right foreground were Gentile Bellini and the male members of his family, ranked in order of age. The hypothesis is implausible, for of Gibbons's group only Jacopo Bellini had been a member and he had died about thirty years earlier. Although the artist had painted a cycle of *istorie* for the Scuola and had received a dowry subvention reserved for needy members for his daughter's marriage (ASV, San Giovanni, Reg. 72), it is improbable that these activities had earned him sufficient status in the confraternity to explain such a prominent inclusion of his family in the *Miracle at San Lorenzo*. Gibbons's notation of a suggestion by H. W. Janson that the painting depicts an actual centennial celebration, held perhaps in 1470 (ibid., p. 57 n. 42) has been picked up by other scholars and repeated as fact. To this date, there has been, however, no documentary substantiation for the notion.

Billanovich (1973), Collins (1973) and, most recently, Meyer zur Capellen (1985) attempted to identify the group as members of the Cornaro family, while J. Bernasconi, in a paper presented at the annual conference of English Art Historians, Manchester, 27 March 1983, proposed the Vendramin family. It is also possible that Gentile depicted himself with the Banca of the Scuola of 1500. Two of the four top officers of that year were members of the Ducal Chancery: the Guardian Grande, Pietro Amadi, and the Vicario, Nicolo de Bernardo (ASV, S. Giov, Reg. 73). They would normally have worn the red togas that we see here.

LIT.: Ridolfi, 1914 edn., I, p. 61; Zanetti, 1771, pp. 58–59; Moschini Marconi, 1955, no. 63, p. 63; Gibbons 1963, pp. 54–58; Collins, 1970, pp. 56–62; idem, 1982c, pp. 201–8; Meyer zur Capellen, 1985, pp. 77–80 and 135.

Pietro Perugino
3. *Deliverance of Andrea Vendramin's Ships (lost)* (1494)

Miracoli della Croce (1590): 'un quadro fatto l'anno 1494. de man di un Perosino, il qual essendo già abbrucciato, è stato ultimamente renovato l'anno 1588. de mano de M. Andrea Visentino.'

Perugino is documented in Venice in 1494 and May–Oct. 1497 (Canuti, 1931, I, p. 121, and II, p. 184). His painting for the Scuola may have been destroyed in the fire of 1567 (doc. 12). Its replacement by Vicentino (not cited by Boschini, Ridolfi or Zanetti) was seen on the window wall in the *Sala della Croce* by Dionisi (1787, p. 20): 'Vi è Andrea Vendramino Confratello della Scola di S. Giovanni Evangelista giacente in letto, ed in sogno implorante la S.S. Croce della sua Scola, a salvezza di una grave disgrazia, da cui gli pareva di essere minacciato, e da un' altra parte del Quadro si vedono due suoi Navigli in grave burrasca in procinto di perdersi, salvati dalla S.S. Croce, che si vede comparsa in loro soccorso; e da un' altro lato, del Quadro stesso compariscono li due Capitani delli detti Navigli, che giungono nella Scola, e si abboccano con il sopra detto Vendramino, esponendogli il prodigio, e la Grazia ricevuta, riconosciuta dalla Reliquia della SS. Croce. Di Andrea Vicentino.'

LIT.: Canuti, 1931, I, p. 121, and II, p. 184; Ballarin, 1978, pp. 237–38; Smyth, 1979, I. p. 231.

Vittore Carpaccio
4. *Healing of the Possessed Man by the Patriarch of Grado (Exorcism)* 1494
Oil on canvas, 365 × 389 cm, cat. n. 566
Color Plates II, XXII; Plate 91

Cut-out for door in lower left-hand corner (0.25 × 1.5 m), awkwardly repaired, probably in the 17th century.

Miracoli della Croce (1590): 'un quadro fatto l'anno 1494. de man de M. Vettor Scarpazza, all'hora ottimo Pittore.'

LIT.: Ridolfi, 1914 edn, I, p. 44; Zanetti, 1771, p. 39; Molmenti and Ludwig, 1907, pp. 189–92; Moschini Marconi, 1955, pp. 96–97; Lauts, 1962, p. 78; Zampetti, 1963a, pp. 84–86; Muraro, 1966, pp. lvi–lxii; Sgarbi, 1979, no. 12.

Giovanni Mansueti
5. *Miracle at the Bridge of San Lio* 1494
Oil on canvas, 318 × 458 cm, cat. n. 564
Color Plates XXI, XLII; Plate 87
Inscription: OPUS / JOANNIS D / MANSUETI / S VENETI / RECTE SENTENTIUM BELLI / NI DISCIPLI

Miracoli della Croce (1590): 'il quadro di questo miracolo, fatto l'anno 1494. de mano de M. Zuane di Mansueti zotto, all'hora perfettissimo Pittore.'

Related drawing: Uffizi, no. 1293 (fig. 85)

LIT.: Ridolfi, 1914 edn, I, pp. 49–50; Zanetti, 1771, p. 43; Moschini Marconi, 1955, p. 134; Tietze and Tietze-Conrat, 1944, p. 69; Miller, 1978, pp. 81–84.

Giovanni Mansueti
6. *Healing of the Daughter of Ser Nicolò Benvegnudo of San Polo* c. 1506
Oil on canvas, 369 × 296 cm, cat. n. 562
Color Plate XXIII; Plate 90

The subject matter of this painting was consistently misunderstood by later critics. It was not specifically attributed to Mansueti in *Miracoli della Croce* (1590), and Ridolfi (followed by Boschini and Zanetti), probably consulting the booklet, looked for a miracle account that matched what he saw in the painting. Instead of the incident involving Benvegnudo's daughter, he chose a tenth miracle that had been added in this edition to the nine cited in the *incunabulum*. It was presented in the form of a letter, dated 1461, from an Antonio Riccio, Cancelliere dell' Arcipelago, telling of a miraculous rescue from a storm at sea. Ridolfi, probably observing a figure in the foreground of the painting who holds a letter, concluded that the scene depicted Riccio at a sort of homecoming party, 'where he is receiving the visits of friends, who celebrate his return to the homeland'.

LIT.: Ridolfi, 1914 edn, I, pp. 50–51; Boschini, 1674, San Polo, p. 38; Zanetti, 1771, p. 43; Moschini Marconi, 1955, p. 137; Miller, 1978, pp. 84–85.

Gentile Bellini
7. *Procession in the Piazza San Marco* 1496
Oil on canvas, 367 × 745 cm, cat. n. 567
Color Plates XII, XVIII, XIX, XXV; Plates 34, 83, 85

Inscription: MCCCCLXXXXVI / GENTILIS BELLINI VENETI EQUITIS CRUCIS / AMORE INCENSUS. OPUS

The inscription was probably repainted. Ridolfi: 'Gentilis Bellinus eques amore incensus crucis MCCCCLXXXXVI.' Zanetti: 'Gentilis Bellini veneti equitis crucis / amore incensi opus MCCCCLXXXXVI.'

Two earlier cuts for doorways, one at each end of the lower edge (L: 72 × 145 cm; R: 70 × 167 cm) have been replaced with canvas inserts and repainted (more convincingly on the right side than on the left).

Miracoli della Croce (1590): 'un quadro, fatto l'anno 1496. de mano de M. Zentil Bellini, in quei tempi singolarissimo Pittore.'

Related drawing: British Museum, 1933–8–3–12 (fig. 83)

LIT.: Ridolfi, 1914 edn, I, p. 58; Zanetti, 1771, pp. 60–61; Tietze and Tietze-Conrat, 1944, p. 70; Moschini Marconi, 1955, pp. 61–63; Collins, 1970, pp. 48–56; Meyer zur Capellen, 1985, pp. 70–77 and 133–34.

Gentile Bellini
8. *Healing of Pietro dei Ludovici* 1501
Oil on canvas, 369 × 259 cm, cat. n. 563
Color Plate XVII; Plate 82

Inscription: GENTILIS BELLINI/VENETI F.

Neither Ridolfi nor Zanetti reported an inscription.

Miracoli della Croce (1590): 'fu fatto un quadro l'anno 1501. fra le due finestre dell'-Albergo, de mano da M. Zentil Bellini...'

A strip (7 × 151 cm) was removed from the bottom and another strip (12 × 259 cm) added at the top (Moschini, 1960).

LIT.: Ridolfi, 1914 edn, I, p. 61; Zanetti, 1771, p. 58; Baumeister, 1934, pp. xxxvi-xl; Moschini Marconi, 1955, pp. 63–64; Collins, 1970, p. 62; Meyer zur Capellen, 1985, pp. 80–81 and 135–36.

Benedetto Diana
9. *Healing of the Son of Alvise Finetti* c. 1505–10
Oil on canvas, 365 × 147 cm, cat. n. 565
Plate 80

Miracoli della Croce (1590) cites this miracle but not the painting. Pignatti's (1981, p. 60) dating to the end of the first decade of the 16th century is credible.

Since Diana's painting is about half the width of the other vertically formatted canvases, some scholars have suggested that it has been radically cut. The question was raised by Boschini's (1674, S. Polo, pp. 37–38) description of the painting: 'vi sono bellisime Architetture, con molte figure, e diversi Confrati, che dispensano danari in elemosina...' In addition to seeing 'many figures' in the work, he misunderstands the subject. Cf. Ridolfi, who saw in it a painter attempting to paint in the style of Giorgione. He described a 'figura d'un giovine, che ha il capello ornato di piume, e l'abito variato di striscie rosse e bianche, appunto alla Giorgionesca.' Bernasconi (1972. pp. 10–13) makes a good case against cutting, while Pignatti (1981) holds that the original painting was wider. It may well have been trimmed, but probably only by a small amount. The present wall space (and its original location, as far as we know) would allow for an addition of about .25 meter width.

LIT.: Ridolfi, 1914 edn, I, p. 41; and Zanetti, 1771, p. 71; Moschini Marconi, 1955, pp. 131–32; Paolucci, 1966, pp. 3–20; Bernasconi, 1972, pp. 10–13.

LITERATURE: MCV, Inc. H222 bis; Vasari, 1550 and 1568, 1966 edn, pp. 428–29; Sansovino, 1581, cc. 100v–101; idem, 1663, I, p. 284; *Miracoli della Croce*, 1590; Boschini, 1664, pp. 292–94; Boschini, 1674, S. Polo, pp. 37–38; Cornaro, 1749, 6, pp. 328–77; Zanetti, 1771, p. 41; G. C. Dionisi, *Sommario de memorie ossia descrizione succinta delli Quadri esistenti nella veneranda Scuola Grande di S. Giovanni Evangelista ed annessa chiesa con li nomi dei loro pittori*, Venice, 1787; Moschini, 1815, II:2, pp. 495–500; Paoletti, 1893, I, p. 57; Moschini Marconi, 1955, pp. 131–32; Schulz, 1966, pp. 89–96; A. Massari, *Giorgio Massari*, 1970, pp. 48–50; Bernasconi, 1972, pp. 19–34; Wurthmann, 1975, pp. 142–52; Puppi and Olivato Puppi, 1977, pp. 218–20; Sohm, 1978, pp. 125–49; Mason Rinaldi, 1978, pp. 293–98; McAndrew, 1980, pp. 144–49 and 364–77; Pignatti, 1981, pp. 48–60; Bernasconi, 1981, pp. 198–202; Brown, 1982, pp. 5–8; Lieberman, 1982, pp. 24–26, and Pls. 67 and 81–85 with text; Zorzi, 1984, pp. 379–82; Pazzi, 1985; Nepi Scire and Valcanover, 1985. See also Cats. VI and VII above.

Measurements from Nepi Scire and Valcanover (1985).

XVI. Arte dei Setaiuoli or Guild of the Silk-weavers

Life of St. Mark c. 1495–99
Color Plate XXXII; Plates 118–20

HISTORY: The Arte dei Setaiuoli was a craft guild, drawing its membership primarily from silk-weavers who had immigrated from Lucca. From the late 15th century, the group held rights to an apsidal chapel in the Church of the Crociferi (later Gesuiti) in the *sestiere* of Cannaregio. It was dedicated to the Virgin Annunciate and St. Mark (Humfrey, 1983, pp. 83 and 106–7).

During the last decade of the 15th century, the chapel was decorated with a small cycle of paintings on wood depicting scenes from the life of St. Mark. No documentation concerning their execution survives, but according to Stringa the program consisted of an altarpiece and four narrative paintings (doc. 1). Boschini reported the same works in the chapel in 1664. But by 1674 only two narrative paintings (by Cima and Mansueti) remained there, and they had been moved to the opposite wall (Boschini, 1674, Cannaregio, p. 11). For later provenance see Humfrey (1983, p. 83).

DOCUMENTS AND SOURCES:
1. 1604. Stringa gives the earliest description of the cycle: 'Paolo Veronese vi fece la Natività di Cristo posta nella cappella dell' altar dell' Annunciata, che giace a man dritta della cappella Maggiore la cui pala è nobilissima per esser stata da Gio. Battista da Conegliano eccellentissimo Pittore dipinta. Vi sono anco di eccellente pittura in questa cappella i quattro quadri molto antichi, ne' quali dipinti, veggonsi alcuni miracoli di S. Marco da Latantio da Rimino l'anno 1499.'
Sansovino-Stringa, 1604, p. 147.
2. 1664. Boschini describes the arrangement in more detail: 'Nella prima Capella, uscendo di Sacrestia, chiamata dell' Annonciata, la Tavola dell' Altare è pure l'Annonciata, di Giovanni Battista Cima da Conegliano; opera gentilissima.
Vi sono poi da un lato quattro quadri, di quattro Autori, nell' uno si vede S. Marco, che sana S. Aniano della ferita della mano; & pure del Conegliano, cosa veramente rara.
Nell'altro, che segue, evvi S. Marco, che predica, & è di mano di Latanzio da Rimini, fatto l'anno 1499. Nel' uno degli altri due sopra questi vè la presa di San Marco: & è di Giovanni Mansueti; l'altro è di autore più antico, & incerto. All'incontro delli detti quadri, vi è la nascita di nostro Signore, di mano di Paolo Veronese cosa signolare.'
Boschini, 1664, pp. 421–22.

ORIGINAL ARRANGEMENT: As Humfrey (1983, pp. 106–7) has shown, the chapel was located to the left of the high altar as we face it. With the light source on the right for XVI.1 and 3, he concluded that the panels would have originally hung in a single row on the left wall. Boschini did place the works on a single wall in 1664, but he seems to indicate that two were placed above (*sopra*) the others. In the Chatsworth drawing, the light source is clearly on the left. If we accept it as a fair model (or copy) of Lattanzio da Rimini's lost painting (see XVI.2 below), we may conclude that the paintings were originally arranged in pairs on each side of the altar and were moved to a single wall to make room for Veronese's *Nativity* at some time before 1604, when Stringa saw them. Their transfer to the right hand wall between 1664 and 1674 (Boschini, 1674, Cannaregio, p. 11) may have been prompted by the desire to offer a better view of Veronese's *Nativity* from the nave of the church.

ORIGINAL CYCLE:

Cima da Conegliano
1. *St. Mark Healing Anianas*
Berlin, Staatliche Museen, cat. n. 15
Oil on poplar, 167 × 137 cm — Plate 118
A 10 cm strip was added at top, and 5.9 cm at bottom; left side cropped c. 6–8 cm (Humfrey, 1983, p. 82).
Humfrey's dating of the panel to 1497–99 is plausible.
LIT.: Ludwig, 1905, pp. 70–71; Coletti, 1959, p. 80; Berlin-Dahlem, 1978, p. 107; Humfrey, 1983, pp. 82–84.

Lattanzio da Rimini
2. *St. Mark Preaching* (lost) — 1499
There is no further mention of the work after Boschini's notice of 1664. It has often been suggested that its composition may be reflected in a drawing once in the Chatsworth Collection [Plate 119] (Tietze and Tietze-Conrat, 1944, I, 181, no. 749).
LIT.: Ludwig, 1905, pp. 30–31.

Giovanni Mansueti
3. *Arrest of St. Mark* — 1499
Collection of the Prince of Liechtenstein, Vaduz
Oil on wood, 164 × 146 cm
Color Plate XXXII; Plate 120
Inscription: IOANES DE MANSVETIS P.
On a *cartellino*: 'Ser Jacò de Simon, Ser Anttò de Uaischo, Ser J de Bevilaqua, Ser Felipò de Belttame, Ser Zuane de Zorzi, Ser Alberto Darin, Ser Fermo de Stefano, Ser Nicholo de Marcho, Ser Michiel Uerzo, Ser Alesio de Andrea, questi son li judexi e li provedador. 1499 adi 18.mazo'
Restoration was begun on this work in 1985.
LIT.: Heinemann, 1965, pp. 150ff; Miller, 1978, p. 91; Reinhold Baumstark, *Masterpieces from the Collection of the Princes of Liechtenstein*, trans. R. Wolf, New York, c. 1980.

4. *Subject and artist unknown* (lost)
The logical subject to complete the narrative sequence would have been the Martyrdom of St. Mark.

Cima da Conegliano
5. *Annunciation*
Leningrad, Hermitage Museum n. 256
Oil and tempera on wood, 143 × 113 cm
LIT.: Humfrey, 1983, pp. 106–8.

LITERATURE: Sansovino, 1663, I, p. 169; Boschini, 1664, pp. 421–22; Boschini, 1674, Cannaregio, p. 11; Humfrey, 1983, pp. 82–4 and 106–8.

XVII. Scuola di San Giorgio degli Schiavoni

Carpaccio
Scenes from the lives of Christ and SS. Jerome, Augustine, George and Tryphon
c. 1502–7
Color Plates XIII, XIV, XXX, XXXVI–XXXVIII; Plates 112, 126, 127, 131

HISTORY: Founded by a group of Dalmatian (or *Schiavoni*) immigrants, the Scuola was approved by the Council of Ten on 19 May 1451. It was dedicated to SS. George and Tryphon, patron saints of Cattaro (Corner, 1749, XII, pp. 388–89; Perocco, 1964, pp. 18–21, and doc. I, pp. 209–14). St. Jerome, another Dalmatian saint, was later added to its dedication. The Priorate of the Order of St. John of Jerusalem (then known as the Knights of Rhodes and later called the Knights of Malta) gave the Scuola land beneath the campanile of San Giovanni del Tempio on which to construct a chapel and altar, as well as meeting-space in the hospice of Santa Caterina, built in the Trecento. The hospice seems to have been closed by that time, but the new confraternity had to share the building with the Priorate and the small Scuola di San Giovanni Battista (Pallucchini and Perocco, 1961, pp. 67–72; Luttrell, 1970, pp. 374–80).
The new Scuola incurred expenses for wall construction and decoration during the period 1451–55, including an altar dedicated to St. George on the ground floor of the old hospice. The room was decorated with a

soffitto painted in red, gold and blue, with a carved and painted wooden relief in the center depicting St. George on horseback flanked by the Angel Gabriel and the Virgin Annunciate at the top, and by tiny figures of SS. Jerome (holding the Scuola building) and Tryphon (holding the town of Cattaro) at the bottom. It remains in the Scuola, now serving as an altar frontal in the *sala* on the *piano nobile* (Pallucchini and Perocco, 1961, p. 47).

Although no documentation survives, Carpaccio's canvases for the Scuola were probably completed between 1502 and 1507 (as claimed by Boschini, 1664, p. 194). In 1502 the Scuola was presented with an important relic of St. George by the patrician Paolo Valaresso, commander of the Venetian fortresses at Modone and Corone when they fell to the Turks in 1499. The donation may have prompted the decoration campaign of painted *istorie*, for two of Carpaccio's paintings (XVII.1 and XVII.4) carry the date 1502 and seem to be among the first completed. Although Perocco suggests five possible patrons, including Valaresso, for the paintings, none can be documented. A coat-of-arms painted on two works (XVII.1 and XVII.2) would seem to offer an important clue, but it has not yet been satisfactorily identified (Pallucchini and Perocco, 1961, pp. 10–12 and 33ff).

A legal battle began, also in 1502, between the Scuola and the Priorate, over 'works in stone and wood' being carried out in the building. The jurisdictional dispute was resolved only in 1518, with a legal clarification and separation between the parts of the building controlled by the two entities. In 1551 the interior of the building was further remodelled and a new facade added. The Scuola borrowed 200 ducats in 1565 to make benches and a new soffit on the upper floor. By 1586 the arrangement of the lower floor with Carpaccio's paintings was probably completed in the form that we see it today, with the exception of the altar structure at the north end of the room which was made in the 17th century (Pallucchini and Perocco, pp. 80–83).

In 1806 the Scuola was faced with extinction under Napoleon's sweeping decree abolishing all of the Venetian *scuole*. However, the Guardian Grande appealed to Prince Eugène Beauharnais, Viceroy of Italy, for an exemption, calling the confraternity 'questo ultimo baluardo degli Schiavoni' and describing its distinct character in the history of Venice. In an unusual concession, Beauharnais revoked the decree and allowed the group to continue as a confraternity. It thus retained its meeting-house and possessions, and Carpaccio's paintings remained in the building for which they were originally intended (Perocco, 1964, p. 52).

DOCUMENTS AND SOURCES:

1. 24 April 1502: The Scuola is given a relic of St. George by Paolo Valaresso, who received it as a death-bed bequest from the Patriarch of Jerusalem.

Scuola di San Giorgio, Mariegola ['La Fraternitade overo Scuola in honore de missier san zorzi e missier san trifon'] (text in Perocco, 1964, doc. III, pp. 215–16; cf. Cornaro, 1749, 12, pp. 391–93). The book is still kept in the Scuola. The confraternity has been publishing the text of the Mariegola by installment in their annual periodical, *Scuola Dalmata dei SS. Giorgio e Trifone* (1973, 1975, 1976 and 1983).

2. 22 June 1502: A papal indulgence is granted for the altar of St. George, directing that it be further adorned and that the brothers should pray before it on the feast-days of SS. George, Tryphon, Jerome and John the Baptist.

Scuola di San Giorgio, Catastico, c. 12b. Cited by Perocco, 1964, pp. 32–33.

3a. 10 July 1503: A dispute which began at some time in 1502 between the Scuola and Prior Sebastiano Michiel over construction work in the building and ownership of the upper floor is adjudicated.

Scuola di S. Giorgio, Catastico, c. 18a. Text in Perocco, 1964, doc. V, pp. 217–19. See also ibid., pp. 31–34 and doc. IV, pp. 216–17; and Pallucchini and Perocco, 1961, pp. 73ff.

3b. 1503 [after 10 July]: A petition presented to the Doge in relation to the legal dispute states that since 1452, the confraternity had 'per ornamento de quella [scuola] speso qualche miaro de Ducati.'

Scuola di San Giorgio, Catastico, cc. 24b–25. Text in Perocco, 1964, doc. VI, pp. 220–21.

4. 5 May 1518: Revived in 1515, the dispute between the Priorate and the Scuola is finally resolved. The latter is given full rights to its portion of the lower floor of the building, although it is not allowed to make modifications there. It was composed of three spaces: the present oratory of the Scuola, probably including a kitchen; the tiny Scuola di S. Giovanni Battista, which occupied most of the present sacristy until 1827; and a passageway behind the sacristy (on the north side) which was to be retained by the Priorate. The Prior was also allowed to remove an altar of St. Catherine from the lower floor.

It was with regard to the upper floor of the building that the Scuola received major concessions. It was to retain full rights to the space that it already occupied and was allowed to add to it an area measuring 3 *passi*, 2 *piedi* [=6 m] in width (excluding wall thickness); and 6 *passi*, 2 *piedi* [=11.2 m] in length (including the wall).

Scuola di San Giorgio, Catastico, cc. 29b–35. Summary in Perocco, 1964, doc. VII, pp. 221–24.

5. 12 Dec. 1551: The Scuola di San Giovanni Battista is asked to contribute 80 ducats for the restoration of the right-hand (east) side of the building where they have their meeting-rooms. They are also authorized to raise the *soffito* of their ground-floor room to match that of the Scuola di San Giorgio which has just been raised by 'piè cinque e mezo in circa' [about 2 m].

Scuola di San Giorgio, Catastico, cc. 101b–102b (Perocco, 1964, pp. 75–77).

6. 1 Dec. 1557: An inventory is made of the contents of the Scuola, giving the earliest surviving reference to Carpaccio's paintings, but omitting the artist's name. The following excerpt includes the complete segment of the list (without omissions) in which all possible references to Carpaccio's *istorie* appear.

> Uno quadro de zoso [giù] della adoration de Cristo al monte.
> Uno quadro de Cristo con l'apostoli.
> Uno quadro de nostra donna.
> Uno quadro de S. hieronimo.
> Uno quadro de S. Agostin.
> Quattro quadri dell'istoria de S. Zorzi.
> Un altar de S. Zorzi.
> Li banchi de zoso atorno l'albergo et il scagno.
> Uno quadro de nostra donna de zoso.
> Un'altar dell' anontiada de suso con quadri tre di sopra doi de nostra donna et uno de S. hieronimo.
> Uno quadro amodo de chiesiola intaiado de nostra Donna.
> Uno quadro grando de S. Zorzi.
> La istoria del martirio de S. Zorzi in doi quadri.

Scuola di San Giorgio, Registro degli Inventari, Cf. Perocco, 1964, doc. IX, pp. 225–29, for a transcription of the complete inventory.

ORIGINAL ARRANGEMENT: The building of Carpaccio's time was substantially remodelled during the last half of the 16th century. According to a document of 1515, the Scuola di San Giorgio shared with the Priorate and the Scuola di San Giovanni Battista a building with overall interior dimensions of 19 × 12 m (Pallucchini and Perocco, 1961, p. 70). This configuration corresponds well enough to Barbari map of 1500, which showed a rectangular structure of two stories. The original placement of Carpaccio's paintings is unknown. Nor is it certain whether they were originally intended to hang together in one room as a single cycle. Molmenti and Ludwig (1907, pp. 116–17) and Perocco assumed that they were originally made for a *sala* on the upper floor. Such a placement is likely, but it should not be taken for granted. Although such was the case in the preceding Scuole Grandi, up to that time the cycles of the other *scuole piccole* were all ground-floor installations. Even before the raising of the ceiling of the lower floor of the Scuola di S. Giorgio by c. 2 m in 1551 (doc. 5), the room still measured about 3 m in height and could have accommodated Carpaccio's canvases above lower wooden benches along the walls. The floor plan of the room would have been essentially the same as the present one (c. 8.25 × 10.6 m).

Although the earlier configuration of the upper floor was very different from the present arrangement, all of Carpaccio's surviving paintings could have been accommodated there as well. Before the agreement of 1518, the total area occupied by the Scuola on the upper floor would have been approximately half that of the present *sala* (c. 12 m wide × 11 m deep), and somewhat less than the present oratory on the lower floor. This space included, moreover, not only a *sala* but two *alberghi*. And yet, even allowing for windows, doors, framing and altarpieces, the available area could have supplied the minimum of about 21.6 meters of running wall-space required by Carpaccio's surviving canvases.

The inventory of 1557 (doc. 6) lists eleven possible *istorie*, citing six (instead of three) paintings of St. George. One of the paintings of St. Jerome (XVII.3 or XVII.4) seems to be omitted, unless it is included with the altar of the Annunciata. St. Tryphon (XVII.9) is not mentioned at all. Perocco (1964, p. 91) suggested that the latter saint could have been mistaken for St. George and that the inventory may have included additional works (such as George's martyrdom) which no longer survive (but cf. Pignatti, 1981, p. 108). The only thing that we can conclude with reasonable certainty from the inventory is the existence in the Scuola in 1557 of at least 7 of the 9 surviving paintings, one of which (Uno quadro de zoso della adoration de Cristo al monte) was in the downstairs room at that time.

The present installation also includes an altarpiece of the Madonna and Child, which was installed in the existing frame only in the 19th century, replacing a 15th-century triptych of SS. George, Jerome and Tryphon. It is attributed by some to Carpaccio's son, Benedetto (Pallucchini and Perocco, 1961, p. 84); and by others, at least tentatively, to Carpaccio (Pignatti, 1981, p. 117). Although the painting is in very poor condition and thus difficult to judge in regard to the paint handling, the composition could well be Carpaccio's.

The surviving narrative paintings may be grouped into four themes: (1). Life of Christ; (2) Life of St. Jerome; (3) Life of St. George; (4) Life of St. Tryphon. The list below follows that order, which appears to coincide with the general sequence of execution with one exception. Pallucchini (1961, p. 49) dated XVII.9 before the other works on the basis of similarities between its architecture and that of the St. Ursula cycle. As far as execution is concerned, it is the weakest of the group, a circumstance that caused Pignatti and others to place it after the other works, as evidence of Carpaccio's declining powers. Pallucchini's argument for the earlier dating is more convincing. Carpaccio's later cycle for the Scuola di San Stefano shows a progression away from the narrative tableau processional movement toward more centralized compositions like those of the life of St. George in the San Giorgio cycle. As Pignatti himself allows, the rather mediocre execution could well have been the responsibility of the workshop, as it was in all likelihood in the case of the Scuola degli Albanesi.

The paintings were restored in 1945–47 by Mauro Pelliciolli (see N. di Carpegna in *Arte Veneta*, 1 [1947], pp. 67–68; V. Moschini in *Burlington Magazine*, 89 [1947], pp. 341; Pallucchini and Perocco, 1961, p. 93). A new restoration is scheduled to begin in the autumn of 1987.

EXISTING CYCLE:
Venice, Scuola di San Giorgio degli Schiavoni
Carpaccio

1. *Calling of Matthew* 1502
Oil and tempera on canvas, 141 × 115 cm
Inscription: C[AR]PAT / IVS [VE]N[E]T[VS] / MDII.

2. *Agony in the Garden*
Oil and tempera on canvas, 141 × 107 cm
Inscription: illegible

3. *St. Jerome and the Lion*
Oil and tempera on canvas, 141 × 211 cm
Color Plate XXX

4. *Funeral of St. Jerome* 1502
Oil and tempera on canvas, 141 × 211 cm
Inscription: VICTOR CARPATIVS / FINGEBAT / MDII

5. *St. Augustine in his Study*
Oil and tempera on canvas, 141 × 211 cm
Color Plates XIII, XIV
Inscription: VICTOR / CARPATHIVS / FINGEBAT

Perocco (1956, p. 223) suggested that Cardinal Bessarion was used as the model for the saint portrayed here, and Roberts (1959, pp. 283–97) first identified the subject of the painting as St. Augustine rather than St. Jerome.

LIT.: Roberts, 1959; E. Lowinsky, 'Epilogue: The Music in "St. Jerome's Study"', *Art Bulletin*, 41 (1959): pp. 298–301; Wazbinski, 1968, pp. 21–29; P. Reutersward, 'The dog in the humanists' study', *Konsthistorisk tidskrift* 50/2 (1981): pp. 53–69; M. Feld, 'Sweynheym and Pannartz, Cardinal Bessarion, Neoplatonism: Renaissance Humanism and Two Early Printers' Choice of Texts', *Harvard Library Bulletin*, 30 (1982): pp. 324–35.

6. *St. George Fighting the Dragon*
Oil and tempera on canvas, 141 × 360 cm
Color Plates XXXVI, XXXVII
Inscription: illegible

7. *Triumph of St. George*
Oil and tempera on canvas, 141 × 360cm
Color Plate XXXVIII; Plates 126, 127
Inscription: illegible
Related drawing: Uffizi, no. 1287 [fig. 128]

8. *St. George Baptizing the Pagans* 1507/8
Oil and tempera on canvas, 141 × 285 cm
Plate 131
Inscription: illegible? or VICTOR CARPA[TIVS] / MDVII (?: effaced on the right side and may read MDVIII).

Cut-out in lower left-hand corner: 103 × 33 cm, now filled.

9. *Miracle of St. Tryphon*
Oil and tempera on canvas, 141 × 300 cm
Plate 112

Trimmed on the left side, but unlikely to be by as much as the 60 cm suggested by Perocco.

LITERATURE: Ridolfi, 1914 edn, p. 47; Sansovino, 1663, p. 47; Boschini, 1664, p. 194; Boschini, 1674, Castello, p. 37; Zanetti, 1771, p. 37; Cornaro, 1749, 12, pp. 388–95; Molmenti and Ludwig, 1907, pp. 111–40; Perocco, 1956, pp. 221–24; Pallucchini and Perocco, 1961; Lauts, 1962, pp. 230–34;

Zampetti, 1963a, pp. 129–97; Perocco, 1964 (essentially repeating the Appendix of Pallucchini and Perocco [1961]); Muraro, 1966, pp. lxxiv-cviii; Wazbinski, 1967, pp. 164–68; Cancogni and Perocco, 1967, pp. 97–101; T. Luttrell, 'The Hospitallers' Hospice of Santa Caterina at Venice: 1358–1451'. *Studi Veneziani* 12 (1970): pp. 374–80; Sgarbi, 1979, cat. nos. 19–26; Pignatti, 1981, pp. 99–117; Gramigna and Perissa, 1981, pp. 38–39.

Measurements for these works given by different scholars vary up to 8 cm in each direction. Those cited here are taken from the most recent publication (Pignatti, 1981, pp. 99–117).

XVIII. Scuola di Santa Maria degli Albanesi

Carpaccio and workshop — c. 1502–8

Life of the Virgin

Color Plates IX, X

HISTORY: Founded on 22 Oct. 1442 by a community of Albanian immigrants, the Scuola di S. M. degli Albanesi was dedicated to the Virgin and S. Gallo. At first it held its meetings in the monastery church of S. Gallo. In 1447 it moved to the Church of San Maurizio, where it established an altar and tomb and took on an additional dedication to the saint of the same name. During the Turkish invasions of Albania, and particularly after the fall of Scutari in 1479, a number of refugees fled to Venice, where they received assistance from the Signoria (Molmenti and Ludwig, 1907, pp. 141–77).

In 1489 the Scuola acquired land adjacent to San Maurizio to build its own meeting-house. Construction of the two-story structure was probably begun in 1497/8 and completed in 1502, when the ceiling of the lower floor was commissioned (Pignatti, 1981, p. 92, with further discussion on the omission of the building from the Barbari map). It was probably around this time that Carpaccio and his workshop began painting a cycle of six *istorie*.

The facade of the building was completed with marble decoration by an unknown sculptor around 1530. The figures of San Gallo, the Madonna and Child and San Maurizio, carved in high relief, are attached above the door and window lintel of the ground floor. Above them, between the windows of the *piano nobile*, is a large plaque in low relief commemorating the sieges of Scutari in 1474 and 1479. The heroes of each battle – Antonio Loredan and Antonio da Lezze respectively – are honored by the inclusion of their coats-of-arms (Molmenti and Ludwig, 1907, pp. 151–53).

Membership dwindled over the next 250 years, and in 1780 the Scuola was terminated and its building given to the Scuola dei Pistori. After the Napoleonic suppression in 1808, the paintings were dispersed (Pignatti, 1981, p. 94; Zorzi, 1984, p. 359).

DOCUMENTS AND SOURCES:

1. 1497. The membership votes 48–9 to construct a new meeting-house with a hospice: 'Nel tempo del discretto et prudente homo sier Bernardino Strazzaruolo Gastaldo . . . che si debbia far fare la Scuola sopra quel terreno della Chiesa di S. Maurizio posto sopra il Campo, con le Casette delli poveri, et assai fratelli della Scuola sporgeranno di l'elimosina per far detta Scuola con l'Hospedaletto, che sara ad honor di Iddio, e della sua Madre Vergine Maria, et di Missier San Gallo, et della nation degli Albanesi, che insin gl'Armeni hanno il suo Hospedaletto, et noi non lo havemo. . .'

   BMV, Cod. It. VII, 737 (=8666), cap. 113:

   'Matricoli della Scola di S. M. e S. Gallo degl' Albanesi in S. Mauritio'. An almost identical copy of the Mariegola is found in ASV, Provedditori di Comun, Reg. U, (relevant passages: ff. 60–75).

2. 1500. Gastaldo Polo di Nicolò Toscano 'fo fato far il soffittato dell'albergo di sopra con sue ruoxe sopra de quadri.'

   ASV, Provveditori di Comun, Reg. U. f. 63; BMV, Cod. It. VII, 737 (=8666), cap. 124.

   Molmenti and Ludwig (1907, p. 149) understood this passage to refer to a carved ceiling with rosettes placed upon square compartments, Pignatti (1981, p. 94) interpreted it to mean a wood ceiling with a rosette pattern, that was to be installed *above the paintings*. He thereupon proposed 1500 as a date *ad quem* – in his opinion the half-way point – for Carpaccio's work in the Scuola. Pignatti's reading, although possible, is unlikely. Normal construction practice would have required the ceiling to have been completed before any paintings were placed in a newly built room. The floor, moreover, seems to have been installed only in the following year (see doc. 3).

3. 1501. Already the new building seems to be insufficient for the needs of the confraternity, for the Gastaldo Alessio Tentore has the upper floor raised in some manner and new terrazzo pavement installed there. An iron grill is made at this time, probably for

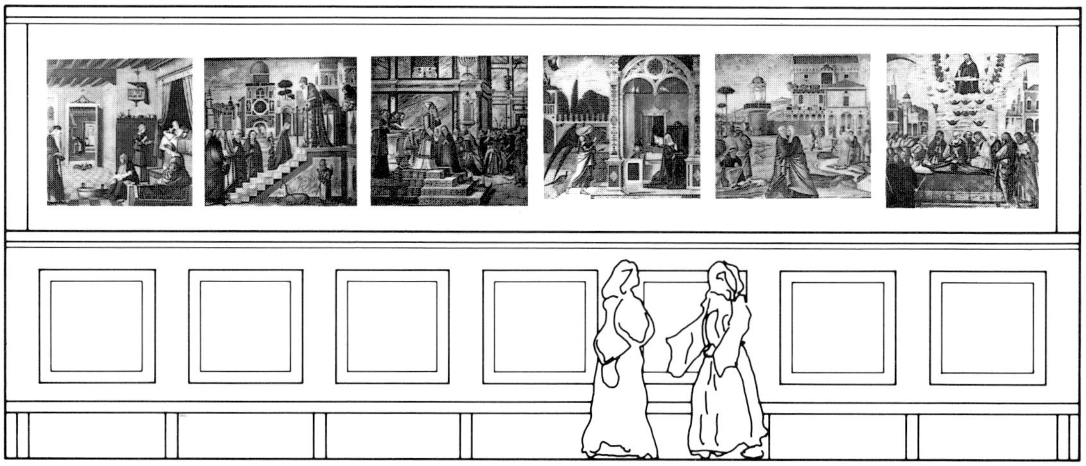

FIG. 3 **Side Wall (West?)**

the door: 'si fece levar la Scuola et terazzar di suso, et battere una Zanca da nuovo' at the cost of 31.5 ducats to the Banca and 22 lire di piccoli to the Scuola.

BMV, MS It. VII, 737 (=8666), cap. 125.

4. 1502. Gastaldo Nicolò de Nicolò delle Taie commissions the ceiling of the room on the lower floor at the expense of the Banca: 'si fece soffittar la soffitta da basso...'

Ibid., cap. 126.

5. 13 May 1502. Nicolò de Nicolò calls for a further small appropriation for the building project: 'fu preso che il Gastaldo con li cinque sindici, et compagni della Banca possano spendere dieci ducati della Scuola per fabricargli.'

Ibid., cap. 128.

6. 10 Mar. 1532. The Banca records having spent 90 ducats on the facade, thus establishing a *terminus ante quem* for the sculptural decoration: 'si attrovano haver speso in fabrica et conzar la Scuola nostra di fuora via con figure, et far Scutari di piera viva come al presente si può vedere...' The facade carries the inscription 'M.D.XXXI.'

Ibid., cap. 158 (Engl. translation in Molmenti and Ludwig, 1907, p. 153).

7. 1 June 1784. Giovan Battista Mengardi, a successor to A. M. Zanetti as official compiler of Venetian paintings, gives the first specific notice of Carpaccio's works *in situ*: 'Ho scoperto nella Scuola dei Pistori a San Maurizio sei quadri eccelenti di Vittor Carpaccio ben degni d'esser posti in Catalogo, e d'esser consegnati a chi spetta per la loro conservazione'. At this time the works were hanging in a row on the left wall. They were listed in the order given below.

ASV, Inquisitori di Stato, B. 909, 'Riferte dell'Ispettore Mengardi G. B., 1779–95', doc. 1, June 1784; cf. ibid., doc. 18 Oct. 1796.

ORIGINAL ARRANGEMENT: The Scuola building still stands with its facade virtually intact on the Calle del Piovan next to the Church of San Maurizio. Now used as a private residence, the interior has undergone changes, but the floor plan given by Perocco (1956, fig. 124) must be close to the original (about 8.1 × 9.4 m). The original location of the paintings was almost certainly in the *albergo di sopra* on the upper floor, where Mengardi saw them hanging together, as shown in Fig. 3, 'all on the left side'. He must have stood with his back to the two windows on the facade, for the light source in all of the paintings is from the left, and faced an altar (undocumented) at the opposite end of the room (cf. Frimmel, 1888, p. 316; Molmenti and Ludwig, 1907, p. 168).

The Albanesi paintings have suffered in critical discourse from comparison with the canvases in the Scuola di S. Giorgio degli Schiavoni, painted around the same time. Most scholars follow Ludwig in crediting Carpaccio in varying degrees with the general composition of the paintings, while attributing the actual execution to his workshop (for a summary of arguments, see Pignatti, 1981, pp. 94–98). It is difficult to argue with such assessments, and yet most of the works have passages of originality which seem to reveal the hand of the master: the Flemish tidiness of the *Birth of the Virgin*; the scholarly inclusion of the Hebrew inscriptions in the *Birth* and the *Marriage*; the graceful angel in the *Annunciation* which recalls that in the *Dream of St. Ursula*; the small child holding a gazelle on the leash in the *Presentation*. Indeed, looking at the paintings in the chronological order of the narrative, we may perceive a decreasing participation of Carpaccio in their execution. He seems to have been very much involved in the *Birth*, and much less so in the *Death of the Virgin*. One senses an increasingly busy artist, whose work in the Scuola di San Giorgio degli Schiavoni drew him away more and more from his commitments with the Albanesi.

The only securely dated work in the cycle is the *Annunciation*, bearing the inscription of 1504. If the paintings were, indeed, executed in chronological order – as they seem to have been – then the first three works may well have been painted between 1502 and 1504, and the last two as late as 1508, as Lauts (1961, p. 234) suggests.

ORIGINAL CYCLE:
Carpaccio

1. *Birth of the Virgin*
Oil on canvas, 126 × 129 cm
Bergamo, Accademia Carrara, n. 731 (155)
Inscription: VICTOR. CARPATIVS. V. FACEBAT (Probably added in 1811 when the work entered the gallery: Pignatti, 1981, p. 95).

2. *Presentation of the Virgin*
Oil on canvas, 130 × 137 cm — Color Plate IX
Milan, Brera, n. 171

3. *Marriage of the Virgin*
Oil on canvas, 130 × 140 cm — Color Plate X
Milan, Brera, n. 169

4. *Annunciation* — 1504
Oil on canvas, 127 × 139 cm
Venice, Galleria Franchetti (Ca' d'Oro) Accad. n. 43
Inscription: 'In tempo de zuan de nicolò zimador e soi compagni. MCCCCCIIII. del mese d'april'
Restored in 1971 by S. Bortoluzzi

5. *Visitation*
Oil on canvas, 128 × 137 cm
Venice, Museo Correr, n. 47
Restored in 1956 by G. Pedrocco

6. *Death of the Virgin*
Oil on canvas, 128 × 133 cm
Venice, Galleria Franchetti (Ca'd'Oro), Accad. n. 49

LITERATURE: Frimmel, 1888, pp. 316ff; Ludwig, 1897, pp. 405–31; Molmenti and Ludwig, 1907, pp. 141–77; Lauts, 1962, pp. 234–35; Zangirolami, 1962; Zampetti, 1963, pp. 199–213; Muraro, 1966, pp. cx–cxxiv; Zorzi, 1984, pp. 359–61; P. Fantelli, 'Niccolò Renieri "pittor fiamengo"', in *Saggi e Memorie di Storia dell'Arte*, 1974, pp. 51–53; Sgarbi, 1979, p. 46; Pignatti, 1981, pp. 89–98; Perissa and Gramigna, 1981, pp. 52–54.

Measurements from Pignatti, 1981, pp. 94–98.

XIX. Scuola Grande di San Marco, Albergo

Life of Saint Mark — 1504–c. 1534

Color Plates XXXIII–XXXV, XLIII; Plates 39, 76, 77, 122, 125, 142, 143

HISTORY: After the fire of 31 March 1485, the brothers of the Scuola di San Marco, by now called a Scuola Grande, took the opportunity to rebuild their meeting-house even more lavishly than before (for earlier campaigns see Cats. VIII and X). The reconstruction was supervised by five *provveditori sopra la fabrica*, a body that had been created to oversee the earlier building campaign of 1437–38. The confraternity was given considerable assistance by the state. On April 16 of the same year, the Senate voted a subvention of 4400 ducats: 2000 ducats to be paid at once with the balance to be paid at the rate of 100 ducats per month for two years. The

Council of Ten granted an exemption from the normal membership limit so that the additional entrance fees could be applied to the project; it also freed the brothers from the obligation to make certain charitable dispensations to the poor. Such extraordinary measures were repeated several times during the period of reconstruction (for a full account, see Sohm, 1982, pp. 79–92 and *passim*; cf. Pignatti, 1981, pp. 132–35).

The new building followed the old plan, with the exception of a 1.7 meter extension in length of the *sala capitolare* and the hall below it. The size and location of the *albergo* remained the same. In November 1489 Pietro Lombardo and Giovanni Buora began the construction and decoration of the facade. Its fabric was complete, along with the lower zone of decoration, when Mauro Codussi was hired as *proto* a year later. During his 4½-year employment, he completed the exterior decoration and designed and supervised the construction of an impressive double-ramped staircase. By 1495, when Codussi was dismissed, the Scuola was in dire financial straits, but the building was virtually complete except for the ceilings of the *piano nobile* (Sohm, 1982, pp. 79–92).

Gentile Bellini first offered to begin the pictorial decoration of the *albergo* in 1492 (doc. 1), when the construction of the staircase and the paving of the lower hall were not yet begun. It would be 12 years before the contract for the first canvas, *St. Mark Preaching in Alexandria* (XIX. 2), was finalized in May 1504 (doc. 2); the commission was followed in November by a decision to install an expensive new ceiling in the *albergo* consisting of 92 compartments, gilded and painted with ultramarine blue, with the lion of St. Mark in relief in the center (Sohm, 1982, doc. 81, p. 278). In the following year Gentile Bellini returned to the Banca to propose a second *istoria* (doc. 3). There is no record of the vote of the Banca on his offer, but the painting was probably never begun. The will that the artist wrote on his deathbed in 1507 mentioned only one work (*St. Mark Preaching*), which he requested his brother Giovanni to complete (doc. 4).

The next documented painting commission appeared in 1515, when Giovanni Bellini was contracted to paint the *Martyrdom of St. Mark* (doc. 8). It was to hang above the entrance portal in the same position as that envisioned in Gentile's offer of 1505 (doc. 3). Giovanni died on 29 Nov. 1516, and the commission was taken over by his assistant Vittore Belliniano who only completed the work in 1526. In 1518, two unspecified canvases were planned for the *albergo* (doc. 9), which were probably the *Healing* and the *Baptism of Anianas* by Mansueti (Humfrey, 1985a, p. 238). When the artist died in 1526/27, he had completed two paintings and a third which was nearly finished except for some portrait heads. His daughter Cecilia was forced to sue the Scuola to accept the latter work and to make the final payment (docs. 12 and 13a–b). In Jan. 1533 the Banca voted to commission 'one or two' canvases to complete the cycle in the *albergo*, and in November of 1534 it was reported that a painting 'will be furnished in a few days' to complete the pictorial decoration (docs. 14–15).

Humfrey's (1985a, pp. 238–39) argument that the *Miracle of St. Mark* (*Sea Storm*) was begun by Palma Vecchio only after Mansueti's death, and was left incomplete when he too died in 1528, is plausible (cf. Sohm, 1979–80). It would help to explain Paris Bordone's completion of the painting and the uncertain language of doc. 14 in which 'one or two' canvases are mentioned.

The fabric of the *albergo* remained essentially unchanged to the end of the Republic. In 1807 the building was made a military hospital. It became the Ospedale Civile under the Austrian government and still serves that function today. It was at this time that Codussi's staircase was destroyed. In 1832 even the facade was dismantled, but it was later reconstructed along with the staircase.

The paintings were dispersed with the suppression of the Scuola. Only one (XIX.7) hangs in the Accademia Galleries. Four of the works were returned to the old *albergo* of the Scuola, now part of the medical library, and are all but inaccessible to the public (see Pignatti, 1981, pp. 145–49).

DOCUMENTS AND SOURCES:

1. 15 July 1492. With his brother Giovanni, Gentile Bellini offers to paint an unspecified number of canvases for the *albergo* to replace those lost in the fire of 1485:

'Inspiradi da inspiration divina piui presto che umana, j nostri chari et amatissimi fradeli, Messer Zentil bellin al presente nostro digniss. vardian da matin, etiam per nome de messer Zuane suo fra.[lo] che al presente non ben se habet simul, et semel, Desiderosi, et avidi de dar principio a le laudevol virtu et opere de larte soa de pictoria, ne j tellari deno esser fatti nel Albergo de questa nostra beneta schuola, et questo si per soa devotion et memoria, como etiam del q. m.° Jac.° bellin olim suo padre, dele chui opere avanti lincendio del bruxar de essa schuola in esso Albergo faceva: Quali se offerisse non per de guadagno, ma solum a fin et effecto chel sia laude e trionfo de lomnipotente dio . . . Die principiar tuta la faza in testa del albergo ditto in un solo tellaro, nel qual se debbi poner quelle historie et opera che per la schuola sera termenado, tamen cum el conseio et parer dej ditti doi fradellj.'

Each artist would receive the modest sum of 50 ducats plus materials for the painting, and after it was completed, each would be commissioned to do other works at the same price: 'Item dapoi fatta ditta opera se obbliga

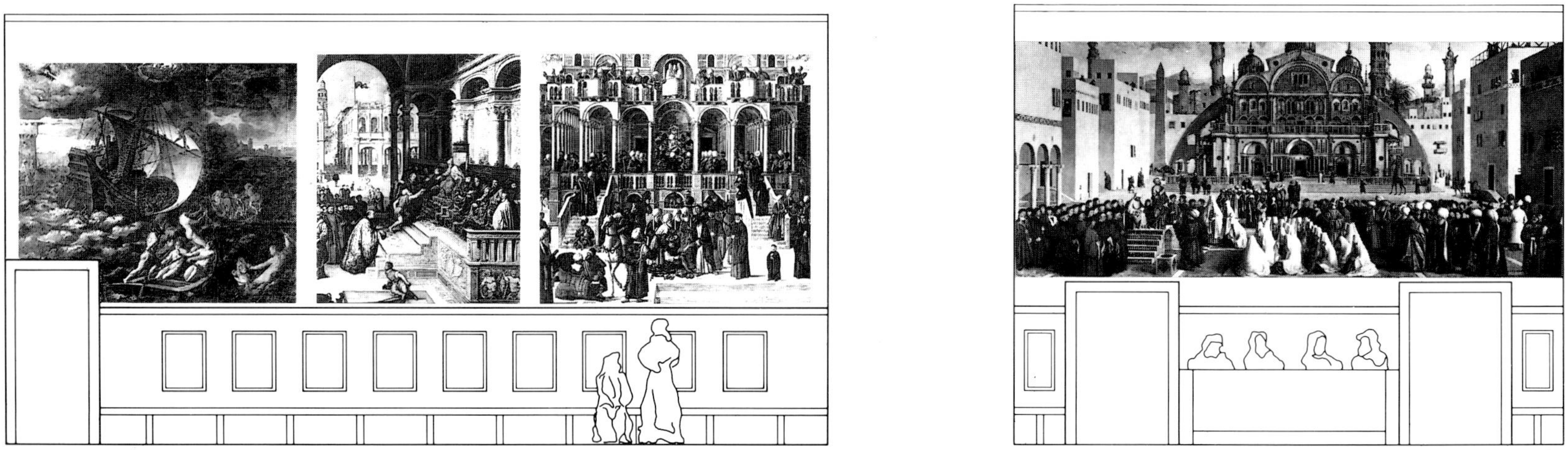

FIG. 4 **North Wall** **East Wall**

far tante altre opere in ditta schuola, dove li sera ordenato che sia oltra la stima...'

No other artist would be allowed to do the work, provided Gentile and his brother kept to their agreement: 'Et acio che tal opera tanto laudevole et degna sia fatta cum presteza et ogni altra solennita, sia etiam prexo, che ad algun altro non possi esser dato ditta opera del dito Albergo a far, ne parte ne niente dun modo j diti fradeli faci el dover suo etc.'

ASV, San Marco, B. 135. Cf. Paoletti, 1894, p. 17. Engl. transl. in Chambers, 1971, pp. 56–57.

2a. 1 May 1504. The Banca votes 8–3 to proceed with the painting campaign: 'Conziosiache messer zentil belin nostro fradelo et al presente vichario ala bancha se offerischa mosso d'amor et carità chel dize aver a questa nostra schuola desideroxo massime de lassar perpetua memoria de sue virtu in dita schuola nostra, far in l'albergo de la dita un teler del mestier suo de pentura che habia a meterse in testa del dito albergo per mezo la porta granda del dito albergo, et habia porto molti partidi sopra de ziò che sono al proposito de dita schuola nostra...'

ASV, S. Marco, Reg. 17, f. 26a. Cf. full text in Molmenti, 1892, pp. 131–32.

2b. 1 May 1504. In another document recording the same transaction, Gentile promises that the painting 'sara de più perfetion e bonta che non e quelo de lalbergo de san Zuane che e sopra la porta del dito...' He is to be paid 25 ducats per year, a sum from which he will pay his own expenses. When completed, the painting will be appraised at 200 or 250 ducats, depending on quality, and Gentile will donate 50 ducats back to the Scuola.

ASV, San Marco, B. 135. Cf. full text in Paoletti, 1894, p. 18.

3. 9 March 1505. Gentile Bellini has made good progress on his first painting: 'fina questo zorno a fato bona partte chome se pol veder...' He thus proposes a second painting for the *albergo*. '...Perho eso messer zentil non senza gran studio a preparato uno zerto modelo in desegnjo che sono una bela fantaxia per dover far uno altro teler segondo quel desegnio, nel dito nostro albergo di sopra dela porta che sara la faxa opoxita a quela dove là prinzipià el primo teler...'

ASV, San Marco, Reg. 17, f. 28a. Cf. full text in Paoletti, 1894, pp. 18–19.

4. 18 Feb. 1507. Gentile Bellini writes his will, in which he leaves a book of drawings made by his father to his brother Giovanni, on condition that he finish the first painting: 'Item volo et ordino atque rogo prefatum Joannem fratrem meum ut sibi placeat complere opus per me inceptum pro dicta scola sancti Marci, quo completo sibi demitto et dari volo librum designorum qui fuit prefati quondam patris nostri ultra mercedem quam habebit a dicta scola, et si nolet perficere dictum opus, volo dictum librum restare in meam commissariam...' Two of his *commissarii* were officers of the Scuola in 1504, when the painting was begun: Guardian Grande Marco Pellegrino and Guardian da Matin Agostino Negro.

ASV, Notarile, Testamenti, Bernardo Cavagnis, B. 271, no. 307. From Molmenti, 1892, pp. 133–34; now in Meyer zur Capellen, 1985, p. 120.

5. 7 Mar. 1507. Provided he deals only with Marco Pellegrino who has been in charge of the commission from the beginning, Giovanni Bellini agrees to the terms of his brother's will: 'essendo romaxo el teller la principiado per la scuola non compido...' The Banca votes 14–0 in favor of the arrangement.

ASV, San Marco, Reg. 17, f. 34a. Cf. full text in Molmenti, 1892, pp. 135–36.

6. 31 Dec. 1507. The chapter votes to raise 1000 ducats and to borrow another 5000 from the Monte Vecchio, in order to install new ceilings in the *albergo* and the chapter hall and complete a new altar.

ASV, San Marco, Reg. 17, ff. 40–41. Cf. Paoletti, 1893, I, p. 106, with the incorrect date of 1504.

7. 1508. A fund-raising effort yields about 115 ducats from 32 members 'per le fabriche del albergo' and 'compir lo adornamento dela Nostra Scolla.'

Ibid., Reg. 77. filza 3, f. 13.

8. 4 July 1515. The Banca votes to continue with the painting cycle and commissions Giovanni Bellini to make 'uno teller de tella sopra el qual se die far depenzer una historia de misser S. Marco: Come essendo in Alexandria el ditto fo strassinato per terra da quelli mori infideli: El qual teller die esser sopra la porta del Albergo grando tra uno muro et laltro per mezo laltro teller depento che se trova sopra la bancha, dove stano el vardian et compagni.'

The painting is to include 'casamenti, figure, animali, et tutto quello achadera a tutte sue spese del ditto missier Zuane si de colori, come de ogni altra cosa in tutta perfection, come se convien a quel luogo: et come rechiede la Excellentia dela virtu del ditto messer Zuanne, meiorando el teller che se trova al incontro el qual fece messer Zentil suo fradello.'

Giovanni will be paid from the income of an account in the Camera de imprestidi in the name of Ser Nicolo Aldioni, which was reserved for the *fabrica* of the Scuola. His contract called for the same price and time limits given to his brother Gentile.

ASV, San Marco, Reg. 17, f. 60. Cf. full text in Paoletti, 1894, p. 14).

9. 24 Oct. 1518. Two unspecified paintings are planned for the *albergo*, along with a decorative revetment for the chapter hall ceiling. 'Per tanto vogliando dar principio al sofito e ligamento de la salla e a doi telleri in lalbergo, havemo deliberato in el tempo nostro dar questi principio azio li successori nostri habiano etiam de tempo in tempo per

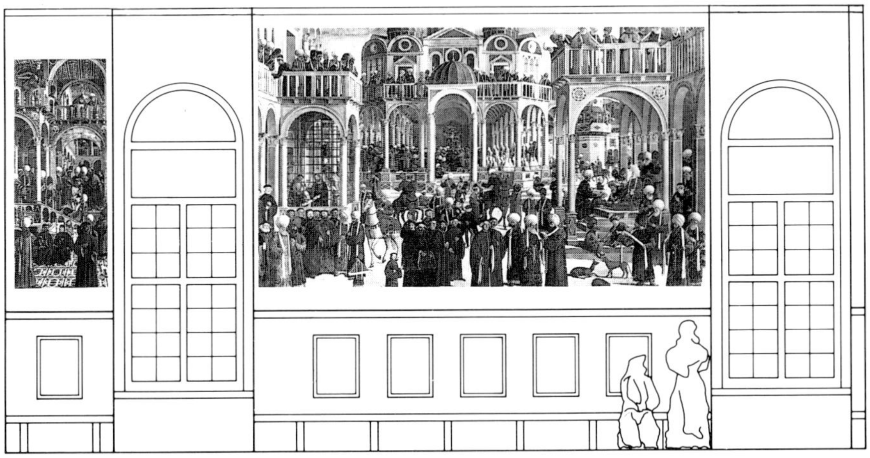

South Wall

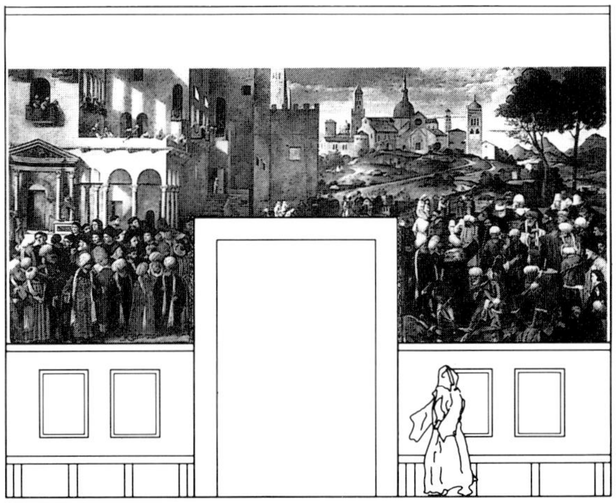

West Wall

far questo et far mur per fecto de quello haveremo facto nuj Et per che questo tal principio non se pol far senza denari.'

ASV, San Marco, Reg. 17, f. 78b. Cf. Sohm, 1982, doc. 92, p. 282. The index in the front of the *busta* lists the *parte* as follows: 'Parte de far il soffitao et legamento della Sala con 2 telleri...'

10. 17 Mar. 1519. Pope Leo X grants an indulgence which classifies all donations to the building fund as Christian alms for pious good works, and grants full remission of sins to all those who visit the meeting-house.

ASV, San Marco, Reg. 75, fasc. 1, f. 9.

11. 2 Aug. 1523. Noting that the Scuola has already received 4000 ducats from the Signoria for rebuilding the meeting-house after the fire of 1485, the Guardian Grande observes the special obligations incurred by the confraternity through its dedication to the patron saint of the city. He calls for a quarter of current income ('i pro de jnprestjdj') to be expended for 'la fabrjcha de ditta schuola sj del sofittado chome dela chapela et de ttelerj ett ttandenda ogni alttra nobeljsima chosa.'

ASV, San Marco, B. 122, fasc. D. c. 38. From Sohm, 1982, doc. 95, pp. 283–84. Cf. ASV, San Marco, Reg. 17, f. 100, and ASV, Consiglio dei Dieci, Parti Miste, Reg. 46, f. 113.

12. 17 Feb. 1529. After Mansueti's death (between 6 Sept 1526 and 26 March 1527: Ludwig, 1905, pp. 66–67), the officers of the Scuola refuse to accept his last canvas for the *albergo* (Cat. XIX. 4). Referring to herself as a 'povera orphana', the artist's daughter, Cecilia, files suit to force payment:

'Anchor che manifestamente si vede per il proccesso formato per lofficio vostro magnifici et excellentissimi Signori Auditori Vechij nela Causa de io Cecilia fo fiola del quondam mistro Zuane di mansueti la qual ho con il guardian dela Scuolla de misser San Marco esser chiaro aprobato per lo medemi non esser sta particularmente fatto ne concluso il marcado del quaro fatto per il ditto quondam mio padre a la ditta Scuola adeo che de rason si dovea stimarlo et tanto darmi di fattura et perche loro dubitano de questo si hanno sforzato dir che il quondam mio padre volceva duc. 133 et loro non si contento et per fugir etiam questo li ha basta lanimo de dir che il ditto quondam mio padre voleva far il quadro et in caso non lo volesseno, tenirlo per lui per suo piacer et hanno fatto una comedia fra loro per far trar le fatiche paterne al vento contra la sua opera non si del dar del denaro come vegnir a veder lopera et farse ritrar quelli dela scuolla et moltre altre sue contrarieta fra loro le qual volendo resechar per essa povera orphana et non haver danari de buttar via li fazo la presente oblation che si voleno farla stimar compita la sara de alchune teste mancha et far de alchuni si voleva far ritrar dela schuolla son contenta star a lopinione de homeni periti et de quanto stimerano me sia dato de contadi jmmediate i danarj mettando a conto quello sara havuto il quondam mio padre, et se non voleno questo sum contenta etiam tuor la summa de j diti duc. 133 et metterli a contto quello lha havuto et compirla et pagarmi le spexe farne. Et si questo etiam non voleno sum contenta tenir il Quadro per mio contto cum questo che i perdino j danari hano dato al ditto quondam mio padre per quel contto per che non saria honesto che io tenisse il quadro, et restituirli anchora i danari essendo sta il povero defuncto sopra la soa fede et in caxo che non voglino aceptar alchun de i dicti parti di le Signorie vostre per justitia, landera la mia sententia, laqual oblation li fazo si al conspecto de quello come ad ogni altro magistrato et conseglio.'

ASV, San Marco, Reg. 133, ff. 6–7. Cf. Sohm, 1982, doc. 101, pp. 285–86.

13a. 6 Mar. 1530: A judgment by the Auditori Vecchii in favor of Mansueti's heirs and against the Scuola is recorded. The document also specifies the Guardian Grande at the time of the original commission as Antonio di Maistri (term in office: 19 March 1525–4 March 1526), giving a *terminus post quem* for the painting. The language of the document is not entirely clear, but it appears that the Scuola must either forfeit its deposit of 30 ducats already paid to the artist if it does not wish to accept the painting; or if it decides to keep it, it must pay the full amount of the contract (130 ducats). It decides to keep the painting, but is still reluctant to pay the judgment in full.

ASV, San Marco, Reg. 18, ff. 51–52. Cf. Ludwig, 1905, p. 66; and Sohm, 1982, doc. 102, p. 286.

13b. 5 Mar. 1531. The Scuola is still quibbling over the exact amount of payment with Mansueti's heirs, but empowers the Guardian Grande to do what seems best to him. The actual placement of the painting is now designated as 'in albergo ttra ttuti duj balchoni...'

ASV, San Marco, Reg. 18, f. 63v. Cf. text in Ludwig, 1905, p. 67. By 5 Nov. 1531, Mansueti's heirs were receiving an assignment of rents from the Scuola to pay off the bill for the painting (ASV, San Marco, B. 83, 'Bottega a San Bartolomeo').

14. 19 Jan. 1532 m.v. (=1533). The Banca and the Zonta [see glossary] vote 22–0 '...far far uno over do telerj che mancha in nel nostro albergo e dar a far al piu hover piuj sufizienttj depentorj che sia posibele aver, azio se fazi tantta degna opera necesaria et onorevole ala nostra squola et quel sara fatto per loro hover per la mazor partte de loro sia valide e forma et ben fatta.'

ASV, San Marco, Reg. 18, f. 84. Cf. Bailo and Biscaro, 1900, pp. 87–88, who transcribed the document with the date 1533, without indicating whether or not it was Venetian style (*more veneto*). Later scholars (Moschini Marconi and Canova) assumed that it was, and incorrectly changed it to 1534.

15. 22 Nov. 1534. An appeal is made for a new carpet, since the decoration of the *albergo* will soon be complete: '...et perche gia lo albergo de la scuola nostra e fornito si de picture conputa al quadro che fra pochi giorni sara fornito etiam de sofitado, spaliere banchali et mancha uno bel tapedo sopra el cancello, quale e necesario per perfecer de ornar esso Albergo.'

ASV, San Marco,. Reg. 18, ff. 106v–107. Cf. Paoletti, 1893, I. p. 107.

ORIGINAL ARRANGEMENT: Despite its transformation into a medical library, the physical fabric of the *albergo* remains essentially unchanged from the late Quattrocento. The first detailed description of the arrangement of the paintings was made by Boschini (1664, pp. 237–38). As Humfrey (1985a, p. 229) rightly observes, it is almost certainly the same as their final disposition in the completed *albergo* of the 1530s.

The paintings, as shown in Fig. 4, are arranged in narrative order, beginning with *St. Mark Healing Anianas* at the east end of the north wall. Humfrey stated that Gentile Bellini's *St. Mark Preaching* was the first episode in the saint's Alexandrian mission according to Voragine's *Golden Legend*. But in the Venetian version of Mark's life written by Bernardo Giustiniani (1772, col. 175), the sequence began with the *St. Mark Healing Anianas*. In this version. St. Mark performed this miracle just after he stepped off the boat from Rome, thus establishing the supernatural primacy of the Christian church: 'Hoc primum Marcus edidit Alexandriae signum, Christi domini exemplum secutus ...' Only after this did Mark preach against the worship of Serapis, the subject of XIX.2 (as Dempsey has shown; see Chapter 11, n. 40 above). Even though the baptism may well have taken place immediately after Anianas's healing, it is only mentioned in retrospect later in the narrative account, after the preaching episode is described.

The room contained no altar, and the Banca sat directly beneath Gentile Bellini's *St. Mark Preaching*, facing the entrance and Belliniano's *Martyrdom*. On the marble lintel above the doorway the original inscription remains: VBI CHARITAS ET AMOR IBI DEVS EST.

ORIGINAL CYCLE:

Giovanni Mansueti
1. *St. Mark Healing Anianas*
Oil on canvas, 376 × 399 cm — Plate 76
Venice, Ospedale Civile, Biblioteca (on deposit), Accad. n. 365
Inscription: IOANNES DE / MANSUETIS FECIT
Below Mark's feet: B. Marcus. Anianum. Sauciatum. Sanat.

Restored by Pelliccioli in 1940, who found that the steps in the lower right corner were part of an addition to the work (*Arti*, 1940–41, p. 67).
LIT.: Moschini Marconi, 1955, no. 146; Miller, 1978, pp. 85–90.

Gentile Bellini
2. *St. Mark Preaching in Alexandria*
Oil on canvas, 347 × 770 cm
Color Plates XXXIV, XXXV, XLIII; Plate 125
Milan, Brera, n. 164

Restored in 1984–85 by Pinin Brambilla, but not yet on display in the gallery in January 1987. See the letter of Carlo Bertelli, the former director of the Brera, in *Giornale dell'Arte*, no. 40, Dec. 1986, p. 38.

Final touches were added by Giovanni Bellini. For his share in the execution, see Chapter 11, n. 27 above. From doc. 8 it appears that the Scuola considered Gentile to be virtually the sole author of the painting.
LIT.: Malaguzzi Valeri, 1908, pp. 76–77; Collins, 1970, pp. 62–70 and 140; Lehmann, 1977; Meyer zur Capellen, 1985, pp. 89–98 and 131–32.

Giovanni Mansueti
3. *St. Mark Baptizing Anianas*
Oil on canvas, 335 × 125 cm
Color Plate XXXIII; Plate 122
Milan, Brera, n. 153
LIT.: Malaguzzi Valeri, 1908, pp. 76–77; Miller, 1978, pp. 85–90.

Giovanni Mansueti
4. *Episodes in the Life of St. Mark* (*Arrest and Trial of St. Mark*)
Oil on canvas, 376 × 612 cm
Plates 77, 123
Venice, Ospedale Civile, Biblioteca (on deposit), Accad. n. 367
Inscription: JOANNES DE MANSUETIS FACIEBAT
Restored by Pelliccioli in 1940 (*Arti*, 1940–41, p. 67).
LIT.: Miller, 1978, pp. 85–90; Moschini Marconi, 1955, no. 145.

Vittore Belliniano
5. *Martyrdom of St. Mark*
Oil on canvas, 362 × 771 cm — Plate 39
Venice, Ospedale Civile, Biblioteca (on deposit), Accad. n. 1071
Inscription: MDXXVI / VICTOR BELLINIANUS

Cut-out for door at lower edge: 158 × 272 cm

Restored by Pellicioli in 1940 (*Arti*, 1940–41, pp. 65ff).
LIT.: Ludwig, 1905, pp. 72–79; Moschini Marconi, 1955, no. 87.

Palma Vecchio and Paris Bordone
6. *Miracle of St. Mark in a Storm at Sea* (also called *Sea Storm*)
Oil on canvas, 360 × 406 cm — Plate 142
Venice, Ospedale Civile, Biblioteca (on deposit) Accad. cat. n. 516

Heavily repainted, the work has suffered from many interventions. The cut-out for a door in the lower left-hand corner was filled in with new canvas and a painting of a sea monster in 1830. See Moschini Marconi, 1962, pp. 165–67; and Pignatti, 1981, p. 147. Restored by Mauro Pelliccioli in 1955 (Moschini, 1957, pp. 77–78).

Once ascribed to Giorgione, but now usually attributed to Palma Vecchio, with the later intervention of Paris Bordone.
LIT.: Moschini Marconi, 1962, pp. 165–67; Sohm, 1979–80, pp. 85–96.

Paris Bordone
7. *Presentation of the Ring to the Doge*
Oil on canvas, 370 × 300 cm — Plate 143
Venice, Accademia, n. 320
Inscription: O PARI DIS / BORDONO
Restored by Pelliciolli in 1958; in restoration in 1986.
LIT.: Bailo and Biscaro, pp. 35–36; Moschini Marconi, 1962, no. 117 (with bibliography); Mariani Canova, 1964, pp. 93–94; Nepi Scire and Valcanover, 1985, p. 97.

LITERATURE: Vasari (1550 and 1568), 1966 edn, pp. 45, 438, 550–51, 624–25; Sansovino, 1581, c. 102; idem, 1663, I, pp. 286–87; Boschini, 1664, pp. 237–38; Boschini, 1674, Castello, pp. 70–71; Molmenti, 1888; Paoletti, 1893, I, pp. 183, 102–7 and 175–77; Paoletti, 1894; Ludwig, 1905; Paoletti, 1929; Moschini Marconi, 1955, pp. 91–92 and 138–39; idem, 1962, pp. 70–72 and 165–68; Wurthmann, 1975; Olivato Puppi and Puppi, 1977, pp. 196ff. and 259ff; McAndrew, 1980, pp. 358–63; Pignatti, 1981, pp. 132–35 and 145–49; Gramigna and Perissa, 1981, pp. 103–8; Sohm, 1982; Lieberman, 1981, Plate 66; W. Sheard, 'The birth of monumental classicizing relief in Venice on the facade of the Scuola di San Marco', in *Interpretazioni Veneziane. Studi di storia dell'arte in onore di Michelangelo Muraro*, ed. D. Rosand, Venice, 1984, pp. 149–74; Humfrey, 1985a. See also Cats. VIII and X.

XX. Scuola di Sant'Alvise

Marco Veglia
Life of St. Alvise (lost) — 1508

HISTORY: The Scuola di Sant'Alvise was a small *scuola di devozione* whose meeting-house was built in 1402 (restored in 1608) next to the church of the same name. Membership was reserved to *cittadini originari*, perhaps in imitation of the powerful Scuole Grandi. Eight canvases with scenes from the life of St. Alvise (St. Louis of Toulouse), painted in tempera by Marco Veglia, were presumably installed in the ground-floor chapel in 1508 (docs. 1 and 2).

The paintings were in poor condition by the end of the 18th century (Zanetti, 1771, p. 44; *Pittura Veneziana*, 1797, II, p. 96). They were dispersed in 1806, following the suppression of the *scuole*, but the meeting-hall still stands (Zorzi, 1984, p. 367).

A painting that carried the inscription 'MARCUS VEGLIA F. ANNO MCCCCCVIII' was noted in 1930 in a private collection in Brussels (V. Moschini, 'Nota su Marco Veglia', *Rivista di Venezia* 9 (1930), pp. 129–33). Painted on a wood support (1.08 × .82 m), it depicted a military encampment with Roman soldiers, horses and tents in the foreground and two women strolling in the background. A fragment of a second work (.57 × .70 m.), painted by the same hand with similiar subject matter, is in storage in the Accademia, Venice (Moschini Marconi, 1955, p. 154). The iconography and wood supports of these works seem to exclude them from the S. Alvise program as described by Sansovino. On the other hand, they would match up nicely with the *Legend of St. Helena and the Invention of the Holy Cross* in the Scuola della Croce (Cat. XXI) if it were not for the presence of the inscription; for none was noted in the sources in connection with that program.

DOCUMENTS AND SOURCES:

1. 1581. Sansovino makes no mention of the Scuola, but writes: 'Nell' estremo della città, parte lietissima per belle contrade, è posto l'antico monistero di S. Luigi habitato da donne monache. . .& Marco Veghia vi lasciò la historia di S. Luigi in diversi quadri di tela dipinti à guazzo.'
Sansovino, 1581, c. 62.

2. 1674. Boschini states that 'nel giro di essa scuola', there are eight paintings in tempera by Marco Veglia, dated 1508, 'con fatti del Santo, con varie figure, ornamenti, & edificij d'Architettura."
Boschini, 1674, Cannaregio, pp. 39–40

LITERATURE:

Sansovino, 1581, c. 62; idem, 1663, p. 175; Zanetti, 1771, p. 44; *Pittura Veneziana*, 1797, II, p. 96; Testi, 1909, II, p. 85; Gramigna and Perissa, 1981, p. 123; Zorzi, 1984, p. 367.

XXI. Scuola della Croce

Legend of St. Helena and the Invention of the Holy Cross (lost) c. 1508

HISTORY: The meeting-house of the Scuola della Croce, a small *scuola di devozione*, was built in 1364 opposite the Church of S. Croce in Luprio on the Campo della Croce in the *sestiere* of the same name. In the early years of the 16th century it was decorated with six or seven paintings in tempera, depicting scenes from the life of St. Helena and the Invention of the Cross. Although they had escaped the attention of Sansovino, in 1674 Boschini recorded six *quadri*, presumably paintings on wood, but was not familiar with the artist (doc. 1). Zanetti cited seven paintings and observed that they were painted in almost the same style as those of Marco Veglia (doc. 2).

The paintings were dispersed after the suppression of the Scuola in 1806 (for their possible survival, see Cat. XX). The building was destroyed a few years later (Zorzi, 1984, p. 370). The site is presently occupied by the gardens of the Palazzo Papadapoli (Sagredo, 1852, p. 25).

DOCUMENTS AND SOURCES:

1. 1674. Boschini listes six *quadri* in the Scuola, 'fatte a tempera, di maniero molto diligente, come se fossero fatte ad oglio: Non si sà l'Autore, ma per esser cose molto belle, se ne fa menzione.'
Boschini, 1674, Santa Croce, p. 5. In a copy once owned by Zanetti (BMV: 122 D. 208), two glosses are found on this page and may be in his hand: 'bellini', written in the margin next to the entry; and at the bottom of the page, 'non c'è nome sicuro.'

2. 1771. As a footnote to his entry on Marco Veglia's works in Sant' Alvise (Cat. XXI above), Zanetti writes: 'Nella Scuola della Croce appresso la Chiesa dell' istesso nome sonovi sette quadri bene assai conservati, contenenti l'invenzione del Santo legno, che sono dipinti quasi nel modo medesimo che quelli del Veglia. Son fatti a tempera.'
Zanetti, 1771, p. 44

LITERATURE: Sansovino, 1581, c. 73v; Boschini, 1674, p. 5; Cornaro, 1749, 9, p. 311; Zanetti, 1771, p. 61; Paganuzzi, *Iconografia delle trenta Parrocchie di Venezia*, Venice, 1821, Plate XIX; Cicogna, 1824–27, I, p. 251; Tassini, 1885, p. 94; Zorzi, 1984, p. 370.

XXII. Scuola di San Stefano

Carpaccio
Life of St. Stephen 1511–c.1520
Color Plates XI, XV, XXXI

HISTORY: The Scuola di San Stefano, founded in 1298, was one of the oldest *scuole di devozione* in Venice. In the early years the group met in the Church of San Stefano, adjacent to the Augustinian convent of the Eremitani. In 1437 the Augustinian friars granted the Scuola a small tract of land opposite the main portal of the church, on which to build its own meeting-house (Molmenti and Ludwig,

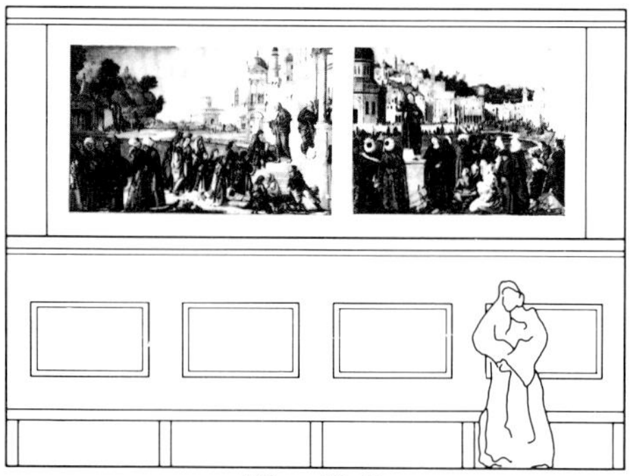
West Wall

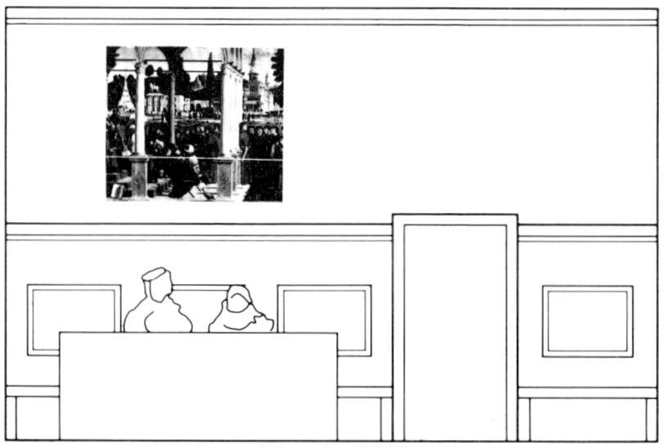
North Wall

1907, pp. 178–79). The building was enlarged in 1476. It was now composed of two stories: a chapel with an altar on the ground floor, and a meeting-room above (doc. 1). In 1506 further decorative embellishment was begun (doc. 2), to be followed by Carpaccio's cycle between 1511–1520. Overlooked by Sansovino, the paintings were first cited in the sources by Ridolfi in 1648 (1914 edn, p. 48).

Eventually drawing many of its members from the wool-working industry, the confraternity was sometimes called the Scuola dei Lanieri. The Scuola declined over the years; in the 18th century part of the meeting-house was rented to a cheese merchant (Zorzi, 1984, p. 376). Five canvases by Carpaccio and an altarpiece were still in the building in 1771 (Zanetti, p. 40), but by 1806 when the Scuola was suppressed, only four narrative paintings remained. These were dispersed and none remains in Venice today (see Pignatti, 1981, p. 123).

DOCUMENTS AND SOURCES:

1. 14 Sept. 1476. The Scuola receives permission from the Augustinian friars to enlarge their meeting-house: '. . . di sotto una Capella per fino alla prima travatura et con uno altare dentro, et di sopra la ditta Capella far la sala insieme con la predetta Scola, la qual fabrica si possi levar in alto discretamente, secondo che si convien all' edificio et che se possa adoperar la mazza con la crose e dopieri inastadi in man tanto che non faci danno alle travamenta.'

The construction is commemorated by an inscription above the entrance portal: 'Divo Stephano Martyrum Principi Pietatis, et devotionis gratia resumpta Fraternitas instauravit Anno Salutis MCCCCLXXVI'.

MCV, Mariegola, no. 3: Scuola di San Stefano (made in 1493). From Molmenti and Ludwig, 1907, p. 179. See also MCV, Cod. Gradenigo-Dolfin 178, 'Frati,' c. 118v.

2. 1506. The Scuola obtains permission from the friars to decorate the meeting-house: 'liberamente ornar lo Altar far le banche attorno et altri concieri milioramenti et ornamenti in essa Capella far come a essi fratelli di ditta scola piacerà per divotione.' No paintings are mentioned, and the citation may refer only to the lower floor, since that was the location of the *capella*.

MCV, Mariegola, no. 3: Scuola di San Stefano, f. 118. From Molmenti and Ludwig, 1907, pp. 179–80. See also MCV, Cod. Gradenigo-Dolfin 178, 'Frati,' cc. 112r ff.

3. 25 Jan. 1564. The paintings are cited in a contract in anticipation of a merger (never completed) between the Scuola di San Stefano and the Scuola di San Teodoro which establishes that: 'li quadri de pitura a oglio della vita del glorioso ms. S. Stefano . . . degni veramente de esser preservati per la loro bellezza' will be placed in the new seat, under a beautiful decorated soffit. The name of the artist is not mentioned.

ASV, Scuola Grande di San Teodoro, Reg. 14, cc. 33–34, from Gallo, 1962, p. 471.

4. 1771. Zanetti gives the fullest description of the works still *in situ*: 'Nella Scuola di Santo Stefano, vicina alla Chiesa dell' istesso Santo sonovi cinque quadri contenenti la vita del Protomartire, e di più la tavola dell'altare con la figura di esso Santo diacono, quella di S. Niccolò da Tolentino, e di S. Tomasso Agostiniano. Si tengono dal Ridolfi delle ultime opere del Carpaccio; e ciò con ragione, poichè dipinte furono, siccome vedesi dal 1511. al 1520. . .

In quattro di essi quadri v'è il nome del Pittore scritto così: *Victor Carpathius Finxit.* (non *Pinxit.*).

Evvi di più nella cornice del primo quadro questa osservabile inscrizione:

Manfredus Lapicida & Collega conspicabilem picturam hanc tempore eorum regiminis posuerunt MDXI.

Evvene un' altra nel quadro vicino col nome di un altro scarpellino, e l'anno MDXIIII; e finalmente nell' ultimo quadro alla sinistra dell' altare si vede l'anno MDXX. e nella cornice MDXXI.'

Zanetti, 1771, p. 40.

ORIGINAL ARRANGEMENT: While the early 16th-century meeting-house still stands, its interior has been thoroughly transformed (the lower floor is now used as a restaurant). Perocco's (1956, p. 224, fig. 125) plan of the present building may give a rough approximation of the earlier one. In their reconstruction of the cycle, Molmenti and Ludwig (1907, pp. 182–83) assumed that the paintings were originally installed on the upper floor, a likely placement considering the fact that part of the building was leased out for retail trade while the Scuola was still in operation. The room was illuminated by two windows in the facade wall facing the Church of San Stefano, and they placed the altar on the opposite wall. Ignoring the lost painting (XXII.4), they put two each on the side walls with the narrative proceeding counter-clockwise from *a cornu evangeli* (left-hand side of the altar). The reconstruction is unsatisfactory for several reasons, although no convincing alternative has since been offered.

Assuming that Zanetti saw the works in their original location, we know that the *Martyrdom* ('ultimo quadro') was immediately to the left of the altar. We might therefore suspect that the paintings were, in fact, placed in clockwise narrative order (as were those in the Scuola di Sant'Orsola and undoubtedly those in the Albanesi), and that the *Ordination*, as the first episode, would have hung to the right of the altar. However, the light source in the paintings is the reverse of what one might expect in such an arrangement if the altar faced the windows, for the light falls from the left in Bissolo's altarpiece and in the first two paintings (XXII.1–2) and from the right in the other three. Although artists often implied the altar as a light source in their paintings, in at least two previous *scuola* cycles (S. Orsola and the Albanesi) Carpaccio seems to have 'illuminated' his paintings from the actual windows.

To my mind, Fig. 5 offers the most satisfactory solution. In it the altar is placed against the facade wall, flanked by two windows and opposite the door leading from a

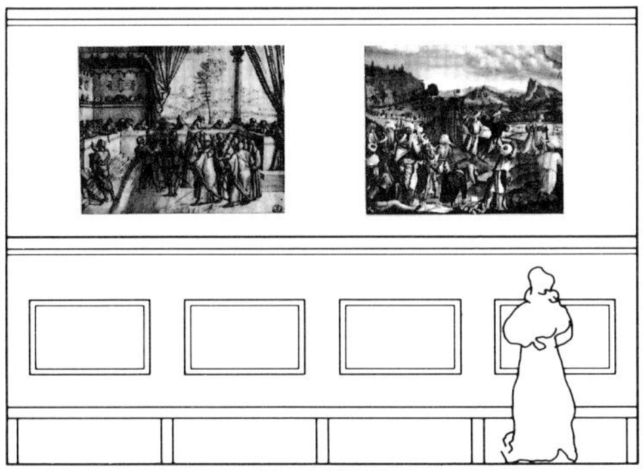

East Wall

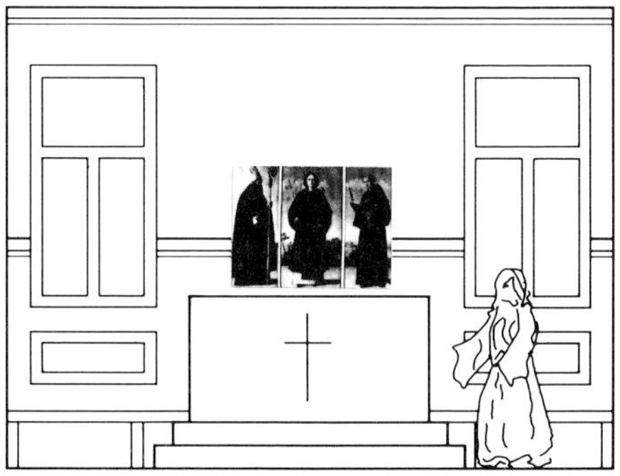

South Wall

staircase, in an arrangement analogous to that of the Scuola di Sant'Orsola. The first two episodes in the narrative would hang on the wall to the right as we face the altar, and the last two on our left. Episode XXII.3 would hang behind us on the wall facing the altar (and probably above the *barca*); its light source and that of the altar would both be consistent, both coming from the left.

The main open question in the critical discourse concerns the relative participation of Carpaccio's workshop. Pignatti (1981, pp. 124–28), who summarizes the arguments, argues for a decline in the artist's powers – particularly obvious in the *Martyrdom* – rather than a growing predominance of collaborators (such as we see the Scuola degli Albanesi). Pignatti's judgment is persuasive, for the *Martyrdom* makes a direct stylistic link to the organ doors in the Cathedral in Capodistria, painted by Carpaccio in 1523 (Cancogni and Perocco, no. 75). Again, here, the works seem to have been executed in narrative order.

ORIGINAL CYCLE:
Carpaccio
1. *Ordination of the Deacons* 1511
Oil on canvas, 148 × 231 cm
Berlin, Staatliche Museen, Gemäldegalerie, n. 23
Inscription: VICTOR CARPATHIVS / FINXIT M.D.XI
For the inscription on the frame, see doc. 3.
LIT.: Berlin-Dahlem, 1978, pp. 94–95.

2. *St. Stephen Preaching in Jerusalem*
Oil on canvas, 148 × 194 cm (measurements from Louvre, *Catalogue sommaire*, 1981)
Color Plate XI
Paris, Louvre, inv. 181
Inscription: illegible

Zanetti (doc. 3) appeared to refer to this work when he wrote: 'Evvene un'altra nel quadro vicino col nome di un altro scarpellino, e l'anno MDXIIII.'

3. *Disputation of St. Stephen* 1514
Oil on canvas, 147 × 172 cm
Color Plates XV, XLI
Milan, Brera, n. 170
Inscription: VICTOR / CARPATHIVS / FINXIT // . M/D.XIIII

4. *Trial of St. Stephen* (lost)

Probably recorded in a charcoal and ink drawing in Florence (Gabinetto dei Disegni, Uffizi, no. 1687F = 22.8 × 27.0 cm), convincingly identified by Von Hadeln as a copy of Carpaccio's finished *modello* for the painting. Attributions for the drawing vary from full autograph by Carpaccio to work of his son, Benedetto.
LIT.: Von Hadeln, 1925, p. 61, pl. 50; Tietze and Tietze-Conrat, 1944, no. A-602; Lauts, 1962, pp. 278–79; Muraro, 1977, pp. 42–43.

5. *Martyrdom of St. Stephen* 1520
Stuttgart, Staatsgalerie, n. 311.
Oil on canvas, 149 × 170 cm
Inscription: VICTOR / CARPA.../ MDXX

Zanetti (doc. 3) reported the date MDXXI on the frame.

Francesco Bissolo
6. *Triptych of the Scuola di San Stefano*
St. Stephen (center: 115 × 58 cm); SS. Augustine (left) and Anthony of Padua (right) (115 × 43 cm each)
Oil on wood
Milan, Brera, n. 158

Zanetti (doc. 3) identified the flanking saints as Thomas Aquinas and Nicholas of Tolentino (cf. Pignatti, 1981, p. 128).

LITERATURE: Ridolfi, 1648, I. p. 48; Cornaro, 1749, 12, p. 305; Boschini, 1674, San Marco, pp. 89–90; Zanetti, 1771, p. 40; Sagredo, 1852, p. 20; Molmenti and Ludwig, 1907, pp. 178–88; Perocco, 1956, p. 224; Lauts, 1962, pp. 235–36; Zampetti, 1963b, pp. 240–60; Muraro, 1966, pp. clxxxii ff.; R. Gallo, 'La Scuola Grande di San Teodoro di Venezia', *Atti dell'Istituto Veneto di Scienze, Lettere ed Arti*, 1962, pp. 470–71; Cancogni and Perocco, 1967, no. 56; Sgarbi, 1978, nos. 36–38; Pignatti, 1981, pp. 119–28; Gramigna and Perissa, 1981, p. 55; Zorzi, 1984, pp. 376–377.

All measurements from Pignatti, 1981, pp. 124–27, unless otherwise noted.

SELECT BIBLIOGRAPHY

MANUSCRIPT SOURCES

Archivio di Stato, Venice:
- Avogaria di Comun
- Capi dei Consiglio dei Dieci, Notatorio
- Cassiere della Bolla Ducale, Grazie del Maggior Consiglio
- Collegio: Ceremoniale, Notatorio
- Commemoriali
- Consiglio dei Dieci: Compilazione Leggi, Comune, Parti Miste
- Inquisitori di Stato
- Inquisitori et revisori sopra le Scuole Grandi
- Maggior Consiglio, Deliberazioni
- Magistrato al Sal, Collegio
- Notarile, Testamenti
- Provveditori al Sal, Notatorio
- Provveditori di Comun
- SS. Giovanni e Paolo
- Scuole Grandi:
  - San Giovanni Evangelista
  - San Marco
  - S. Maria della Carità
  - S. Maria della Misericordia
- Scuole piccole e suffragi:
  - Scuola di Sant'Orsola
- Senato: Secreta, Terra

Biblioteca Nazionale Marciana, Venice:

CODICI ITALIANI, CLASSE VII
- no. 125 (=7460): 'Cronache venete.'
- no. 165 (=8867): 'Memorie della famiglia Freschi.'
- no. 341 (=8623): 'Storia delle famiglie cittadinesche di Venezia.'
- no. 737 (=8666): 'Mariegola, Scuola di S. M. degli Albanese.'
- no. 1667 (=8459): 'Elenco degli ordinari, estraordinari, segretari de pregadi e cancellieri grandi dal secolo XIII fino al XVII.'

Biblioteca del Museo Civico Correr, Venice:

CODICI CORRER
- Cons. IX D 1-1/5: Giuseppe Tassini, 'Cittadini Veneziani.'
- I, no. 383 (=1497): 'Il libro della leggenda degli Apostoli Pietro e Paolo, di S. Albano e della venuta a Venezia di Papa Alexandro III.'
- no. 1391: 'Matrimonio Veneto.'

CODICI CICOGNA
- no. 2156: 'Cronaca di famiglie cittadine.'
- no. 2653: 'Dispacci al Senato e ad altri di Ser Bortolomio Minio Provveditor e Capitanio a Napoli a Romania dal MCCCCLXXIX al MCCCCL-XXXIII.'
- no. 2987–88: 'Miscellanea antica.' Fasc. 17: 'Passio et translatio quedamque miraculagliossimi Marci evangelisti.'
- no. 3063: 'Materie ecclesiastiche veneziane.'

CODICI GRADENIGO-DOLFIN
- no. 83: 'Corona seconda della veneta republica.'
- no. 192: 'Cittadini veneti.'
- no. 194: 'Scole Grandi.'

MARIEGOLE
- no. 3, Scuola di San Stefano.
- no. 19, Scuola di San Marco: 'Inventarii.'
- no. 68, Scuola di Santa Marina.
- no. 83, Scuola di San Marco.
- no. 113, Scuola di San Gerolamo.

Scuola di San Giorgio degli Schiavoni, Venice:
- Mariegola
- Catastico

Seminario Patriarcale, Venice:
- Cod. 950: Jacopo d'Albizzotto Guidi, 'El sommo della condizione e stato e principio della città de Vinegia e di suo territorio.'

PRINTED MATERIAL BEFORE 1800

Alberti, Leon Battista. *On Painting and On Sculpture. The Latin Texts of De Pictura and De Statua*, edited by Cecil Grayson. London, 1972.

Bardi, Girolamo. *Dichiaratione di tutte le istorie, che si contengono nei quadri posti novamente nelle Sale dello Scrutinio, & del Gran Consiglio, del Palagio Ducale della Serenissima Republica*. Venice, 1587a.

———. *Vittoria navale ottenuta della republica venetiana contra Othone, figliuolo di Federico primo imperadore; per la restitutione di Alessandro terzo, pontefice massimo, venuto à Venetia*. Venice, 1587b

Biondo, Flavio. *Historiae ab inclinatione... Romanorum imperii decades*. Basel, 1531.

Bonincontro da Bovi, 'Historia de discordia et persecutione quam habuit Ecclesia cum Imperatore Federico Barbarossa tempore Alexandri III. Sum. Pont., et demum de pace facta Venetiis et habita inter eos'. In Sanudo, *Vite dei Dogi*, edited by Giovanni Monticolo, in *Rerum Italicarum Scriptores*, new series, 22:4, pp. 374–410.

Boschini, Marco. *Le minere della pittura veneziana*. Venice, 1664.

———. *Le ricche minere della pittura veneziana*. Venice, 1674.

Brasca, Santo. *Viaggio in Terrasanta 1480, con l'itinerario di Gabriele Capodilista*, edited by Anna Laura Momigliano Lepschy. Milan, 1966.

Breydenbach, Bernhard von. *Opusculum Sanctarum peregrinationum ad sepulcrum Christi venerandum*. Mainz, 1486. Facsimile edition: *Die Reise ins Heilige Land*, edited by Elisabeth Geck. Wiesbaden, 1977.

[Casola, Pietro]. *Canon Pietro Casola's Pilgrimage to Jerusalem in the Year 1494*, edited and translated by Mary Margaret Newett. Manchester, 1907.

Commynes, Philippe de. *Mémoires*, edited by M. Dupont. 3 vols., Paris, 1840–47.
Contarini, Gasparo. *De magistratibus et republica Venetorum libri quinque*. Basel, 1547. Translated by Lewes Lewkenor, *The Commonwealth and Government of Venice*, London, 1599.
Cornaro, Flaminio. *Ecclesiae Venetae*. 13 vols. and supplementa, Venice, 1749.
______. *Notizie storiche delle chiese e monasteri di Venezia e di Torcello*... Padua, 1758.
Cotrugli, Benedetto. *Della mercatura e del mercante perfetto*. Venice, 1573.
Fabri, Felix. *Evagatorium in Terrae Sanctae, Arabiae et Egypti Peregrinationem*, edited by C. D. Hassler. 3 vols., Stuttgart, 1843.
______. *The Wanderings of*..., translated by A. Stewart. Palestine Pilgrims' Texts Society, vols. 7–10, London, 1896.
Facio, Bartolomeo. *De viris illustribus*. Florence, 1745.
Foresti, Jacopo Filippo. *Supplementum Chronicarum*. Venice, 1486.
Gabrieli, Angelo, *Libellus hospitalis munificentiae venetorum in excipienda Anna Regina Hungariae*. Venice, 1502. Reprinted in Latin and Italian by Francesco Testa. *Per le faustissime nozze Negri-Stecchini*. Padua, 1837.
Giannotti, Donato. *Libro de la Republica de Vinitiani*. Rome, 1542.
Giustiniani, Bernardo. *De origine urbis venetiarum rebusque gestis a venetis*...*Adjectis tribus libris de Divi Marci Evangelistae Vita, ejus Translatione e Sepulturae Loco*, edited by J. Graevius. In *Thesaurus Antiquitatem et Historiarum Italiae*, 5:1, Louvain, 1772.
Guylforde, Sir Richard. *The Pylgrymage of*...*to the Holy Land, A. D. 1506*, edited by H. Ellis. The Camden Society, no. 51, London, 1851.
Harff, Arnold von. *The Pilgrimage of*...*1496 to 1499*, translated and edited by M. Letts. London, 1946.
Lezze, Donado da. *Historia turchesca, 1300–1514*, ed. I. Ursu. Bucharest, 1909.
Lorenzi, G. *Monumenti per servire alla storia del Palazzo Ducale di Venezia*. Parte I dal 1253 al 1600. Venice, 1868.
Malipiero, Domenico. *Annali veneti, dall'anno 1457 al 1500*, edited by A. Sagredo. In *Archivio storico italiano*, 1st series 7:1–2 (1843–44).
Martino da Canal. *Les estoires de Venise. Cronaca veneziana in lingua francese dalle origini al 1275*, edited by Alberto Limentani. Florence, 1972.
[Michiel, Marcantonio]. *The Anonimo*, edited by G. C. Williamson. New York, 1969.
Miracoli della croce santissima della scuola Grande di S. Giovanni Evangelista. Venice, 1590.
Morosini, Domenico. *De bene instituta re publica*, edited by C. Finzi. Milan, 1969.
Pagani, Zaccaria. *Voyage du magnifique et très illustre chevalier et procurateur de saint-marc Domenico Trevisan*. In Jean Thenaud, *Le voyage d'Outremer (Egypte, Mont Sinay, Palestine) suivi de La Relation de l'Ambassade de Domenico Trevisan auprès du Soudan d'Egypte, 1512*, edited by C. Schefer. Paris, 1884.
Della pittura veneziana. Trattato in cui osservasi l'ordine del Boschini, e si conserva la dottrina, e le definizioni dello Zanetti. 2 vols. Venice, 1797.
Priuli, Girolamo. *I Diarii*, edited by Arturo Segre and Roberto Cessi. In *Rerum Italicarum Scriptores*, new series, vol. 24, pt. 3, Bologna, 1912–41.
Questi sono i miracoli delasantissima croce dela scola de misier san zuane evangelista. N.p., n.d. [Museo Civico Correr, Inc. H222 bis.]
Ramusio, G. Battista. *Delle navigationi et viaggi*. 3 vols., Venice, 1559, with many later editions.
[Rannusio, Paolo] Rhamnusii, P. *De bello Constantinopolitano et imperatoribus Comnenis per Venetos et Gallos restitutis, MCCIV, libri sex*. Venice, 1604.
Ridolfi, Carlo. *Le meraviglie dell'arte Ovvero le vite degli illustri pittori veneti e dello stato*, edited by Detlev von Hadeln. Berlin, 1914; reprint (2 vols.), Rome, 1965.
Sabellico, Marcantonio. *De Venetae urbis situ*. Venice, 1490. Reprinted in *Thesaurus Antiquitatem et Historiarum Italiae*, vol. 5:1, edited by J. Graevius, Louvain, 1772.
[Sansovino, Francesco]. *Delle cose notabili che sono in Venetia*. Venice, 1604.
Sansovino, Francesco. *Venetia città nobilissima et singolare descritta in XIIII libri*. Venice, 1581; with additions by Giovanni Stringa, Venice, 1604; with additions by Giustiniano Martinioni, Venice, 1663.
Sanudo, Marin. *I commentarii della guerra di Ferrara*, edited by P. Bettio, Venice, 1829.
______. *De origine, situ et magistratibus urbis Venetae ovvero La Città di Venetia (1493–1530)*, edited by A. Caracciolo Aricò. Milan, 1980.
______. *I Diarii*, edited by R. Fulin et al. 58 vols., Venice, 1879–1903.
______. *L'Itinerario di Marin Sanudo per la terraferma veneziana nell'anno MCCCCLXXXIII*. Padua, 1847.
______. *La spedizione di Carlo VIII in Italia*, edited by R. Fulin, Venice, 1883.
______. *Vitae Ducum Venetorum*, edited by L. Muratori. In *Rerum Italicarum Scriptores*, old series, 22, Milan, 1733.
______. *Le vite dei dogi*, edited by G. Monticolo and G. Carducci. In *Rerum Italicarum Scriptores*, new series, 22:4, Città di Castello and Bologna, 1900–1902.
Savonarola, Michele da. *Libellus de magnificus ornamentus regie civitatis Padue*, edited by A. Segarizzi. In *Rerum Italicarum Scriptores*, new series, 24:15, Città di Castello, 1902.
Travels to Tana and Persia by Josafa Barbaro and Ambrogio Contarini, translated by W. Thomas and S. Roy, and edited by Lord Stanley of Alderley. Hakluyt Society, 49:1–2, London, 1873.
Vasari, Giorgio. *Le vite de' più eccellenti pittori, scultori ed architettori nelle Redazioni di 1550 e 1568*, edited by R. Bettarini and P. Barocchi. 4 vols., Florence, 1966.
I viaggi in Persia degli ambasciatori veneti Barbaro e Contarini, edited by L. Lockhart, R. Morozzo della Rocca and M. F. Tiepolo. *Il Nuovo Ramusio*, VII, Rome, 1973.
Voragine, Jacobus da. *The Golden Legend*, translated by G. Ryan and H. Ripperger. New York, 1941.
Zanetti, Anton Maria. *Della pittura veneziana e delle opere pubbliche de veneziani maestri libri V*. Venice, 1771.

SECONDARY SOURCES

Alberigo, G. 'Contributi alla storia delle confraternite dei disciplinati e della spiritualità laicale nei secc. XV e XVI'. In *Il Movimento dei Disciplinati nel Settimo Centenario dal suo inizio (Perugia-1260)*, Deputazione di storia patria per l'Umbria, no. 9. Perugia, 1960.
Alpers, Svetlana. 'Ekphrasis and Aesthetic Attitudes in Vasari's Lives'. *Journal of the Warburg and Courtauld Institutes* 23 (1960): pp. 190–215.
Amat di S. Filippo, P. *Biografia dei viaggiatori italiani*. Rome, 1881.
Ames-Lewis, Francis. *Drawing in Early Renaissance Italy*. New Haven and London, 1981.
Ames-Lewis, Francis and Wright, Joanne. *Drawing in the Italian Renaissance*

Workshop. London, 1983.
Arslan, Edoardo. *Gothic Architecture in Venice*. London, 1971.
Babinger, Franz. *Johannes Darius (1414–1494) Sachwalter Venedigs im Morgenland und sein griechischer Umkreis*, Bayerischer Akademie der Wissenschaften, phil.-hist. Klasse, Sitzungsberichte, Heft 5. Munich, 1961.
______. *Mehmed the Conqueror and His Times*, translated by R. Manheim and edited by W. Hickman. Princeton, 1978.
Bailo, Luigi and Biscaro, Gerolamo. *Della Vita e delle Opere di Paris Bordon*. Treviso, 1900.
Ballarin, Alessandro. 'Una nuova prospettiva su Giorgione: La ritrattistica degli anni 1500–1503'. In *Giorgione: Atti del Convegno Internazionale di Studio per il 5° centenario della nascita, 29–31 maggio 1978*, Castelfranco Veneto, 1979.
Bardon, Francoise. 'De la passio à la peinture: analyse historique du récit verbal de la légende d'Ursule'. *Revue belge d'archéologie et d'histoire d'art* 52 (1983): pp. 43–79.
______. *La peinture narrative de Carpaccio dans le cycle de Ste Ursule*, Istituto Veneto di Scienze, Lettere ed Arti. Memorie Classe di Scienze Morali, Lettere ed Arti. 39, fasc. IV, 1985.
Baron, Hans. 'Early Renaissance Venetian Chronicles: Their History and a Manuscript in the Newberry Library'. In Baron, *From Petrarch to Bruni*, Chicago and London, 1968.
Barthes, Roland. 'An Introduction to the Structural Analysis of Narrative'. *New Literary History* 6 (1975): pp. 237–72.
Bassi, Elena. 'Appunti per la storia del Palazzo Ducale di Venezia'. *Critica d'Arte* 51 (1962a): pp. 25–38; 52 (1962b): pp. 41–53.
______. 'Il Palazzo Ducale nel '400'. *Bollettino del Centro internationale di studi di architettura Andrea Palladio* 6:2 (1964): pp. 181–87.
Bassi, Elena and Trincanato, Egle Renata. *Il Palazzo Ducale nella storia e nell'arte di Venezia*. Milan, 1960.
Baumeister, Engelbert. 'Unbekannte Studienblätter von Gentile Bellini für 'Das Wunder der Kreuzesreliquie' in der Scuola di San Giovanni Evangelista'. *Münchner Jahrbuch der bildenden Kunst* 11 (1934): pp. xxxvi-xl.
Baxandall, Michael. 'A Dialogue on Art from the Court of Leonello d'Este. Angelo Decembrio's *De Politia Litteraria Pars LXVIII*'. *Journal of the Warburg and Courtauld Institutes* 26 (1963): pp. 304–26.
______. *Giotto and the Orators*. Oxford, 1971.
______. 'Guarino, Pisanello and Chrysoloras'. *Journal of the Warburg and Courtauld Institutes* 28 (1965): pp. 183–204.
______. *Painting and Experience in Fifteenth Century Italy*. Oxford, 1972.
Belting, Hans. 'The New Role of Narrative in the Public Painting of the Trecento Historia and Allegory'. *Studies in the History of Art* 16 (1985): pp. 151–68.
Berchet, F. 'La Sala del Maggior Consiglio'. *Atti del R. Istituto Veneto di Scienze, Lettere ed Arti* 59 (1899/1900): pp. 949–61.
[Berlin-Dahlem.] *Catalogue of Paintings, Picture Gallery, Staatliche Museen Preussischer Kulturbesitz*. 2nd rev. edition, translated by L. Parshall. Berlin-Dahlem, 1978.
Berenson, Bernard. *Italian Pictures of the Renaissance. Venetian School*. 2 vols., London, 1957.
Bernasconi, John. 'The Cycle of the Relic of the Cross from the Scuola Grande di S. Giovanni Evangelista'. M.A. report, Courtauld Institute, 1972.
______. 'The Dating of the Cycle of the Miracles of the Cross from the Scuola di San Giovanni Evangelista'. *Arte Veneta* 35 (1981): pp. 198–202.
Bertolotti, A. *Artisti in relazione coi Gonzaga duchi di Mantova nei secoli XVI e XVII*. Modena, 1885.
Bevilacqua, E. 'Geografi e cosmografi'. In *Storia della cultura veneta dal primo Quattrocento al Concilio di Trento*, 3/II, edited by G. Arnaldi and M. Pastore Stocchi. Vicenza, 1980.
Billanovich, E. 'Note per la storia della pittura nel Veneto'. *Italia medioevale e umanistica* 16 (1973): pp. 359–89.
Bistort, Giulio. *Il magistrato alle pompe nella republica di Venezia: Studio storico*. Miscellanea di storia veneta, 3rd series, Vol. V. Venice, 1912.
Borsook, Eve. *The Mural Painters of Tuscany*. Rev. ed. London, 1980.
Braghirolli, W. 'Carteggio di Isabella intorno ad un quadro di Giambellino'. *Archivio Veneto* 13 (1877): pp. 376–83.
Branca, Vittorio. 'Ermolao Barbaro and Late Quattrocento Venetian Humanism'. In *Renaissance Venice*, edited by J. R. Hale. London, 1973.
______. 'L'umanesimo veneziano alla fine del Quattrocento Ermolao Barbaro e il suo circolo'. In *Storia della cultura veneta dal primo Quattrocento al Concilio di Trento*, 3/I, edited by G. Arnaldi and M. Pastore Stocchi. Vicenza, 1980.
Branca, Vittorio and Weiss, Roberto. 'Carpaccio e l'iconografia del più grande umanista veneziano (Ermolao Barbaro)'. *Arte Veneta* 17 (1963): pp. 35–40.
Brejon de Lavergnée, A. and Thiebaut, D. *Catalogue sommaire illustré des peintures du musée du Louvre: II Italie, Espagne, Allemagne, Grande-Bretagne et divers*. Paris, 1981.
Brilliant, Richard. *Visual Narratives. Storytelling in Etruscan and Roman Art*. Ithaca, 1984.
Brown, Patricia Fortini. 'Honor and Necessity: The Dynamics of Patronage in the Confraternities of Renaissance Venice'. *Studi Veneziani* 14 (1987): pp. 179–212.
______. 'An Incunabulum of the Miracles of the True Cross of the Scuola Grande di San Giovanni Evangelista.' *Bollettino dei Civici Musei Veneziani d'arte e di storia*, new series, 27:1–4 (1982): pp. 5–8.
______. 'Painting and History in Renaissance Venice'. *Art History* 7 (1984): pp. 263–94.
Cadorin, Giuseppe. *Pareri di XV architetti e notizie storiche intorno al Palazzo Ducale di Venezia*. Venice, 1858.
Cancogni, Manlio, ed. *L'opera completa del Carpaccio*, with notes by Guido Perocco. Classici dell' arte, no. 13. Milan, 1967.
Canuti, F. *Il Perugino*. 2 vols., Siena, 1931.
Caracciolo Aricò, Angela. 'Marin Sanudo il Giovane, Precursore di Francesco Sansovino'. *Lettere Italiane* (1979): pp. 419–37.
Carile, Antonio. 'Aspetti della cronachistica veneziana nei secoli XIII e XIV'. In *La storiografia veneziana fino al secolo XVI*, pp. 75–126, edited by A. Pertusi. Civiltà veneziana, Saggi, no. 18. Florence, 1970.
______. *La cronachistica veneziana (XIII-XVI secolo) di fronte alla spartizione della Romania nel 1204*. Florence, 1969.
Castelfranchi-Vegas, Liana. *Italia e Fiandra nella pittura del Quattrocento*. Milan, 1983.
Cecchetti, Bartolomeo. 'Libri, scuole, maestri, sussidi allo studio in Venezia nei secoli XIV e XV'. *Archivio veneto*, new series, 32 (1886): pp. 325–63.
______. *La vita dei veneziani nel 1300*. Venice, 1885. Reprint Bologna: Arnaldo Forni, 1980.
Cessi, Roberto. *Rialto: L'isola-il ponte-il mercato*. Bologna, 1934.
Chambers, D. S. *Patrons and Artists in the Italian Renaissance*. Columbia, S.C., 1971.
Chastel, André. *A Chronicle of Italian Renaissance Painting*. Ithaca, 1983.
Chojnacki, Stanley. 'In Search of the Venetian Patriciate: Families and Factions in the Fourteenth Century'. In *Renaissance Venice*, edited by J. R. Hale. London, 1973.
Christiansen, Keith. *Gentile da Fabriano*. Ithaca, 1982.

———. 'Venetian Painting of the Early Quattrocento'. *Apollo* 125 (March 1987): pp. 166–77.
Cicogna, Emmanuele. *Breve notizia intorno alla origine della Confraternità di San Giovanni Evangelista in Venezia*. Venice, 1885.
———. *Delle inscrizioni veneziane*. 6 vols., Venice, 1824–27.
Cochrane, Eric. *Historians and Historiography in the Italian Renaissance*. Chicago and London, 1981.
Coletti, L. *Cima da Conegliano*. Venice, 1959.
Collins, Howard. 'The cyclopean vision of Jacopo Bellini'. *Pantheon* 40 (1982a): pp. 300–3.
———. 'Gentile Bellini: A Monograph and Catalogue of Works'. Ph.D. dissertation. University of Pittsburgh, 1970.
———. 'Major narrative paintings of Jacopo Bellini.' *Art Bulletin* 64 (1982b): pp. 466–72.
———. 'Time, Space and Gentile Bellini's *The Miracle of the Cross at the Ponte San Lorenzo* (Portraits of Catherina Cornaro and Pietro Bembo)'. *Gazette des Beaux-Arts*, 6th series, 100 (1982c): pp. 201–8.
Collobi, Licia. 'Lazzaro Bastiani'. *Critica d'Arte* 4–5 part 2 (1939–40): pp. 33–53.
Conti, A. 'Un ambasciata del 1512, da Gentile Bellini a Benedetto Diana'. In *Per Maria Cionini Visani, Scritti d'amici*. Turin, 1977.
Cozzi, Gaetano. 'Authority and the Law in Renaissance Venice'. In *Renaissance Venice*, edited by J. Hale. London, 1973.
———. 'Cultura politica e religione nella 'pubblica storiografia' veneziana del '500'. *Bolletino dell' Istituto di Storia della Società e dello Stato Veneziano* 5–6 (1963–64): pp. 215–94.
———. 'Domenico Morosini e il *De bene instituta re publica*'. *Studi veneziani* 12 (1970a): pp. 405–58.
———. 'La Donna, l'amore e Tiziano'. In *Tiziano e Venezia: Convegno internazionale di studi, Venezia, 1976*. Vicenza, 1980.
———. 'Marin Sanudo il Giovane: Dalla cronaca alla storia'. In *La storiografia veneziana fino al secolo XVI*, edited by A. Pertusi. Civiltà veneziana, Saggi, no. 18. Florence. 1970b.
Cozzi, Gaetano and Knapton, Michael. *Storia della Repubblica di Venezia. Dalla guerra di Chioggia alla riconquista della Terraferma*. Turin, 1986.
Cracco, Giorgio. *Società e stato nel medioevo veneziano (secolo XII–XIV)*. Florence, 1967.
———. *Un 'altro mondo'. Venezia nel medioevo. Dal secolo XI al secolo XIV*. Turin, 1986.
Crowe, J. and Cavalcaselle, G. *A History of Painting in North Italy*, edited by T. Borenius. 3 vols., London, 1912.
Damisch, Hubert. 'Le théatre de peinture'. In *Interpretazioni veneziane. Studi di storia dell'arte in onore di Michelangelo Muraro*, edited by David Rosand. Venice, 1984.
Davies, Martin, *The Earlier Italian Schools*. 2nd rev. ed., London, 1961. Reprint London, 1986.
Davis, Margaret Daly. 'Carpaccio and the Perspective of Regular Bodies'. In *La prospettiva rinascimentale*, edited by M. Dalai Emiliani. Florence, 1980.
Degenhart, Bernhard. *Pisanello*. Vienna, 1941.
Degenhart, Bernhard and Schmitt, Annegrit. *Corpus der italienischen Zeichnungen, 1300–1450. Teil II. Venedig. Addenda zu Sud- und Mittelitalien*. 3 vols., Berlin, 1980.
Degenhart, Bernhard and Schmitt, Annegrit. *Jacopo Bellini. The Louvre Book of Drawings*. New York, 1984.
Della Rovere, Antonio. 'Vittore Carpaccio. Arrivo di Ercole I e di Alfonso I d'Este a Venezia'. *Rassegna d'Arte* 2 (1902): pp. 33–36.
Dempsey, Charles. 'Renaissance Hieroglyphic Studies and Gentile Bellini's *St. Mark Preaching in Alexandria*'. In *Hermeticism and the Renaissance. Intellectual History and the Occult in Early Modern Europe*, edited by Ingrid Merkel and Allen Debus. Folger Shakespeare Library. London and Toronto, 1987 (forthcoming).
Demus, Otto. *The Church of San Marco in Venice: History, Architecture, Sculpture*. Dumbarton Oaks Studies, no. 6. Washington, 1960.
———. *The Mosaics of San Marco*. 4 vols., Chicago and London, 1984.
———. 'Oriente e Occidente nell'arte veneta del Duecento'. In *La civiltà veneziana del secolo di Marco Polo*. Florence, 1955.
Dionisotti. Carlo. 'La guerra d'Oriente nella letteratura veneziana del Cinquecento'. In *Venezia e l'Oriente fra tardo Medioevo e Rinascimento*, edited by A. Pertusi. Venice, 1966.
Donazzolo, P. *I viaggiatori veneti minori. Studio bio-bibliografico*. Rome, 1927.
Escher, Konrad. 'Die grossen Gemäldefolgen im Dogenpalast in Venedig und ihre inhaltliche Bedeutung für den Barock'. *Repertorium für Kunstwissenschaft* 41 (1919): pp. 87–125.
Fasoli, Gina. 'Liturgia e cerimoniale ducale'. In *Venezia e il levante fino al secolo XV*, I: pp. 261–95, edited by A. Pertusi. Florence, 1973.
———. 'Nascita di un mito'. In *Studi storici in onore di Gioacchino Volpe* I: pp. 445–79. Florence, 1958.
Favaro, Elena. *L'arte dei pittori in Venezia e i suoi statuti*. Florence, 1975.
Fedalto, Giorgio. 'Stranieri a Venezia e a Padova'. In *Storia della cultura veneta dal primo Quattrocento al Concilio di Trento*, 3/I, edited by G. Arnaldi and M. Pastore Stocchi. Vicenza, 1980.
Finlay, Robert. *Politics in Renaissance Venice*. New Brunswick, 1980.
Fiocco, Giuseppe. *Carpaccio*. Rome, 1930.
———. 'Vista da vicino: La Predica di San Marco di Gentile e Giovanni Bellini'. *Emporium* 88 (1938): pp. 6–16.
Fletcher, Jennifer F. 'Marcantonio Michiel, 'che ha veduto assai'. *The Burlington Magazine* 123 (1981a): pp. 602–8.
———. 'Marcantonio Michiel: his friends and collection'. *The Burlington Magazine* 123 (1981b): pp. 453–67.
———. Review of Francoise Bardon, *La peinture narrative de Carpaccio dans le cycle de Ste Ursule*. In *The Burlington Magazine* 128 (1986): pp. 427–28.
———. 'Sources of Carpaccio in German Woodcuts', *The Burlington Magazine* 115 (1973): pp. 599.
Flores D'Arcais, Francesca. *Guariento*. Padua, 1974.
Fogolari, Gino. 'Processione veneziane'. *Dedalo* 5 (1924–25): pp. 775–94.
Foscari, L. 'Autoritratti di Maestri della Scuola Veneziana'. *Rivista di Venezia* 12 (1933): pp. 247–62.
Fossi Todorow, M. *I disegni del Pisanello e della sua cerchia*. Florence, 1966.
Franzoi, Umberto. *Storia e leggenda del Palazzo Ducale di Venezia*. Verona, 1982.
Frimmel, Theodor. Review of P. Molmenti, *Il Carpaccio e il Tiepolo*. Turin, 1885. In *Repertorium für Kunstwissenschaft* 11 (1888): pp. 316ff.
Gallo, Rodolfo. 'La Scuola di Sant'Orsola, i teleri del Carpaccio e la tomba di Gentile e Giovanni Bellini'. *Bollettino dei Musei Civici Veneziani* 8 (1963): pp. 1–24.
———. 'I teleri di Giambellino della Sala del Maggior Consiglio'. *Vernice* 4 (1949): pp. 31–32.
Geanakoplos, Deno. *Greek Scholars in Venice: Studies in the Dissemination of Greek Learning from Byzantium to the West*. Cambridge, Mass., 1962
———. *Byzantine East and Latin West: Two Worlds of Christendom in Middle Ages and Renaissance*. New York, 1966.
Ghinzoni, P. 'Federico III Imperatore a Venezia (7 al 19 Febbrajo 1469)'. *Archivio Veneto* 37 (1889): pp. 133–53.

Gibbons, Felton. 'Giovanni Bellini's Topographical Landscapes'. In *Studies in Late Medieval and Renaissance Painting in Honor of Millard Meiss*, I: pp. 174–84, edited by I. Lavin and J. Plummer. New York, 1977.

———. 'New Evidence for the Birth Dates of Gentile and Giovanni Bellini'. *Art Bulletin* 45 (1963): pp. 54–58.

———. 'Practices in Giovanni Bellini's Workshop'. *Pantheon* 23 (1965): pp. 146–55.

Gilbert, Creighton. Review of Lionello Puppi, *Bartolomeo Montagna*. In *Art Bulletin* 49 (1967): pp. 184–88.

Gilbert, Felix. 'Humanism in Venice'. In *Florence and Venice: Comparisons and Relations*, vol. 1, Quattrocento, edited by Sergio Bertelli, Nicolai Rubinstein and Craig Hugh Smyth. Florence, 1979.

———. *The Pope, his Banker and Venice*. Cambridge, Mass., 1980.

———. 'Venice in the Crisis of the League of Cambrai'. In *Renaissance Venice*, edited by J.R. Hale. London, 1973.

Gilles de la Tourette, F. *L'Orient e les Peintres de Venise*. Paris, 1924.

Goffen, Rona. *Piety and Patronage in Renaissance Venice: Bellini and Titian and the Franciscans*. New Haven, 1986.

Gramigna Dian, Silvia and Perissa Torrini, Annalisa. *Scuole di arti, mestieri e devozione a Venezia*. Venice, 1981.

Gronau, Georg. *Die Kunstlerfamilie Bellini*. Bielefeld and Leipzig, 1909.

Grubb, James. 'When Myths Lose Power: Four Decades of Venetian Historiography'. *Journal of Modern History* 58 (1986): pp. 43–94.

Grundmann, H. *Movimenti religiosi nel medioevo*, translated by M. Ausserhofer and L. Santini. Bologna, 1974.

Hadeln, Detlev Freiherr von. *Venezianische Zeichnungen der Hochrenaissance*. Berlin, 1925a.

———. *Venezianische Zeichnungen des Quattrocento*. Berlin, 1925b.

Hartt, Frederick. 'The Earliest Works of Andrea del Castagno'. *Art Bulletin* 41 (1959): pp. 225–36.

Heinemann, Fritz. 'Spätwerke des Giovanni Mansueti'. *Arte Veneta* 19 (1965): pp. 150–52.

———. 'Vittore Carpaccio in Dogenpalast'. *Kunstchronik* 16 (1963): pp. 237–46.

Herald, Jacqueline. *Renaissance Dress in Italy, 1400–1500*. London, 1981.

Hope, Charles. 'Titian's Role as Official Painter to the Venetian Republic'. In *Tiziano e Venezia*, Vicenza, 1980.

Howard, Deborah. *The Architectural History of Venice*. London, 1980.

Humfrey, Peter. 'The Bellinesque Life of St. Mark cycle for the Scuola Grande di San Marco in Venice in its original arrangement'. *Zeitschrift für Kunstgeschichte* 48 (1985a): pp. 225–42.

———. *Cima da Conegliano*. Cambridge, 1983.

———. 'The Life of St. Jerome cycle from the Scuola di San Gerolamo in Cannaregio'. *Arte Veneta* 39 (1985b): pp. 41–46.

Humfrey, Peter and MacKenney, Richard. 'Venetian trade guilds as patrons of art in the renaissance'. *The Burlington Magazine* 128 (1986): pp. 317–30.

Huse, Norbert. *Studien zu Giovanni Bellini*. Berlin, 1972.

Huse, Norbert and Wolters, Wolfgang. *Venedig. Die Kunst der Renaissance. Architektur, Skulptur, Malerei, 1460–1590*. Munich, 1986.

Joost-Gaugier, Christiane. 'Considerations Regarding Jacopo Bellini's place in the Venetian Renaissance'. *Arte Veneta* 28 (1974): pp. 21–38.

———. *Jacopo Bellini. Selected Drawings*. New York, 1980.

———. 'Jacopo Bellini and the Theatre of his Time'. *Paragone* 27, nr. 325 (1977a): pp. 70–80.

———. 'Jacopo Bellini's Interest in Perspective and its Iconographical Significance'. *Zeitschrift für Kunstgeschichte* 38 (1975): pp. 1–28.

———. 'The Tuscanization of Jacopo Bellini'. *Acta Historiae Artium* 23 (1977b): pp. 95–112 and 291–313.

Jorga, Nicolai. *Philippe de Mézières 1327–1405 et la croisade au XIVe siècle*. Paris, 1896.

Kemp, Martin. 'From 'Mimesis' to 'Fantasia': the Quattrocento Vocabulary of Creation, Inspiration and Genius in the Visual Arts'. *Viator* 8 (1977): pp. 347–98.

———. *Leonardo da Vinci. The Marvellous Works of Nature and Man*. Cambridge, Mass., 1981.

King, Margaret. 'The Patriciate and the Intellectuals: Power and Ideas in Quattrocento Venice'. *Societas* 5:4 (1975): pp. 295–312.

———. *Venetian Humanism in an Age of Patrician Dominance*. Princeton, 1986.

Kurz, Otto. 'Mamluk Heraldry and Interpretatio Christiana'. In *Studies in Memory of Gaston Wiet*. Jerusalem, 1977.

Labalme, Patricia. *Bernardo Giustiniani, a Venetian of the Quattrocento*. Rome, 1969.

Lane, Frederick C. 'The enlargement of the Great Council of Venice'. In *Florilegium Historiale. Essays Presented to Wallace K. Ferguson*, edited by J. Rowe and W. Stockdale. Toronto, 1971.

———. *Venice. A Maritime Republic*. Baltimore, 1973.

Lauts, Jan. *Carpaccio*. London, 1962.

Lecoq, Anne-Marie. 'La 'Città festeggiante' Les fêtes publiques au XVe et XVIe siècles'. *Revue de l'Art* 33 (1976): pp. 83–100.

———. '"Finxit". Le peintre comme "fictor" au XVIe siècle'. *Bibliothèque d' Humanisme et Renaissance* 37 (1975): pp. 225–43.

Lehmann, Phyllis. *Cyriacus of Ancona's Egyptian Visit and its Reflections in Gentile Bellini and Hieronymus Bosch*. Locust Valley, N.Y., 1977.

Levi d'Ancona, Mirella. 'Giustino del fu Gherardino da Forlì e gli affreschi perduti del Guariento nel Palazzo Ducale di Venezia'. *Arte Veneta* 21 (1967): pp. 34–44.

Lieberman, Ralph. *Renaissance Architecture in Venice*. New York, 1982.

Lightbown, Ronald. *Mantegna*. Berkeley and Los Angeles, 1986.

Limentani, Alberto. 'Martino da Canal, la basilica di San Marco e le arti figurative'. In *Mélanges offerts à René Crozet*, pp. 1177–90. Poitiers, 1966.

Logan, Oliver. *Culture and Society in Venice, 1470–1790*. London, 1972.

Longhi, Roberto. *Viatico per cinque secoli di pittura veneziana*. Florence, 1952.

Lorenzetti, Giulio. *La 'Scuola Grande' di S. Giovanni Evangelista*. Venice, 1929.

Lowry, Martin. 'The social world of Nicholas Jenson and John of Cologne'. *La Bibliofilia* 83 (1981): pp. 193–218.

———. *The World of Aldus Manutius. Business and Scholarship in Renaissance Venice*. Oxford, 1979.

Lucchetta, Giuliano. 'L'Oriente Mediterraneo nella cultura di Venezia tra il Quattro e il Cinquecento'. In *Storia della cultura veneta dal primo Quattrocento al Concilio di Trento*, 3/II, edited by G. Arnaldi and M. Pastore Stocchi. Vicenza, 1980a.

———. 'Viaggiatori e racconti di viaggi nel Cinquecento'. In *Storia della cultura veneta dal primo Quattrocento al Concilio di Trento*, 3/II, edited by G. Arnaldi and M. Pastore Stocchi. Vicenza, 1980b.

Ludwig, Gustav. 'Archivalische Beiträge zur Geschichte der venezianischen Malerei'. *Jahrbuch der k. preussischen Kunstsammlungen* 26, Beiheft (1905): pp. 1–159.

———. 'Vittore Carpaccio. I. La Scuola degli Albanese in Venezia'. *Archivio storico dell'arte*, 2nd series, 3, fasc. 6 (1897): pp. 405–31.

Luzio, A. 'Disegni topografici e pitture dei

Bellini'. *Archivio storico dell'arte* 1, fasc. 7 (1888): p. 276.
Magagnato, L. 'Il momento architettonico di tre pittori veneti del tardo Quattrocento'. *Bollettino del Centro Internazionale di Studi d'Architettura Andrea Palladio* 6 (1964): pp. 228–38.
———. 'A proposito delle architetture del Carpaccio'. *Comunità* 17, no. 111 (1963): pp. 70–81.
Malaguzzi Valeri, F. *Catalogo della R. Pinacoteca di Brera*. Bergamo, 1908.
Mallett, Michael. 'Diplomacy and War in Later Fifteenth-Century Italy'. *Proceedings of the British Academy* 67 (1981): pp. 267–88.
Mallett, Michael and Hale, J. R. *The Military Organization of a Renaissance State, Venice c. 1400–1617*. Cambridge, 1983.
Marshall, David. 'Carpaccio, Saint Stephen, and the Topography of Jerusalem'. *Art Bulletin* 66 (1984): pp. 619–20.
Mariani Canova, Giordana. *Paris Bordone*. Venice, 1964.
Martineau, Jane and Hope, Charles, eds. *The Genius of Venice, 1500–1600*. London, 1983.
Maschio, Ruggiero. 'Le Scuole Grandi a Venezia'. In *Storia della cultura veneta dal primo Quattrocento al Concilio di Trento*, 3/III, edited by G. Arnaldi and M. Pastore Stocchi. Vicenza, 1981.
Mas-Latrie, L. de. 'Testaments d'artistes vénitiens'. *Bibliothèque de l'École des Chartes* 5 (1869): pp. 204–9.
Mason Rinaldi, Stefania. 'Contributi d'Archivio per la decorazione pittorica della Scuola di S. Giovanni Evangelista'. *Arte Veneta* 32 (1978): pp. 293–301.
Mayer, L. *Mamluk Costume. A Survey*. Geneva, 1952.
McAndrew, John. *Venetian Architecture of the Early Renaissance*. Boston, 1980.
Meiss, Millard. 'Jan van Eyck and the Italian Renaissance'. In *Venezia e l'Europa. Atti del XVIII Congresso internazionale di Storia dell'Arte*. Venice, 1956.
Mercati, G. *Ultimi contributi alla storia degli Umanisti, II: Pescennio Francesco Negro*. Rome, 1939.
Meyer zur Capellen, Jürg. 'Bellini in der Scuola Grande di San Marco'. *Zeitschrift für Kunstgeschichte* 43 (1980): pp. 104–8.
———. *Gentile Bellini*. Stuttgart, 1985.
Miller, Sanda. 'Giovanni Mansueti: a little master of the Venetian Quattrocento'. *Révue Roumaine d'histoire de l'art*, ser. beaux-arts 15 (1978): pp. 77–115.
Moffitt, John. 'Anastasis-Templum: 'Subject or Non-subject' in an Architectural Representation by Jacopo Bellini?' *Paragone* no. 391 (1982): pp. 3–24.
Molmenti, Pompeo. *La storia di Venezia nella vita privata*. 3 vols., 7th edition. Bergamo, 1928.
———. 'I pittori Bellini'. *Archivio veneto* 36 (1888): pp. 219–36. Reprinted in Molmenti, *Studi e ricerche di storia e d'arte*, pp. 109–36. Turin and Rome, 1892.
Molmenti, Pompeo and Ludwig, Gustav. *The Life and Works of Vittorio Carpaccio*, translated by R. Cust. London, 1907.
Mommsen, Theodor. 'Petrarch and the Decoration of the Sala Virorum Illustrium in Padua'. *Art Bulletin* 34 (1952): pp. 95–116.
Monti, G. *Le confraternite medievali dell'Alta e Media Italia*. 2 vols., Venice, 1927.
Moore, Sally and Myerhoff, Barbara. *Secular Ritual*. Amsterdam, 1977.
Moretti, Lino. 'Ambienti dogali'. In *I Dogi*, edited by Gino Benzoni, Milan, 1982.
Moschetti, Andrea. 'Il "Paradiso" del Guariento nel Palazzo Ducale di Venezia.' *L'Arte* 7 (1904): pp. 394–97.
Moschini, Guido. *Guida per la città di Venezia*. 4 vols., Venice, 1815.
Moschini, V. 'Altri restauri alle gallerie di Venezia'. *Bollettino d'Arte* 45 (1960): pp. 353–65.
———. 'Nuovi allestimenti e restauri alle gallerie di Venezia'. *Bollettino d'Arte* 42 (1957): pp. 74–83.
Moschini Marconi, Sandra. *Gallerie dell' Accademia di Venezia: Opere d'Arte dei secoli XIV e XV*. Rome 1955.
———. *Gallerie dell'Accademia di Venezia: Opere d'Arte di secolo XVI*. Rome, 1962.
Muir, Edward. *Civic Ritual in Renaissance Venice*. Princeton, 1981.
———. 'Images of Power: Art and Pageantry in Renaissance Venice'. *American Historical Review* 84 (1979): pp. 16–52.
Muraro, Maria Teresa. 'La Festa a Venezia e le sue manifestazioni rappresentative: Le Compagnie della Calza e le Momarie'. In *Storia della cultura veneta dal primo Quattrocento fino al Concilio di Trento*, 3/III: pp. 315–41, edited by G. Arnaldi and M. Pastore Stocchi. Vicenza, 1981.
———. 'Le lieu des spectacles (publics ou privés) à Venise du XVe au XVIe siècles'. In *Le lieu théâtral à la Renaissance*, edited by J. Jacquot. Paris, 1964.
Muraro, Michelangelo. *Carpaccio*. Florence, 1966.
———. *I disegni di Vittore Carpaccio*. Florence, 1977.
———. *Paolo da Venezia*. University Park and London, 1970.
———. *Pitture murali nel Veneto e tecnica dell'affresco*. Venice, 1960.
———. 'The Statutes of the Venetian 'Arti' and the Mosaics of the Mascoli Chapel'. *Art Bulletin* 43 (1961): pp. 263–74.
———. 'Vittore Carpaccio o il Teatro in Pittura'. In *Studi sul teatro veneto fra Rinascimento ed età Barocca*, pp. 7–19, edited by Maria Teresa Muraro. Florence, 1971.
Neff, Mary. 'A citizen in the service of the patrician state: the career of Zaccaria de' Freschi'. *Studi veneziani*, new series, 5 (1981): pp. 33–62.
Newett, Mary Margaret. 'The Sumptuary Laws of Venice in the Fourteenth and Fifteenth Centuries'. In *Historical Essays by Members of the Owens College, Manchester*, edited by T. Tout and J. Tait. Manchester, 1907.
Paccagnini, Giovanni. *Pisanello e il ciclo cavalleresco di Mantova*. Milan, 1972.
Padoan Urban, Lina. 'La festa della Sensa nelle arte e nell'iconografia'. *Studi veneziani* 10 (1968): pp. 291–311.
———. 'Gli spettacoli urbani e l'Utopia'. *Architettura e Utopia nella Venezia del Cinquecento*. Milan, 1980.
Il Palazzo Ducale di Venezia, edited by Alvise Zorzi, Elena Bassi, Terisio Pignatti and Camillo Semanzato. Turin, 1971.
Pallucchini, Rodolfo. *La pittura veneziana del Trecento*. Venice and Rome, 1964.
———. *I Teleri del Carpaccio in San Giorgio degli Schiavoni*, appendix by G. Perocco. Milan, 1961.
———. *I Vivarini*. Venice, n.d. [1962].
Pallucchini, Rodolfo and Rossi, Paola. *Tintoretto. Le opere sacre e profane*. Milan, 1982.
Panofsky, Erwin. *Early Netherlandish Painting*. 2 vols., New York, 1971.
Paoletti, Pietro. *L'Architettura e la scultura del Rinascimento in Venezia*. 2 vols. in 3, Venice, 1893.
———. *Raccolta di documenti inediti per servire alla storia della pittura veneziana nei secoli XV e XVI*. 2 vols., Padua, 1894–95.
———. *La Scuola Grande di San Marco*. Venice, 1929.
Paoletti, Pietro, and Ludwig, Gustav. 'Neue archivalische Beiträge zur Geschichte der venezianischen Malerei'. *Repertorium für Kunstwissenschaft* 22 (1899): pp. 255–78 and 427–57.
Paolucci, A. 'Benedetto Diana'. *Paragone* no. 199 (1966): pp. 3–20.
Pavan, Elisabeth. 'Imaginaire et Politique: Venise et la Mort à la fin du Moyen Age'. *Mélanges de l'École Francaise de Rome*, Moyen Age-Temps Modern, 93 (1981): pp. 467–93.
Pazzi, Piero. *La Chiesa di San Giovanni Evangelista a Venezia*. Venice, 1985.

Perocco, Guido. *Carpaccio nella Scuola di S. Giorgio degli Schiavoni.* 1964. Reprint, Venice, 1975.
______. 'La Scuola di S. Giorgio degli Schiavoni'. In *Venezia e l'Europa. Atti del XVIII Congresso internazionale di Storia dell'Arte, 1955*, pp. 221–24. Venice, 1956.
______. *Tutta la pittura del Carpaccio.* Milan, 1960.
Pertusi, Agostino. 'Gli inizi della storiografia umanistica nel Quattrocento'. In *La storiografia veneziana fino al secolo XVI. Aspetti e problemi*, pp. 269–332, edited by A. Pertusi. Florence, 1970.
______. 'Quedam regalia insignia. Ricerche sulle insegne del potere ducale a Venezia durante il Medioevo.' *Studi veneziani* 7 (1965): pp. 3–123.
______. 'L'umanesimo greco dalla fine del secolo XIV agli inizi del secolo XVI'. In *Storia della Cultura Veneta dal primo Quattrocento fino al Concilio di Trento*, 3/I, edited by G. Arnaldi and M. Pastore Stocchi. Vicenza, 1980.
Pesaro, C. 'Un'ipotesi sulle date di partecipazione di tre artisti veneziani alla decorazione della Sala del Maggior Consiglio nella prima metà del Quattrocento'. *Bollettino dei Musei Civici Veneziani* 23 (1978): pp. 44–56.
Piazza San Marco: l'architettura, la storia, le funzioni, edited by G. Samona, U. Franzoi and E. R. Trincanato. Padua. 1970.
Pignatti, Terisio. *Carpaccio.* Brescia, 1970.
______. 'Cinque secoli di pittura veneziana'. In *Il Palazzo Ducale di Venezia*, pp. 91–168. Turin, 1971.
______, ed. *Le scuole di Venezia.* Milan, 1981.
______. *Veronese.* Venice, 1976.
Pincus, Debra. *The Arco Foscari. The Building of a Triumphal Gateway in Fifteenth Century Venice.* New York 1976.
Planicsig, Leo. 'Jacopo und Gentile Bellini (Neue Beiträge zu ihrem Werk)'. *Jahrbuch der Kunsthistorische Sammlungen Wien* 2 (1928): pp. 41–62.
Pope-Hennessey, John. *Italian Renaissance Sculpture.* 2nd rev. edn, Oxford, 1986.
______. *Paolo Uccello.* London, 1950.
______. *The Portrait in the Renaissance.* London and New York, 1966.
Pouncey, Philip. 'The Miraculous Cross in Titian's "Vendramin Family"'. *Journal of the Warburg and Courtauld Institutes* 2 (1938–39): pp. 191–93.
Povoledo, Elena. 'Scène et mise en scène à Venise dans la première moitié du XVI siècle'. In *Actes du XIe Stage International de Tours*, pp. 75–99. Paris, 1972.
Preto, Paolo. *Venezia e i Turchi.* Florence, 1975.
Pullan, Brian. 'Natura e carattere delle Scuole'. In *Le scuole di Venezia*, pp. 9–26, edited by T. Pignatti. Milan, 1981.
______. *Rich and Poor in Renaissance Venice.* Cambridge, Mass., 1971.
Puppi, Lionello. *Bartolommeo Montagna.* Venice, 1962.
______. 'Verso Gerusalemme'. *Arte Veneta* 32 (1978): pp. 73–78.
Puppi, Lionello and Olivato Puppi, Loredana. *Mauro Codussi.* Milan, 1977.
Raby, Julian. 'Cyriacus of Ancona and the Ottoman Sultan Mehmed II'. *Journal of the Warburg and Courtauld Institutes* 43 (1980a): pp. 242–46.
______. 'El Gran Turco: Mehmed the Conqueror as Patron of the Arts of Christendom'. D.Phil. thesis, Faculty of Oriental Studies, Oxford University, 1980b.
______. *Venice, Durer and the Oriental Mode.* The Hans Huth Memorial Studies I, London, 1982.
Renier-Michiel, Giustina. *Origine delle feste veneziane.* 6 vols. in 3, Venice, 1829.
Renosto, Renata. 'La Capella di Sant'Orsola a Venezia'. *Bollettino dei musei civici veneziani* 8, fasc. 2–3 (1963): pp. 37–50.
Ricci, Corrado, *Jacopo Bellini e i suoi libri di disegni.* 2 vols., Florence, 1908.
Roberts, Helen. 'St. Augustine in "St. Jerome's Study": Carpaccio's Painting and its Legendary Source'. *Art Bulletin* 41 (1959): pp. 283–97.
Robertson, Giles. *Giovanni Bellini.* Oxford, 1968.
Romanelli, Giandomenico. 'Ritrattistica dogale: ombre, immagini e volti'. In *I Dogi*, edited by Gino Benzoni. Milan, 1982.
Rosand, David. *Painting in Cinquecento Venice: Titian, Veronese, Tintoretto.* New Haven and London, 1982.
Roskill, Mark. *Dolce's 'Aretino' and Venetian Art Theory of the Cinquecento.* New York, 1968.
Rossi, V. 'Jacopo d'Albizzotto Guidi e il suo poema inedito su Venezia'. *Nuovo archivio veneto* 5 (1893): pp. 397–451.
Rouillard, C. D. 'A Reconsideration of "La Reception de l'Ambassadeur Domenico Trevisan au Caire, École de Gentile Bellini," at the Louvre, as an "Audience de Venetiens a Damas"'. *Gazette des Beaux-Arts*, 6th series 82 (1973): pp. 297–304.
Ruggiero, Guido. *Violence in Early Renaissance Venice.* New Brunswick, 1980.
Ruskin, John. *St. Mark's Rest.* 2nd edn, London, 1894.
Sagredo, A. *Degli edifici consacrati al culto divino in Venezia o distrutti o mutati d'uso nella prima metà del secolo XIX.* Venice, 1852.
Sauvaget, J. 'Une ancienne représentation de Damas au Musée du Louvre'. *Bulletin d'études orientales* 11 (1945–46): pp. 5–12.
Sbriziolo, Lia. 'Le confraternite veneziane di devozione. Saggio bibliografico e premesse storiografiche'. *Rivista di storia della Chiesa in Italia* 21 (1967): pp. 167–97 and 502–42.
______. 'Per la storia delle confraternite veneziane: dalle deliberazioni miste (1310–1476) del Consiglio dei Dieci. *Scolae comunes*, artigiane e nazionali'. *Atti dell'Istituto Veneto di Scienze, Lettere ed Arti*, Classe di scienze morali 126 (1967–68): pp. 404–42.
______. Per la storia delle confraternite veneziane: dalle deliberazioni miste (1310–1476) del Consiglio dei Dieci. Le scuole dei battuti'. In *Studi in onore di Gilles Gerard Meersseman* II: pp. 715–64. Padua, 1970.
Schlosser, Julius von. 'Ein Veronesisches Bilderbuch und die höfische Kunst des XIV. Jahrhunderts'. *Jahrbuch der Kunsthistorischen Sammlungen des Allerhöchsten Kaiserhauses* 16 (1895): pp. 144ff.
Juergen Schulz. 'Jacopo de' Barbari's View of Venice: Map Making, City Views, and Moralized Geography Before the Year 1500'. *Art Bulletin* 60 (1978): pp. 425–74.
______. 'The Printed Plans and Panoramic Views of Venice (1486–1797)'. *Saggi e Memorie di Storia dell'Arte* 7 (1970).
______. 'Tintoretto and the First Competition for the Ducal Palace "Paradise"'. *Arte Veneta* 34 (1980): pp. 112–26.
______. 'Titian's Ceiling in the Scuola di San Giovanni Evangelista'. *Art Bulletin* 48 (1966): pp. 89–94.
______. *Venetian Painted Ceilings of the Renaissance.* Berkeley and Los Angeles, 1968.
Serres, Michel. *Esthétiques sur Carpaccio.* Paris, 1975.
Sgarbi, Vittorio. *Ca' Dario.* Milan, 1984.
______. *Carpaccio.* Bologna, 1979.
Sheard, Wendy Stedman. 'Sanudo's List of Notable Things in Venetian Churches and the Date of the Vendramin Tomb'. *Yale Italian Studies* 1 (1977): pp. 219–68.
Sinding-Larsen, Staale. 'Christ in the Council Hall: Studies in the Religious Iconography of the Venetian Republic.' In *Acta ad archaeologiam et artium historiam pertinentia*, Vol. 5. Rome, 1974.
______. 'L'immagine della Repubblica di Venezia. Programmi decorativi di Palazzo Ducale'. In *Architettura e Utopia nella Venezia del Cinquecento.* Venice, 1980.

Smith, Christine. 'Cyriacus of Ancona's Seven Drawings of Hagia Sophia'. *Art Bulletin* 69 (1987): pp. 16–32.
Smyth, Craig Hugh. 'Venice and the Emergence of the High Renaissance in Florence'. In *Florence and Venice. Comparisons and Relations*, Vol. 1, Quattrocento, edited by Sergio Bertelli, Nicolai Rubinstein and Craig Hugh Smyth. Florence, 1979.
Sohm, Philip. 'Palma Vecchio's Sea Storm: A Political Allegory'. *Révue d'art canadienne / Canadian Art Review* 6 (1979–80): pp. 85–96.
———. *The Scuola Grande di San Marco, 1437–1550. The Architecture of a Venetian Lay Confraternity*. New York and London, 1982.
———. 'The Staircases of the Venetian Scuole Grandi and Mauro Codussi'. *Architectura* 8 (1978): pp. 125–49.
Southard. Edith. *The Frescoes in Siena's Palazzo Pubblico, 1289–1539: Studies in Imagery and Relations to Other Communal Palaces in Tuscany*. New York, 1974.
Steer, John. *Alvise Vivarini*. London, 1982.
Tafuri, Manfredo. 'La "nuova Costantinopoli." La rappresentazione della "renovatio" nella Venezia dell' Umanesimo (1450–1509)'. *Rassegna* 9 (1983): pp. 25–38.
———, ed. *'Renovatio urbis.' Venezia nell'età di Andrea Gritti (1523–1538)*. Rome, 1984.
Tenenti, Alberto. 'The Sense of Space and Time in the Venetian World of the Fifteenth and Sixteenth Centuries'. In *Renaissance Venice*, edited by J. R. Hale. London, 1973.
———. 'L'uso scenografico degli spazi pubblici: 1490–1580'. In *Tiziano e Venezia: Convegno Internazionale di Studi, Venezia, 1976*, pp. 21–26. Venice, 1980.
Testi, Laudadeo. *La storia della pittura veneziana*. 2 vols., Bergamo, 1909.
Thuasne, L. *Gentile Bellini et Sultan Mohammed II*. Paris, 1888.
Tietze, Hans. 'Master and Workshop in the Venetian Renaissance'. *Parnassus* 11 (1939): pp. 34ff.
Tietze, Hans and Tietze-Conrat, Erika. *The Drawings of the Venetian Painters*. New York, 1944.
Tietze-Conrat, Erika. 'Decorative Paintings of the Venetian Renaissance Reconstructed from Drawings'. *Art Quarterly* 3 (1940): pp. 15–39.
Trebbi, Giuseppe. 'La cancelleria veneta nei secoli XVI e XVII'. *Annali della Fondazione Luigi Einaudi* 14: pp. 65–125. Turin, 1980.
Trexler, Richard. *Public Life in Renaissance Florence*. New York, 1980.
———. 'Ritual Behavior in Florence: the Setting'. *Medievalia et Humanistica* 4 (1973): pp. 125–44.
Trincanato, Egle Renata. 'Il Palazzo Ducale'. In *Piazza S. Marco, l'architettura, la storia, le funzioni*. Padua, 1970.
Tucci, Ugo. 'Mercenti, viaggiatori, pellegrini nel Quattrocento'. In *Storia della cultura veneta dal primo Quattrocento al Concilio di Trento*, 3/II: pp. 317–353, edited by G. Arnaldi and M. Pastore Stocchi. Vicenza, 1980.
———. 'The Psychology of the Venetian Merchant in the Sixteenth Century'. In *Renaissance Venice*, edited by J. R. Hale. London, 1973.
Turner, Victor. 'Social Dramas and Stories about Them'. In *On Narrative*, edited by W. J. T. Mitchell. Chicago, 1981.
Urbani de Gheltof, G. M. *Guida storico-artistica della Scuola di S. Giovanni Evangelista in Venezia*. Venice, 1895.
Valcanover, Francesco. *The Galleries of the Accademia*. Venice, 1981.
Venturi, A. *Pisanello*. Rome, 1939.
———. *Le Vite di Gentile da Fabriano e il Pisanello*. Florence, 1896.
Venturi, Lionello. 'Le compagnie della calza (sec. XV–XVI)'. *Nuovo archivio veneto*, 3rd series 16 (1908): pp. 161–221; and 17 (1909): pp. 140–233.
Vertova, L. *Carpaccio*. Milan and Florence, 1952.
Villa, Massimo. 'Gentile e la politica del "sembiante" a Stambul'. In *Venezia e i Turchi. Scontri e confronti di due civiltà*. Milan, 1985.
Walter, Christopher. 'Papal Political Imagery in the Medieval Lateran Palace'. *Cahiers Archéologiques* 20 (1970): pp. 169ff.
Wazbinski, Zygmunt. 'Autour de Carpaccio'. *L'information d'histoire de l'art* 7 (1967): pp. 164–68.
———. 'Portrait d'un amateur d'art de la Renaissance'. *Arte Veneta* 32 (1968): pp. 21–29.
Weissman, Ronald. *Ritual Brotherhood in Renaissance Florence*. New York, 1982.
Wethey, Harold. *The Paintings of Titian*. 3 vols., London, 1969.
White, Hayden. 'The Value of Narrativity in the Representation of Reality'. In *On Narrative*, edited by W. J. T. Mitchell. Chicago and London, 1981.
Wickhoff, Franz. 'Der Saal des grossen Rathes zu Venedig in seinem alten Schmucke'. *Repertorium für Kunstwissenschaft* 6 (1883): pp. 1–37.
Wieruszowski, Helene. 'Art and the Commune in the Time of Dante'. *Speculum* 19 (1944): pp. 19–33.
Winter, Irene. 'After the Battle is Over: The Stele of the Vultures and the Beginning of Historical Narrative in the Art of the Ancient Near East'. *Studies in the History of Art* 16 (1985): pp. 11–34.
———. 'Royal Rhetoric and the Development of Historical Narrative in Neo-Assyrian Reliefs'. *Studies in Visual Communication* 7:2 (1981): pp. 2–38.
Wolters, Wolfgang. *Der Bilderschmuck des Dogenpalastes. Untersuchungen zur Selbstdarstellung der Republik Venedig im 16. Jahrhundert*. Wiesbaden, 1983.
———. 'Der Programmentwurf zur Dekoration des Dogenpalastes nach dem Brand von 20 Dezember 1577'. *Mitteilungen des kunsthistorischen Institutes in Florenz* 12 (1966): pp. 271–318.
Wurthmann, William. 'The Scuole Grandi and Venetian Art, 1260–c.1500'. Ph.D. dissertation, University of Chicago, 1975.
Zampetti, Pietro. 'L'Oriente del Carpaccio'. In *Venezia e l'Oriente fra Tardo Medioevo e Rinascimento*, edited by Agostino Pertusi. Venice, 1966a.
———. 'Per la Scuola di Sant' Orsola'. *Bollettino dei musei civici veneziani* 8, fasc. 2–3 (1963a): pp. 25–28.
———. 'Una veduta cinquecentesca del Duomo di Ancona'. *Le Arti* (1941–42): pp. 211ff.
———. *Vittore Carpaccio*. Catalogo della mostra, Venezia-Palazzo Ducale, 15 June–6 Oct. 1963. Venice, 1963b.
———. *Vittore Carpaccio*. Venice, 1966b.
Zangirolami, C. *Storia delle chiese rapinate e distrutte*. Venice, 1962.
Zanotto, Francesco. *Il Palazzo Ducale di Venezia*. 5 vols., Venice, 1858.
———. *Pinacoteca della I. R. Accademia Veneta delle Belle Arti*. 2 vols., Venice, 1834.
Zorzi, Alvise. *Venezia scomparsa*. 1973. 2nd edn, 2 vols in 1, Milan, 1984.
Zorzi, Ludovico. 'Elementi per la visualizzione della scena veneta prima del Palladio'. *Studi sul teatro veneto fra Rinascimento ed età Barocca*, edited by Maria Teresa Muraro. Florence, 1971.
———. 'L'imagine di Roma e la rappresentazione dell'antico secondo Vittore Carpaccio'. In *Roma e l'antico nell'arte e nella cultura del Cinquecento*, edited by Marcello Fagiolo. Rome, 1985.
———. *Il teatro e la città: saggi sulla scena italiana*. Turin, 1977.

Index

All monuments and institutions are in Venice, unless otherwise noted. Main entries in the Catalogue are indicated in **boldface** type: e.g., **Cat. II, 259–60**